BOLLINGEN SERIES XX

THE COLLECTED WORKS

OF

C. G. JUNG

VOLUME 6

EDITORS

SIR HERBERT READ

MICHAEL FORDHAM, M.D., M.R.C.P.

GERHARD ADLER, PH.D.

WILLIAM MCGUIRE, *executive editor*

PSYCHOLOGICAL
TYPES

C. G. JUNG

A REVISION BY R. F. C. HULL

OF THE TRANSLATION BY H. G. BAYNES

BOLLINGEN SERIES XX

PRINCETON UNIVERSITY PRESS

Second printing, 1974

First PRINCETON/BOLLINGEN PAPERBACK printing,
with corrections, 1976

Ninth printing, 1990

THIS EDITION IS BEING PUBLISHED IN THE
UNITED STATES OF AMERICA BY PRINCETON
UNIVERSITY PRESS AND IN ENGLAND BY
ROUTLEDGE & KEGAN PAUL, LTD. IN THE
AMERICAN EDITION, ALL THE VOLUMES
COMPRISING THE COLLECTED WORKS CON-
STITUTE NUMBER XX IN BOLLINGEN SERIES.
THE PRESENT VOLUME IS NUMBER 6 OF THE
COLLECTED WORKS AND WAS THE SIXTEENTH
TO APPEAR.

Except for the appendix, originally published in German as *Psychologische Typen*, Rascher Verlag, Zurich, 1921. Including appendix, published as volume
6 in the *Gesammelte Werke*, Rascher
Verlag, Zurich, 1960; 2nd edition, 1967.
The H. G. Baynes translation of *Psychological Types* was published in 1923 by
Kegan Paul, London, and Harcourt,
Brace and Co., New York.

ISBN 0-691-01813-8 (paperback edn.)
ISBN 0-691-09770-4 (hardcover edn.)

18   17   16   15   14   13   12

LIBRARY OF CONGRESS CATALOGUE CARD NUMBER: 75-156

MANUFACTURED IN THE U. S. A.

EDITORIAL NOTE

Jung was engaged in the preparatory work for *Psychological Types* during his so-called "fallow period," from 1913 to 1917 or 1918, a time of intense preoccupation with the images of his own unconscious, which he describes in the sixth and seventh chapters of *Memories, Dreams, Reflections*. As he wrote: "This work sprang originally from my need to define the ways in which my outlook differed from Freud's and Adler's. In attempting to answer this question, I came across the problem of types; for it is one's psychological type which from the outset determines and limits a person's judgment. My book, therefore, was an effort to deal with the relationship of the individual to the world, to people and things. It discussed the various aspects of consciousness, the various attitudes the conscious mind might take toward the world, and thus constitutes a psychology of consciousness regarded from what might be called a clinical angle."

Psychologische Typen was published by Rascher Verlag, of Zurich, in 1921. It was translated into English by H. G. Baynes (1882–1943), who during 1919–22 was Jung's assistant in Zurich and subsequently became one of the most prominent British analytical psychologists. His translation, subtitled "The Psychology of Individuation," was published in 1923 by Kegan Paul in London and Harcourt, Brace in New York. Some 22,000 copies of the Baynes version were sold. Translations have also appeared in Dutch, French, Greek, Italian, Japanese, Portuguese, Russian, Spanish,* and Swedish.

By 1950, the Swiss edition had gone through seven reprintings (some 15,000 copies), with little revision. The work was published as Band 6 in the *Gesammelte Werke* in 1960; for that edition the text was slightly revised, partly with the help of the author, quotations and references were checked and corrected, and a definition of the "self," formulated by Professor Jung for the edition, was added. In the original the "self" had

---

* See infra, Foreword to the Argentine Edition.

figured under the concept of the ego. In accordance with the previously announced plan of the *Collected Works* in English, an appendix was added containing an important preliminary study for the present book, a lecture delivered at the Psychoanalytical Congress in Munich, 1913, entitled "A Contribution to the Study of Psychological Types," and three other short works on typology (1925, 1928, 1936). A corrected edition of Band 6 appeared in 1967.

The present volume is one of the last to appear in the *Collected Works*. Owing to the continued availability of the Baynes translation in Great Britain and the United States, and the fact that Jung never subjected this work to revision (other than in minor details), the Editors have given precedence to issuing other volumes of which translations were lacking or inadequate.

The *Gesammelte Werke* version, in its second, corrected edition, is the basis of the present translation. The paragraph numbering of the Swiss and English editions differs, chiefly because it is the policy of the *Collected Works* to print quotations in smaller type and not number them as paragraphs. Furthermore, some of the very long paragraphs in the Swiss text have been broken up. For the convenience of readers who wish to compare passages in the two editions, a table of comparative paragraph numbers is given in the back of this volume.

The numbers of the Definitions fail to correspond among the various editions, owing to the vagaries of alphabetical order.

When quoted translations contain modifications, the indication "Cf." is given in the pertinent footnote. Grateful acknowledgment is made for permission to quote as follows: to Pantheon Books, a Division of Random House, Inc., for Lawrence Grant White's translation of the *Divine Comedy*; to Penguin Books Ltd., for Philip Wayne's translation of Goethe's *Faust*; to Oxford University Press, New York, and Faber and Faber, Ltd., for Louis MacNeice's translation of *Faust*.

The Editors wish to acknowledge their gratitude to the late A.S.B. Glover, who contributed research assistance, various translations of Latin quotations, and wide-ranging advice, to this as all the other volumes in the edition.

TABLE OF CONTENTS

vii

FOREWORD TO THE FIRST SWISS EDITION

This book is the fruit of nearly twenty years' work in the domain of practical psychology. It grew gradually in my thoughts, taking shape from the countless impressions and experiences of a psychiatrist in the treatment of nervous illnesses, from intercourse with men and women of all social levels, from my personal dealings with friend and foe alike, and, finally, from a critique of my own psychological peculiarity.

It is not my intention to burden the reader with case material; my concern is rather to show how the ideas I have abstracted from my practical work can be linked up, both historically and terminologically, with an existing body of knowledge. I have done this not so much from a need for historical justification as from a desire to bring the experiences of a medical specialist out of their narrow professional setting into a more general context, a context which will enable the educated layman to derive some profit from them. I would never have embarked upon this amplification, which might easily be misunderstood as an encroachment upon other spheres, were I not convinced that the psychological views presented in this book are of wide significance and application, and are therefore better treated in a general frame of reference than left in the form of a specialized scientific hypothesis.

With this aim in view I have confined myself to examining the ideas of comparatively few workers in this field, and have refrained from mentioning all that has already been said concerning our problem in general. Apart from the fact that even an approximately complete catalogue of the relevant material and opinions would far exceed my powers, such a compilation would not make any fundamental contribution to the discussion and development of the problem. Without regret, therefore, I have omitted much that I have collected in the course of the years, and confined myself as far as possible to essentials. A valuable document that was of very great help to me has also had to be sacrificed. This is a bulky correspondence which I exchanged with my friend Dr. Hans Schmid[1], of Basel, on the question of types. I owe a great deal of clarification to this interchange of ideas, and much of it, though of course in altered and greatly revised form, has gone into my book. The correspondence belongs essentially to the preparatory stage of the work, and its inclusion would create more confusion than clarity. Nevertheless, I owe it to the labours of my friend to express my thanks to him here.

C. G. JUNG

Küsnacht/Zurich
Spring, 1920

FOREWORD TO THE SEVENTH SWISS EDITION

This new edition appears unaltered, which is not to say that the book is not in need of further additions, improvements, and supplementary material. In particular, the somewhat terse descriptions of the types could have been expanded. Also, a consideration of works on typology by psychologists since this book first appeared would have been desirable. But the present scope of the book is already so great that it ought not to be augmented unless urgently necessary. Moreover, there is little practical purpose in making the problems of typology still more complicated when not even the elements have been properly understood. Critics commonly fall into the error of assuming that the types were, so to speak, fancy free and were forcibly imposed on the empirical material. In face of this

---

[1] [Swiss psychotherapist and former pupil of Jung's; died 1932. The correspondence (1915–16) was brought to light in 1966 by Schmid's daughter, Marie-Jeanne Boller-Schmid, who had been Jung's secretary from 1932 to 1952. The correspondence was discontinued early in 1916 at Jung's request. After careful consideration we concur with his view that its inclusion (e.g., in an Appendix to this volume) "would create more confusion than clarity"; nor, on account of its prolixity, is it included in *Coll. Works*, vol. 18. A remarkable personal codicil to a letter to Schmid, written on November 6, 1915, too valuable and moving to pass into oblivion, is, however, included in *C. G. Jung: Letters*, vol. 1. Cf. also Jung's obituary for Schmid, *Coll. Works*, vol. 18, pars. 1713ff. —EDITORS.]

assumption I must emphasize that my typology is the result of many years of practical experience—experience that remains completely closed to the academic psychologist. I am first and foremost a doctor and practising psychotherapist, and all my psychological formulations are based on the experiences gained in the hard course of my daily professional work. What I have to say in this book, therefore, has, sentence by sentence, been tested a hundredfold in the practical treatment of the sick and originated with them in the first place. Naturally, these medical experiences are accessible and intelligible only to one who is professionally concerned with the treatment of psychic complications. It is therefore not the fault of the layman if certain of my statements strike him as strange, or if he thinks my typology is the product of idyllically undisturbed hours in the study. I doubt, however, whether this kind of ingenuousness is a qualification for competent criticism.

September 1937   C. G. Jung

FOREWORD TO THE EIGHTH SWISS EDITION

The new edition again appears unaltered in essentials, but this time many small, long-necessary corrections have been made in the details. Also a new index has been compiled. I am especially indebted to Mrs. Lena Hurwitz-Eisner for this irksome work.

June 1949   C. G. Jung

FOREWORD TO THE ARGENTINE EDITION[1]

No book that makes an essentially new contribution to knowledge enjoys the privilege of being thoroughly understood. Perhaps it is most difficult of all for new psychological insights to make any headway. A psychology that is grounded on experience always touches upon personal and intimate matters and thus arouses everything that is contradictory and unclarified in the human psyche. If one is plunged, as I am for professional reasons, into the chaos of psychological opinions, prejudices, and susceptibilites, one gets a profound and indelible impression of the diversity of individual psychic dispositions, tendencies, and convictions, while on the other hand one increasingly feels the need for some kind of order among the chaotic multiplicity of points of view. This need calls for a critical orientation and for general principles and criteria, not too specific in their formulation, which may serve as *points de repère* in sorting out the empirical material. What I have attempted in this book is essentially a critical psychology.

This fundamental tendency in my work has often been overlooked, and far too many readers have succumbed to the error of thinking that Chapter X ("General Description of the Types") represents the essential content and purpose of the book, in the sense that it provides a system of classification and a practical guide to a good judgment of human character. Indeed, even in medical circles the opinion has got about that my method of treatment consists in fitting patients into this system and giving them corresponding "advice." This regrettable misunderstanding completely ignores the fact that this kind of classification is nothing but a childish parlour game, every bit as futile as the division of mankind into brachycephalics and dolichocephalics. My typology is far rather a critical apparatus serving to sort out and organize the welter of empirical material, but not in any sense to stick labels on people at first sight.

[1] [*Tipos psicológicos*, translated by Ramón de la Serna (Buenos Aires, 1936).]

xiv

It is not a physiognomy and not an anthropological system, but a critical psychology dealing with the organization and delimitation of psychic processes that can be shown to be typical. For this reason I have placed the general typology and the Definitions at the end of the book, after having described, in chapters I to IX, the processes in question with the help of various examples. I would therefore recommend the reader who really wants to understand my book to immerse himself first of all in chapters II and V. He will gain more from them than from any typological terminology superficially picked up, since this serves no other purpose than a totally useless desire to stick on labels.

It is now my pleasant duty to express my sincerest thanks to Madame Victoria Ocampo for her great help in securing the publication of this book, and to Señor Ramón de la Serna for his work of translation.

Küsnacht/Zurich   C. G. JUNG
October 1934

PSYCHOLOGICAL TYPES

Plato and Aristotle! These are not merely two systems, they are types of two distinct human natures, which from time immemorial, under every sort of disguise, stand more or less inimically opposed. The whole medieval world in particular was riven by this conflict, which persists down to the present day, and which forms the most essential content of the history of the Christian Church. Although under other names, it is always of Plato and Aristotle that we speak. Visionary, mystical, Platonic natures disclose Christian ideas and the corresponding symbols from the fathomless depths of their souls. Practical, orderly, Aristotelian natures build out of these ideas and symbols a fixed system, a dogma and a cult. Finally the Church embraces both natures, one of them entrenched in the clergy and the other in monasticism, but both keeping up a constant feud.

—Heine, *Deutschland*, I

INTRODUCTION

1   In my practical medical work with nervous patients I have long been struck by the fact that besides the many individual differences in human psychology there are also typical differences. Two types especially become clear to me; I have termed them the introverted and the extraverted types.

2   When we consider the course of human life, we see how the fate of one individual is determined more by the objects of his interest, while in another it is determined more by his own inner self, by the subject. Since we all swerve rather more towards one side or the other, we naturally tend to understand everything in terms of our own type.

3   I mention this circumstance at once in order to avoid possible misunderstandings. It will be apparent that it is one which considerably aggravates the difficulty of a general description of types. I must presume unduly upon the goodwill of the reader if I may hope to be rightly understood. It would be relatively simple if every reader knew to which category he belonged. But it is often very difficult to find out whether a person belongs to one type or the other, especially in regard to oneself. In respect of one's own personality one's judgment is as a rule extraordinarily clouded. This subjective clouding of judgment is particularly common because in every pronounced type there is a special tendency to compensate the one-sidedness of that type, a tendency which is biologically purposive since it strives constantly to maintain the psychic equilibrium. The compensation gives rise to secondary characteristics, or secondary types, which present a picture that is extremely difficult to interpret, so difficult that one is inclined to deny the existence of types altogether and to believe only in individual differences.

4   I must emphasize this difficulty in order to justify certain peculiarities in my presentation. It might seem as if the simplest way would be to describe two concrete cases and to dis-

3

sect them side by side. But everyone possesses both mechanisms, extraversion as well as introversion, and only the relative predominance of one or the other determines the type. Hence, in order to throw the picture into the necessary relief, one would have to retouch it rather vigorously, and this would amount to a more or less pious fraud. Moreover, the psychological reactions of a human being are so complicated that my powers of description would hardly suffice to draw an absolutely correct picture. From sheer necessity, therefore, I must confine myself to a presentation of principles which I have abstracted from a wealth of facts observed in many different individuals. In this there is no question of a *deductio a priori*, as it might appear; it is rather a deductive presentation of empirically gained insights. These insights will, I hope, help to clarify a dilemma which, not only in analytical psychology but in other branches of science as well, and especially in the personal relations of human beings with one another, has led and still continues to lead to misunderstanding and discord. For they explain how the existence of two distinct types is actually a fact that has long been known: a fact that in one form or another has struck the observer of human nature or dawned upon the brooding reflection of the thinker, presenting itself to Goethe's intuition, for instance, as the all-embracing principle of systole and diastole. The names and concepts by which the mechanisms of extraversion and introversion have been grasped are extremely varied, and each of them is adapted to the standpoint of the observer in question. But despite the diversity of the formulations the fundamental idea common to them all constantly shines through: in one case an outward movement of interest towards the object, and in the other a movement of interest away from the object to the subject and his own psychological processes. In the first case the object works like a magnet upon the tendencies of the subject; it determines the subject to a large extent and even alienates him from himself. His qualities may become so transformed by assimilation to the object that one might think it possessed some higher and decisive significance for him. It might almost seem as if it were an absolute determinant, a special purpose of life or fate that he should abandon himself wholly to the object. But in the second case the subject is and remains the centre of every interest. It looks, one might say, as though all the life-energy were ultimately seeking the subject, and thus continually prevented the object from exercising any overpowering influence. It is as though the energy were flowing away from the object, and the subject were a magnet drawing the object to itself.

5   It is not easy to give a clear and intelligible description of this two-way relationship to the object without running the risk of paradoxical formulations which would create more confusion than clarity. But in general one could say that the introverted standpoint is one which sets the ego and the subjective psychological process above the object and the objective process, or at any rate seeks to hold its ground against the object. This attitude, therefore, gives the subject a higher value than the object, and the object accordingly has a lower value. It is of secondary importance; indeed, sometimes the object represents no more than an outward token of a subjective content, the embodiment of an idea, the idea being the essential thing. If it is the embodiment of a feeling, then again the feeling is the main thing and not the object in its own right. The extraverted standpoint, on the contrary, subordinates the subject to the object, so that the object has the higher value. In this case the subject is of secondary importance, the subjective process appearing at times as no more than a disturbing or superfluous appendage of objective events. It is clear that the psychology resulting from these contrary standpoints must be classed as two totally different orientations. The one sees everything in terms of his own situation, the other in terms of the objective event.

6   These contrary attitudes are in themselves no more than correlative mechanisms: a diastolic going out and seizing of the object, and a systolic concentration and detachment of energy from the object seized. Every human being possesses both mechanisms as an expression of his natural life-rhythm, a rhythm which Goethe, surely not by chance, described physiologically in terms of the heart's activity. A rhythmical alternation of both forms of psychic activity would perhaps correspond to the normal course of life. But the complicated outer conditions under which we live and the even more complicated conditions of our individual psychic make-up seldom permit

a completely undisturbed flow of psychic energy. Outer circumstances and inner disposition frequently favour one mechanism and restrict or hinder the other. One mechanism will naturally predominate, and if this condition becomes in any way chronic a *type* will be produced; that is, an habitual attitude in which one mechanism predominates permanently, although the other can never be completely suppressed since it is an integral part of the psychic economy. Hence there can never be a pure type in the sense that it possesses only one mechanism with the complete atrophy of the other. A typical attitude always means merely the relative predominance of one mechanism.

7   The hypothesis of introversion and extraversion allows us, first of all, to distinguish two large groups of psychological individuals. Yet this grouping is of such a superficial and general nature that it permits no more than this very general distinction. Closer investigation of the individual psychologies that fall into one group or the other will at once show great differences between individuals who nevertheless belong to the same group. If, therefore, we wish to determine wherein lie the differences between individuals belonging to a definite group, we must take a further step. Experience has taught me that in general individuals can be distinguished not only according to the broad distinction between introversion and extraversion, but also according to their basic psychological functions. For in the same measure as outer circumstances and inner disposition cause either introversion or extraversion to predominate, they also favour the predominance of one definite basic function in the individual. I have found from experience that the basic psychological functions, that is, functions which are genuinely as well as essentially different from other functions, prove to be *thinking, feeling, sensation,* and *intuition.* If one of these functions habitually predominates, a corresponding type results. I therefore distinguish a thinking, a feeling, a sensation, and an intuitive type. *Each of these types may moreover be either introverted or extraverted,* depending on its relation to the object as we have described above. In my preliminary work on psychological types[1] I did not carry out

1 "A Contribution to the Study of Psychological Types" (1913), infra, Appendix, pars. 858ff., and "The Psychology of the Unconscious Processes," *Collected Papers*

this differentiation, but identified the thinking type with the introvert and the feeling type with the extravert. A deeper study of the problem has shown this equation to be untenable. In order to avoid misunderstandings, I would ask the reader to bear in mind the differentiation I have developed here. For the sake of clarity, which is essential in such complicated matters, I have devoted the last chapter of this book to the definition of my psychological concepts.

---

on Analytical Psychology (2nd edn., 1917), pp. 391 ff. [The latter section, on types, was subsequently revised and appears as ch. IV ("The Problem of the Attitude-Type") of the first of the *Two Essays on Analytical Psychology*. Cf. also "The Structure of the Unconscious" (1916), in ibid., pars. 462, n. 8, and 482.—EDITORS.]

THE PROBLEM OF TYPES IN THE HISTORY
OF CLASSICAL AND MEDIEVAL THOUGHT

1. PSYCHOLOGY IN THE CLASSICAL AGE:
THE GNOSTICS, TERTULLIAN, ORIGEN

8   So long as the historical world has existed there has always been psychology, but an objective psychology is only of
recent growth. We could say of the science of former times
that in proportion to the lack of objective psychology there is
an increase in the rate of subjectivity. Hence, though the works
of the ancients are full of psychology, only little of it can be
described as objective psychology. This may be due in no small
measure to the peculiar character of human relationships in
classical and medieval times. The ancients had, so to speak, an
almost entirely biological valuation of their fellow-men; this is
everywhere apparent in their habits of life and in the legislation of antiquity. The medieval man, in so far as his value judgments found any expression at all, had on the contrary a
metaphysical valuation of his fellows, and this had its source
in the idea of the imperishable value of the human soul. This
metaphysical valuation, which may be regarded as compensatory to the standpoint of antiquity, is just as unfavourable as
the biological one so far as a *personal* valuation is concerned,
which alone can form the basis of an objective psychology.

9   Although not a few people think that a psychology can be
written *ex cathedra*, nowadays most of us are convinced that
an objective psychology must be founded above all on observation and experience. This foundation would be ideal if only
it were possible. The ideal and aim of science do not consist
in giving the most exact possible description of the facts—
science cannot compete as a recording instrument with the
camera and the gramophone—but in establishing certain laws,

which are merely abbreviated expressions for many diverse processes that are yet conceived to be somehow correlated. This aim goes beyond the purely empirical by means of the *concept*, which, though it may have general and proved validity, will always be a product of the subjective psychological constellation of the investigator. In the making of scientific theories and concepts many personal and accidental factors are involved. There is also a personal equation that is psychological and not merely psychophysical. We see colours but not wave-lengths. This well-known fact must nowhere be taken to heart more seriously than in psychology. The effect of the personal equation begins already in the act of observation. *One sees what one can best see oneself.* Thus, first and foremost, one sees the mote in one's brother's eye. No doubt the mote is there, but the beam sits in one's own eye—and may considerably hamper the act of seeing. I mistrust the principle of "pure observation" in so-called objective psychology unless one confines oneself to the eye-pieces of chronoscopes and tachistoscopes and suchlike "psychological" apparatus. With such methods one also guards against too embarrassing a yield of empirical psychological facts.

10 But the personal equation asserts itself even more in the presentation and communication of one's own observations, to say nothing of the interpretation and abstract exposition of the empirical material. Nowhere is the basic requirement so indispensable as in psychology that the observer should be adequate to his object, in the sense of being able to see not only subjectively but also objectively. The demand that he should see *only* objectively is quite out of the question, for it is impossible. We must be satisfied if he does not see *too* subjectively. That the subjective observation and interpretation accord with the objective facts proves the truth of the interpretation only in so far as the latter makes no pretence to be generally valid, but valid only for that area of the object which is being considered. To this extent it is just the beam in one's own eye that enables one to detect the mote in one's brother's eye. The beam in one's own eye, as we have said, does not prove that one's brother has no mote in his. But the impairment of one's own vision might easily give rise to a general theory that all motes are beams.

9

11   The recognition and taking to heart of the subjective determination of knowledge in general, and of psychological knowledge in particular, are basic conditions for the scientific and impartial evaluation of a psyche different from that of the observing subject. These conditions are fulfilled only when the observer is sufficiently informed about the nature and scope of his own personality. He can, however, be sufficiently informed only when he has in large measure freed himself from the levelling influence of collective opinions and thereby arrived at a clear conception of his own individuality.

12   The further we go back into history, the more we see personality disappearing beneath the wrappings of collectivity. And if we go right back to primitive psychology, we find absolutely no trace of the concept of an individual. Instead of individuality we find only collective relationship or what Lévy-Bruhl calls *participation mystique*. The collective attitude hinders the recognition and evaluation of a psychology different from the subject's, because the mind that is collectively oriented is quite incapable of thinking and feeling in any other way than by projection. What we understand by the concept "individual" is a relatively recent acquisition in the history of the human mind and human culture. It is no wonder, therefore, that the earlier all-powerful collective attitude prevented almost completely an objective psychological evaluation of individual differences, or any scientific objectification of individual psychological processes. It was owing to this very lack of psychological thinking that knowledge became "psychologized," i.e., filled with projected psychology. We find striking examples of this in man's first attempts at a philosophical explanation of the cosmos. The development of individuality, with the consequent psychological differentiation of man, goes hand in hand with the de-psychologizing work of objective science.

13   These reflections may explain why objective psychology has such a meagre source in the material handed down to us from antiquity. The differentiation of the four temperaments, which we took over from the ancients, hardly rates as a psychological typology since the temperaments are scarcely more than psychophysical colourings. But this lack of information does not mean that we can find no trace in classical literature

of the effects of the psychological pairs of opposites we are discussing.

14 Gnostic philosophy established three types, corresponding perhaps to three of the basic psychological functions: thinking, feeling, and sensation. The *pneumatikoi* could be correlated with thinking, the *psychikoi* with feeling, and the *hylikoi* with sensation. The inferior rating of the *psychikoi* was in accord with the spirit of Gnosticism, which, unlike Christianity, insisted on the value of knowledge. The Christian principles of love and faith kept knowledge at a distance. In the Christian sphere the *pneumatikoi* would accordingly get the lower rating, since they were distinguished merely by the possession of Gnosis, i.e., knowledge.

15 Type differences should also be borne in mind when we consider the long and perilous struggle which the Church from its earliest beginnings waged against Gnosticism. Owing to the predominantly practical trend of early Christianity the intellectual hardly came into his own, except when he followed his fighting instincts by indulging in polemical apologetics. The rule of faith was too strict and allowed no freedom of movement. Moreover, it was poor in positive intellectual content. It boasted of few ideas, and though these were of immense practical value they were a definite obstacle to thought. The intellectual was much worse hit by the *sacrificium intellectus* than the feeling type. It is therefore understandable that the vastly superior intellectual content of Gnosis, which in the light of our present mental development has not lost but has considerably gained in value, must have made the greatest possible appeal to the intellectual within the Church. For him it held out in very truth all the temptations of this world. Docetism in particular caused grave trouble to the Church with its contention that Christ possessed only an apparent body and that his whole earthly existence and passion had been merely a semblance. In this contention the purely intellectual element predominates at the expense of human feeling.

16 Perhaps the struggle with Gnosis is most vividly presented to us in two figures who were of the utmost significance not only as Church Fathers but as personalities. These are Tertullian and Origen, who lived towards the end of the second century. Schultz says of them:

One organism is able to take in nourishment and assimilate it almost completely into its own nature; another with equal persistence eliminates it with every sign of passionate resistance. Thus Origen on one side, and Tertullian on the other, reacted in diametrically opposite ways to Gnosis. Their reaction is not only characteristic of the two personalities and their philosophical outlook; it is of fundamental significance with regard to the position of Gnosis in the spiritual life and religious currents of that age.[1]

17   Tertullian was born in Carthage somewhere about A.D. 160. He was a pagan, and he abandoned himself to the lascivious life of his city until about his thirty-fifth year, when he became a Christian. He was the author of numerous writings wherein his character, which is our especial interest, is unmistakably displayed. Most clearly of all we see his unparalleled noble-hearted zeal, his fire, his passionate temperament, and the profundity of his religious understanding. He was a fanatic, brilliantly one-sided in his defence of a recognized truth, possessed of a matchless fighting spirit, a merciless opponent who saw victory only in the total annihilation of his adversary, his language a flashing blade wielded with ferocious mastery. He was the creator of the Church Latin that lasted for more than a thousand years. It was he who coined the terminology of the early Church. "Once he had seized upon a point of view, he had to follow it through to its ultimate conclusion as though lashed by the legions of hell, even when right had long since ceased to be on his side and all reasonable order lay in shreds before him."[2] His impassioned thinking was so inexorable that again and again he alienated himself from the very thing for which he had given his heart's blood. Accordingly his ethical code was bitterly severe. Martyrdom he commanded to be sought and not shunned; he permitted no second marriage, and required the permanent veiling of persons of the female sex. Gnosis, which in reality is a passion for thinking and knowing, he attacked with unrelenting fanaticism, together with philosophy and science which differed from it so little. To him is ascribed the sublime confession: *Credo quia absurdum est* (I believe because it is absurd). This does not altogether accord with historical fact, for he merely said: "And the Son of God

[1] *Dokumente der Gnosis,* p. xxix.
[2] Ibid., p. xxv.

died, which is immediately credible because it is absurd. And buried he rose again, which is certain because it is impossible."[3]

18   Thanks to the acuteness of his mind, he saw through the poverty of philosophical and Gnostic knowledge, and contemptuously rejected it. He invoked against it the testimony of his own inner world, his own inner realities, which were one with his faith. In shaping and developing these realities he became the creator of those abstract conceptions which still underlie the Catholic system of today. The irrational inner reality had for him an essentially dynamic nature; it was his principle, his foundation in face of the world and of all collectively valid and rational science and philosophy. I quote his own words:

I summon a new witness, or rather a witness more known than any written monument, more debated than any system of life, more published abroad than any promulgation, greater than the whole of man, yea that which constitutes the whole of man. Approach then, O my soul, whether you be something divine and eternal, as many philosophers believe—the less then will you lie—or not wholly divine, because mortal, as Epicurus alone contends—the less then ought you to lie—whether you come from heaven or are born of earth, whether compounded of numbers or of atoms, whether you have your beginning with the body or are later joined to it; what matter indeed whence you come and how you make man to be what he is, a reasonable being, capable of perception and of knowledge. But I summon you not, O soul, as proclaiming wisdom, trained in the schools, conversant with libraries, fed and nourished in the academies and pillared halls of Athens. No, I would speak with you, O soul, as wondrous simple and unlearned, awkward and inexperienced, such as you are for those who possess nothing else but you, even as you come from the alleys, from the street-corners, and from the workshops. It is just your unknowingness that I need.[4]

19   The self-mutilation performed by Tertullian in the *sacrificium intellectus* led him to an unqualified recognition of the irrational inner reality, the true rock of his faith. The necessity of the religious process which he sensed in himself he crystallized in the incomparable formula *anima naturaliter christiana*

[3] "Et mortuus est dei filius, prorsus credibile est, quia ineptum est. Et sepultus resurrexit; certum est, quia impossibile est" (*De carne Christi*, 5). Cf. *Treatise on the Incarnation*, p. 19.

[4] *De Testimonio animae*, 1. Cf. *The Writings of Tertullian*, I, p. 132.

(the soul is by nature Christian). With the *sacrificium intellectus* philosophy and science, and hence also Gnosis, fell to the ground. In the further course of his life the qualities I have described became exacerbated. When the Church was driven to compromise more and more with the masses, he revolted against it and became a follower of the Phrygian prophet Montanus, an ecstatic, who stood for the principle of absolute denial of the world and complete spiritualization. In violent pamphlets he now began to assail the policy of Pope Calixtus I, and this together with his Montanism put him more or less outside the pale of the Church. According to a report of Augustine, he even quarrelled with Montanism later and founded a sect of his own.

20   Tertullian is a classic example of introverted thinking. His very considerable and keenly developed intellect was flanked by an unmistakable sensuality. The psychological process of development which we call specifically Christian led him to the sacrifice, the amputation, of the most valuable function—a mythical idea that is also found in the great and exemplary symbol of the sacrifice of the Son of God. His most valuable organ was the intellect and the clarity of knowledge it made possible. Through the *sacrificium intellectus* the way of purely intellectual development was closed to him; it forced him to recognize the irrational dynamism of his soul as the foundation of his being. The intellectuality of Gnosis, the specifically rational stamp it gave to the dynamic phenomena of the soul, must have been odious to him, for that was just the way he had to forsake in order to acknowledge the principle of feeling.

21   In Origen we may recognize the absolute opposite of Tertullian. He was born in Alexandria about A.D. 185. His father was a Christian martyr. He himself grew up in that quite unique mental atmosphere where the ideas of East and West mingled. With an intense yearning for knowledge he eagerly absorbed all that was worth knowing, and accepted everything, whether Christian, Jewish, Hellenistic, or Egyptian, that the teeming intellectual world of Alexandria offered him. The pagan philosopher Porphyry, a pupil of Plotinus, said of him: "His outward life was that of a Christian and against the law; but in his opinions about material things and the Deity he

thought like a Greek, and introduced Greek ideas into foreign fables."[5]

22   His self-castration had taken place sometime before A.D. 211; his inner motives for this may be guessed, but historically they are not known to us. Personally he was of great influence, and had a winning speech. He was constantly surrounded by pupils and a whole host of amanuenses who gathered up the precious words that fell from the revered master's lips. As an author he was extraordinarily prolific and he developed into a great teacher. In Antioch he even delivered lectures on theology to the Emperor's mother Mammaea. In Caesarea he was the head of a school. His teaching activities were frequently interrupted by his extensive journeyings. He possessed an extraordinary erudition and had an astounding capacity for careful investigation. He hunted up old biblical manuscripts and earned special merit for his textual criticism. "He was a great scholar, indeed the only true scholar the early Church possessed," says Harnack. In complete contrast to Tertullian, Origen did not cut himself off from the influence of Gnosticism; on the contrary, he even channelled it, in attenuated form, into the bosom of the Church, or such at least was his aim. Indeed, judging by his thought and fundamental views, he was himself almost a Christian Gnostic. His position in regard to *faith* and *knowledge* is described by Harnack in the following psychologically significant words:

The Bible is equally needful to both: the believers receive from it the facts and commandments they need, while the Gnostics decipher thoughts in it and gather from it the powers which guide them to the contemplation and love of God—whereby all material things, through spiritual interpretation (allegorical exegesis, hermeneutics), seem to be melted into a cosmos of ideas, until at last everything is surmounted and left behind as a stepping-stone, while only this remains: the blessed and abiding relationship of the God-created creaturely soul to God (*amor et visio*).[6]

23   His theology as distinguished from Tertullian's was essentially philosophical; it fitted neatly into the framework of Neo-

[5] [Cf. Harnack, *A History of Dogma*, I, p. 357; Eusebius, *The Ecclesiastical History and the Martyrs of Palestine*, I, p. 192.]
[6] [Reference cannot be traced.—EDITORS.]

platonic philosophy. In Origen the two worlds of Greek philosophy and Gnosis on the one hand, and Christian ideas on the other, interpenetrate in a peaceful and harmonious whole. But this daring, perspicacious tolerance and fair-mindedness led Origen, too, to the fate of condemnation by the Church. Actually the final condemnation took place only posthumously, after Origen as an old man had been tortured in the persecution of the Christians under Decius and had subsequently died from the effects of the torture. Pope Anastasius I pronounced the condemnation in 399, and in 543 his heretical teachings were anathematized at a synod convoked by Justinian, which judgment was upheld by later councils.

24   Origen is a classic example of the extraverted type. His basic orientation was towards the object; this showed itself in his scrupulous regard for objective facts and their conditions, as well as in the formulation of that supreme principle: *amor et visio Dei*. The Christian process of development encountered in Origen a type whose ultimate foundation was the relation to the object—a relation that has always symbolically expressed itself in sexuality and accounts for the fact that there are certain theories today which reduce all the essential psychic functions to sexuality too. Castration was therefore an adequate expression of the sacrifice of the most valuable function. It is entirely characteristic that Tertullian should perform the *sacrificium intellectus*, whereas Origen was led to the *sacrificium phalli*, because the Christian process demands a complete abolition of the sensual tie to the object; in other words, it demands the sacrifice of the hitherto most valued function, the dearest possession, the strongest instinct. Considered biologically, the sacrifice serves the interests of domestication, but psychologically it opens a door for new possibilities of spiritual development through the dissolution of old ties.

25   Tertullian sacrificed the intellect because it bound him most strongly to worldliness. He fought against Gnosis because for him it represented a deviation into intellectuality, which at the same time involved sensuality. In keeping with this fact we find that in reality Gnosticism also was divided into two schools: one school striving after a spirituality that exceeded all bounds, the other losing itself in an ethical anarchism, an

absolute libertinism that shrank from no lewdness and no depravity however atrocious and perverse. A definite distinction was made between the Encratites, who practised continence, and the Antitactae or Antinomians, who were opposed to law and order, and who in obedience to certain doctrines sinned on principle and purposely gave themselves up to unbridled debauchery. To the latter school belong the Nicolaitans, Archontics, etc., and the aptly named Borborians. How closely the seeming contraries lay side by side is shown by the example of the Archontics, for this same sect was divided into an Encratite and an Antinomian school, both of which pursued their aims logically and consistently. If anyone wants to know what are the ethical consequences of intellectualism pushed to the limit and carried out on a grand scale, let him study the history of Gnostic morals. He will then fully understand the *sacrificium intellectus*. These people were also consistent in practice and carried their crazy ideas to absurd lengths in their actual lives.

26   Origen, by mutilating himself, sacrificed his sensual tie to the world. For him, evidently, the specific danger was not the intellect but feeling and sensation, which bound him to the object. Through castration he freed himself from the sensuality that was coupled with Gnosticism; he could then surrender without fear to the treasures of Gnostic thought, whereas Tertullian through his sacrifice of the intellect turned away from Gnosis but also reached a depth of religious feeling that we miss in Origen. "In one way he was superior to Origen," says Schultz, "because in his deepest soul he lived every one of his words; it was not reason that carried him away, like the other, but the heart. Yet in another respect Tertullian stands far behind him, inasmuch as he, the most passionate of all thinkers, was on the verge of rejecting knowledge altogether, for his battle against Gnosis was tantamount to a complete denial of human thought."[7]

27   We see here how, in the Christian process, the original type has actually become reversed: Tertullian, the acute thinker, becomes the man of feeling, while Origen becomes the scholar and loses himself in intellectuality. Logically, of course,

[7] *Dokumente der Gnosis*, p. xxvii.

it is quite easy to put it the other way round and say that Tertullian had always been the man of feeling and Origen the intellectual. Apart from the fact that the difference of type is not thereby done away with but exists as before, the reversal does not explain how it comes that Tertullian saw his most dangerous enemy in the intellect, and Origen in sexuality. One could say they were both deceived, adducing as evidence the fatal outcome of both lives by way of argument. If that were the case, one would have to assume that they both sacrificed the less important thing, and that both of them made a crooked bargain with fate. That is certainly a point of view whose validity should be recognized in principle. Are there not just such slyboots among primitives who approach their fetish with a black hen under the arm, saying; "See, here is thy sacrifice, a beautiful black pig." I am, however, of the opinion that the depreciatory method of explanation, notwithstanding the unmistakable relief which the ordinary mortal feels in dragging down something great, is not under all circumstances the correct one, even though it may appear to be very "biological." From what we can personally know of these two great figures in the realm of the spirit, we must say that their whole nature was so sincere that their conversion to Christianity was neither an underhand trick nor a fraud, but had both reality and truthfulness.

28   We shall not be digressing if we take this opportunity to try to grasp the psychological meaning of this rupture of the natural course of instinct, which is what the Christian process of sacrifice appears to be. From what has been said it follows that conversion signifies at the same time a transition to another attitude. This also makes it clear from what source the impelling motive for conversion comes, and how far Tertullian was right in conceiving the soul as *naturaliter Christiana*. The natural course of instinct, like everything in nature, follows the line of least resistance. One man is rather more gifted here, another there; or again, adaptation to the early environment of childhood may demand relatively more reserve and reflection or relatively more empathy and participation, according to the nature of the parents and the circumstances. In this way a certain preferential attitude is built up automatically, resulting in different types. Since every man, as a relatively stable

being, possesses all the basic psychological functions, it would be a psychological necessity with a view to perfect adaptation that he should also employ them in equal measure. For there must be a reason why there are different modes of psychological adaptation: evidently one alone is not enough, since the object seems to be only partially comprehended when, for example, it is something that is merely thought or merely felt. A one-sided ("typical") attitude leaves a deficiency in the adaptive performance which accumulates during the course of life, and sooner or later this will produce a disturbance of adaptation that drives the subject toward some kind of compensation. But the compensation can be obtained only by means of an amputation (sacrifice) of the hitherto one-sided attitude. This results in a temporary accumulation of energy and an overflow into channels not used consciously before though lying ready unconsciously. The adaptive deficiency, which is the *causa efficiens* of the process of conversion, is subjectively felt as a vague sense of dissatisfaction. Such an atmosphere prevailed at the turning-point of our era. A quite astonishing need of redemption came over mankind, and brought about that unparalleled efflorescence of every sort of possible and impossible cult in ancient Rome. Nor was there any lack of advocates of "living life to the full," who operated with arguments based on the science of that day instead of with biological ones. They, too, could never be done with speculations as to why mankind was in such a bad way. Only, the causalism of that epoch, as compared with our science, was considerably less restricted; they could hark back far beyond childhood to cosmogony, and numerous systems were devised proving that what had happened in the remote abyss of time was the source of insufferable consequences for mankind.

29   The sacrifice that Tertullian and Origen carried out was drastic—too drastic for our taste—but it was in keeping with the spirit of the age, which was thoroughly concretistic. Because of this spirit the Gnostics took their visions as absolutely real, or at least as relating directly to reality, and for Tertullian the reality of his feeling was objectively valid. The Gnostics projected their subjective inner perception of the change of attitude into a cosmogonic system and believed in the reality of its psychological figures.

19

30   In my book *Wandlungen und Symbole der Libido*[8] I left
the whole question open as to the origin of the peculiar course
the libido took in the Christian process of development. I spoke
of a splitting of libido into two halves, each directed against
the other. The explanation of this is to be found in a one-sided
psychological attitude so extreme that compensations from the
unconscious became an urgent necessity. It is precisely the
Gnostic movement in the early centuries of our era that most
clearly demonstrates the breakthrough of unconscious contents
at the moment of compensation. Christianity itself signified the
collapse and sacrifice of the cultural values of antiquity, that
is, of the classical attitude. At the present time it is hardly
necessary to remark that it is a matter of indifference whether
we speak of today or of that age two thousand years ago.

2. THE THEOLOGICAL DISPUTES OF THE ANCIENT CHURCH

31   It is more than probable that the contrast of types will also
be found in the history of the schisms and heresies that were
so frequent in the disputes of the early Church. The Ebionites
or Jewish Christians, who were probably identical with the
primitive Christians generally, believed in the exclusive
humanity of Christ and held him to be the son of Mary and
Joseph, only subsequently receiving his consecration through
the Holy Ghost. On this point the Ebionites were diametrically
opposed to the Docetists. The effects of this opposition endured long after. The conflict came to light again in an altered
form—which, though doctrinally attenuated, had an even
graver effect on Church politics—about the year 320 in the
Arian heresy. Arius denied the formula propounded by the
orthodox Church: τῷ Πατρὶ ὁμοούσιος (of one substance
with the Father), in favour of τῷ Πατρὶ ὁμοιούσιος (of
like substance with the Father). When we examine more
clearly the history of the great Arian controversy concerning
homoousia and *homoiousia* (the complete identity as against
the similarity of Christ's substance with God), it seems to us
that *homoiousia* definitely puts the accent on the sensuous and

8 [1911–12; first translated as *Psychology of the Unconscious* (1916); revised
edition (1952) retitled *Symbols of Transformation*.]

humanly perceptible, in contrast to the purely conceptual and abstract standpoint of *homoousia*. In the same way it would appear to us that the revolt of the Monophysites (who upheld the absolute unity of Christ's nature) against the Dyophysite formula of the Council of Chalcedon (which upheld the inseparable duality of Christ, his human and divine nature coexisting in one body) once more asserted the standpoint of the abstract and inconceivable as against the sensuous and naturalistic formula of the Dyophysites.

32   At the same time it becomes overwhelmingly clear to us that, in the Arian movement as in the Monophysite dispute, although the subtle dogmatic question was the main issue for the minds that originally conceived it, this was not so for the great mass of people who took part in the controversy. Even in those early days so subtle a question had no motivating force with the masses, who were stirred rather by the problems and claims of political power that had nothing to do with differences of theological opinion. If type differences had any significance at all here, it was merely because they provided catchwords that gave a flattering label to the crude instincts of the mass. But this should in no way blind us to the fact that, for those who kindled the quarrel, *homoousia* and *homoiousia* were a very serious matter. For concealed within it, both historically and psychologically, lay the Ebionite creed of a purely human Christ with only relative ("apparent") divinity, and the Docetist creed of a purely divine Christ with only apparent corporeality. And beneath this level in turn lies the great psychological schism. The one position attaches supreme value and importance to the sensuously perceptible, whose subject, though it may not always be human and personal, is nevertheless always a projected human sensation; the other maintains that the chief value lies with the abstract and extrahuman, whose subject is the function; in other words, with the objective process of nature, that runs its course determined by impersonal law, beyond human sensation, of which it is the actual foundation. The former standpoint overlooks the function in favour of the function-complex, if man may be so regarded; the latter overlooks man as the indispensable subject in favour of the function. Each standpoint denies the principal value of the other. The more resolutely the adherents of either stand-

21

point identify themselves with it, the more they strive, with the best intentions perhaps, to force it on the other, and thereby violate the other's supreme value.

33   Another aspect of the type conflict appears in the Pelagian controversy at the beginning of the fifth century. The experience so profoundly felt by Tertullian, that man cannot avoid sin even after baptism, grew with Augustine—who in many ways was not unlike Tertullian—into that thoroughly characteristic, pessimistic doctrine of original sin, whose essence consists in the concupiscence[9] inherited from Adam. Over against the fact of original sin there stood, according to Augustine, the redeeming grace of God, with the institution of the Church ordained by his grace to administer the means of salvation. In this scheme of things the value of man stands very low. He is really nothing but a miserable rejected creature, who is delivered over to the devil under all circumstances, unless through the medium of the Church, the sole means of salvation, he is made a participator of the divine grace. Not only man's value, but his moral freedom and his self-determination crumbled away accordingly, with the result that the value and significance of the Church as an *idea* were so much the more enhanced, as was altogether in keeping with Augustine's explicit programme in the *Civitas Dei*.

34   Against such a stifling conception there rises ever anew the feeling of man's freedom and moral value—a feeling that will not long endure suppression whether by insight however searching, or logic however keen. The rightness of the feeling of human value found its defenders in Pelagius, a British monk, and Celestius, his pupil. Their teaching was founded on the moral freedom of man as a given fact. It is characteristic of the psychological kinship existing between the Pelagian standpoint and the Dyophysite view that the persecuted Pelagians found an advocate in Nestorius, the Metropolitan of Constantinople. Nestorius stressed the separation of the two natures of Christ in contrast to the Cyrillian doctrine of the φυσικὴ ἕνωσις, physical oneness of Christ as the God-man. Also, Nestorius definitely did not want Mary to be understood as the Θεοτόκος (God-bearer), but merely as the Χριστοτόκος (Christ-

[9] We would rather say untamed libido, which, in the form of *heimarmene* (compulsion of the stars, or fate), leads man into wrongdoing and corruption.

bearer). With some justification he even called the idea that Mary was the mother of God heathenish. From him originated the Nestorian controversy, which finally ended with the secession of the Nestorian Church.

3. THE PROBLEM OF TRANSUBSTANTIATION

35   With the immense political upheavals of that age, the collapse of the Roman Empire, and the decay of ancient civilization, these controversies likewise passed into oblivion. But when, after several centuries, a state of stability was again reached, the psychological differences also reappeared in their characteristic ways, tentatively at first but becoming ever more intense with advancing civilization. No longer was it the problems that had thrown the early Church into an uproar; new forms had been devised, but underneath them the same psychology was concealed.

36   About the middle of the ninth century the Abbot Paschasius Radbertus appeared on the scene with a treatise on the Communion, in which he propounded the doctrine of the transubstantiation, i.e., the assertion that the wine and holy wafer become transformed into the actual blood and body of Christ. As is well known, this view became a dogma, according to which the transformation is accomplished *vere, realiter, substantialiter* (in truth, in reality, in substance). Although the "accidentals," the bread and wine, preserve their outward aspect, they are substantially the flesh and blood of Christ. Against this extreme concretization of a symbol Ratramnus, a monk of the same monastery where Radbertus was abbot, ventured to raise some opposition. However, Radbertus found a more resolute opponent in Scotus Erigena, one of the great philosophers and daring thinkers of the early Middle Ages, who, as Hase says in his *History of the Christian Church*, towered so high and solitary above his time that his doctrines were not sufficiently understood to be condemned by the Church until the thirteenth century. As abbot of Malmesbury, he was butchered by his own monks about the year 889. Scotus Erigena, for whom true philosophy was also true religion, was no blind follower of authority and the "once accepted" because,

unlike the majority of his age, he himself could think. He set reason above authority, very unseasonably perhaps but in a way that assured him the acclaim of later centuries. Even the Church Fathers, who were considered to be above discussion, he held as authorities only in so far as the treasures of human reason were contained in their writings. Thus he also held that the Communion was nothing more than a commemoration of that last supper which Jesus celebrated with his disciples, a view in which all reasonable men in every age will concur. Scotus Erigena, clear and humanistic as he was in his thinking, and however little disposed to detract from the significance and value of the sacred ceremony, was not attuned to the spirit of his age and the desires of the world around him, a fact that might, indeed, be inferred from his assassination by his own comrades of the cloister. Because he could think rationally and logically success did not come to him; instead, it fell to Radbertus, who assuredly could not think, but who "transubstantiated" the symbolic and meaningful and made it coarse and sensual, attuned as he obviously was to the spirit of his age, which was all for the concretization of religious experiences.

37   Again in this controversy we can easily recognize the basic elements we have already met in the disputes discussed earlier: the abstract standpoint that abhors any contamination with the concrete object, and the concretistic that is turned towards the object.

38   Far be it from us to pronounce, from the intellectual standpoint, a one-sided, depreciatory judgment on Radbertus and his achievement. Although to the modern mind this dogma must appear simply absurd, we should not be misled on that account into declaring it historically worthless. Certainly it is a showpiece for every collection of human aberrations, but that does not establish its worthlessness *eo ipso*. Before passing judgment, we must carefully examine what this dogma accomplished in the religious life of that epoch, and what our age still owes indirectly to its effect. It must not be overlooked, for instance, that it is precisely the belief in the reality of this miracle that demands a detachment of the psychic process from the purely sensual, and this cannot remain without influence on the psychic process itself. Directed thinking becomes absolutely impossible when the sensual has too high a thresh-

old value. Because its value is too high it constantly intrudes into the psyche, where it disrupts and destroys the function of directed thinking which is based on the exclusion of everything incompatible with thought. From this elementary consideration follows the practical importance of rites and dogmas that prove their value not only from this point of view but from a purely opportunistic and biological one, not to speak of the immediate, specifically religious effects accruing to individuals from a belief in this dogma. Highly as we esteem Scotus Erigena, the less is it permitted to despise the achievement of Radbertus. But what we may learn from this example is that the thinking of the introvert is incommensurable with the thinking of the extravert, since the two forms of thinking, as regards their determinants, are wholly and fundamentally different. We might perhaps say that the thinking of the introvert is *rational*, while that of the extravert is *programmatic*.

39   These arguments, I wish particularly to emphasize, do not pretend to have said anything decisive about the individual psychology of our two protagonists. What we know of Scotus Erigena personally—it is little enough—is not sufficient for us to make a sure diagnosis of his type. What we do know speaks in favour of the introverted type. Of Radbertus we know next to nothing. We know only that he said something that contradicted ordinary human thinking, but with surer logic of feeling surmised what his age was prepared to accept as suitable. This would speak in favour of the extraverted type. For insufficient knowledge we must suspend judgment on both personalities, since, particularly in the case of Radbertus, the matter might well be decided quite differently. He might equally well have been an introvert, but with limited reasoning powers that in no way rose above the conceptions of his milieu, and with a logic so lacking in originality that it was just sufficient to draw the obvious conclusion from the premises already laid down in the writings of the Church Fathers. Conversely, Scotus Erigena might as well have been an extravert, if it could be shown that he lived in a milieu that was distinguished in any case by common sense and that considered a corresponding assertion suitable and desirable. But this has in no sense been demonstrated. On the other hand, we do know how great was the yearning of that age for the reality of religious miracles. To an age so

constituted, the views of Scotus Erigena must have seemed cold and deadening, whereas the assertion of Radbertus must have been felt as life-promoting, since it concretized what everyone desired.

4. NOMINALISM AND REALISM

40   The Communion controversy of the ninth century was merely the signal for a much greater controversy that divided the minds of men for centuries and had incalculable consequences. This was the conflict between nominalism and realism. By nominalism is meant that school which asserted that the so-called universals, namely generic or universal concepts such as beauty, goodness, animal, man, etc., are nothing but *nomina*, names, or words, derisively called *flatus vocis*. Anatole France says: "What is thinking? And how does one think? We think with words; that in itself is sensual and brings us back to nature. Think of it! A metaphysician has nothing with which to construct his world system except the perfected cries of monkeys and dogs."[10] This is extreme nominalism, as it is when Nietzsche says that reason is "speech metaphysics."

41   Realism, on the contrary, affirms the existence of universals *ante rem*, and holds that general concepts exist in themselves after the manner of Platonic ideas. In spite of its ecclesiastical associations, nominalism is a sceptical tendency that denies the separate existence characteristic of abstractions. It is a kind of scientific scepticism coupled with the most rigid dogmatism. Its concept of reality necessarily coincides with the sensuous reality of things; their individuality represents the real as opposed to the abstract idea. Strict realism, on the contrary, transfers the accent on reality to the abstract, the idea, the universal, which it posits before the thing (*ante rem*).

a. The Problem of Universals in Antiquity

42   As our reference to the doctrine of Platonic ideas shows, we are dealing with a conflict that reaches very far back in time. Certain envenomed remarks in Plato concerning "grey-bearded schoolboys" and the "mentally poverty-stricken" are

10 *Le Jardin d'Epicure*, p. 8o.

innuendos aimed at the adherents of two allied schools of philosophy that were at odds with the Platonic spirit, these being the Cynics and the Megarians. Antisthenes, the leader of the former school, although by no means a stranger to the Socratic ambiance and even a friend of Xenophon, was nevertheless avowedly inimical to Plato's beautiful world of ideas. He even wrote a pamphlet against Plato, in which he scurrilously changed Plato's name to Σάθων. Σάθων means 'boy' or 'man,' but under his sexual aspect, since σάθων comes from σάθη, 'penis,' 'cock'; whereby Antisthenes, through the time-honoured method of projection, delicately suggests what cause he is defending against Plato. For Origen, as we saw, this was also a prime cause, the very devil whom he sought to lay low by means of self-castration, in order to pass without hindrance into the richly furnished world of ideas. Antisthenes, however, was a pre-Christian pagan, and for him what the phallus has stood for from time immemorial as the acknowledged symbol was of heartfelt interest, namely the delights of the senses—not that he was alone in this, for as we know it affected the whole Cynic school, whose cry was "Back to Nature!" There were plenty of reasons that might have thrust his concrete feeling and sensation into the foreground; he was before everything a proletarian, who made a virtue of his envy. He was no ἰθαγενής, no thoroughbred Greek. He was an outsider, and he taught outside too, before the gates of Athens, where he flaunted his proletarian behaviour, a model of Cynic philosophy. Moreover, the whole school was composed of proletarians, or at least of people on the fringe, all of whom indulged in corrosive criticism of the traditional values.

43 After Antisthenes one of the most prominent members of the school was Diogenes, who conferred on himself the title of Κύων, 'dog,' and whose tomb was adorned by a dog in Parian marble. Despite his warm love of man, for his whole nature was suffused with human understanding, he nonetheless pitilessly satirized everything that the men of his time held sacred. He ridiculed the horror that gripped the spectator in the theatre at the sight of Thyestes' repast,[11] or the incestuous tragedy

---

[11] [Thyestes, son of Pelops, in the course of a struggle for the kingdom with his brother Atreus, was given, unknown to himself, the flesh of his own children to eat.—EDITORS.]

of Oedipus; anthropophagy was not so bad, since human flesh can claim no exceptional position among meats, and furthermore the mishap of an incestuous affair is not such a disaster after all, as the instructive example of our domestic animals makes plain to us. In many respects the Megarian school was akin to the Cynics. Was not Megara the unsuccessful rival of Athens? After a most promising start, when Megara rose to prominence through the founding of Byzantium and Hyblaeaic Megara in Sicily, internal squabbles broke out, after which Megara sickened and wasted away, and was in every respect outstripped by Athens. Loutish peasant wit was known in Athens as "Megarian jesting." This envy, which in the defeated is imbibed with the mother's milk, might explain not a little that is characteristic of Megarian philosophy. Like that of the Cynics, it was thoroughly nominalistic and utterly opposed to the realism of Plato's ideology.

44   Another leading figure in this school was Stilpon of Megara, about whom the following characteristic anecdote is related. One day Stilpon came to Athens and saw on the Acropolis the wondrous statue of Pallas Athene made by Phidias. A true Megarian, he remarked that it was not the daughter of Zeus but of Phidias. This jest catches the whole spirit of Megarian thinking, for Stilpon taught that generic concepts are without reality and objective validity. Anyone, therefore, who speaks of "man" speaks of nobody, because he is designating οὔτε τόνδε οὔτε τόνδε (neither this nor that). Plutarch ascribes to him the statement ἕτερον ἑτέρου μὴ κατηγορεῖσθαι (one thing can affirm nothing concerning [the nature of] another).[12] The teaching of Antisthenes was very similar. The oldest exponent of this type of propositional thinking seems to have been Antiphon of Rhamnos, a sophist and contemporary of Socrates. One of his propositions runs: "A man who perceives long objects neither sees the length with his eyes nor can perceive it with his mind."[13] The denial of the substantiality of generic concepts follows directly from this proposition. Naturally the whole position of Platonic ideas is undermined by this type of thinking, for with Plato it is just the ideas that have eternal and immutable validity, while the "real" and the

12 Plutarch, *Adversus Colotem*, 22.
13 [Cf. Gomperz, *Greek Thinkers*, I, p. 434.]

"many" are merely their fugitive reflections. From the realist standpoint, the Cynic-Megarian critique breaks down generic concepts into purely sophisticated and descriptive nomina lacking any substantiality, and lays the accent on the individual thing.

45   This manifest and fundamental opposition was clearly conceived by Gomperz[14] as the problem of *inherence* and *predication*. When, for instance, we speak of "warm" and "cold," we speak of warm and cold things, to which "warm" and "cold" belong as attributes, predicates, or assertions. The assertion refers to something perceived and actually existing, namely to a warm or a cold body. From a plurality of similar cases we abstract the concepts of "warmth" and "coldness," which again we immediately connect in our thoughts with something concrete, thing-like. Thus "warmth" and "coldness" are thing-like for us because of the reverberation of sense-perception in the abstraction. It is extremely difficult for us to strip the abstraction of its "thingness," for there naturally clings to every abstraction the thing it is abstracted from. In this sense the thingness of the predicate is actually an *a priori*. If we now pass to the next higher generic concept, "temperature," we still have no difficulty in perceiving its thingness, which, though it has lost its definiteness for the senses, nevertheless retains the quality of representability that adheres to every sense-perception. If we then ascend to a very much higher generic concept, such as "energy," its thing-like character quite disappears, and with it, to a certain extent, goes the quality of representability. At this point the conflict arises about the "nature" of energy: whether energy is purely conceptual and abstract, or whether it is something "real." The learned nominalist of our day is quite convinced that energy is nothing but a name, a mere counter in our mental calculus; but in spite of this, in our everyday speech we treat energy as though it were thing-like, thus sowing in our heads the greatest confusion from the standpoint of the theory of knowledge.

46   The thing-likeness of the purely conceptual, which creeps so naturally into the process of abstraction and brings about the "reality" of the predicate or the abstract idea, is no artificial product, no arbitrary hypostatizing of a concept, but a natural

14 Ibid., II, pp. 175ff.

necessity. It is not that the abstract idea is arbitrarily hypostatized and transplanted into a transcendental world of equally artificial origin; the actual historical process is quite the reverse. Among primitives, for instance, the imago, the psychic reverberation of the sense-perception, is so strong and so sensuously coloured that when it is reproduced as a spontaneous memory-image it sometimes even has the quality of an hallucination. Thus when the memory-image of his dead mother suddenly reappears to a primitive, it is as if it were her ghost that he sees and hears. We only "think" of the dead, but the primitive actually perceives them because of the extraordinary sensuousness of his mental images. This explains the primitive's belief in ghosts and spirits; they are what we quite simply call "thoughts." When the primitive "thinks," he literally has visions, whose reality is so great that he constantly mistakes the psychic for the real. Powell says: "The confusion of confusions is that universal habit of savagery—the confusion of the objective with the subjective."[15] Spencer and Gillen observe: "What a savage experiences during a dream is just as real to him as what he sees when he is awake."[16] What I myself have seen of the psychology of the Negro completely endorses these findings. From this basic fact of the psychic realism and autonomy of the image vis-à-vis the autonomy of the sense-perception springs the belief in spirits, and not from any need of explanation on the part of the primitive, which is merely imputed to him by Europeans. For the primitive, thought is visionary and auditory, hence it also has the character of revelation. Thus the sorcerer, the visionary, is always the thinker of the tribe, who brings about the manifestation of the spirits or gods. This also explains the magical effect of thought; it is as good as the deed, just because it is real. In the same way the word, the outer covering of thought, has a "real" effect because it calls up "real" memory-images. Primitive superstition surprises us only because we have largely succeeded in de-sensualizing the psychic image; we have learnt to think abstractly—always, of course, with the above-mentioned limitations. Nevertheless, as anybody who is engaged in the practice of analytical psychology knows, even "educated" European patients constantly need re-

[15] "Sketch of the Mythology of the North American Indians," p. 20.
[16] *The Northern Tribes of Central Australia*, p. 451.

minding that thinking is not doing—one patient because he believes that to think something is enough, another because he
feels he must not think something or he would immediately
have to go and do it.

47   How easily the primitive reality of the psychic image reappears is shown by the dreams of normal people and the hallucinations that accompany mental derangement. The mystics
even endeavour to recapture the primitive reality of the imago
by means of an artificial introversion, in order to counterbalance extraversion. There is an excellent example of this in the
initiation of the Mohammedan mystic Tewekkul-Beg, by
Molla-Shah. Tewekkul-Beg relates:

> After these words he called me to seat myself opposite to him, while
> still my senses were as though bemused, and commanded me to
> create his own image in my inner self; and after he had bound my
> eyes, he bade me gather all the forces of the soul into my heart. I
> obeyed, and in the twinkling of an eye, by divine favour and with
> the spiritual succour of the Sheik, my heart was opened. I beheld
> there in my innermost self something resembling an overturned
> bowl; when this vessel was righted, a feeling of boundless joy
> flooded through my whole being. I said to the Master: "From this
> cell, in which I am seated before you, I behold within me a true vi-
> sion, and it is as though another Tewekkul-Beg were seated before
> another Molla-Shah."[17]

The Master explained this to him as the first phenomenon of
his initiation. Other visions soon followed, once the way to the
primitive image of the real had been opened.

48   The reality of the predicate is given *a priori* since it has
always existed in the human mind. Only by subsequent criticism is the abstraction deprived of the quality of reality. Even
in Plato's time the belief in the magical reality of verbal concepts was so great that it was worth the philosopher's while to
devise traps or fallacies by which he was able, through the
absolute significance of words, to elicit an absurd reply. A simple example is the Enkekalymmenos (veiled man) fallacy devised by the Megarian philosopher Eubulides: "Can you recognize your father? — Yes. Can you recognize this veiled man?
— No. You contradict yourself; this veiled man is your father.
Thus you can recognize your father and at the same time not

[17] Buber, *Ekstatische Konfessionen*, pp. 31f.

recognize him." The fallacy merely lies in this, that the person questioned naïvely assumes the word "recognize" refers in all cases to the same objective fact, whereas in reality its validity is restricted to certain definite cases. The Keratines (horned man) fallacy is based on the same principle: "What you have not lost, you still have. You have not lost horns, therefore you have horns." Here too the fallacy lies in the naïveté of the subject, who assumes in the premise a specific fact. With the help of this method it could be convincingly shown that the absolute significance of words was an illusion. As a result, the reality of the generic concept, which in the form of the Platonic idea had a metaphysical existence and exclusive validity, was put in jeopardy. Gomperz says:

Men were not as yet possessed of that distrust of language which animates us moderns and frequently causes us to see in words a far from adequate expression of the facts. On the contrary, there was a simple and unsuspecting faith that the range of an idea and the range of the word roughly corresponding to it must in every case exactly coincide.[18]

49   In view of this magical, absolute significance of words, which presupposes that words also imply the objective behaviour of things, the Sophist critique was very much in place. It offered a striking proof of the impotence of language. In so far as ideas are merely names—a supposition that remains to be proved—the attack upon Plato was justified. But generic concepts cease to be mere names when they designate the similarities or conformities of things. The question then arises whether these conformities are objective realities or not. These conformities actually exist, hence the generic concept also corresponds with some kind of reality. It contains as much reality as does the exact description of a thing. The generic concept differs from the description only in that it describes or designates the conformities of things. The weakness, therefore, lies neither in the generic concept nor in the Platonic idea, but in its verbal expression, which obviously under no circumstances adequately reproduces either the thing or the conformity. The nominalist attack on the doctrine of ideas was thus in principle an unwarrantable encroachment, and Plato's exasperated counterstroke was fully justified.

[18] Cf. *Greek Thinkers*, II, p. 193.

50   According to Antisthenes, the principle of inherence consists in this, that not only can no kind of predicate be asserted of a subject which differs from it, but no predicate at all. Antisthenes granted as valid only those predicates that were identical with the subject. Apart from the fact that such statements of identity ("sweet is sweet") affirm nothing at all and are, therefore, meaningless, the weakness of the principle of inherence is that a statement of identity has also nothing to do with the thing: the word "grass" has no connection with the thing "grass." The principle of inherence suffers just as much from the old word-fetishism, which naïvely supposes that the word coincides with the thing. So when the nominalist tells the realist: "You are dreaming—you think you are dealing with things, but all the time you are fighting verbal chimeras!" the realist can answer the nominalist in precisely the same words; for neither is the nominalist dealing with things in themselves but with the words he has put in the place of things. Even when he uses a separate word for each individual thing, they are always only words and not the things themselves.

51   Now though the idea of energy is admittedly a mere verbal concept, it is nevertheless so extraordinarily real that your Electricity Company pays dividends out of it. The board of directors would certainly allow no metaphysical argument to convince them of the unreality of energy. "Energy" designates simply the conformity of the phenomena of force—a conformity that cannot be denied and that daily gives striking proof of its existence. So far as a thing is real, and a word conventionally designates that thing, the word also acquires reality-significance. And so far as the conformity of things is real, the generic concept designating that conformity likewise acquires reality-significance, a significance that is neither greater nor less than that of the word designating the individual thing. The shifting of the accent of value from one side to the other is a matter of individual attitude and the psychology of the time. Gomperz was also aware of these underlying psychological factors in Antisthenes, and brings out the following points:

Sound common sense, a resistance to all dreamy enthusiasm, perhaps also the strength of individual feeling that endows the personality and hence, probably, the individual's whole character with

33

the stamp of complete reality—these may well have been among the forces that swelled the tide of reaction.[19]

To this we might add the envy of a man without full rights of citizenship, a proletarian, a man upon whom fate had bestowed but little beauty, and who at best could only climb to the heights by demolishing the values of others. This was especially characteristic of the Cynic, who must forever be carping at others, and to whom nothing was sacred if it happened to belong to somebody else; he even had no compunction about destroying the peace of the home if he might seize an occasion to parade his invaluable advice.

52   To this essentially critical attitude of mind Plato's world of ideas with their eternal reality stands diametrically opposed. It is evident that the psychology of the man who fashioned that world had an orientation altogether foreign to the carping, corrosive judgments described above. From the world of multiplicity Plato's thinking abstracted and created synthetic constructive concepts, which designate and express the general conformities of things as that which truly exists. Their invisible and suprahuman quality is the direct opposite of the concretism of the principle of inherence, which would reduce the stuff of thought to the unique, the individual, the objective. This attempt is just as impossible as the exclusive acceptance of the principle of predication, which would exalt what has been affirmed of many isolated things to an eternally existing substance above all decay. Both forms of judgment are justifiable, as both are naturally present in every man. This is best seen, in my view, from the fact that the very founder of the Megarian school, Eucleides of Megara, established an "All-oneness" that was immeasurably far above the individual and particular. For he linked together the Eleatic principle of "being" with "good," so that for him "being" and "good" were identical. As opposed to this there was only "non-existing evil." This optimistic All-oneness was, of course, nothing but a generic concept of the highest order, one that simply included "being" but at the same time contradicted all evidence, far more so even than the Platonic ideas. With this concept Eucleides produced a compensation for the negatively critical

19 Cf. ibid., pp. 181f.

dissolution of constructive judgments into mere verbalities. His All-oneness was so remote and so vague that it utterly failed to express the conformity of things; it was no type at all, but rather the product of a desire for a unity that would embrace the disordered multitude of individual things. This desire forces itself on all those who pay homage to extreme nominalism, in so far as they make any attempt to escape from their negatively critical attitude. Hence it is not uncommon to find in people of this sort an idea of fundamental uniformity that is superlatively improbable and arbitrary. It is manifestly impossible to base oneself entirely on the principle of inherence. Gomperz pertinently observes:

Attempts of this nature are foredoomed to failure in every age. Their success was completely out of the question in an age that was destitute of historical understanding, and in which there was next to no insight into the deeper problems of psychology. It was not a mere risk, it was an absolute certainty that the more patent and palpable, but on the whole less important, values would thrust into the background others of greater moment, though less easily discerned. In taking the brute and the savage for a model in their efforts to lop off the excrescences of civilization, men laid a destroying hand upon much that was the fruit of an ascending process of development which must be measured in myriads of years.[20]

53   Constructive judgment—which, unlike inherence, is based on the conformity of things—has created general ideas that must be counted among the highest values of civilization. Even if these ideas relate only to the dead, we are nevertheless still bound to them by threads which, as Gomperz says, have gained an almost unbreakable strength. He continues:

Thus it is with the body bereft of life; but things which never possessed life may also have a claim on our forbearance, our reverence, even our self-sacrificing devotion; for example, statues, graves, the soldier's flag. And if we do violence to our nature, if we succeed in breaking by main force the bonds of association, we lapse into savagery, we suffer injury in our own souls by the loss of all those feelings which, so to speak, clothe the hard bedrock of naked reality with a garniture of verdant life. On the maintenance of these overgrowths of sentiment, on the due treasuring of acquired values, depend all the refinement, the beauty, and the grace of life, all

[20] Cf. ibid., pp. 167f.

ennobling of the animal instincts, together with all enjoyment and the pursuit of art—all, in short, that the Cynics set themselves to root up without scruple and without pity. There is, no doubt, a limit—so much we may readily concede to them and their not inconsiderable imitators of the present day—beyond which we cannot allow ourselves to be ruled by the principle of association without incurring the charge of that same folly and superstition which quite certainly grew out of the unlimited sway of that principle.[21]

54   We have gone so thoroughly into the problem of inherence and predication not only because this problem was revived in the nominalism and realism of the Scholastics but because it has never yet been finally set at rest and presumably never will be. For here again the question at issue is the typical opposition between the abstract standpoint, where the decisive value lies with the mental process itself, and the personal thinking and feeling which, consciously or unconsciously, underlie orientation by the objects of sense. In the latter case the mental process is simply a means for accentuating the personality. It is small wonder that it was precisely the proletarian philosophy that adopted the principle of inherence. Wherever sufficient reasons exist for laying the emphasis on personal feeling, thinking and feeling necessarily become negatively critical through lack of positive creative energy, which is all diverted to personal ends; they become a mere analytical organ that reduces everything to the concrete and particular. The resultant accumulation of disordered particulars is at best subordinated to a vague feeling of All-oneness, the wishful character of which is plain to see. But when the accent lies on the mental process, the product of the mind's activity is exalted above the disordered multiplicity as an *idea*. The idea is depersonalized as much as possible, while personal feeling passes over almost entirely into the mental process, which it hypostatizes.

55   Before proceeding further we might inquire whether the psychology of the Platonic doctrine of ideas justifies us in the supposition that Plato may personally have belonged to the introverted type, and whether the psychology of the Cynics and Megarians allows us to count such figures as Antisthenes, Diogenes, and Stilpon among the extraverts. Put in this form,

21 Cf. ibid., p. 168.

the question is absolutely impossible to answer. An extremely careful examination of Plato's authentic writings considered as *documents humains* might perhaps enable one to conclude to which type he belonged, but I for my part would not venture to pronounce any positive judgment. If someone were to furnish evidence that Plato belonged to the extraverted type, it would not surprise me. What has been handed down concerning the others is so very fragmentary that in my opinion a decision is out of the question. Since the two types of thinking we have been discussing depend on a displacement of the accent of value, it is of course equally possible that in the case of the introvert personal feeling may, for various reasons, be pushed into the foreground and will subordinate thinking, so that his thinking becomes negatively critical. For the extravert, the accent of value lies on his relation to the object as such, and not necessarily on his personal relation to it. When the relation to the object occupies the foreground, the mental process is already subordinate; but, if it concerns itself exclusively with the nature of the object and avoids the admixture of personal feeling, it does not possess a destructive character. We have, therefore, to class the particular conflict between the principles of inherence and predication as a special case, which in the further course of our investigation will be examined more thoroughly. The special nature of this case lies in the positive and negative parts played by personal feeling. When the type (generic concept) reduces the individual thing to a shadow, the type has acquired the reality of a collective idea. But when the value of the individual thing abolishes the type (generic concept), anarchic disintegration is at work. Both positions are extreme and unfair, but they form a contrasting picture whose clear outlines, by their very exaggeration, throw into relief features which, in a milder and more covert form, are also inherent in the nature of the introverted and extraverted types, even in the case of individuals in whom personal feeling is not pushed into the foreground. For instance, it makes a considerable difference whether the mental function is master or servant. The master thinks and feels differently from the servant. Even the most far-reaching abstraction of the personal in favour of the general value can never quite eliminate the personal admixtures. And in so far as these exist, thinking and

37

feeling will contain destructive tendencies that come from the self-assertion of the person in the face of unfavourable social conditions. But it would surely be a great mistake if, for the sake of personal tendencies, we were to reduce the traditional universal values to personal undercurrents. That would be pseudo-psychology, but it nevertheless exists.

b. The Problem of Universals in Scholasticism

56 The problem of the two forms of judgment remained unsolved because—*tertium non datur.* Porphyry handed down the problem to the Middle Ages thus: "As regards universal and generic concepts, the real question is whether they are substantial or merely intellectual, whether corporeal or incorporeal, whether separate from sensible things or in and around them."[22] The Scholastics took up the problem in this form. They started with the Platonic view, the *universalia ante rem,* the universal idea as the pattern or exemplar above all individual things and altogether detached from them, existing ἐν οὐρανίῳ τόπῳ, 'in a heavenly place.' As the wise Diotima says to Socrates in the dialogue on beauty:

> Nor again will this beauty appear to him like the beauty of a face or hands or anything else corporeal, or like the beauty of a thought or a science, or like beauty which has its seat in something other than itself, be it a living thing or the earth or the sky or anything else whatever; he will see it as absolute, existing alone with itself, unique, eternal, and all other beautiful things as partaking of it, yet in such manner that, while they come into being and pass away, it neither undergoes any increase or diminution nor suffers any change.[23]

57 Opposed to the Platonic form, as we saw, was the critical assumption that generic concepts are mere words. Here the real is *prius,* the ideal *posterius.* This view was designated *universalia post rem.* Between the two conceptions stood the

---

22 Cf. *The Organon, or Logical Treatises of Aristotle, with the Introduction of Porphyry,* II, pp. 609f.

23 *Symposium,* 211B (trans. Hamilton), pp. 93f. [In similar contexts, Jung cited from Plato the phrase "a supra-celestial place" or "a place beyond the skies," which is from *Phaedrus* 247C. See "The Structure of the Psyche," par. 336; "Psychological Aspects of the Mother Archetype," par. 149; "Transformation Symbolism in the Mass," par. 430; "Flying Saucers," par. 621.—EDITORS.]

moderate, realistic view of Aristotle which we might call *universalia in re*, that form (εἶδος) and matter coexist. The Aristotelian standpoint is a concretistic attempt at mediation fully in accord with Aristotle's nature. As against the transcendentalism of his teacher Plato, whose school afterwards relapsed into Pythagorean mysticism, Aristotle was entirely a man of reality—of classical reality, one should add, which contained much in concrete form that later ages abstracted and added to the inventory of the human mind. His solution reflected the concretism of classical common sense.

58   These three forms also reveal the structure of medieval opinion in the great controversy about universals, which was the quintessence of Scholasticism. It cannot be my task—even if I were competent—to probe more deeply into the details of this controversy. I must content myself with hints for the purpose of general orientation. The dispute began with the views of Johannes Roscellinus towards the end of the eleventh century. Universals were for him nothing but *nomina rerum*, names of things, or, as tradition says, *flatus vocis*. For him there were only individual things. He was, as Taylor aptly observes, "strongly held by the reality of individuals."[24] To think of God, too, as only individual was the next obvious conclusion, though actually it dissolved the Trinity into three separate persons, so that Roscellinus arrived at tritheism. This was intolerable to the prevailing realism of the times, and in 1092 his views were condemned by a synod at Soissons. The opposing side was represented by William of Champeaux, the teacher of Abelard, an extreme realist but of Aristotelian complexion. According to Abelard, he taught that one and the same thing existed in its totality and at the same time in separate individual things. There were no essential differences between individual things, but merely a multitude of "accidentals." By this concept the actual differences between things were explained as fortuitous, just as in the dogma of transubstantiation the bread and wine, as such, were only "accidentals."

59   On the realist side there was also Anselm of Canterbury, the father of Scholasticism. A true Platonist, the universals resided for him in the divine Logos. It is in this spirit that we must understand the psychologically important proof of God

[24] *The Mediaeval Mind*, II, p. 340.

advanced by Anselm, which is known as the ontological proof. This proof demonstrates the existence of God from the idea of God. Fichte formulates it trenchantly as follows: "The existence of the idea of an Absolute in our consciousness proves the real existence of this Absolute."[25] Anselm held that the concept of a Supreme Being present in the intellect also implied the quality of existence (*non potest esse in intellectu solo*). He continued: "So, then, there truly is a being than which a greater cannot be thought—so truly that it cannot even be thought of as not existing. And thou art this being, O Lord our God."[26] The logical weakness of the ontological argument is so obvious that it even requires a psychological explanation to show how a mind like Anselm's could advance such an argument. The immediate cause is to be sought in psychological disposition of realism in general, namely in the fact that there was not only a certain class of men but, in keeping with the current of the age, also certain groups of men for whom the accent of value lay on the idea, so that the idea represented for them a higher reality or value for life than the reality of individual things. Hence it seemed simply impossible to suppose that what to them was most valuable and significant should not *really* exist. Indeed, they had the most striking proof of its efficacy in their own hands, since their whole lives, their thinking and feeling, were entirely oriented by this point of view. The invisibility of an idea mattered little in comparison with its extraordinary efficacy, which was indeed a reality. They had an ideal, and not a sensual, concept of the real.

60   A contemporary opponent of Anselm's, Gaunilo, raised the objection that the oft-recurring idea of the Islands of the Blessed (based on Homer's land of the Phaeacians, *Odyssey*, VIII) does not necessarily prove their actual existence. This objection is palpably reasonable. Similar objections were raised in the course of the centuries, though they did nothing to prevent the ontological argument surviving even down to quite recent times, it being espoused in the nineteenth century

---

25 *Psychologie*, II, p. 120.

26 "Sic ergo vere est aliquid, quo majus cogitari non potest, ut nec cogitari possit non esse, et hoc es tu, Domine Deus Noster" (*Proslogion*, trans. Fairweather, p. 74).

by Hegel, Fichte, and Lotze. Such contradictory statements cannot be ascribed to some peculiar defect in the logic of these thinkers or to an even greater delusion on one side or the other. That would be absurd. Rather is it a matter of deep-seated psychological differences which must be acknowledged and clearly stated. The assumption that only *one* psychology exists or only *one* fundamental psychological principle is an intolerable tyranny, a pseudo-scientific prejudice of the common man. People always speak of man and his "psychology" as though there were "nothing but" that psychology. In the same way one always talks of "reality" as though it were the only one. Reality is simply what works in a human soul and not what is assumed by certain people to work there, and about which prejudiced generalizations are wont to be made. Even when this is done in a scientific spirit, it should not be forgotten that science is not the *summa* of life, that it is actually only one of the psychological attitudes, only one of the forms of human thought.

61   The ontological argument is neither argument nor proof, but merely the psychological demonstration of the fact that there is a class of men for whom a definite idea has efficacy and reality—a reality that even rivals the world of perception. The sensualist brags about the undeniable certainty of his reality, and the idealist insists on his. Psychology has to resign itself to the existence of these two (or more) types, and must at all costs avoid thinking of one as a misconception of the other; and it should never seriously try to reduce one type to the other, as though everything "other" were merely a function of the one. This does not mean that the scientific axiom known as Occam's razor—"explanatory principles should not be multiplied beyond the necessary"—should be abrogated. But the need for a plurality of psychological explanatory principles still remains. Aside from the arguments already adduced in favour of this, our eyes ought to have been opened by the remarkable fact that, notwithstanding the apparently final overthrow of the ontological proof by Kant, there are still not a few post-Kantian philosophers who have taken it up again. And we are today just as far or perhaps even further from an understanding of the pairs of opposites—idealism / realism, spiritualism /

materialism, and all the subsidiary questions they raise—than were the men of the early Middle Ages, who at least had a common philosophy of life.

62   There can surely be no logical argument that appeals to the modern intellect in favour of the ontological proof. The ontological argument in itself has really nothing to do with logic; in the form in which Anselm bequeathed it to history it is a subsequently intellectualized or rationalized *psychological fact*, and naturally this could never have come about without begging the question and sundry other sophistries. But it is just here that the unassailable validity of the argument shows itself—in the fact that it exists, and that the *consensus gentium* proves it to be a fact of universal occurrence. It is the fact that has to be reckoned with, not the sophistry of its proof. The mistake of the ontological argument consists simply and solely in its trying to argue logically, when in reality it is very much more than a merely logical proof. The real point is that it is a psychological fact whose existence and efficacy are so overwhelmingly clear that no sort of argumentation is needed to prove it. The *consensus gentium* proves that, in the statement "God *is*, because he is thought," Anselm was right. It is an obvious truth, indeed nothing but a statement of identity. The "logical" argumentation about it is quite superfluous, and false to boot, inasmuch as Anselm wanted to establish his idea of God as a concrete reality. He says: "Without doubt, therefore, there exists, both in the understanding and in reality [*in intellectu et in re*], something than which a greater cannot be thought."[27] For the Scholastics, the concept *res* was something that existed on the same level as thought. Thus Dionysius the Areopagite, whose writings exercised a considerable influence on early medieval philosophy, distinguished the categories *entia rationalia, intellectualia, sensibilia, simpliciter existentia*. For Thomas Aquinas, *res* was *quod est in anima* (what is in the soul) as well as *quod est extra animam* (what is outside the soul).[28] This remarkable equation allows us to discern the primitive "thing-likeness" (*res* = "reality") of thought in the conceptions of that time. It is a state of mind that makes the psychology of

[27] Ibid.

[28] *Scriptum supra libros Sententiarum magistri Petri Lombardi*, I, dist. 25, qu. 1, art. 4 (ed. Mandonnet, I, p. 612).

42

the ontological proof readily understandable. The hypostatizing of the idea was not at all an essential step, but was implicit as a reverberation of the primitive sensuousness of thought. Gaunilo's counter-argument was psychologically unsatisfactory, for although, as the *consensus gentium* proves, the idea of the Islands of the Blessed frequently occurs, it is unquestionably less effective than the idea of God, which consequently acquires a higher reality-value.

63   Later writers who took up the ontological argument again all fell, at least in principle, into Anselm's error. Kant's reasoning should be final. We will therefore briefly outline it. He says:

The concept of an absolutely necessary being is a concept of pure reason, that is, a mere idea the objective reality of which is very far from being proved by the fact that reason requires it. . . . But the unconditioned necessity of judgments is not the same as an absolute necessity of things. The absolute necessity of the judgment is only a conditioned necessity of the thing, or of the predicate in the judgment.[29]

64   Immediately prior to this Kant shows, as an example of a necessary judgment, that a triangle must have three angles. He is referring to this proposition when he continues:

The above proposition does not declare that three angles are absolutely necessary, but that, under the condition that there is a triangle (that is, that a triangle is given), three angles will necessarily be found in it. So great, indeed, is the power of illusion exercised by this logical necessity that, by the simple device of forming an *a priori* concept of a thing in such a manner as to include existence within the scope of its meaning, we have supposed ourselves to have justified the conclusion that because existence necessarily belongs to the object of this concept—always under the condition that we posit the thing as given (as existing)—we are also of necessity, in accordance with the law of identity, required to posit the existence of its object, and that this being is therefore itself absolutely necessary—and this, to repeat, for the reason that the existence of this being has already been thought in a concept which is assumed arbitrarily and on condition that we posit its object.[30]

29 *Critique of Pure Reason* (trans. Kemp Smith), pp. 500f.
30 Ibid., pp. 510f.

65   The "power of illusion" referred to here is nothing else than the primitive, *magical power of the word*, which likewise mysteriously inhabits the concept. It needed a long process of development before man recognized once and for all that the word, the *flatus vocis*, does not always signify a reality or bring it into being. The fact that certain men have realized this has not by any means been able to uproot in every mind the power of superstition that dwells in formulated concepts. There is evidently something in this "instinctive" superstition that refuses to be exterminated, because it has some sort of justification which till now has not been sufficiently appreciated. In like manner the false conclusion creeps into the ontological argument, through an illusion which Kant now proceeds to elucidate. He begins with the assertion of "absolutely necessary subjects," the conception of which is inherent in the concept of existence, and which therefore cannot be dismissed without inner contradiction. This conception would be that of the "supremely real being":

It is declared that it possesses all reality, and that we are justified in assuming that such a being is possible. . . . Now the "all reality" includes existence; existence is therefore contained in the concept of a thing that is possible. If, then, this thing is rejected, the internal possibility of the thing is rejected—which is self-contradictory . . . in that case either the thought, which is in us, is the thing itself, or we have presupposed an existence as belonging to the realm of the possible, and have then, on that pretext, inferred its existence from its internal possibility—which is nothing but a miserable tautology.[31]

Being is evidently not a real predicate; that is, it is not a concept of something which could be added to the concept of a thing. It is merely the positing of a thing, or of certain of its determinants. In logical usage, it is merely the copula of a judgment. The proposition "God is omnipotent" contains two concepts, each of which has its object—God and omnipotence. The little word "is" adds no new predicate, but only serves to posit the predicate *in its relation* to the subject. If, now, we take the subject (God) with all its predicates (among which is omnipotence) and say "God is" or "There is a God," we attach no new predicate to the concept of God, but only posit the subject in itself with all its predicates, and indeed posit it as being an *object* that stands in relation to my *concept*. The content

[31] Ibid., p. 503.

of both must be one and the same; nothing can have been added to the concept, which expresses merely what is possible, by my thinking its object (through the expression "it is") as given absolutely. Otherwise stated, the real contains no more than the merely possible. A hundred real thalers do not contain a cent more than a hundred possible thalers. . . . My financial position is, however, affected very differently by a hundred real thalers than it is by the mere concept of them (that is, of their possibility).[32]

Whatever, therefore, and however much, our concept of an object may contain, we must go outside it, if we are to ascribe existence to the object. In the case of objects of the senses, this takes place through their connection with some one of our perceptions, in accordance with empirical laws. But in dealing with objects of pure thought, we have no means whatsoever of knowing their existence, since it would have to be known in a completely *a priori* manner. Our consciousness of all existence (whether immediately through perception, or mediately through inferences which connect something with perception) belongs exclusively to the unity of experience; any [alleged] existence outside this field, while not indeed such as we can declare to be absolutely impossible, is of the nature of an assumption which we can never be in a position to justify.[33]

66   This detailed reminder of Kant's fundamental exposition seems to me necessary, because it is precisely here that we find the clearest division between *esse in intellectu* and *esse in re.* Hegel cast the reproach at Kant that one could not compare the concept of God with an imaginary hundred thalers. But, as Kant rightly pointed out, logic strips away all content, for it would no longer be logic if a content were to prevail. From the standpoint of logic, there is, as always, no *tertium* between the logical either-or. But between *intellectus* and *res* there is still *anima,* and this *esse in anima* makes the whole ontological argument superfluous. Kant himself, in his *Critique of Practical Reason,* made an attempt on a grand scale to evaluate the *esse in anima* in philosophical terms. There he introduces God as a postulate of practical reason resulting from the *a priori* recognition of "respect for moral law necessarily directed towards the highest good, and the consequent supposition of its objective reality."[34]

67   The *esse in anima,* then, is a psychological fact, and the

---

32 Ibid., pp. 504f.   33 Ibid., p. 506.
34 Cf. *Critique of Practical Reason,* pp. 226f.

only thing that needs ascertaining is whether it occurs but once, often, or universally in human psychology. The datum which is called "God" and is formulated as the "highest good" signifies, as the term itself shows, the supreme psychic value. In other words it is a concept upon which is conferred, or is actually endowed with, the highest and most general significance in determining our thoughts and actions. In the language of analytical psychology, the God-concept coincides with the particular ideational complex which, in accordance with the foregoing definition, concentrates in itself the maximum amount of libido, or psychic energy. Accordingly, the actual God-concept is, psychologically, completely different in different people, as experience testifies. Even as an idea God is not a single, constant being, and still less so in reality. For, as we know, the highest value operative in a human soul is variously located. There are men "whose God is the belly" (Phil. 3 : 19), and others for whom God is money, science, power, sex, etc. The whole psychology of the individual, at least in its essential aspects, varies according to the localization of the highest good, so that a psychological theory based exclusively on one fundamental instinct, such as power or sex, can explain no more than secondary features when applied to an individual with a different orientation.

c. Abelard's Attempt at Conciliation

68   It is not without interest to inquire how the Scholastics themselves attempted to settle the dispute about universals and to create a balance between the typical opposites that were divided by the *tertium non datur*. This attempt was the work of Abelard, that unhappy man who burned with love for Héloise and who paid for his passion with the loss of his manhood. Anyone acquainted with the life of Abelard will know how intensely his own soul harboured those separated opposites whose philosophical reconciliation was for him such a vital issue. De Rémusat in his book[35] characterizes him as an eclectic, who criticized and rejected every accepted theory of universals but freely borrowed from them what was true and tenable. Abelard's writings, so far as they relate to the uni-

35 *Abélard.*

versals controversy, are difficult and confusing, because the author was constantly engaged in weighing every argument and aspect of the case. It is precisely because he considered none of the accepted standpoints right, but always sought to comprehend and conciliate the contrary view, that he was never properly understood even by his own pupils. Some understood him as a nominalist, others as a realist. This misunderstanding is characteristic: it is much easier to think in terms of one definite type, because in it one can remain logical and consistent, than it is to think in terms of both types, since the intermediate position is lacking. Realism as well as nominalism if pursued consistently lead to precision, clarity, uniformity. But the weighing and balancing of opposites lead to confusion and, so far as the types are concerned, to an unsatisfactory conclusion, since the solution is completely satisfying neither to the one nor to the other. De Rémusat has collected from Abelard's writings a whole series of almost contradictory assertions on the subject, and exclaims: "Must we suppose that one man's head contained so vast and incoherent a collection of teachings? Is Abelard's philosophy a chaos?"[36]

69   From nominalism Abelard took over the truth that universals are words, in the sense that they are intellectual conventions expressed by language, and also the truth that a thing in reality is never a universal but always an individual fact. From realism he took over the truth that genera and species are combinations of individual facts and things by reason of their unquestionable similarities. For him the intermediate position was *conceptualism*. This is to be understood as a function which apprehends the individual objects perceived, classifies them into genera and species by reason of their similarities, and thus reduces their absolute multiplicity to a relative unity. However indisputable the multiplicity and diversity of individual things may be, the existence of similarities, which makes their combination possible in a concept, is equally beyond dispute. For anyone who is psychologically so constituted as to perceive chiefly the similarity of things, the inclusive concept is, as it were, given from the start; it forcibly obtrudes itself with the undeniable actuality of a sense-perception. But for one who is psychologically so constituted as to perceive

[36] Ibid., II, p. 119.

chiefly the diversity of things, their similarity is not clearly given; what he sees is their difference, which forces itself upon him with as much actuality as similarity does upon the other.

70   It seems as if *empathy into* the object were the psychological process which brings the distinctiveness of the object into more than usually clear focus, and as if *abstraction from* the object were the psychological process most calculated to blind one's eyes to the distinctiveness of individual things in favour of their general similarity, which is the actual foundation of the idea. Empathy and abstraction combined produce the function that underlies the concept of conceptualism. It is grounded, therefore, on the only psychological function that has any real possibility of bringing nominalism and realism together on the middle way.

71   Although the Scholastics knew how to wax grandiloquent on the subject of the soul, there was as yet no psychology, which is one of the youngest of the sciences. If a psychology had existed at that time, Abelard would surely have made *esse in anima* his mediatory formula. De Rémusat clearly discerned this when he said:

In pure logic, universals are only the terms of a conventional language. In physics, which for him is transcendent rather than experimental, and is his real ontology, genera and species are based on the way in which beings are really produced and formed. Finally, between his pure logic and his physics there is a kind of mediatory or half-way science—we may call it psychology—in which Abelard examines how our concepts come into being, and retraces the whole intellectual genealogy of beings, a picture or symbol of their hierarchy and their real existence.[37]

72   The *universalia ante rem* and *post rem* remained a matter of controversy for every century that followed, even though they cast aside their scholastic gown and appeared under a new guise. Fundamentally it was the same old problem. Sometimes the attempted solution veered towards realism, sometimes towards nominalism. The scientism of the nineteenth century gave the problem a push once more towards the nominalist side after the early philosophy of that century had done full justice to realism. The opposites are no longer so far apart as

[37] Ibid., p. 112.

they were in Abelard's day. We have a psychology, a mediatory science, and this alone is capable of uniting the idea and the thing without doing violence to either. This capacity inheres in the very nature of psychology, though no one would contend that psychology so far has accomplished this task. One has to agree with De Rémusat:

Abelard, then, has triumphed; for in spite of the serious limitations which a discerning critique discovers in the nominalism or conceptualism imputed to him, his view is really the modern view in its first form. He heralds it, foretells it, he is its promise. The light that silvers the horizon at dawn is that of the star, as yet invisible, which is about to give light to the world.[38]

73   If one disregards the existence of psychological types, and also the fact that the truth of the one is the error of the other, then Abelard's labours will mean nothing but one scholastic sophistry the more. But if we acknowledge the existence of the two types, Abelard's efforts must appear to us of the greatest importance. He sought the mediatory position in the *sermo*, by which he meant not so much a "discourse" as a formal proposition joined to a definite meaning—in fact, a definition requiring several words for its meaning to be established. He did not speak of *verbum*, for in the nominalist sense this was nothing more than a *vox*, a *flatus vocis*. Indeed, it is the great psychological achievement of both classical and medieval nominalism that it completely abolished the primitive, magical, mystical identity of the word with the thing—too completely for the type of man who has his foothold not in things but in the abstraction of the idea from things. Abelard's horizon was too wide for him to have overlooked the value of nominalism in this sense. For him the word was indeed a *vox*, but the *sermo*, as he understood it, was something more; it carried with it a fixed meaning, it described the common factor, the idea—what in fact has been thought and perceptively discerned about things. In the *sermo* the universal lived, and there alone. It is readily understandable, therefore, that Abelard was counted among the nominalists, though this was incorrect because the universal was for him a greater reality than a *vox*.

74   The expression of his conceptualism must have been diffi-

[38] Ibid., p. 140.

cult enough for Abelard, as he had necessarily to construct it out of contradictions. An epitaph in an Oxford manuscript gives us, I think, a profound glimpse into the paradoxical nature of his teaching:

He taught what words signify in relation to things,
And that words denote things by signification;
He corrected the errors about genera and species,
And taught that genera and species were matters of words alone,
And made it clear that genera and species were sermones.
. . .
Thus he proved that both "living thing" and "no living thing" are
each a genus,
And "man" and "no man" both rightly called species.[39]

75   The opposites can hardly be expressed otherwise than in paradoxes, in so far as an expression is striven for that is based in principle on one standpoint, in Abelard's case the intellectual. We must not forget that the radical difference between nominalism and realism is not purely logical and intellectual, but a psychological one, which in the last resort amounts to a typical difference of psychological attitude to the object as well as to the idea. The man who is oriented to the idea apprehends and reacts from the standpoint of the idea. But the man who is oriented to the object apprehends and reacts from the standpoint of sensation. For him the abstract is of secondary importance, since what must be thought about things seems to him relatively inessential, while for the former it is just the reverse. The man who is oriented to the object is by nature a nominalist—"name is sound and smoke" (Faust)—in so far as he has not yet learnt to compensate his object-oriented attitude. Should this happen, he will become, if he has the necessary equipment, a hair-splitting logician, unequalled for meticulous-

[39] "Hic docuit voces cum rebus significare,
Et docuit voces res significando notare;
Errores generum correxit, ita specierum.
Hic genus et species in sola voce locavit,
Et genus et species sermones esse notavit.
. . .
Sic animal nullumque animal genus esse probatur.
Sic et homo et nullus homo species vocitatur."
Ms. by Godfrey, Prior of St. Swithin's, Winchester. Bodleian Library, Ms. Digby 65 (13th cent.), fol. 7.

ness, methodicalness, and dullness. The idea-oriented man is by nature logical; that is why, when all is said and done, he can neither understand nor appreciate textbook logic. Compensation of his type makes him, as we saw from Tertullian, a man of passionate feeling, though his feelings still remain under the spell of his ideas. Conversely, the man who is a logician by compensation remains, along with his ideas, under the spell of the object.

76   These reflections bring us to the shadow-side of Abelard's thought. His attempted solution was one-sided. If the conflict between nominalism and realism had been merely a matter of logical-intellectual argumentation, it would be incomprehensible why nothing except a paradoxical end-formulation was possible. But since it was essentially a psychological conflict, a one-sided logical-intellectual formulation had to end in paradox: "Thus both man and no man are rightly called species." Logical-intellectual expression is simply incapable, even in the form of the *sermo*, of providing the mediatory formula that will be fair to the real nature of the two opposing psychological attitudes, for it derives exclusively from the abstract side and lacks all recognition of concrete reality.

77   Every logical-intellectual formulation, however perfect it may be, strips the objective impression of its vitality and immediacy. It must do this in order to arrive at any formulation whatever. But then just that is lost which seems to the extravert the most important of all—the relation to the object. There is no possibility, therefore, of finding any satisfactory, reconciling formula by pursuing the one or the other attitude. And yet, even if his mind could, man cannot remain thus divided, for the split is not a mere matter of some off-beat philosophy, but the daily repeated problem of his relation to himself and to the world. And because this is basically the problem at issue, the division cannot be resolved by a discussion of the nominalist and realist arguments. For its solution a third, mediating standpoint is needed. *Esse in intellectu* lacks tangible reality, *esse in re* lacks mind. Idea and thing come together, however, in the human psyche, which holds the balance between them. What would the idea amount to if the psyche did not provide its living value? What would the thing be worth if the psyche withheld from it the determining force of the sense-impres-

sion? What indeed is reality if it is not a reality in ourselves, an *esse in anima*? Living reality is the product neither of the actual, objective behaviour of things nor of the formulated idea exclusively, but rather of the combination of both in the living psychological process, through *esse in anima*. Only through the specific vital activity of the psyche does the sense-impression attain that intensity, and the idea that effective force, which are the two indispensable constituents of living reality.

78   This autonomous activity of the psyche, which can be explained neither as a reflex action to sensory stimuli nor as the executive organ of eternal ideas, is, like every vital process, a continually creative act. The psyche creates reality every day. The only expression I can use for this activity is *fantasy*. Fantasy is just as much feeling as thinking; as much intuition as sensation. There is no psychic function that, through fantasy, is not inextricably bound up with the other psychic functions. Sometimes it appears in primordial form, sometimes it is the ultimate and boldest product of all our faculties combined. Fantasy, therefore, seems to me the clearest expression of the specific activity of the psyche. It is, pre-eminently, the creative activity from which the answers to all answerable questions come; it is the mother of all possibilities, where, like all psychological opposites, the inner and outer worlds are joined together in living union. Fantasy it was and ever is which fashions the bridge between the irreconcilable claims of subject and object, introversion and extraversion. In fantasy alone both mechanisms are united.

79   Had Abelard probed deeply enough to discern the psychological difference between the two standpoints, he would logically have had to enlist the aid of fantasy in developing his mediating formula. But in the world of science, fantasy is just as much taboo as feeling. Once, however, we recognize the underlying opposition as a psychological one, psychology will be obliged to acknowledge not only the standpoint of feeling but the mediating standpoint of fantasy as well. But here comes the great difficulty: fantasy is for the most part a product of the unconscious. Though it undoubtedly includes conscious elements, it is none the less an especial characteristic of fantasy that it is essentially involuntary and, by reason of its

strangeness, directly opposed to the conscious contents. It has these qualities in common with the dream, though the latter of course is involuntary and strange in a much higher degree.

80   The relation of the individual to his fantasy is very largely conditioned by his relation to the unconscious in general, and this in turn is conditioned in particular by the spirit of the age. According to the degree of rationalism that prevails, the individual will be more disposed or less to have dealings with the unconscious and its products. Christianity, like every closed system of religion, has an undoubted tendency to suppress the unconscious in the individual as much as possible, thus paralyzing his fantasy activity. Instead, religion offers stereotyped symbolic concepts that are meant to take the place of his unconscious once and for all. The symbolic concepts of all religions are recreations of unconscious processes in a typical, universally binding form. Religious teaching supplies, as it were, the final information about the "last things" and the world beyond human consciousness. Wherever we can observe a religion being born, we see how the doctrinal figures flow into the founder himself as revelations, in other words as concretizations of his unconscious fantasy. The forms welling up from his unconscious are declared to be universally valid and thus replace the individual fantasies of others. The evangelist Matthew has preserved for us a fragment of this process from the life of Christ: in the story of the temptation we see how the idea of kingship rises out of the founder's unconscious in the visionary form of the devil, who offers him power over all the kingdoms of the earth. Had Christ misunderstood the fantasy and taken it concretely, there would have been one madman the more in the world. But he rejected the concretism of his fantasy and entered the world as a king to whom the kingdoms of *heaven* are subject. He was therefore no paranoiac, as the result also proved. The views advanced from time to time from the psychiatric side concerning the morbidity of Christ's psychology are nothing but ludicrous rationalistic twaddle, with no comprehension whatever of the meaning of such processes in the history of mankind.

81   The form in which Christ presented the content of his unconscious to the world became accepted and was declared valid for all. Thereafter all individual fantasies became otiose

53

and worthless, and were persecuted as heretical, as the fate of
the Gnostic movement and of all later heresies testifies. The
prophet Jeremiah is speaking just in this vein when he warns
(ch. 23):

16. Thus saith the Lord of hosts, Hearken not unto the words of
the prophets that prophesy unto you: they make you vain: they
speak a vision of their own heart, and not out of the mouth of the
Lord.

25. I have heard what the prophets said that prophesy lies in my
name, saying, I have dreamed, I have dreamed.

26. How long shall this be in the heart of the prophets that
prophesy lies? yea, they are prophets of the deceit of their own
heart;

27. Which think to cause my people to forget my name by their
dreams which they tell every man to his neighbour, as their fathers
have forgotten my name for Baal.

28. The prophet that hath a dream, let him tell a dream; and he
that hath my word, let him speak my word faithfully. What is the
chaff to the wheat? saith the Lord.

82   Similarly, we see in early Christianity how the bishops
zealously strove to stamp out the activity of the individual unconscious among the monks. The archbishop Athanasius of
Alexandria in his biography of St. Anthony gives us particularly valuable insights in this respect. By way of instruction to
his monks, he describes the apparitions and visions, the perils
of the soul, which befall those that pray and fast in solitude.
He warns them how cleverly the devil disguises himself in
order to bring saintly men to their downfall. The devil is, of
course, the voice of the anchorite's own unconscious, in revolt
against the forcible suppression of his nature. I give a number
of excerpts from this rather inaccessible book.[40] They show
very clearly how the unconscious was systematically suppressed and devalued.

There is a time when we see no man and yet the sound of the working of the devils is heard by us, and it is like the singing of a song
in a loud voice; and there are times when the words of the Scriptures are heard by us, just as if a living man were repeating them,
and they are exactly like the words which we should hear if a man

---

[40] "Life of St. Anthony," in *The Paradise or Garden of the Holy Fathers,* compiled by Athanasius, Archbishop of Alexandria, and others (trans. E. A. W.
Budge), I, pp. 3–76.

were reading the Book. And it also happens that they [the devils] rouse us up to the night prayer, and incite us to stand up; and they make apparent unto us also the similitudes of monks and the forms of those who mourn; and they draw nigh unto us as if they had come from a long way off, and they begin to utter words like unto these, that they may make lax the understanding of those who are little of soul:—"It is now a law unto all creation that we love desolation, but we were unable, by reason of God, to enter into our houses when we came unto them, and to do fair things." And when they are unable to work their will by means of a scheme of this kind, they depart from this kind of deceit unto another, and say: "How now is it possible for thee to live? For thou hast sinned and committed iniquity in many things. Thinkest thou, that the Spirit hath not revealed unto me what hath been done by thee, or that I know not that thou hast done such and such a thing?" If therefore a simple brother hear these things, and feel within himself that he has done even as the Evil One has said, and he be not acquainted with his craftiness, his mind shall be troubled straightway, and he shall fall into despair and turn backwards.

It is then, O my beloved, unnecessary for us to be terrified at these things, and we have need to fear only when the devils multiply the speaking of the things *which are true* and then we must rebuke them severely. . . . Let us then take heed that we incline not our hearing to their words, even though they be words of truth which they utter; for it would be a disgrace unto us that those who have rebelled against God should become our teachers. And let us, O my brethren, arm ourselves with the armour of righteousness, and let us put on the helmet of redemption, and in the time of contending let us shoot out from a believing mind spiritual arrows as from a bow which is stretched. For they [the devils] are nothing at all, and even if they were, their strength has in it nothing which would enable it to resist the might of the Cross.[41]

And again on another occasion

there appeared unto me a devil of an exceedingly haughty and insolent appearance, and he stood up before me with the tumultuous noise of many people, and he dared to say unto me: "I, even I, am the power of God," and "I, even I, am the Lord of the worlds." And he said unto me: "What dost thou wish me to give thee? Ask, and thou shalt receive." Then I blew a puff of wind at him, and I rebuked him in the name of Christ. . . .

And on another occasion, when I was fasting, the crafty one appeared to me in the form of a brother monk carrying bread, and he

41 Ibid., pp. 24f.

began to speak unto me words of counsel, saying, "Rise up, and stay thy heart with bread and water, and rest a little from thine excessive labours, for thou art a man, and howsoever greatly thou mayest be exalted thou art clothed with a mortal body and thou shouldest fear sickness and tribulations." Then I regarded his words, and I held my peace and refrained from giving an answer. And I bowed myself down in quietness, and I began to make supplications in prayer, and I said: "O Lord, make Thou an end of him, even as Thou hast been wont to do him away at all times." And as I concluded my words he came to an end and vanished like dust, and went forth from the door like smoke.

Now on one occasion Satan approached the house one night and knocked at the door, and I went out to see who was knocking, and I lifted up mine eyes and saw the form of an exceedingly tall and strong man; and, having asked him "Who art thou?," he answered and said unto me: "I am Satan." And after this I said unto him: "What seekest thou?" and he answered unto me: "Why do the monks and the anchorites, and the other Christians revile me, and why do they at all times heap curses upon me?" And having clasped my head firmly in wonder at his mad folly, I said unto him: "Wherefore dost thou give them trouble?" Then he answered and said unto me: "It is not I who trouble them, but it is they who trouble themselves. For there happened to me on a certain occasion that which did happen to me, and had I not cried out to them that I was the Enemy, his slaughters would have come to an end for ever. I have therefore no place to dwell in and not one glittering sword, and not even people who are really subject unto me, for those who are in service to me hold me wholly in contempt; and moreover, I have to keep them in fetters, for they do not cleave to me because they esteem it right to do so, and they are ever ready to escape from me in every place. The Christians have filled the whole world, and behold, even the desert is filled full with their monasteries and habitations. Let them then take good heed to themselves when they heap abuse upon me."

Then, wondering at the grace of our Lord I said unto him: "How doth it happen that whilst thou hast been a liar on every other occasion, at this present the truth is spoken by thee? And how is it that thou speakest the truth now when thou art wont to utter lies? It is indeed true that when Christ came into this world, thou wast brought down to the lowest depths, and that the root of thine error was plucked up from the earth." And when Satan heard the name of Christ his form vanished and his words came to an end.[42]

42 Ibid., pp. 33ff.

83   These quotations show how, with the help of the general belief, the unconscious of the individual was rejected despite the fact that it transparently spoke the truth. There are in the history of the mind especial reasons for this rejection, but it is not incumbent on us to discuss them here. We must be content with the fact that the unconscious was suppressed. Psychologically, the suppression consists in a withdrawal of libido. The libido thus gained promotes the growth and development of the conscious attitude, with the result that a new picture of the world is gradually built up. The undoubted advantages accruing from this process naturally consolidate the new attitude. It is, therefore, not surprising that the psychology of our time is characterized by a predominantly unfavourable attitude towards the unconscious.

84   It is easy to understand why all sciences have excluded the standpoints of both feeling and fantasy, and indeed it was absolutely necessary for them to do so. They are sciences for that very reason. How is it then with psychology? If it is to be regarded as a science, it must do the same. But will it then do justice to its material? Every science ultimately seeks to formulate and express its material in abstractions; thus psychology could, and actually does, grasp the processes of feeling, sensation, and fantasy in abstract intellectual form. This treatment certainly establishes the rights of the abstract intellectual standpoint, but not the claims of other quite possible psychological points of view. These others can receive only a bare mention in a scientific psychology; they cannot emerge as independent scientific principles. Science is under all circumstances an affair of the intellect, and the other psychological functions are subordinated to it as objects. The intellect is the sovereign of the scientific realm. But it is another matter when science steps over into the realm of its practical application. The intellect, which was formerly king, is now merely a minister—a scientifically refined instrument it is true, but still only a tool; no longer an end in itself, but merely a precondition. The intellect, and along with it science, is now placed at the service of a creative power and purpose. Yet this is still "psychology" although no longer science; it is psychology in the wider meaning of the word, a psychological activity of a creative nature, in which creative fantasy is given prior place.

57

Instead of using the term "creative fantasy," it would be just as true to say that in practical psychology of this kind the leading role is given to *life* itself; for while it is undoubtedly fantasy, procreative and productive, which uses science as a tool, it is the manifold demands of external reality which in turn stimulate the activity of creative fantasy. Science as an end in itself is assuredly a high ideal, yet its consistent fulfilment brings about as many "ends in themselves" as there are sciences and arts. Naturally this leads to a high differentiation and specialization of the particular functions concerned, but also to their detachment from the world and from life, as well as to a multiplication of specialized fields which gradually lose all connection with one another. The result is an impoverishment and desiccation not merely in the specialized fields but also in the psyche of every man who has differentiated himself up or sunk down to the specialist level. Science must prove her value for life; it is not enough that she be mistress, she must also be the maid. By so serving she in no way dishonours herself.

85   Although science has granted us insight into the irregularities and disturbances of the psyche, thus meriting our profound respect for her intrinsic intellectual gifts, it would nevertheless be a grave mistake to impute to her an absolute aim which would incapacitate her from being simply an instrument. For when we approach the actual business of living from the side of the intellect and science, we immediately come up against barriers that shut us out from other, equally real provinces of life. We are therefore compelled to acknowledge that the universality of our ideal is a limitation, and to look round for a *spiritus rector* which, bearing in mind the claims of a fuller life, can offer us a greater guarantee of psychological universality than the intellect alone can compass. When Faust exclaims "feeling is all," he is expressing merely the antithesis of the intellect, and so only goes to the other extreme; he does not achieve that totality of life and of his own psyche in which feeling and thinking are united in a third and higher principle. This higher third, as I have already indicated, can be understood either as a practical goal or as the creative fantasy that creates the goal. The goal of totality can be reached neither by science, which is an end in itself, nor by feeling, which lacks

the visionary power of thought. The one must lend itself as an auxiliary to the other, yet the opposition between them is so great that a bridge is needed. This bridge is already given us in creative fantasy. It is not born of either, for it is the mother of both—nay more, it is pregnant with the child, that final goal which unites the opposites.

86   If psychology remains for us only a science, we do not penetrate into life—we merely serve the absolute aim of science. It leads us, certainly, to a knowledge of the objective situation, but it always opposes every other aim but its own. The intellect remains imprisoned in itself just so long as it does not willingly sacrifice its supremacy by recognizing the value of other aims. It shrinks from the step which takes it out of itself and which denies its universal validity, since from the standpoint of the intellect everything else is *nothing but fantasy*. But what great thing ever came into existence that was not first fantasy? Inasmuch as the intellect rigidly adheres to the absolute aim of science it cuts itself off from the springs of life. For it fantasy is nothing but a wish dream, and herein is expressed all that depreciation of fantasy which for science is so welcome and so necessary. Science as an end in itself is inevitable so long as the development of science is the sole question at issue. But this at once becomes an evil when it is a question of life itself demanding development. Thus it was an historical necessity in the Christian process of culture that unbridled fantasy should be suppressed, just as it was also necessary, though for different reasons, that fantasy should be suppressed in our age of natural science. It must not be forgotten that creative fantasy, if not restrained within just bounds, can degenerate into the rankest of growths. But these bounds are never artificial limitations imposed by the intellect or by rational feeling; they are boundaries set by necessity and irrefutable reality.

87   The tasks of every age differ, and it is only in retrospect that we can discern with certainty what had to be and what should not have been. In the momentary present the conflict of opinions will always rage, for "war is the father of all."[43] History alone decides the issue. Truth is not eternal, it is a

43 Heraclitus, fr. 44, in Burnet, *Early Greek Philosophy*, p. 136.

programme to be fulfilled. The more "eternal" a truth is, the more lifeless it is and worthless; it says nothing more to us because it is self-evident.

88   How fantasy is assessed by psychology, so long as this remains merely science, is illustrated by the well-known views of Freud and Adler. The Freudian interpretation reduces fantasy to causal, elementary, instinctive processes. Adler's conception reduces it to the elementary, final aims of the ego. Freud's is a psychology of instinct, Adler's an ego-psychology. Instinct is an impersonal biological phenomenon. A psychology founded on instinct must by its very nature neglect the ego, since the ego owes its existence to the *principium individuationis*, i.e., to individual differentiation, whose isolated character removes it from the realm of general biological phenomena. Although biological instinctive processes also contribute to the formation of the personality, individuality is nevertheless essentially different from collective instincts; indeed, it stands in the most direct opposition to them, just as the individual as a personality is always distinct from the collective. His essence consists precisely in this distinction. Every ego-psychology must necessarily exclude and ignore just the collective element that is bound to a psychology of instinct, since it describes that very process by which the ego becomes differentiated from collective drives. The characteristic animosity between the adherents of the two standpoints arises from the fact that either standpoint necessarily involves a devaluation and disparagement of the other. So long as the radical difference between ego-psychology and the psychology of instinct is not recognized, either side must naturally hold its respective theory to be universally valid. This is not to say that a psychology of instinct could not devise a theory of the ego-process. It can very well do so, but in a way which to the ego-psychologist looks too much like a negation of his theory. Hence we find that with Freud the "ego-instincts" do occasionally emerge, but for the most part they eke out a very modest existence. With Adler, on the other hand, it would seem as though sexuality were the merest vehicle, which in one way or another serves the elementary aims of power. The Adlerian principle is the safeguarding of personal power which is superimposed on the collective instincts. With Freud it is instinct that makes the ego

serve its purposes, so that the ego appears as a mere function of instinct.

89   The scientific tendency in both is to reduce everything to their own principle, from which their deductions in turn proceed. In the case of fantasies this operation is particularly easy to accomplish because, unlike the functions of consciousness, they are not adapted to reality and therefore do not have an objectively oriented character, but express purely instinctive as well as pure ego-tendencies. Anyone who adopts the standpoint of instinct will have no difficulty in discovering in them the "wish-fulfillment," the "infantile wish," the "repressed sexuality." And the man who adopts the standpoint of the ego can just as easily discover those elementary aims concerned with the security and differentiation of the ego, since fantasies are mediating products between the ego and the instincts. Accordingly they contain elements of both sides. Interpretation from either side is always somewhat forced and arbitrary, because one side is always suppressed. Nevertheless, a demonstrable truth does on the whole emerge; but it is only a partial truth that can lay no claim to general validity. Its validity extends only so far as the range of its principle. But in the domain of the other principle it is invalid.

90   Freudian psychology is characterized by one central idea, the repression of incompatible wish-tendencies. Man appears as a bundle of wishes which are only partially adaptable to the object. His neurotic difficulties are due to the fact that environmental influences, education, and objective conditions put a considerable check on the free expression of instinct. Other influences, productive of moral conflicts or infantile fixations that compromise later life, emanate from the father and mother. The original instinctive disposition is a fundamental datum which undergoes disturbing modifications mainly through objective influences; hence the most untrammelled expression of instinct in respect of suitably chosen objects would appear to be the needful remedy. Adler's psychology, on the other hand, is characterized by the central concept of ego-superiority. Man appears primarily as an ego-point which must not under any circumstances be subordinated to the object. While the craving for the object, the fixation on the object, and the impossible nature of certain desires for the object play a para-

mount role with Freud, with Adler everything is directed to the superiority of the subject. Freud's repression of instinct in respect of the object corresponds to the security of the subject in Adler. For Adler the remedy is the removal of the security that isolates the subject; for Freud it is the removal of the repression that makes the object inaccessible.

91   The basic formula with Freud is therefore sexuality, which expresses the strongest relation between subject and object; with Adler it is the power of the subject, which secures him most effectively against the object and guarantees him an impregnable isolation that abolishes all relationships. Freud would like to ensure the undisturbed flow of instinct towards its object; Adler would like to break the baleful spell of the object in order to save the ego from suffocating in its own defensive armour. Freud's view is essentially extraverted, Adler's introverted. The extraverted theory holds good for the extraverted type, the introverted theory for the introverted type. Since a pure type is a product of a wholly one-sided development it is also necessarily unbalanced. Overaccentuation of the one function is synonymous with repression of the other.

92   Psychoanalysis fails to remove this repression just in so far as the method it employs is oriented according to the theory of the patient's own type. Thus the extravert, in accordance with his theory, will reduce the fantasies rising out of his unconscious to their instinctual content, while the introvert will reduce them to his power aims. The gains resulting from such an analysis merely increase the already existing imbalance. This kind of analysis simply reinforces the existing type and renders any mutual understanding between the two types impossible. On the contrary the gap is widened, both without and within. An inner dissociation arises, because portions of other functions coming to the surface in unconscious fantasies, dreams, etc., are each time devalued and again repressed. On these grounds a certain critic was justified up to a point when he described Freud's as a neurotic theory, though the tinge of malice in this statement is merely intended to absolve us from the duty of seriously coming to grips with the problem. The standpoints of Freud and Adler are equally one-sided and characteristic only of one type.

93   Both theories reject the principle of imagination since they

reduce fantasies to something else and treat them merely as a semiotic[44] expression. In reality fantasies mean much more than that, for they represent at the same time the other mechanism—of repressed extraversion in the introvert, and of repressed introversion in the extravert. But the repressed function is unconscious, and hence undeveloped, embryonic, and archaic. In this condition it cannot be united with the higher level of the conscious function. The unacceptable nature of fantasy derives chiefly from this peculiarity of the unrecognized, unconscious function. For everyone whose guiding principle is adaptation to external reality, imagination is for these reasons something reprehensible and useless. And yet we know that every good idea and all creative work are the offspring of the imagination, and have their source in what one is pleased to call infantile fantasy. Not the artist alone, but every creative individual whatsoever owes all that is greatest in his life to fantasy. The dynamic principle of fantasy is *play*, a characteristic also of the child, and as such it appears inconsistent with the principle of serious work. But without this playing with fantasy no creative work has ever yet come to birth. The debt we owe to the play of imagination is incalculable. It is therefore short-sighted to treat fantasy, on account of its risky or unacceptable nature, as a thing of little worth. It must not be forgotten that it is just in the imagination that a man's highest value may lie. I say "may" advisedly, because on the other hand fantasies are also valueless, since in the form of raw material they possess no realizable worth. In order to unearth the treasures they contain they must be developed a stage further. But this development is not achieved by a simple analysis of the fantasy material; a synthesis is also needed by means of a constructive method.[45]

94   It remains an open question whether the opposition between the two standpoints can ever be satisfactorily resolved in intellectual terms. Although in one sense Abelard's attempt

[44] I say "semiotic" in contradistinction to "symbolic." What Freud terms symbols are no more than *signs* for elementary instinctive processes. But a *symbol* is the best possible expression for something that cannot be expressed otherwise than by a more or less close analogy.

[45] Jung, "On Psychological Understanding," pars. 391 ff., and *Two Essays on Analytical Psychology*, pars. 121 ff.

must be rated very highly, in practice no consequences worth mentioning have resulted from it, for he was unable to establish any mediatory psychological principle beyond conceptualism or "sermonism," which is merely a revised edition, altogether one-sided and intellectual, of the ancient Logos conception. The Logos, as mediator, had of course this advantage over the *sermo*, that in its human manifestation it also did justice to man's non-intellectual aspirations.

95   I cannot, however, rid myself of the impression that Abelard's brilliant mind, which so fully comprehended the great Yea and Nay of life, would never have remained satisfied with his paradoxical conceptualism, and would not have renounced a further creative effort, if the impelling force of passion had not been lost to him through his tragic fate. In confirmation of this we need only compare conceptualism with what the great Chinese philosophers Lao-tzu and Chuang-tzu, or the poet Schiller, made of this same problem.

5. THE HOLY COMMUNION CONTROVERSY BETWEEN LUTHER AND ZWINGLI

96   Of the later dissensions that stirred men's minds, Protestantism and the Reformation movement should really receive our first attention. Only, this phenomenon is of such complexity that it would first have to be resolved into many separate psychological processes before it could become an object of analytical investigation. But this lies outside my competence. I must therefore content myself with selecting a specific instance of that great dispute, namely the Holy Communion controversy between Luther and Zwingli. The dogma of transubstantiation, mentioned earlier, was sanctioned by the Lateran Council of 1215, and thenceforward became an established article of faith, in which tradition Luther grew up. Although the notion that a ceremony and its concrete performance have an objective redemptory significance is really quite unevangelical, since the evangelical movement was actually directed against the values of Catholic institutions, Luther was nevertheless unable to free himself from the immediately effective sensuous impression in the taking of bread and wine. He was

unable to perceive in it a mere sign; the sensuous reality and the immediate experience of it were for him an indispensable religious necessity. He therefore claimed the actual presence of the body and blood of Christ in the Communion. "In and beneath" the bread and wine he received the body and blood of Christ. For him the religious significance of the immediate experience of the object was so great that his imagination was spellbound by the concretism of the material presence of the sacred body. All his attempts at explanation are under the spell of this fact: the body of Christ is present, albeit "nonspatially." According to the doctrine of so-called *con*substantiation, the actual substance of the sacred body was also really present beside the bread and wine. The ubiquity of Christ's body, which this assumption postulated, proved especially discomforting to human intelligence and was later replaced by the concept of *volipresence*, which means that God is present wherever he wills to be. But Luther, unperturbed by all these difficulties, held unswervingly to the immediate experience of the sensuous impression and preferred to thrust aside all the scruples of human reason with explanations that were either absurd or at best unsatisfying.

97   It can hardly be supposed that it was merely the force of tradition that made Luther determined to cling to this dogma, for he of all people gave abundant proof of his ability to throw aside traditional forms of belief. Indeed, we should not go far wrong in assuming that it was rather the actual contact with the "real" and material in the Communion, and the feeling-value of this contact for Luther himself, that prevailed over the evangelical principle, which maintained that the word was the sole vehicle of grace and not the ceremony. For Luther the word certainly had redeeming power, but the partaking of the Communion was also a mediator of grace. This, I repeat, must have been only an apparent concession to the institutions of the Catholic Church; in reality it was an acknowledgement, demanded by Luther's own psychology, of the fact of feeling grounded upon the immediate sense-impression.

98   In contrast to the Lutheran standpoint, Zwingli championed a purely symbolic conception of the Communion. What really mattered for him was a "spiritual" partaking of the body and blood of Christ. This standpoint is characterized by reason

65

and by an ideal conception of the ceremony. It had the advantage of not violating the evangelical principle, and at the same time it avoided all hypotheses contrary to reason. However, it did scant justice to the thing that Luther wished to preserve—the reality of the sense-impression and its particular feeling-value. Zwingli, it is true, also administered the Communion, and like Luther partook of the bread and wine, but his conception contained no formula that could adequately reproduce the unique sensory and feeling-value of the object. Luther provided a formula for this, but it was contrary to reason and to the evangelical principle. From the standpoint of sensation and feeling this matters little, and indeed rightly so, for the idea, the principle, is just as little concerned with the sensation of the object. In the last resort, both points of view are mutually exclusive.

99   Luther's formulation favours the extraverted conception of things, while Zwingli's favours the ideal standpoint. Although Zwingli's formula does no violence to feeling and sensation, merely offering an ideal conception, it nevertheless appears to leave room for the efficacy of the object. But it seems as though the extraverted standpoint—Luther's—is not content with just leaving room for the object; it also demands a formulation in which the ideal subserves the sensory, exactly as the ideal formulation demands the subservience of feeling and sensation.

100   At this point, with the consciousness of having done no more than pose the question, I close this chapter on the problem of types in the history of classical and medieval thought. I lack the competence to treat so difficult and far-reaching a problem in any way exhaustively. If I have succeeded in conveying to the reader some idea of the existence of typical differences of standpoint, my purpose will have been achieved. I need hardly add that I am aware that none of the material here touched upon has been dealt with conclusively. I must leave this task to those who command a wider knowledge of the subject than myself.

II

SCHILLER'S IDEAS ON THE TYPE PROBLEM

1. LETTERS ON THE AESTHETIC EDUCATION OF MAN

a. The Superior and the Inferior Functions

101   So far as I have been able to ascertain with my somewhat limited knowledge, Friedrich Schiller seems to have been the first to attempt a conscious differentiation of typical attitudes on a large scale and to give a detailed account of their peculiarities. This important endeavour to present the two mechanisms in question, and at the same time to discover a possible way of reconciling them, is to be found in his essay first published in 1795: "Über die ästhetische Erziehung des Menschen." The essay consists of a number of letters which Schiller addressed to the Duke of Holstein-Augustenburg.[1]

102   Schiller's essay, by its profundity of thought, psychological penetration, and wide view of a possible psychological solution of the conflict, prompts me to a rather lengthy discussion and evaluation of his ideas, for it has never yet been their lot to be treated in such a context. The service rendered by Schiller from our psychological point of view, as will become clear in the course of our exposition, is by no means inconsiderable, for he offers us carefully worked out lines of approach whose value we, as psychologists, are only just beginning to appreciate. My undertaking will not be an easy one, for I may well be accused of putting a construction on Schiller's ideas which his actual words do not warrant. Although I shall try to quote his actual words at every essential point, it may not be altogether possible to introduce his ideas into the present context without putting certain interpretations and constructions

[1] All quotations are from the translation by Snell, *On the Aesthetic Education of Man.*

upon them. This is a possibility I must not overlook, but on the other hand we must remember that Schiller himself belonged to a definite type, and was therefore compelled, even in spite of himself, as I am, to give a one-sided presentation of his ideas. The limitations of our views and our knowledge are nowhere more apparent than in psychological discussions, where it is almost impossible for us to project any other picture than the one whose main outlines are already laid down in our own psyche.

103   From various characteristics I have come to the conclusion that Schiller belongs to the introverted type, whereas Goethe—if we disregard his overriding intuition—inclines more to the extraverted side. We can easily discover Schiller's own image in his description of the idealistic type. Because of this identification, an inevitable limitation is imposed on his formulations, a fact we must never lose sight of if we wish to gain a fuller understanding. It is owing to this limitation that the one function is presented by Schiller in richer outline than the other, which is still imperfectly developed in the introvert, and just because of its imperfect development it must necessarily have certain inferior characteristics attached to it. At this point the author's exposition requires our criticism and correction. It is evident, too, that this limitation of Schiller's impelled him to use a terminology which lacks general applicability. As an introvert he had a better relation to ideas than to things. The relation to ideas can be more emotional or more reflective according to whether the individual belongs more to the feeling or to the thinking type. And here I would request the reader, who may perhaps have been led by my earlier publications to identify feeling with extraversion and thinking with introversion, to bear in mind the definitions given in Chapter XI of this book. By the introverted and extraverted types I distinguish two general classes of men, which can be further subdivided into function-types, i.e., thinking, feeling, sensation, and intuitive types. Hence an introvert can be either a thinking or a feeling type, since feeling as well as thinking can come under the supremacy of the idea, just as both can be dominated by the object.

104   If, then, I consider that Schiller, in his nature and particularly in his characteristic opposition to Goethe, corresponds to

the introverted type, the question next arises as to which sub-division he belongs. This is hard to answer. Without doubt intuition plays a great role with him; we might on this account, or if we regard him exclusively as a poet, reckon him an in-tuitive. But in the letters on the aesthetic education of man it is unquestionably Schiller the thinker who confronts us. Not only from these, but from his own repeated admissions, we know how strong the reflective element was in Schiller. Conse-quently we must shift his intuitiveness very much towards the side of thinking, thus approaching him also from the angle of the psychology of the *introverted thinking* type. It will, I hope, become sufficiently clear from what follows that this hypothesis is in accord with reality, for there are not a few passages in Schiller's writings that speak distinctly in its favour. I would, therefore, beg the reader to remember that the hypothesis I have just advanced underlies my whole argument. This re-minder seems to me necessary because Schiller approaches the problem from the angle of his own inner experience. In view of the fact that another psychology, i.e., another type of man, would have approached the same problem in quite another way, the very broad formulation which Schiller gives might be regarded as a subjective bias or an ill-considered generaliza-tion. But such a judgment would be incorrect, since there ac-tually is a large class of men for whom the problem of the sep-arated functions is exactly the same as it was for Schiller. If, therefore, in the ensuing argument I occasionally emphasize Schiller's one-sidedness and subjectivity, I do not wish to de-tract from the importance and general validity of the problem he has raised, but rather to make room for other formulations. Such criticisms as I may occasionally offer have more the char-acter of a transcription into another language which will re-lieve Schiller's formulation of its subjective limitations. My argument, nevertheless, follows Schiller's very closely, since it is concerned much less with the general question of introver-sion and extraversion—which exclusively engaged our atten-tion in Chapter I—than with the *typical conflict of the intro-verted thinking type.*

105   Schiller concerns himself at the very outset with the ques-tion of the cause and origin of the separation of the two func-tions. With sure instinct he hits on the differentiation of the

individual as the basic motive. "It was culture itself that inflicted this wound upon modern humanity."[2] This one sentence shows Schiller's wide grasp of the problem. The breakdown of the harmonious cooperation of psychic forces in instinctive life is like an ever open and never healing wound, a veritable Amfortas' wound, because the differentiation of one function among several inevitably leads to the hypertrophy of the one and the neglect and atrophy of the others:

I do not fail to appreciate the advantages to which the present generation, considered as a unity and weighed in the scales of reason, may lay claim in the face of the best of antiquity, but it has to enter the contest in close order and let whole compete with whole. What individual modern will emerge to contend in single combat with the individual Athenian for the prize of humanity? Whence comes this disadvantageous relation of individuals in spite of all the advantages of the race?[3]

106   Schiller places the responsibility for this decline of the modern individual on culture, that is, on the differentiation of functions. He next points out how, in art and learning, the intuitive and the speculative minds have become estranged, and how each has jealously excluded the other from its respective field of application:

By confining our activity to a single sphere we have handed ourselves over to a master who is not infrequently to end up by suppressing the rest of our capacities. While in one place a luxuriant imagination ravages the hard-earned fruits of the intellect, in another the spirit of abstraction stifles the fire at which the heart might have warmed itself and the fancy been enkindled.[4]

If the community makes the function the measure of a man, if it respects in one of its citizens only memory, in another a tabulating intellect, in a third only mechanical skill; if, indifferent to character, it here lays stress upon knowledge alone, and there pardons the profoundest darkness of the intellect so long as it co-exists with a spirit of order and a law-abiding demeanour—if at the same time it requires these special aptitudes to be exercised with an intensity proportionate to the loss of extensity which it permits in the individuals concerned—can we then wonder that the remaining aptitudes of the mind become neglected in order to bestow every attention upon the only one which brings honour and profit?[5]

2 Ibid., p. 39.   3 Ibid.   4 Ibid.   5 Ibid., pp. 40f.

107   There is volume indeed in these thoughts of Schiller's. It is understandable that Schiller's generation, who with their imperfect knowledge of the Greek world judged the Greeks by the grandeur of the works they left behind them, should also have overestimated them beyond all measure, since the peculiar beauty of Greek art is due not least to its contrast with the milieu from which it arose. The advantage enjoyed by the Greek was that he was less differentiated than modern man, if indeed one is disposed to regard that as an advantage—for the disadvantage of such a condition must be equally obvious. The differentiation of functions was assuredly not the result of human caprice, but, like everything else in nature, of necessity. Could one of those late admirers of the "Grecian heaven" and Arcadian bliss have visited the earth as an Attic helot, he might well have surveyed the beauties of Greece with rather different eyes. Even if it were true that the primitive conditions of the fifth century before Christ gave the individual a greater opportunity for an all-round development of his qualities and capacities, this was possible only because thousands of his fellow men were cramped and crippled by circumstances that were all the more wretched. A high level of individual culture was undoubtedly reached by certain exemplary personalities, but a collective culture was quite unknown to the ancient world. This achievement was reserved for Christianity. Hence it comes about that, as a mass, the moderns can not only measure up to the Greeks, but by every standard of collective culture easily surpass them. On the other hand, Schiller is perfectly right in his contention that our individual culture has not kept pace with our collective culture, and it has certainly not improved during the hundred and twenty years that have passed since Schiller wrote. Quite the reverse—for, if we had not strayed even further into the collective atmosphere so detrimental to individual development, the violent reactions personified by Stirner or Nietzsche would scarcely have been needed as a corrective. Schiller's words, therefore, still remain valid today.

108   Just as the ancients, with an eye to individual development, catered to the well-being of an upper class by an almost total suppression of the great majority of the common people (helots, slaves), the Christian world reached a condition of col-

lective culture by transferring this same process, as far as possible, to the psychological sphere *within* the individual himself —raising it, one might say, to the subjective level. As the chief value of the individual was proclaimed by Christian dogma to be an imperishable soul, it was no longer possible for the inferior majority of the people to be suppressed in actual fact for the freedom of a more valuable minority. Instead, the more valuable function within the individual was preferred above the inferior functions. In this way the chief importance was attached to the one valued function, to the detriment of all the rest. Psychologically this meant that the external form of society in classical civilization was transferred into the subject, so that a condition was produced within the individual which in the ancient world had been external, namely a dominating, privileged function which was developed and differentiated at the expense of an inferior majority. By means of this psychological process a collective culture gradually came into existence, in which the "rights of man" were guaranteed for the individual to an immeasurably greater degree than in antiquity. But it had the disadvantage of depending on a subjective slave culture, that is to say on a transfer of the old mass enslavement into the psychological sphere, with the result that, while collective culture was enhanced, individual culture was degraded. Just as the enslavement of the masses was the open wound of the ancient world, so the enslavement of the inferior functions is an ever-bleeding wound in the psyche of modern man.

109   "One-sidedness in the exercise of powers, it is true, inevitably leads the individual into error, but the race to truth,"[6] says Schiller. The privileged position of the superior function is as detrimental to the individual as it is valuable to society. This detrimental effect has reached such a pitch that the mass organizations of our present-day culture actually strive for the complete extinction of the individual, since their very existence depends on a mechanized application of the privileged functions of individual human beings. It is not man who counts, but his one differentiated function. Man no longer appears as man in our collective culture: he is merely represented by a function, what is more he identifies himself completely with this function and denies the relevance of the other inferior func-

[6] Cf. p. 44.

tions. Thus modern man is debased to a mere function, because it is this that represents a collective value and alone guarantees a possible livelihood. But, as Schiller clearly sees, a differentiation of function could have come in no other way:

There was no other way of developing the manifold capacities of man than by placing them in opposition to each other. This antagonism of powers is the great instrument of culture, but it is only the instrument; for as long as it persists, we are only on the way towards culture.[7]

110   According to this view the present state of our warring capacities would not be a state of culture, but only a stage on the way. Opinions will, of course, be divided about this, for by culture one man will understand a state of collective culture, while another will regard this state merely as *civilization*[8] and will expect of culture the sterner demands of individual development. Schiller is, however, mistaken when he allies himself exclusively with the second standpoint and contrasts our collective culture unfavourably with that of the individual Greek, since he overlooks the defectiveness of the civilization of that time, which makes the unlimited validity of that culture very questionable. Hence no culture is ever really complete, for it always swings towards one side or the other. Sometimes the cultural ideal is extraverted, and the chief value then lies with the object and man's relation to it: sometimes it is introverted, and the chief value lies with subject and his relation to the idea. In the former case, culture takes on a collective character, in the latter an individual one. It is therefore easy to understand how under the influence of Christianity, whose principle is Christian love (and by counter-association, also its counterpart, the violation of individuality), a collective culture came about in which the individual is liable to be swallowed up because individual values are depreciated on principle. Hence there arose in the age of the German classicists that extraordinary yearning for the ancient world which for them was a symbol of individual culture, and on that account was for the most part very much overvalued and often grossly

[7] Ibid., p. 43.

[8] [For the Germanic distinction between culture and civilization, see *The Practice of Psychotherapy*, par. 227, n. 10.—TRANS.]

idealized. Not a few attempts were even made to imitate or re-capture the spirit of Greece, attempts which nowadays appear to us somewhat silly, but must none the less be appreciated as forerunners of an individual culture.

111   In the hundred and twenty years that have passed since Schiller wrote his letters, conditions with respect to individual culture have gone from bad to worse, since the interest of the individual is invested to a far greater extent in collective occupations, and therefore much less leisure is left over for the development of individual culture. Hence we possess today a highly developed collective culture which in organization far exceeds anything that has gone before, but which for that very reason has become increasingly injurious to individual culture. There is a deep gulf between what a man is and what he represents, between what he is as an individual and what he is as a collective being. His function is developed at the expense of his individuality. Should he excel, he is merely identical with his collective function; but should he not, then, though he may be esteemed as a function in society, his individuality is wholly on the level of his inferior, undeveloped functions, and he is simply a barbarian, while in the former case he has happily deceived himself as to his actual barbarism. This one-sidedness has undoubtedly brought society advantages that should not be underestimated, and acquisitions that could have been gained in no other way, as Schiller finely observes:

Only by concentrating the whole energy of our spirit in one single focus, and drawing together our whole being into one single power, do we attach wings, so to say, to this individual power and lead it by artifice far beyond the bounds which nature seems to have imposed upon it.[9]

112   But this one-sided development must inevitably lead to a reaction, since the suppressed inferior functions cannot be indefinitely excluded from participating in our life and development. The time will come when the division in the inner man must be abolished, in order that the undeveloped may be granted an opportunity to live.

113   I have already indicated that the process of differentiation in cultural development ultimately brings about a dissociation

9 Cf. Snell, p. 44.

74

of the basic functions of the psyche, going far beyond the differentiation of individual capacities and even encroaching on the sphere of the psychological attitude in general, which governs the way in which those capacities are employed. At the same time, culture effects a differentiation of the function that already enjoys a better capacity for development through heredity. In one man it is the capacity for thought, in another feeling, which is particularly amenable to development, and therefore, impelled by cultural demands, he will concern himself in special degree with developing an aptitude to which he is already favourably disposed by nature. Its cultivation does not mean that the function in question has an *a priori* claim to any particular proficiency; on the contrary, one might say, it presupposes a certain delicacy, lability, pliability, on which account the highest individual value is not always to be sought or found in this function, but rather, perhaps, only the highest collective value, in so far as this function is developed for a collective end. It may well be, as I have said, that beneath the neglected functions there lie hidden far higher individual values which, though of small importance for collective life, are of the greatest value for individual life, and are therefore vital values that can endow the life of the individual with an intensity and beauty he will vainly seek in his collective function. The differentiated function procures for him the possibility of a collective existence, but not that satisfaction and *joie de vivre* which the development of individual values alone can give. Their absence is often sensed as a profound lack, and the severance from them is like an inner division which, with Schiller, one might compare with a painful wound. He goes on to say:

Thus, however much may be gained for the world as a whole by this fragmentary cultivation of human powers, it is undeniable that the individuals whom it affects suffer under the curse of this universal aim. Athletic bodies are certainly developed by means of gymnastic exercises, but only through the free and equable play of the limbs is beauty formed. In the same way the exertion of individual talents certainly produces extraordinary men, but only their even tempering makes full and happy men. And in what relation should we stand to past and future ages if the cultivation of human nature made such a sacrifice necessary? We should have been the bondslaves of humanity, we should have drudged for it for centuries on end, and branded upon our mutilated nature the shameful traces of this servitude—in order that a later generation might devote itself in blissful indolence to the care of its moral health, and develop the free growth of its humanity! But can man really be destined to neglect himself for any end whatever? Should Nature be able, by her designs, to rob us of a completeness which Reason prescribes to us by hers? It must be false that the cultivation of individual powers necessitates the sacrifice of their totality; or however much the law of Nature did have that tendency, *we must be at liberty to restore by means of a higher Art this wholeness in our nature which Art has destroyed.*[10]

114   It is evident that Schiller in his personal life had a profound sense of this conflict, and that it was just this antagonism in himself that generated a longing for the coherence or homogeneity which should bring deliverance to the suppressed functions languishing in servitude and a restoration of harmonious living. This idea is also the *leit-motif* of Wagner's *Parsifal,* and it is given symbolic expression in the restoration of the missing spear and the healing of the wound. What Wagner tried to say in artistic terms Schiller laboured to make clear in his philosophical reflections. Although it is nowhere openly stated, the implication is clear enough that his problem revolved round the resumption of a classical mode of life and view of the world; from which one is bound to conclude that he either overlooked the Christian solution or deliberately ignored it. In any case his spiritual eye was focussed more on the beauty of antiquity than on the Christian doctrine of redemption, which, nevertheless, has no other aim than what Schiller himself strove for—the deliverance from evil. The heart of man is "filled with raging battle," says Julian the Apostate in his discourse on King Helios;[11] and with these words he aptly characterizes not only himself but his whole age—the inner laceration of late antiquity which found expression in an unexampled, chaotic confusion of hearts and minds, and from which the Christian doctrine promised deliverance. What Christianity offered was not, of course, a solution but a breaking free, a detachment of the one valuable function from all the other

[10] Ibid., pp. 44f. My italics.
[11] Oratio IV, *In regem solem.* Cf. Julian, *Works* (L.C.L.), I, p. 389.

functions which, at that time, made an equally peremptory claim to government. Christianity offered one definite direction to the exclusion of all others. This may have been the essential reason why Schiller passed over in silence the possibility of salvation offered by Christianity. The pagan's close contact with nature seemed to promise just that possibility which Christianity did not offer:

Nature in her physical creation indicates to us the way we should pursue in moral creation. Not until the struggle of elementary powers in the lower organizations has been assuaged does she rise to the noble formation of the physical man. In the same way the strife of elements in the ethical man, the conflict of blind instincts, must first be allayed, and the crude antagonism within him must have ceased, before we may dare to promote his diversity. On the other hand, the independence of his character must be assured, and subjection to alien despotic forms have given place to a decent freedom, before we can submit the multiplicity in him to the unity of the ideal.[12]

115   Thus it is not to be a detachment or redemption of the inferior function, but an acknowledgement of it, a coming to terms with it, that unites the opposites on the path of nature. But Schiller feels that the acceptance of the inferior function might lead to a "conflict of blind instincts," just as, conversely, the unity of the ideal might re-establish the supremacy of the valuable function over the less valuable ones and thereby restore the original state of affairs. The inferior functions are opposed to the superior, not so much in their essential nature as because of their momentary form. They were originally neglected and repressed because they hindered civilized man from attaining his aims. But these consist of one-sided interests and are by no means synonymous with the perfection of human individuality. If that were the aim, these unacknowledged functions would be indispensable, and as a matter of fact they do not by nature contradict it. But so long as the cultural aim does not coincide with the ideal of perfecting the human individuality, these functions are subject to depreciation and some degree of repression. The conscious acceptance of repressed functions is equivalent to an internal civil war; the opposites, previously restrained, are unleashed and the "independence

[12] Snell, p. 46.

of character" is abolished forthwith. This independence can be attained only by a settlement of the conflict, which appears to be impossible without despotic jurisdiction over the opposing forces. In that way freedom is compromised, and without it the building up of a morally free personality is equally impossible. But if freedom is preserved, one is delivered over to the conflict of instincts:

> Terrified of the freedom which always declares its hostility to their first attempts, men will in one place throw themselves into the arms of a comfortable servitude, and in another, driven to despair by a pedantic tutelage, they will break out into the wild libertinism of the natural state. Usurpation will plead the weakness of human nature, insurrection its dignity, until at length the great sovereign of all human affairs, blind force, steps in to decide the sham conflict of principles like a common prize-fight.[13]

116   The contemporary revolution in France gave this statement a living, albeit bloody background: begun in the name of philosophy and reason, with a soaring idealism, it ended in blood-drenched chaos, from which arose the despotic genius of Napoleon. The Goddess of Reason proved herself powerless against the might of the unchained beast. Schiller felt the defeat of reason and truth and therefore had to postulate that truth herself should become a *power*:

> If she has hitherto displayed so little of her conquering power, the fault lies not so much with the intellect that knew not how to unveil her, as with the heart that shut her out, and with the instinct that would not serve her. Whence arises this still universal sway of prejudice, this intellectual darkness, beside all the light that philosophy and experience have shed? *The age is enlightened,* that is to say knowledge has been discovered and publicly disseminated, which would at least suffice to set right our practical principles. The spirit of free enquiry has scattered the delusions which for so long barred the approach to truth, and is undermining the foundations upon which fanaticism and fraud have raised their thrones. Reason has been purged of the illusions of the senses and of deceitful sophistry, and philosophy itself, which first caused us to forsake Nature, is calling us loudly and urgently back to her bosom—why is it that we still remain barbarians?[14]

[13] Ibid., p. 47.
[14] Cf. ibid., pp. 48f.

117   We feel in these words of Schiller the proximity of the French Enlightenment and the fantastic intellectualism of the Revolution. "The age is enlightened"—what an overvaluation of the intellect! "The spirit of free enquiry has scattered the delusions"—what rationalism! One is vividly reminded of the Proktophantasmist in *Faust*: "Vanish at once, you've been explained away!" Even though the men of that age were altogether too prone to overestimate the importance and efficacy of reason, quite forgetting that if reason really possessed such a power, she had long had the amplest opportunity to demonstrate it, the fact should not be overlooked that not all the influential minds of the age thought that way; consequently this soaring flight of rationalistic intellectualism may equally well have sprung from a particularly strong subjective development of this same propensity in Schiller himself. In him we have to reckon with a predominance of intellect, not at the expense of his poetic intuition but at the cost of feeling. To Schiller himself it seemed as though there were a perpetual conflict in him between imagination and abstraction, that is, between intuition and thinking. Thus he wrote to Goethe (August 31, 1794):

This is what gave me, especially in early years, a certain awkwardness both in the realm of speculation and in that of poetry; as a rule the poet would overtake me when I would be a philosopher, and the philosophic spirit hold me when I would be a poet. Even now it happens often enough that the power of imagination disturbs my abstraction, and cold reasoning my poetry.[15]

118   His extraordinary admiration for Goethe's mind, and his almost feminine empathy and sympathy with his friend's intuition, to which he so often gives expression in his letters, spring from a piercing awareness of this conflict, which he must have felt doubly hard in comparison with the almost perfect synthesis of Goethe's nature. This conflict was due to the psychological fact that the energy of feeling lent itself in equal measure to his intellect and to his creative imagination. Schiller seems to have suspected this, for in the same letter to Goethe he makes the observation that no sooner has he begun

[15] Goethe, *Briefwechsel mit Schiller in den Jahren 1794–1805*, in *Werke* (ed. Beutler), XX, p. 20.

to "know and to use" his moral forces, which should set proper limits to imagination and intellect, than a physical illness threatens to undermine them. As has been pointed out already, it is characteristic of an imperfectly developed function to withdraw itself from conscious control and, thanks to its own autonomy, to get unconsciously contaminated with other functions. It then behaves like a purely dynamic factor, incapable of differentiated choice, an impetus or surcharge that gives the conscious, differentiated function the quality of being carried away or coerced. In one case the conscious function is transported beyond the limits of its intentions and decisions, in another it is arrested before it attains its aim and is diverted into a side-track, and in a third it is brought into conflict with the other conscious functions—a conflict that remains unresolved so long as the unconscious contaminating and disturbing force is not differentiated and subjected to conscious control. We may safely conjecture that the exclamation "Why is it that we are still barbarians?" was rooted not merely in the spirit of the age but in Schiller's subjective psychology. Like other men of his time, he sought the root of the evil in the wrong place; for barbarism never did and never does consist in reason or truth having so little effect but in expecting from them far too much, or even in ascribing such efficacy to reason out of a superstitious overvaluation of "truth." Barbarism consists in one-sidedness, lack of moderation—bad measure in general.

119 From the spectacular example of the French Revolution, which had just then reached the climax of terror, Schiller could see how far the sway of the Goddess of Reason extended, and how far the unreasoning beast in man was triumphant. It was doubtless these contemporary events that forced the problem on Schiller with particular urgency; for it often happens that, when a problem which is at bottom personal, and therefore apparently subjective, coincides with external events that contain the same psychological elements as the personal conflict, it is suddenly transformed into a general question embracing the whole of society. In this way the personal problem acquires a dignity it lacked hitherto, since the inner discord always has something humiliating and degrading about it, so that one sinks into an ignominious condition both within and without, like a state dishonoured by civil war. It is this that makes one

shrink from displaying before the public a purely personal conflict, provided of course that one does not suffer from an overdose of self-esteem. But if the connection between the personal problem and the larger contemporary events is discerned and understood, it brings a release from the loneliness of the purely personal, and the subjective problem is magnified into a general question of our society. This is no small gain as regards the possibility of a solution. For whereas only the meagre energies of one's conscious interest in one's own person were at the disposal of the personal problem, there are now assembled the combined forces of collective instinct, which flow in and unite with the interests of the ego; thus a new situation is brought about which offers new possibilities of a solution. For what would never have been possible to the personal power of the will or to courage is made possible by the force of collective instinct; it carries a man over obstacles which his own personal energy could never overcome.

120   We may therefore conjecture that it was largely the impressions of contemporary events that gave Schiller the courage to undertake this attempt to solve the conflict between the individual and the social function. The same antagonism was also deeply felt by Rousseau—indeed it was the starting-point for his work *Emile, ou l'éducation* (1762). We find there several passages that are of interest as regards our problem:

The citizen is but the numerator of a fraction, whose value depends on its denominator; his value depends on the whole, that is, on the community. Good social institutions are those best fitted to make a man unnatural, to exchange his independence for dependence, to merge the unit in the group.[16]

He who would preserve the supremacy of natural feelings in social life knows not what he asks. Ever at war with himself, hesitating between his wishes and his duties, he will be neither a man nor a citizen. He will be of no use to himself nor to others.[17]

121   Rousseau opens his work with the famous sentence: "Everything as it leaves the hands of the Author of things is good; everything degenerates under the hands of man."[18] This statement is characteristic not only of Rousseau but of the whole epoch.

[16] *Emile* (trans. Foxley), p. 7.   [17] Ibid., p. 8.
[18] Cf. ibid., p. 5.

122   Schiller likewise looks back, not of course to Rousseau's
natural man—and here lies the essential difference—but to the
man who lived "under a Grecian heaven." This retrospective
orientation is common to both and is inextricably bound up
with an idealization and overvaluation of the past. Schiller,
marvelling at the beauties of antiquity, forgets the actual everyday Greek, and Rousseau mounts to dizzy heights with the sentence: "The natural man is wholly himself; he is an integral
unity, an absolute whole,"[19] quite forgetting that the natural
man is thoroughly collective, i.e., just as much in others as in
himself, and is anything rather than a unity. Elsewhere Rousseau says:

We grasp at everything, we clutch on to everything, times, places,
men, things; all that is, all that will be, matters to each of us; we
ourselves are but the least part of ourselves. We spread ourselves,
so to speak, over the whole world, and become sensitive over this
whole vast expanse. . . . Is it nature which thus bears men so far
from themselves?[20]

123   Rousseau is deceived; he believes this state of affairs is a
recent development. But it is not so; we have merely become
conscious of it recently; it was always so, and the more so the
further we descend into the beginnings of things. For what
Rousseau describes is nothing but that primitive collective
mentality which Lévy-Bruhl has aptly termed *participation
mystique*. This suppression of individuality is nothing new, it
is a relic of that archaic time when there was no individuality
whatever. So it is not by any means a recent suppression we
are dealing with, but merely a new sense and awareness of the
overwhelming power of the collective. One naturally projects
this power into the institutions of Church and State, as though
there were not already ways and means enough of evading
even moral commands when occasion offered! In no sense do
these institutions possess the omnipotence ascribed to them, on
account of which they are from time to time assailed by in-
novators of every sort; the suppressive power lies unconsciously in ourselves, in our own barbarian collective mentality. To the collective psyche every individual development is
hateful that does not directly serve the ends of collectivity.

19 Cf. ibid., p. 7.   20 Cf. ibid., p. 46.

82

Hence although the differentiation of the one function, about which we have spoken above, is a development of an individual value, it is still so largely determined by the views of the collective that, as we have seen, it becomes injurious to the individual himself.

124   It was their imperfect knowledge of earlier conditions of human psychology that led both our authors into false judgments about the values of the past. The result of this false judgment is a belief in the illusory picture of an earlier, more perfect type of man, who somehow fell from his high estate. Retrospective orientation is itself a relic of pagan thinking, for it is a well-known characteristic of the archaic and barbarian mentality that it imagined a paradisal Golden Age as the forerunner of the present evil times. It was the great social and spiritual achievement of Christianity that first gave man hope for the future, and promised him some possibility of realizing of his ideals.[21] The emphasizing of this retrospective orientation in the more recent development of the mind may be connected with the phenomenon of that widespread regression to paganism which has made itself increasingly felt ever since the Renaissance.

125   To me it seems certain that this retrospective orientation must also have a decided influence on the choice of the methods of human education. The mind thus oriented is ever seeking support in some phantasmagoria of the past. We could make light of this were it not that the knowledge of the conflict between the types and the typical mechanisms compels us to look round for something that would establish their harmony. As we shall see from the following passages, this is also what Schiller had at heart. His fundamental thought is expressed in these words, which sum up what we have just said:

Let some beneficent deity snatch the infant betimes from his mother's breast, nourish him with the milk of a better age and suffer him to grow up to full maturity under that far-off Grecian heaven. Then when he has become a man, let him return, a stranger, to his own century; not to gladden it by his appearance, but rather, terrible like Agamemnon's son, to cleanse it.[22]

21 Indications of this are already to be found in the Greek mysteries.
22 Cf. Snell, p. 51.

126　　The predilection for the Grecian prototype could hardly be expressed more clearly. But in this stern formulation one can also glimpse a limitation which impels Schiller to a very essential broadening of perspective:

He will indeed take his material from the present age, but his form he will borrow from a nobler time—nay, from beyond all time, from the absolute unchangeable unity of his being.[23]

Schiller clearly felt that he must go back still further, to some primeval heroic age where men were still half divine. He continues:

Here, from the pure aether of his daemonic nature, gushes down the well-spring of Beauty, untainted by the corruption of generations and ages which wallow in the dark eddies far below.[24]

Here we have the beautiful illusion of a Golden Age when men were still gods and were ever refreshed by the vision of eternal beauty. But here, too, the poet has overtaken Schiller the thinker. A few pages further on the thinker gets the upper hand again:

It must indeed set us thinking when we find that in almost every epoch of history when the arts are flourishing and taste prevails, humanity is in a state of decline, and cannot produce a single example where a high degree and wide diffusion of aesthetic culture among a people has gone hand in hand with political freedom and civic virtue, fine manners with good morals, or polished behaviour with truth.[25]

127　　In accordance with this familiar and in every way undeniable experience those heroes of olden time must have led a none too scrupulous life, and indeed not a single myth, Greek or otherwise, claims that they ever did anything else. All that beauty could revel in its existence only because there was as yet no penal code and no guardian of public morals. With the recognition of the psychological fact that living beauty spreads her golden shimmer only when soaring above a reality full of misery, pain, and squalor, Schiller cuts the ground from under his own feet; for he had undertaken to prove that what was

23 Cf. ibid., pp. 51f.　　　　　24 Cf. ibid., p. 52.
25 Cf. ibid , p. 58.

divided would be united by the vision, enjoyment, and creation of the beautiful. Beauty was to be the mediator which
should restore the primal unity of human nature. On the contrary, all experience goes to show that beauty needs her opposite as a condition of her existence.

128   As before it was the poet, so now it is the thinker that carries Schiller away: he *mistrusts* beauty, he even holds it
possible, arguing from experience, that she may exercise a deleterious influence:

> Whenever we turn our gaze in the ancient world, we find taste and
> freedom mutually avoiding each other, and Beauty establishing her
> sway only on the ruins of heroic virtues.[26]

This insight, gained by experience, can hardly sustain the claim
that Schiller makes for beauty. In the further pursuit of his
theme he even gets to the point where he depicts the reverse
side of beauty with an all too glaring clarity:

> If then we keep solely to what experience has taught us hitherto
> about the influence of Beauty, we cannot certainly be much en-
> couraged in the development of feelings which are so dangerous to
> the true culture of mankind; and we should rather dispense with
> the melting power of Beauty, even at the risk of coarseness and aus-
> terity, than see ourselves, for all the advantages of refinement, con-
> signed to her enervating influence.[27]

29   The quarrel between the poet and the thinker could surely
be composed if the thinker took the words of the poet not
literally but *symbolically*, which is how the tongue of the poet
desires to be understood. Can Schiller have misunderstood
himself? It would almost seem so, otherwise he could not argue
thus against himself. The poet speaks of a spring of unsullied
beauty which flows beneath every age and generation, and is
constantly welling up in every human heart. It is not the man
of Greek antiquity whom the poet has in mind, but the old
pagan in ourselves, that bit of eternally unspoiled nature and
pristine beauty which lies unconscious but living within us,
whose reflected splendour transfigures the shapes of the past,
and for whose sake we fall into the error of thinking that those

[26] Ibid., p. 59.   [27] Ibid., p. 59

heroes actually possessed the beauty we seek. It is the archaic man in ourselves, who, rejected by our collectively oriented consciousness, appears to us as hideous and unacceptable, but who is nevertheless the bearer of that beauty we vainly seek elsewhere. This is the man the poet Schiller means, but the thinker mistakes him for his Greek prototype. What the thinker cannot deduce logically from his evidential material, what he labours for in vain, the poet in symbolic language reveals as the promised land.

130   From all this it is abundantly clear that any attempt to equalize the one-sided differentiation of the man of our times has to reckon very seriously with an acceptance of the inferior, because undifferentiated, functions. No attempt at mediation will be successful if it does not understand how to release the energies of the inferior functions and lead them towards differentiation. This process can take place only in accordance with the laws of energy, that is, a gradient must be created which offers the latent energies a chance to come into play.

131   It would be a hopeless task—which nevertheless has often been undertaken and as often has foundered—to transform an inferior function directly into a superior one. It would be as easy to make a *perpetuum mobile*. No lower form of energy can simply be converted into a higher form unless a source of higher value simultaneously lends its support; that is, the conversion can be accomplished only at the expense of the superior function. But under no circumstances can the initial value of the higher form of energy be attained by the lower forms as well or be resumed by the superior function: an equalization at some intermediate level must inevitably result. For every individual who identifies with his one differentiated function, this entails a descent to a condition which, though balanced, is of a definitely lower value as compared with the initial value. This conclusion is unavoidable. All education that aspires to the unity and harmony of man's nature has to reckon with this fact. In his own fashion, Schiller draws the same conclusion, but he struggles against accepting its consequences, even to the point where he has to renounce beauty. But when the thinker has uttered his harsh judgment, the poet speaks again:

But perhaps experience is not the tribunal before which such a question is to be decided, and before we allow any weight to its testimony it must first be established, beyond doubt, that it is the self-same Beauty about which we are speaking and against which those examples testify.[28]

132   It is evident that Schiller is here attempting to stand above experience; in other words he bestows on beauty a quality which experience does not warrant. He believes that "Beauty must be exhibited as a necessary condition of humanity,"[29] that is, as a necessary, compelling category; therefore he speaks also of a purely intellectual concept of beauty, and of a "transcendental way" that removes us from "the round of appearances and from the living presence of things." "Those who do not venture out beyond actuality will never capture Truth."[30] His subjective resistance to what experience has shown to be the ineluctable downward way impels Schiller to press the logical intellect into the service of feeling, forcing it to come up with a formula that makes the attainment of the original aim possible after all, despite the fact that its impossibility has already been sufficiently demonstrated.

133   A similar violation is committed by Rousseau in his assumption that whereas dependence on nature does not involve depravity, dependence on man does, so that he can arrive at the following conclusion:

If the laws of nations, like the laws of nature, could never be broken by any human power, dependence on men would become dependence on things; all the advantages of a state of nature could be combined with all the advantages of social life in the commonwealth. The liberty which preserves a man from vice would be united with the morality which raises him to virtue.[31]

On the basis of these reflections he gives the following advice:

Keep the child dependent solely on things, and you will have followed the order of nature in the progress of his education. . . . Do not make him sit still when he wants to run about, nor run when he wants to stay quiet. If we did not spoil our children's wills by our blunders, their desires would be free from caprice.[32]

134   The misfortune is that never under any circumstances are the laws of nations in such concord with those of nature that the civilized state is at the same time the natural state. If such

[28] Ibid.   [29] Ibid., p. 60.   [30] Cf. ibid.
[31] *Emile* (trans. Foxley), p. 49.   [32] Cf. ibid., p. 50.

concord is to be conceived as possible at all, it can be conceived only as a compromise in which neither state could attain its ideal but would remain far below it. Whoever wishes to attain one or the other of the ideals will have to rest content with Rousseau's own formulation: "You must choose between making a man or a citizen, you cannot make both at once."[33]

135   Both these necessities exist in us: nature and culture. We cannot only be ourselves, we must also be related to others. Hence a way must be found that is not a mere rational compromise; it must be a state or process that is wholly consonant with the living being, "a highway and a holy way," as the prophet says, "a straight way, so that fools shall not err therein."[34] I am therefore inclined to give the poet in Schiller his due, though in this case he has encroached somewhat violently on the thinker, for rational truths are not the last word, there are also irrational ones. In human affairs, what appears impossible by way of the intellect has often become true by way of the irrational. Indeed, all the greatest transformations that have ever befallen mankind have come not by way of intellectual calculation, but by ways which contemporary minds either ignored or rejected as absurd, and which only long afterwards were recognized because of their intrinsic necessity. More often than not they are never recognized at all, for the all-important laws of mental development are still a book with seven seals.

136   I am, however, little inclined to concede any particular value to the philosophical gesturings of the poet, for in his hands the intellect is a deceptive instrument. What the intellect can achieve it has already achieved in this case; it has uncovered the contradiction between desire and experience. To persist, then, in demanding a solution of this contradiction from philosophical thinking is quite useless. And even if a solution could finally be thought out, the real obstacle would still confront us, for the solution does not lie in the possibility of thinking it or in the discovery of a rational truth, but in the discovery of a way which real life can accept. There has never been any lack of suggestions and wise precepts. If it were only a question of that, mankind would have had the finest oppor-

[33] Cf. ibid., p. 7.   [34] Isaiah 35:8.

tunity of reaching the heights in every respect at the time of Pythagoras. That is why what Schiller proposes must not be taken in a literal sense but, as I have said, as a symbol, which in accordance with Schiller's philosophical proclivities appears under the guise of a philosophical concept. Similarly, the "transcendental way" which Schiller sets out to tread must not be understood as a piece of critical ratiocination based on knowledge, but symbolically as the way a man always follows when he encounters an obstacle that cannot be overcome by reason, or when he is confronted with an insoluble task. But in order to find and follow this way, he must first have lingered a long time with the opposites into which his former way forked. The obstacle dams up the river of his life. Whenever a damming up of libido occurs, the opposites, previously united in the steady flow of life, fall apart and henceforth confront one another like antagonists eager for battle. They then exhaust themselves in a prolonged conflict the duration and upshot of which cannot be foreseen, and from the energy which is lost to them is built that third thing which is the beginning of the new way.

137   In accordance with this law, Schiller now devotes himself to a profound examination of the nature of the opposites at work. No matter what obstacle we come up against—provided only it be a difficult one—the discord between our own purpose and the refractory object soon becomes a discord in ourselves. For, while I am striving to subordinate the object to my will, my whole being is gradually brought into relationship with it, following the strong libido investment which, as it were, draws a portion of my being across into the object. The result of this is a partial identification of certain portions of my personality with similar qualities in the object. As soon as this identification has taken place, the conflict is transferred into my own psyche. This "introjection" of the conflict with the object creates an inner discord, making me powerless against the object and also releasing affects, which are always symptomatic of inner disharmony. The affects, however, prove that I am sensing myself and am therefore in a position—if I am not blind—to apply my attention to myself and to follow up the play of opposites in my own psyche.

138   This is the way that Schiller takes. The discord he finds is

not between the State and the individual, but, at the beginning of the eleventh letter, he conceives it as the duality of "person and condition,"[35] that is, as the ego and its changing states of affect. For whereas the ego has a relative constancy, its relatedness, or proneness to affect, is variable. Schiller thus tries to grasp the discord at its root. And as a matter of fact the one side of it is the conscious ego-function, while the other side is the ego's relation to the collective. Both determinants are inherent in human psychology. But the various types will each see these basic facts in a different light. For the introvert the idea of the ego is the continuous and dominant note of consciousness, and its antithesis for him is relatedness or proneness to affect. For the extravert, on the contrary, the accent lies more on the continuity of his relation to the object and less on the idea of the ego. Hence for him the problem is different. This point must be borne in mind as we follow Schiller's further reflections. When, for instance, he says that the "person" reveals itself "in the eternally constant ego, and in this alone,"[36] this is viewed from the standpoint of the introvert. From the standpoint of the extravert we would have to say that the person reveals itself simply and solely in its relatedness, in the function of relationship to the object. For only with the introvert is the "person" exclusively the ego; with the extravert it lies in his affectivity and not in the affected ego. His ego is, as it were, of less importance than his affectivity, i.e., his relatedness. The extravert discovers himself in the fluctuating and changeable, the introvert in the constant. The ego is not "eternally constant," least of all in the extravert, who pays little attention to it. For the introvert, on the other hand, it has too much importance; he therefore shrinks from every change that is at all liable to affect his ego. Affectivity for him can be something positively painful, while for the extravert it must on no account be missed. Schiller at once reveals himself as an introvert in the following formulation:

To remain constantly himself throughout all change, to turn every perception into experience, that is, into the unity of knowledge, and to make each of his manifestations in time a law for all time, that is the rule which is prescribed for him by his rational nature.[37]

[35] Snell, p. 60.   [36] Cf. ibid., p. 61.   [37] Ibid., p. 62.

139   The abstracting, self-contained attitude is evident; it is even made the supreme rule of conduct. Every occurrence must at once be raised to the level of an experience, and from the sum of these experiences a law for all time must instantly emerge; though the other attitude, that no occurrence should become an experience lest it produce laws that might hamper the future, is equally human.

140   It is altogether in keeping with Schiller's attitude that he cannot think of God as *becoming*, but only as *eternally being*; hence with unerring intuition he recognizes the "godlikeness" of the introverted ideal state:

Man conceived in his perfection would accordingly be the constant unity which amidst the tides of change remains eternally the same. . . .[38] Beyond question man carries the potentiality for divinity within himself.[39]

141   This conception of the nature of God ill accords with his Christian incarnation and with similar Neoplatonic views of the mother of the gods and of her son who descends as the demiurge into creation.[40] But it is clear what is the function to which Schiller attributes the highest value, divinity: it is the constancy of the idea of the ego. The ego that abstracts itself from affectivity is for him the most important thing, consequently this is the idea he has differentiated most, as is the case with every introvert. His god, his highest value, is the abstraction and conservation of the ego. For the extravert, on the contrary, the god is the experience of the object, complete immersion in reality; hence a god who became man is more sympathetic to him than an eternal, immutable lawgiver. These views, if I may anticipate a little, are valid only for the *conscious* psychology of the types. In the unconscious the relations are reversed. Schiller seems to have had an inkling of this: although with his conscious mind he believes in an immutably existing God, yet the way to divinity is revealed to him through the *senses*, through affectivity, through the living process of change. But for him this is a function of secondary importance, and to the extent that he identifies with his ego

[38] Ibid.   [39] Ibid., p. 63.

[40] Cf. the discourse of Julian the Apostate on the mother of the gods, *Works*, I, pp. 462ff.

and abstracts it from change, his conscious attitude also becomes entirely abstract, while his affectivity, his relatedness to the object, necessarily lapses into the unconscious.

142   From the abstracting attitude of consciousness, which in pursuit of its ideal makes an experience of every occurrence and from the sum of experience a law, a certain limitation and impoverishment result which are characteristic of the introvert. Schiller clearly sensed this in his relation to Goethe, for he felt Goethe's more extraverted nature as something objectively opposed to himself.[41] Of himself Goethe significantly says:

As a contemplative man I am an arrant realist, so that I am capable of desiring nothing from all the things that present themselves to me, and of wishing nothing added to them. I make no sort of distinction among objects beyond whether they interest me or not.[42]

Concerning Schiller's effect upon him, Goethe very characteristically says:

If I have served you as the representative of certain objects, you have led me from a too rigorous observation of external things and their relations back into myself. You have taught me to view the many-sidedness of the inner man with more justice.[43]

143   In Goethe, on the other hand, Schiller finds an often accentuated complement or fulfillment of his own nature, at the same time sensing the difference, which he indicates in the following way:

Expect of me no great material wealth of ideas, for that is what I find in you. My need and endeavour is to make much out of little, and, if ever you should realize my poverty in all that men call acquired knowledge, you will perhaps find that in some ways I may have succeeded. Because my circle of ideas is smaller, I traverse it more quickly and oftener, and for that reason can make better use of what small ready cash I own, creating through the form a diversity which is lacking in the content. You strive to simplify your great world of ideas, while I seek variety for my small possessions.

---

[41] Letter to Goethe, January 5, 1798 (Beutler, XX, p. 485).
[42] Letter to Schiller, April 27, 1798 (p. 564).
[43] Letter to Schiller, January 6, 1798 (pp. 486f.).

You have a kingdom to rule, and I only a somewhat numerous family of ideas which I would like to expand into a little universe.[44]

144   If we subtract from this statement a certain feeling of inferiority that is characteristic of the introvert, and add to it the fact that the "great world of ideas" is not so much ruled by the extravert as he himself is subject to it, then Schiller's plaint gives a striking picture of the poverty that tends to develop as the result of an essentially abstracting attitude.

145   A further result of the abstracting attitude of consciousness, and one whose significance will become more apparent in the course of our exposition, is that the unconscious develops a compensating attitude. For the more the relation to the object is restricted by abstraction (because too many "experiences" and "laws" are made), the more insistently does a craving for the object develop in the unconscious, and this finally expresses itself in consciousness as a compulsive sensuous tie to the object. The sensuous relation to the object then takes the place of a feeling relation, which is lacking, or rather suppressed, because of abstraction. Characteristically, therefore, Schiller regards the *senses*, and not *feelings*, as the way to divinity. His ego makes use of thinking, but his affections, his feelings, make use of sensation. Thus for him the schism is between spirituality in the form of thinking, and sensuousness in the form of affectivity or feeling. For the extravert the situation is reversed: his relation to the object is highly developed, but his world of ideas is sensory and concrete.

146   Sensuous feeling, or rather the feeling that is present in the sensuous state, is collective. It produces a relatedness or proneness to affect which always puts the individual in a state of *participation mystique*, a condition of partial identity with the sensed object. This identity expresses itself in a compulsive dependence on that object, and in turn, after the manner of a vicious circle, causes in the introvert an intensification of abstraction for the purpose of abolishing the burdensome dependence and the compulsion it evokes. Schiller recognized this peculiarity of sensuous feeling:

So long as he merely senses, merely desires and acts from mere appetite, man is still nothing but *world*.

[44] Letter to Goethe, August 31, 1794 (p. 19).

But since the introvert cannot go on abstracting indefinitely in order to escape being affected, he sees himself forced in the end to give shape to externals. Schiller goes on:

> Thus in order not to be merely world, he must impart form to matter; he must externalize all within, and shape everything without. Both tasks, in their highest fulfilment, lead back to the concept of divinity from which I started.[45]

147   This is an important point. Let us suppose the sensuously felt object to be a human being—will he accept this prescription? Will he permit himself to be shaped as though the person to whom he is related were his creator? Man is certainly called upon to play the god on a small scale, but ultimately even inanimate things have a divine right to their own existence, and the world ceased to be chaos long ago when the first hominids began to sharpen stones. It would indeed be a dubious undertaking if every introvert wanted to externalize his limited world of ideas and to shape the external world accordingly. Such attempts happen daily, but the individual suffers, and rightly so, under this "godlikeness."

148   For the extravert, Schiller's formula should run: "Internalize all without and shape everything within." This was the reaction that, as we saw, Schiller evoked in Goethe. Goethe supplies a telling parallel to this when he writes to Schiller:

> On the other hand in every sort of activity I am, one might almost say, completely idealistic: I ask nothing at all from objects, but instead I demand that everything shall conform to my conceptions.[46]

This means that when the extravert thinks, things go just as autocratically as when the introvert acts upon the external world.[47] The formula can therefore hold good only when an almost perfect state has been reached, when in fact the introvert has attained a world of ideas so rich and flexible and capable of expression that it no longer forces the object on to a procrustean bed, and the extravert such an ample knowledge of

---

[45] Cf. Snell, p. 63.

[46] Letter to Schiller, April 27, 1798 (p. 564).

[47] I would like to emphasize that everything I say in this chapter about the extravert and introvert applies only to the types we are discussing: the intuitive, extraverted feeling type represented by Goethe, and the intuitive, introverted thinking type represented by Schiller.

and respect for the object that it no longer gives rise to a caricature when he operates with it in his thinking. Thus we see that Schiller bases his formula on the highest possible criterion and so makes almost prohibitive demands on the psychological development of the individual—assuming that he is thoroughly clear in his own mind what his formula means in every particular.

149   Be that as it may, it is at least fairly clear that the formula "Externalize all within and shape everything without" is the ideal of the conscious attitude of the introvert. It is based, on the one hand, on the assumption of an ideal range of his inner conceptual world, of the formal principle, and, on the other, on the assumption of the possibility of an ideal application of the sensuous principle, which then no longer appears as affectivity, but as an active potency. So long as man is "sensuous" he is "nothing but world," and "in order not to be merely world he must impart form to matter." This implies a reversal of the passive, receptive, sensuous principle. Yet how can such a reversal come about? That is the whole point. It can scarcely be supposed that a man can give his world of ideas that extraordinary range which would be necessary in order to impose a congenial form on the material world, and at the same time convert his affectivity, his sensuous nature, from a passive to an active state in order to bring it up to the level of his world of ideas. Somewhere or other man must be related, must be subject to something, otherwise he would be really godlike. One is forced to conclude that Schiller would let it go so far that violence was done to the object. But that would be to concede to the archaic, inferior function an unlimited right to existence, which as we know Nietzsche, at least in theory, actually did. This conclusion is by no means applicable to Schiller, since, so far as I am aware, he nowhere consciously expressed himself to this effect. His formula has instead a thoroughly naïve and idealistic character, quite consistent with the spirit of his time, which was not yet vitiated by that deep distrust of human nature and of human truth which haunted the epoch of psychological criticism inaugurated by Nietzsche.

150   Schiller's formula could be carried out only by applying a ruthless power standpoint, with never a scruple about justice for the object nor any conscientious examination of its own

competence. Only under such conditions, which Schiller certainly never contemplated, could the inferior function participate in life. In this way the archaic elements, naïve and unconscious and decked in the glamour of mighty words and fair gestures, also came bursting through and helped to build our present "civilization," concerning the nature of which humanity is at this moment in some measure of disagreement. The archaic power instinct, hitherto hidden behind the façade of civilized living, finally came to the surface in its true colours, and proved beyond question that we are "still barbarians." For it should not be forgotten that, in the same measure as the conscious attitude may pride itself on a certain godlikeness by reason of its lofty and absolute standpoint, an unconscious attitude develops with a godlikeness oriented downwards to an archaic god whose nature is sensual and brutal. The enantiodromia of Heraclitus ensures that the time will come when this *deus absconditus* shall rise to the surface and press the God of our ideals to the wall. It is as though men at the close of the eighteenth century had not really seen what was taking place in Paris, but lingered on in an aesthetic, enthusiastic, or trifling attitude in order to delude themselves about the real meaning of that glimpse into the abysses of human nature.

> In that nether world is terror,
> And man shall not tempt the gods.
> Let him never yearn to see
> What they veil with night and horror![48]

151   When Schiller lived, the time for dealing with that nether world had not yet come. Nietzsche at heart was much nearer to it; to him it was certain that we were approaching an epoch of unprecedented struggle. He it was, the only true pupil of Schopenhauer, who tore through the veil of naïveté and in his *Zarathustra* conjured up from the nether region ideas that were destined to be the most vital content of the coming age.

b. Concerning the Basic Instincts

152   In this twelfth letter Schiller comes to grips with the two basic instincts, to which he devotes a detailed description. The "sensuous" instinct is concerned with "setting man within the

[48] Schiller, *The Diver*.

bounds of time and turning him into matter."[49] This instinct demands

that there be change, so that time should have a content. This state of merely filled time is called *sensation*.

Man in this state is nothing but a unit of magnitude, a filled moment of time—or rather, he is not even that, for his personality is extinguished so long as sensation rules him and time whirls him along.

With unbreakable bonds this instinct chains the upward-striving spirit to the world of sense, and summons abstraction from its unfettered wanderings in the infinite back into the confines of the present.[50]

153   It is entirely characteristic of Schiller's psychology that he should conceive the expression of this instinct as *sensation*, and not as active, sensuous *desire*. This shows that for him sensuousness has the character of *reactiveness*, of affectivity, which is altogether typical of the introvert. An extravert would undoubtedly emphasize the element of desire. It is further significant that it is this instinct which demands *change*. The idea wants changelessness and eternity. Whoever lives under the supremacy of the idea strives for permanence; hence everything that pushes towards change must be opposed to the idea. In Schiller's case it is feeling and sensation, which as a rule are fused together on account of their undeveloped state. Schiller does not in fact discriminate sufficiently between feeling and sensation as the following passage proves:

Feeling can only say: this is true for this subject and at this moment; another moment another subject may come and revoke the statement of the present sensation.[51]

154   This passage clearly shows that for Schiller feeling and sensation are actually interchangeable terms, and it reveals an inadequate evaluation and differentiation of feeling as distinct from sensation. Differentiated feeling can establish universal values as well as those that are merely specific and individual. But it is true that the "feeling-sensation" of the introverted thinking type, because of its passive and reactive character, is purely specific; it can never rise above the individual case, by which alone it is stimulated, to an abstract comparison of all

[49] Snell, p. 64.   [50] Cf. ibid., p. 64f.   [51] Cf. ibid., p. 66.

cases, since with the introverted thinking type this duty is performed not by the feeling function but by the thinking function. Conversely, with the introverted feeling type, feeling attains an abstract and universal character and can establish universal and permanent values.

155   From a further analysis of Schiller's description we find that "feeling-sensation" (by which term I mean the characteristic fusion of the two in the introverted thinking type) is the function with which the ego does not declare itself identical. It has the character of something inimical and foreign, that "extinguishes" the personality, whirls it away, setting the subject outside himself and alienating him from himself. Hence Schiller likens it to affect, which sets a man "beside himself" (= extraverted). When one has collected oneself he says this is called, "just as correctly, going into oneself [= introverted], that is, returning to one's ego, re-establishing the personality."[52] From this it is quite evident that it seems to Schiller as though "feeling-sensation" does not really belong to the person, but is a rather precarious accessory "to which a firm will may triumphantly oppose its demands."[53] But to the extravert it is just this side of him which seems to constitute his true nature; it is as if he were actually himself only when he is being affected by the object—as we can well understand when we consider that for him the relation to the object is his superior, differentiated function, to which abstract thinking and feeling are just as much opposed as they are indispensable to the introvert. The thinking of the extraverted feeling type is just as prejudiced by the sensuous instinct as is the feeling of the introverted thinking type. For both it means extreme restriction to the material and specific. Living through the object also has its "unfettered wanderings in the infinite," and not abstraction alone, as Schiller thinks.

156   By excluding sensuousness from the concept and scope of the "person" Schiller is able to assert that the "person, being an absolute and indivisible unity, can never be at variance with itself."[54] This unity is a desideratum of the intellect, which would like to preserve the subject in its most ideal integrity; hence as the superior function it must exclude the ostensibly

[52] Ibid., p. 65n.   [53] P. 65.   [54] P. 66.

inferior function of sensuousness. The result is that very mutilation of human nature which is the motive and starting-point of Schiller's quest.

157 Since, for Schiller, feeling has the quality of "feeling-sensation" and is therefore merely specific, the supreme value, a really eternal value, is naturally assigned to formative thought, or what Schiller calls the "formal instinct":[55]

> But when once thought pronounces: *that is*, it decides for ever and aye, and the validity of its pronouncement is vouched for by the personality itself, which defies all change.[56]

One cannot refrain from asking: Do the meaning and value of the personality really lie only in what is permanent? May it not be that change, becoming, and development represent actually higher values than mere "defiance" of change?[57] Schiller continues:

> When therefore the formal instinct holds sway, and the pure object acts within us, there is the highest expansion of being, all barriers disappear, and from a unit of magnitude to which the needy senses confined him, man has risen to a unity of idea embracing the whole realm of phenomena. By this operation we are no more in time, but time, with its complete and infinite succession, is in us. We are no longer individuals, but species; the judgment of all minds is pronounced by our own, the choice of all hearts is represented by our deed.[58]

158 There can be no doubt that the thinking of the introvert aspires to this Hyperion; it is only a pity that the "unity of idea" is the ideal of such a very limited class of men. Thinking is merely a function which, when fully developed and exclusively obeying its own laws, naturally sets up a claim to universal validity. Only one part of the world, therefore, can be grasped by thinking, another part only by feeling, a third only through sensation, and so on. That is probably why there are different psychic functions; for, biologically, the psychic system can be understood only as a system of adaptation, just as eyes exist presumably because there is light. Thinking can claim only a third or a fourth part of the total significance, although

---

[55] The "formal instinct" is equivalent to the "power of thought" for Schiller.
[56] P. 66.   [57] Later on Schiller himself criticizes this point.
[58] Cf. p. 67.

in its own sphere it possesses exclusive validity—just as sight is the exclusively valid function for the perception of light waves, and hearing for that of sound waves. Consequently a man who puts the unity of idea on a pinnacle, and for whom "feeling-sensation" is something antipathetic to his personality, can be compared to a man who has good eyes but is totally deaf and suffers from anaesthesia.

159   "We are no longer individuals, but species": certainly, if we identify ourselves exclusively with thinking, or with any one function whatsoever; for then we are collective beings with universal validity although quite estranged from ourselves. Outside this quarter-psyche, the three other quarters languish in the darkness of repression and inferiority. "Is it nature which thus bears men so far from themselves?" we might ask with Rousseau—nature, or is it not rather our own psychology, which so barbarously overvalues the one function and allows itself to be swept away by it? This impetus is of course a piece of nature too, that untamed instinctive energy before which the differentiated type recoils if ever it should "accidentally" manifest itself in an inferior function instead of in the ideal function, where it is prized and honoured as a divine afflatus. As Schiller truly says:

But your individuality and your present need will be swept away by change, and what you now ardently desire will one day become the object of your abhorrence.[59]

160   Whether the untamed, extravagant, disproportionate energy shows itself in sensuality—in *abjectissimo loco*—or in an overestimation and deification of the most highly developed function, it is at bottom the same: barbarism. But naturally one has no insight into this so long as one is still hypnotized by the *object* of the deed and ignores *how* it is done.

161   Identification with the one differentiated function means that one is in a collective state—not, of course, identical with the collective, as is the primitive, but collectively adapted so far as "the judgment of all minds is pronounced by our own" and our thought and speech exactly conform to the general expectations of those whose thinking is differentiated and adapted to the same degree. Furthermore, "the choice of all hearts is represented by our deed" so far as we think and do

59 P. 66.

as all desire it to be thought and done. And in fact everyone thinks and believes that it is the best and most desirable thing when there is the maximum of identity with the one differentiated function, for that brings the most obvious social advantages, but at the same time the greatest disadvantages to those lesser developed sides of our human nature, which sometimes constitute a large part of our individuality. Schiller goes on:

Once we assert the primary, and therefore necessary, antagonism of the two instincts, there is really no other means of preserving the unity in man except by the absolute subordination of the sensuous instinct to the rational. But the only result of that is mere uniformity, not harmony, and man still remains for ever divided.[60]

Because it is difficult to remain true to our principles amidst all the ardour of the feelings, we adopt the more comfortable expedient of making the character more secure by blunting them; for it is infinitely easier to keep calm in the face of an unarmed adversary than to master a spirited and active foe. In this operation, then, consists for the most part what we call the forming of a human being; and that in the best sense of the term, as signifying the cultivation of the inner, not merely the outward, man. A man so formed will indeed be secured against being crude Nature, and from appearing as such; but he will at the same time be armed by his principles against every sensation of Nature, so that humanity can reach him as little from without as from within.[61]

162   Schiller was also aware that the two functions, thinking and affectivity (feeling-sensation), can take one another's place, which happens, as we saw, when one function is privileged:

He can assign to the passive function [feeling-sensation] the intensity which the active function requires, forestall the formal by means of the material instinct, and make the receptive faculty the determining one. Or he can assign to the active function [positive thinking] the extensity which is proper to the passive, forestall the material instinct by means of the formal, and substitute the determining for the receptive faculty. In the first case he will never be himself, in the second he will never be anything else. Consequently, in both cases he is neither the one nor the other, and is therefore a nonentity.[62]

163   In this very remarkable passage much is contained that we have already discussed. When the energy of positive thinking

60 Cf. p. 68n.   61 Cf. p. 71n.   62 Cf. p. 70.

is supplied to feeling-sensation, which would amount to a reversal of the introverted thinking type, the qualities of undifferentiated, archaic feeling-sensation become paramount: the individual relapses into an extreme relatedness, or identity with the sensed object. This state is one of *inferior extraversion*, an extraversion which, as it were, detaches the individual entirely from his ego and dissolves him into archaic collective ties and identifications. He is then no longer "himself," but sheer relatedness, identical with the object and therefore without a standpoint. The introvert instinctively feels the greatest resistance to this condition, which is no guarantee that he will not unconsciously fall into it. It should on no account be confused with the extraversion of the extraverted type, inclined as the introvert is to make this mistake and to display for this extraversion the same contempt which, at bottom, he always feels for his own.[63] Schiller's second instance, on the other hand, is the purest illustration of the introverted thinking type, who by amputating his inferior feeling-sensations condemns himself to sterility, to a state in which "humanity can reach him as little from without as from within."

164   Here again it is obvious that Schiller is writing, as always, only from the standpoint of the introvert. The extravert, whose ego resides not in thinking but in the feeling relation to the object, actually finds himself through the object, whereas the introvert loses himself in it. But when the extravert proceeds to introvert, he arrives at a state of inferior relatedness to collective ideas, an identity with collective thinking of an archaic, concretistic kind, which one might call *sensation-thinking*. He loses himself in this inferior function just as much as the introvert in his inferior extraversion. Hence the extravert has the same repugnance, fear, or silent contempt for introversion as the introvert for extraversion.

165   Schiller senses this opposition between the two mechanisms—in his case between sensation and thinking, or, as he puts it, "matter and form," "passivity and activity"[64]—as *unbridgeable*.

---

[63] To avoid misunderstandings, I should like to observe that this contempt does not apply to the object, at least not as a rule, but to the relation to it.

[64] That is, between affectivity and *active* thinking, in contrast to the *reactive* thinking previously referred to.

The distance between matter and form, between passivity and
activity, between sensation and thought, is infinite, and the two
cannot conceivably be reconciled. The two conditions are opposed
to each other and can never be made one.[65]

But both instincts want to exist, and as "energies"—Schiller's
own very modern word for them—they need and demand a
"depotentiation."[66]

The material instinct and the formal are equally earnest in their
demands, since in cognition the one relates to the reality, the other
to the necessity, of things.[67]
   But this depotentiation of the sensuous instinct should never be
the effect of a physical incapacity and a blunting of sensation which
everywhere merits nothing but contempt; it must be an act of freedom, an activity of the person, tempering the sensual by its moral
intensity. . . . For sense must lose only to the advantage of mind.[68]

It follows, then, that mind must lose only to the advantage of
sense. Schiller does not actually say this, but it is surely implied when he continues:

Just as little should the depotentiation of the formal instinct be the
effect of spiritual incapacity and a feebleness of thought and will
that would degrade humanity. Abundance of sensations must be its
glorious source; sensuousness itself must maintain its territory with
triumphant power, and resist the violence which by its usurping
activity the mind would inflict upon it.[69]

166   With these words Schiller acknowledges the equal rights
of sensuousness and spirituality. He concedes to sensation the
right to its own existence. But at the same time we can see in
this passage the outlines of a still deeper thought: the idea of
a "reciprocity" between the two instincts, a community of interest, or, in modern language, a *symbiosis* in which the waste
products of the one would be the food supply of the other.

We have now reached the conception of a reciprocal action between
the two instincts, of such a kind that the operation of the one at the
same time establishes and restricts the operation of the other, and
each reaches its highest manifestation precisely through the activity
of the other.[70]

65 Cf. Snell, p. 88.   66 Cf. p. 72.   67 Cf. p. 78.
68 Cf. p. 72.   69 Cf. ibid.   70 Cf. p. 73.

167   Hence, if we follow out this idea, their opposition must not be conceived as something to be done away with, but on the contrary as something useful and life-promoting that should be preserved and strengthened. This is a direct attack on the predominance of the one differentiated and socially valuable function, since that is the prime cause of the suppression and depletion of the inferior functions. It would amount to a slave rebellion against the heroic ideal which compels us to sacrifice everything else for the sake of the one. If this principle, which, as we saw, was developed in particularly high degree by Christianity for the spiritualizing of man, and then proved equally effective in furthering his materialistic ends, were once finally broken, the inferior functions would find a natural release and would demand, rightly or wrongly, the same recognition as the differentiated function. The complete opposition between sensuousness and spirituality, or between the feeling-sensation and thinking of the introverted thinking type, would then be openly revealed. But, as Schiller says, this complete opposition also entails a reciprocal limitation, equivalent psychologically to an abolition of the power principle, i.e., to a renunciation of the claim to a universally valid standpoint on the strength of one differentiated and adapted collective function.

168   The direct outcome of this renunciation is *individualism*,[71] that is, the need for a realization of individuality, a realization of man as he *is*. But let us hear how Schiller tries to tackle the problem:

This reciprocal relation of the two instincts is purely a task of reason, which man will be able to solve fully only through the perfection of his being. It is in the truest sense of the term the idea of his humanity, and consequently something infinite to which he can approach ever nearer in the course of time, without ever reaching it.[72]

71 Individualism. [The positive definition of individualism, given here, which is similar to the definition of individuation (cf. par. 757), is in marked contrast to the negative aspect stressed in par. 433 and especially par. 761: "A real conflict with the collective norm arises only when an individual way is raised to a norm, which is the actual aim of extreme individualism. Naturally this aim is pathological and inimical to life. It has, accordingly, nothing to do with individuation." This fundamental distinction between individualism and individuation is expanded upon in *Two Essays*, pars. 267–8.—EDITORS.]

72 Cf. p. 73.

169   It is a pity that Schiller is so conditioned by his type, otherwise it could never have occurred to him to look upon the co-operation of the two instincts as a "task of reason," for opposites are not to be united rationally: *tertium non datur*—that is precisely why they are called opposites. It must be that Schiller understands by reason something other than *ratio*, some higher and almost mystical faculty. In practice, opposites can be united only in the form of a compromise, or *irrationally,* some new thing arising between them which, although different from both, yet has the power to take up their energies in equal measure as an expression of both and of neither. Such an expression cannot be contrived by reason, it can only be created through living. As a matter of fact Schiller means just this, as we can see from the following passage:

> But if there were cases when [man] had this twofold experience at the same time, when he was at once conscious of his freedom and sensible of his existence, when he at once felt himself as matter and came to know himself as mind, he would in such cases, and positively in them alone, have a complete intuition of his humanity, and the object which afforded him this intuition would serve him as a symbol of his accomplished destiny.[73]

Thus if a man were able to live both faculties or instincts at the same time, i.e., thinking by sensing and sensing by thinking, then, out of that experience (which Schiller calls the object), a *symbol* would arise which would express his accomplished destiny, i.e., his individual way on which the Yea and Nay are united.

170   Before we take a closer look at the psychology of this idea, it would be as well for us to ascertain how Schiller conceives the nature and origin of the symbol:

> The object of the sensuous instinct . . . may be called *life* in its widest meaning; a concept that signifies all material being, and all that is directly present to the senses. The object of the formal instinct . . . may be called *form*, both in the figurative and in the literal sense; a concept that includes all formal qualities of things and all their relations to the intellectual faculties.[74]

171   The object of the mediating function, therefore, according to Schiller, is "living form," for this would be precisely a symbol in which the opposites are united; "a concept that serves

---

[73] Cf. pp. 73f.   [74] Cf. p. 76.

to denote all aesthetic qualities of phenomena and, in a word, what we call *Beauty* in the widest sense of the term."[75] But the symbol presupposes a function that creates symbols, and in addition a function that understands them. This latter function takes no part in the creation of the symbol, it is a function in its own right, which one could call symbolic thinking or symbolic understanding. The essence of the symbol consists in the fact that it represents in itself something that is not wholly understandable, and that it hints only intuitively at its possible meaning. The creation of a symbol is not a rational process, for a rational process could never produce an image that represents a content which is at bottom incomprehensible. To understand a symbol we need a certain amount of intuition which apprehends, if only approximately, the meaning of the symbol that has been created, and then incorporates it into consciousness. Schiller calls the symbol-creating function a third instinct, the *play* instinct; it bears no resemblance to the two opposing functions, but stands between them and does justice to both their natures—always provided (a point Schiller does not mention) that sensation and thinking are *serious* functions. But there are many people for whom neither function is altogether serious, and for them seriousness must occupy the middle place instead of play. Although elsewhere Schiller denies the existence of a third, mediating, basic instinct,[76] we will nevertheless assume, though his conclusion is somewhat at fault, his intuition to be all the more accurate. For, as a matter of fact, something does stand between the opposites, but in the pure differentiated type it has become invisible. In the introvert it is what I have called feeling-sensation. On account of its relative repression, the inferior function is only partly attached to consciousness; its other part is attached to the unconscious. The differentiated function is the most fully adapted to external reality; it is essentially the reality-function; hence it is as much as possible shut off from any admixture of fantastic elements. These elements, therefore, become associated with the inferior functions, which are similarly repressed. For this reason the sensation of the introvert, which is usually sentimental, has a very strong tinge of unconscious fantasy. *The third element, in which the opposites merge, is fantasy activity,*

75 Ibid.   76 P. 67.

which is creative and receptive at once. This is the function Schiller calls the play instinct, by which he means more than he actually says. He exclaims: "For, to declare it once and for all, man plays only when he is in the full sense of the word a man, and he is only wholly man when he is playing." For him the object of the play instinct is beauty. "Man shall only *play* with Beauty, and only with *Beauty* shall he play."[77]

172   Schiller was in fact aware what it might mean to give first place to the play instinct. As we have seen, the release of repression brings a collision between the opposites, causing an equalization that necessarily results in a lowering of the value that was highest. For culture, as we understand it today, it is certainly a catastrophe when the barbarian side of the European comes uppermost, for who can guarantee that such a man, when he begins to play, will make the aesthetic temper and the enjoyment of genuine beauty his goal? That would be an entirely unjustifiable anticipation. From the inevitable lowering of the cultural level a very different result is to be expected. Schiller rightly says:

The aesthetic play instinct will then be hardly recognizable in its first attempts, as the sensuous instinct is incessantly intervening with its headstrong caprice and its savage appetite. Hence we see crude taste first seizing on what is new and startling, gaudy, fantastic, and bizarre, on what is violent and wild, and avoiding nothing so much as simplicity and quietude.[78]

173   From this we must conclude that Schiller was aware of the dangers of this development. It also follows that he himself could not acquiesce in the solution found, but felt a compelling need to give man a more substantial foundation for his humanity than the somewhat insecure basis which a playful aesthetic attitude can offer him. And that must indeed be so. For the opposition between the two functions, or function groups, is so great and so inveterate that play alone would hardly suffice to counterbalance the full gravity and seriousness of this conflict. *Similia similibus curantur*—a third factor is needed, which at least can equal the other two in seriousness. With the attitude of play all seriousness must vanish, and this opens the way for what Schiller calls an "unlimited determinability."[79] Sometimes

[77] Cf. p. 80.   [78] Cf. p. 135.   [79] Cf. infra, pars. 185f.

instinct will allow itself to be allured by sensation, sometimes by thinking; now it will play with objects, now with ideas. But in any case it will not play exclusively with beauty, for then man would be no longer a barbarian but already aesthetically educated, whereas the question at issue is: How is he to emerge from the state of barbarism? Above all else, therefore, it must definitely be established where man actually stands in his innermost being. *A priori* he is as much sensation as thinking; he is in opposition to himself, hence he must stand somewhere in between. In his deepest essence he must be a being who partakes of both instincts, yet may also differentiate himself from them in such a way that, though he must suffer them and in some cases submit to them, he can also use them. But first he must differentiate himself from them, as from natural forces to which he is subject but with which he does not declare himself identical. On this point Schiller says:

Moreover, this indwelling of the two fundamental instincts in no way contradicts the absolute unity of the mind, provided only that we distinguish it in itself from both instincts. Both certainly exist and operate within it, but the mind itself is neither matter nor form, neither sensuousness nor reason.[80]

174   Here, it seems to me, Schiller has put his finger on something very important, namely, *the possibility of separating out an individual nucleus*, which can be at one time the subject and at another the object of the opposing functions, though always remaining distinguishable from them. This separation is as much an intellectual as a moral judgment. In one case it comes about through thinking, in another through feeling. If the separation is unsuccessful, or if it is not made at all, a dissolution of the individuality into pairs of opposites inevitably follows, since it becomes identical with them. A further consequence is disunion with oneself, or an arbitrary decision in favour of one or the other side, together with a violent suppression of its opposite. This train of thought is a very ancient one, and so far as I know its most interesting formulation, psychologically speaking, may be found in Synesius, the Christian bishop of Ptolemais and pupil of Hypatia. In his book *De insomniis* he assigns to the *spiritus phantasticus* practically the

[80] Cf. p. 94.

same psychological role as Schiller to the play instinct and I to creative fantasy; only his mode of expression is not psychological but metaphysical, an ancient form of speech which is not suitable for our purpose. He says of this spirit: "The fantastic spirit is the medium between the eternal and the temporal, and in it we are most alive."[81] It unites the opposites in itself; hence it also participates in instinctive nature right down to the animal level, where it becomes instinct and arouses daemonic desires:

For this spirit borrows anything that is suitable to its purpose, taking it from both extremes as it were from neighbours, and so unites in one essence things that dwell far apart. For Nature has extended the reach of fantasy through her many realms, and it descends even to the animals, which do not yet possess reason. . . . It is itself the intelligence of the animal, and the animal understands much through this power of fantasy. . . . All classes of demons derive their essence from the life of fantasy. For they are in their whole being imaginary, and are images of that which happens within.

175   Indeed, from the psychological point of view demons are nothing other than intruders from the unconscious, spontaneous irruptions of unconscious complexes into the continuity of the conscious process. Complexes are comparable to demons which fitfully harass our thoughts and actions; hence in antiquity and the Middle Ages acute neurotic disturbances were conceived as possession. Thus, when the individual consistently takes his stand on one side, the unconscious ranges itself on the other and rebels—which is naturally what struck the Neoplatonic and Christian philosophers most, since they represented the standpoint of exclusive spirituality. Particularly valuable is Synesius' reference to the imaginary nature of demons. It is, as I have already pointed out, precisely the fantastic element that becomes associated in the unconscious with the repressed functions. Hence, if the individuality (as we might call the "individual nucleus" for short) fails to differentiate itself from the opposites, it becomes identical with them and is inwardly torn

---

81 [No page references are given in the German text for these quotations. Jung used a Latin translation by Ficino, cited in the Bibliography. For the longer passage, as translated from the original Greek, cf. *The Essays and Hymns of Synesius* (trans. FitzGerald), II, pp. 334f.—EDITORS.]

asunder, so that a state of agonizing disunion arises. Synesius expresses this as follows:

> Thus this animal spirit, which devout men have also called the spiritual soul, becomes both idol and god and demon of many shapes. In this also does the soul exhibit her torment.

176   By participating in the instinctive forces the spirit becomes a "god and demon of many shapes." This strange idea becomes immediately intelligible when we remember that in themselves sensation and thinking are collective functions, into which the individuality (or mind, according to Schiller) is dissolved by non-differentiation. It becomes a collective entity, i.e., godlike, since God is a collective idea of an all-pervading essence. In this state, says Synesius, "the soul exhibits her torment." But deliverance is won through differentiation; for, he continues, when the spirit becomes "moist and gross" it sinks into the depths, i.e., gets entangled with the object, but when purged through pain it becomes "dry and hot" and rises up again, for it is just this fiery quality that differentiates it from the humid nature of its subterranean abode.

177   Here the question naturally arises: By virtue of what power does that which is indivisible, i.e., the in-dividual, defend himself against the divisive instincts? That he can do this by means of the play instinct even Schiller, at this point, no longer believes; it must be something serious, some considerable power, that can effectively detach the individuality from both the opposites. From one side comes the call of the highest value, the highest ideal; from the other the allure of the strongest desire. Schiller says:

> Each of these two fundamental instincts, as soon as it is developed, strives by its nature and by necessity towards satisfaction; but just because both are necessary and both are yet striving towards opposite objectives, this twofold compulsion naturally cancels itself out, and the *will* preserves complete freedom between them both. Thus it is the will which acts as a power against both instincts, but neither of the two can of its own accord act as a power against the other. . . . There is in man no other power but his will, and only that which abolishes man, death and every destroyer of consciousness, can abolish this inner freedom.[82]

[82] Cf. Snell, p. 94.

178   That the opposites must cancel each other is *logically* correct, but *practically* it is not so, for the instincts are in mutual, active opposition and cause a temporarily insoluble conflict. The will could indeed decide the issue, but only if we anticipate the very condition that must first be reached. However, the problem of how man is to emerge from barbarism is not yet solved, neither is that condition established which alone could impart to the will a direction that would be fair to both opposites and so unite them. It is truly a sign of the barbarian state that the will is determined unilaterally by one function, for the will must have some content, some aim, and how is this aim set? How else than by an antecedent psychic process which through an intellectual or an emotional judgment, or a sensuous desire, provides the will with both a content and an aim? If we allow sensuous desire to be a motive of the will, we act in accordance with one instinct against our rational judgment. Yet if we leave it to our rational judgment to settle the dispute, then even the fairest arbitration will always be based on that, and will give the formal instinct priority over the sensuous. In any event, the will is determined more from this side or from that, so long as it depends for its content on one side or the other. But, to be really able to settle the conflict, it must be grounded on an intermediate state or process, which shall give it a content that is neither too near nor too far from either side. According to Schiller, this must be a *symbolic* content, since the mediating position between the opposites can be reached only by the symbol. The reality presupposed by one instinct is different from the reality of the other. To the other it would be quite unreal or bogus, and vice versa. This dual character of real and unreal is inherent in the symbol. If it were only real, it would not be a symbol, for it would then be a real phenomenon and hence unsymbolic. Only that can be symbolic which embraces both. And if it were altogether unreal, it would be mere empty imagining, which, being related to nothing real, would not be a symbol either.

179   The rational functions are, by their very nature, incapable of creating symbols, since they produce only rationalities whose meaning is determined unilaterally and does not at the same time embrace its opposite. The sensuous functions are equally unfitted to create symbols, because their products too

are determined unilaterally by the object and contain only themselves and not their opposites. To discover, therefore, that impartial basis for the will, we must appeal to another authority, where the opposites are not yet clearly separated but still preserve their original unity. Manifestly this is not the case with consciousness, since the whole essence of consciousness is *discrimination*, distinguishing ego from non-ego, subject from object, positive from negative, and so forth. The separation into pairs of opposites is entirely due to conscious differentiation; only consciousness can recognize the suitable and distinguish it from the unsuitable and worthless. It alone can declare one function valuable and the other non-valuable, thus bestowing on one the power of the will while suppressing the claims of the other. But, where no consciousness exists, where purely unconscious instinctive life still prevails, there is no reflection, no *pro et contra*, no disunion, nothing but simple happening, self-regulating instinctivity, living proportion. (Provided, of course, that instinct does not come up against situations to which it is unadapted, in which case blockage, affects, confusion, and panic arise.)

180   It would, therefore, be pointless to call upon consciousness to decide the conflict between the instincts. A conscious decision would be quite arbitrary, and could never supply the will with a symbolic content that alone can produce an irrational solution of a logical antithesis. For this we must go deeper; we must descend into the foundations of consciousness which have still preserved their primordial instinctivity—that is, into the unconscious, where all psychic functions are indistinguishably merged in the original and fundamental activity of the psyche. The lack of differentiation in the unconscious arises in the first place from the almost direct association of all the brain centres with each other, and in the second from the relatively weak energic value of the unconscious elements.[83] That they possess relatively little energy is clear from the fact that an unconscious element at once ceases to be subliminal as soon as it acquires a stronger accent of value; it then rises above the threshold of consciousness, and it can do this only by virtue of the energy accruing to it. It becomes a "lucky idea" or "hunch,"

[83] Cf. Nunberg, "On the Physical Accompaniments of Association Processes," in Jung (ed.), *Studies in Word-Association*, pp. 531ff.

or, as Herbart calls it, a "spontaneously arising presentation." The strong energic value of the conscious contents has the effect of intense illumination, whereby their differences become clearly perceptible and any confusion between them is ruled out. In the unconscious, on the contrary, the most heterogeneous elements possessing only a vague analogy can be substituted for one another, just because of their low luminosity and weak energic value. Even heterogeneous sense-impressions coalesce, as we see in "photisms" (Bleuler) or in colour hearing. Language, too, contains plenty of these unconscious contaminations, as I have shown in the case of sound, light, and emotional states.[84]

181   The unconscious, then, might well be the authority we have to appeal to, since it is a neutral region of the psyche where everything that is divided and antagonistic in consciousness flows together into groupings and configurations. These, when raised to the light of consciousness, reveal a nature that exhibits the constituents of one side as much as the other; they nevertheless belong to neither but occupy an independent middle position. It is this position that constitutes both their value and their non-value for consciousness. They are worthless in so far as nothing clearly distinguishable can be perceived from their configuration, thus leaving consciousness embarrassed and perplexed; but valuable in so far as it is just their undifferentiated state that gives them that symbolic character which is essential to the content of the mediating will.

182   Thus, besides the will, which is entirely dependent on its content, man has a further auxiliary in the unconscious, that maternal womb of creative fantasy, which is able at any time to fashion symbols in the natural process of elementary psychic activity, symbols that can serve to determine the mediating will. I say "can" advisedly, because the symbol does not of its own accord step into the breach, but remains in the unconscious just so long as the energic value of the conscious contents exceeds that of the unconscious symbol. Under normal conditions this is always the case; but under abnormal conditions a reversal of value sets in, whereby the unconscious acquires a higher value than the conscious. The symbol then rises to the surface without, however, being taken up by the will

[84] Cf. *Symbols of Transformation*, pars. 233ff.

and the executive conscious functions, since these, on account of the reversal of value, have now become *subliminal*. The unconscious, on the other hand, has become *supraliminal*, and an abnormal state, a psychic disturbance, has supervened.

183   Under normal conditions, therefore, energy must be artificially supplied to the unconscious symbol in order to increase its value and bring it to consciousness. This comes about (and here we return again to the idea of differentiation provoked by Schiller) through a differentiation of the self[85] from the opposites. This differentiation amounts to a detachment of libido from both sides, in so far as the libido is disposable. For the libido invested in the instincts is only in part freely disposable, just so far in fact as the power of the will extends. This is represented by the amount of energy which is at the "free" disposal of the ego. The will then has the self as a possible aim, and it becomes the more possible the more any further development is arrested by the conflict. In this case, the will does not decide between the opposites, but purely for the self, that is, the disposable energy is withdrawn into the self—in other words, it is *introverted*. The introversion simply means that the libido is retained by the self and is prevented from taking part in the conflict of opposites. Since the way outward is barred to it, it naturally turns towards thought, where again it is in dan-

---

[85] [A preliminary formulation of the "self" first occurs in "The Structure of the Unconscious" (1916), *Two Essays* (1966 edn.), par. 512: "The unconscious personal contents constitute the *self*, the *unconscious or subconscious* ego." Thereafter the self does not appear to have been mentioned in Jung's writings until the publication of *Psychological Types*, and even as late as the 1950 Swiss edition it is at one point (p. 123) used interchangeably with the ego. This has been corrected in *Ges. Werke* (p. 95), where "Selbst" (self) is deleted. (In the Baynes version confusion is made worse confounded because throughout this whole passage "Ich"=ego is more often than not translated as "self," which Jung used only at that one point. Cf. Baynes, pp. 115–17, with pars. 138–41 of the present edition.) Thus, in par. 183, the "self" appears for the first time as an entity distinct from the ego, though it is evident from the context that the term also has an affinity with the "individual nucleus" which can be differentiated from the opposing functions or opposites (par. 174). In par. 175, however, the "individual nucleus" is abbreviated into the "individuality." The relation between the self and individuality is developed later, in *Two Essays*. Cf. par. 266: ". . . in so far as 'individuality' embraces our innermost, last, and incomparable uniqueness, it also implies becoming one's own self." Par. 404: "The self is our life's goal, for it is the completest expression of that fateful combination we call individuality."—EDITORS.]

ger of getting entangled in the conflict. The act of differentiation and introversion involves the detachment of disposable libido not merely from the outer object but also from the inner object, the thought. The libido becomes wholly objectless, it is no longer related to anything that could be a content of consciousness, and it therefore sinks into the unconscious, where it automatically takes possession of the waiting fantasy material, which it thereupon activates and forces to the surface.

184   Schiller's term for the symbol, "living form," is happily chosen, because the constellated fantasy material contains images of the psychological development of the individuality in its successive states—a sort of preliminary sketch or representation of the onward way between the opposites. Although it may frequently happen that the discriminating activity of consciousness does not find much in these images that can be immediately understood, these intuitions nevertheless contain a living power which can have a determining effect on the will. But the determining of the will has repercussions on both sides, so that after a while the opposites recover their strength. The renewed conflict again demands the same treatment, and each time a further step along the way is made possible. This function of mediation between the opposites I have termed the *transcendent function*, by which I mean nothing mysterious, but merely a combined function of conscious and unconscious elements, or, as in mathematics, a common function of real and imaginary quantities.[86]

185   Besides the will—whose importance should not on that account be denied—we also have creative fantasy, an irrational, instinctive function which alone has the power to supply the will with a content of such a nature that it can unite the opposites. This is the function that Schiller intuitively apprehended as the source of symbols; but he called it the "play instinct" and could therefore make no further use of it for the motivation of the will. In order to obtain a content for the will

[86] I must emphasize that I am here presenting this function only in principle. Further contributions to this very complex problem, concerning in particular the fundamental importance of the way in which the unconscious material is assimilated into consciousness, will be found in "The Structure of the Unconscious" and "The Psychology of the Unconscious Processes." [These were subsequently expanded into *Two Essays on Analytical Psychology*. Cf. also "The Transcendent Function."—EDITORS.]

he reverted to the intellect and thus allied himself to one side only. But he comes surprisingly close to our problem when he says:

The sway of sensation must therefore be destroyed before the law [i.e., of the rational will] can be set up in its place. So it is not enough for something to begin which previously did not exist; something must first cease which previously did exist. Man cannot pass directly from sensation to thinking; he must take a step backwards, since only by the removal of one determinant can its opposite appear. In order, therefore, to exchange passivity for self-dependence, an inactive determinant for an active one, he must be momentarily free from all determinacy and pass through a state of pure determinability. Consequently, he must somehow return to that negative state of sheer indeterminacy in which he existed before anything at all made an impression on his senses. But that state was completely empty of content, and it is now a question of uniting an equal indeterminacy with an equally unlimited determinability possessing the greatest possible fulness of content, since something positive is to result directly from this condition. The determinacy which he received by means of sensation must therefore be preserved, because he must not lose hold of reality; but at the same time it must, in so far as it is a limitation, be removed, because an unlimited determinability is to make its appearance.[87]

186   With the help of what has been said above, this difficult passage can be understood easily enough if we bear in mind that Schiller constantly tends to seek a solution in the rational will. Making allowance for this fact, what he says is perfectly clear. The "step backwards" is the differentiation from the contending instincts, the detachment and withdrawal of libido from all inner and outer objects. Here, of course, Schiller has the sensuous object primarily in mind, since, as we have said, his constant aim is to get across to the side of rational thinking, which seems to him an indispensable factor in determining the will. Nevertheless, he is still driven by the necessity of abolishing all determinacy, and this also implies detachment from the inner object, the thought—otherwise it would be impossible to achieve that complete indeterminacy and emptiness of content which is the original state of unconsciousness, with no discrim-

[87] Cf. Snell, p. 98.

ination of subject and object. It is obvious that Schiller means a process which might be formulated as an *introversion into the unconscious.*

187   "Unlimited determinability" clearly means something very like the unconscious, a state in which everything acts on everything else without distinction. This empty state of consciousness must be united with the "greatest possible fulness of content." This fulness, the counterpart of the emptiness of consciousness, can only be the content of the unconscious, since no other content is given. Schiller is thus expressing the union of conscious and unconscious, and from this state "something positive is to result." This "positive" something is for us a symbolic determinant of the will. For Schiller it is a "mediatory condition," by which the union of sensation and thinking is brought about. He also calls it a "mediatory disposition" where sensuousness and reason are simultaneously active; but just because of that each cancels the determining power of the other and their opposition ends in negation. This cancelling of the opposites produces a void, which we call the unconscious. Because it is not determined by the opposites, this condition is susceptible to every determinant. Schiller calls it the "aesthetic condition."[88] It is remarkable that he overlooks the fact that sensuousness and reason cannot both be "active" in this condition, since, as he himself says, they are already cancelled by mutual negation. But, since something must be active and Schiller has no other function at his disposal, the pairs of opposites must, according to him, become active again. Their activity is there all right, but since consciousness is "empty," it must necessarily be in the unconscious.[89] But this concept was unknown to Schiller—hence he contradicts himself at this point. His mediating aesthetic function would thus be the equivalent of our symbol-forming activity (creative fantasy). Schiller defines the "aesthetic character" of a thing as its relation to "the totality of our various faculties, without being a specific object for any single one of them."[90] Instead of this vague definition, he would perhaps have done better to return to his earlier concept of the symbol; for the symbol has the

88 Ibid., p. 99.
89 As Schiller says, "man in the aesthetic condition is a cipher" (p. 101).
90 Cf. p. 99n.

quality of being related to all psychic functions without being a specific object for any single one. Having now reached this "mediatory disposition," Schiller perceives that "it is henceforth possible for man, by the way of nature, to make of himself what he will—the freedom to be what he ought to be is completely restored to him."[91]

188 Because by preference Schiller proceeds rationally and intellectually, he falls a victim to his own conclusion. This is already demonstrated in his choice of the word "aesthetic." Had he been acquainted with Indian literature, he would have seen that the *primordial image* which floated before his mind's eye had a very different character from an "aesthetic" one. His intuition seized on the unconscious model which from time immemorial has lain dormant in our mind. Yet he interpreted it as "aesthetic," although he himself had previously emphasized its symbolic character. The primordial image I am thinking of is that particular configuration of Eastern ideas which is condensed in the *brahman-atman* teaching of India and whose philosophical spokesman in China is Lao-tzu.

189 The Indian conception teaches liberation from the opposites, by which are to be understood every sort of affective state and emotional tie to the object. Liberation follows the withdrawal of libido from all contents, resulting in a state of complete introversion. This psychological process is, very characteristically, known as *tapas*, a term which can best be rendered as "self-brooding." This expression clearly pictures the state of meditation without content, in which the libido is supplied to one's own self somewhat in the manner of incubating heat. As a result of the complete detachment of all affective ties to the object, there is necessarily formed in the inner self an equivalent of objective reality, or a complete identity of inside and outside, which is technically described as *tat tvam asi* (that art thou). The fusion of the self with its relations to the object produces the identity of the self (*atman*) with the essence of the world (i.e., with the relations of subject to object), so that the identity of the inner with the outer *atman* is cognized. The concept of *brahman* differs only slightly from that of *atman*, for in *brahman* the idea of the self is not explicitly given; it is, as it

[91] Cf. p. 101.

were, a general indefinable state of identity between inside and outside.

190   Parallel in some ways with *tapas* is the concept of yoga, understood not so much as a state of meditation as a conscious technique for attaining the *tapas* state. Yoga is a method by which the libido is systematically "introverted" and liberated from the bondage of opposites. The aim of *tapas* and yoga alike is to establish a mediatory condition from which the creative and redemptive element will emerge. For the individual, the psychological result is the attainment of *brahman*, the "supreme light," or *ananda* (bliss). This is the whole purpose of the redemptory exercises. At the same time, the process can also be thought of as a cosmogonic one, since *brahman-atman* is the universal Ground from which all creation proceeds. The existence of this myth proves, therefore, that creative processes take place in the unconscious of the yogi which can be interpreted as new adaptations to the object. Schiller says:

As soon as it is light in man, it is no longer night without. As soon as it is hushed within him, the storm in the universe is stilled, and the contending forces of nature find rest between lasting bounds. No wonder, then, that age-old poetry speaks of this great event in the inner man as though it were a revolution in the world outside him.[92]

191   Yoga introverts the relations to the object. Deprived of energic value, they sink into the unconscious, where, as we have shown, they enter into new relations with other unconscious contents, and then reassociate themselves with the object in new form after the completion of the *tapas* exercise. The transformation of the relation to the object has given the object a new face. It is as though newly created; hence the cosmogonic myth is an apt symbol for the outcome of the *tapas* exercise. The trend of Indian religious practice being almost exclusively introverted, the new adaptation to the object has of course little significance; but it still persists in the form of an unconsciously projected, doctrinal cosmogonic myth, though without leading to any practical innovations. In this respect the Indian religious attitude is the diametrical opposite

[92] Cf. p. 120.

of the Christian, since the Christian principle of love is extraverted and positively demands an object. The Indian principle makes for riches of knowledge, the Christian for fulness of works.

192   The *brahman* concept also contains the concept of *rta*, right order, the orderly course of the world. In *brahman*, the creative universal essence and universal Ground, all things come upon the right way, for in it they are eternally dissolved and recreated; all development in an orderly way proceeds from *brahman*. The concept of *rta* is a stepping-stone to the concept of *tao* in Lao-tzu. *Tao* is the right way, the reign of law, the middle road between the opposites, freed from them and yet uniting them in itself. The purpose of life is to travel this middle road and never to deviate towards the opposites. The ecstatic element is entirely absent in Lao-tzu; its place is taken by sublime philosophic lucidity, an intellectual and intuitive wisdom obscured by no mystical haze—a wisdom that represents what is probably the highest attainable degree of spiritual superiority, as far removed from chaos as the stars from the disorder of the actual world. It tames all that is wild, without denaturing it and turning it into something higher.

193   It could easily be objected that the analogy between Schiller's train of thought and these apparently remote ideas is very far-fetched. But it must not be forgotten that not so long after Schiller's time these same ideas found a powerful spokesman through the genius of Schopenhauer and became intimately wedded to Germanic mind, never again to depart from it. In my view it is of little importance that whereas the Latin translation of the Upanishads by Anquetil du Perron (published 1801–2) was available to Schopenhauer, Schiller took at least no conscious note of the very meagre information that was available in his time.[93] I have seen enough in my own practical experience to know that no direct communication is needed in the formation of affinities of this kind. We see something very similar in the fundamental ideas of Meister Eckhart and also, in some respects, of Kant, which display a quite astonishing affinity with those of the Upanishads, though there is not the faintest trace of any influence either direct or indirect. It is the same as with myths and symbols, which can arise autochtho-

[93] Schiller died in 1805.

120

nously in every corner of the earth and yet are identical, because they are fashioned out of the same worldwide human unconscious, whose contents are infinitely less variable than are races and individuals.

194   I also feel it necessary to draw a parallel between Schiller's ideas and those of the East because in this way Schiller's might be freed from the all too constricting mantle of aestheticism.[94] Aestheticism is not fitted to solve the exceedingly serious and difficult task of educating man, for it always presupposes the very thing it should create—the capacity to love beauty. It actually hinders a deeper investigation of the problem, because it always averts its face from anything evil, ugly, and difficult, and aims at pleasure, even though it be of an edifying kind. Aestheticism therefore lacks all moral force, because *au fond* it is still only a refined hedonism. Certainly Schiller is at pains to introduce an absolute moral motive, but with no convincing success since, just because of his aesthetic attitude, it is impossible for him to see the consequences which a recognition of the other side of human nature would entail. The conflict thus engendered involves such confusion and suffering for the individual that, although the spectacle of beauty may with luck enable him to repress its opposite again, he still does not escape from it, so that, even at best, the old condition is re-established. In order to help him out of this conflict, another attitude than the aesthetic is needed. This is shown nowhere more clearly than in the parallel with Oriental ideas. The religious philosophy of India grasped this problem in all its profundity and showed the kind of remedy needed to solve the conflict. What is needed is a supreme moral effort, the greatest self-denial and sacrifice, the most intense religious austerity and true saintliness.

195   Schopenhauer, despite his regard for the aesthetic, most emphatically pointed out just this side of the problem. But we must not delude ourselves that the words "aesthetic," "beauty," etc. had the same associations for Schiller as they have for us. I am not, I think, putting it too strongly when I say that for him "beauty" was a *religious ideal*. Beauty was his

[94] I use "aestheticism" as an abbreviated expression for an "aesthetic view of world." I do not mean aestheticism in the pejorative sense of a sentimental pose or fashionable fad, which might perhaps be connoted by that word.

religion. His "aesthetic mood" might equally well be called "devoutness." Without definitely expressing anything of that kind, and without explicitly characterizing his central problem as a religious one, Schiller's intuition none the less arrived at the religious problem. It was, however, the religious problem of the primitive, which he even discussed at some length in his letters, though without following out this line of thought to the end.

196   It is worth noting that in the further course of his argument the question of the play instinct retires into the background in favour of the aesthetic mood, which seems to have acquired an almost mystical value. This, I believe, is no accident, but has a quite definite cause. Often it is the best and most profound ideas in a man's work which most obstinately resist a clear formulation, even though they are hinted at in various places and should therefore really be ripe enough for a lucid synthesis to be possible. It seems to me that we are faced with some such difficulty here. To the concept of an aesthetic mood as a mediating creative state Schiller himself brings thoughts which at once reveal its depth and seriousness. And yet, quite as clearly, he picks on the play instinct as the long-sought mediating activity. Now it cannot be denied that these two concepts are in some sort opposed, since play and seriousness are scarcely compatible. Seriousness comes from a profound inner necessity, but play is its outward expression, the face it turns to consciousness. It is not, of course, a matter of *wanting* to play, but of *having* to play; a playful manifestation of fantasy from inner necessity, without the compulsion of circumstance, without even the compulsion of the will.[95] *It is serious play.* And yet it is certainly play in its outward aspect, as seen from the standpoint of consciousness and collective opinion. That is the ambiguous quality which clings to everything creative.

197   If play expires in itself without creating anything durable

[95] Cf. "Über die notwendigen Grenzen beim Gebrauch schöner Formen" (Cottasche Ausgabe, XVIII), p. 195: "For since, in the man of aesthetic refinement, the imagination, even in its free play, is governed by law, and the senses permit themselves enjoyment only with the consent of reason, the reciprocal favour is required that in the seriousness of its law-making reason shall be governed in the interests of the imagination, and not command the will without the consent of the sensuous instincts."

and vital, it is only play, but in the other case it is called creative work. Out of a playful movement of elements whose interrelations are not immediately apparent, patterns arise which
an observant and critical intellect can only evaluate afterwards.
The creation of something new is not accomplished by the intellect, but by the play instinct acting from inner necessity. The
creative mind plays with the object it loves.

198   Hence it is easy to regard every creative activity whose potentialities remain hidden from the multitude as play. There
are, indeed, very few artists who have not been accused of playing. With the man of genius, which Schiller certainly was, one
is inclined to let this label stick. But he himself wanted to go
beyond the exceptional man and his nature, and to reach the
common man, that he too might share the help and deliverance
which the creative artist, acting from inner necessity, cannot
escape anyway. But the possibility of extending such a viewpoint
to the education of the common man is not guaranteed in advance, or at least it would seem not to be.

199   To resolve this question we must appeal, as in all such cases,
to the testimony of the history of human thought. But first we
must once more be clear in our own minds from what angle
we are approaching the question. We have seen how Schiller
demands a detachment from the opposites even to the point
of a complete emptying of consciousness, in which neither sensations, nor feelings, nor thoughts, nor intentions play any sort
of role. The condition striven for is one of undifferentiated
consciousness, a consciousness in which, by the depotentiation
of energic values, all contents have lost their distinctiveness.
But real consciousness is possible only when values facilitate a
discrimination of contents. Where discrimination is lacking, no
real consciousness can exist. Accordingly such a state might be
called "unconscious," although the possibility of consciousness
is present all the time. It is a question of an *abaissement du
niveau mental* (Janet), which bears some resemblance to the
yogic and trance states of hysterical *engourdissement*.

200   So far as I know, Schiller never expressed any views concerning the actual technique—if one may use such a word—
for inducing the "aesthetic mood." The example of the Juno
Ludovici that he mentions incidentally in his letters[96] testifies

96 Snell, p. 81.

to a state of "aesthetic devotion" consisting in a complete surrender to, and empathy for, the object of contemplation. But
such a state of devotion lacks the essential characteristics of being without any content or determinant. Nevertheless, in conjunction with other passages, this example shows that the idea
of devotion or devoutness was constantly present in Schiller's
mind.[97] This brings us back to the religious problem, but at
the same time it gives us a glimpse of the actual possibility of
extending Schiller's viewpoint to the common man. *For religious devotion is a collective phenomenon that does not depend on individual endowment.*

201   There are, however, yet other possibilities. We have seen
that the empty state of consciousness, the unconscious condition, is brought about by the libido sinking into the unconscious. In the unconscious feeling-toned contents lie dormant
memory-complexes from the individual's past, above all the
parental complex, which is identical with the childhood complex in general. Devotion, or the sinking of libido into the
unconscious, reactivates the childhood complex so that the
childhood reminiscences, and especially the relations with the
parents, become suffused with life. The fantasies produced by
this reactivation give rise to the birth of father and mother
divinities, as well as awakening the childhood relations with
God and the corresponding childlike feelings. Characteristically, it is *symbols* of the parents that become activated and
by no means always the images of the real parents, a fact
which Freud explains as repression of the parental imago
through resistance to incest. I agree with this interpretation,
yet I believe it is not exhaustive, since it overlooks the extraordinary significance of this *symbolic substitution*. Symbolization
in the shape of the God-image is an immense step beyond the
concretism, the sensuousness, of memory, since, through
acceptance of the "symbol" as a real symbol, the regression to the
parents is instantly transformed into a progression, whereas it
would remain a regression if the symbol were to be interpreted merely as a *sign* for the actual parents and thus robbed
of its independent character.[98]

[97] Ibid.: "While the womanly god demands our veneration, the godlike woman
kindles our love."

[98] *Symbols of Transformation*, esp. pars. 180, 329ff.

202   Humanity came to its gods by accepting the reality of the symbol, that is, it came to the *reality of thought*, which has made man lord of the earth. Devotion, as Schiller correctly conceived it, is a regressive movement of libido towards the primordial, a diving down into the source of the first beginnings. Out of this there rises, as an image of the incipient progressive movement, the symbol, which is a condensation of all the operative unconscious factors—"living form," as Schiller says, and a God-image, as history proves. It is therefore no accident that he should seize on a divine image, the Juno Ludovici, as a paradigm. Goethe makes the divine images of Paris and Helen float up from the tripod of the Mothers[99]—on the one hand the rejuvenated pair, on the other the symbol of a process of inner union, which is precisely what Faust passionately craves for himself as the supreme inner atonement. This is clearly shown in the ensuing scene as also from the further course of the drama. As we can see from the example of Faust, the vision of the symbol is a pointer to the onward course of life, beckoning the libido towards a still distant goal —but a goal that henceforth will burn unquenchably within him, so that his life, kindled as by a flame, moves steadily towards the far-off beacon. This is the specific life-promoting significance of the symbol, and such, too, is the meaning and value of religious symbols. I am speaking, of course, not of symbols that are dead and stiffened by dogma, but of living symbols that rise up from the creative unconscious of the living man.

203   The immense significance of such symbols can be denied only by those for whom the history of the world begins with the present day. It ought to be superfluous to speak of the significance of symbols, but unfortunately this is not so, for the spirit of our time thinks itself superior to its own psychology. The moralistic and hygienic temper of our day must always know whether such and such a thing is harmful or useful, right or wrong. A real psychology cannot concern itself with such queries; to recognize how things are in themselves is enough.

204   The symbol-formation resulting from "devotion" is another of those collective religious phenomena that do not depend on

[99] *Faust, Part Two* (trans. Wayne) Act 1, "Baronial Hall," pp. 83ff. [For the tripod see also p. 79.]

individual endowment. So in this respect too we may assume the possibility of extending Schiller's viewpoint to the common man. I think that at least its theoretical possibility for human psychology in general has now been sufficiently demonstrated. For the sake of completeness and clarity I should add that the question of the relation of the symbol to consciousness and the conscious conduct of life has long occupied my mind. I have come to the conclusion that, in view of its great significance as an exponent of the unconscious, too light a value should not be set on the symbol. We know from daily experience in the treatment of neurotic patients what an eminently practical importance the interventions from the unconscious possess. The greater the dissociation, i.e., the more the conscious attitude becomes alienated from the individual and collective contents of the unconscious, the more harmfully the unconscious inhibits or intensifies the conscious contents. For quite practical reasons, therefore, the symbol must be credited with a not inconsiderable value. But if we grant it a value, whether great or small, the symbol acquires a conscious motive force—that is, it is *perceived*, and its unconscious libido-charge is thereby given an opportunity to make itself felt in the conscious conduct of life. Thus, in my view, a practical advantage of no small consequence is gained, namely, the *collaboration of the unconscious,* its participation in the conscious psychic performance, and hence the elimination of disturbing influences from the unconscious.

205   This common function, the relation to the symbol, I have termed the *transcendent function.* I cannot at this point submit this question to a thorough investigation, as it would be absolutely necessary to bring together all the material that comes up as a result of the activity of the unconscious. The fantasies hitherto described in the specialist literature give no conception of the symbolic creations we are concerned with. There are, however, not a few examples of such fantasies in *belles-lettres*; but these, of course, are not observed and reported in their "pure" state—they have undergone an intensive "aesthetic" elaboration. From all these examples I would single out two works of Meyrink for special attention: *The Golem* and *Das grüne Gesicht.* I must reserve the treatment of this aspect of the problem for a later investigation.

206   Although these observations concerning the mediatory
state were prompted by Schiller, we have already gone far beyond his conceptions. In spite of his having discerned the opposites in human nature with such keen insight, he remained
stuck at an early stage in his attempt at a solution. For this
failure, it seems to me, the term "aesthetic mood" is not without
blame. Schiller makes the "aesthetic mood" practically identical with "beauty," which of its own accord precipitates our
sentiments into this mood.[100] Not only does he blend cause with
effect, he also, in the teeth of his own definition, gives the state
of "indeterminacy" an unequivocally determined character by
equating it with beauty. From the very outset, therefore, the
edge is taken off the mediating function, since beauty immediately prevails over ugliness, whereas it is equally a question of
ugliness. We have seen that Schiller defines a thing's "aesthetic
character" as its relation to "the totality of our various faculties."[101] Consequently "beautiful" cannot coincide with "aesthetic," since our various faculties also vary aesthetically: some
are beautiful, some ugly, and only an incorrigible idealist and
optimist could conceive the "totality" of human nature as simply beautiful. To be quite accurate, human nature is simply
what it is; it has its dark and its light sides. The sum of all
colours is grey—light on a dark background or dark on light.

207   This conceptual flaw also accounts for the fact that it remains far from clear *how* this mediatory condition is to be
brought about. There are numerous passages which state unequivocally that it is called into being by "the enjoyment of
pure beauty." Thus Schiller says:

Whatever flatters our senses in immediate sensation opens our soft
and sensitive nature to every impression, but it also makes us in the
same measure less capable of exertion. What braces our intellectual
powers and invites us to abstract concepts strengthens our mind for
every kind of resistance, but also hardens it proportionately, and
deprives us of sensibility just as much as it helps us towards a
greater spontaneity. For that very reason the one no less than the
other must in the end necessarily lead to exhaustion. . . . On the
other hand, when we have abandoned ourselves to the enjoyment
of pure beauty, we are at such a moment masters in equal degree of
our passive and active powers, and shall turn with equal facility

[100] Cf. Snell, p. 99n.   [101] Cf. ibid.

to seriousness or to play, to rest or to movement, to compliance or to resistance, to abstract thought or to contemplation.[102]

208   This statement is in direct contradiction to the earlier definitions of the "aesthetic condition," where man was to be "empty," a "cipher," "undetermined," whereas here he is in the highest degree determined by beauty ("abandoned" to it). But it is not worth while pursuing this question further with Schiller. Here he comes up against a barrier common both to himself and his time which it was impossible for him to overstep, for everywhere he encountered the invisible "Ugliest Man," whose discovery was reserved for our age by Nietzsche.

209   Schiller was intent on making the sensuous man into a rational being "by first making him aesthetic."[103] He himself says that "we must first alter his nature,"[104] "we must subject man to form even in his purely physical life,"[105] "he must carry out his physical determination . . . according to the laws of Beauty,"[106] "on the neutral plane of physical life man must start his moral life,"[107] "though still within his sensuous limits he must begin his rational freedom,"[108] "he must already be imposing the law of his will upon his inclinations,"[109] "he must learn to desire more *nobly*."[110]

210   That "must" of which our author speaks is the familiar "ought" which is always invoked when one can see no other way. Here again we come up against the inevitable barriers. It would be unfair to expect one individual mind, were it never so great, to master this gigantic problem which times and nations alone can solve, and even then by no conscious purpose, but only as fate would have it.

211   The greatness of Schiller's thought lies in his psychological observation and in his intuitive grasp of the things observed. There is yet another of his trains of thought I would like to mention, as it deserves special emphasis. We have seen that the mediatory condition is characterized as producing "something positive," namely the symbol. The symbol unites antithetical elements within its nature; hence it also unites the antithesis between real and unreal, because on the one hand it is a

102 Cf. pp. 103f.   103 P. 109.   104 P. 110.
105 Ibid.   106 Cf. ibid   107 Cf. p. 112.
108 Cf. ibid.   109 Ibid.   110 Ibid.

psychic reality (on account of its efficacy), while on the other it corresponds to no physical reality. It is *reality* and *appearance* at once. Schiller clearly emphasizes this in order to append an apologia for appearance, which is in every respect significant:

Extreme stupidity and extreme intelligence have a certain affinity with each other, in that both seek only the *real* and are wholly insensible to mere *appearance*. Only through the immediate presence of an object in the senses is stupidity shaken from its repose, and intelligence is granted its repose only through relating its concepts to the data of experience; in a word, stupidity cannot rise above reality and intelligence cannot remain below truth. In so far, then, as the need for reality and attachment to the real are merely the results of deficiency, it follows that indifference to reality and interest in appearance are a true enlargement of humanity and a decisive step towards culture.[111]

212   When speaking earlier of an assignment of value to the symbol, I showed the practical advantages of an appreciation of the unconscious. We exclude an unconscious disturbance of the conscious functions when we take the unconscious into our calculations from the start by paying attention to the symbol. It is well known that the unconscious, when not realized, is ever at work casting a false glamour over everything, a false appearance: *it appears to us always on objects*, because everything unconscious is projected. Hence, when we can apprehend the unconscious as such, we strip away the false appearance from objects, and this can only promote truth. Schiller says:

Man exercises this human right to sovereignty in the *art of appearance,* and the more strictly he here distinguishes between *mine* and *thine,* the more carefully he separates form from being, and the more independence he learns to give to this form, the more he will not merely extend the realm of Beauty but even secure the boundaries of Truth; for he cannot cleanse appearance from reality without at the same time liberating reality from appearance.[112]

To strive after absolute appearance demands greater capacity for abstraction, more freedom of heart, more vigour of will than man needs if he confines himself to reality, and he must already have put this behind him if he wishes to arrive at appearance.[113]

[111] Cf. p. 125.   [112] Cf. p. 127.   [113] P. 131.

2. A DISCUSSION ON NAÏVE AND SENTIMENTAL POETRY

213   For a long time it seemed to me as though Schiller's division of poets into *naïve* and *sentimental*[114] were a classification that accorded with the type psychology here expounded. After mature reflection, however, I have come to the conclusion that this is not so. Schiller's definition is very simple: "The naïve poet *is* Nature, the sentimental poet *seeks* her." This simple formula is beguiling, since it postulates two different kinds of relation to the object. It is therefore tempting to say: He who seeks or desires Nature as an object does not possess her, and such a man would be an introvert; while conversely, he who already is Nature, and therefore stands in the most intimate relation with the object, would be an extravert. But a rather forced interpretation such as this would have little in common with Schiller's point of view. His division into naïve and sentimental is one which, in contrast to our type division, is not in the least concerned with the individual mentality of the poet, but rather with the character of his creative activity, or of its product. The same poet can be sentimental in one poem, naïve in another. Homer is certainly naïve throughout, but how many of the moderns are not, for the most part, sentimental? Evidently Schiller felt this difficulty, and therefore asserted that the poet was conditioned by his time, not as an individual but as a poet. He says:

All real poets will belong either to the naïve or sentimental, depending on whether the conditions of the age in which they flourish, or accidental circumstances, exert an influence on their general make-up and on their passing emotional mood.[115]

214   Consequently it is not a question of fundamental types for Schiller, but of certain characteristics or qualities of the individual product. Hence it is at once obvious that an introverted poet can, on occasion, be just as naïve as he is sentimental. It therefore follows that to identify naïve and sentimental respectively with extravert and introvert would be quite beside the point so far as the question of *types* is concerned. Not so, however, so far as it is a question of *typical mechanisms*.

[114] "Über naive und sentimentalische Dichtung" (Cottasche Ausgabe, XVIII), pp. 205ff.
[115] P. 236.

a. The Naïve Attitude

215   I will first present the definitions which Schiller gives of this attitude. As has already been said, the naïve poet is "Nature." He "simply follows Nature and sensation and confines himself to the mere copying of reality."[116] "With naïve poetry we delight in the living presence of objects in our imagination."[117] "Naïve poetry is a boon of Nature. It is a lucky throw, needing no improvement when it succeeds, but fit for nothing when it fails."[118] "The naïve genius has to do everything through his nature; he can do little through his freedom, and he will accomplish his idea only when Nature works in him from inner necessity."[119] Naïve poetry is "the child of life and unto life it returns."[120] The naïve genius is wholly dependent on "experience," on the world, with which he is in "direct touch." He "needs succour from without."[121] For the naïve poet the "common nature" of his surroundings can "become dangerous," because "sensibility is always more or less dependent on the external impression, and only a constant activity of the productive faculty, which is not to be expected of human nature, would be able to prevent mere matter from exercising at times a blind power over his sensibility. But whenever this happens, the poetic feeling will be commonplace."[122] "The naïve genius allows Nature unlimited sway in him."[123]

216   From these definitions the dependence of the naïve poet on the object is especially clear. His relation to the object has a compelling character, because he introjects the object—that is, he unconsciously identifies with it or has, as it were, an *a priori* identity with it. Lévy-Bruhl describes this relation to the object as *participation mystique*. This identity always derives from an analogy between the object and an unconscious content. One could also say that the identity comes about through the projection of an unconscious association by analogy with the object. An identity of this kind has a compelling character too, because it expresses a certain quantity of libido which, like all libido operating from the unconscious, is not at the disposal of consciousness and thus exercises a compulsion on its con-

---

116 Ibid., p. 248. 117 P. 250n. 118 P. 303.
119 P. 304. 120 P. 303. 121 P. 305.
122 Pp. 307f. 123 P. 314.

tents. The attitude of the naïve poet is, therefore, in a high degree conditioned by the object; the object operates independently in him, as it were; it fulfils itself in him because he himself is identical with it. He lends his expressive function to the object and represents it in a certain way, not in the least actively or intentionally, but because it represents itself that way in him. He is himself Nature: Nature creates in him the product. He "allows Nature unlimited sway in him." Supremacy is given to the object. To this extent the naïve attitude is extraverted.

b. The Sentimental Attitude

217   The sentimental poet *seeks* Nature. He "reflects on the impression objects make on him, and on that reflection alone depends the emotion with which he is exalted, and which likewise exalts us. Here the object is related to an idea, and on this relation alone depends his poetic power."[124] He "is always involved with two opposing ideas and sensations, with reality as finite, and with the idea as infinite: the mixed feeling he arouses always bears witness to this dual origin."[125] "The sentimental mood is the result of an effort to reproduce the naïve sensation, the content of it, even under conditions of reflection."[126] "Sentimental poetry is the product of abstraction."[127] "As a result of his effort to remove every limitation from human nature, the sentimental genius is exposed to the danger of abolishing human nature altogether; not merely mounting, as he must and should, above every fixed and limited reality to absolute possibility: which is to *idealize*, but even transcending possibility itself: which is to *fantasize*. . . . The sentimental genius abandons reality in order to soar into the world of ideas and rule his material with absolute freedom."[128]

218   It is easy to see that the sentimental poet, contrasted with the naïve, is characterized by a reflective and abstract attitude to the object. *He reflects on the object by abstracting himself from it.* He is, as it were, separated from the object *a priori* as soon as his work begins; it is not the object that operates in him, he himself is the operator. He does not, however, work in towards himself, but out beyond the object. He is distinct from

[124] P. 249.　　　[125] P. 250.　　　[126] P. 301 n.
[127] P. 303.　　　[128] P. 314.

132

the object, not identical with it; he seeks to establish *his* relation to it, to "rule his material." From his distinction from the object comes that sense of duality which Schiller refers to; for the sentimental poet draws his creativity from two sources: from the object and/or his perception of it, and from himself. For him the external impression of the object is not something absolute, but material which he handles as directed by his own contents. He thus stands above the object and yet has a relation to it—not a relation of mere impressionability or receptivity, but one in which by his own free choice he bestows value or quality on the object. His is therefore an introverted attitude.

219   By characterizing these two attitudes as extraverted and introverted we have not, however, exhausted Schiller's conception. Our two mechanisms are merely basic phenomena of a rather general nature, which only vaguely indicate what is specific about those attitudes. To understand the naïve and sentimental types we must enlist the help of two further functions, *sensation* and *intuition*. I shall discuss these in greater detail at a later stage of our investigation. I only wish to say at this point that the naïve is characterized by a preponderance of sensation, and the sentimental by a preponderance of intuition. Sensation creates ties to the object, it even pulls the subject into the object; hence the "danger" for the naïve type consists in his vanishing in it altogether. Intuition, being a perception of one's own unconscious processes, withdraws one from the object; it mounts above it, ever seeking to rule its material, to shape it, even violently, in accordance with one's own subjective viewpoint, though without being aware of doing so. The danger for the sentimental type, therefore, is a complete severance from reality and a vanishing in the fluid fantasy world of the unconscious.

c. The Idealist and the Realist

220   In the same essay Schiller's reflections lead him to postulate two fundamental psychological types. He says:

This brings me to a very remarkable psychological antagonism among men in an age of progressive culture, an antagonism which, because it is radical and grounded in the innate emotional constitution, is the cause of a sharper division among men than the random conflict of interests could ever bring about; which robs the poet and artist of all hope of making a universal appeal and giving pleasure to every one—although this is his task; which makes it impossible for the philosopher, in spite of every effort, to be universally convincing—although this is implied in the very idea of philosophy; and which, finally, will never permit a man in practical life to see his mode of behaviour universally applauded: in short, an antagonism which is to blame for the fact that no work of the mind and no deed of the heart can have a decisive success with one class of men without incurring the condemnation of the other. This antagonism is, without doubt, as old as the beginning of culture, and to the end it can hardly be otherwise, save in rare individual cases, such as have always existed and, it is to be hoped, will always exist. But although it lies in the very nature of its operations that it frustrates every attempt at a settlement, because no party can be brought to admit either a deficiency on his own side or a reality on the other's, yet there is always profit enough in following up such an important antagonism to its final source, thus at least reducing the actual point at issue to a simpler formulation.[129]

221   It follows conclusively from this passage that by observing the antagonistic mechanisms Schiller arrived at a conception of two psychological types which claim the same significance in his scheme of things as I ascribe to the introverted and extraverted in mine. With regard to the reciprocal relation of the two types postulated by me I can endorse almost word for word what Schiller says of his. In agreement with what I said earlier, Schiller proceeds from the mechanism to the type, by "isolating from the naïve and the sentimental character alike the poetic quality common to both."[130] If we perform this operation too, subtracting the creative genius from both, then what is left to the naïve is his attachment to the object and its autonomy in the subject, and to the sentimental his superiority over the object, which expresses itself in his more or less arbitrary judgment or treatment of it. Schiller continues:

After this nothing remains of the [naïve], on the theoretical side, but a sober spirit of observation and a fixed dependence on the uniform testimony of the senses; and, on the practical, a resigned submission to the exigencies of Nature. . . . Of the sentimental character nothing remains, on the theoretical side, but a restless spirit of speculation that insists on the absolute in every act of cognition, and, on the practical, a moral rigorism that insists on the absolute in

[129] Pp. 329f.   [130] P. 331.

every act of the will. Whoever counts himself among the former can be called a *realist*, and, among the latter, an *idealist*.[131]

222   Schiller's further observations on his two types relate almost exclusively to the familiar phenomena of the realist and idealist attitudes and are therefore without interest for our investigation.

[131] Ibid.

III

THE APOLLINIAN AND THE DIONYSIAN

223   The problem discerned and partially worked out by Schiller was taken up again in a new and original way by Nietzsche in his book *The Birth of Tragedy* (1871). This early work is more nearly related to Schopenhauer and Goethe than to Schiller. But it at least appears to share Schiller's aestheticism and Hellenism, while having pessimism and the motif of deliverance in common with Schopenhauer and unlimited points of contact with Goethe's *Faust*. Among these connections, those with Schiller are naturally the most significant for our purpose. Yet we cannot pass over Schopenhauer without paying tribute to the way in which he gave reality to those dawning rays of Oriental wisdom which appear in Schiller only as insubstantial wraiths. If we disregard his pessimism which springs from the contrast with the Christian's enjoyment of faith and certainty of redemption, Schopenhauer's doctrine of deliverance is seen to be essentially Buddhist. He was captivated by the East. This was undoubtedly a reaction against our Occidental atmosphere. It is, as we know, a reaction that still persists today in various movements more or less completely oriented towards India. For Nietzsche this pull towards the East stopped in Greece. Also, he felt Greece to be the midpoint between East and West. To this extent he maintains contact with Schiller— but how utterly different is his conception of the Greek character! He sees the dark foil upon which the serene and golden world of Olympus is painted:

In order to make life possible, the Greeks had to create those gods from sheer necessity. . . . They knew and felt the terror and frightfulness of existence; to be able to live at all, the Greeks had to interpose the shining, dream-born Olympian world between themselves and that dread. That tremendous mistrust of the titanic pow-

136

ers of Nature, Moira pitilessly enthroned above all knowledge, the vulture of Prometheus the great friend of man, the awful fate of the wise Oedipus, the family curse of the Atrides that drove Orestes to matricide . . . all this dread was ever being conquered anew by the Greeks with the help of that visionary, intermediate world of the Olympians, or was at least veiled and withdrawn from sight.[1]

That Greek "serenity," that smiling heaven of Hellas seen as a shimmering illusion hiding a sombre background—this insight was reserved for the moderns, and is a weighty argument against moral aestheticism.

224   Here Nietzsche takes up a standpoint differing significantly from Schiller's. What one might have guessed with Schiller, that his letters on aesthetic education were also an attempt to deal with his own problems, becomes a complete certainty in this work of Nietzsche's: it is a "profoundly personal" book. Whereas Schiller begins to paint light and shade almost timorously and in pallid hues, apprehending the conflict in his own psyche as "naïve" versus "sentimental," and excluding everything that belongs to the background and abysmal depths of human nature, Nietzsche has a profounder grasp and spans an opposition which, in one aspect, is no whit inferior to the dazzling beauty of Schiller's vision, while its other aspect reveals infinitely darker tones that certainly enhance the effect of the light but allow still blacker depths to be divined.

225   Nietzsche calls his fundamental pair of opposites the *Apollinian* and the *Dionysian*. We must first try to picture to ourselves the nature of this pair. For this purpose I shall select a number of quotations which will enable the reader, even though unacquainted with Nietzsche's work, to form his own judgment and at the same time to criticize mine.

We shall have gained much for the science of aesthetics when once we have perceived not only by logical inference, but by the immediate certainty of intuition, that the continuous development of art is bound up with the duality of the Apollinian and the Dionysian, in much the same way as generation depends on the duality of the sexes, involving perpetual conflicts with only periodic reconciliations.[2]

---

[1] Cf. *The Birth of Tragedy* (trans. Haussmann), pp. 31ff. [The extracts appear here in modified form.—TRANS.]   [2] Ibid., p. 21.

From the two deities of the arts, Apollo and Dionysus, we derive our knowledge that a tremendous opposition existed in the Greek world, both as to their origin and their aim, between the Apollinian art of the shaper and the non-figurative Dionysian art of music. These two very different impulses run side by side, for the most part openly at variance, each continually rousing the other to new and mightier births, in order to perpetuate in them the warring antagonism that is only seemingly bridged by the common term "Art"; until finally, by a metaphysical miracle of the Hellenic "will," they appear paired one with the other, and from this mating the equally Apollinian and Dionysian creation of Attic tragedy is at last brought to birth.[3]

226   In order to characterize these two "impulses" more closely, Nietzsche compares the peculiar psychological states they give rise to with those of *dreaming* and *intoxication*. The Apollinian impulse produces the state comparable to dreaming, the Dionysian the state comparable to intoxication. By "dreaming" Nietzsche means, as he himself says, essentially an "inward vision," the "lovely semblance of dream-worlds."[4] Apollo "rules over the beautiful illusion of the inner world of fantasy," he is "the god of all shape-shifting powers."[5] He signifies measure, number, limitation, and subjugation of everything wild and untamed. "One might even describe Apollo himself as the glorious divine image of the *principium individuationis*."[6]

227   The Dionysian impulse, on the other hand, means the liberation of unbounded instinct, the breaking loose of the unbridled dynamism of animal and divine nature; hence in the Dionysian rout man appears as a satyr, god above and goat below.[7] The Dionysian is the horror of the annihilation of the *principium individuationis* and at the same time "rapturous delight" in its destruction. It is therefore comparable to intoxication, which dissolves the individual into his collective instincts and components—an explosion of the isolated ego through the world. Hence, in the Dionysian orgy, man finds man: "alienated Nature, hostile or enslaved, celebrates once more her feast of reconciliation with her prodigal son—Man."[8] Each feels himself "not only united, reconciled, merged with his neighbour, but one with him."[9] His individuality is entirely

3 Ibid., pp. 21f.   4 P. 23.   5 P. 24.
6 P. 25.   7 Pp. 63ff.   8 P. 26.
9 P. 27. Cf. infra, par. 230.

obliterated. "Man is no longer the artist, he has become the work of art."[10] "All the artistry of Nature is revealed in the ecstasies of intoxication."[11] Which means that the creative dynamism, libido in instinctive form, takes possession of the individual as though he were an object and uses him as a tool or as an expression of itself. If it is permissible to conceive the natural creature as a "work of art," then of course man in the Dionysian state has become a natural work of art too; but in so far as the natural creature is decidedly not a work of art in the ordinary sense of the word, he is nothing but sheer Nature, unbridled, a raging torrent, not even an animal that is restricted to itself and the laws of its being. I must emphasize this point for the sake of clarity in the ensuing discussion, since for some reason Nietzsche has omitted to make it clear, and has consequently shed a deceptive aesthetic veil over the problem, which at times he himself has involuntarily to draw aside. Thus, in connection with the Dionysian orgies, he says:

Practically everywhere the central point of these festivals lay in exuberant sexual licence, which swamped all family life and its venerable traditions; the most savage bestialities of nature were unleashed, including that atrocious amalgam of lust and cruelty which has always seemed to me the true witch's broth.[12]

228   Nietzsche considers the reconciliation of the Delphic Apollo with Dionysus a symbol of the reconciliation of these opposites in the breast of the civilized Greek. But here he forgets his own compensatory formula, according to which the gods of Olympus owe their splendour to the darkness of the Greek psyche. By this token, the reconciliation of Apollo and Dionysus would be a "beautiful illusion," a desideratum evoked by the need of the civilized Greek in his struggle with his own barbarian side, the very element that broke out unchecked in the Dionysian rout.

229   Between the religion of a people and its actual mode of life there is always a compensatory relation, otherwise religion would have no practical significance at all. Beginning with the highly moral religion of the Persians and the notorious dubiousness, even in antiquity, of Persian habits of life, right down to our own "Christian" era, when the religion of love assisted

---

[10] P. 27.   [11] Ibid.   [12] P. 30.

at the greatest blood-bath in the world's history—wherever we turn this rule holds true. We may therefore infer from the symbol of the Delphic reconciliation an especially violent split in the Greek character. This would also explain the longing for deliverance which gave the mysteries their immense significance for the social life of Greece, and which was completely overlooked by the early admirers of the Greek world. They were content with naïvely attributing to the Greeks everything they themselves lacked.

230   Thus in the Dionysian state the Greek was anything but a "work of art"; on the contrary, he was gripped by his own barbarian nature, robbed of his individuality, dissolved into his collective components, made one with the collective unconscious (through the surrender of his individual aims), and one with "the genius of the race, even with Nature herself."[13] To the Apollinian side which had already achieved a certain amount of domestication, this intoxicated state that made man forget both himself and his humanity and turned him into a mere creature of instinct must have been altogether despicable, and for this reason a violent conflict between the two impulses was bound to break out. Supposing the instincts of civilized man were let loose! The culture-enthusiasts imagine that only sheer beauty would stream forth. This error is due to a profound lack of psychological knowledge. The dammed-up instinctual forces in civilized man are immensely destructive and far more dangerous than the instincts of the primitive, who in a modest degree is constantly living out his negative instinct. Consequently no war of the historical past can rival in grandiose horror the wars of civilized nations. It will have been the same with the Greeks. It was just their living sense of horror that gradually brought about a reconciliation of the Apollinian with the Dionysian—"through a metaphysical miracle," as Nietzsche says. This statement, as well as the other where he says that the antagonism between them is "only seemingly bridged by the common term 'Art,' " must constantly be borne in mind, because Nietzsche, like Schiller, had a pronounced tendency to credit art with a mediating and redeeming role. The problem then remains stuck in aesthetics—the ugly is also "beautiful," even beastliness and evil shine forth

13 P. 32.

enticingly in the false glamour of aesthetic beauty. The artistic nature in both Schiller and Nietzsche claims a redemptive significance for itself and its specific capacity for creation and expression.

231   Because of this, Nietzsche quite forgets that in the struggle between Apollo and Dionysus and in their ultimate reconciliation the problem for the Greeks was never an aesthetic one, but was essentially religious. The Dionysian satyr festival, to judge by all the analogies, was a kind of totem feast involving a regressive identification with the mythical ancestors or directly with the totem animal. The cult of Dionysus had in many places a mystical and speculative streak, and in any case exercised a very strong religious influence. The fact that Greek tragedy arose out of an originally religious ceremony is at least as significant as the connection of our modern theatre with the medieval Passion play, which was exclusively religious in origin; we are not permitted, therefore, to judge the problem under its purely aesthetic aspect. Aestheticism is a modern bias that shows the psychological mysteries of the Dionysus cult in a light in which they were assuredly never seen or experienced by the ancients. With Nietzsche as with Schiller the religious viewpoint is entirely overlooked and is replaced by the aesthetic. These things obviously have their aesthetic side and it should not be neglected.[14] Nevertheless, if medieval Christianity is understood only aesthetically its true character is falsified and trivialized, just as much as if it were viewed exclusively from the historical standpoint. A true understanding is possible only on a common ground—no one would wish to maintain that the nature of a railway bridge is adequately understood from a purely aesthetic angle. In adopting the view that the antagonism between Apollo and Dionysus is purely a question of conflicting artistic impulses, the problem is shifted to the aesthetic sphere in a way that is both historically and materially unjustified, and is subjected to a partial approach which can never do justice to its real content.

14 Aestheticism can, of course, take the place of the religious function. But how many things are there that could not do the same? What have we not come across at one time or another as a substitute for the absence of religion? Even though aestheticism may be a very noble substitute, it is nevertheless only a compensation for the real thing that is lacking. Moreover, Nietzsche's later "conversion" to Dionysus best shows that the aesthetic substitute did not stand the test of time.

232   This shifting of the problem must doubtless have its psychological cause and purpose. The advantages of such a procedure are not far to seek: the aesthetic approach immediately converts the problem into a picture which the spectator can contemplate at his ease, admiring both its beauty and its ugliness, merely re-experiencing its passions at a safe distance, with no danger of becoming involved in them. The aesthetic attitude guards against any real participation, prevents one from being personally implicated, which is what a religious understanding of the problem would mean. The same advantage is ensured by the historical approach—an approach which Nietzsche himself criticized in a series of very valuable essays.[15] The possibility of taking such a tremendous problem —"a problem with horns," as he calls it—merely aesthetically is of course very tempting, for its religious understanding, which in this case is the only adequate one, presupposes some actual experience of it which modern man can rarely boast of. Dionysus, however, seems to have taken his revenge on Nietzsche, as we can see from "An Attempt at Self-Criticism," which dates from 1886 and was added as a preface to the reissue that year of *The Birth of Tragedy*:

What is a Dionysian? In this book may be found an answer: a "knowing one" speaks here, the votary and disciple of his god.[16]

But that was not the Nietzsche who wrote *The Birth of Tragedy*; at that time he was a votary of aestheticism, and he became a Dionysian only at the time of writing *Zarathustra* and that memorable passage with which he concludes "An Attempt at Self-Criticism":

Lift up your hearts, my brethren, high, higher! And forget not the legs! Lift up your legs also, you good dancers, and better still if also you stand on your heads![17]

233   Nietzsche's profound grasp of the problem in spite of his aesthetic defences was already so close to the real thing that his later Dionysian experience seems an almost inevitable consequence. His attack on Socrates in *The Birth of Tragedy* is aimed at the rationalist, who proves himself impervious to Dio-

---

[15] *Thoughts Out of Season*, Part 2: "The Use and Abuse of History."
[16] *Complete Works*, I, p. 6.   [17] Ibid., p. 15.

nysian orgiastics. This outburst is in line with the analogous error into which the aesthete always falls: he holds himself aloof from the problem. But even at that time, in spite of his aestheticism, Nietzsche had an inkling of the real solution when he said that the antagonism was not bridged by art but by "a metaphysical miracle of the Hellenic 'will.'" He puts "will" in inverted commas, which, considering how strongly he was at that time influenced by Schopenhauer, we might well interpret as a reference to concept of the metaphysical Will. "Metaphysical" has for us the psychological connotation "unconscious." If, then, we replace "metaphysical" in Nietzsche's formula by "unconscious," the desired key to the problem would be an unconscious "miracle." A "miracle" is irrational, hence the act is an unconscious irrational happening, shaping itself without the assistance of reason and conscious purpose. It happens of itself, it just grows, like a phenomenon of creative Nature, and not from any clever trick of human wit; it is the fruit of yearning expectation, of faith and hope.

234   At this point I must leave the problem for the time being, as we shall have occasion to discuss it more fully later. Let us turn instead to a closer examination of the Apollinian and Dionysian for their psychological qualities. First we will consider the Dionysian. From Nietzsche's description it is immediately apparent that an unfolding is meant, a streaming outwards and upwards, a diastole, as Goethe called it; a motion embracing the whole world, as Schiller also describes it in his "Ode to Joy":

> Approach, ye millions, and embrace!
> To the whole world my kiss shall swell!
> . . .
>
> All the world may draughts of joy
> From the breasts of Nature take;
> Good and ill alike employ
> Pains to trace joy's rosy wake.
> Kisses gave she and the grape,
> And the faithful, lifelong friend;
> Even the worm its joy can shape,
> Heavenwards the cherubs wend.[18]

18 Cf. *Poems* (trans. Arnold-Forster), p. 61.

This is Dionysian expansion. It is a flood of overpowering universal feeling which bursts forth irresistibly, intoxicating the senses like the strongest wine. It is intoxication in the highest sense of the word.

235 In this state the psychological function of sensation, whether it be sensory or affective, participates to the highest degree. It is an extraversion of all those feelings which are inextricably bound up with sensation, for which reason we call it feeling-sensation. What breaks out in this state has more the character of pure affect, something instinctive and blindly compelling, that finds specific expression in an affection of the bodily sphere.

236 In contrast to this, the Apollinian is a perception of inner images of beauty, of measure, of controlled and proportioned feelings. The comparison with dreaming clearly indicates the character of the Apollinian state: it is a state of introspection, of contemplation turned inwards to the dream world of eternal ideas, and hence a state of introversion.

237 So far the analogy with our mechanisms is unarguable. But if we were to be content with the analogy, it would be a limitation of outlook that does violence to Nietzsche's concepts by putting them on a Procrustean bed.

238 We shall see in the course of our investigation that the state of introversion, if habitual, always entails a differentiation of the relation to the world of ideas, while habitual extraversion involves a similar differentiation of the relation to the object. We see nothing of this differentiation in Nietzsche's two concepts. Dionysian feeling has the thoroughly archaic character of affective sensation. It is therefore not pure feeling, abstracted and differentiated from instinct and becoming a mobile element, which, in the extraverted type, is obedient to the dictates of reason and lends itself to them as their willing instrument. Similarly, Nietzsche's conception of introversion is not that pure, differentiated relation to ideas which has freed itself from the perception of inner images whether sensuously determined or creatively produced, and has become a contemplation of pure and abstract forms. The Apollinian mode is an inner perception, and intuition of the world of ideas. The parallel with dreaming clearly shows that Nietzsche thinks of this state as on the one hand merely perceptive and on the other merely eidetic.

239 These characteristics are individual peculiarities which we must not import into our conception of the introverted or extraverted attitude. In a man whose attitude is predominantly reflective, the Apollinian perception of inner images produces an elaboration of the perceived material in accordance with the nature of intellectual thinking. In other words, it produces ideas. In a man whose attitude is predominated by feeling a similar process results: a "feeling through" of the images and the production of a feeling-toned idea, which may coincide in essentials with an idea produced by thinking. Ideas, therefore, are just as much feelings as thoughts, examples being the idea of the fatherland, freedom, God, immortality, etc. In both elaborations the principle is a rational and logical one. But there is also a quite different standpoint, from which the rational and logical elaboration is not valid. This is the *aesthetic* standpoint. In introversion it dwells on the *perception* of ideas, it develops intuition, the inner vision; in extraversion it dwells on sensation and develops the senses, instinct, affectivity. From this standpoint, thinking is not the principle of an inner perception of ideas, and feeling just as little; instead, thinking and feeling are mere derivatives of inner perception and outer sensation.

240 Nietzsche's concepts thus lead us to the principles of a third and a fourth psychological type, which one might call "aesthetic" types as opposed to the rational types (thinking and feeling). These are the intuitive and sensation types. Both of them have the mechanisms of introversion and extraversion in common with the rational types, but they do not—like the thinking type—differentiate the perception and contemplation of inner images into thought, nor—like the feeling type—differentiate the affective experience of instinct and sensation into feeling. On the contrary, the intuitive raises unconscious perception to the level of a differentiated function, by which he also achieves his adaptation to the world. He adapts by means of unconscious directives, which he receives through an especially sensitive and sharpened perception and interpretation of dimly conscious stimuli. To describe such a function is naturally very difficult on account of its irrational and quasi-unconscious character. In a sense one might compare it to the daemon of Socrates—with the qualification, however, that the strongly rationalistic attitude of Socrates repressed the intuitive function as far as possible, so that it had to make itself felt

in the form of concrete hallucinations since it had no direct access to consciousness. But this is not the case with the intuitive type.

241   The sensation type is in every respect the converse of the intuitive. He relies almost exclusively on his sense impressions, and his whole psychology is oriented by instinct and sensation. He is therefore entirely dependent on external stimuli.

242   The fact that it is just the psychological functions of intuition on the one hand and sensation and instinct on the other that Nietzsche emphasizes must be characteristic of his own personal psychology. He must surely be reckoned an intuitive with leanings towards introversion. As evidence of the former we have his pre-eminently intuitive-artistic manner of production, of which *The Birth of Tragedy* is very characteristic, while his masterpiece *Thus Spake Zarathustra* is even more so. His aphoristic writings express his introverted intellectual side. These, in spite of a strong admixture of feeling, display a pronounced critical intellectualism in the manner of the intellectuals of the eighteenth century. His lack of rational moderation and conciseness argues for the intuitive type in general. Under these circumstances it is not surprising that in his early work he unwittingly sets the facts of his personal psychology in the foreground. This is quite in accord with the intuitive attitude, which perceives the outer primarily through the medium of the inner, sometimes even at the expense of reality. By means of this attitude he also gained deep insight into the Dionysian qualities of his unconscious, the crude forms of which, so far as we know, reached the surface of his consciousness only after the outbreak of his illness, although they had previously revealed their presence in various erotic allusions. It is extremely regrettable, therefore, from the standpoint of psychology, that the fragmentary writings—so significant in this respect—which were found in Turin after the onset of his malady should have met with destruction in deference to moral and aesthetic scruples.

IV

THE TYPE PROBLEM IN HUMAN CHARACTER

1. GENERAL REMARKS ON JORDAN'S TYPES

243   Continuing my chronological survey of previous contributions to this interesting problem of psychological types, I now come to a small and rather odd work, my acquaintance with which I owe to my esteemed colleague Dr. Constance Long, of London: *Character as Seen in Body and Parentage*, by Furneaux Jordan, F.R.C.S.

244   In this little book of one hundred and twenty-six pages, Jordan describes in the main two characterological types, the definition of which is of interest to us in more than one respect. Although—to anticipate slightly—the author is really concerned with only one half of our types, thinking and feeling, he nevertheless introduces the standpoint of the other half, the intuitive and sensation types, and blends the two together. I will first let the author speak for himself in his introductory definition:

There are two generic fundamental biases in character . . . two conspicuous types of character (with a third, an intermediate one) . . . one in which the tendency to action is extreme and the tendency to reflection slight, and another in which the proneness to reflection greatly predominates and the impulse for action is feebler. Between the two extremes are innumerable gradations; it is sufficient to point only to a third type . . . in which the powers of reflection and action tend to meet in more or less equal degree. . . . In an intermediate class may also be placed the characters which tend to eccentricity, or in which other possibly abnormal tendencies predominate over the emotional and non-emotional.[1]

245   It is clear from this definition that Jordan contrasts reflection, or thinking, with action. It is readily understandable that

[1] P. 5.

147

an observer of men, not probing too deeply, would first be struck by the contrast between reflective and active natures, and would therefore tend to define the observed antithesis in those terms. The simple reflection, however, that activity is not necessarily the product of mere impulse, but can also proceed from thinking, would make it seem necessary to carry the definition a stage further. Jordan himself reaches this conclusion, for on page 6 he introduces a further element which for us has a particular value, the element of feeling. He states here that the active type is less passionate, while the reflective temperament is distinguished by its passionate feelings. Hence he calls his types the "less impassioned" and the "more impassioned." Thus the element he overlooked in his introductory definition subsequently acquires the status of a fixed term. But what mainly distinguishes his conception from ours is that he makes the "less impassioned" type active and the "more impassioned" inactive.

247   This combination seems to me unfortunate, since highly passionate and profound natures exist which at the same time are very energetic and active, and conversely, there are less passionate and superficial natures which are in no way distinguished by activity, not even by the low form of activity that consists in being busy. In my view, his otherwise valuable conception would have gained much in clarity if he had left the factors of activity and inactivity altogether out of account, as belonging to a quite different point of view, although in themselves they are important characterological determinants.

246   It will be seen from the arguments which follow that the "less impassioned and more active" type describes the extravert, and the "more impassioned and less active" type the introvert. Either can be active or inactive without changing his type, and for this reason the factor of activity should, in my opinion, be ruled out as a main characteristic. As a determinant of secondary importance, however, it still plays a role, since the whole nature of the extravert appears more mobile, more full of life and activity than that of the introvert. But this quality entirely depends on the phase in which the individual momentarily finds himself vis-à-vis the external world. An introvert in an extraverted phase appears active, while an extravert in an introverted phase appears passive. Activity itself, as

a fundamental trait of character, can sometimes be introverted; it is then all directed inwards, developing a lively activity of thought or feeling behind an outward mask of profound repose. Or else it can be extraverted, showing itself a vigorous action while behind the scenes there stands a firm unmoved thought or untroubled feeling.

248   Before we examine Jordan's arguments more closely, I must, for greater clarity, stress yet another point which, if not borne in mind, may give rise to confusion. I remarked at the beginning of this book that in my earlier publications I identified the introvert with the thinking and the extravert with the feeling type. As I have said before, it became clear to me only later that introversion and extraversion are to be distinguished as general basic attitudes from the function-types. These two attitudes may be recognized with the greatest ease, while it requires considerable experience to distinguish the function-type. At times it is uncommonly difficult to find out which function holds prior place. The fact that the introvert, because of his abstracting attitude, naturally has a reflective and contemplative air is misleading. One is inclined to assume that in him the primacy falls to thinking. The extravert, on the contrary, naturally displays many immediate reactions, which easily lead one to conjecture a predominance of feeling. These suppositions are deceptive, since the extravert may well be a thinking, and the introvert a feeling type. Jordan describes in general merely the introvert and the extravert. But, when he goes into details, his description becomes misleading, because traits of different function-types are blended together which a more thorough examination of the material would have kept apart. In its general outline, however, the picture of the introverted and extraverted attitudes is unmistakable, so that the nature of the two basic attitudes can plainly be discerned.

249   The characterization of types in terms of affectivity seems to me the really important aspect of Jordan's work. We have already seen that the reflective, contemplative nature of the introvert is compensated by a condition in which instinct and sensation are unconscious and archaic. We might even say this is just why he is introverted: he has to rise above his archaic, impulsive nature to the safe heights of abstraction in order to dominate from there his unruly and turbulent affects. This

point of view is not at all wide of the mark in many cases. We might also say, conversely, that the affective life of the extravert, being less deeply rooted, lends itself more readily to differentiation and domestication than his unconscious, archaic thinking and feeling, and that this fantasy life of his can have a dangerous influence on his personality. Hence he is always the one who seeks life and experience as busily and abundantly as possible in order not to have to come to himself and face his evil thoughts and feelings. These observations, which can easily be verified, help to explain an otherwise paradoxical passage in Jordan, where he says (p. 6) that in the "less impassioned" (= extraverted) temperament the intellect predominates and has an unusually large share in the regulation of life, whereas in the "reflective" (= introverted) temperament it is affects that claim the greater importance.

250   At first glance, this view would seem to fly in the face of my assertion that the "less impassioned" type corresponds to the extravert. But closer scrutiny proves that this is not so, since the reflective character, the introvert, though certainly *trying* to deal with his unruly affects, is in reality more influenced by his passions than the man whose life is consciously guided by desires oriented to objects. The latter, the extravert, tries to get away with this all the time, but is forced to experience how his subjective thoughts and feelings constantly stand in his way. He is far more influenced by his psychic inner world than he suspects. He cannot see it himself, but the people around him, if observant, will always detect the personal purpose in his striving. Hence his golden rule should always be to ask himself: "What am I really after? What is my secret intention?" The other, the introvert, with his conscious thought-out intentions, always overlooks what the people around him see only too clearly, that his intentions are really subservient to powerful impulses, lacking both aim and object, and are in a high degree influenced by them. The observer and critic of the extravert is liable to take the parade of thinking and feeling as a thin covering that only imperfectly conceals a cold and calculated personal aim. Whereas the man who tries to understand the introvert will readily conclude that vehement passions are only with difficulty held in check by apparent sophistries.

251   Either judgment is both true and false. It is *false* when the conscious standpoint, or consciousness itself, is strong enough to offer resistance to the unconscious; but it is *true* when a weaker conscious standpoint encounters a strong unconscious and eventually has to give way to it. Then the motive that was kept in the background breaks through: in one case the egoistic aim, in the other the unsubdued passion, the elemental affect, that throws every consideration to the winds.

252   These reflections enable us to discern Jordan's mode of observation: he is evidently preoccupied with the affectivity of the observed type, hence his nomenclature: "less impassioned," "more impassioned." When, therefore, from the standpoint of affect, he conceives the introvert as the more impassioned, and the extravert as the less impassioned and even as the intellectual type, he displays a peculiar kind of discernment which one must describe as *intuitive*. I have already pointed out that Jordan blends the standpoint of the rational types with that of the "aesthetic" types.[2] So when he characterizes the introvert as passionate and the extravert as intellectual he is obviously seeing the two types from the unconscious side, that is, he *perceives them through the medium of his own unconscious*. He observes and cognizes intuitively, and this must always be the case, more or less, with a practical observer of men.

253   But however true and profound such an apprehension may sometimes be, it suffers from one very important limitation: it overlooks the living reality of the person observed, since it always judges him by his unconscious mirror-image instead of by his actual appearance. This error is inseparable from all intuition, and reason has always been at loggerheads with it on that account, only grudgingly admitting its right to exist despite the fact that in many cases the objective rightness of the intuition cannot be denied. Thus Jordan's formulations accord on the whole with reality, though not with reality as it is understood by the rational types, but with the reality which for them is unconscious. Naturally these conditions are calculated to confuse all judgment of the observed and to make agreement about it all the more difficult. One should therefore

2 [Cf. supra, par. 240, where the intuitive and sensation types are called the "aesthetic" types.—EDITORS.]

not quarrel over the nomenclature but should stick exclusively to the observable differences. Although I, in accordance with my nature, express myself quite differently from Jordan, we are—allowing for certain divergences—nevertheless at one in our classification of the observed material.

254   Before going on to discuss Jordan's typology, I should like to return for a moment to the third or "intermediate" type which he postulates. Under this heading he includes on the one hand characters that are entirely balanced, and on the other those that are unbalanced or "eccentric." It will not be superfluous to recall at this point the classification of the Valentinian school, according to which the *hylic* man is inferior to the psychic and the pneumatic man. The hylic man corresponds by definition to the sensation type, whose ruling determinants are supplied by the senses. The sensation type possesses neither differentiated thinking nor differentiated feeling, but his sensuousness is well developed. This, as we know, is also the case with the primitive. The instinctive sensuousness of the primitive has its counterpart in the spontaneity of his psychic processes: his mental products, his thoughts, just appear to him, as it were. It is not he who makes them or thinks them—he is not capable of that—they make themselves, they happen to him, they even confront him as hallucinations. Such a mentality must be termed intuitive, for intuition is the instinctive perception of an emergent psychic content. Although the principal psychological function of the primitive is as a rule sensation, the less conspicuous compensatory function is intuition. On the higher levels of civilization, where one man has thinking more more or less differentiated and another feeling, there are also quite a number who have developed intuition to a high degree and can employ it as the essentially determining function. From these we get the intuitive type. It is my belief, therefore, that Jordan's intermediate group can be resolved into the sensation and intuitive types.

2. SPECIAL DESCRIPTION AND CRITICISM OF JORDAN'S TYPES

255   As regards the general characterization of the two types, Jordan emphasizes (p. 17) that the more impassioned type includes far fewer prominent and striking personalities than the

less impassioned. This assertion derives from the fact that Jordan identifies the active type with the less impassioned, which in my opinion is inadmissible. But if we discount this error, it is certainly true that the behaviour of the less impassioned or extraverted type makes him more conspicuous than the more impassioned or introverted type.

a. The Introverted Woman
("The More Impassioned Woman")

256   We will first summarize the chief points in Jordan's discussion of the introverted woman:

She has quiet manners, and a character not easy to read: she is occasionally critical, even sarcastic, but though bad temper is sometimes noticeable, she is not habitually fitful, or restless, or captious, or censorious, nor is she a "nagging" woman. She diffuses an atmosphere of repose, and unconsciously she consoles and heals, but under the surface emotions and passions lie dormant. Her emotional nature matures slowly. As she grows older the charm of her character increases. She is "sympathetic," i.e., she brings insight and experience to bear on the problems of others. Yet the very worst characters are found among the more impassioned women. They are the cruellest stepmothers. They make most affectionate wives and mothers, but their passions and emotions are so strong that these frequently hold reason in subjection or carry it away with them. They love too much, but they also hate too much. Jealousy can make wild beasts of them. Stepchildren, if hated by them, may even be done to death. If evil is not in the ascendant, morality itself is associated with deep feeling, and may take a profoundly reasoned and independent course which will not always fit itself to conventional standards. It will not be an imitation or a submission; not a bid for a reward here or hereafter. It is only in intimate relations that the excellences and drawbacks of the impassioned woman are seen. Here she unfolds herself; here are her joys and sorrows, here her faults and weaknesses are seen, perhaps slowness to forgive, implacability, sullenness, anger, jealousy, or degraded uncontrolled passions. She is charmed with the moment, and less apt to think of the comfort and welfare of the absent. She is disposed to forget others and forget time. If she is affected, her affectation is less an imitation than a pronounced change of manners and speech with changing shades of thought and especially of feeling. In social life she tends to be the same in all circles. In both domestic and social life she is as a rule not difficult to please, she spontaneously appreciates, congratulates, and praises. She can soothe the mentally bruised and encourage the unsuccessful. She rises to the high and stoops to the low, she is the sister and playmate of all nature. Her judgment is mild and lenient. When she reads she tries to grasp the inmost thought and deepest feeling of the book; she reads and re-reads the book, marks it freely, and turns down its corners.[3]

257   From this description it is not difficult to recognize the introverted character. But it is, in a certain sense, one-sided, because the chief stress is laid on feeling, without considering the one characteristic to which I attach special value—the *conscious inner life*. Jordan mentions in passing that the introverted woman is "contemplative" (p. 18), but he does not pursue the matter further. His description, however, seems to me a confirmation of my comments on his mode of observation. It is chiefly the outward behaviour constellated by feeling, and the expressions of passion that strike him; he does not probe into the conscious life of this type. He never mentions that the inner life plays an altogether decisive role in the introvert's conscious psychology. Why, for example, does the introverted woman read so attentively? Because above everything else she loves to understand and grasp ideas. Why is she restful and soothing? Because she usually keeps her feelings to herself, expressing them in her thoughts instead of unloading them on others. Her unconventional morality is backed by deep reflection and convincing inner feelings. The charm of her quiet and intelligent character depends not merely on a peaceful attitude, but on the fact that one can talk with her reasonably and coherently, and that she is able to appreciate the value of her partner's argument. She does not interrupt him with impulsive exclamations, but accompanies his meaning with her thoughts and feelings, which none the less remain steadfast, never yielding to the opposing argument.

258   This compact and well-developed ordering of the conscious psychic contents is a stout defence against a chaotic and passionate emotional life of which the introvert is very often

[3] Pp. 17ff. [Although printed as quoted matter, this and the following two extracts (pars. 261, 265) are a mixture of Jung's own summary and direct quotation. It would not be possible to quote Jordan verbatim without adding a great deal of irrelevant material. For the sake of easier reading, suspension points have been omitted. Only the extract in par. 269 is a direct quotation.—EDITORS.]

aware, at least in its personal aspect: she fears it because she knows it too well. She meditates about herself, and is therefore outwardly calm and can acknowledge and accept others without overwhelming them with praise or blame. But because her emotional life would devastate these good qualities, she rejects as far as possible her instincts and affects, though without mastering them. In contrast, therefore, to her logical and well-knit consciousness, her affective life is elemental, confused, and ungovernable. It lacks the true human note, it is out of proportion, irrational, a *phenomenon of nature* that breaks through the human order. It lacks any kind of palpable afterthought or purpose, so at times it is purely destructive, a raging torrent that neither intends destruction nor avoids it, ruthless and necessary, obedient only to its own laws, a process that is its own fulfillment. Her good qualities depend on her thinking, which by its tolerant or benevolent outlook has succeeded in influencing or restraining one part of her instinctive life, though without being able to embrace and transform the whole. The introverted woman is far less conscious of the full range of her affectivity than she is of her rational thoughts and feelings. Her affectivity is much less mobile than her intellectual content; it is, as it were, viscous and curiously inert, therefore hard to change; it is persevering, hence her unconscious steadiness and equability, but also her self-will and her occasional unreasonable inflexibility in things that touch her emotions.

259 These reflections may explain why any judgment on the introverted woman in terms of affectivity alone is incomplete and unfair in good and bad alike. If Jordan finds the vilest characters among introverted women, this, in my opinion, is due to the fact that he lays too great a stress on affectivity, as if passion alone were the mother of all evil. We can torture children to death in other ways than the merely physical. And, conversely, that wondrous wealth of love in the introverted woman is not by any means always her own possession; she is more often possessed by it and cannot choose but love, until one day a favourable opportunity occurs, when suddenly, to the amazement of her partner, she displays an inexplicable coldness. The emotional life of the introverted woman is generally her weak side, it is not absolutely trustworthy. She

deceives herself about it; others also are deceived and disappointed in her if they rely too much on her emotionality. Her mind is more to be relied on, because more adapted. Her affect is too close to sheer untamed nature.

b. The Extraverted Woman
("The Less Impassioned Woman")

260   Let us now turn to Jordan's description of the "less impassioned" woman. Here too I must reject everything the author has confused by the introduction of activity, since this admixture is only calculated to make the typical character less recognizable. Thus when he speaks of a certain "quickness" of the extravert, this does not mean vivacity or activity, but merely the mobility of active psychological processes.

261   Of the extraverted woman Jordan says:

She is marked by activity, vivacity, quickness, and opportuneness rather than by persistence or consistency. Her life is almost wholly occupied with little things. She goes even further than Lord Beaconsfield in the belief that unimportant things are not very unimportant, and important things not very important. She likes to dwell on the way her grandmother did things, and how her grandchildren will do them, and on the universal degeneracy of human beings and affairs. Her daily wonder is how things would go on if she were not there to look after them. She is frequently invaluable in social movements. She expends her energies in household cleanliness, which is the end and aim of existence to not a few women. Frequently she is "idea-less, emotionless, restless and spotless." Her emotional development is usually precocious, and at eighteen she is little less wise than at twenty-eight or forty-eight. Her mental outlook usually lacks range and depth, but it is clear from the first. When intelligent, she is capable of taking a leading position. In society she is kindly, generous and hospitable. She judges her neighbours and friends, forgetful that she is herself being judged, but she is active in helping them in misfortune. Deep passion is absent in her, love is simply preference, hatred merely dislike, and jealousy only injured pride. Her enthusiasm is not sustained, and she is more alive to the beauty of poetry than she is to its passion and pathos. Her beliefs and disbeliefs are complete rather than strong. She has no convictions, but she has no misgivings. She does not believe, she adopts, she does not disbelieve, she ignores. She never enquires and she never doubts. In large affairs she defers to authority; in small affairs she jumps to conclusions. In the detail of her own little world, whatever is, is wrong: in the larger world outside, whatever is, is right. She instinctively rebels against carrying the conclusions of reason into practice.

At home she shows quite a different character from the one seen in society. With her, marriage is much influenced by ambition, or a love of change, or obedience to well-recognized custom and a desire to be "settled in life," or from a sincere wish to enter a greater sphere of usefulness. If her husband belongs to the impassioned type, he will love children more than she does.

In the domestic circle, her least pleasing characteristics are evident. Here she indulges in disconnected, disapproving comment, and none can foresee when there will be a gleam of sunshine through the cloud. The unemotional woman has little or no self-analysis. If she is plainly accused of habitual disapproval she is surprised and offended, and intimates that she only desires the general good, "but some people do not know what is good for them." She has one way of doing good to her family, and quite another way where society is concerned. The household must always be ready for social inspection. Society must be encouraged and propitiated. Its upper section must be impressed and its lower section kept in order. Home is her winter, society her summer. If the door but opens and a visitor is announced, the transformation is instant.

The less emotional woman is by no means given to asceticism; respectability and orthodoxy do not demand it of her. She is fond of movement, recreation, change. Her busy day may open with a religious service, and close with a comic opera. She delights, above all, to entertain her friends and to be entertained by them. In society she finds not only her work and her happiness, but her rewards and her consolations. She believes in society, and society believes in her. Her feelings are little influenced by prejudice, and as a rule she is "reasonable." She is very imitative and usually selects good models, but is only dimly conscious of her imitations. The books she reads must deal with life and action.[4]

262   This familiar type of woman is extraverted beyond a doubt. Her whole demeanour indicates a character that by its very nature must be called extraverted. The continual criticizing, which is never based on real reflection, is an extraversion of a fleeting impression that has nothing to do with real thinking. I remember a witty aphorism I once read somewhere: "Thinking is difficult, therefore let the herd pass judgment!" Reflection demands time above everything: hence the man who

4 Pp. 9ff.

reflects has no opportunity for continual criticism. Incoherent and inconsequential criticism, dependent on tradition and authority, reveals the absence of any independent reflection; similarly the lack of self-criticism and the dearth of independent ideas betray a defect in the function of judgment. The absence of inner mental life in this type comes out much more clearly than its presence in the introverted type described earlier. From this sketch one might easily conclude that there is just as great or even greater a lack of affectivity, for it is obviously superficial, shallow, almost spurious, because the ulterior motive always bound up with it or discernible behind it makes the affective output practically worthless. I am, however, inclined to assume that our author is undervaluing here, just as much as he overvalued in the former case. In spite of an occasional admission of good qualities, the type on the whole comes out of it very badly. I believe this is due to a bias on the part of the author. It is usually enough to have had bitter experiences with one or more representatives of the same type for one's taste to be spoiled for all of them. One must not forget that, just as the good sense of the introverted woman depends on a careful accommodation of her mental contents to the general thinking, the affectivity of the extraverted woman possesses a certain lability and shallowness because it is adapted to the ordinary life of human society. It is thus a socially differentiated affectivity with an incontestable general value, which compares very favourably with the heavy, sultry, passionate affect of the introvert. This differentiated affectivity has sloughed off everything chaotic and pathetic and become a disposable function of adaptation, even though it be at the expense of the inner mental life, which is conspicuous by its absence. It none the less exists in the unconscious, and moreover in a form corresponding to the passion of the introvert, i.e., it is in an undeveloped, archaic, infantile state. Working from the unconscious, the undeveloped mentality supplies the affective output with contents and hidden motives that cannot fail to make a bad impression on the critical observer, although they may be unperceived by the uncritical eye. The disagreeable impression that the constant perception of thinly veiled egoistic motives has on the observer makes him only too prone to forget the actual reality and adapted usefulness of the affective output displayed. All that is easy-going, unforced, temperate, harmless, and superficial in life would disappear if there were no differentiated affects. One would either be stifled in perpetual pathos or engulfed in the yawning abyss of repressed passion. If the social function of the introvert concentrates mainly on individuals, it is usually true that the extravert promotes the life of the community, which also has a right to exist. For this extraversion is needed, because it is first and foremost the bridge to one's neighbour.

263   As we all know, the expression of affect works by suggestion, whereas the mind can operate only indirectly, after arduous translation into another medium. The affects required by the social function need not be at all deep, otherwise they beget passion in others, and passion upsets the life and wellbeing of society. Similarly, the adapted, differentiated mentality of the introvert has extensity rather than intensity; hence it is not disturbing and provocative but reasonable and calming. But, just as the introvert causes trouble by the violence of his passions, the extravert irritates by his half-unconscious thoughts and feelings, incoherently and abruptly applied in the form of tactless and unsparing judgments on his fellow men. If we were to make a collection of such judgments and tried to construct a psychology out of them, they would build up into an utterly brutal outlook, which in chilling savagery, crudity, and stupidity rivals the murderous affectivity of the introvert. Hence I cannot subscribe to Jordan's view that the very worst characters are to be found among passionate introverted natures. Among extraverts there is just as much inveterate wickedness. But whereas introverted passion expresses itself in brutal actions, the vulgarity of the extravert's unconscious thoughts and feelings commits crimes against the soul of the victim. I do not know which is worse. The drawback in the former case is that the deed is visible, while the latter's vulgarity of mind is concealed behind the veil of acceptable behaviour. I would like, however, to stress the social thoughtfulness of this type, his active concern for the general welfare, as well as a decided tendency to give pleasure to others. The introvert as a rule has these qualities only in his fantasies.

264   Differentiated affects have the further advantage of charm and elegance. They spread about them an air that is aesthetic and beneficial. A surprising number of extraverts practise an

art—chiefly music—not so much because they are specially qualified for it as from a desire to make their contribution to social life. Nor is their fault-finding always unpleasant or altogether worthless. Very often it is no more than a well-adapted educative tendency which does a great deal of good. Equally, their dependence on the judgment of others is not necessarily a bad thing, as it often conduces to the suppression of extravagances and pernicious excesses which in no way further the life and welfare of society. It would be altogether unjustifiable to maintain that one type is in any respect more valuable than the other. The types are mutually complementary, and their differences generate the tension that both the individual and society need for the maintenance of life.

c. The Extraverted Man
("The Less Impassioned Man")

265   Of the extraverted man Jordan says:

He is fitful and uncertain in temper and behaviour, given to petulance, fuss, discontent and censoriousness. He makes depreciatory judgments on all and sundry, but is ever well satisfied with himself. His judgment is often at fault and his projects often fail, but he never ceases to place unbounded confidence in both. Sidney Smith, speaking of a conspicuous statesman of his time, said he was ready at any moment to command the Channel Fleet or amputate a limb. He has an incisive formula for everything that is put before him—either the thing is not true, or everybody knows it already. In his sky there is not room for two suns. If other suns insist on shining, he has a curious sense of martyrdom.

He matures early. He is fond of administration, and is often an admirable public servant. At the committee of his charity he is as much interested in the selection of its washer-woman as in the selection of its chairman. In company he is usually alert, to the point, witty, and apt at retort. He resolutely, confidently, and constantly shows himself. Experience helps him and he insists on getting experience. He would rather be the *known* chairman of a committee of three than the *unknown* benefactor of a nation. When he is less gifted he is probably not less self-important. Is he busy? He believes himself to be energetic. Is he loquacious? He believes himself to be eloquent.

He rarely puts forth new ideas, or opens new paths, but he is quick to follow, to seize, to apply, to carry out. His natural tendency is to ancient, or at least accepted, forms of belief and policy. Special circumstances may sometimes lead him to contemplate with admiration the audacity of his own heresy. Not rarely the less emotional intellect is so lofty and commanding that no disturbing influence can hinder the formation of broad and just views in all the provinces of life. His life is usually characterized by morality, truthfulness, and high principle; sometimes his desire to produce an immediate effect however leads to later trouble.

If, in public assembly, adverse fates have given him nothing to do,—nothing to propose, or second, or support, or amend, or oppose—he will rise and ask for some window to be closed to keep out a draught, or, which is more likely, that one be opened to let in more air; for, physiologically, he commonly needs much air as well as much notice. He is especially prone to do what he is not asked to do—what, perhaps, he is not best fitted to do; nevertheless he constantly believes that the public sees him as he wishes it to see him, as he sees himself—a sleepless seeker of the public good. He puts others in his debt, and he cannot go unrewarded. He may, by well-chosen language, move his audience although he is not moved himself. He is probably quick to understand his time or at least his party; he warns it of impending evil, organizes its forces, deals smartly with its opponents. He is full of projects and prophecies and bustle. Society must be pleased if possible; if it will not be pleased it must be astonished; if it will neither be pleased nor astonished it must be pestered and shocked. He is a saviour by profession and as an acknowledged saviour is not ill pleased with himself. We can of ourselves do nothing right—but we can believe in him, dream of him, thank God for him, and ask him to address us.

He is unhappy in repose, and rests nowhere long. After a busy day he must have a pungent evening. He is found in the theatre, or concert, or church, or the bazaar, at the dinner, or conversazione or club, or all these, turn and turn about. If he misses a meeting, a telegram announces a more ostentatious call.[5]

266   From this description, too, the type can easily be recognized. But, perhaps even more than in the description of the extraverted woman, there emerges, in spite of occasional appreciative touches, an element of depreciation that amounts to caricature. It is due partly to the fact that this method of description cannot hope to be fair to the extraverted nature in general, because it is virtually impossible for the intellectual approach to put the specific value of the extravert in the right

[5] Pp. 26ff.

light. This is much more possible with the introvert, because his essential reasonableness and his conscious motivation can be expressed in intellectual terms as readily as his passions can and the actions resulting from them. With the extravert, on the other hand, the specific value lies in his relation to the object. It seems to me that only life itself can grant the extravert the just dues that intellectual criticism cannot give him. Life alone reveals his values and appreciates them. We can, of course, establish that the extravert is socially useful, that he has made great contributions to the progress of human society, and so on. But any analysis of his resources and motives will always yield a negative result, because his specific value lies in the reciprocal relation to the object and not in himself. The relation to the object is one of those imponderables that an intellectual formulation can never grasp.

267   Intellectual criticism cannot help proceeding analytically and bringing the observed type to full clarity by pinning down its motives and aims. But this, as we have said, results in a picture that amounts to a caricature of the psychology of the extravert, and anyone who believes he has found the right attitude to an extravert on the basis of such a description would be astonished to see how the actual personality turns the description into a mockery. Such a one-sided view of things makes any adaptation to the extravert impossible. In order to do him justice, *thinking* about him must be altogether excluded, while for his part the extravert can properly adapt to the introvert only when he is prepared to accept his mental contents in themselves regardless of their practical utility. Intellectual analysis cannot help attributing to the extravert every conceivable design, stratagem, ulterior motive, and so forth, though they have no actual existence but at most are shadowy effects leaking in from the unconscious background.

268   It is certainly true that the extravert, if he has nothing else to say, will at least demand that a window be open or shut. But who notices, who is struck by it? Only the man who is trying to account for all the possible reasons and intentions behind such an action, who reflects, dissects, puts constructions on it, while for everyone else this little stir vanishes in the general bustle of life without their seeing in it anything sinister or remarkable. But this is just the way the psychology of the

extravert manifests itself: it is part and parcel of the happenings of daily human life, and it signifies nothing more than that, neither better nor worse. But the man who reflects sees further and—so far as actual life is concerned—sees crooked, though his vision is sound enough as regards the unconscious background of the extravert's thought. He does not see the positive man, but only his *shadow*. And the shadow proves the judgment right at the expense of the conscious, positive man. For the sake of understanding, it is, I think, a good thing to detach the man from his shadow, the unconscious, otherwise the discussion is threatened with an unparalleled confusion of ideas. One sees much in another man that does not belong to his conscious psychology, but is a gleam from his unconscious, and one is deluded into attributing the observed quality to his conscious ego. Life and fate may do this, but the psychologist, to whom knowledge of the structure of the psyche and the possibility of a better understanding of man are of the deepest concern, must not. A clear differentiation of the conscious man from his unconscious is imperative, since only by the assimilation of conscious standpoints will clarity and understanding be gained, but never by a process of reduction to the unconscious backgrounds, sidelights, quarter-tones.

d. The Introverted Man
("The More Impassioned Man")

269   Of the introverted man Jordan says:

He may spend his evenings in pleasure from a genuine love of it; but his pleasures do not change every hour, and he not driven to them from mere restlessness. If he takes part in public work he is probably invited to do so from some special fitness; or it may be that he has at heart some movement—beneficent or mischievous—which he wishes to promote. When his work is done he willingly retires. He is able to see what others can do better than he; and he would rather that his cause should prosper in other hands than fail in his own. He has a hearty word of praise for his fellow-workers. Probably he errs in estimating too generously the merits of those around him. He is never, and indeed cannot be, an habitual scold. . . . Men of profound feeling and illimitable pondering tend to suspense or even hesitation; they are never the founders of religions; never leaders of religious movements; they neither receive nor deliver divine messages. They are moreover never so supremely confi-

163

dent as to what is error that they burn their neighbours for it; never so confident that they possess infallible truth that, although not wanting in courage, they are prepared to be burnt in its behalf.[6]

270   To me it seems significant that in his chapter on the introverted man Jordan says no more in effect than what is given in the above excerpts. What we miss most of all is a description of the passion on account of which the introvert is called "impassioned" in the first place. One must, of course, be cautious in making diagnostic conjectures, but this case seems to invite the supposition that the introverted man has received such niggardly treatment for subjective reasons. After the elaborately unfair description of the extraverted type, one might have expected an equal thoroughness in the description of the introvert. Why is it not forthcoming?

271   Let us suppose that Jordan himself is on the side of the introverts. It would then be intelligible that a description like the one he gives of his opposite number with such pitiless severity would hardly have suited his book. I would not say from lack of objectivity, but rather from lack of knowledge of his own shadow. The introvert cannot possibly know or imagine how he appears to his opposite type unless he allows the extravert to tell him to his face, at the risk of having to challenge him to a duel. For as little as the extravert is disposed to accept Jordan's description as an amiable and apposite picture of his character is the introvert inclined to let his picture be painted by an extraverted observer and critic. The one would be as depreciatory as the other. Just as the introvert who tries to get hold of the nature of the extravert invariably goes wide of the mark, so the extravert who tries to understand the other's inner life from the standpoint of externality is equally at sea. The introvert makes the mistake of always wanting to derive the other's actions from the subjective psychology of the extravert, while the extravert can conceive the other's inner life only as a consequence of external circumstances. For the extravert an abstract train of thought must be a fantasy, a sort of cerebral mist, when no relation to an object is in evidence. And as a matter of fact the introvert's brain-weavings are often nothing more. At all events a lot more could be said of the in-

6 Pp. 35f., 40f.

troverted man, and one could draw a shadow portrait of him no less complete and no less unfavourable than the one Jordan drew of the extravert.

272   His observation that the introvert's love of pleasure is "genuine" seems to me important. This appears to be a peculiarity of introverted feeling in general: it is genuine because it is there of itself, rooted in the man's deeper nature; it wells up out of itself, having itself as its own aim; it will serve no other ends, lending itself to none, and is content to be an end in itself. This hangs together with the spontaneity of any archaic and natural phenomenon that has never yet bowed to the ends and aims of civilization. Rightly or wrongly, or at any rate without regard to right or wrong, suitability or unsuitability, the affective state bursts out, forcing itself on the subject even against his will and expectation. There is nothing about it that suggests a calculated motivation.

273   I do not wish to discuss the remaining chapters of Jordan's book. He cites historical personalities as examples, presenting numerous distorted points of view which all derive from the fallacy already referred to, of introducing the criterion of active and passive and mixing it up with the other criteria. This leads to the frequent conclusion that an active personality must be reckoned a passionless type and, conversely, that a passionate nature must be passive. I seek to avoid this error by excluding the factor of activity as a criterion altogether.

274   To Jordan, however, belongs the credit for having been the first, so far as I know, to give a relatively appropriate character sketch of the emotional types.

V

THE TYPE PROBLEM IN POETRY

Carl Spitteler: *Prometheus and Epimetheus*

1. INTRODUCTORY REMARKS ON SPITTELER'S TYPOLOGY

275   If, besides the themes offered to the poet by the complications of emotional life, the type problem did not also play a significant role, it would almost amount to a proof that the problem did not exist. But we have already seen how in Schiller this problem stirred the poet in him as deeply as the thinker. In this chapter we shall turn our attention to a poetic work based almost exclusively on the type problem: Carl Spitteler's *Prometheus and Epimetheus*, published in 1881.

276   I have no wish to declare at the outset that Prometheus, the "forethinker," stands for the introvert, and Epimetheus, the man of action and "afterthinker," for the extravert. The conflict between these two figures is essentially a struggle between the introverted and extraverted lines of development in one and the same individual, though the poet has embodied it in two independent figures and their typical destinies.

277   There can be no mistaking the fact that Prometheus exhibits introverted character traits. He presents the picture of a man introverted to his inner world, true to his "soul." He expresses his nature perfectly in the reply he gives to the angel:

> But it does not lie with me to judge of the face of my soul, for lo, she is my Lady and Mistress, and she is my God in joy and sorrow, and all that I am, I owe to her alone. And so I will share my honour with her, and, if needs must, I am ready to forego it altogether.[1]

[1] *Prometheus and Epimetheus* (trans. Muirhead), pp. 22f.

166

278   Prometheus surrenders himself, come honour or dishonour, to his soul, that is, to the function of relation to the inner world. That is why the soul has a mysterious, metaphysical character, precisely on account of her relation to the unconscious. Prometheus concedes her an absolute significance, as mistress and guide, in the same unconditional manner in which Epimetheus surrenders himself to the world. He sacrifices his individual ego to the soul, to the relation with the unconscious as the matrix of eternal images and meanings, and becomes de-individualized, because he has lost the counterweight of the persona,[2] the function of relation to the external object. With this surrender to his soul Prometheus loses all connection with the surrounding world, and hence also the very necessary corrective offered by external reality. But this loss cannot be reconciled with the nature of the real world. Therefore an angel appears to Prometheus, evidently a representative of the powers-that-be; in psychological terms, he is the projected image of a tendency aiming at adaptation to reality. The angel accordingly says to Prometheus:

It shall come to pass, if you do not prevail and free yourself from your froward soul, that you shall lose the great reward of many years, and the joy of your heart, and all the fruits of your richly endowed mind.[3]

And again:

You shall be cast out on the day of your glory on account of your soul, for she knows no god and obeys no law, and nothing is sacred to her pride, either in heaven or on earth.[4]

279   Because Prometheus has a one-sided orientation to his soul, all tendencies to adapt to the external world are repressed and sink into the unconscious. Consequently, if perceived at all, they appear as not belonging to his own personality but as projections. There would seem to be a contradiction in the fact that the soul, whose cause Prometheus has espoused and whom he has, as it were, fully assimilated into consciousness, appears at the same time as a projection. But since the soul, like the

---

[2] Jung, *Two Essays on Analytical Psychology*, pars. 243ff., 254ff., 305ff.
[3] Cf. Muirhead, p. 23.   [4] Cf. ibid., p. 22.

persona, is a function of relationship, it must consist in a certain sense of two parts—one part belonging to the individual, and the other adhering to the object of relationship, in this case the unconscious. Unless one frankly subscribes to von Hartmann's philosophy, one is generally inclined to grant the unconscious only a conditional existence as a psychological factor. On epistemological grounds, we are at present quite unable to make any valid statement about the objective reality of the complex psychological phenomenon we call the unconscious, just as we are in no position to say anything valid about the essential nature of real things, for this lies beyond our psychological ken. On the grounds of practical experience, however, I must point out that, in relation to the activity of consciousness, the contents of the unconscious lay the same claim to reality on account of their obstinate persistence as do the real things of the external world, even though this claim must appear very improbable to a mind that is "outer-directed." It must not be forgotten that there have always been many people for whom the contents of the unconscious possessed a greater reality than the things of the outside world. The history of human thought bears witness to both realities. A more searching investigation of the human psyche shows beyond question that there is in general an equally strong influence from both sides on the activity of consciousness, so that, psychologically, we have a right on purely empirical grounds to treat the contents of the unconscious as just as *real* as the things of the outside world, even though these two realities are mutually contradictory and appear to be entirely different in their natures. But to subordinate one reality to the other would be an altogether unjustifiable presumption. Theosophy and spiritualism are just as violent in their encroachments on other spheres as materialism. We have to accommodate ourselves to our psychological capacities, and be content with that.

280   The peculiar reality of unconscious contents, therefore, gives us the same right to describe them as *objects* as the things of the outside world. Now just as the persona, being a function of relationship, is always conditioned by the external object and is anchored as much in it as in the subject, so the soul, as a function of relationship to the inner object, is represented by that object; hence she is always distinct from the

subject in one sense and is actually perceived as something different. Consequently, she appears to Prometheus as something quite separate from his individual ego. In the same way as a man who surrenders entirely to the outside world still has the world as an object distinct from himself, the unconscious world of images behaves as an object distinct from the subject even when a man surrenders to it completely. And, just as the unconscious world of mythological images speaks indirectly, through the experience of external things, to the man who surrenders wholly to the outside world, so the real world and its demands find their way indirectly to the man who has surrendered wholly to the soul; for no man can escape both realities. If he is intent only on the outer reality, he must live his myth; if he is turned only towards the inner reality, he must dream his outer, so-called real life. Accordingly the soul says to Prometheus:

I told you I was a wayward goddess, who would lead you astray on untrodden paths. But you would not listen to me, and now it has come to pass according to my words: for my sake they have robbed you of the glory of your name and stolen from you your life's happiness.[5]

281   Prometheus refuses the kingdom the angel offers him, which means that he refuses to adapt to things as they are because his soul is demanded from him in exchange. The subject, Prometheus, is essentially human, but his soul is of a quite different character. She is daemonic, because the inner object, the suprapersonal, collective unconscious with which she is connected as the function of relationship, gleams through her. The unconscious, considered as the historical background of the human psyche, contains in concentrated form the entire succession of engrams (imprints) which from time immemorial have determined the psychic structure as it now exists. These engrams are nothing other than function-traces that typify, on average, the most frequently and intensively used functions of the human psyche. They present themselves in the form of mythological motifs and images, appearing often in identical form and always with striking similarity among all races; they can also be easily verified in the unconscious material of mod-

[5] Cf. p. 38.

ern man. It is therefore understandable that decidedly animal traits or elements should appear among the unconscious contents side by side with those sublime figures which from ancient times have been man's companions on the road of life. The unconscious is a whole world of images whose range is as boundless as that of the world of "real" things. Just as the man who has surrendered entirely to the outside world encounters it in the form of some intimate and beloved being through whom, should his destiny lie in extreme devotion to a personal object, he will experience the whole ambivalence of the world and of his own nature, so the other, who has surrendered to the soul, will encounter her as a daemonic personification of the unconscious, embodying the totality, the utter polarity and ambivalence of the world of images. These are borderline phenomena that overstep the norm; hence the normal, middle-of-the-road man knows nothing of these cruel enigmas. They do not exist for him. It is always only a few who reach the rim of the world, where its mirror-image begins. For the man who always stands in the middle the soul has a human and not a dubious, daemonic character, neither does his neighbour appear to him in the least problematical. Only complete surrender to one world or the other evokes their ambivalence. Spitteler's intuition caught a soul-image which would have appeared to a less profound nature at most in a dream:

And while he thus bore himself in the frenzy of his ardour, a strange quiver played about her lips and face, and her eyelids flickered, opening and closing quickly. And behind the soft and delicate fringe of her eyelashes something menacing lurked and prowled, like the fire that steals through a house maliciously and stealthily, or like the tiger that winds through the jungle, showing amid the dark leaves glimpses of its striped and yellow body.[6]

282   The life-line that Prometheus chooses is unmistakably introverted. He sacrifices all connection with the present in order to create by forethought a distant future. It is very different with Epimetheus: he realizes that his aim is the world and what the world values. Therefore he says to the angel:

But now my desire is for truth and my soul lies in my hand, and if it please you, pray give me a conscience that I may mind my "p's" and "q's" and everything that is just.[7]

6 Cf. p. 38.   7 Cf. p. 24.

Epimetheus cannot resist the temptation to fulfil his own destiny and submit to the "soulless" point of view. This alliance with the world is immediately rewarded:

And it came to pass that as Epimetheus stood upon his feet, he felt his stature was increased and his courage firmer, and all his being was at one with itself, and all his feeling was sound and mightily at ease. And thus he strode with bold steps through the valley, following the straight path as one who fears no man, with free and open bearing, like a man inspired by the contemplation of his own right-doing.[8]

283   He has, as Prometheus says, bartered his soul for the "p's" and "q's".[9] He has lost his soul—to his brother's gain. He has followed his extraversion, and, because this orients him to the external object, he is caught up in the desires and expectations of the world, seemingly at first to his great advantage. He has become an extravert, after having lived many solitary years under the influence of his brother as an *extravert falsified by imitating the introvert*. This kind of involuntary "simulation dans le caractère" (Paulhan) is not uncommon. His conversion to true extraversion is therefore a step towards "truth" and brings him a just reward.

284   Whereas Prometheus, through the tyrannical claims of his soul, is hampered in every relation to the external object and has to make the cruellest sacrifices in the service of the soul, Epimetheus is armed with an effective shield against the danger that most threatens the extravert—the danger of complete surrender to the external object. This protection consists in a conscience that is backed by the traditional "right ideas," that is, by the not-to-be-despised treasures of worldly wisdom, which are employed by public opinion in much the same way as the judge uses the penal code. This provides Epimetheus with a protective barrier that restrains him from surrendering to the object as boundlessly as Prometheus does to his soul. This is forbidden him by his conscience, which deputizes for his soul. When Prometheus turns his back on the world of men and their codified conscience, he plays into the hands of his cruel soul-mistress and her caprices, and only after endless suffering does he atone for his neglect of the world.

8 Cf. ibid.
9 [Literally, *-heit* and *-keit*.—TRANS.]

285   The prudent restraint of a blameless conscience puts such a bandage over Epimetheus' eyes that he must blindly live his myth, but ever with the sense of doing right, because he always does what is expected of him, and with success ever at his side, because he fulfils the wishes of all. That is how men desire to see their king, and thus Epimetheus plays his part to the inglorious end, never forsaken by the spine-stiffening approval of the public. His self-assurance and self-righteousness, his unshakable confidence in his own worth, his indubitable "right-doing" and good conscience, present an easily recognizable portrait of the extraverted character as depicted by Jordan. Let us hear how Epimetheus visits the sick Prometheus, desiring to heal his sufferings:

When all was set in order, King Epimetheus stepped forward supported by a friend on either side, greeted Prometheus, and spoke to him these well-meant words: "I am heartily sorry for you, Prometheus, my dear brother! But nonetheless take courage, for look, I have a salve here which is a sure remedy for every ill and works wondrously well in heat and in frost, and moreover can be used alike for solace as for punishment."

So saying, he took his staff and tied the box of ointment to it, and reached it carefully and with all due solemnity towards his brother. But as soon as he saw and smelt the ointment, Prometheus turned away his head in disgust. At that the King changed his tone, and shouted and began to read his brother a lesson with great zest: "Of a truth it seems you have need of yet greater punishment, since your present fate does not suffice to teach you."

And as he spoke, he drew a mirror from the folds of his robe, and made everything clear to him from the beginning, and waxed very eloquent and knew all his faults.[10]

286   This scene is a perfect illustration of Jordan's words: "Society must be pleased if possible; if it will not be pleased, it must be astonished; if it will neither be pleased nor astonished, it must be pestered and shocked."[11] In the East a rich man proclaims his rank by never showing himself in public unless supported by two slaves. Epimetheus affects this pose in order to make an impression. Well-doing must at the same time be com-

[10] Cf. pp. 108f.
[11] *Character as Seen in Body and Parentage*, p. 31. [Cf. supra, par. 265.]

bined with admonition and moral instruction. And, as that does not produce an effect, the other must at least be horrified by the picture of his own baseness. Everything is aimed at creating an impression. There is an American saying that runs: "In America two kinds of men make good—the man who can *do*, and the man who can *bluff*." Which means that pretence is sometimes just as successful as actual performance. An extravert of this kind prefers to work by *appearance*. The introvert tries to do it by *force* and *misuses* his work to that end.

287 　 If we fuse Prometheus and Epimetheus into one personality, we should have a man outwardly Epimethean and inwardly Promethean—an individual constantly torn by both tendencies, each seeking to get the ego finally on its side.

2. A COMPARISON OF SPITTELER'S WITH GOETHE'S PROMETHEUS

288 　 It is of considerable interest to compare this conception of Prometheus with Goethe's. I believe I am justified in the conjecture that Goethe belongs more to the extraverted than to the introverted type, while Spitteler would seem to belong to the latter. Only an exhaustive examination and analysis of Goethe's biography would be able to establish the rightness of this supposition. My conjecture is based on a variety of impressions, which I refrain from mentioning here for lack of sufficient evidence to support them.

289 　 The introverted attitude need not necessarily coincide with the figure of Prometheus, by which I mean that the traditional Prometheus can be interpreted quite differently. This other version is found, for instance, in Plato's *Protagoras*, where the bestower of vital powers on the creatures the gods have created out of fire and water is not Prometheus but Epimetheus. Here, as in the myth, Prometheus (conforming to classical taste) is the crafty and inventive genius. There are two versions of Prometheus in Goethe's works. In the "Prometheus Fragment" of 1773 Prometheus is the defiant, self-sufficient, godlike, god-disdaining creator and artist. His soul is Minerva, daughter of Zeus. The relation of Prometheus to Minerva is very like the relation of Spitteler's Prometheus to his soul:

From the beginning thy words have been celestial light to me!
Always as though my soul spoke to herself
Did she reveal herself to me,
And in her of their own accord
Sister harmonies rang out.
And when I deemed it was myself,
A goddess spoke,
And when I deemed a goddess was speaking,
It was myself.
So it was between thee and me,
So fervently one.
Eternal is my love for thee![12]

And again:

As the twilight glory of the departed sun
Hovers over the gloomy Caucasus
And encompasses my soul with holy peace,
Parting, yet ever present with me,
So have my powers waxed strong
With every breath drawn from thy celestial air.[13]

290   So Goethe's Prometheus, too, is dependent on his soul. The resemblance between this relationship and that of Spitteler's Prometheus to his soul is very striking. The latter says to his soul:

And though I be stripped of all, yet am I rich beyond all measure so long as you alone remain with me, and name me "my friend" with your sweet mouth, and the light of your proud and gracious countenance go not from me.[14]

291   But for all the similarity of the two figures and their relations with the soul, one essential difference remains. Goethe's Prometheus is a creator and artist, and Minerva inspires his clay images with life. Spitteler's Prometheus is suffering rather than creative; only his soul is creative, but her work is secret and mysterious. She says to him in farewell:

And now I depart from you, for a great work awaits me, a work of immense labour, and I must hasten to accomplish it.[15]

292   It would seem that, with Spitteler, the Promethean creativity falls to the soul, while Prometheus himself merely suffers the

12 *Werke* (ed. Beutler), IV, pp. 188f.   13 Ibid., p. 189.
14 Cf. Muirhead, p. 38.   15 Cf. ibid., p. 41.

174

pangs of the creative soul within him. But Goethe's Prometheus is self-activating, he is essentially and exclusively creative, defying the gods out of the strength of his own creative power:

> Who helped me
> Against the pride of the Titans?
> Who saved me from death?
> And slavery?
> Did you not do it all alone,
> O ardent, holy heart?[16]

293   Epimetheus in this fragment is only sparingly sketched, he is thoroughly inferior to Prometheus, an advocate of collective feeling who can only understand the service of the soul as "obstinacy." He says to Prometheus:

> You stand alone!
> You in your obstinacy know not that bliss
> When the gods, you, and all that you have,
> Your world, your heaven,
> Are enfolded in one embracing unity.[17]

294   Such indications as are to be found in the Prometheus fragments are too sparse to enable us to discern the character of Epimetheus. But Goethe's delineation of Prometheus shows a typical difference from the Prometheus of Spitteler. Goethe's Prometheus creates and works outwards into the world, he peoples space with the figures he has fashioned and his soul has animated, he fills the earth with the offspring of his creativeness, he is at once the master and teacher of man. But with the Prometheus of Spitteler everything goes inwards and vanishes in the darkness of the soul's depths, just as he himself disappears from the world of men, even wandering from the narrow confines of his homeland as though to make himself the more invisible. In accordance with the principle of compensation in analytical psychology, the soul, the personification of the unconscious, must then be especially active, preparing a work that is not yet visible. Besides the passage already quoted, there is in Spitteler a full description of this expected compensatory process. We find it in the Pandora interlude.

[16] From another Prometheus fragment, *Werke*, I, p. 321.
[17] *Werke*, IV, p. 188.

295   Pandora, that enigmatical figure in the Prometheus myth, is in Spitteler's version the divine maiden who lacks every relation with Prometheus but the very deepest. This conception is based on a version of the myth in which the woman who enters into relation with Prometheus is either Pandora or Athene. The Prometheus of mythology has his soul-relation with Pandora or Athene, as in Goethe. But, in Spitteler, a noteworthy departure is introduced, though it is already indicated in the historical myth, where Prometheus and Pandora are contaminated with Hephaestus and Athene. In Goethe, the Prometheus-Athene version is given preference. In Spitteler, Prometheus is removed from the divine sphere and granted a soul of his own. But his divinity and his original relation with Pandora in the myth are preserved as a cosmic counterplot, enacted independently in the celestial sphere. The happenings in the other world are what takes place on the further side of consciousness, that is in the unconscious. The Pandora interlude, therefore, is an account of what goes on in the unconscious during the sufferings of Prometheus. When Prometheus vanishes from the world, destroying every link that binds him to mankind, he sinks into his own depths, and the only thing around him, his only object, is himself. He has become "godlike," for God is by definition a Being who everywhere reposes in himself and by virtue of his omnipresence has himself always and everywhere for an object. Naturally Prometheus does not feel in the least godlike—he is supremely wretched. After Epimetheus has come to spit upon his misery, the interlude in the other world begins, and that naturally is just at the moment when all Prometheus' relations to the world are suppressed to the point of extinction. Experience shows that at such moments the contents of the unconscious have the best opportunity to assert their independence and vitality, so much so that they may even overwhelm consciousness.[18] Prometheus' condition in the unconscious is reflected in the following scene:

And on the dark morning of that very day, in a still and solitary meadow above all the worlds, wandered God, the creator of all life, pursuing the accursed round in obedience to the strange nature of his mysterious and grievous sickness.

[18] "The Content of the Psychoses" and *Two Essays on Analytical Psychology*, pars. 221 ff., 250ff.

For because of this sickness, he could never make an end of the weariness of his walk, might never find rest on the path of his feet, but ever with measured tread, day after day, year after year, must make the round of the still meadow, with plodding steps, bowed head, furrowed brow, and distorted countenance, his beclouded gaze turned always towards the midpoint of the circle.

And when today as on all other days he made the inevitable round and his head sank deeper for sorrow and his steps dragged the more for weariness and the wellspring of his life seemed spent by the sore vigils of the night, there came to him through night and early dawn Pandora, his youngest daughter, who with uncertain step demurely approached the hallowed spot, and stood there humbly at his side, greeting him with modest glance, and questioning him with lips that held a reverential silence.[19]

296   It is evident at a glance that God has caught the sickness of Prometheus. For just as Prometheus makes all his passion, his whole libido flow inwards to the soul, to his innermost depths, dedicating himself entirely to his soul's service, so God pursues his course round and round the pivot of the world and exhausts himself exactly like Prometheus, who is near to self-extinction. All his libido has gone into the unconscious, where an equivalent must be prepared; for libido is energy, and energy cannot disappear without a trace, but must always produce an equivalent. This equivalent is Pandora and the gift she brings to her father: a precious jewel which she wants to give to mankind to ease their sufferings.

297   If we translate this process into the human sphere of Prometheus, it would mean that while Prometheus lies suffering in his state of "godlikeness," his soul is preparing a work destined to alleviate the sufferings of mankind. His soul wants to get to men. Yet the work which his soul actually plans and carries out is not identical with the work of Pandora. Pandora's jewel is an unconscious mirror-image that *symbolizes* the real work of the soul of Prometheus. The text shows unmistakably what the jewel signifies: it is a *God-redeemer*, a renewal of the sun.[20] The sickness of God expresses his longing for rebirth, and to this end his whole life-force flows back into the centre of the self, into the depths of the unconscious, out of which life

[19] Cf. Muirhead, p. 113.
[20] For the motifs of the jewel and rebirth, see *Symbols of Transformation*, Part II, chs. IV and V.

is born anew. That is why the appearance of the jewel in the world is described in a way that reflects the imagery of the birth of the Buddha in the *Lalita-Vistara*:[21] Pandora lays the jewel beneath a walnut-tree, just as Maya bears her child under a fig-tree:

In the midnight shade beneath the tree it glows and sparkles and flames evermore, and, like the morning star in the dark sky, its diamond lightning flashes afar.

And the bees also, and the butterflies, which danced over the flowery mead, hurried up, and played and rocked around the wonder-child . . . and the larks dropped down sheer from the upper air, all eager to pay homage to the new and lovelier sun-countenance, and as they drew near and beheld the dazzling radiance, their hearts swooned . . .

And, enthroned over all, fatherly and benign, the chosen tree with his giant crown and heavy mantle of green, held his kingly hands protectingly over the faces of his children. And his many branches bent lovingly down and bowed themselves towards the earth as though they wished to screen and ward off alien glances, jealous that they alone might enjoy the unearned grace of the gift; while all the myriads of gently moving leaves fluttered and trembled with rapture, murmuring in joyous exultation a soft, clear-voice chorus in rustling accord: "Who could know what lies hidden beneath this lowly roof, or guess the treasure reposing in our midst!"[22]

298   So Maya, when her hour was come, bore her child beneath the *plaksa* tree, which bowed its crown shelteringly to earth. From the incarnate Bodhisattva an immeasurable radiance spread through the world; gods and all nature took part in the birth. At his feet there grew up an immense lotus, and standing in the lotus he scanned the world. Hence the Tibetan prayer: *Om mani padme hum* (Om! Behold the jewel in the lotus). And the moment of rebirth found the Bodhisattva beneath the chosen *bodhi* tree, where he became the Buddha, the Enlightened One. This rebirth or renewal was attended by the same light-phenomena, the same prodigies of nature and apparitions of gods, as the birth.

299   In Spitteler's version, the inestimable treasure gets lost in the kingdom of Epimetheus, where only conscience reigns and

21 [Trans. Rajendralala Mitra, ch. VI, esp. p. 94.]
22 Cf. Muirhead, pp. 130f.

not the soul. Raging over the stupidity of Epimetheus, the angel upbraids him: "And had you no soul, that like the dumb and unreasoning beasts you hid from the wondrous divinity?"[23]

300   It is clear that Pandora's jewel symbolizes a renewal of God, a new God, but this takes place in the divine sphere, i.e., in the unconscious. The intimations of the process that filter through into consciousness are not understood by the Epimethean principle, which governs the relation to the world. This is elaborated by Spitteler in the ensuing sections,[24] where we see how the world of consciousness with its rational attitude and orientation to objects is incapable of appreciating the true value and significance of the jewel. Because of this, it is irretrievably lost.

301   The renewed God signifies a regenerated attitude, a renewed possibility of life, a recovery of vitality, because, psychologically speaking, God always denotes the highest value, the maximum sum of libido, the fullest intensity of life, the optimum of psychological vitality. But in Spitteler the Promethean attitude proves to be just as inadequate as the Epimethean. The two tendencies get dissociated: the Epimethean attitude is adapted to the world as it actually is, but the Promethean is not, and for that reason it has to work for a renewal of life. It also produces a new attitude to the world (symbolized by the jewel given to mankind), though this does not find favour with Epimetheus. Nevertheless, we recognize in Pandora's gift a symbolic attempt to solve the problem discussed in the chapter on Schiller's *Letters*—the problem of uniting the differentiated with the undifferentiated function.

302   Before proceeding further with this problem, we must turn back to Goethe's Prometheus. As we have seen, there are unmistakable differences between the creative Prometheus of Goethe and the suffering figure presented by Spitteler. Another and more important difference is the relation to Pandora. In Spitteler, Pandora is a duplicate of the soul of Prometheus belonging to the other world, the sphere of the gods; in Goethe she is entirely the creature and daughter of the Titan, and thus absolutely dependent on him. The relation of Goethe's Prome-

---

[23] Cf. p. 161. Spitteler depicts the famous "conscience" of Epimetheus as a little animal. It corresponds to the animal's opportunist instinct.

[24] Muirhead, pp. 135ff.

theus with Minerva puts him in the place of Vulcan, and the fact that Pandora is wholly his creature, and does not figure as a being of divine origin, makes him a creator-god and removes him altogether from the human sphere. Hence Prometheus says:

> And when I deemed it was myself,
> A goddess spoke,
> And when I deemed a goddess was speaking,
> It was myself.

303   With Spitteler, on the other hand, Prometheus is stripped of divinity, even his soul is only an unofficial daemon; his divinity is hypostatized, quite detached from everything human. Goethe's version is classical to this extent: it emphasizes the divinity of the Titan. Accordingly Epimetheus too must diminish in stature, whilst in Spitteler he emerges as a much more positive character. Now in Goethe's "Pandora" we are fortunate in possessing a work which conveys a far more complete portrait of Epimetheus than the fragment we have been discussing. Epimetheus introduces himself as follows:

> For me day and night are not clearly divided,
> Always I carry the old evil of my name:
> My progenitors named me Epimetheus.
> Brooding on the past with its hasty actions,
> Glancing back, troubled in thought,
> To the melancholy realm of fugitive forms
> Interfluent with the opportunities of past days.
> Such bitter toil was laid on my youth
> That turning impatiently towards life
> I seized heedlessly the present moment
> And won tormenting burdens of fresh care.[25]

304   With these words Epimetheus reveals his nature: he broods over the past, and can never free himself from Pandora, whom (according to the classical myth) he has taken to wife. He cannot rid himself of her memory-image, although she herself has long since deserted him, leaving him her daughter Epimeleia (Care), but taking with her Elpore (Hope). Epimetheus is portrayed so clearly that we are at once able to recognize what

25 "Pandora," *Werke*, VI, p. 407.

psychological function he represents. While Prometheus is still the same creator and modeller, who daily rises early from his couch with the same inexhaustible urge to create and to set his stamp on the world, Epimetheus is entirely given up to fantasies, dreams, and memories, full of anxious misgivings and troubled deliberations. Pandora appears as the creature of Hephaestus, rejected by Prometheus but chosen by Epimetheus for a wife. He says of her: "Even the pains which such a treasure brings are pleasure." Pandora is to him a precious jewel, the supreme value:

> And forever she is mine, the glorious one!
> From her I have received supreme delight.
> I possessed Beauty, and Beauty enfolded me,
> Splendidly she came in the wake of the spring.
> I knew her, I caught her, and then it was done.
> Clouding thoughts vanished like mist,
> She raised me from earth and up to heaven.
> You seek for words worthy to praise her,
> You would extol her, she wanders already on high.
> Set your best beside her, you'll see it is bad.
> Her words bewilder, yet she is right.
> Struggle against her, she'll win the fight.
> Faltering to serve her, you're still her slave.
> Kindness and love she loves to fling back.
> What avails high esteem? She will strike it down.
> She sets her goal and wings on her way.
> If she blocks your path, she at once holds you up.
> Make her an offer and she'll raise your bid,
> You'll give riches and wisdom and all in the bargain.
> She comes down to earth in a thousand forms,
> Hovering the waters, striding the meadows.
> Divinely proportioned she dazzles and thrills,
> Her form ennobling the content within,
> Lending it and herself the mightiest power.
> She came radiant with youth and the flesh of woman.[26]

305   For Epimetheus, as these verses clearly show, Pandora has the value of a soul-image—she stands for his soul; hence her divine power, her unshakable supremacy. Whenever such attributes are conferred upon a personality, we may conclude

[26] Ibid., pp. 429f.

with certainty that such a personality is a *symbol-carrier*, or an image of projected unconscious contents. For it is the contents of the unconscious that have the supreme power Goethe has described, incomparably characterized in the line: "Make her an offer and she'll raise your bid." In this line the peculiar emotional reinforcement of conscious contents by association with analogous contents of the unconscious is caught to perfection. This reinforcement has in it something daemonic and compelling, and thus has a "divine" or "devilish" effect.

306   We have already described Goethe's Prometheus as extraverted. It is still the same in his "Pandora," although here the relation of Prometheus with the soul, the unconscious feminine principle, is missing. To make up for this, Epimetheus emerges as the introvert turned to the inner world. He broods, he calls back memories from the grave of the past, he "reflects." He differs absolutely from Spitteler's Epimetheus. We could therefore say that in Goethe's "Pandora" the situation suggested in his earlier fragment has actually come about. Prometheus represents the extraverted man of action, and Epimetheus the brooding introvert. This Prometheus is, in extraverted form, what Spitteler's is in introverted form. In Goethe's "Pandora" he is purely creative for collective ends—he sets up a regular factory in his mountain, where articles of use for the whole world are produced. He is cut off from his inner world, which relation devolves this time on Epimetheus, i.e., on the secondary and purely reactive thinking and feeling of the extravert which possess all the characteristics of the undifferentiated function. Thus it comes about that Epimetheus is wholly at the mercy of Pandora, because she is in every respect superior to him. This means, psychologically, that the unconscious Epimethean function of the extravert, namely that fantastic, brooding, ruminative fancy, is intensified by the intervention of the soul. If the soul is coupled with the less differentiated function, one must conclude that the superior, differentiated function is too collective; it is the servant of the collective conscience (Spitteler's "p's" and "q's") and not the servant of freedom. Whenever this is so—and it happens very frequently—the less differentiated function or the "other side" is reinforced by a pathological egocentricity. The extravert then fills up his spare time with melancholic or hypochondriacal brooding and

may even have hysterical fantasies and other symptoms,[27] while the introvert grapples with compulsive feelings of inferiority[28] which take him unawares and put him in a no less dismal plight.

307 The resemblance between the Prometheus of "Pandora" and the Prometheus of Spitteler ends here. He is merely a collective itch for action, so one-sided that it amounts to a repression of eroticism. His son Phileros ('lover of Eros') is simply erotic passion; for, as the son of his father, he must, as is often the case with children, re-enact under unconscious compulsion the unlived lives of his parents.

308 The daughter of Pandora and Epimetheus, the man who always broods afterwards on his unthinking actions, is fittingly named Epimeleia, Care. Phileros loves Epimeleia, and thus the guilt of Prometheus in rejecting Pandora is expiated. At the same time, Prometheus and Epimetheus become reconciled when the industriousness of Prometheus is shown to be nothing but unadmitted eroticism, and Epimetheus' constant broodings on the past to be rational misgivings which might have checked the unremitting productivity of Prometheus and kept it within reasonable bounds.

309 This attempt of Goethe's to find a solution, which appears to have evolved from his extraverted psychology, brings us back to Spitteler's attempt, which we left for the time being in order to discuss Goethe's Prometheus.

310 Spitteler's Prometheus, like his God, turns away from the world, from the periphery, and gazes inwards to the centre, the "narrow passage"[29] of rebirth. This concentration or introversion pipes the libido into the unconscious. The activity of the unconscious is increased—the psyche begins to "work" and creates a product that wants to get out of the unconscious into consciousness. But consciousness has two attitudes: the Promethean, which withdraws the libido from the world, introverting without giving out, and the Epimethean, constantly giving out and responding in a soulless fashion, fascinated by the claims

[27] This may be compensated by an outburst of sociability or by an intensive social round in the eager pursuit of which forgetfulness is sought.

[28] Sometimes compensated by a morbid and feverish activity which likewise serves the purpose of repression.

[29] Cf. *Symbols of Transformation*, par. 417, end of quotation.

of external objects. When Pandora makes her gift to the world it means, psychologically, that an unconscious product of great value is on the point of reaching the extraverted consciousness, i.e., it is seeking a relation to the real world. Although the Promethean side, or in human terms the artist, intuitively apprehends the great value of the product, his personal relations to the world are so subordinated to the tyranny of tradition that it is appreciated merely as a work of art and not taken for what it actually is, a symbol that promises a renewal of life. In order to transform it from a purely aesthetic interest into a living reality, it must be assimilated into life and actually lived. But when a man's attitude is mainly introverted and given to abstraction, the function of extraversion is inferior, in the grip of collective restraints. These restraints prevent the symbol created by the psyche from living. The jewel gets lost, but one cannot really live if "God," the supreme vital value that is expressed in the symbol, cannot become a living fact. Hence the loss of the jewel signifies at the same time the beginning of Epimetheus' downfall.

311 And now the enantiodromia begins. Instead of taking for granted, as every rationalist and optimist is inclined to do, that a good state will be followed by a better, because everything tends towards an "ascending development," Epimetheus, the man of blameless conscience and universally acknowledged moral principles, makes a pact with Behemoth and his evil host, and even the divine children entrusted to his care are bartered to the devil.[30] Psychologically, this means that the collective, undifferentiated attitude to the world stifles a man's highest values and becomes a destructive force, whose influence increases until the Promethean side, the ideal and abstract attitude, places itself at the service of the soul's jewel and, like a true Prometheus, kindles for the world a new fire. Spitteler's Prometheus has to come out of his solitude and tell men, even at the risk of his life, that they are in error, and where they err. He must acknowledge the pitilessness of truth, just as Goethe's Prometheus has to experience in Phileros the pitilessness of love.

312 That the destructive element in the Epimethean attitude is actually this traditional and collective restraint is shown in

[30] Cf. infra, pars. 456ff.

Epimetheus' raging fury against the "little lamb," an obvious caricature of traditional Christianity. In this outburst of affect something breaks through that is familiar to us from the Ass Festival in *Zarathustra*. It is the expression of a contemporary tendency.

313   Man is constantly inclined to forget that what was once good does not remain good eternally. He follows the old ways that once were good long after they have become bad, and only with the greatest sacrifices and untold suffering can he rid himself of this delusion and see that what was once good is now perhaps grown old and is good no longer. This is so in great things as in small. The ways and customs of childhood, once so sublimely good, can hardly be laid aside even when their harmfulness has long since been proved. The same, only on a gigantic scale, is true of historical changes of attitude. A collective attitude is equivalent to a religion, and changes of religion constitute one of the most painful chapters in the world's history. In this respect our age is afflicted with a blindness that has no parallel. We think we have only to declare an accepted article of faith incorrect and invalid, and we shall be psychologically rid of all the traditional effects of Christianity or Judaism. We believe in enlightenment, as if an intellectual change of front somehow had a profounder influence on the emotional processes or even on the unconscious. We entirely forget that the religion of the last two thousand years is a psychological attitude, a definite form and manner of adaptation to the world without and within, that lays down a definite cultural pattern and creates an atmosphere which remains wholly uninfluenced by any intellectual denials. The change of front is, of course, symptomatically important as an indication of possibilities to come, but on the deeper levels the psyche continues to work for a long time in the old attitude, in accordance with the laws of psychic inertia. Because of this, the unconscious was able to keep paganism alive. The ease with which the spirit of antiquity springs to life again can be observed in the Renaissance, and the readiness of the vastly older primitive mentality to rise up from the past can be seen in our own day, perhaps better than at any other epoch known to history.

314   The more deeply rooted the attitude, the more violent will be the attempts to shake it off. "Écrasez l'infâme," the cry of

the Age of Enlightenment, heralded the religious upheaval
started off by the French Revolution, and this religious upheaval was nothing but a basic readjustment of attitude,
though it lacked universality. The problem of a general change
of attitude has never slept since that time; it cropped up again
in many prominent minds of the nineteenth century. We have
seen how Schiller sought to master it, and in Goethe's treatment of Prometheus and Epimetheus we see yet another attempt to effect some sort of union between the more highly
differentiated function, which corresponds to the Christian
ideal of favouring the good, and the less differentiated function, whose repression corresponds to the Christian ideal of
rejecting the evil.[31] In the symbols of Prometheus and Epimetheus, the difficulty that Schiller sought to master philosophically and aesthetically is clothed in the garment of a classical
myth. Consequently, something happens which, as I pointed
out earlier, is a typical and regular occurrence: when a man
meets a difficult task which he cannot master with the means
at his disposal, a retrograde movement of libido automatically
sets in, i.e., a regression. The libido draws away from the problem of the moment, becomes introverted, and reactivates in the
unconscious a more or less primitive analogue of the conscious
situation. This law determined Goethe's choice of a symbol:
Prometheus was the saviour who brought light and fire to mankind languishing in darkness. Goethe's deep scholarship could
easily have picked on another saviour, so that the symbol he
chose is not sufficient as an explanation. It must lie rather in
the classical spirit, which at the turn of the eighteenth century
was felt to contain a compensatory value and was given expression in every possible way—in aesthetics, philosophy, morals,
even politics (Philhellenism). It was the paganism of antiquity,
glorified as "freedom," "naïveté," "beauty," and so on, that met
the yearnings of that age. These yearnings, as Schiller shows
so clearly, sprang from a feeling of imperfection, of spiritual
barbarism, of moral servitude, of drabness. This feeling in its
turn arose from a one-sided evaluation of everything Greek,

[31] Cf. Goethe's "Geheimnisse," *Werke*, III, pp. 273-83. Here the Rosicrucian
solution is attempted: the union of Dionysus and Christ, rose and cross. The
poem leaves one cold. One cannot pour new wine into old bottles.

and from the consequent fact that the psychological dissociation between the differentiated and the undifferentiated functions became painfully evident. The Christian division of man into two halves, one valuable and one depraved, was unbearable to the superior sensibilities of that age. Sinfulness stumbled on the idea of an everlasting natural beauty, in the contemplation of which the age reached back to an earlier time when the idea of sinfulness had not yet disrupted man's wholeness, when the heights and depths of human nature could still dwell together in complete naïveté without offending moral or aesthetic susceptibilities.

315   But the attempt at a regressive Renaissance shared the fate of the "Prometheus Fragment" and "Pandora": it was stillborn. The classical solution would no longer work, because the intervening centuries of Christianity with their profound spiritual upheavals could not be undone. So the penchant for the antique gradually petered out in medievalism. This process sets in with Goethe's *Faust*, where the problem is seized by both horns. The divine wager between good and evil is accepted. Faust, the medieval Prometheus, enters the lists with Mephistopheles, the medieval Epimetheus, and makes a pact with him. And here the problem becomes so sharply focussed that one can see that Faust and Mephisto are the same person. The Epimethean principle, which always thinks backwards and reduces everything to the primal chaos of "interfluent forms" (par. 303), condenses into the devil whose evil power threatens everything living with the "devil's cold fist" and would force back the light into the maternal darkness whence it was born. The devil everywhere displays a true Epimethean thinking, a thinking in terms of "nothing but" which reduces All to Nothing. The naïve passion of Epimetheus for Pandora becomes the diabolical plot of Mephistopheles for the soul of Faust. And the cunning foresight of Prometheus in turning down the divine Pandora is expiated in the tragedy of Gretchen and the yearning for Helen, with its belated fulfillment, and in the endless ascent to the Heavenly Mothers ("The Eternal Feminine / Leads us upward and on").

316   The Promethean defiance of the accepted gods is personified in the figure of the medieval magician. The magician

187

has preserved in himself a trace of primitive paganism;[32] he possesses a nature that is still unaffected by the Christian dichotomy and is in touch with the still pagan unconscious, where the opposites lie side by side in their original naïve state, beyond the reach of "sinfulness" but liable, if assimilated into conscious life, to beget evil as well as good with the same daemonic energy ("Part of that power which would / Ever work evil yet engenders good"). He is a destroyer but also a saviour, and such a figure is pre-eminently suited to become the symbolic bearer of an attempt to resolve the conflict. Moreover the medieval magician has laid aside the classical naïveté which was no longer possible, and become thoroughly steeped in the Christian atmosphere. The old pagan element must at first drive him into a complete Christian denial and mortification of self, because his longing for redemption is so strong that every avenue has to be explored. But in the end the Christian attempt at a solution fails too, and it then transpires that the possibility of redemption lies precisely in the obstinate persistence of the old pagan element, because the anti-Christian symbol opens the way for an acceptance of evil. Goethe's intuition thus grasped the problem in all its acuteness. It is certainly significant that the more superficial attempts at a solution—the "Prometheus Fragment," "Pandora," and the Rosicrucian compromise, a blend of Dionysian joyousness and Christian self-sacrifice—remained uncompleted.

317   Faust's redemption began at his death. The divine, Promethean character he had preserved all his life fell away from him only at death, with his rebirth. Psychologically, this means that the Faustian attitude must be abandoned before the individual can become an integrated whole. The figure that first appeared as Gretchen and then on a higher level as Helen, and was finally exalted as the Mater Gloriosa, is a symbol whose many meanings cannot be discussed here. Suffice to say that it is the same primordial image that lies at the heart of Gnosticism, the image of the divine harlot—Eve, Helen, Mary, Sophia-Achamoth.

---

[32] Very often it is the older folk-elements that possess magical powers. In India it is the Nepalese, in Europe the gypsies, and in Protestant areas the Capuchins.

3. THE SIGNIFICANCE OF THE UNITING SYMBOL

318   If, from the vantage point we have now gained, we glance once more at Spitteler's presentation of the problem, we are immediately struck by the fact that the pact with evil[33] came about by no design of Prometheus but because of the thoughtlessness of Epimetheus, who possesses a merely collective conscience but has no power of discrimination with regard to the things of the inner world. As is invariably the case with a standpoint oriented to the object, it allows itself to be determined exclusively by collective values and consequently overlooks what is new and unique. Current collective values can certainly be measured by an objective criterion, but only a free and individual assessment—a matter of living feeling—can give the true measure of something newly created. It also needs a man who has a "soul" and not merely relations to objects.

319   The downfall of Epimetheus begins with the loss of the new-born God-image. His morally unassailable thinking, feeling, and acting in no way prevent the evil and destructive element from creeping in and gaining the upper hand. The invasion of evil signifies that something previously good has turned into something harmful. Spitteler is here expressing the idea that the ruling moral principle, although excellent to begin with, in time loses its essential connection with life, since it no longer embraces life's variety and abundance. What is rationally correct is too narrow a concept to grasp life in its totality and give it permanent expression. The divine birth is an event altogether outside the bounds of rationality. Psychologically, it proclaims the fact that a new symbol, a new expression of life at its most intense, is being created. Every Epimethean man, and everything Epimethean in man, prove incapable of comprehending this event. Yet, from that moment, the highest intensity of life is to be found only in this new direction. Every other direction gradually drops away, dissolved in oblivion.

---

[33] [The pact with Behemoth (supra, par. 311), described in section 5 (infra, pars. 456ff.). The reader may find it helpful to read the whole of section 5 at this point, as it also describes (pars. 450ff.) the fate of the redeeming symbol, the jewel whose loss was mentioned earlier (pars. 300, 310).—EDITORS.]

320   The new life-giving symbol springs from Prometheus' love for his soul-mistress, a daemonic figure indeed. One can therefore be certain that, interwoven with the new symbol and its living beauty, there will also be the element of evil, for otherwise it would lack the glow of life as well as beauty, since life and beauty are by nature morally neutral. That is why the Epimethean, collective mentality finds nothing estimable in it. It is completely blinded by its one-sided moral standpoint, which is identical with the "little lamb." The raging of Epimetheus when he turns against the "little lamb" is merely "Écrasez l'infâme" in new form, a revolt against established Christianity, which was incapable of understanding the new symbol and so giving life a new direction.

321   This bare statement of the case might leave us entirely cold were there no poets who could fathom and read the collective unconscious. They are always the first to divine the darkly moving mysterious currents and to express them, as best they can, in symbols that speak to us. They make known, like true prophets, the stirrings of the collective unconscious or, in the language of the Old Testament, "the will of God," which in the course of time must inevitably come to the surface as a collective phenomenon. The redemptive significance of the deed of Prometheus, the downfall of Epimetheus, his reconciliation with his soul-serving brother, and the vengeance Epimetheus wreaks on the "little lamb"—recalling in its cruelty the scene between Ugolino and Archbishop Ruggieri[34]—prepare a solution of the conflict that entails a sanguinary revolt against traditional collective morality.

322   In a poet of modest capacity we may assume that the pinnacle of his work does not transcend his personal joys, sorrows, and aspirations. But Spitteler's work entirely transcends his personal destiny. For this reason his solution of the problem is not an isolated one. From here to Zarathustra, the breaker of the tables, is only a step. Stirner had also joined the company in the wake of Schopenhauer, who was the first to conceive the theory of "world negation." Psychologically, "world" means how I see the world, my attitude to the world; thus the

---

[34] Dante, *Inferno*, XXXII.

world can be conceived as "my will" and "my idea."[35] In itself the world is indifferent. It is my Yes and No that create the differences. Negation, therefore, is itself an attitude to the world, a particularly Schopenhauerian attitude that on the one hand is purely intellectual and rational, and on the other a profound feeling of mystical identity with the world. This attitude is introverted; it suffers therefore from its typological antithesis. But Schopenhauer's work by far transcends his personality. It voices what was obscurely thought and felt by many thousands. Similarly with Nietzsche: his *Zarathustra*, in particular, brings to light the contents of the collective unconscious of our time, and in him we find the same distinguishing features: iconoclastic revolt against the conventional moral atmosphere, and acceptance of the "Ugliest Man," which leads to the shattering unconscious tragedy presented in *Zarathustra*. But what creative minds bring up out of the collective unconscious also actually exists, and sooner or later must make its appearance in collective psychology. Anarchism, regicide, the constant increase and splitting off of a nihilistic element on the extreme Left, with a programme absolutely hostile to culture—these are phenomena of mass psychology, which were long ago adumbrated by poets and creative thinkers.

323   We cannot, therefore, afford to be indifferent to the poets, since in their principal works and deepest inspirations they create from the very depths of the collective unconscious, voicing aloud what others only dream. But though they proclaim it aloud, they fashion only a symbol in which they take aesthetic pleasure, without any consciousness of its true meaning. I would be the last to dispute that poets and thinkers have an educative influence on their own and succeeding generations, but it seems to me that their influence consists essentially in the fact that they voice rather more clearly and resoundingly what all men know, and only to the extent that they express this universal unconscious "knowledge" have they an educative or seductive effect. The poet who has the greatest and most immediately suggestive effect is the one who knows how to express the most superficial levels of the unconscious in a suitable form.

35 [A reference to Schopenhauer's *Die Welt als Wille und Vorstellung.*—EDITORS.]

But the more deeply the vision of the creative mind penetrates, the stranger it becomes to mankind in the mass, and the greater is the resistance to the man who in any way stands out from the mass. The mass does not understand him although unconsciously living what he expresses; not because the poet proclaims it, but because the mass draws its life from the collective unconscious into which he has peered. The more thoughtful of the nation certainly comprehend something of his message, but, because his utterance coincides with processes already going on in the mass, and also because he anticipates their own aspirations, they hate the creator of such thoughts, not out of malice, but merely from the instinct of self-preservation. When his insight into the collective unconscious reaches a depth where its content can no longer be grasped in any conscious form of expression, it is difficult to decide whether it is a morbid product or whether it is incomprehensible because of its extraordinary profundity. An imperfectly understood yet deeply significant content usually has something morbid about it. And morbid products are as a rule significant. But in both cases the approach to it is difficult. The fame of these creators, if it ever arrives at all, is posthumous and often delayed for several centuries. Ostwald's assertion that a genius today is misunderstood at most for a decade is confined, one must hope, to the realm of technological discoveries, otherwise such an assertion would be ludicrous in the extreme.

324   There is another point of particular importance to which I feel I ought to draw attention. The solution of the problem in *Faust*, in Wagner's *Parsifal*, in Schopenhauer, and even in Nietzsche's *Zarathustra*, is *religious*. It is therefore not surprising that Spitteler too is drawn towards a religious setting. When a problem is grasped as a religious one, it means, psychologically, that it is seen as something very important, of particular value, something that concerns the whole man, and hence also the unconscious (the realm of the gods, the other world, etc.). With Spitteler the religious background is of such luxuriance that the specifically religious problem loses in depth, though gaining in mythological richness and archaism. The lush mythological texture makes the work difficult to approach, as it shrouds the problem from clear comprehension and obscures its solution. The abstruse, grotesque, somewhat

tasteless quality that always attaches to this kind of mythological embroidery checks the flow of empathy, alienates one from the meaning of the work, and gives the whole a rather disagreeable flavour of a certain kind of originality that manages to escape being psychically abnormal only by its meticulous attention to detail. Nevertheless, this mythological profusion, however tiresome and unpalatable it may be, has the advantage of allowing the symbol plenty of room to unfold, though in such an unconscious fashion that the conscious wit of the poet is quite at a loss to point up its meaning, but devotes itself exclusively to mythological proliferation and its embellishment. In this respect Spitteler's poem differs from both *Faust* and *Zarathustra*: in these works there is a greater conscious participation by the authors in the meaning of the symbol, with the result that the mythological profusion of *Faust* and the intellectual profusion of *Zarathustra* are pruned back in the interests of the desired solution. Both *Faust* and *Zarathustra* are, for this reason, far more satisfying *aesthetically* than Spitteler's Prometheus, though the latter, as a more or less faithful reflection of actual processes of the collective unconscious, has a deeper *truth*.

325 *Faust* and *Zarathustra* are of very great assistance in the individual mastery of the problem, while Spitteler's *Prometheus and Epimetheus*, thanks to the wealth of mythological material, affords a more general insight into it and the way it appears in collective life. What, first and foremost, is revealed in Spitteler's portrayal of unconscious religious contents is the *symbol of God's renewal*, which was subsequently treated at greater length in his *Olympian Spring*. This symbol appears to be intimately connected with the opposition between the psychological types and functions, and is obviously an attempt to find a solution in the form of a renewal of the general attitude, which in the language of the unconscious is expressed as a renewal of God. This is a well-known primordial image that is practically universal; I need only mention the whole mythological complex of the dying and resurgent god and its primitive precursors all the way down to the re-charging of fetishes and churingas with magical force. It expresses a transformation of attitude by means of which a new potential, a new manifestation of life, a new fruitfulness, is created. This latter

analogy explains the well-attested connection between the renewal of the god and seasonal and vegetational phenomena. One is naturally inclined to assume that seasonal, vegetational, lunar, and solar myths underlie these analogies. But that is to forget that a myth, like everything psychic, cannot be solely conditioned by external events. Anything psychic brings its own internal conditions with it, so that one might assert with equal right that the myth is purely psychological and uses meteorological or astronomical events merely as a means of expression. The whimsicality and absurdity of many primitive myths often makes the latter explanation seem far more appropriate than any other.

326   The psychological point of departure for the god-renewal is an increasing split in the deployment of psychic energy, or libido. One half of the libido is deployed in a Promethean direction, the other half in the Epimethean. Naturally this split is a hindrance not only in society but also in the individual. As a result, the vital optimum withdraws more and more from the opposing extremes and seeks a middle way, which must naturally be irrational and unconscious, just because the opposites are rational and conscious. Since the middle position, as a function of mediation between the opposites, possesses an irrational character and is still unconscious, it appears projected in the form of a mediating god, a Messiah. In our more primitive, Western forms of religion—primitive because lacking insight— the new bearer of life appears as a God or Saviour who, in his fatherly love and solicitude or from his own inner resolve, puts an end to the division as and when it suits him and for reasons we are not fitted to understand. The childishness of this conception needs no stressing. The East has for thousands of years been familiar with this process and has founded on it a psychological doctrine of salvation which brings the way of deliverance within man's ken and capacity. Thus the religions of India and China, and particularly Buddhism which combines the spheres of both, possess the idea of a redemptive middle way of magical efficacy which is attainable by means of a conscious attitude. The Vedic conception is a conscious attempt to find release from the pairs of opposites in order to reach the path of redemption.

a. The Brahmanic Conception of the Problem of Opposites

327   The Sanskrit term for pairs of opposites in the psychological sense is *dvandva*. It also means pair (particularly man and woman), strife, quarrel, combat, doubt. The pairs of opposites were ordained by the world-creator. The *Laws of Manu* says:[36]

> Moreover, in order to distinguish actions, he separated merit from demerit, and he caused the creatures to be affected by the pairs of opposites, such as pain and pleasure.

As further pairs of opposites, the commentator Kulluka names desire and anger, love and hate, hunger and thirst, care and folly, honour and disgrace. The *Ramayana* says: "This world must suffer under the pairs of opposites for ever."[37] Not to allow oneself to be influenced by the pairs of opposites, but to be *nirdvandva* (free, untouched by the opposites), to raise oneself above them, is an essentially ethical task, because deliverance from the opposites leads to redemption.

328   In the following passages I give a series of examples:

> When by the disposition [of his heart] he becomes indifferent to all objects, he obtains eternal happiness both in this world and after death. He who has in this manner gradually given up all attachments and is freed from all pairs of opposites reposes in Brahman alone.[38]

> The Vedas speak of the three *gunas*; but do you, O Arjuna, be indifferent to the three *gunas*, indifferent to the opposites, ever steadfast in courage.[39]

---

[36] *Sacred Books of the East*, XXV, p. 13. [Since the existing English translations of the Sanskrit texts quoted in sections *a*, *b*, and *c* often differ widely from one another, and also from the German sources used by the author, both in meaning and in readability, the quotations given here are for the most part composites of the English and German versions, and in general lean towards the latter. For the purpose of comparison, standard translations are cited in the footnotes; full details are given in the bibliography.—TRANS.]

[37] [Source in the *Ramayana* untraceable.—EDITORS.]

[38] Cf. *The Laws of Manu, SBE*, XXV, p. 212.

[39] The famous exhortation of Krishna, *Bhagavad Gita* 2.45. [The three *gunas* are the qualities or constituents of organic matter: *tamas* (darkness, inertia), *rajas* (passion, impurity, activity), *sattva* (purity, clarity, harmony).—TRANSLATOR.]

Then [in deepest meditation, *samadhi*] comes the state of being untroubled by the opposites.[40]

There he shakes off his good deeds and his evil deeds. His dear relatives succeed to the good deeds; those not so dear, to the evil deeds. Then, just as one driving a chariot looks down upon the two chariot wheels, so he looks down upon day and night, so upon good deeds and evil deeds, and upon all the pairs of opposites. Being freed from good and from evil, the knower of Brahman enters into Brahman.[41]

One entering into meditation must be a master over anger, attachment to the world, and the desires of the senses, free from the pairs of opposites, void of self-seeking, empty of expectation.[42]

Clothed with dust, housed under the open sky, I will make my lodging at the root of a tree, surrendering all things loved as well as unloved, tasting neither grief nor pleasure, forfeiting blame and praise alike, neither cherishing hope, nor offering respect, free from the opposites, with neither fortune nor belongings.[43]

He who remains the same in living as in dying, in fortune as in misfortune, whether gaining or losing, loving or hating, will be liberated. He who covets nothing and despises nothing, who is free from the opposites, whose soul knows no passion, is in every way liberated. . . . He who does neither right nor wrong, renouncing the merit and demerit acquired in former lives, whose soul is tranquil when the bodily elements vanish away, he will be liberated.[44]

A thousand years I have enjoyed the things of sense, while still the craving for them springs up unceasingly. These I will therefore renounce, and direct my mind upon Brahman; indifferent to the opposites and free from self-seeking, I will roam with the wild.[45]

Through forbearance towards all creatures, through the ascetic life, through self-discipline and freedom from desire, through the vow and the blameless life, through equanimity and endurance of the opposites, man will partake of the bliss of Brahman, which is without qualities.[46]

[40] *Yogasutra* of Patanjali. Deussen, *Allgemeine Geschichte der Philosophie*, I, Part 3, p. 511.

[41] *Kaushitaki Upanishad* 1.4. Cf. Hume, *The Thirteen Principal Upanishads*, pp. 304f.

[42] *Tejobindu Upan.* 3. Cf. *Minor Upanishads*, p. 17.

[43] *Mahabharata* 1.119.8f. Cf. Dutt trans., I, p. 168.

[44] Ibid. 14.19.4f. Cf. Dutt, XIV, p. 22.

[45] *Bhagavata Purana* 9.19.18f. Cf. *Brihadaranyaka Upan.* 3.5, in Hume, p. 112: "When he has become disgusted both with the non-ascetic state and with the ascetic state, then he becomes a Brahman."

[46] *Bhagavata Purana* 4.22.24.

Free from pride and delusion, with the evils of attachment conquered, faithful always to the highest Atman, with desires extinguished, untouched by the opposites of pain and pleasure, they go, undeluded, towards that imperishable place.[47]

329   As is clear from these quotations, it is external opposites, such as heat and cold, that must first be denied participation in the psyche, and then extreme fluctuations of emotion, such as love and hate. Fluctuations of emotion are, of course, the constant concomitants of all psychic opposites, and hence of all conflicts of ideas, whether moral or otherwise. We know from experience that the emotions thus aroused increase in proportion as the exciting factor affects the individual as a whole. The Indian purpose is therefore clear: it wants to free the individual altogether from the opposites inherent in human nature, so that he can attain a new life in Brahman, which is the state of redemption and at the same time God. It is an irrational union of opposites, their final overcoming. Although Brahman, the world-ground and world-creator, created the opposites, they must nevertheless be cancelled out in it again, for otherwise it would not amount to a state of redemption. Let me give another series of examples:

Braham is *sat* and *asat*, being and non-being, *satyam* and *asatyam*, reality and irreality.[48]

There are two forms of Brahman: the formed and the formless, the mortal and the immortal, the stationary and the moving, the actual and the transcendental.[49]

That Person, the maker of all things, the great Self, seated forever in the heart of man, is perceived by the heart, by the thought, by the mind; they who know that become immortal. When there is no darkness [of ignorance] there is neither day nor night, neither being nor not-being.[50]

In the imperishable, infinite, highest Brahman, two things are hidden: knowing and not-knowing. Not-knowing perishes, knowing is immortal; but he who controls both knowing and not-knowing is another.[51]

---

[47] *Garuda Purana* 16.110. Cf. *Sacred Books of the Hindus*, XXVI, p. 167.
[48] Deussen, *Geschichte der Philosophie*, I, Part 2, p. 117.
[49] *Brihadaranyaka Upan.* 2.3.1. Cf. Hume, p. 97.
[50] *Shvetashvatara Upan.* 4.17–8. Cf. Hume, p. 405.
[51] *Shvet. Upan.* 5.1. Cf. Hume, p. 406.

That Self, smaller than small, greater than great, is hidden in the heart of this creature here. Man becomes free from desire and free from sorrow when by the grace of the Creator he beholds the glory of the Self. Sitting still he walks afar; lying down he goes everywhere. Who but I can know the God who rejoices and rejoices not?[52]

> Unmoving, the One is swifter than the mind.
> Speeding ahead, it outruns the gods of the senses.
> Past others running, it goes standing.
> . . .
> It moves. It moves not.
> Far, yet near.
> Within all,
> Outside all.[53]

Just as a falcon or an eagle, after flying to and fro in space, wearies, and folds its wings, and drops down to its eyrie, so this Person (*purusha*) hastens to that state where, asleep, he desires no desires and sees no dream.

This, verily, is that form of his which is beyond desire, free from evil, without fear. As a man in the embrace of a beloved woman knows nothing of a without and within, so this Person, in the embrace of the knowing Self, knows nothing of a without and within. This, verily, is that form of his in which all desire is satisfied, Self his sole desire, which is no desire, without sorrow.

An ocean of seeing, one without a second, he becomes whose world is Brahman. . . . This is man's highest achievement, his greatest wealth, his final goal, his utmost joy.[54]

> That which moves, that which flies and yet stands still,
> That which breathes yet draws no breath,
>   that which closes the eyes,
> That, many-formed, sustains the whole earth,
> That, uniting, becomes One only.[55]

330   These quotations show that Brahman is the union and dissolution of all opposites, and at the same time stands outside them as an irrational factor. It is therefore wholly beyond cognition and comprehension. It is a divine entity, at once the self (though to a lesser degree than the analogous Atman concept)

[52] *Katha Upan.* 2.20–1. Cf. Hume, pp. 349ff.
[53] *Isha Upan.* 4–5. Cf. Hume, pp. 362f. [Last two lines perhaps: "immanent, transcendent."—TRANSLATOR.]
[54] *Brihad. Upan.* 4.3.19, 21, 32. Cf. Hume, pp. 136ff.
[55] *Atharva Veda* 10.8.11. Cf. Whitney/Lanman trans., VIII, p. 597.

and a definite psychological state characterized by isolation from the flux of affects. Since suffering is an affect, release from affects means deliverance. Deliverance from the flux of affects, from the tension of opposites, is synonymous with the way of redemption that gradually leads to Brahman. Brahman is thus not only a state but also a process, a *durée créatrice*. It is therefore not surprising that it is expressed in the Upanishads by means of the symbols I have termed libido symbols.[56] In the following section I give some examples of these.

b. *The Brahmanic Conception of the Uniting Symbol*

331   When it is said that Brahman was first born in the East, it means that each day Brahman is born in the East like yonder sun.[57]

Yonder man in the sun is Parameshtin, Brahman, Atman.[58]

Brahman is a light like the sun.[59]

As to that Brahman, it is yonder burning disk.[60]

First was Brahman born in the East.
From the horizon the Gracious One appears in splendour;
He illumines the forms of this world, the deepest, the highest,
He is the cradle of what is and is not.
Father of the luminaries, *begetter* of the treasure,
He entered many-formed into the spaces of the air.
They glorify him with hymns of praise,
Making the youth that is Brahman increase by Brahman.[61]
Brahman brought forth the gods, Brahman created the world.[62]

332   In this last passage, I have italicized certain characteristic points which make it clear that Brahman is not only the producer but the produced, the ever-becoming. The epithet "Gracious One" (*vena*), here bestowed on the sun, is elsewhere applied to the seer who is endowed with the divine light, for, like the Brahman-sun, the mind of the seer traverses "earth and

---

[56] *Symbols of Transformation*, pars. 204ff.
[57] *Shatapatha Brahmana* 14.1.3, 3. Cf. *SBE*, XLIV, pp. 459f.
[58] *Taittiriya Aranyaka* 10.63.15.
[59] *Vajasanayi Samhita* 23.48. Cf. Griffith trans., p. 215.
[60] *Shatapatha Brahmana* 8.5.3, 7. Cf. *SBE*, XLIII, p. 94.
[61] [One meaning of Brahman is prayer, hymn, sacred knowledge, magic formula. Cf. par. 336.—TRANSLATOR.]
[62] *Taittiriya Brahmana* 2.8.8, 8ff.

heaven contemplating Brahman."[63] The intimate connection, indeed identity, between the divine being and the self (Atman) of man is generally known. I give an example from the *Atharva Veda*:

> The disciple of Brahman gives life to both worlds.
> In him all the gods are of one mind.
> He contains and sustains earth and heaven,
> His *tapas* is food even for his teacher.
> To the disciple of Brahman there come, to visit him,
> Fathers and gods, singly and in multitudes,
> And he nourishes all the gods with his *tapas*.[64]

333   The disciple of Brahman is himself an incarnation of Brahman, whence it follows that the essence of Brahman is identical with a definite psychological state.

> The sun, set in motion by the gods, shines unsurpassed yonder.
> From it came the Brahma-power, the supreme Brahman,
> And all the gods, and what makes them immortal.
> The disciple of Brahman upholds the splendour of Brahman,
> Interwoven in him are the hosts of the gods.[65]

334   Brahman is also *prana*, the breath of life and the cosmic principle; it is *vayu*, wind, which is described in the *Brihadaranyaka Upanishad* (3, 7) as "the thread by which this world and the other world and all things are tied together, the Self, the inner controller, the immortal."

> He who dwells in man, he who dwells in the sun, are the same.[66]

Prayer of the dying:

> The face of the Real
> Is covered with a golden disk.
> Open it, O sun,
> That we may see the nature of the Real.
> . . .
> Spread thy rays, and gather them in!

[63] *Atharva Veda* 10.5.1.
[64] Ibid. [For *tapas* (self-incubation) see *Symbols of Transformation*, pars. 588ff.]
[65] *Atharva Veda* 11.5.23f. Cf. Whitney/Lanman trans., VIII, pp. 639f.
[66] *Taittiriya Upan.* 2.8. Cf. Hume, p. 289.

The light which is thy fairest form,
I see it.
That Person who dwells yonder, in the sun, is myself.
May my breath go to the immortal wind
When my body is consumed to ash.[67]

And this light which shines above this heaven, higher than all, on top of everything, in the highest world, beyond which there are no other worlds, this same is the light which is in man. And of this we have tangible proof, when we perceive by touch the heat here in the body.[68]

As a grain of rice, or a grain of barley, or a grain of millet, or the kernel of a grain of millet, is this golden Person in the heart, like a flame without smoke, greater than the earth, greater than the sky, greater than space, greater than all these worlds. That is the soul of all creatures, that is myself. Into that I shall enter on departing hence.[69]

335   Brahman is conceived in the *Atharva Veda* as the vitalistic-principle, the life force, which fashions all the organs and their respective instincts:

Who planted the seed within him, that he might spin the thread of generation? Who assembled within him the powers of the mind, gave him voice and the play of features?[70]

336   Even man's strength comes from Brahman. It is clear from these examples, which could be multiplied indefinitely, that the Brahman concept, by virtue of all its attributes and symbols, coincides with that of a dynamic or creative principle which I have termed libido. The word Brahman means prayer, incantation, sacred speech, sacred knowledge (*veda*), holy life, the sacred caste (the Brahmans), the Absolute. Deussen stresses the prayer connotation as being especially characteristic.[71] The word derives from *barh* (cf. L. *farcire*), 'to swell,'[72]

---

[67] *Brihad. Upan.* 5.15. Cf. Hume, p. 157.

[68] *Chhandogya Upan.* 3.13.7. Cf. Hume, p. 209.

[69] *Shatapatha Brahmana* 10.6.3. Cf. *SBE*, XLIII, p. 400. [Cf. *Chhandogya Upan.* 3.14.3–4; Hume, p. 209.—TRANSLATOR.]

[70] *Atharva Veda* 10.2.17. Cf. Whitney/Lanman trans., VIII, p. 569.

[71] Deussen, I, Part 1, pp. 240ff.

[72] Also confirmed by the reference to Brahman, or breath (*prana*), as *matarisvan*, 'he who swells in the mother,' in *Atharva Veda* 11.4.15. Cf. Whitney/Lanman trans., VIII, p. 63.

whence "prayer" is conceived as "the upward-striving will of man towards the holy, the divine." This derivation indicates a particular psychological state, a specific concentration of libido, which through overflowing innervations produces a general state of tension associated with the feeling of swelling. Hence, in common speech, one frequently uses images like "overflowing with emotion," "unable to restrain oneself," "bursting" when referring to such a state. ("What filleth the heart, goeth out by the mouth.") The yogi seeks to induce this concentration or accumulation of libido by systematically withdrawing attention (libido) both from external objects and from interior psychic states, in a word, from the opposites. The elimination of sense-perception and the blotting out of conscious contents enforce a lowering of consciousness (as in hypnosis) and an activation of the contents of the unconscious, i.e., the primordial images, which, because of their universality and immense antiquity, possess a cosmic and suprahuman character. This accounts for all those sun, fire, flame, wind, breath similes that from time immemorial have been symbols of the procreative and creative power that moves the world. As I have made a special study of these libido symbols in my book *Symbols of Transformation*, I need not expand on this theme here.

337   The idea of a creative world-principle is a projected perception of the living essence in man himself. In order to avoid all vitalistic misunderstandings, one would do well to regard this essence in the abstract, as simply *energy*. On the other hand, the hypostatizing of the energy concept after the fashion of modern physicists must be rigorously rejected. The concept of energy implies that of polarity, since a current of energy necessarily presupposes two different states, or poles, without which there can be no current. Every energic phenomenon (and there is no phenomenon that is not energic) consists of pairs of opposites: beginning and end, above and below, hot and cold, earlier and later, cause and effect, etc. The inseparability of the energy concept from that of polarity also applies to the concept of libido. Hence libido symbols, whether mythological or speculative in origin, either present themselves directly as opposites or can be broken down into opposites. I have already referred in my earlier work to this inner splitting of libido, thereby provoking considerable resistance, unjustifi-

ably, it seems to me, because the direct connection between a libido symbol and the concept of polarity is sufficient justification in itself. We find this connection also in the concept or symbol of Brahman. Brahman as a combination of prayer and primordial creative power, the latter resolving itself into the opposition of the sexes, occurs in a remarkable hymn of the *Rig Veda* (10.31.6):

> And this prayer of the singer, spreading afar,
> Became the bull which existed before the world was.
> The gods are nurslings of the same brood,
> Dwelling together in Asura's mansion.
> What was the wood, what was the tree,
> Out of which heaven and earth were fashioned?
> These two stand fast and never grow old,
> They have sung praises to many a dawn and morning.
> There is no other thing greater than he,
> The bull, supporter of earth and heaven.
> He makes his skin a filter purifying the rays,
> When as Surya his bay horses bear him along.
> As the arrow of the sun he illumines the broad earth,
> As the wind scatters the mist he storms through the world.
> With Mitra and Varuna he comes anointed with ghee,
> As Agni in the firesticks he shoots out splendour.
> Driven to him, the cow once barren brought forth,
> The moveless thing she created moved, pasturing freely.
> She bore the son who was older than the parents.[73]

338   The polarity of the creative world principle is represented in another form in the *Shatapatha Brahmana* (2.2.4):

In the beginning, Prajapati[74] was this world alone. He meditated: How can I propagate myself? He travailed, he practised *tapas*; then he begat Agni (fire) out of his mouth,[75] and because he begat him out of his mouth, Agni is a devourer of food.
    Prajapati meditated: As a devourer of food I have begotten this

[73] [The above rendering is a composite of the Deussen version (Jung, *Gesammelte Werke*, 6, p. 217) translated by Baynes in the 1923 edn. (p. 251) of the present volume, and the Griffith version in *The Hymns of the Rigveda*, II, p. 426. The interested reader would do well to compare all four versions.—TRANSLATOR.]

[74] Prajapati is the cosmic creative principle = libido. *Taittiriya Samhita* 5.5.2, 1: "After he had created them, Prajapati instilled love into all his creatures." Cf. Keith trans., II, p. 441.

[75] The begetting of fire in the mouth has remarkable connections with speech. Cf. *Symbols of Transformation*, pars. 208ff.

Agni out of myself, but there is nothing else beside myself that he may devour. For the earth at that time was quite barren, there were no herbs and no trees, and this thought was heavy upon him.

Then Agni turned upon him with gaping maw. His own greatness spoke to him: Sacrifice! Then Prajapati knew: My own greatness has spoken to me. And he sacrificed.

Thereupon that rose up which shines yonder (the sun); thereupon that rose up which purifies all things here (the wind). Thus Prajapati, by offering sacrifice, propagated himself, and at the same time saved himself from death, who as Agni would have devoured him.

339 Sacrifice always means the renunciation of a valuable part of oneself, and through it the sacrificer escapes being devoured. In other words, there is no transformation into the opposite, but rather equilibration and union, from which arises a new form of libido: sun and wind. Elsewhere the *Shatapatha Brahmana* says that one half of Prajapati is mortal, the other immortal.[76]

340 In the same way as he divides himself into bull and cow, Prajapati also divides himself into the two principles *manas* (mind) and *vac* (speech):

This world was Prajapati alone, *vac* was his self, and *vac* his second self. He meditated: This *vac* I will send forth, and she shall go hence and pervade all things. Then he sent forth *vac*, and she went and filled the universe.[77]

This passage is of especial interest in that speech is conceived as a creative, extraverted movement of libido, a diastole in Goethe's sense. There is a further parallel in the following passage:

In truth Prajapati was this world, and with him was *vac* his second self. He copulated with her; she conceived; she went forth out of him, and made these creatures, and once again entered into Prajapati.[78]

341 In *Shatapatha Brahmana* 8.1.2, 9 the role attributed to *vac* is a prodigious one: "Truly *vac* is the wise Vishvakarman, for by *vac* was this whole world made." But at 1.4.5, 8–11 the question of primacy between *manas* and *vac* is decided differently:

[76] Cf. the Dioscuri motif in *Symbols of Transformation*, par. 294.
[77] *Pañcavimsha Brahmana* 20.14.12. Cf. *Bibliotheca Indica*, vol. 252, pp. 145f.
[78] Weber, *Indische Studien*, IX, p. 477, as in Deussen, I, Part 1, p. 206.

Now it happened that Mind and Speech strove for priority one with the other. Mind said: I am better than you, for you speak nothing that I have not first discerned. Then Speech said: I am better than you, for I announce what you have discerned and make it known.

They went to Prajapati for judgment. Prajapati decided in favour of Mind, saying to Speech: Truly Mind is better than you, for you copy what Mind does and run in his tracks; moreover it is the inferior who is wont to imitate his betters.

342   These passages show that the principles into which the world-creator divides himself are themselves divided. They were at first contained in Prajapati, as is clear from the following:

Prajapati desired: I wish to be many, I will multiply myself. Then he meditated silently in his Mind, and what was in his Mind became *brihat* (song). He bethought himself: This embryo of me is hidden in my body, through Speech I will bring it forth. Then he created Speech.[79]

343   This passage shows the two principles as psychological functions: *manas* an introversion of libido begetting an inner product, *vac* a function of exteriorization or extraversion. This brings us to another passage relating to Brahman:

When Brahman had entered into that other world, he bethought himself: How can I extend myself through these worlds? And he extended himself twofold through these worlds, by Form and Name.

These two are the two monsters of Brahman; whoever knows these two monsters of Brahman, becomes a mighty monster himself. These are the two mighty manifestations of Brahman.[80]

344   A little later, Form is defined as *manas* ("*manas* is form, for through *manas* one knows it is this form") and Name as *vac* ("for through *vac* one grasps the name"). Thus the two "mighty monsters" of Brahman turn out to be mind and speech, two psychic functions by which Brahman can "extend himself" through both worlds, clearly signifying the function of "relationship." The forms of things are "apprehended" or "taken in" by introverting through *manas*; names are given to things by

[79] *Pañcavimsha Brahmana* 7.6.
[80] *Shatapatha Brahmana* 11.2.3. Cf. *SBE*, XXVI, pp. 27f.

extraverting through *vac*. Both involve relationship and adaptation to objects as well as their assimilation. The two "monsters" are evidently thought of as personifications; this is indicated by their other name, *yaksha* ('manifestation') for *yaksha* means much the same as a daemon or superhuman being. Psychologically, personification always denotes the relative autonomy of the content personified, i.e., its splitting off from the psychic hierarchy. Such contents cannot be voluntarily reproduced; they reproduce themselves spontaneously, or else withdraw themselves from consciousness in the same way.[81] A dissociation of this kind occurs, for instance, when an incompatibility exists between the ego and a particular complex. As we know, it is observed most frequently when the latter is a sexual complex, but other complexes can get split off too, for instance the power-complex, the sum of all those strivings and ideas aiming at the acquisition of personal power. There is, however, another form of dissociation, and that is the splitting off of the conscious ego, together with a selected function, from the other components of the personality. This form of dissociation can be defined as an identification of the ego with a particular function or group of functions. It is very common in people who are too deeply immersed in one of their psychic functions and have differentiated it into their sole conscious means of adaptation.

345   A good literary example of such a man is Faust at the beginning of the tragedy. The other components of his personality approach him in the shape of the poodle, and later as Mephistopheles. Although Mephistopheles, as is perfectly clear from many of his associations, also represents the sexual complex, it would in my view be a mistake to explain him as a split-off complex and declare that he is nothing but repressed sexuality. This explanation is too narrow, because Mephistopheles is far more than sexuality—he is also power; in fact, he is practically the whole life of Faust, barring that part of it which is taken up with thinking and research. The result of the pact with the devil makes this very evident. What undreamt-of possibilities of power unfold themselves before the rejuvenated Faust! The correct explanation, therefore, would seem to be

[81] [Jung, "A Review of the Complex Theory."—EDITORS.]

that Faust identified with one function and got split off as Mephistopheles from his personality as a whole. Subsequently, Wagner the thinker also gets split off from Faust.

346   A *conscious* capacity for one-sidedness is a sign of the highest culture, but *involuntary* one-sidedness, i.e., the inability to be anything but one-sided, is a sign of barbarism. Hence the most one-sided differentiations are found among semi-barbarous people—for instance, certain aspects of Christian asceticism that are an affront to good taste, and parallel phenomena among the yogis and Tibetan Buddhists. For the barbarian, this tendency to fall a victim to one-sidedness in one way or another, thus losing sight of his total personality, is a great and constant danger. The Gilgamesh epic, for example, begins with this conflict. The one-sidedness of the barbarian takes the form of daemonic compulsion; it has something of the character of going berserk or running amok. In all cases it presupposes an atrophy of instinct that is not found in the true primitive, for which reason he is in general still free from the one-sidedness of the cultural barbarian.

347   Identification with one particular function at once produces a tension of opposites. The more compulsive the one-sidedness, and the more untamed the libido which streams off to one side, the more daemonic it becomes. When a man is carried away by his uncontrolled, undomesticated libido, he speaks of daemonic possession or of magical influences. In this sense *manas* and *vac* are indeed mighty demons, since they work mightily upon men. All things that produced powerful effects were once regarded as gods or demons. Thus, among the Gnostics, the mind was personified as the serpent-like *Nous*, and speech as *Logos*. *Vac* bears the same relation to Prajapati as Logos to God. The sort of demons that introversion and extraversion may become is a daily experience for us psychotherapists. We see in our patients and can feel in ourselves with what irresistible force the libido streams inwards or outwards, with what unshakable tenacity an introverted or extraverted attitude can take root. The description of *manas* and *vac* as "mighty monsters of Brahman" is in complete accord with the psychological fact that at the instant of its appearance the libido divides into two streams, which as a rule alternate periodically but at times may appear simultaneously

in the form of a conflict, as an outward stream opposing an inward stream. The daemonic quality of the two movements lies in their ungovernable nature and overwhelming power. This quality, however, makes itself felt only when the instinct of the primitive is already so stunted as to prevent a natural and purposive counter-movement to one-sidedness, and culture not sufficiently advanced for man to tame his libido to the point where he can follow its introverting or extraverting movement of his own free will and intention.

c. The Uniting Symbol as the Principle of Dynamic Regulation

348   In the foregoing passages from Indian sources we have followed the development of a redemptive principle from the pairs of opposites and have traced their origin to the same creative principle, thereby gaining an insight into a regular psychological occurrence which was found to be compatible with the concepts of modern psychology. The impression that this occurrence is a regular one is confirmed by the Indian sources themselves, since they identify Brahman with *rta*. What is *rta*? *Rta* means established order, regulation, destiny, sacred custom, statute, divine law, right, truth. According to the etymological evidence its root meaning is: ordinance, (right) way, direction, course (to be followed). That which is ordained by *rta* fills the whole world, but the particular manifestations of *rta* are in those processes of nature which always remain constant and arouse the idea of regular recurrence: "By the ordinance of *rta* the heaven-born dawn was lighted." "In obedience to *rta*" the Ancient Ones who order the world "made the sun to mount into the heavens," who himself is "the burning countenance of *rta*." Around the heavens circles the year, the twelve-spoked wheel of *rta* that never ages. Agni is called the offspring of *rta*. In the doings of man, *rta* operates as moral law, which ordains truth and the straight way. "Whoso follows *rta*, finds a fair and thornless path to walk in."

349   In so far as they represent a magical repetition or reenactment of cosmic events, *rta* also figures in religious rites. As the rivers flow in obedience to *rta* and the crimson dawn is set ablaze, so "under the harness[82] of *rta*" is the sacrifice kin-

---

[82] Allusion to the horse, indicating the dynamic nature of *rta*.

dled; on the path of *rta*, Agni offers sacrifice to the gods. "Free from magic, I invoke the gods; with *rta* I do my work, and shape my thought," says the sacrificer. Although *rta* does not appear personified in the Vedas, according to Bergaigne[83] a suggestion of concrete existence undoubtedly attaches to it. Since *rta* expresses the direction of events, there are "paths of *rta*," "charioteers[84] of *rta*," "ships of *rta*," and on occasion the gods appear as parallels. For instance, the same is said of *rta* as of Varuna, the sky-god. Mitra also, the ancient sun-god, is brought into relation with *rta*. Of Agni it is said: "Thou shalt become Varuna, if thou strivest after *rta*."[85] The gods are the guardians of *rta*.[86] Here are some of the most important associations:

Rta is Mitra, for Mitra is Brahman and *rta* is Brahman.[87]

By giving the cow to the Brahmans, one gains all the worlds, for in her is contained *rta*, Brahman, and *tapas* also.[88]

Prajapati is named the first-born of *rta*.[89]

The gods followed the laws of *rta*.[90]

He who has seen the hidden one (Agni), draws nigh to the streams of *rta*.[91]

O wise one of *rta*, know *rta*! Bore for *rta*'s many streams.[92]

350   The "boring" refers to the worship of Agni, to whom this hymn is dedicated. (Agni is here called "the red bull of *rta*.") In the worship of Agni, the fire obtained by boring is used as a magic symbol of the regeneration of life. Boring for the streams of *rta* obviously has the same significance; the streams

---

[83] [Cf. *La Religion védique*, III, index I, s.v. *rita*.—EDITORS.]

[84] Agni is called the charioteer of *rta*. Cf. *Vedic Hymns*, SBE, XLVI, p. 158, 7 (*Rig Veda* 1.143.7), p. 160, 3 (*Rig Veda* 1.144.3), p. 229, 8 (*Rig Veda* 3.2.8).

[85] Oldenberg, "Zur Religion und Mythologie des Veda," pp. 167ff., and *Die Religion des Veda*, pp. 194ff. For this reference I am indebted to Prof. E. Abegg, Zurich.

[86] Deussen, *Geschichte der Philosophie*, I, Part 1, p. 92.

[87] *Shatapatha Brahmana* 4.1.4, 10. Cf. *SBE*, XXVI, p. 272.

[88] *Atharva Veda* 10.10.33. Cf. Whitney/Lanman trans., II, p. 608.

[89] Ibid., 12.1.61. Cf. Whitney/Lanman trans., II, p. 671.

[90] *Rig Veda* 1.65.3. (*Vedic Hymns*, SBE, XLVI, p. 54.)

[91] 1.67.7. (Cf. p. 61.)

[92] 4.12.2. (Cf. p. 393.)

of life rise to the surface again, libido is freed from its bonds.[93] The effect produced by the ritual fire-boring, or by the recital of hymns, is naturally regarded by believers as the magical effect of the object; in reality it is an "enchantment" of the subject, an intensification of vital feeling, an increase and release of life force, a restoration of psychic potential:

> Though he [Agni] slinks away, the prayer goes straight to him. They [the prayers] have led forth the flowing streams of rta.[94]

351   The revival of vital feeling, of this sense of streaming energy, is in general compared to a spring gushing from its source, to the melting of the iron-bound ice of winter in springtime, or to the breaking of a long drought by rain.[95] The following passage takes up this theme:

> The lowing milch-cows of rta were overflowing, their udders full. The streams, imploring from afar the favour of the gods, have broken through the midst of the rock with their floods.[96]

The imagery clearly suggests a state of energic tension, a damming up of libido and its release. Rta appears here as the bestower of blessing in the form of "lowing milch cows" and as the ultimate source of the released energy.

352   The aforementioned image of rain as a release of libido is borne out in the following passage:

> The mists fly, the clouds thunder. When he who is swollen with the milk of rta is led on the straight path of rta, Aryaman, Mitra, and Varuna who wanders over the earth, fill the leathern sack (= cloud) in the womb of the lower (world?).[97]

It is Agni, swollen with the milk of rta, who is likened to the lightning that bursts forth from the massed clouds heavy with

[93] Release of libido is obtained through ritual work. The release puts the libido at the disposal of consciousness, where it becomes domesticated. From an instinctive, undomesticated state it is converted into a state of disposability. The following passage is an illustration of this: "The rulers, the bountiful lords, brought him (Agni) forth by their power out of the depths, out of the bull's shape." *Rig Veda* 1.141.3. (Cf. *Vedic Hymns*, p. 147.)

[94] *Rig Veda* 1.141.1. (Cf. ibid.)

[95] Cf. *The Song of Tishtriya (Tir Yasht)*, in *Symbols of Transformation*, pars. 395 and 439, n. 47.

[96] *Rig Veda* 1.73.6. (Cf. *Vedic Hymns*, p. 88.)

[97] 1.79.2–3. (Cf. p. 103.)

rain. Here again *rta* appears as the actual source of energy, whence Agni also is born, as expressly mentioned in the *Vedic Hymns*.[98]

They have greeted with shouts the streams of *rta*, which were hidden at the birthplace of the god, at his seat. There did he drink when he dwelt dispersed in the womb of the waters.[99]

353   This confirms what we have said about *rta* as the source of libido where the god dwells and whence he is brought forth in the sacred ceremonies. Agni is the positive manifestation of the latent libido; he is accomplisher or fulfiller of *rta*, its "charioteer"; he harnesses the two long-maned red mares of *rta*.[100] He even holds *rta* like a horse, by the bridle.[101] He brings the gods to mankind, their power and blessing; they represent definite psychological states in which the vital feelings and energies flow with greater freedom and joy. Nietzsche has captured this state in his verses:

> You with your fiery lances
> Shatter the ice-bound soul of me,
> Till with high hope it advances
> Rushing and roaring into the sea.[102]

354   The following invocation echoes this theme:

May the divine gates, the increasers of *rta*, open themselves . . . that the gods may come forth. May Night and Dawn . . . the young mothers of *rta*, sit down together on the sacrificial grass.[103]

The analogy with the sunrise is unmistakable. *Rta* appears as the sun, since it is from night and dawn that the young sun is born.

355   There is no need, I think, of further examples to show that the concept of *rta* is a libido-symbol like sun, wind, etc. Only, *rta* is less concretistic and contains the abstract element of fixed direction and regularity, the idea of a predetermined, ordered path or process. It is, therefore, a kind of philosophical libido symbol that can be directly compared with the Stoic concept of *heimarmene*. For the Stoics *heimarmene* had the significance of creative, primal heat, and at the same time it

---

[98] Ibid., p. 161, 7.   [99] 1.144.2. (Cf. p. 160, 2.)
[100] 3.6 (p. 244, 6) and 4.2 (p. 316, 3).
[101] Ibid., p. 382.   [102] Cf. *The Joyful Wisdom*, p. 211.
[103] *Rig Veda* 1.142.6. (Cf. *Vedic Hymns*, p. 153, 8.)

was a predetermined, regular process (hence its other meaning: "compulsion of the stars").[104] Libido as psychic energy naturally has these attributes too; the concept of energy necessarily includes the idea of a regulated process, since a process always flows from a higher potential to a lower. It is the same with the libido concept, which signifies nothing more than the energy of the life process. Its laws are the laws of vital energy. Libido as an energy concept is a quantitative formula for the phenomena of life, which are naturally of varying intensity. Like physical energy, libido passes through every conceivable transformation; we find ample evidence of this in the fantasies of the unconscious and in myths. These fantasies are primarily self-representations of energic transformation processes, which follow their specific laws and keep to a definite "path." This path is the line or curve representing the optimal discharge of energy and the corresponding result in work. Hence it is simply the expression of flowing and self-manifesting energy. The path is *rta*, the right way, the flow of vital energy or libido, the predetermined course along which a constantly self-renewing current is directed. This path is also fate, in so far as a man's fate depends on his psychology. It is the path of our destiny and of the law of our being.

356   It would be quite wrong to assert that such a direction or tendency is nothing more than naturalism, meaning a complete surrender to one's instincts. This presupposes that the instincts have a constant "downward" tendency, and that naturalism amounts to an unethical sliding down an inclined plane. I have nothing against such an interpretation of naturalism, but I am bound to observe that the man who is left to his own devices, and has therefore every opportunity for sliding downwards, as for instance the primitive, not only has a moral code but one which in the severity of its demands is often considerably more exacting than our civilized morality. It makes no difference if good and evil mean one thing for the primitive and another for us; his naturalism leads to law-giving—that is the chief point. Morality is not a misconception invented by some vaunting Moses on Sinai, but something inherent in the laws of life and fashioned like a house or a ship or any other cultural instrument. The natural flow of libido, this same middle path, means

104 [Cf. *Symbols of Transformation*, pars. 102, 644.—TRANSLATOR.]

complete obedience to the fundamental laws of human nature, and there can positively be no higher moral principle than harmony with natural laws that guide the libido in the direction of life's optimum. The vital optimum is not to be found in crude egoism, for fundamentally man is so constituted that the pleasure he gives to his neighbour is something essential to him. Nor can the optimum be reached by an unbridled craving for individualistic supremacy, because the collective element in man is so powerful that his longing for fellowship would destroy all pleasure in naked egoism. The optimum can be reached only through obedience to the tidal laws of the libido, by which systole alternates with diastole—laws which bring pleasure and the necessary limitations of pleasure, and also set us those individual life tasks without whose accomplishment the vital optimum can never be attained.

357   If the attainment of the middle path consisted in a mere surrender to instinct, as the bewailers of "naturalism" suppose, the profoundest philosophical speculation that the human mind has ever known would have no *raison d'être*. But, as we study the philosophy of the Upanishads, the impression grows on us that the attainment of this path is not exactly the simplest of tasks. Our Western superciliousness in the face of these Indian insights is a mark of our barbarian nature, which has not the remotest inkling of their extraordinary depth and astonishing psychological accuracy. We are still so uneducated that we actually need laws from without, and a task-master or Father above, to show us what is good and the right thing to do. And because we are still such barbarians, any trust in the laws of human nature seems to us a dangerous and unethical naturalism. Why is this? Because under the barbarian's thin veneer of culture the wild beast lurks in readiness, amply justifying his fear. But the beast is not tamed by locking it up in a cage. *There is no morality without freedom.* When the barbarian lets loose the beast within him, that is not freedom but bondage. Barbarism must first be vanquished before freedom can be won. This happens, in principle, when the basic root and driving force of morality are felt by the individual as constituents of his own nature and not as external restrictions. How else is man to attain this realization but through the conflict of opposites?

213

d. The Uniting Symbol in Chinese Philosophy

358   The idea of a middle way between the opposites is to be found also in China, in the form of *tao*. The concept of *tao* is usually associated with the name of the philosopher Lao-tzu, born 604 B.C. But this concept is older than the philosophy of Lao-tzu. It is bound up with the ancient folk religion of Taoism, the "way of Heaven," a concept corresponding to the Vedic *rta*. The meanings of *tao* are as follows: way, method, principle, natural force or life force, the regulated processes of nature, the idea of the world, the prime cause of all phenomena, the right, the good, the moral order. Some translators even translate it as God, not without some justification, it seems to me, since *tao*, like *rta*, has a tinge of substantiality.

359   I will first give a number of passages from the *Tao Te Ching*, Lao-tzu's classic:

> Was Tao the child of something else? We cannot tell.
> But as a substanceless image it existed before the Ancestor.[105]

> There was something formless yet complete,
> That existed before heaven and earth;
> Without sound, without substance,
> Dependent on nothing, unchanging,
> All pervading, unfailing,
> One may think of it as the mother of all things under heaven.
> Its true name we do not know;
> "Way" is the name that we give it.[106]

360   In order to characterize its essential quality, Lao-tzu likens it to water:

> The highest good is like that of water. The goodness of water is that it benefits the ten thousand creatures; yet itself does not scramble, but is content with the [low] places that all men disdain. It is this that makes water so near to the Way.[107]

The idea of a "potential" could not be better expressed.

---

[105] Waley, trans., *The Way and Its Power*, p. 146. [This and the next quotation, unfortunately, contradict Jung's statement that *tao* has a tinge of substantiality.—TRANSLATOR.]
[106] Ibid., p. 174.
[107] P. 151.

214

He that is without desire sees its essence,
He that clings to desire sees only its outward form.[108]

361   The affinity with the fundamental Brahmanic ideas is unmistakable, though this does not necessarily imply direct contact. Lao-tzu was an entirely original thinker, and the primordial image underlying *rta-brahman-atman* and *tao* is as universal as man, appearing in every age and among all peoples as a primitive conception of energy, or "soul force," or however else it may be called.

He who knows the Always-so has room in him for everything;
He who has room in him for everything is without prejudice.
To be without prejudice is to be kingly;
To be kingly is to be of heaven;
To be of heaven is to be in Tao.
Tao is forever, and he that possesses it,
Though his body ceases, is not destroyed.[109]

362   Knowledge of *tao* therefore has the same redeeming and uplifting effect as the knowledge of *brahman*. Man becomes one with *tao*, with the unending *durée créatrice* (if we may compare this concept of Bergson's with its older congener), for *tao* is also the stream of time. It is irrational, inconceivable:

Tao is a thing impalpable, incommensurable.[110]
For though all creatures under heaven are the products
    of [Tao as] Being,
Being itself is the product of [Tao as] Not-Being.[111]
Tao is hidden and nameless.[112]

It is obviously an irrational union of opposites, a symbol of what is and is not.

The Valley Spirit never dies;
It is named the mysterious Female.
And the door of the mysterious Female
Is the base from which heaven and earth sprang.[113]

363   *Tao* is the creative process, begetting as the father and bringing forth as the mother. It is the beginning and end of all creatures.

---

108 [Trans. from author's German. Cf. Waley, p. 141.]   109 P. 162.
110 P. 170.   111 P. 192.   112 P. 193.   113 P. 149.

He whose actions are in harmony with *Tao* becomes one with *Tao*.[114]

Therefore the perfected sage liberates himself from the opposites, having seen through their connection with one another and their alternation. Therefore it is said:

> When your work is done, then withdraw.
> Such is heaven's way.[115]
> He [the perfected sage] cannot either be drawn into
>   friendship or repelled,
> Cannot be benefited, cannot be harmed,
> Cannot be either raised or humbled.[116]

364   Being one with *tao* resembles the state of infancy:

> Can you keep the unquiet physical soul from straying, hold fast
>   to the Unity, and never quit it?
> Can you, when concentrating your breath, make it soft like that
>   of a little child?[117]

> He who knows the male, yet cleaves to what is female,
> Becomes like a ravine, receiving all things under heaven;
> And being such a ravine,
> He knows all the time a power that he never calls upon in vain.
> This is returning to the state of infancy.[118]

> The impunity of that which is fraught with this power
> May be likened to that of an infant.[119]

365   This psychological attitude is, as we know, an essential condition for obtaining the kingdom of heaven, and this in its turn—all rational interpretations notwithstanding—is the central, irrational symbol whence the redeeming effect comes. The Christian symbol merely has a more social character than the related conceptions of the East. These are directly connected with age-old dynamistic ideas of a magical power emanating from people and things or—at a higher level of development—from gods or a divine principle.

366   According to the central concepts of Taoism, *tao* is divided into a fundamental pair of opposites, *yang* and *yin*. *Yang* signifies warmth, light, maleness; *yin* is cold, darkness, femaleness. *Yang* is also heaven, *yin* earth. From the *yang* force

---

[114] [Trans. from author's German. Cf. Waley, p. 172.]   [115] P. 153.
[116] P. 210.   [117] P. 153.   [118] P. 178.   [119] P. 209.

arises *shen*, the celestial portion of the human soul, and from the *yin* force comes *kwei*, the earthly part. As a microcosm, man is a reconciler of the opposites. Heaven, man, and earth form the three chief elements of the world, the *san-tsai*.

367   The picture thus presented is an altogether primitive idea which we find in similar forms elsewhere, as for instance in the West African myth where Obatala and Odudua, the first parents (heaven and earth), lie together in a calabash until a son, man, arises between them. Hence man as a microcosm uniting the world opposites is the equivalent of an irrational symbol that unites the psychological opposites. This primordial image of man is in keeping with Schiller's definition of the symbol as "living form."

368   The division of the psyche into a *shen* (or *hwan*) soul and a *kwei* (or *p'o*) soul is a great psychological truth. This Chinese conception is echoed in the well-known passage from *Faust*:

> Two souls, alas, are housed within my breast,
> And each will wrestle for the mastery there.
> The one has passion's craving crude for love,
> And hugs a world where sweet the senses rage;
> The other longs for pastures fair above,
> Leaving the murk for lofty heritage.[120]

369   The existence of two mutually antagonistic tendencies, both striving to drag man into extreme attitudes and entangle him in the world, whether on the material or spiritual level, sets him at variance with himself and accordingly demands the existence of a counterweight. This is the "irrational third," *tao*. Hence the sage's anxious endeavour to live in harmony with *tao*, lest he fall into the conflict of opposites. Since *tao* is irrational, it is not something that can be got by the will, as Lao-tzu repeatedly emphasizes. This lends particular significance to another specifically Chinese concept, *wu-wei*. *Wu-wei* means "not-doing" (which is not to be confused with "doing nothing"). Our rationalistic "doing," which is the greatness as well as the evil of our time, does not lead to *tao*.

370   The aim of Taoist ethics, then, is to find deliverance from the cosmic tension of opposites by a return to *tao*. In this connection we must also remember the "sage of Omi," Nakae

---

[120] *Faust, Part One* (trans. Wayne), p. 67.

Toju,[121] an outstanding Japanese philosopher of the seventeenth century. Basing himself on the teaching of the Chu-hi school, which had migrated from China, he established two principles, *ri* and *ki*. *Ri* is the world soul, *ki* is the world stuff. *Ri* and *ki* are, however, the same because they are both attributes of God and therefore exist only in him and through him. God is their union. Equally, the soul embraces both *ri* and *ki*. Toju says of God: "As the essence of the world, God embraces the world, but at the same time he is in our midst and even in our bodies." For him God is a universal self, while the individual self is the "heaven" within us, something supra-sensible and divine called *ryochi*. *Ryochi* is "God within us" and dwells in every individual. It is the true self. Toju distinguishes a true from a false self. The false self is an acquired personality compounded of perverted beliefs. We might define this false self as the *persona*, that general idea of ourselves which we have built up from experiencing our effect upon the world around us and its effect upon us. The persona is, in Schopenhauer's words, how one *appears* to oneself and the world, but not what one *is*. What one is, is one's individual self, Toju's "true self" or *ryochi*. *Ryochi* is also called "being alone" or "knowing alone," clearly because it is a condition related to the essence of the self, beyond all personal judgments conditioned by external experience. Toju conceives *ryochi* as the summum bonum, as "bliss" (*brahman* is bliss, *ananda*). It is the light which pervades the world—a further parallel with *brahman*, according to Inouye. It is love for mankind, immortal, all-knowing, good. Evil comes from the will (shades of Schopenhauer!). *Ryochi* is the self-regulating function, the mediator and uniter of the opposites, *ri* and *ki*; it is in fullest accord with the Indian idea of the "wise old man who dwells in the heart." Or as Wang Yang-ming, the Chinese father of Japanese philosophy, says: "In every heart there dwells a *sejin* (sage). Only, we do not believe it firmly enough, and therefore the whole has remained buried."[122]

* * *

[121] Inouye, "Die japanische Philosophie," in *Allg. Geschichte der Phil.*, pp. 84f.

[122] Ibid., p. 85. [Cf. Wang Yang-ming, *Instructions for Practical Living*, trans. Chan, sec. 207, pp. 193f.]

371   From[123] this point of view it is not so difficult to see what the primordial image was that helped to solve the problem in Wagner's *Parsifal*. Here the suffering is caused by the tension of opposites represented by the Grail and the power of Klingsor, who has taken possession of the holy spear. Under the spell of Klingsor is Kundry, symbolizing the instinctive life-force or libido that Amfortas lacks. Parsifal rescues the libido from the state of restless, compulsive instinctuality, in the first place because he does not succumb to Kundry, and in the second because he does not possess the Grail. Amfortas has the Grail and suffers for it, because he lacks libido. Parsifal has nothing of either, he is *nirdvandva*, free from the opposites, and is therefore the redeemer, the bestower of healing and renewed vitality, who unites the bright, heavenly, feminine symbol of the Grail with the dark, earthly, masculine symbol of the spear. The death of Kundry may be taken as the liberation of libido from its naturalistic, undomesticated form (cf. the "bull's shape," par. 350, n. 93), which falls away as a lifeless husk, while the energy bursts forth as a new stream of life in the glowing of the Grail.

372   By his renunciation of the opposites (unwilling though this was, at least in part), Parsifal caused a blockage of libido that created a new potential and thus made a new manifestation of energy possible. The undeniable sexual symbolism might easily lead to the one-sided interpretation that the union of spear and Grail merely signifies a release of sexuality. The fate of Amfortas shows, however, that sexuality is not the point. On the contrary, it was his relapse into a nature-bound, brutish attitude that was the cause of his suffering and brought about the loss of his power. His seduction by Kundry was a symbolic act, showing that it was not sexuality that dealt him his wound so much as an attitude of nature-bound compulsion, a supine submission to the biological urge. This attitude expresses the supremacy of the animal part of our psyche. The sacrificial wound that is destined for the beast strikes the man who is

123 [The following four paragraphs, though coming abruptly after the excursus on Chinese symbolism, may be taken as a bridge-passage to the Western solution of the problem of opposites discussed in section 4. This passage is of direct relevance to the interpretation and derivation of the *vas*/Grail symbol in pars. 394–401.—EDITORS.]

overcome by the beast—for the sake of man's further development. The fundamental problem, as I have pointed out in *Symbols of Transformation*, is not sexuality *per se*, but the domestication of libido, which concerns sexuality only so far as it is one of the most important and most dangerous forms of libidinal expression.

373　　If, in the case of Amfortas and the union of spear and Grail, only the sexual problem is discerned, we get entangled in an insoluble contradiction, since the thing that harms is also the thing that heals. Such a paradox is true and permissible only when one sees the opposites as united on a higher plane, when one understands that it is not a question of sexuality, either in this form or in that, but purely a question of the attitude by which every activity, including the sexual, is regulated. Once again I must emphasize that the practical problem in analytical psychology lies deeper than sexuality and its repression. The latter point of view is no doubt very valuable in explaining the infantile and therefore morbid part of the psyche, but as an explanatory principle for the whole of the psyche it is quite inadequate. What lies behind sexuality or the power instinct is the *attitude* to sexuality or to power. In so far as an attitude is not merely an intuitive (i.e., unconscious and spontaneous) phenomenon but also a conscious function, it is, in the main, a *view of life*. Our conception of all problematical things is enormously influenced, sometimes consciously but more often unconsciously, by certain collective ideas that condition our mentality. These collective ideas are intimately bound up with the view of life and the world of the past centuries or epochs. Whether or not we are conscious of this dependence has nothing to do with it, since we are influenced by these ideas through the very air we breathe. Collective ideas always have a religious character, and a philosophical idea becomes collective only when it expresses a primordial image. Their religious character derives from the fact that they express the realities of the collective unconscious and are thus able to release its latent energies. The great problems of life, including of course sex, are always related to the primordial images of the collective unconscious. These images are balancing or compensating factors that correspond to the problems which life confronts us with in reality.

374   This is no matter for astonishment, since these images are deposits of thousands of years of experience of the struggle for existence and for adaptation. Every great experience in life, every profound conflict, evokes the accumulated treasure of these images and brings about their inner constellation. But they become accessible to consciousness only when the individual possesses so much self-awareness and power of understanding that he also reflects on what he experiences instead of just living it blindly. In the latter event he actually lives the myth and the symbol without knowing it.

4. THE RELATIVITY OF THE SYMBOL

a. The Worship of Woman and the Worship of the Soul

375   The Christian principle which unites the opposites is the *worship of God*, in Buddhism it is the *worship of the self* (self-development), while in Spitteler and Goethe it is the *worship of the soul* symbolized by the *worship of woman*. Implicit in this categorization is the modern individualistic principle on the one hand, and on the other a primitive poly-daemonism which assigns to every race, every tribe, every family, every individual its specific religious principle.

376   The medieval background of *Faust* has a quite special significance because there actually was a medieval element that presided over the birth of modern individualism. It began, it seems to me, with the worship of woman, which strengthened the man's soul very considerably as a psychological factor, since the worship of woman meant worship of the soul. This is nowhere more beautifully and perfectly expressed than in Dante's *Divine Comedy*.

377   Dante is the spiritual knight of his lady; for her sake he embarks on the adventure of the lower and upper worlds. In this heroic endeavour her image is exalted into the heavenly, mystical figure of the Mother of God—a figure that has detached itself from the object and become the personification of a purely psychological factor, or rather, of those unconscious contents whose personification I have termed the *anima*. Canto XXXIII of the *Paradiso* expresses this culminating point of Dante's psychic development in the prayer of St. Bernard:

> O Virgin Mother, daughter of thy Son,
> Humbler and more exalted than all others,
> Predestined object of the eternal will!
> Thou gavest such nobility to man
> That He who made mankind did not disdain
> To make Himself a creature of His making.

Verses 22–27, 29–33, 37–39 also allude to this development:

> This man, who from the nethermost abyss
> Of all the universe, as far as here,
> Has seen the spiritual existences,
> Now asks thy grace, so thou wilt grant him strength
> That he may with his eyes uplift himself
> Still higher toward the ultimate salvation.
>
> . . .
>
> I . . . proffer to thee
> All my prayers—and pray they may suffice—
> That thou wilt scatter from him every cloud
> Of his mortality, with thine own prayers,
> So that the bliss supreme may be revealed.
>
> . . .
>
> May thy protection quell his human passions!
> Lo, Beatrice and many a blessed soul
> Entreat thee, with clasped hands, to grant my wish![124]

378   The very fact that Dante speaks here through the mouth of St. Bernard is an indication of the transformation and exaltation of his own being. The same transformation also happens to Faust, who ascends from Gretchen to Helen and from Helen to the Mother of God; his nature is altered by repeated figurative deaths (Boy Charioteer, homunculus, Euphorion), until finally he attains the highest goal as Doctor Marianus. In that form Faust utters his prayer to the Virgin Mother:

> Pavilioned in the heaven's blue,
> Queen on high of all the world,
> For the holy sight I sue,
> Of the mystery unfurled.
> Sanction what in man may move
> Feelings tender and austere,
> And with glow of sacred love
> Lifts him to thy presence near.

[124] *The Divine Comedy* (trans. L. G. White), p. 187.

Souls unconquerable rise
If, sublime, thou will it;
Sinks that storm in peaceful wise
If thy pity still it.
Virgin, pure in heavenly sheen,
Mother, throned supernal,
Highest birth, our chosen Queen,
Godhead's peer eternal.

. . .

O contrite hearts, seek with your eyes
The visage of salvation;
Blissful in that gaze, arise,
Through glad regeneration.
Now may every pulse of good
Seek to serve before thy face,
Virgin, Queen of Motherhood,
Keep us, Goddess, in thy grace.[125]

379   We might also mention in this connection the symbolic attributes of the Virgin in the Litany of Loreto:

Mater amabilis	Lovable Mother
Mater admirabilis	Wonderful Mother
Mater boni consilii	Mother of good counsel
Speculum justitiae	Mirror of justice
Sedes sapientiae	Seat of wisdom
Causa nostrae laetitiae	Cause of our gladness
Vas spirituale	Vessel of the spirit
Vas honorabile	Vessel of honour
Vas insigne devotionis	Noble vessel of devotion
Rosa mystica	Mystical rose
Turris Davidica	Tower of David
Turris eburnea	Tower of ivory
Domus aurea	House of gold
Foederis arca	Ark of the covenant
Janua coeli	Gate of heaven
Stella matutina	Morning star[126]

380   These attributes reveal the functional significance of the Virgin Mother image: they show how the soul-image (anima) affects the conscious attitude. She appears as a vessel of devotion, a source of wisdom and renewal.

[125] *Faust, Part Two* (trans. Wayne), pp. 284f., 288.
[126] [From the *Rituale Romanum*, trans. here by A. S. B. Glover.]

223

381   We find this characteristic transition from the worship of woman to the worship of the soul in an early Christian document, the *Shepherd* of Hermas, who flourished about A.D. 140. This book, written in Greek, consists of a number of visions and revelations describing the consolidation of the new faith. The book, long regarded as canonical, was nevertheless rejected by the Muratori Canon. It begins as follows:

> The man who reared me sold me to a certain Rhoda in Rome. After many years, I made her acquaintance again and began to love her as a sister. One day I saw her bathing in the Tiber, and gave her my hand and helped her out of the water. When I saw her beauty I thought in my heart: "How happy I would be if I had a wife of such beauty and distinction." This was my only thought, and no other, no, not one.[127]

382   This experience was the starting-point for the visionary episode that followed. Hermas had apparently served Rhoda as a slave; then, as often happened, he obtained his freedom, and met her again later, when, probably as much from gratitude as from delight, a feeling of love stirred in his heart, though so far as he was aware it had merely the character of brotherly love. Hermas was a Christian, and moreover, as the text subsequently reveals, he was at that time already the father of a family, circumstances which would readily explain the repression of the erotic element. Yet the peculiar situation, doubtless provocative of many problems, was all the more likely to bring the erotic wish to consciousness. It is, in fact, expressed quite clearly in the thought that he would have liked Rhoda for a wife, though, as Hermas is at pains to emphasize, it is confined to this simple statement since anything more explicit and more direct instantly fell under a moral ban and was repressed. It is abundantly clear from what follows that this repressed libido wrought a powerful transformation in his unconscious, for it imbued the soul-image with life and brought about a spontaneous manifestation:[128]

127 [This and the following extracts were translated by an unknown hand (possibly by Baynes) from the German source used by the author. For an alternative version see *The Shepherd of Hermas* (trans. Kirsopp Lake), in *The Apostolic Fathers*, vol. 2.—TRANSLATOR.] Cf. ibid., p. 7.

128 Cf. ibid., pp. 7–9.

After a certain time, as I journeyed unto Cumae, praising God's creation in its immensity, beauty, and power, I grew heavy with sleep. And a spirit caught me up, and led me away through a pathless region where a man may not go. For it was a place full of crevices and torn by water-courses. I made my passage over the river and came upon even ground, where I threw myself upon my knees, and prayed to God, confessing my sins. While I thus prayed, the heavens opened and I beheld that lady for whom I yearned, who greeted me from heaven and said: "Hail to thee, Hermas!" While my eyes dwelt upon her, I spake, saying: "Mistress, what doest thou there?" And she answered: "I was taken up, in order to charge thee with thy sins before the Lord." I said unto her: "Dost thou now accuse me?" "No," said she, "yet hearken now unto the words I shall speak unto thee. For God, who dwelleth in heaven, and hath created the existing out of the non-existing, and hath magnified it and brought it to increase for the sake of His Holy Church, is wroth with thee, because thou has sinned against me." I answered and spake unto her: "How have I sinned against thee? When and where spake I ever an evil word unto thee? Have I not looked upon thee as a goddess? Have I not ever treated thee like a sister? Wherefore, O lady, dost thou falsely charge me with such evil and unclean things?" She smiled and said unto me: "The desire of sin arose in thy heart. Or is it not indeed a sin in thine eyes for a just man to cherish a sinful desire in his heart? Verily is it a sin," said she, "and a great one. For the just man striveth after what is just."

383   Solitary wanderings are, as we know, conducive to daydreaming and reverie. Presumably Hermas, on his way to Cumae, was thinking of his mistress; while thus engaged, the repressed erotic fantasy gradually pulled his libido down into the unconscious. Sleep overcame him, as a result of this lowering of the intensity of consciousness, and he fell into a somnambulant or ecstatic state, which itself was nothing but a particularly intense fantasy that completely captivated his conscious mind. It is significant that what then came to him was not an erotic fantasy; instead he is transported as it were to another land, represented in fantasy as the crossing of a river and a journey through a pathless country. The unconscious appears to him as an upper world in which events take place and men move about exactly as in the real world. His mistress appears before him not in an erotic fantasy but in "divine" form, seem-

225

ing to him like a goddess in heaven. The repressed erotic impression has activated the latent primordial image of the goddess, i.e., the archetypal soul-image. The erotic impression has evidently become united in the collective unconscious with archaic residues which have preserved from time immemorial the imprint of vivid impressions of the nature of woman— woman as mother and woman as desirable maid. Such impressions have immense power, as they release forces, both in the child and in the adult man, which fully merit the attribute "divine" i.e., something irresistible and absolutely compelling. The recognition of these forces as daemonic powers can hardly be due to moral repression, but rather to a self-regulation of the psychic organism which seeks by this change of front to guard against loss of equilibrium. For if, in face of the overwhelming might of passion, which puts one human being wholly at the mercy of another, the psyche succeeds in building up a counterposition so that, at the height of passion, the boundlessly desired object is unveiled as an idol and man is forced to his knees before the divine image, then the psyche has delivered him from the curse of the object's spell. He is restored to himself again and, flung back on himself, finds himself once more between gods and men, following his own path and subject to his own laws. The awful fear that haunts the primitive, his terror of everything impressive, which he at once senses as magic, as though it were charged with magical power, protects him in a purposive way against that most dreaded of all possibilities, loss of soul, with its inevitable sequel of sickness and death.

384   Loss of soul amounts to a tearing loose of part of one's nature; it is the disappearance and emancipation of a complex, which thereupon becomes a tyrannical usurper of consciousness, oppressing the whole man. It throws him off course and drives him to actions whose blind one-sidedness inevitably leads to self-destruction. Primitives are notoriously subject to such phenomena as running amok, going berserk, possession, and the like. The recognition of the daemonic character of passion is an effective safeguard, for it at once deprives the object of its strongest spell, relegating its source to the world of demons, i.e., to the unconscious, whence the force of passion actually springs. Exorcistic rites, whose aim is to bring back

the soul and release it from enchantment, are similarly effective in causing the libido to flow back into the unconscious.

385   This mechanism obviously worked in the case of Hermas. The transformation of Rhoda into a divine mistress deprived the actual object of her provocative and destructive power and brought Hermas under the law of his own soul and its collective determinants. Thanks to his abilities and connections, Hermas no doubt had a considerable share in the spiritual movements of his age. At that very time his brother Pius occupied the episcopal see at Rome. Hermas, therefore, was probably qualified to collaborate in the great task of his time to a greater degree than he, as a former slave, may have consciously realized. No able mind could for long have withstood the contemporary task of spreading Christianity, unless of course the barriers and peculiarities of race assigned him a different function in the great process of spiritual transformation. Just as the external conditions of life force a man to perform a social function, so the collective determinants of the psyche impel him to socialize ideas and convictions. By transforming a possible social *faux pas* into the service of his soul after having been wounded by the dart of passion, Hermas was led to accomplish a social task of a spiritual nature, which for that time was surely of no small importance.

386   In order to fit him for this task, it was clearly necessary that his soul should destroy the last possibility of an erotic attachment to the object, as this would have meant dishonesty towards himself. By consciously denying any erotic wish, Hermas merely demonstrated that it would be more agreeable for him if the erotic wish did not exist, but it by no means proved that he actually had no erotic intentions and fantasies. Therefore his sovereign lady, the soul, mercilessly revealed to him the existence of his sin, thus releasing him from his secret bondage to the object. As a "vessel of devotion" she took over the passion that was on the point of being fruitlessly lavished upon her. The last vestige of this passion had to be eradicated if the contemporary task was to be accomplished, and this consisted in delivering man from sensual bondage, from the state of primitive *participation mystique*. For the man of that age this bondage had become intolerable. The spiritual function had to be differentiated in order to restore the psychic equi-

librium. All philosophical attempts to do this by achieving "equanimity," most of which concentrated on the Stoic doctrine, came to grief because of their rationalism. Reason can give a man equilibrium only if his reason is already an equilibrating organ. But for how many individuals and at what periods of history has it been that? As a rule, a man needs the opposite of his actual condition to force him to find his place in the middle. For the sake of mere reason he can never forgo the sensuous appeal of the immediate situation. Against the power and delight of the temporal he must set the joy of the eternal, and against the passion of the sensual the ecstasy of the spiritual. The undeniable reality of the one must be matched by the compelling power of the other.

387   Through insight into the actual existence of his erotic desire, Hermas was able to acknowledge this metaphysical reality. The sensual libido that had previously clung to the concrete object now passed to his soul-image and invested it with the reality which the object had claimed exclusively for itself. Consequently his soul could speak to good effect and successfully enforce her demands.

388   After his conversation with Rhoda, her image vanishes and the heavens close. In her stead there now appears an "old woman in shining garments," who informs Hermas that his erotic desire is a sinful and foolish defiance of a venerable spirit, but that God is angry with him not so much on that account as because he tolerates the sins of his family. In this adroit fashion the libido is drawn away entirely from the erotic desire and in a flash is directed to the social task. An especial refinement is that the soul has discarded the image of Rhoda and taken on the appearance of an old woman, thus allowing the erotic element to recede into the background. It is later revealed to Hermas that this old woman is the Church; the concrete and personal has resolved itself into an abstraction, and the idea acquires a reality it had never before possessed. The old woman then reads to him from a mysterious book attacking heathens and apostates, but whose exact meaning he is unable to grasp. Subsequently we learn that the book sets forth a mission. Thus his sovereign lady presents him with his task, which as her knight he is pledged to accomplish. Nor is the trial of virtue lacking. For, not long after, Hermas has a vision

in which the old woman reappears, promising to return about the fifth hour in order to explain the revelation. Whereupon Hermas betook himself into the country to the appointed place, where he found a couch of ivory, set with a pillow and a cover of fine linen.

As I beheld these things lying there, I was sore amazed, and a quaking fell upon me and my hair stood on end, and a dreadful fear befell me, because I was alone in that place. But when I came once more to myself, I remembered the glory of God and took new courage; I knelt down and again confessed my sins unto God, as I had done before. Then she drew near with six young men, the which also I had seen before, and stood beside me and listened while I prayed and confessed my sins unto God. And she touched me and said: "Hermas, have done with all thy prayers and the reciting of thy sins. Pray also for righteousness, whereby thou mayest bear some of it with thee to thy house." And she raised me up by the hand and led me to the couch, and said unto the young men: "Go and build!" And when the youths were gone and we were alone, she said unto me: "Sit thee here!" I said unto her: "Mistress, let the aged first be seated." She said: "Do as I said unto thee and be thou seated." But, when I made as though to seat myself upon her right hand, she motioned me with a gesture of the hand to be seated upon her left.

As I wondered thereat, and was troubled, that I might not sit upon the right side, she said unto me: "Why art thou grieved, Hermas? The seat upon the right is for those who are already well-pleasing to God and have suffered for the Name. But to thee there lacketh much before thou canst sit with them. Yet remain as heretofore in thy simplicity, and thou shalt surely sit with them, and thus shall it be for all who shall have accomplished the work which those wrought, and endured what they suffered."[129]

389   In this situation, it would have been very easy for Hermas to give way to an erotic misunderstanding. The rendezvous has about it the feeling of a trysting-place in a "beautiful and sequestered spot," as he puts it. The rich couch waiting there is a fatal reminder of Eros, so that the terror which overcame Hermas at the sight of it is quite understandable. Clearly he must fight vigorously against these erotic associations lest he fall into a mood far from holy. He does not appear to have recognized the temptation for what it was, unless perhaps it is

[129] Cf. ibid., pp. 27ff.

tacitly admitted in the description of his terror, a touch of honesty that came more easily to the man of that time than to the man of today. For in that age man was more closely in touch with his own nature than we are, and was therefore in a position to perceive his natural reactions directly and to recognize what they were. In the case of Hermas, the confession of his sins may very well have been prompted by unholy sensations. At all events, the ensuing question as to whether he shall sit on the right hand or the left leads to a moral reprimand from his mistress. For although signs coming from the left were regarded as favourable in the Roman auguries, the left side, for both the Greeks and the Romans, was on the whole inauspicious, as the double meaning of the word "sinister" shows. But the question raised here of left and right has nothing to do with popular superstitions and is clearly of Biblical origin, referring to Matthew 25:33: "And he shall set the sheep on his right hand, but the goats on the left." Because of their guileless and gentle nature, sheep are an allegory of the good, while the unruly and lascivious nature of goats makes them an image of evil. By assigning him a seat on the left, his mistress tactfully reveals to him her understanding of his psychology.

390   When Hermas has taken his seat on her left, rather sadly, as he records, his mistress shows him a visionary scene which unrolls itself before his eyes. He beholds how the youths, assisted by ten thousand other men, build a mighty tower whose stones fit together without seams. This seamless tower, of indestructible solidity, signifies the Church, so Hermas is given to understand. *His mistress is the Church, and so is the tower.* We have seen already in the Litany of Loreto that the Virgin is named "tower of David" and "tower of ivory." The same or a similar association seems to be made here. The tower undoubtedly has the meaning of something solid and secure, as in Psalm 61:4: "For thou hast been a shelter for me, and a strong tower from the enemy." Any resemblance to the tower of Babel would involve an intense inner contradiction and must be excluded, but there may nevertheless be echoes of it, since Hermas, in company with every other thoughtful mind of that epoch, must have suffered much from the depressing spectacle of the ceaseless schisms and heretical disputes of the early Church. Such an impression may even have been his

main reason for writing these confessions, an inference supported by the fact that the mysterious book that was revealed to him inveighed against heathens and apostates. The same confusion of tongues that frustrated the building of the tower of Babel almost completely dominated the Church in the early centuries, demanding desperate efforts on the part of the faithful to overcome the chaos. Since Christendom at that time was far from being one flock under one shepherd, it was only natural that Hermas should long for the "shepherd," the *poimen*, as well as for some solid and stable structure, the "tower," that would unite in one inviolable whole the elements gathered from the four winds, the mountains and seas.

391   Earth-bound desire, sensuality in all its forms, attachment to the lures of this world, and the incessant dissipation of psychic energy in the world's prodigal variety, are the main obstacle to the development of a coherent and purposive attitude. Hence the elimination of this obstacle must have been one of the most important tasks of the time. It is therefore not surprising that, in the *Shepherd* of Hermas, it is the mastering of this task that is unfolded before our eyes. We have already seen how the original erotic stimulus and the energy it released were canalized into the personification of the unconscious complex, becoming the figure of Ecclesia, the old woman, whose visionary appearance demonstrates the spontaneity of the underlying complex. We learn, moreover, that the old woman now turns into a tower, since the tower is also the Church. This transformation is unexpected, because the connection between the tower and the old woman is not immediately apparent. But the attributes of the Virgin in the Litany of Loreto will put us on the right track, for there we find, as already mentioned, the tower associated with the Virgin Mother. This attribute has its source in the Song of Songs 4:4: "Thy neck is like the tower of David builded for an armoury," and 7:4: "Thy neck is a tower of ivory." Similarly 8:10: "I am a wall, and my breasts like towers."

392   The Song of Songs, as we know, was originally a love poem, perhaps a wedding song, which was denied canonical recognition even by Jewish scholars until very late. Mystical interpretation, however, has always loved to conceive the bride as Israel and the bridegroom as Jehovah, impelled by a sound

instinct to turn even erotic feelings into a relationship between God and the chosen people. Christianity appropriated the Song of Songs for the same reason, interpreting the bridegroom as Christ and the bride as the Church. To the psychology of the Middle Ages this analogy had an extraordinary appeal, and it inspired the quite unabashed Christ-eroticism of the Christian mystics, some of the best examples of which are supplied by Mechtild of Magdeburg. The Litany of Loreto was conceived in this spirit. It derived certain attributes of the Virgin directly from the Song of Songs, as in the case of the tower symbol. The rose, too, was used as one of her attributes even at the time of the Greek Fathers, together with the lily, which likewise appear in the Song of Songs (2:1): "I am the rose of Sharon, and the lily of the valleys." Images much used in the medieval hymns are the "enclosed garden" and the "sealed fountain" (Song of Songs 4:12: "A garden inclosed is my sister, my spouse; a spring shut up, a fountain sealed"). The unmistakably erotic nature of these images was explicitly accepted as such by the Fathers. Thus St. Ambrose interprets the "enclosed garden" as virginity.[130] In the same way, he[131] compares Mary with the ark of bulrushes in which Moses was found:

By the ark of bulrushes is meant the Blessed Virgin. Therefore his mother prepared the ark of bulrushes wherein Moses was placed, because the wisdom of God, which is the Son of God, chose blessed Mary the virgin and formed in her womb a man to whom he might become joined in unity of person.[132]

393   St. Augustine employs the simile (frequently used by later writers) of the *thalamus*, bridal chamber, for Mary, again in an expressly anatomical sense: "He chose for himself a chaste bridal chamber, where the bridegroom was joined to the bride,"[133] and: "He issued forth from the bridal chamber, that is from the virginal womb."[134]

130 *De institutione virginis*, cap. 9 (Migne, *P.L.*, vol. 16, col. 321).

131 [A. S. B. Glover, who made the following translation, points out that this *Sermo* is by *pseudo*-Ambrose. See bibliography *s.v.* Ambrose.—EDITORS.]

132 *Expositio beati Ambrosii Episcopi super Apocalypsin*, Visio III, cap. 6, p. 38.

133 [A. S. B. Glover was unable to locate this quotation.—EDITORS.]

134 *Sermo* 192 (Migne, *P.L.*, vol. 38, col. 1013).

394   The interpretation of *vas* as the womb may therefore be taken as certain when St. Ambrose says in confirmation of St. Augustine: "Not of earth but of heaven did he choose for himself this vessel, through which he should descend to sanctify the temple of shame."[135] The designation σκεῦος (vessel) is not uncommon with the Greek Fathers. Here again there is probably an allusion to the Song of Songs, for although the designation *vas* does not appear in the Vulgate text, we find instead the image of the goblet and of drinking (7:2): "Thy navel is like a round goblet, which wanteth not liquor; thy belly is like a heap of wheat set about with lilies." The meaning of the first sentence has a parallel in the *Meisterlieder der Kolmarer Handschrift*, where Mary is compared with the widow's cruse of oil (I Kings:17:9ff.): ". . . Zarephath in the land of Zidon, whither Elijah was sent to a widow who should feed him; my body is fitly compared with hers, for God sent the prophet unto me, to change for us our time of famine."[136] With regard to the second, St. Ambrose says: "In the womb of the virgin grace increased like a heap of wheat and the flowers of the lily, even as it generated the grain of wheat and the lily."[137] In Catholic sources[138] very far-fetched passages are drawn into this vessel symbolism, as for instance Song of Songs 1:1 (DV): "Let him kiss me with the kiss of his mouth: for thy *breasts* are better than wine," and even Exodus 16:33: "Take a *pot*, and put an omer full of manna therein, and lay it up before the Lord, to be kept for your generations."

395   These associations are so contrived that they argue against rather than for the Biblical origin of the vessel symbolism. In favour of an extra-Biblical source is the fact that the medieval hymns to Mary brazenly borrowed their imagery from everywhere, so that everything that was in any way precious became associated with her. The fact that the vessel symbol is very old —it stems from the third to fourth century—is no argument against its secular origin, since even the Fathers had a weakness for non-Biblical, pagan imagery; for instance Tertullian,[139]

---

135 *De institutione virginis*, cap. 5 (Migne, *P.L.*, vol. 16, col. 313).

136 Ed. Bartsch, p. 216.

137 *De institutione virginis*, cap. 14 (Migne, *P.L.*, vol. 16, col. 327).

138 E.g., Salzer, *Sinnbilder und Beiworte Mariens*.

139 *Adversus Judaeos*, XIII (Migne, *P.L.*, vol. 2, col. 635): "That virgin earth, not yet watered by the rains nor fecundated by showers."

Augustine,[140] and others compared the Virgin with the unde-filed earth and the unploughed field, not without a sidelong glance at the Kore of the mysteries.[141] Such comparisons were based on pagan models, as Cumont has shown to be the case with the ascension of Elijah in the early medieval illustrated manuscripts, which keep closely to the Mithraic prototype. In many of its rites the Church followed the pagan model, not least in making the birth of Christ coincide with the birth of the *sol invictus,* the invincible sun. St. Jerome compares the Virgin with the sun as the mother of the light.

396   These non-Biblical allegories can have their source only in pagan conceptions still current at that time. It is therefore only just, when considering the vessel symbol, to call to mind the well-known and widespread Gnostic symbolism of the vessel. A great many incised gems have been preserved from that time which bear the symbol of a pitcher with remarkable winged bands, at once recalling the uterus with the *ligamenta lata.* This vessel is called the "vase of sins,"[142] in contrast with the hymns to Mary in which she is extolled as the "vessel of virtue." King[143] contests the former interpretation as arbitrary and agrees with Köhler[144] that the cameo-image (principally Egyptian) refers to the pots on the water-wheels that drew up water from the Nile to irrigate the fields; this would also ex-plain the peculiar bands which clearly served for fastening the pot to the water-wheel. The fertilizing function of the pot was, as King notes, expressed as the "fecundation of Isis by the seed of Osiris." Often there is on the vessel a winnowing bas-ket, probably with reference to the "mystical winnowing basket of Iakchos," or λῖκνον, the figurative birthplace of the grain of wheat, symbolizing fertility.[145] There used to be a Greek marriage ceremony in which a winnowing basket filled with

---

[140] *Sermones,* 189, II (Migne, *P.L.,* vol. 38, col. 1006): "Truth is arisen from the earth, because Christ is born of a virgin."

[141] Cf. Jung, "The Psychological Aspects of the Kore."

[142] Jacques Matter, *Histoire critique du gnosticisme.* [As cited by King, *The Gnostics and Their Remains,* p. 111.]

[143] King, ibid.

[144] [Possibly H.K.E. von Köhler, "Einleitung über die Gemmen mit dem Namen der Künstler."—EDITORS.]

[145] *Symbols of Transformation,* pars. 528ff.

fruit was placed on the head of the bride, an obvious fertility charm.

397   This interpretation of the vessel is supported by the ancient Egyptian view that everything originated from the primal water, Nu or Nut, who was also identified with the Nile or the ocean. Nu is written with three pots, three water signs, and the sign for heaven. A hymn to Ptah-Tenen says: "Maker of grain, which cometh forth from him in his name Nu the Aged, who maketh fertile the watery mass of heaven, and maketh to come forth the water on the mountains to give life to men and women."[146] Wallis Budge drew my attention to the fact that the uterus symbolism exists today in the southern hinterland of Egypt in the form of rain and fertility charms. Occasionally it still happens that the natives in the bush kill a woman and take out her uterus for use in magical rites.[147]

398   When one considers how strongly the Church Fathers were influenced by Gnostic ideas in spite of their resistance to these heresies,[148] it is not inconceivable that we have in the symbolism of the vessel a pagan relic that proved adaptable to Christianity, and this is all the more likely as the worship of Mary was itself a vestige of paganism which secured for the Christian Church the heritage of the Magna Mater, Isis, and other mother goddesses. The image of the *vas Sapientiae*, vessel of wisdom, likewise recalls its Gnostic prototype, Sophia.

399   Official Christianity, therefore, absorbed certain Gnostic elements that manifested themselves in the worship of woman and found a place for them in an intensified worship of Mary. I have selected the Litany of Loreto as an example of this process of assimilation from a wealth of equally interesting material. The assimilation of these elements to the Christian symbol nipped in the bud the psychic culture of the man; for his soul, previously reflected in the image of the chosen mistress, lost its individual form of expression through this absorption. Consequently, any possibility of an individual differentiation of the soul was lost when it became repressed in the collective worship. Such losses generally have unfortunate

---

[146] Budge, *The Gods of the Egyptians*, I, p. 511.

[147] Talbot, *In the Shadow of the Bush*, pp. 67, 74ff.

[148] [Jung, *Aion*, chs. V and XIII.—EDITORS.]

consequences, and in this case they soon made themselves felt. Since the psychic relation to woman was expressed in the collective worship of Mary, the image of woman lost a value to which human beings had a natural right. This value could find its natural expression only through individual choice, and it sank into the unconscious when the individual form of expression was replaced by a collective one. In the unconscious the image of woman received an energy charge that activated the archaic and infantile dominants. And since all unconscious contents, when activated by dissociated libido, are projected upon external objects, the devaluation of the real woman was compensated by daemonic traits. She no longer appeared as an object of love, but as a persecutor or witch. The consequence of increasing Mariolatry was the witch hunt, that indelible blot on the later Middle Ages.

400   But this was not the only consequence. The splitting off and repression of a valuable progressive tendency resulted in a quite general activation of the unconscious. This activation could find no satisfying expression in collective Christian symbols, for an adequate expression always takes an individual form. Thus the way was paved for heresies and schisms, against which the only defence available to the Christian consciousness was fanaticism. The frenzied horror of the Inquisition was the product of over-compensated doubt, which came surging up from the unconscious and finally gave rise to one of the greatest schisms of the Church—the Reformation.

401   If I have dwelt rather longer on the symbolism of the vessel than my readers might have expected, I have done so for a definite reason, because I wanted to elucidate the psychological relations between the worship of woman and the legend of the Grail, which was so essentially characteristic of the early Middle Ages. The central religious idea in this legend, of which there are numerous variants, is the holy vessel, which, it must be obvious to everyone, is a thoroughly non-Christian image, whose origin is to be sought in extra-canonical sources.[149] From the material I have cited, it seems to me a

149 Further evidence of the pagan root of the vessel symbolism is the "magic cauldron" of Celtic mythology. Dagda, one of the benevolent gods of ancient Ireland, possesses such a cauldron, which supplies everybody with food according to his needs or merits. The Celtic god Bran likewise possesses a cauldron of renewal. It has even been suggested that the name Brons, one of the figures in the

genuine relic of Gnosticism, which either survived the extermination of heresies because of a secret tradition, or owed its revival to an unconscious reaction against the domination of official Christianity. The survival or unconscious revivification of the vessel symbol is indicative of a strengthening of the feminine principle in the masculine psychology of that time. Its symbolization in an enigmatic image must be interpreted as a spiritualization of the eroticism aroused by the worship of woman. But spiritualization always means the retention of a certain amount of libido, which would otherwise be immediately squandered in sexuality. Experience shows that when the libido is retained, one part of it flows into the spiritualized expression, while the remainder sinks into the unconscious and activates images that correspond to it, in this case the vessel symbol. The symbol lives through the restraint imposed upon certain forms of libido, and in turn serves to restrain these forms. The dissolution of the symbol means a streaming off of libido along the direct path, or at any rate an almost irresistible urge for its direct application. But the living symbol exorcises this danger. A symbol loses its magical or, if you prefer, its redeeming power as soon as its liability to dissolve is recognized. To be effective, a symbol must be by its very nature unassailable. It must be the best possible expression of the prevailing world-view, an unsurpassed container of meaning; it must also be sufficiently remote from comprehension to resist all attempts of the critical intellect to break it down; and finally, its aesthetic form must appeal so convincingly to our feelings that no argument can be raised against it on that score. For a certain time the Grail symbol clearly fulfilled these requirements, and to this fact it owed its vitality, which, as the example of Wagner shows, is still not exhausted today, even though our age and our psychology strive unceasingly for its dissolution.[150]

Grail legend, is derived from Bran. Alfred Nutt considers that Bran, lord of the cauldron, and Brons are steps in the transformation of the Celtic Peredur Saga into the quest of the Holy Grail. It would seem, therefore, that Grail motifs already existed in Celtic mythology. I am indebted to Dr. Maurice Nicoll, of London, for this information.

[150] [Pars. 399–400 = *Ges. Werke* 6, par. 447, which there follows our par. 401.— EDITORS.]

402   Let us now recapitulate this rather lengthy discussion and see what insights have been gained. We began with the vision of Hermas, in which he saw a tower being built. The old woman, who at first had declared herself to be the Church, now explains that the tower is a symbol of the Church. Her significance is thus transferred to the tower, and it is with this that the whole remaining part of the text is concerned. For Hermas it is only the tower that matters, and no longer the old woman, let alone Rhoda. The detachment of libido from the real object, its concentration on the symbol and canalization into a symbolic function, is complete. The idea of a universal and undivided Church, expressed in the symbol of a seamless and impregnable tower, has become an unshakable reality in the mind of Hermas. The detachment of libido from the object transfers it into the subject, where it activates the images lying dormant in the unconscious. These images are archaic forms of expression which become symbols, and these appear in their turn as equivalents of the devalued objects. This process is as old as mankind, for symbols may be found among the relics of prehistoric man as well as among the most primitive human types living today. Symbol-formation, therefore, must obviously be an extremely important biological function. As the symbol can come alive only through the devaluation of the object, it is evident that the purpose it serves is to deprive the object of its value. If the object had an absolute value, it would be an absolute determining factor for the subject and would abolish his freedom of action absolutely, since even a relative freedom could not coexist with absolute determination by the object. Absolute relation to the object is equivalent to a complete exteriorization of the conscious processes; it amounts to an identity of subject and object which would render all cognition impossible. In a milder form this state still exists today among primitives. The projections we so often encounter in practical analysis are only residues of this original identity of subject and object.

403   The elimination of cognition and conscious experience resulting from such a state means a considerable impairment of the capacity for adaptation, and this weights the scales heavily against man, who is already handicapped by his nat-

ural defencelessness and the helplessness of his young. But it also produces a dangerous inferiority in the realm of affect, because an identity of feeling with the object means, firstly, that any object whatsoever can affect the subject to any degree, and secondly, any affect on the part of the subject immediately includes and violates the object. An incident in the life of a bushman may illustrate what I mean. A bushman had a little son whom he loved with the tender monkey-love characteristic of primitives. Psychologically, this love is completely auto-erotic—that is to say, the subject loves himself in the object. The object serves as a sort of erotic mirror. One day the bushman came home in a rage; he had been fishing, and had caught nothing. As usual the little fellow came running to meet him, but his father seized hold of him and wrung his neck on the spot. Afterwards, of course, he mourned for the dead child with the same unthinking abandon that had brought about his death.

404   This is a good example of the object's identity with a passing affect. Obviously this kind of mentality is inimical to any protective tribal organization and to the propagation of the species, and must therefore be repressed and transformed. This is the purpose the symbol serves, and to this end it came into being. It draws libido away from the object, devalues it, and bestows the surplus libido on the subject. This surplus exerts its effect upon the unconscious, so that the subject finds himself placed between an inner and an outer determinant, whence arises the possibility of choice and relative subjective freedom.

405   Symbols always derive from archaic residues, from racial engrams (imprints), about whose age and origin one can speculate much although nothing definite can be determined. It would be quite wrong to try to derive symbols from personal sources, for instance from repressed sexuality. Such a repression can at most supply the amount of libido required to activate the archaic engram. The engram, however, corresponds to an inherited mode of functioning which owes its existence not to centuries of sexual repression but to the differentiation of instinct in general. The differentiation of instinct was and still is a biological necessity; it is not peculiar to the human

species but manifests itself equally in the sexual atrophy of the worker-bee.

406   I have used the vessel symbolism as an illustration of the way symbols are derived from archaic conceptions. Just as we found the primitive notion of the uterus at the root of this symbol, we may conjecture a similar derivation in the case of the tower. The tower belongs in all probability to the category of phallic symbols in which the history of symbolism abounds. The fact that the tower, presumably symbolizing erection, appears at the very moment when Hermas has to repress his erotic fantasies at the sight of the alluring couch is not surprising. We have seen that other symbolic attributes of the Virgin and the Church are unquestionably erotic in origin, as already attested by their derivation from the Song of Songs, and that they were expressly so interpreted by the Church Fathers. The tower symbol in the Litany of Loreto has the same source and may therefore have a similar underlying meaning. The attribute "ivory" is undoubtedly erotic in origin, since it is an allusion to the tint and texture of the skin (Song of Songs 5:14: "His belly is as bright ivory"). But the tower itself is also found in an unmistakably erotic context in 8:10: "I am a wall, and my breasts like towers," which obviously refers to the jutting-out breasts with their full and elastic consistency. "His legs are as pillars of marble" (5:15), "thy neck is as a tower of ivory" (7:4), "thy nose is as the tower of Lebanon" (7:4), are equally obvious allusions to something slender and projecting. These attributes originate in tactile sensations which are transferred from the organ to the object. Just as a gloomy mood seems grey, and a joyous one bright and colourful, so also the sense of touch is influenced by subjective sexual sensations (in this case the sensation of erection) whose qualities are transferred to the object. The erotic psychology of the Song of Songs uses the images aroused in the subject for the purpose of enhancing the object's value. Ecclesiastical psychology employs these same images in order to guide the libido towards a figurative object, while the psychology of Hermas exalts the unconsciously activated image into an end in itself, using it to embody ideas that were of supreme importance for the minds of that time, namely, the consolidation and organization of the newly won Christian attitude and view of the world.

b. The Relativity of the God-concept in Meister Eckhart

407   The process of transformation which Hermas experienced represents on a small scale what took place on a large scale in the early medieval psychology: a new revelation of woman and the development of the feminine symbol of the Grail. Hermas saw Rhoda in a new light, and the libido thus set free transformed itself under his hands into the fulfilment of his social task.

408   It is, I think, characteristic of our psychology that we find on the threshold of the new age two figures who were destined to exert an immense influence on the hearts and minds of the younger generation: Wagner, the prophet of love, whose music runs the whole gamut of feeling from Tristan down to incestuous passion, then up again from Tristan to the sublime spirituality of Parsifal; and Nietzsche, the prophet of power and of the triumphant will for individuality. Wagner, in his last and loftiest utterance, harked back to the Grail legend, as Goethe did to Dante, but Nietzsche seized on the idea of a master caste and a master morality, an idea embodied in many a fair-haired hero and knight of the Middle Ages. Wagner broke the bonds that fettered love, Nietzsche shattered the "tables of values" that cramp individuality. Both strove after similar goals while at the same time creating irremediable discord; for where love is, power cannot prevail, and where power prevails, love cannot reign.

409   The fact that three of the greatest minds of Germany should fasten on early medieval psychology in their most important works is proof, it seems to me, that that age has left behind a question which still remains to be answered. It may be well, therefore, to examine this question a little more closely. I have the impression that the mysterious something that inspired the knightly orders (the Templars, for instance), and that seems to have found expression in the Grail legend, may possibly have been the germ of a new orientation to life, in other words, a nascent symbol. The non-Christian or Gnostic character of the Grail symbol takes us back to the early Christian heresies, those germinating points in which a whole world of audacious and brilliant ideas lay hidden. In Gnosticism we see man's unconscious psychology in full flower, almost per-

verse in its luxuriance; it contained the very thing that most strongly resisted the *regula fidei*, that Promethean and creative spirit which will bow only to the individual soul and to no collective ruling. Although in crude form, we find in Gnosticism what was lacking in the centuries that followed: a belief in the efficacy of individual revelation and individual knowledge. This belief was rooted in the proud feeling of man's affinity with the gods, subject to no human law, and so overmastering that it may even subdue the gods by the sheer power of Gnosis. In Gnosis are to be found the beginnings of the path that led to the intuitions of German mysticism, so important psychologically, which came to flower at the time of which we are speaking.

410   The question now before us focuses our attention on the greatest thinker of that age, Meister Eckhart. Just as signs of a new orientation are apparent in chivalry, so, in Eckhart, we are confronted with new ideas, ideas having the same *psychic* orientation that impelled Dante to follow the image of Beatrice into the underworld of the unconscious and that inspired the singers who sang the lore of the Grail.

411   Nothing is known, unfortunately, of Eckhart's personal life that would explain how he was led to his knowledge of the soul. But the meditative air with which he says in his discourse on repentance, "And still today one seldom finds that people come to great things without they first go somewhat astray,"[151] permits the inference that he wrote from personal experience. Strangely appealing is Eckhart's sense of an inner affinity with God, when contrasted with the Christian sense of sin. We feel ourselves transported back into the spacious atmosphere of the Upanishads. Eckhart must have experienced a quite extraordinary enhancement of the value of the soul, i.e., of his own inner being, that enabled him to rise to a purely psychological and relativistic conception of God and of his relation to man. This discovery and painstaking exposition of the relativity of God to man and the soul seem to me one of the most important landmarks on the way to a psychological understanding of religious phenomena, serving at the same time to liberate the religious function from the cramping limitations of intellectual

[151] Cf. Evans, *Meister Eckhart*, II, p. 19.

criticism, though this criticism, of course, must not be denied its dues.

412   We now come to the main theme of this chapter—the relativity of the symbol. The "relativity of God," as I understand it, denotes a point of view that does not conceive of God as "absolute," i.e., wholly "cut off" from man and existing outside and beyond all human conditions, but as in a certain sense dependent on him; it also implies a reciprocal and essential relation between man and God, whereby man can be understood as a function of God, and God as a psychological function of man. From the empirical standpoint of analytical psychology, the God-image is the symbolic expression of a particular psychic state, or function, which is characterized by its absolute ascendency over the will of the subject, and can therefore bring about or enforce actions and achievements that could never be done by conscious effort. This overpowering impetus to action (so far as the God-function manifests itself in acts), or this inspiration that transcends conscious understanding, has its source in an accumulation of energy in the unconscious. The accumulated libido activates images lying dormant in the collective unconscious, among them the God-image, that engram or imprint which from the beginning of time has been the collective expression of the most overwhelmingly powerful influences exerted on the conscious mind by unconscious concentrations of libido.

413   Hence, for our psychology, which as a science must confine itself to empirical data within the limits set by cognition, God is not even relative, but a function of the unconscious—the manifestation of a dissociated quantum of libido that has activated the God-image. From the metaphysical point of view God is, of course, absolute, existing in himself. This implies his complete detachment from the unconscious, which means, psychologically, a complete unawareness of the fact that God's action springs from one's own inner being. The relativity of God, on the other hand, means that a not inconsiderable portion of the unconscious processes is registered, at least indirectly, as a psychological content. Naturally this insight is possible only when more attention than usual is paid to the psyche, with the consequence that the contents of the unconscious are withdrawn from projection into objects and become

endowed with a conscious quality that makes them appear as belonging to the subject and as subjectively conditioned.

414   This was what happened with the mystics, though it was not the first time that the idea of God's relativity had appeared. It is found in principle and in the very nature of things among primitives. Almost everywhere on the lower human levels the idea of God has a purely dynamic character; God is a divine force, a power related to health, to the soul, to medicine, to riches, to the chief, a power that can be captured by certain procedures and employed for the making of things needful for the life and well-being of man, and also to produce magical or baneful effects. The primitive feels this power as much within him as outside him; it is as much his own life force as it is the "medicine" in his amulet, or the mana emanating from his chief. Here we have the first demonstrable conception of an all-pervading spiritual force. Psychologically, the efficacy of the fetish, or the prestige of the medicine-man, is an unconscious subjective evaluation of those objects. Their power resides in the libido which is present in the subject's unconscious, and it is perceived in the object because whenever unconscious contents are activated they appear in projection.

415   The relativity of God in medieval mysticism is, therefore, a regression to a primitive condition. In contrast, the related Eastern conceptions of the individual and supra-individual *atman* are not so much a regression to the primitive as a continuous development out of the primitive in a typically Eastern way that still manages to preserve the efficacy of the primitive principle. The regression to the primitive is not surprising, in view of the fact that every vital form of religion organizes one or the other primitive tendency in its ceremonials or its ethics, thereby securing for itself those secret instinctive forces that conduce to the perfecting of human nature in the religious process. This reversion to the primitive, or, as in India, the uninterrupted connection with it, keeps man in touch with Mother Earth, the prime source of all power. Seen from the heights of a differentiated point of view, whether rational or ethical, these instinctive forces are "impure." But life itself flows from springs both clear and muddy. Hence all excessive "purity" lacks vitality. A constant striving for clarity and differentiation means a proportionate loss of vital intensity, precisely because the muddy elements are excluded. Every re-

newal of life needs the muddy as well as the clear. This was evidently perceived by the great relativist Meister Eckhart when he said:

For this reason God is willing to bear the brunt of sins and often winks at them, mostly sending them to those whom he has destined for great things. Behold! Who was dearer and nearer to our Lord than the apostles? Not one of them but fell into mortal sin; all were mortal sinners. In the Old Testament and in the New he has shown this to be true of those who afterwards were far the dearest to him; and still today one seldom finds that people come to great things without they first go somewhat astray.[152]

416   Both on account of his psychological perspicacity and his deep religious feeling and thought, Meister Eckhart was the most brilliant exponent of that critical movement within the Church which began towards the end of the thirteenth century. I would like to quote a few of his sayings to illustrate his relativistic conception of God:

For man is truly God, and God is truly man.[153]

Whereas he who has not God as such an inner possession, but with every means must fetch him from without, in this thing or in that, where he is then sought for in vain, in all manner of works, people, or places; verily such a man has him not, and easily something comes to trouble him. And it is not only evil company that troubles him, but also the good, not only the street, but also the church, not only vile words and deeds, but the good as well. For the hindrance lies within himself, because in him God has not yet become the world. Were God that to him, then all would be well and good with him in every place and with all people, always possessing God.[154]

417   This passage is of particular psychological interest, as it exemplifies something of the primitive idea of God outlined above. "Fetching God from without" is the equivalent of the primitive view that *tondi*[155] can be got from outside. With Eckhart, it may be merely a figure of speech, but the original meaning nevertheless glimmers through. At any rate it is clear

---

152 Cf. Evans, pp. 18f.   153 Ibid., I, p. 188.
154 Cf. ibid., II, p. 8.
155 The libido concept of the Bataks. Cf. Warneck, *Die Religion der Batak.* *Tondi* is the magic force round which every thing turns. [Cf. "On Psychic Energy," par. 125.—EDITORS.]

that Eckhart understands God as a psychological value. This is proved by the words "and easily something comes to trouble him." For, when God is outside, he is necessarily projected into objects, with the result that all objects acquire a surplus value. But whenever this happens, the object exerts an overpowering influence over the subject, holding him in slavish dependence. Eckhart is evidently referring to this subjection to the object, which makes the world appear in the role of God, i.e., as an absolutely determining factor. Hence he says that for such a person "God has not yet become the world," since for him the world has taken the place of God. The subject has not succeeded in detaching and introverting the surplus value from the object, thus turning it into an inner possession. Were he to possess it in himself, he would have God (this same value) continually as an object, so that God would have become the world. In the same passage Eckhart says:

> He that is right in his feeling is right in any place and in any company, but if he is wrong he finds nothing right wherever or with whom he may be. For a man of right feeling has God with him.[156]

A man who has this value in himself is everywhere at ease; he is not dependent on objects—not for ever needing and hoping to get from the object what he lacks himself.

418   From all this it should be sufficiently clear that, for Eckhart, God is a psychological or, to be more accurate, a *psychodynamic* state.

> . . . by this kingdom of God we understand the soul, for the soul is of like nature with the Godhead. Hence all that has been said here of the kingdom of God, how God is himself the kingdom, may be said with equal truth of the soul. St. John says, "All things were made by him." This is to be understood of the soul, for the soul is all things. The soul is all things because she is an image of God, and as such she is also the kingdom of God. . . . So much, says one Master, is God in the soul, that his whole divine nature depends upon her. It is a higher state for God to be in the soul than for the soul to be in God. The soul is not blissful because she is in God, she is blissful because God is in her. Rely upon it, God himself is blissful in the soul.[157]

156 Cf. Evans, II, p. 7.

157 Cf. ibid., I, p. 270. [The last sentence contains an untranslatable play on words: "Gott ist selig (blissful) in der Seele (soul)."—TRANSLATOR.]

419   Looked at historically, the soul, that many-faceted and much-interpreted concept, refers to a psychological content that must possess a certain measure of autonomy within the limits of consciousness. If this were not so, man would never have hit on the idea of attributing an independent existence to the soul, as though it were some objectively perceptible thing. It must be a content in which spontaneity is inherent, and hence also partial unconsciousness, as with every autonomous complex. The primitive, as we know, usually has several souls —several autonomous complexes with a high degree of spontaneity, so that they appear as having a separate existence (as in certain mental disorders). On a higher level the number of souls decreases, until at the highest level of culture the soul resolves itself into the subject's general awareness of his psychic activities and exists only as a term for the totality of psychic processes. This absorption of the soul into consciousness is just as much a characteristic of Eastern as it is of Western culture. In Buddhism everything is dissolved into consciousness; even the *samskaras*, the unconscious formative forces, must be transformed through religious self-development.

420   As against this historical evolution of the idea of the soul, analytical psychology opposes the view that the soul does not coincide with the totality of the psychic functions. We define the soul on the one hand as the relation to the unconscious, and on the other as a personification of unconscious contents. From the civilized standpoint it may seem deplorable that personifications of unconscious contents still exist, just as a man with a differentiated consciousness might well lament the existence of contents that are still unconscious. But since analytical psychology is concerned with man as he is and not with man as he would like to be, we have to admit that those same phenomena which impel the primitive to speak of "souls" still go on happening, just as there are still countless people among civilized nations who believe in ghosts. We may believe as much as we please in the doctrine of the "unity of the ego," according to which there can be no such things as autonomous complexes, but Nature herself does not bother in the least about our abstract theories.

421   If the "soul" is a personification of unconscious contents, then, according to our previous definition, God too is an uncon-

scious content, a personification in so far as he is thought of as personal, and an image or expression of something in so far as he is thought of as dynamic. God and the soul are essentially the same when regarded as personifications of an unconscious content. Meister Eckhart's view, therefore, is purely psychological. So long as the soul, he says, is only in God, she is not blissful. If by "blissful" one understands a state of intense vitality, it follows from the passage quoted earlier that this state does not exist so long as the dynamic principle "God," the libido, is projected upon objects. For, so long as God, the highest value, is not in the soul, it is somewhere outside. God must be withdrawn from objects and brought into the soul, and this is a "higher state" in which God himself is "blissful." Psychologically, this means that when the libido invested in God, i.e., the surplus value that has been projected, is recognized as a projection,[158] the object loses its overpowering significance, and the surplus value consequently accrues to the individual, giving rise to a feeling of intense vitality, a new potential. God, life at its most intense, then resides in the soul, in the unconscious. But this does not mean that God has become completely unconscious in the sense that all idea of him vanishes from consciousness. It is as though the supreme value were shifted elsewhere, so that it is now found inside and not outside. Objects are no longer autonomous factors, but God has become an autonomous psychic complex. An autonomous complex, however, is always only partially conscious, since it is associated with the ego only in limited degree, and never to such an extent that the ego could wholly comprehend it, in which case it would no longer be autonomous. Henceforth the determining factor is no longer the overvalued object, but the unconscious. The determining influences are now felt as coming from within oneself, and this feeling produces a oneness of being, a relation between conscious and unconscious, in which of course the unconscious predominates.

422   We must now ask ourselves, whence comes this "blissful"

---

[158] The recognition of something as a projection should never be understood as a purely intellectual process. Intellectual insight dissolves a projection only when it is ripe for dissolution. But when it is not, it is impossible to withdraw libido from it by an intellectual judgment or by an act of the will.

feeling, this ecstasy of love?[159] In this Brahman-like state of *ananda*, with the supreme value lying in the unconscious, there is a drop in the conscious potential, the unconscious becomes the determining factor, and the ego almost entirely disappears. It is a state strongly reminiscent of that of the child on the one hand, and of the primitive on the other, who is likewise influenced in the highest degree by the unconscious. We can safely say that the restoration of the earlier paradisal state is the cause of this blissfulness. But we have still to find out why this original state is so peculiarly blissful. The feeling of bliss accompanies all those moments when one feels borne along by the current of life, when what was dammed up can flow off without restraint, when there is no need to do this thing or that thing with a conscious effort in order to find a way out or to achieve a result. We have all known situations or moods when "things go of themselves," when we no longer need to manufacture all sorts of wearisome conditions for our joy or pleasure. The time of childhood is the unforgettable emblem of this joy, which, unperturbed by things without, pours in a warm flood from within. "Childlikeness" is therefore a symbol of that unique inner condition on which "blissfulness" depends. To be like a child means to possess a treasury of accumulated libido which can constantly stream forth. The libido of the child flows into things; in this way he gains the world, then by degrees loses himself in the world (to use the language of religion) through a gradual over-valuation of things. The growing dependence on things entails the necessity of sacrifice, i.e., the withdrawal of libido, the severance of ties. The intuitive teachings of religion seek by this means to gather the energy together again; indeed, religion portrays this process of re-collection in its symbols. Actually, the over-valuation of the object as compared with the low value of the subject produces a retrograde current that would bring the libido quite naturally back to the subject were it not for the obstructing power of consciousness. Everywhere among primitives we find religious practice harmonizing with nature, because the primitive is able to follow his instinct without difficulty, now in one

[159] "Energy is eternal delight": Blake, "The Marriage of Heaven and Hell," *The Complete Writings* (ed. Keynes), p. 149.

direction and now in another. His religious practices enable him to recreate the magical power he needs, or to recover the soul that was lost to him during the night.

423   The aim of the great religions is expressed in the injunction "not of this world," and this implies the inward movement of libido into the unconscious. Its withdrawal and introversion create in the unconscious a concentration of libido which is symbolized as the "treasure," as in the parables of the "pearl of great price" and the "treasure in the field." Eckhart interprets the latter as follows:

Christ says, "The kingdom of heaven is like a treasure hid in a field." This field is the soul, wherein lies hidden the treasure of the divine kingdom. In the soul, therefore, are God and all creatures blessed.[160]

424   This interpretation agrees with our psychological argument: the soul is a personification of the unconscious, where lies the treasure, the libido which is immersed in introversion and is allegorized as God's kingdom. This amounts to a permanent union with God, a living in his kingdom, in that state where a preponderance of libido lies in the unconscious and determines conscious life. The libido concentrated in the unconscious was formerly invested in objects, and this made the world seem all-powerful. God was then "outside," but now he works from within, as the hidden treasure conceived as God's kingdom. If, then, Eckhart reaches the conclusion that the soul is itself God's kingdom, it is conceived as a function of relation to God, and God would be the power working within the soul and perceived by it. Eckhart even calls the soul the *image of God*.

425   It is evident from the ethnological and historical material that the soul is a content that belongs partly to the subject and partly to the world of spirits, i.e., the unconscious. Hence the soul always has an earthly as well as a rather ghostly quality. It is the same with magical power, the divine force of primitives, whereas on the higher levels of culture God is entirely separate from man and is exalted to the heights of pure ideality. But the soul never loses its intermediate position. It must

160 Cf. Evans, I, p. 271.

therefore be regarded as a function of relation between the subject and the inaccessible depths of the unconscious. The determining force (God) operating from these depths is reflected by the soul, that is, it creates symbols and images, and is itself only an image. By means of these images the soul conveys the forces of the unconscious to consciousness; it is both receiver and transmitter, an organ for perceiving unconscious contents. What it perceives are symbols. But symbols are shaped energies, determining ideas whose affective power is just as great as their spiritual value. When, says Eckhart, the soul is in God it is not "blissful," for when this organ of perception is overwhelmed by the divine *dynamis* it is by no means a happy state. But when God is in the soul, i.e., when the soul becomes a vessel for the unconscious and makes itself an image or symbol of it, this is a truly happy state. The happy state is a *creative* state, as we see from the following noble words:

If any should ask me, Wherefore do we pray, wherefore do we fast, wherefore do we do all manner of good works, wherefore are we baptized, wherefore did God become man, I would answer, So that God may be born in the soul and the soul again in God. Therefore were the Holy Scriptures written. Therefore did God create the whole world, that God might be born in the soul and the soul again in God. The innermost nature of all grain is wheat, and of all metal, gold, and of all birth, Man![161]

426   Here Eckhart states bluntly that God is dependent on the soul, and at the same time, that the soul is the birthplace of God. This latter sentence can readily be understood in the light of our previous reflections. The organ of perception, the soul, apprehends the contents of the unconscious, and, as the creative function, gives birth to its *dynamis* in the form of a symbol.[162] The soul gives birth to images that from the rational standpoint of consciousness are assumed to be worthless. And so they are, in the sense that they cannot immediately be turned to account in the objective world. The first possibility

[161] Cf. ibid., p. 81.

[162] According to Eckhart, the soul is as much the comprehender as the comprehended. Evans, I, p. 389.

of making use of them is *artistic*, if one is in any way gifted in that direction;[163] a second is *philosophical speculation*;[164] a third is *quasi-religious*, leading to heresy and the founding of sects; and a fourth way of employing the *dynamis* of these images is to squander it in every form of licentiousness. As we noted at the beginning (par. 25), the latter two modes of application were especially apparent in the Encratitic (ascetic) and Antitactic (anarchic) schools of Gnosticism.

427   The conscious realization of these images is, however, of indirect value from the point of view of adaptation to reality, in that one's relation to the surrounding world is thereby freed from admixtures of fantasy. Nevertheless, their main value lies in promoting the subject's happiness and well-being, irrespective of external circumstances. To be adapted is certainly an ideal, but adaptation is not always possible. There are situations in which the only adaptation is patient endurance. This form of passive adaptation is made easier by an elaboration of the fantasy-images. I say "elaboration" because at first the fantasies are merely raw material of doubtful value. They have to be worked on and put in a form best calculated to yield the maximum benefit. This is a matter of technique, which it would not be appropriate to discuss here. I will only say, for clarity's sake, that there are two methods of treatment: 1. the reductive, and 2. the synthetic. The former traces everything back to primitive instincts, the latter develops the material into a process for differentiating the personality. The two methods are complementary, for reduction to instinct leads back to reality, indeed to an over-valuation of reality and hence to the necessity of sacrifice. The synthetic method elaborates the symbolic fantasies resulting from the introversion of libido through sacrifice. This produces a new attitude to the world, whose very difference offers a new potential. I have termed this transition to a new attitude the transcendent function.[165] In the regenerated attitude the libido that was formerly sunk in the unconscious emerges in the form of some positive achievement. It is equivalent to a renewal of life, which Eckhart symbolizes by

[163] Literary examples are E. T. A. Hoffmann, Meyrink, Barlach (*Der tote Tag*), and, on a higher level, Spitteler, Goethe, Wagner.

[164] E.g., Nietzsche's *Zarathustra*.

[165] See infra, par. 828. Cf. also "The Transcendent Function."

God's birth. Conversely, when the libido is withdrawn from external objects and sinks into the unconscious, the soul is born again in God. This state, as he rightly observes, is not a blissful one,[166] because it is a negative act, a turning away from life and a descent to the *deus absconditus*, who possesses qualities very different from those of the God who shines by day.

428   Eckhart speaks of God's birth as a continual process. As a matter of fact, the process in question is a psychological one that unconsciously repeats itself almost continually, though we are conscious of it only when it swings towards the extreme. Goethe's idea of a systole and diastole seems to have hit the mark intuitively. It may well be a question of a vital rhythm, of fluctuations of vital forces, which as a rule go on unconsciously. This may also explain why the existing terminology for such a process is in the main either religious or mythological, since these formulas refer primarily to unconscious psychological facts and not, as the scientific interpreters of myths often assert, to the phases of the moon or other meteorological phenomena. And because it is pre-eminently a question of unconscious processes, we have the greatest difficulty, as scientists, in extricating ourselves at least so far from the language of metaphor as to reach the level of metaphor used by other sciences. Reverence for the great mysteries of Nature, which the language of religion seeks to express in symbols hallowed by their antiquity, profound significance, and beauty, will not suffer from the extension of psychology to this domain, to which science has hitherto found no access. We only shift the symbols back a little, shedding a little light on their darker reaches, but without succumbing to the erroneous notion that we have created anything more than merely a new symbol for the same enigma that perplexed all ages before us. Our science is a language of metaphor too, but in practice it works better than the old mythological hypothesis, which used concretisms as a means of expression, and not, as we do, concepts.

By being created, the soul created God, for he did not exist until the soul was made. A little while since and I declared, I am the

166 Eckhart says: "Therefore do I turn back once more to myself, there do I find the deepest places, deeper than hell itself; for even from there does my wretchedness drive me. Nowhere can I escape myself! Here I will set me down and here I will remain." Cf. Evans, I, p. 389.

cause that God is God! God is gotten of the soul, his Godhead he has of himself.[167]

God comes into being and passes away.[168]

Because all creatures declare him, God comes into being. While yet I abode in the ground and the depths of Godhead, in its flood and source, none asked me whither I went or what I did; none was there who could have questioned me. But when I flowed forth, all creatures declared God. . . . And why did they not declare the God-head? All that is in Godhead is one, and of that there is nothing to declare. Only God does; Godhead does nothing, there is nothing it can do, and never has it looked for anything to do. God and God-head are as different as doing and non-doing. When I come home again in God, I do nothing more in myself, so this my breaking through is much more excellent than my first going out. For truly it is I who bring all creatures out of their own into my mind and make them one in me. When I come back into the ground and the depths of Godhead, into its flood and source, none asks me whence I came or whither I went. None missed me. God passes away.[169]

429   We see from these passages that Eckhart distinguishes between God and Godhead. Godhead is All, neither knowing nor possessing itself, whereas God is a function of the soul, just as the soul is a function of Godhead. Godhead is obviously all-pervading creative power or, in psychological terms, self-generating creative instinct, that neither knows nor possesses itself, comparable to Schopenhauer's universal Will. But God appears as issuing forth from Godhead and the soul. Like every creature, the soul "declares" him: he exists in so far as the soul distinguishes itself from the unconscious and perceives its *dynamis,* and he ceases to exist as soon as the soul is immersed in the "flood and source" of unconscious *dynamis.* Thus Eckhart says:

When I flowed out from God, all things declared, "God is!" Now this cannot make me blessed, for thereby I acknowledge myself a creature. But in my breaking through I stand empty in the will of God, and empty also of God's will, and of all his works, even of God himself—then I am more than all creatures, then I am neither God nor creature: I am what I was, and that I shall remain, now and ever more! Then I receive a thrust which carries me above all angels. By this thrust I become so rich that God cannot suffice me,

[167] Cf. ibid., p. 410.   [168] Cf. ibid., p. 143.   [169] Cf. ibid.

despite all that he is as God and all his godly works; for in this breakthrough I receive what God and I have in common. I am what I was, I neither increase nor diminish, for I am the unmoved mover that moves all things. Here God can find no more place in man, for man by his emptiness has won back that which he eternally was and ever shall remain.[170]

430   The "flowing out" means a realization of the unconscious content and the unconscious *dynamis* in the form of an *idea* born of the soul. This is an act of conscious differentiation from the unconscious *dynamis*, a separation of the ego as subject from God (= *dynamis*) as object. By this act God "becomes." But when the "breakthrough" abolishes this separation by cutting the ego off from the world, and the ego again becomes identical with the unconscious *dynamis*, God disappears as an object and dwindles into a subject which is no longer distinguishable from the ego. In other words the ego, as a late product of differentiation, is reunited with the dynamic All-oneness (the *participation mystique* of primitives). This is the immersion in the "flood and source." The numerous analogies with Eastern ideas are immediately apparent, and they have been elaborated by writers more qualified than myself. In the absence of direct transmission this parallelism proves that Eckhart was thinking from the depths of the collective psyche which is common to East and West. This universal foundation, for which no common historical background can be made answerable, underlies the primitive mentality with its energic conception of God.

431   The return to primeval nature and mystic regression to the psychic conditions of prehistory are common to all religions in which the impelling *dynamis* has not yet petrified into an abstract idea but is still a living experience, no matter whether this be expressed in ceremonies of identification with the totem among the Australian aborigines[171] or in the ecstasies of the Christian mystics. As a result of this retrograde process the original state of identity with God is re-established and a new potential is produced. However improbable such a state may be, it is a profoundly impressive experience which, by revivi-

---

170 Cf. p. 221.
171 Spencer and Gillen, *The Northern Tribes of Central Australia.*

fying the individual's relation to God as an object, creates the world anew.

432   In speaking of the relativity of the God-symbol, we would be failing in our duty if we omitted to mention that solitary poet whose tragic fate it was to find no relation either to his own times or to his own inner vision: Angelus Silesius.[172] What Eckhart laboured to express with a great effort of thought, and often in barely intelligible language, Angelus Silesius sings in touchingly intimate verses, which portray the relativity of God with naïve simplicity. His verses speak for themselves:

> I know that without me
> God can no moment live;
> Were I to die, then He
> No longer could survive.
>
> God cannot without me
> A single worm create;
> Did I not share with Him
> Destruction were its fate.
>
> I am as great as God,
> And He is small like me;
> He cannot be above,
> Nor I below Him be.
>
> In me is God a fire
> And I in Him its glow;
> In common is our life,
> Apart we cannot grow.
>
> God loves me more than Self
> My love doth give His weight,
> Whate'er He gives to me
> I must reciprocate.
>
> He's God and man to me,
> To Him I'm both indeed;
> His thirst I satisfy,
> He helps me in my need.
>
> This God, who feels for us,
> Is to us what we will;
> And woe to us, if we
> Our part do not fulfil.

[172] [Johann Scheffler, mystic and doctor, 1624–1677.—EDITORS.]

God is whate'er He is,
I am what I must be;
If you know one, in sooth,
You know both Him and me.

I am not outside God,
Nor leave I Him afar;
I am His grace and light,
And He my guiding star.

I am the vine, which He
Doth plant and cherish most;
The fruit which grows from me
Is God, the Holy Ghost.

I am God's child, His son,
And He too is my child;
We are the two in one,
Both son and father mild.

To illuminate my God
The sunshine I must be;
My beams must radiate
His calm and boundless sea.[173]

433   It would be absurd to suppose that such audacious ideas as these and Meister Eckhart's are nothing but figments of conscious speculation. Such thoughts are always profoundly significant historical phenomena, borne along on the unconscious currents of the collective psyche. Below the threshold of consciousness, thousands of other nameless ones are ranged behind them with similar thoughts and feelings, ready to open the gates of a new age. In these bold ideas we hear the voice of the collective psyche, which with imperturbable assurance and the finality of a natural law brings about spiritual transformation and renewal. The unconscious currents reached the surface at the time of the Reformation. The Reformation largely did away with the Church as the dispenser of salvation and established once more the personal relation to God. The culminating point in the objectification of the God-concept had now been passed, and from then on it became more and more

[173] From the "Cherubinischer Wandersmann" in Scheffler's *Sämmtliche Poetische Werke* (ed. Rosenthal), I, pp. 5ff. [The twelve stanzas do not constitute one continuous poem, but are respectively aphorisms Nos. I,8; I,96; I,10; I,11; I,18; I,224; III,140; I,212; I,106; II,122; I,256; I,115.—EDITORS.]

subjective. The logical consequence of this subjectifying process is a splitting up into sects, and its most extreme outcome is individualism, representing a new form of detachment from the world, the immediate danger of which is re-submersion in the unconscious *dynamis*. The cult of the "blond beast" stems from this development, besides much else that distinguishes our age from others. But whenever this submersion in instinct occurs, it is compensated by a growing resistance to the chaos of sheer dynamism, by a need for form and order. Diving down into the maelstrom, the soul must create the symbol that captures and expresses this dynamism. It is this process in the collective psyche that is felt or intuited by poets and artists whose main source of creativity is their perception of unconscious contents, and whose intellectual horizon is wide enough to discern the crucial problems of the age, or at least their outward aspects.

5. THE NATURE OF THE UNITING SYMBOL IN SPITTELER

434   Spitteler's *Prometheus* marks a psychological turning point: it illustrates the splitting apart of pairs of opposites that were once united. Prometheus, the artist, the servant of the soul, disappears from the world of men; while society itself, in obedience to a soulless moral routine, is delivered over to Behemoth, symbolizing the inimical, the destructive effect of an obsolete ideal. At the right moment Pandora, the soul, creates the saving jewel in the unconscious, but it does not benefit mankind because men fail to appreciate it. The change for the better comes about only through the intervention of Prometheus, who through insight and understanding brings first a few, and then many, individuals to their senses. It can hardly be doubted that this work of Spitteler's has its roots in the intimate life of its creator. But if it consisted only in a poetic elaboration of purely personal experiences, it would lack general validity and permanent value. It achieves both because it is not merely personal but is concerned with Spitteler's own experience of the collective problems of our time. On its first appearance it was bound to meet with the apathetic indifference of the public, for in any age the vast majority of men are

called upon to preserve and praise the *status quo*, thus helping to bring about the disastrous consequences which the creative spirit had sought to avert.

435 One important question still remains to be discussed, and that is the nature of this jewel, or symbol of renewed life, which the poet senses will bring joy and deliverance. We have already documented the "divine" nature of the jewel, and this clearly means that it contains possibilities for a new release of energy, for freeing the libido bound in the unconscious. The symbol always says: in some such form as this a new manifestation of life will become possible, a release from bondage and world-weariness. The libido that is freed from the unconscious by means of the symbol appears as a rejuvenated god, or actually as a new god; in Christianity, for instance, Jehovah is transformed into a loving Father with a higher and more spiritual morality. The motif of the god's renewal is universal and may be assumed to be familiar to most readers. Speaking of the redeeming power of the jewel, Pandora says: "I have heard of a race of men, full of sorrow and deserving of pity, and I have thought of a gift with which, if you graciously approve, I may assuage or solace their many sufferings."[174] The leaves of the tree that shelters the "wonder-child" sing: "For here is the presence, and here is bliss, and here is grace."[175]

436 The message of the wonder-child is love and joy, a paradisal state just as it was at the birth of Christ; while the greeting by the sun-goddess[176] and the miracle that all men, however far away, became "good" and were blessed at the moment of this birth[177] are attributes to the birth of the Buddha. From the "divine blessing" I will excerpt only this one significant passage: "May every man meet again those images he once beheld as a child in the shimmering dream of the future."[178] This is an affirmation that childhood fantasies strive for fulfilment; the images are not lost, but come again in ripe manhood and should be fulfilled. As Old Kule says in Barlach's *Der tote Tag*:

When I lie here at night, and the pillows of darkness weigh me down, at times there presses about me a light that resounds, visible

[174] Cf. *Prometheus and Epimetheus* (trans. Muirhead), p. 114.
[175] Ibid., p. 131.
[176] Ibid., pp. 135f.   [177] P. 132.   [178] Cf. ibid.

to my eyes and audible to my ears; and there about my bed stand
the lovely forms of a better future. Stiff they are as yet, but of a
radiant beauty, still sleeping; but he who shall awaken them would
make for the world a fairer face. He would be a hero who could do
that. . . . They stand not in the sun and nowhere are they lit by the
sun. But sometime they shall and must come forth from the night.
What a master-work that would be, to raise them up to the sun!
There they would live.[179]

437   Epimetheus, too, as we shall see, longs for the image, the
jewel; in his discourse on the statue of Herakles (the hero!)
he says: "This is the meaning of the statue . . . that a jewel shall
ripen over our heads, a jewel we must win."[180] But when the
jewel is rejected by Epimetheus and is brought to the priests,
they sing in just the same strain as Epimetheus did when he
longed for it: "O come, O God, with thy grace," only to repudiate and revile in the very next instant the heavenly jewel that
is offered them. The verses of the hymn sung by the priests can
easily be recognized as the Protestant hymn:

> Living Spirit, once again
> Come, Thou true eternal God!
> Nor thy power descend in vain,
> Make us ever Thine abode;
> So shall Spirit, joy and light
> Dwell in us, where all was night.
>
> . . .
>
> Spirit Thou of strength and power,
> Thou new Spirit God hath given,
> Aid us in temptation's hour,
> Make us perfect Thou for heaven.
> Arm us in the battle field,
> Leave us never there to yield.[181]

438   This hymn bears out our earlier argument. It is wholly in
keeping with the rationalistic nature of Epimethean creatures
that the same priests who sing this hymn should reject the new
spirit of life, the new symbol. Reason must always seek the so-

---

[179] Pp. 30f.

[180] Cf. *Prometheus and Epimetheus*, pp. 140f.

[181] *Lyra Germanica: Second Series*. Trans. from the *Gesangbuch der evange-
lisch-reformierten Kirchen der deutschsprachigen Schweiz* by Catherine Winkworth, pp. 53f.

lution in some rational, consistent, logical way, which is certainly justifiable enough in all normal situations but is entirely inadequate when it comes to the really great and decisive questions. It is incapable of creating the symbol, because the symbol is irrational. When the rational way proves to be a *cul de sac*—as it always does after a time—the solution comes from the side it was least expected. ("Can there any good thing come out of Nazareth?"[182]) Such is the psychological law underlying the Messianic prophecies, for instance. The prophecies themselves are projections of events foreshadowed in the unconscious. Because the solution is irrational, the coming of the Saviour is associated with an irrational and impossible condition: the pregnancy of a virgin (Isaiah 7:14). This prophecy, like many another, can be taken in two ways, as in *Macbeth* (IV, 1):

> Macbeth shall never vanquished be until
> Great Birnam wood to high Dunsinane hill
> Shall come against him.

439   The birth of the Saviour, the redeeming symbol, occurs just when one is least expecting it, and in the most improbable of places. Thus Isaiah says (53:1–3):

Who hath believed our report? and to whom is the arm of the Lord revealed?
   For he shall grow up before him as a tender plant, and as a root out of a dry ground: he hath no form nor comeliness; and when we shall see him, there is no beauty that we should desire him.
   He is despised and rejected of men; a man of sorrows, and acquainted with grief; and we hid as it were our faces from him; he was despised, and we esteemed him not.

440   Not only does the redeeming power come from the place where nothing is expected, it also appears in a form that has nothing to recommend it from the Epimethean point of view. Spitteler can hardly have borrowed consciously from the Bible when describing the rejection of the symbol, or we would note it in his words. It is more likely that he drew on the same depths from which prophets and creative artists call up the redeeming symbol.

182 John 1:46.

441   The coming of the Saviour signifies a union of opposites:

> The wolf also shall dwell with the lamb, and the leopard shall lie down with the kid; and the calf and the young lion and the fatling together; and a little child shall lead them.
> And the cow and the bear shall feed; their young ones shall lie down together: and the lion shall eat straw like the ox.
> And the sucking child shall play on the hole of the asp, and the weaned child shall put his hand on the cockatrice' den.[183]

442   The nature of the redeeming symbol is that of a child[184] (the "wonder-child" of Spitteler)—childlikeness or lack of prior assumptions is of the very essence of the symbol and its function. This childlike attitude necessarily brings with it another guiding principle in place of self-will and rational intentions, as overwhelmingly powerful in effect as it is divine. Since it is of an irrational nature, the new guiding principle appears in miraculous form:

> For unto us a child is born, unto us a son is given; and the government shall be on his shoulder; and his name shall be called Wonderful, Counsellor, The mighty God, The everlasting Father, the Prince of Peace.[185]

443   These honorific titles reproduce the essential qualities of the redeeming symbol. Its "divine" effect comes from the irresistible *dynamis* of the unconscious. The saviour is always a figure endowed with magical power who makes the impossible possible. The symbol is the middle way along which the opposites flow together in a new movement, like a watercourse bringing fertility after a long drought. The tension that precedes solution is likened in Isaiah to pregnancy:

> Like as a woman with child, that draweth near the time of her delivery, is in pain, and crieth out in her pangs, so we have been in thy sight, O Lord.
> We have been with child, we have been in pain, we have as it were brought forth wind; we have not wrought any deliverance in the earth; neither have the inhabitants of the world fallen.
> Thy dead men shall live, together with my dead body shall they arise.[186]

[183] Isaiah 11:6ff.
[184] Jung, "The Psychology of the Child Archetype."
[185] Isaiah 9:6.   [186] Isaiah 26:17-19.

444   Through the act of deliverance what was inert and dead comes to life; in psychological terms, the functions that have lain fallow and unfertile, and were unused, repressed, undervalued, despised, etc., suddenly burst forth and begin to live. It is precisely the least valued function that enables life, which was threatened with extinction by the differentiated function, to continue.[187] This motif recurs in the New Testament idea of the ἀποκατάστασις πάντων, restitution of all things (Acts 3:21), which is a more highly developed form of that worldwide version of the hero myth where the hero, on his exit from the belly of the whale, brings with him not only his parents but the whole company of those previously swallowed by the monster—what Frobenius calls the "universal slipping out."[188] The connection with the hero myth is preserved in Isaiah three verses later:

> In that day the Lord with his sore and great and strong sword shall punish leviathan the piercing serpent, even leviathan that crooked serpent; and he shall slay the dragon that is in the sea.[189]

445   With the birth of the symbol, the regression of libido into the unconscious ceases. Regression is converted into progression, the blockage starts to flow again, and the lure of the maternal abyss is broken. When Old Kule in Barlach's *Der tote Tag* says that he who awakened the sleeping images would be a hero, the mother replies: "He must first bury his mother."[190] I have fully documented the motif of the "mother dragon" in my earlier work,[191] so I may spare myself a repetition of it here. The blossoming of new life and fruitfulness where all was arid before is described in Isaiah 35:5ff.:

> Then the eyes of the blind shall be opened, and the ears of the deaf shall be unstopped.
> Then shall the lame man leap up as an hart, and the tongue of the

---

[187] Supra, pars. 111ff.

[188] *Das Zeitalter des Sonnengottes*. Cf. *Symbols of Transformation*, par. 309.

[189] Isaiah 27:1.

[190] P. 30. [Cf. Neumann, *The Origins and History of Consciousness*, pp. 165ff., 174, 186.—EDITORS.]

[191] *Symbols of Transformation*, Part II, chs. V and VII, esp. pars. 394, 379ff., 580. In Spitteler, the parallel of the slaying of Leviathan is the overpowering of Behemoth.

dumb sing: for in the wilderness shall waters break out, and streams in the desert.

And the parched ground shall become a pool, and the thirsty land springs of water: in the habitations of dragons, where each lay, shall be grass with reeds and rushes.

And an highway shall be there, and a way, and it shall be called the way of holiness; the unclean shall not pass over it. And this shall be unto you a straight way, so that fools shall not err therein.

The redeeming symbol is a highway, a way upon which life can move forward without torment and compulsion.

446   Hölderlin says in "Patmos":

> Near is God
> And hard to apprehend.
> But where danger is, there
> Arises salvation also.

That sounds as though the nearness of God were a danger, i.e., as though the concentration of libido in the unconscious were a danger to conscious life. And indeed this is so, for the more the libido is invested—or, to be more accurate, invests itself— in the unconscious, the greater becomes its influence or potency: all the rejected, disused, outlived functional possibilities that have been lost for generations come to life again and begin to exert an ever-increasing influence on the conscious mind, despite its desperate struggles to gain insight into what is happening. The saving factor is the symbol, which embraces both conscious and unconscious and unites them. For while the consciously disposable libido gets gradually used up in the differentiated function and is replenished more and more slowly and with increasing difficulty, the symptoms of inner disunity multiply and there is a growing danger of inundation and destruction by the unconscious contents, but all the time the symbol is developing that is destined to resolve the conflict. The symbol, however, is so intimately bound up with the dangerous and menacing aspect of the unconscious that it is easily mistaken for it, or its appearance may actually call forth evil and destructive tendencies. At all events the appearance of the redeeming symbol is closely connected with destruction and devastation. If the old were not ripe for death, nothing new would appear; and if the old were not injuriously blocking the way for the new, it could not and need not be rooted out.

447   This natural combination of psychological opposites is
found in Isaiah, where we are told that a virgin shall conceive
and bear a son, who shall be called Immanuel (7:14). Significantly, Immanuel (the redeeming symbol) means "God with
us," i.e., union with the latent *dynamis* of the unconscious.
The verses which immediately follow show what this union
portends:

For before the child shall know to refuse the evil and choose the
good, the land that thou abhorrest shall be forsaken of both her
kings.

And the Lord said to me, Take thee a great book, and write in it
with a man's pen: *Hasten to take the spoils, quickly take the prey.*[192]
. . . And I went to the prophetess, and she conceived, and bore a
son. And the Lord said to me: Call his name, *Hasten to take the
spoils, quickly take the prey.* For before the child know how to cry,
My father, My mother, the riches of Damascus and the spoil of
Samaria shall be taken away before the king of Assyria.

Forasmuch as this people refuseth the waters of Shiloah that go
softly . . . behold the Lord will bring upon them the waters of the
river, strong and many, even the king of Assyria, and all his glory;
and he shall come up over all his channels, and go over all his
banks, and he shall pass through Judah; he shall overflow and go
over, and he shall reach even to the neck; and the stretching out of
his wings shall fill the breadth of thy land, O Immanuel.[193]

448   I have shown in my earlier work[194] that the birth of the
god is threatened by the dragon, by the danger of inundation,
and infanticide. Psychologically, this means that the latent
dynamis of the unconscious may burst forth and overwhelm
consciousness. For Isaiah the danger is the foreign king, who
rules over a powerful and hostile country. The problem for
him is not, of course, psychological, but concrete because of its
complete projection. With Spitteler, on the contrary, the problem is a psychological one from the start, and hence detached
from the object, but it is none the less expressed in a form that
closely resembles Isaiah's, even though it may not have been
consciously borrowed.

449   The birth of the saviour is equivalent to a great catastro-

---

192 8:1 and 3 (AV): Maher-shalal-hash-baz.
193 Isaiah 7:16; 8:1, 3, 4; 8:6–8 (AV and DV, mod.).
194 *Symbols of Transformation*, Part II, chs. V–VII.

phe, because a new and powerful life springs up just where there had seemed to be no life and no power and no possibility of further development. It comes streaming out of the unconscious, from that unknown part of the psyche which is treated as nothing by all rationalists. From this discredited and rejected region comes the new afflux of energy, the renewal of life. But what is this discredited and rejected source of vitality? It consists of all those psychic contents that were repressed because of their incompatibility with conscious values—everything hateful, immoral, wrong, unsuitable, useless, etc., which means everything that at one time or another appeared so to the individual concerned. The danger now is that when these things reappear in a new and wonderful guise, they may make such an impact on him that he will forget or repudiate all his former values. What he once despised now becomes the supreme principle, and what was once truth now becomes error. This reversal of values is similar to the devastation of a country by floods.

450   Thus, in Spitteler, Pandora's heavenly gift brings evil to the country and its inhabitants, just as in the classical myth diseases streamed forth to ravage the land when Pandora opened her box. To understand why this should be so we must examine the nature of the symbol. The first to find the jewel were the peasants, as the shepherds were the first to greet the Saviour. They turned it about in their hands, "until in the end they were utterly dumbfounded by its bizarre, immoral, illicit appearance."[195] When they brought it to Epimetheus to examine, his conscience (which he kept in a wardrobe) sprang to the floor and hid itself under the bed in great alarm, "with impossible suspicions."

Like a crab goggling wickedly and malevolently brandishing its crooked claws, Conscience peered out from under the bed, and the nearer Epimetheus pushed the image, the further Conscience shrank back with gesticulations of disgust. And so it sulked there silently, uttering not a word or syllable, in spite of all the king's entreaties and petitions and inducements.[196]

451   Conscience, evidently, found the new symbol acutely distasteful. The king, therefore, bade the peasants bear the jewel to the priests.

[195] Cf. *Prometheus and Epimetheus*, p. 136.   [196] Cf. ibid., p. 142.

But hardly had Hiphil-Hophal [the high priest] glanced at the face of the image than he shuddered with disgust, and crossing his arms over his forehead as though to ward off a blow, he shouted: "Away with this mockery! For it is opposed to God and carnal is its heart and insolence flashes from its eyes."[197]

452   The peasants then brought the jewel to the academy, but the professors found it lacked "feeling and soul, and moreover it wanted in gravity, and above all had no guiding thought."[198] In the end the goldsmith found the jewel to be spurious and of common stuff. On the marketplace, where the peasants tried to get rid of it, the police descended on the image and cried out:

Is there no heart in your body and no conscience in your soul? How dare you expose before the eyes of all this stark, shameless, wanton piece of nakedness? . . . And now, away with you at once! And woe betide you if the sight of it has polluted our innocent children and lily-white wives![199]

453   The symbol is described by the poet as bizarre, immoral, illicit, outraging our moral feelings and our ideas of the spiritual and divine; it appeals to sensuality, is wanton, and liable to endanger public morals by provoking sexual fantasies. These attributes define something that is blatantly opposed to our moral values and aesthetic judgment because it lacks the higher feeling-values, and the absence of a "guiding thought" suggests the irrationality of its intellectual content. The verdict "opposed to God" might equally well be "anti-Christian," since this episode is set neither in antiquity nor in the East. By reason of its attributes, the symbol stands for the inferior functions, for psychic contents that are not acknowledged. Although it is nowhere stated, it is obvious that the "image" is of a naked human body—a "living form." It expresses the complete freedom to be what one is, and also the duty to be what one is. It is a symbol of man as he might be, the perfection of moral and aesthetic beauty, moulded by nature and not by some artificial ideal. To hold such an image before the eyes of present-day man can have no other effect than to release everything in him that lies captive and unlived. If only half of him is civilized and the other half barbarian, all his barbarism will be aroused, for a man's hatred is always concentrated on the

[197] Cf. p. 144.   [198] Cf. p. 146.   [199] Cf. p. 149.

thing that makes him conscious of his bad qualities. Hence the fate of the jewel was sealed the moment it appeared in the world. The dumb shepherd lad who first found it was half cudgelled to death by the enraged peasants, who in the end "hurled" the jewel into the street. Thus the redeeming symbol runs its brief but typical course. The parallel with the Passion is unmistakable, and the jewel's saviour-nature is further borne out by the fact that it appears only once every thousand years. The appearance of a saviour, a Saoshyant, or a Buddha is a rare phenomenon.

454   The end of the jewel is mysterious: it falls into the hands of a wandering Jew. "It was not a Jew of this world, and his clothes seemed to us exceedingly strange."[200] This peculiar Jew can only be *Ahasuerus*, who did not accept the actual Redeemer, and now, as it were, steals his image. The story of Anasuerus is a late Christian legend, which cannot be traced back earlier than the thirteenth century.[201] Psychologically, it sprang from a component of the personality or a charge of libido that could find no outlet in the Christian attitude to life and the world and was therefore repressed. The Jews were always a symbol for this, hence the persecution mania against the Jews in the Middle Ages. The idea of ritual murder is a projection, in acute form, of the rejection of the Redeemer, for one always sees the mote in one's own eye as the beam in one's brother's. The ritual murder idea also plays a part in Spitteler's story—the Jew steals the wonder-child from heaven. It is a mythologized projection of a dim realization that the workings of the Redeemer are constantly being frustrated by the presence of an unredeemed element in the unconscious. This unredeemed, untamed, barbarian element, which can only be held on a chain and cannot be allowed to run free, is projected upon those who have never accepted Christianity. There is an unconscious awareness of this intractable element whose existence we don't like to admit—hence the projection. In reality it is a part of ourselves that has contrived to escape the Christian process of domestication. The restlessness of the wandering Jew is a concretization of this unredeemed state.

200 Ibid., p. 164.
201 König, *Ahasver*. [Cf. *Symbols of Transformation*, par. 282.—EDITORS.]

455   The unredeemed element at once attracts to itself the new light, the energy of the new symbol. This is another way of expressing what we said earlier (pars. 449ff.) about the effect the symbol has on the psyche as a whole. It arouses all the repressed and unacknowledged contents, just as it provoked the "guardians of the marketplace" in Spitteler; and it has the same effect on Hiphil-Hophal, who, because of his unconscious resistance to his own religion, immediately emphasizes the ungodliness and carnality of the new symbol. The affect displayed in the rejection of the jewel equals the amount of repressed libido. With the moral degradation of the pure gift of heaven and its conversion into the lurid fantasies of the priests and police the ritual murder is complete. The appearance of the symbol has, nevertheless, not been entirely valueless. Although not accepted in its pure form, it is devoured by the archaic and undifferentiated forces of the unconscious (symbolized by Behemoth), assiduously supported by conscious morality and ideas of beauty. Thereupon the enantiodromia begins, the transformation of the hitherto valued into the worthless, and of the former good into the bad.

456   The kingdom of the good, ruled over by Epimetheus, had long been at enmity with the kingdom of Behemoth.[202] Behemoth and Leviathan are the two famous monsters of Jehovah from the Book of Job, symbolizing his mighty strength. As crude animal symbols they represent similar psychological forces in human nature.[203] Jehovah declaims (Job 40:10ff., DV):

> Behold Behemoth whom I made with thee. He eateth grass
> like an ox.
> His strength is in his loins, and his force in the navel of his belly.
> He setteth up his tail like a cedar: the sinews of his
> testicles are wrapped together.[204]
> His bones are like pipes of brass, his gristle like plates of iron.
> He is the beginning of the ways of God . . .

457   One should read these words attentively. This sheer *dynamis* is "the beginning of the ways of God," that is, of Jehovah, who in the New Testament sloughs off this form and

[202] Spitteler, p. 179.

[203] Cf. *Symbols of Transformation*, pars. 87ff. Also Schärf, *Satan in the Old Testament*, pp. 51, 127.

[204] Spitteler—significantly enough—makes Astarte the daughter of Behemoth.

ceases to be a nature-god. This means, psychologically, that the animal side of the libido stored up in the unconscious is permanently held in check by the Christian attitude; one half of God is repressed, or written down to man's debit account, and is ultimately consigned to the domain of the devil. Hence, when the unconscious *dynamis* starts welling up and "the ways of God" begin, God appears in the form of Behemoth.[205] One might even say that God presents himself in the devil's shape. These moral evaluations are optical illusions, however: the life force is beyond moral judgment. Meister Eckhart says:

> So if I say God is good, it is not true: *I* am good, God is not good. I go further: I am better than God! For only what is good can become better, and only what is better can become the best. God is not good, therefore he cannot become better; and since he cannot become better he cannot become the best. These three: good, better, best, are infinitely remote from God, who is above all.[206]

458   The immediate effect of the redeeming symbol is the union of opposites: the ideal realm of Epimetheus becomes one with the kingdom of Behemoth. That is to say, moral consciousness enters into a dangerous alliance with the unconscious contents and the libido associated with them. The "divine children," the highest values of humanity without which man would be an animal, are now entrusted to the care of Epimetheus. But the union with his unconscious opposite brings with it the danger of devastation and inundation—the values of consciousness are liable to be swamped by the unconscious *dynamis*. Had the jewel, the symbol of natural morality and beauty, been accepted at its face value instead of serving merely to stir up all the filthiness in the background of our "moral" culture, the divine children would not have been imperilled despite the alliance with Behemoth, for Epimetheus would always have been able to discriminate between the valuable and the worthless. But because the symbol appeared unacceptable to his one-sided, rationalistic, warped mentality, every standard of value fails. When the union of opposites nevertheless takes place on a higher plane, the danger of inundation and destruction necessarily follows because, characteristically, the antagonistic

205 Cf. Flournoy, "Une Mystique moderne."
206 Cf. Evans, I, p. 246.

tendencies get smuggled in under the cover of "correct ideas." Even the evil and pernicious can be rationalized and made to look aesthetic. Thus the conscious values are exchanged for sheer instinctuality and stupidity—one after another, the divine children are handed over to Behemoth. They are devoured by savage, barbarian tendencies that were formerly unconscious; hence Behemoth and Leviathan set up an *invisible whale* as a symbol of their power, while the corresponding symbol of the Epimethean realm is the *bird*. The whale, a denizen of the deep, is a well-known symbol of the devouring unconscious;[207] the bird, an inhabitant of the bright realm of the air, is a symbol of conscious thought,[208] of the (winged) ideal, and of the Holy Ghost (dove).

459   The final extinction of the good is prevented by the intervention of Prometheus. He delivers Messias, the last of the divine children, from the power of his enemy. Messias becomes heir to the divine kingdom, while Prometheus and Epimetheus, the personifications of the divided opposites, now united, withdraw to the seclusion of their "native valley." Both are relieved of sovereignty—Epimetheus because he was forced to renounce it, Prometheus because he never strove for it. In psychological terms, introversion and extraversion cease to dominate as exclusive principles, and consequently the psychic dissociation also ceases. In their stead a new function appears, symbolized by the divine child Messias, who had long lain sleeping. Messias is the mediator, the symbol of a new attitude in which the opposites are united. He is a child, a boy, the *puer aeternus* of the ancient prototype, heralding the rebirth and restitution (apocatastasis) of all that is lost. What Pandora brought to earth in the form of an image, and, being rejected of men, became the cause of their undoing, is fulfilled in him. This combination of symbols is frequently met with in analytical practice: a symbol emerging in dreams is rejected for the very reasons we have described, and even provokes an antagonistic reaction corresponding to the invasion of Behemoth. As a result of this conflict, the personality is levelled down to the basic characteristics that have been present since

---

[207] For further documentation see *Symbols of Transformation*, pars. 309ff., 375ff., 538n.

[208] [Cf. *Psychology and Alchemy*, par. 305.—EDITORS.]

birth, and that keep the mature personality in touch with the childhood sources of energy. But as Spitteler shows, the great danger is that instead of the symbol being accepted, the archaic instincts it arouses will be rationalized and put at the disposal of the traditional ways of thinking.

460   The English mystic William Blake says: "These two classes of men are always upon earth . . . the Prolific and the Devouring. . . . Religion is an endeavour to reconcile the two."[209] With these words of Blake, which summarize so simply the fundamental ideas of Spitteler and the whole of our previous discussion, I would like to close this chapter. If I have unduly expanded it, it was because I wanted to do full justice to the profusion of stimulating ideas that Spitteler offers us in *Prometheus and Epimetheus*, just as Schiller did in his *Letters*. I have, so far as possible, confined myself to essentials; indeed, I have had to pass over a large number of problems which would have to be considered in a comprehensive exposition of the material.

[209] "The Marriage of Heaven and Hell," *The Complete Writings of William Blake* (ed. Keynes), p. 155.

VI

THE TYPE PROBLEM IN PSYCHOPATHOLOGY

461   We now come to the work of a psychiatrist who made an attempt to single out two types from among the bewildering variety of mental disturbances that are generally grouped under the heading "psychopathic inferiority." This very extensive group includes all psychopathic borderline states that cannot be reckoned among the psychoses proper; that is, all the neuroses and all degenerate states such as intellectual, moral, affective, and other psychic inferiorities.

462   This attempt was made by Otto Gross, who in 1902 published a theoretical study entitled *Die zerebrale Sekundärfunktion*. It was the basic hypothesis of this work that led him to the conception of two psychological types.[1] Although the empirical material discussed by him is taken from the domain of psychopathic inferiority, there is no reason why the insights gained should not be carried over into the wider field of normal psychology. The unbalanced psychic state gives the investigator an almost exaggeratedly clear view of certain psychic phenomena which, very often, can only be dimly perceived within the limits of the normal. The abnormal state sometimes acts like a magnifying glass. Gross himself, in his final chapter, also extends his conclusions to a wider domain, as we shall see.

463   By the "secondary function" Gross understands a cerebral cell-process that comes into action after the "primary function" has taken place. The primary function would correspond to the actual performance of the cell, namely, the production of a positive psychic process, for example an idea. This performance is an energic process, presumably a discharge of chemical tension; in other words, it is a process of chemical decomposi-

---

[1] Gross gives a revised though essentially unaltered account of his types in his book *Über psychopathische Minderwertigkeiten*, pp. 27ff.

tion. After this acute discharge, which Gross calls the primary function, the secondary function comes into action. It is a process of recovery, a rebuilding through assimilation. This function will require for its operation a longer or shorter period depending on the intensity of the preceding discharge of energy. During this time the condition of the cell has altered; it is now in a state of stimulation, and this cannot remain without influence on the subsequent psychic processes. Processes that are especially highly-toned and charged with affect require an especially intense discharge of energy, and hence an especially prolonged period of recovery governed by the secondary function. The effect of the secondary function on the psychic process in general consists, according to Gross, in its specific and demonstrable influence on the subsequent course of association, in the sense that it restricts the choice of associations to the "theme" or "leading idea" represented by the primary function. And indeed, in my own experimental work (which was corroborated by several of my pupils), I was able to demonstrate statistically that *perseveration* followed in the train of ideas with a high feeling-tone.[2] My pupil Eberschweiler, in an investigation of language components,[3] has demonstrated this same phenomenon in assonances and agglutinations. Further, we know from experiences in pathology how frequently perseverations occur in the case of severe cerebral lesions, apoplexies, tumours, atrophic and other degenerative states. Such perseverations may well be ascribed to this retarded process of recovery. Gross' hypothesis thus has much to recommend it.

464   It is therefore only natural to ask whether there may not be individuals, or even types, in whom the period of recovery, the secondary function, lasts longer than in others, and if so, whether certain characteristic psychologies may not be traceable to this. A short secondary function, clearly, will influence far fewer consecutive associations in a given period of time than a long one. Hence the primary function can operate much more frequently. The psychological picture in such a case would show a constant and rapidly renewed readiness for action and reaction, a kind of *distractibility*, a tendency to

[2] *Studies in Word-Association.*
[3] "Untersuchungen über die sprachliche Komponente der Assoziation."

superficial associations and a lack of deeper, more concise ones, and a certain incoherence so far as an association is expected to be significant. On the other hand many new themes will crowd up in a given unit of time, though not at all intense or clearly focussed, so that heterogeneous ideas of varying value appear on the same niveau, thus giving the impression of a "levelling of ideas" (Wernicke). This rapid succession of primary functions necessarily precludes any real experience of the affective value of the ideas *per se*, with the result that the affectivity cannot be anything other than superficial. But, at the same time, this makes rapid adaptations and changes of attitude possible. The actual thought-process, or process of abstraction, naturally suffers when the secondary function is curtailed in this way, since abstraction requires a sustained contemplation of several initial ideas and their after-effects, and therefore a longer secondary function. Without this, there can be no intensification and abstraction of an idea or group of ideas.

465   The rapid recovery of the primary function produces a higher reactivity, extensive rather than intensive, leading to a prompt grasp of the immediate present in its superficial aspects, though not of its deeper meanings. A person of this type gives the impression of having an uncritical or unprejudiced attitude; we are struck by his readiness to oblige and by his understanding, or again we may find in him an unaccountable lack of consideration, tactlessness, and even brutality. That too facile gliding over the deeper meanings evokes the impression of blindness to everything not lying immediately on the surface. His quick reactivity has the appearance of presence of mind, of audacity to the point of foolhardiness, which from lack of criticism actually turns out to be an inability to realize danger. His rapidity of action looks like decisiveness; more often than not it is just blind impulse. Interference in other people's affairs is taken as a matter of course, and this comes all the more easily because of his ignorance of the emotional value of an idea or action and its effect on his fellow men. The ever renewed readiness for action has an adverse effect on the assimilation of perceptions and experiences; as a rule, memory is considerably impaired, because, in general, the associations that can be most readily be reproduced are those that have

become massively interlinked with others. Those that are relatively isolated become quickly submerged; for this reason it is infinitely more difficult to remember a series of meaningless, disconnected words than a poem. Excitability and an enthusiasm that soon fades are further characteristics of this type, also a certain lack of taste due to the rapid succession of heterogeneous contents and a failure to appreciate their differing emotional values. His thinking has more the character of a representation and orderly arrangement of contents than that of abstraction and synthesis.

466   In describing this type with a short secondary function I have followed Gross in all essentials, here and there transcribing it in terms of normal psychology. Gross calls this type "inferiority with shallow consciousness." If the excessively crass features are toned down to the normal, we get an overall picture in which the reader will easily recognize Jordan's "less emotional" type, i.e., the extravert. Gross deserves full credit for being the first to set up a simple and consistent hypothesis to account for this type.

467   Gross calls the opposite type "inferiority with contracted consciousness." In this type the secondary function is particularly intense and prolonged. It therefore influences the consecutive associations to a higher degree than in the other type. We may also suppose an intensified primary function, and hence a more extensive and complete cell-performance than with the extravert. A prolonged and intensified secondary function would be the natural consequence of this. As a result of this prolongation, the after-effect of the initial idea persists for a longer period. From this we get what Gross calls a "contractive effect": the choice of associations follows the path of the initial idea, resulting in a fuller realization or *approfondissement* of the "theme." The idea has a lasting influence, the impression goes deep. One disadvantage of this is that the associations are restricted to a narrow range, so that thinking loses much of its variety and richness. Nevertheless, the contractive effect aids synthesis, since the elements that have to be combined remain constellated long enough to make their abstraction possible. This restriction to one theme enriches the associations that cluster round it and consolidates one particular complex of ideas, but at the same time the complex is shut

off from everything extraneous and finds itself in isolation, a phenomenon which Gross (borrowing from Wernicke) calls "sejunction." One result of the sejunction of the complex is a multiplication of groups of ideas (or complexes) that have no connection with one another or only quite a loose one. Outwardly such a condition shows itself as a disharmonious or, as Gross calls it, a "sejunctive" personality. The isolated complexes exist side by side without any reciprocal influence; they do not interact, mutually balancing and correcting each other. Though firmly knit in themselves, with a logical structure, they are deprived of the correcting influence of complexes with a different orientation. Hence it may easily happen that a particularly strong and therefore particularly isolated and uninfluenceable complex becomes an "over-valued idea,"[4] a dominant that defies all criticism and enjoys complete autonomy, until it finally becomes an all-controlling factor manifesting itself as "spleen." In pathological cases it turns into an obsessive or paranoid idea, absolutely unshakable, that rules the individual's entire life. His whole mentality is subverted, becoming "deranged." This conception of the growth of a paranoid idea may also explain why, during the early stages, it can sometimes be corrected by suitable psychotherapeutic procedures which bring it into connection with other complexes that have a broadening and balancing influence.[5] Paranoiacs are very wary of associating disconnected complexes. They feel things have to remain neatly separated, the bridges between the complexes are broken down as much as possible by an over-precise and rigid formulation of the content of the complex. Gross calls this tendency "fear of association."[6]

468   The rigid inner cohesion of such a complex hampers all attempts to influence it from outside. The attempt is successful only when it is able to bind the complex to another complex as firmly and logically as it is bound in itself. The multiplication

[4] Elsewhere (*Psychopath. Minderw.*, p. 41) Gross draws a distinction, rightly, in my opinion, between the "over-valued idea" and what he calls the "over-valued complex." The latter is characteristic not only of this type, as Gross thinks, but also of the other. The "conflict complex" always has considerable value because of its high feeling-tone, no matter in which type it may appear.

[5] Bjerre, "Zur Radikalbehandlung der chronischen Paranoia," pp. 795ff.

[6] *Psychopath. Minderw.*, p. 40.

of insufficiently connected complexes naturally results in rigid seclusion from the outside world and a corresponding accumulation of libido within. Hence we regularly find an extraordinary concentration on inner processes, either on physical sensations or on intellectual processes, depending on whether the subject belongs to the sensation or to the thinking type. The personality seems inhibited, absorbed or distracted, "sunk in thought," intellectually lopsided, or hypochondriacal. In every case there is only a meagre participation in external life and a distinct tendency to solitude and fear of other people, often compensated by a special love of animals or plants. To make up for this, the inner processes are particularly active, because from time to time complexes which hitherto had little or no connection with one another suddenly "collide," thereby stimulating the primary function to intense activity which, in its turn, releases a prolonged secondary function that amalgamates the two complexes. One might think that all complexes would at some time or other collide in this way, thus producing a general uniformity and cohesion of psychic contents. Naturally, this wholesome result could only come about if in the meantime all change in external life were arrested. But since this is not possible, fresh stimuli continually arrive and initiate secondary functions, which intersect and confuse the inner lines. Accordingly this type has a decided tendency to fight shy of external stimuli, to keep out of the way of change, to stop the steady flow of life until all is amalgamated within. Pathological cases show this tendency too; they hold aloof from everything and try to lead the life of a recluse. But only in mild cases will the remedy be found in this way. In all severe ones, the only remedy is to reduce the intensity of the primary function, but this is a chapter in itself, and one which we have already touched on in our discussion of Schiller's *Letters*.

469   It is clear that this type is distinguished by quite peculiar phenomena in the realm of affect. We have seen how the subject realizes the associations set in motion by the initial idea. He carries out a full and coherent association of the material relevant to the theme, i.e., he associates all material that is not already linked to other complexes. When a stimulus hits on a complex, the result is either a violent explosion of affect, or, if

the isolation of the complex is complete, it is entirely negative. But should realization take place, all the affective values are unleashed; there is a strong emotional reaction with a prolonged after-effect. Very often this cannot be seen from outside, but it bores in all the deeper. The emotional reverberations prey on the subject's mind and make him incapable of responding to new stimuli until the emotion has faded away. An accumulation of stimuli becomes unbearable, so he wards them off with violent defence reactions. Whenever there is a marked accumulation of complexes, a chronic attitude of defence usually develops, deepening into mistrust and in pathological cases into persecution mania.

470   The sudden explosions, alternating with defensiveness and periods of taciturnity, can give the personality such a bizarre appearance that such people become an enigma to everyone in their vicinity. Their absorption in themselves leaves them at a loss when presence of mind or swift action is demanded. Embarrassing situations often arise from which there seems no way out—one reason the more for shunning society. Moreover the occasional outbursts of affect play havoc with their relations to others, and, because of their embarrassment and helplessness, they feel incapable of retrieving the situation. This awkwardness in adapting leads to all sorts of unfortunate experiences which inevitably produce a feeling of inferiority or bitterness, and even of hatred that is readily directed at those who were the actual or supposed authors of their misfortunes. Their affective inner life is very intense, and the manifold emotional reverberations linger on as an extremely fine gradation and perception of feeling-tones. They have a peculiar emotional sensitivity, revealing itself to the outside world as a marked timidity and uneasiness in the face of emotional stimuli, and in all situations that might evoke them. This touchiness is directed primarily against the emotional conditions in their environment. All brusque expressions of opinion, emotional declarations, playing on the feelings, etc., are avoided from the start, prompted by the subject's fear of his own emotion, which in turn might start off a reverberating impression he might not be able to master. This sensitivity may easily develop over the years into melancholy, due to the feeling of being cut off from life. In fact, Gross considers melancholy to be especially char-

acteristic of this type.[7] He also emphasizes that the realization of affective values easily leads to emotional judgments, to "taking things too seriously." The prominence given in this picture to inner processes and the emotional life at once reveals the introvert. Gross's description is much fuller than Jordan's sketch of the "impassioned type," though the latter, in its main features, must be identical with the type described by Gross.

471 In chapter V of his book Gross observes that, within the limits of the normal, both types of inferiority represent *physiological differences of individuality*. The shallow extensive or the narrow intensive consciousness is therefore a difference of character.[8] According to Gross, the type with a shallow consciousness is essentially practical, because of his rapid adaptation to circumstances. His inner life does not predominate, having no part to play in the formation of the "great ideational complexes." "They are energetic propagandists for their own personality, and, on a higher level, they also work for the great ideas handed down from the past."[9] Gross asserts that the emotional life of this type is primitive, though at a higher level it becomes organized through "the taking over of ready-made ideals from outside." In this way, Gross says, his activity can become "heroic," but "it is always banal." "Heroic" and "banal" scarcely seem compatible with one another. But Gross shows us at once what he means: in this type the connection between the erotic complex and the other complexes of ideas, whether aesthetic, ethical, philosophical, or religious, which make up the contents of consciousness, is not sufficiently developed. Freud would say that the erotic complex has been repressed. For Gross the marked presence of this connection is the "authentic sign of a superior nature" (p. 61). It requires for its development a prolonged secondary function, because a synthesis of the contents can be achieved only through *approfondissement* and their prolonged retention in consciousness. The taking over of conventional ideals may force sexuality into socially useful paths, but it "never rises above the level of triviality." This somewhat harsh judgment becomes explicable in the light of the extraverted character: the extravert orients

[7] Ibid., p. 37.

[8] *Die zerebrale Sekundärfunktion*, pp. 58f.

[9] Cf. supra, par. 265, Jordan's remarks on the Extraverted Man.

himself exclusively by external data, so that his psychic activity consists mainly in his preoccupation with such things. Hence little or nothing is left over for the ordering of his inner life. It has to submit as a matter of course to determinants accepted from without. Under these circumstances, no connection between the more highly and the less developed functions can take place, for this demands a great expense of time and trouble; it is a lengthy and difficult labour of self-education which cannot possibly be achieved without introversion. But the extravert lacks both time and inclination for this; moreover he is hampered by the same unconcealed distrust of his inner world which the introvert feels for the outer world.

472   One should not imagine, however, that the introvert, thanks to his greater synthetizing capacity and ability to realize affective values, is thereby equipped to complete the synthesis of his own individuality without further ado—in other words, to establish once and for all a harmonious connection between the higher and lower functions. I prefer this formulation to Gross's, which maintains that it is solely a question of sexuality, for it seems to me that other instincts besides sex are involved. Sexuality is of course a very frequent form of expression for crude and untamed instincts, but so too is the striving for power in all its manifold aspects. Gross coined the term "sejunctive personality" for the introvert in order to emphasize the peculiar difficulty this type has in integrating his complexes. His synthetizing capacity merely serves in the first place to build up complexes that, so far as possible, are isolated from each other. But such complexes positively hinder the development of a higher unity. Thus the sexual complex, or the egoistic striving for power, or the search for pleasure, remains just as isolated and unconnected with other complexes in the introvert as in the extravert. I remember the case of an introverted, highly intellectual neurotic who spent his time alternating between the loftiest flights of transcendental idealism and the most squalid suburban brothels, without any conscious admission of a moral or aesthetic conflict. The two things were utterly distinct as though belonging to different spheres. The result, naturally, was an acute compulsion neurosis.

473   We must bear this criticism in mind when following Gross's account of the type with intensive consciousness. Intensive

consciousness is, as Gross says, "the foundation of the intro-spective individuality." Because of the strong contractive effect, external stimuli are always regarded from the stand-point of some idea. Instead of the impulse towards practical life there is a "drive for inwardness." "Things are conceived not as individual phenomena but as partial ideas or com-ponents of the great ideational complexes." This view accords with what we said earlier in our discussion of the nominalist and realist standpoints and the Platonic, Megarian, and Cynic schools in antiquity. It is easy to see from Gross's argument what the difference is between the two standpoints: the [extra-verted] man with the short secondary function has many loosely connected primary functions operating in a given space of time, so that he is struck more particularly by the individual phenomenon. For him universals are only names lacking real-ity. But for the [introverted] man with the prolonged second-ary function, the inner facts, abstractions, ideas, or universals always occupy the foreground; for him they are the only true realities, to which he *must* relate all individual phenomena. He is therefore by nature a realist (in the Scholastic sense). Since, for the introvert, the way he thinks about things always takes precedence over the perception of externals, he is inclined to be a relativist.[10] Harmony in his surroundings gives him espe-cial pleasure;[11] it reflects his own inner urge to harmonize his isolated complexes. He avoids all "uninhibited behaviour" be-cause it might easily lead to disturbing stimuli (explosions of affect must of course be excepted). His social *savoir faire* is poor because of his absorption in his inner life. The predomi-nance of his own ideas prevents him from taking over the ideas or ideals of others. The intense inner elaboration of the com-plexes gives them a pronounced individual character. "The emotional life is frequently of no use socially, but is always individual."[12]

474   We must subject this statement to a thorough criticism, for it contains a problem which, in my experience, always gives rise to the greatest misunderstandings between the types. The introverted intellectual, whom Gross obviously has in mind here, outwardly shows as little feeling as possible, he entertains logically correct views and tries to do the right things in the

[10] *Die zerebrale Sekundärfunktion*, p. 63.
[11] Ibid., p. 64.   [12] Ibid., p. 65.

first place because he has a natural distaste for any display of feeling and in the second because he is fearful lest by incorrect behaviour he should arouse disturbing stimuli, the affects of his fellow men. He is afraid of disagreeable affects in others because he credits others with his own sensitiveness; furthermore, he is always distressed by the quickness and volatility of the extravert. He bottles up his feeling inside him, so that it sometimes swells into a passion of which he is only too painfully aware. His tormenting emotions are well known to him. He compares them with the feelings displayed by others, principally, of course, with those of the extraverted feeling type, and finds that his "feelings" are quite different from those of other men. Hence he gets round to thinking that his feelings (or, more correctly, emotions) are unique or, as Gross says, "individual." It is natural that they should differ from the feelings of the extraverted feeling type, because the latter are a differentiated instrument of adaptation and therefore lack the "genuine passion" which characterizes the deeper feelings of the introverted thinking type. But passion, as an elemental instinctive force, possesses little that is individual—it is something common to all men. Only what is differentiated can be individual. In the case of intense emotions, type differences are instantly obliterated in the "human-all-too-human." In my view, the extraverted feeling type has really the chief claim to individualized feeling, because his feelings are differentiated; but he falls into the same delusion in regard to his thinking. He has thoughts that torment him. He compares them with the thoughts expressed by the other people around him, chiefly those of the introverted thinking type. He discovers that his thoughts have little in common with them; he may therefore regard them as individual and himself, perhaps, as an original thinker, or he may repress his thoughts altogether, since no one else thinks the same. In reality they are thoughts which everybody has but are seldom uttered. In my view, therefore, Gross's statement springs from a subjective delusion, though one that is the general rule.

475   "The heightened contractive power enables one to get absorbed in things to which no immediate vital interest is attached."[13] Here Gross hits on an essential feature of the intro-

[13] Ibid.

verted mentality: the introvert delights in elaborating his thoughts for their own sake, regardless of external reality. This is both an advantage and a danger. It is a great advantage to be able to develop a thought into an abstraction, freed from the confines of the senses. The danger is that it will be removed altogether from the sphere of practical applicability and lose its vital value. The introvert is always in danger of getting too far away from life and of viewing things too much under their symbolic aspect. This is also stressed by Gross. The extravert is in no better plight, though for him matters are different. He has the capacity to curtail the secondary function to such an extent that he experiences practically nothing but a succession of positive primary functions: he is nowhere attached to anything, but soars above reality in a kind of intoxication; things are no longer seen as they are but are used merely as stimulants. This capacity is an advantage in that it enables him to manoeuvre himself out of many difficult situations ("he who hesitates is lost"), but, since it so often leads to inextricable chaos, it finally ends in catastrophe.

476 From the extraverted type Gross derives what he calls the "civilizing genius," and from the introverted type the "cultural genius." The former he equates with "practical achievement," the latter with "abstract invention." In the end Gross expresses his conviction that our age stands in especial need of the contracted, intensive consciousness, in contrast to former ages when consciousness was shallower and more extensive. "We delight in the ideal, the profound, the symbolic. Through simplicity to harmony—that is the art of the highest culture."[14]

477 Gross wrote these words in 1902. And now? If one were to express an opinion at all, one would have to say that we obviously need both civilization *and* culture,[15] a shortening of the secondary function for the one, and its prolongation for the other. We cannot create one without the other, and we must admit, unfortunately, that modern humanity lacks both. Where there is too much of the one there is too little of the other, if we want to put it more cautiously. The continual harping on progress has by now become rather suspect.

14 Ibid., pp. 68f.
15 [Cf. supra, par. 110, n. 8.—TRANSLATOR.]

478   In conclusion I would like to remark that Gross's views coincide substantially with my own. Even my terms "extraversion" and "introversion" are justified in the light of his conceptions. It only remains for us to make a critical examination of Gross's basic hypothesis, the concept of the secondary function.

479   It is always a risky business to frame physiological or "organic" hypotheses with respect to psychological processes. There was a regular mania for this at the time of the great successes in brain research, and the hypothesis that the pseudopodia of the brain-cells withdrew during sleep is by no means the most absurd of those that were taken seriously and deemed worthy of "scientific" discussion. People were quite justified in speaking of a veritable "brain mythology." I have no desire to treat Gross's hypothesis as another "brain myth"—its empirical value is too great for that. It is an excellent working hypothesis, and one that has received due recognition in other quarters as well. The concept of the secondary function is as simple as it is ingenious. It enables one to reduce a very large number of complex psychic phenomena to a satisfying formula—phenomena whose diversity would have resisted simple reduction and classification under any other hypothesis. It is indeed such a happy one that, as always, one is tempted to overestimate its range of application. This, unfortunately, is rather limited. We will entirely disregard the fact that the hypothesis in itself is only a postulate, since no one has ever seen a secondary function of the brain cells, and no one could demonstrate how and why it has in principle the same contractive effect on subsequent associations as the primary function, which is by definition essentially different from the secondary function. There is a further fact which in my opinion carries even greater weight: the psychological attitude in one and the same individual can change its habits in a very short space of time. But if the duration of the secondary function has a physiological or organic character, it must surely be regarded as more or less constant. It could not then be subject to sudden change, for such changes are never observed in a physiological or organic character, pathological changes excepted. But, as I have pointed out more than once, introversion and extraversion are not traits of *character* at all but *mechanisms*, which can, as it

were, be switched on or off at will. Only from their habitual predominance do the corresponding characters develop. The predilection one way or the other no doubt depends on the inborn disposition, but this is not always the decisive factor. I have frequently found environmental influences to be just as important. In one case in my experience, it even happened that a man with markedly extravert behaviour, while living in close proximity to an introvert, changed his attitude and became quite introverted when he later came into contact with a pronounced extraverted personality. I have repeatedly observed how quickly personal influences can alter the duration of the secondary function even in a well-defined type, and how the previous condition re-establishes itself as soon as the alien influence is removed.

480   With such experiences in mind, we should, I think, direct our attention more to the nature of the primary function. Gross himself lays stress on the special prolongation of the secondary function in the wake of strongly feeling-toned ideas,[16] thus showing its dependence on the primary function. There is, in fact, no plausible reason why one should base a theory of types on the duration of the secondary function; it could be based just as well on the *intensity of the primary function*, since the duration of the secondary function is obviously dependent on the intensity of the cell-performance and on the expenditure of energy. It might be objected that the duration of the secondary function depends on the rapidity of cell recovery, and that there are individuals with especially prompt cerebral assimilation as opposed to others who are less favoured. In that case the brain of the extravert must possess a greater capacity for cell recovery than that of the introvert. But such a very improbable assumption lacks all proof. What is known to us of the actual causes of the prolonged secondary function is limited to the fact that, leaving pathological conditions aside, the special intensity of the primary function results, quite logically, in a prolongation of the secondary function. That being so, the real problem would lie with the primary function and might be resolved into the question: how comes it that in one person the primary function is intense,

16 Ibid., p. 12. See also *Psychopath. Minderw.*, pp. 30, 37.

while in another it is weak? By shifting the problem to the primary function, we have to account for its varying intensity, which does indeed alter very rapidly. It is my belief that this is an energic phenomenon, dependent on a general *attitude*.

481   The intensity of the primary function seems to me directly dependent on the degree of tension in the propensity to act. If the psychic tension is high, the primary function will be particularly intense and will produce corresponding results. When with increasing fatigue the tension slackens, distractibility and superficiality of association appear, and finally "flight of ideas," a condition characterized by a weak primary and a short secondary function. The general psychic tension (if we discount physiological causes, such as relaxation, etc.) is dependent on extremely complex factors, such as mood, attention, expectancy, etc., that is to say, on value judgments which in their turn are the resultants of all the antecedent psychic processes. By these judgments I mean not only logical judgments but also judgments of feeling. Technically, the general tension could be expressed in the energic sense as *libido,* but in its psychological relation to consciousness we must express it in terms of *value.* An intense primary function is a manifestation of libido, i.e., it is a highly charged energic process. But it is also a psychological value; hence we term the trains of association resulting from it valuable in contrast to those which are the result of a weak contractive effect, and these are valueless because of their superficiality.

482   A tense attitude is in general characteristic of the introvert, while a relaxed, easy attitude distinguishes the extravert.[17] Exceptions, however, are frequent, even in one and the same individual. Give an introvert a thoroughly congenial, harmonious milieu, and he relaxes into complete extraversion, so that one begins to wonder whether one may not be dealing with an extravert. But put an extravert in a dark and silent room, where all his repressed complexes can gnaw at him, and he will get into such a state of tension that he will jump at the slightest stimulus. The changing situations of life can have the same effect of momentarily reversing the type, but the basic

---

[17] This tension or relaxation can sometimes be perceived even in the muscle tone. Usually one can see it in the facial expression.

attitude is not as a rule permanently altered. In spite of occasional extraversion the introvert remains what he was before, and the extravert likewise.

483   To sum up: the primary function is in my view more important than the secondary. The intensity of the primary function is the decisive factor. It depends on the general psychic tension, i.e., on the amount of accumulated, disposable libido. The factors determining this accumulation are the complex resultants of all the antecedent psychic states—mood, attention, affect, expectancy, etc. Introversion is characterized by general tension, an intense primary function and a correspondingly long secondary function; extraversion by general relaxation, a weak primary function and a correspondingly short secondary function.

VII

THE TYPE PROBLEM IN AESTHETICS

484   It stands to reason that every province of the human mind directly or indirectly concerned with psychology will have its contribution to make to the problem under discussion. Now that we have listened to the philosopher, the poet, the observer of men and the physician, let us hear what the aesthetician has to say.

485   Aesthetics by its very nature is applied psychology and has to do not only with the aesthetic qualities of things but also —and perhaps even more—with the psychological question of the aesthetic attitude. A fundamental problem like the contrast between introversion and extraversion could not long escape the attention of the aesthetician, because the way in which art and beauty are sensed by different individuals differs so widely that one could not fail to be struck by it. Aside from the numerous individual peculiarities of attitude, some of them more or less unique, there are two basic antithetical forms which Worringer has described as *abstraction* and *empathy (Einfühlung)*.[1] His definition of empathy derives principally from Lipps. For Lipps, empathy is "the objectification of myself in an object distinct from myself, no matter whether the thing objectified merits the name 'feeling' or not." "By apperceiving an object, I experience, as though issuing from it or inherent in it as something apperceived, an impulse towards a particular mode of inner behaviour. This has the appearance of being communicated to me by the object."[2] Jodl interprets it as follows:

The sensuous image produced by the artist not only serves to bring to our minds kindred experiences by the laws of association. Since

[1] *Abstraction and Empathy* (trans. Bullock).
[2] *Leitfaden der Psychologie*, pp. 193f.

289

it is subject to the general law of externalization[3] and appears as something outside ourselves, we simultaneously project into it the inner processes it evokes in us, thereby endowing it with aesthetic animation [*Beseelung*]—a term that may be preferred to *Einfühlung* because, in this introjection of one's own inner state into the image, it is not feeling alone that is involved, but inner processes of all kinds.[4]

486   Wundt reckons empathy among the elementary processes of assimilation.[5] It is therefore a kind of perceptive process, characterized by the fact that, through feeling, some essential psychic content is projected into the object, so that the object is assimilated to the subject and coalesces with him to such an extent that he feels himself, as it were, in the object. This happens when the projected content is associated to a higher degree with the subject than with the object. He does not, however, feel himself projected into the object; rather, the "empathized" object appears animated to him, as though it were speaking to him of its own accord. It should be noted that in itself projection is usually an unconscious process not under conscious control. On the other hand it is possible to imitate the projection consciously by means of a conditional sentence —for instance, "if you were my father"—thus bringing about the situation of empathy. As a rule, the projection transfers unconscious contents into the object, for which reason empathy is also termed "transference" (Freud) in analytical psychology. Empathy, therefore, is a form of extraversion.

487   Worringer defines the aesthetic experience of empathy as follows: "Aesthetic enjoyment is objectified self-enjoyment."[6] Consequently, only a form one can empathize with is beautiful. Lipps says: "Only so far as this empathy extends are forms beautiful. Their beauty is simply my ideal having free play in them."[7] According to this, any form one cannot empathize with would be ugly. But here the theory of empathy reaches its limitations, for, as Worringer points out, there are art-forms to which the empathetic attitude cannot be applied. Specifi-

[3] By externalization Jodl means the localizing of sense-perception in space. We neither hear sounds in the ear nor see colours in the eye, but in the spatially localized object. Jodl, *Lehrbuch der Psychologie*, II, p. 223.

[4] Ibid., p. 396.

[5] *Grundzüge der physiologischen Psychologie*, III, p. 191.

[6] *Abstraction and Empathy*, p. 5.   [7] *Aesthetik*, p. 247.

cally, one might mention the oriental and exotic art-forms as examples. In the West, long tradition has established "natural beauty and verisimilitude" as the criterion of beauty in art, since this is the criterion and essential character of Graeco-Roman and occidental art in general (with the exception of certain stylized medieval forms).

488   Since antiquity, our general attitude to art has always been empathic, and for this reason we designate as beautiful only those things we can empathize with. If the art-form is opposed to life, if it is inorganic or abstract, we cannot feel our own life in it. "What I feel myself into is life in general," says Lipps. We can empathize only with organic form—form that is true to nature and has the will to live. And yet another art-principle undoubtedly exists, a style that is opposed to life, that denies the will to live, but nevertheless lays a claim to beauty. When art produces life-denying, inorganic, abstract forms, there can no longer be any question of the will to create arising out of the need for empathy; it is rather a need that is directly opposed to empathy—in other words, a tendency to suppress life. Worringer says: "This counter-pole to the need for empathy appears to us to be the urge to abstraction."[8] As to the psychology of this urge to abstraction, Worringer continues:

Now, what are the psychic preconditions for the urge to abstraction? Among those peoples where it exists we must look for them in their feeling about the world, in their psychic attitude towards the cosmos. Whereas the precondition for the urge to empathy is a happy pantheistic relationship of confidence between man and the phenomena of the external world, the urge to abstraction is the outcome of a great inner uneasiness inspired in man by these phenomena, and its religious counterpart is the strongly transcendental colouring of all ideas. We might describe this state as an immense spiritual dread of space. When Tibullus says, *primum in mundo fecit deus timorem* [the first thing God made in the world was fear],[9] this same feeling of fear may also be assumed to be the root of artistic creation.[10]

[8] *Abstraction and Empathy*, p. 14.

[9] [Worringer was mistaken about both the author and the quotation. The above words cannot be traced in Tibullus. But the following may be found in Statius (*Thebaid*, Book 3, line 661): "Primus in orbe deos fecit timor" (fear was what first brought gods into the world). This, obviously, expresses the sense of Worringer's argument.—EDITORS.]

[10] Cf. *Abstraction and Empathy*, p. 15.

489   It is indeed true that empathy presupposes a subjective attitude of confidence, or trustfulness towards the object. It is a readiness to meet the object halfway, a subjective assimilation that brings about a good understanding between subject and object, or at least simulates it. A passive object allows itself to be assimilated subjectively, but its real qualities are in no way altered in the process; they are merely veiled, and may even be violated, because of the transference. Empathy can create similarities and seemingly common qualities which have no real existence in themselves. It is understandable, therefore, that the possibility of another kind of aesthetic relation to the object must also exist, an attitude that does not go to meet the object halfway, but rather withdraws from it and seeks to secure itself against the influence of the object by creating in the subject a psychic activity whose function it is to neutralize the effect of the object.

490   Empathy presupposes that the object is, as it were, empty, and seeks to imbue it with life. Abstraction, on the other hand, presupposes that the object is alive and active, and seeks to withdraw from its influence. The abstracting attitude is centripetal, i.e., introverting. Worringer's conception of abstraction therefore corresponds to the introverted attitude. It is significant that Worringer describes the influence of the object as fear or dread. The abstracting attitude endows the object with a threatening or injurious quality against which it has to defend itself. This seemingly *a priori* quality is doubtless a projection, but a negative one. We must therefore suppose that abstraction is preceded by an unconscious act of projection which transfers negative contents to the object.

491   Since empathy, like abstraction, is a conscious act, and since the latter is preceded by an unconscious projection, we may reasonably ask whether an unconscious act may not also precede empathy. As the essence of empathy is the projection of subjective contents, it follows that the preceding unconscious act must be the opposite—a neutralizing of the object that renders it inoperative. In this way the object is emptied, so to speak, robbed of its spontaneous activity, and thus made a suitable receptacle for subjective contents. The empathizing subject wants to feel his own life in the object; hence the independence of the object and the difference between it and the subject must not be too great. As a result of the unconscious act

that precedes empathy, the sovereignty of the object is depotentiated, or rather it is overcompensated, because the subject immediately gains ascendency over the object. This can only happen unconsciously, through an unconscious fantasy that either devalues and depotentiates the object or enhances the value and importance of the subject. Only in this way can that difference of potential arise which empathy needs in order to convey subjective contents into the object.

492   The man with the abstracting attitude finds himself in a frighteningly animated world that seeks to overpower and smother him. He therefore withdraws into himself, in order to think up a saving formula calculated to enhance his subjective value at least to the point where he can hold his own against the influence of the object. The man with the empathetic attitude finds himself, on the contrary, in a world that needs his subjective feeling to give it life and soul. He animates it with himself, full of trust; but the other retreats mistrustfully before the daemonism of objects, and builds up a protective anti-world composed of abstractions.

493   If we recall what was said in the preceding chapter, it is easy to see that empathy corresponds to the mechanism of extraversion, and abstraction to that of introversion. "The great inner uneasiness inspired in man by the phenomena of the external world" is nothing other than the introvert's fear of all stimuli and change, occasioned by his deeper sensitivity and powers of realization. His abstractions serve the avowed purpose of confining the irregular and changeable within fixed limits. It goes without saying that this essentially magical procedure is found in full flower in the art of primitives, whose geometrical patterns have a magical rather than an aesthetic value. Worringer rightly says of Oriental art:

> Tormented by the confusion and flux of the phenomenal world, these people were dominated by an immense need for repose. The enjoyment they sought in art consisted not so much in immersing themselves in the things of the outside world and finding pleasure there, as in raising the individual object out of its arbitrary and seemingly fortuitous existence, immortalizing it by approximation to abstract forms, and so finding a point of repose amid the ceaseless flux of appearances.[11]

These abstract, regular forms are not merely the highest, they are

11 Cf. ibid., p. 16.

the only forms in which man may find repose in face of the monstrous confusion of the world.[12]

494   As Worringer says, it is precisely the Oriental art-forms and religions that display this abstracting attitude to the world. To the Oriental, therefore, the world must appear very different from what it does to the Occidental, who animates it with his empathy. For the Oriental, the object is imbued with life from the start and has ascendency over him; therefore he withdraws into a world of abstraction. For an illuminating insight into the Oriental attitude, we may turn to the "Fire Sermon" of the Buddha:

All is on fire. The eye and all the senses are on fire, with the fire of passion, the fire of hate, the fire of delusion; the fire is kindled by birth, old age, and death, by pain and lamentation, by sorrow, suffering, and despair. . . . The whole world is in flames, the whole world is wrapped in smoke, the whole world is consumed by fire, the whole world trembles.[13]

495   It is this fearful and sorrowful vision of the world that forces the Buddhist into his abstracting attitude, just as, according to legend, a similar impression started the Buddha on his life's quest. The dynamic animation of the object as the impelling cause of abstraction is strikingly expressed in the Buddha's symbolic language. This animation does not come from empathy, but from an unconscious projection that actually exists *a priori*. The term "projection" hardly conveys the real meaning of this phenomenon. Projection is really an act that happens, and not a condition existing *a priori*, which is what we are obviously dealing with here. It seems to me that Lévy-Bruhl's *participation mystique* is more descriptive of this condition, since it aptly formulates the primordial relation of the primitive to the object. His objects have a dynamic animation, they are charged with soul-stuff or soul-force (and not always possessed of souls, as the animist theory supposes), so that they have a direct psychic effect upon him, producing what is practically a dynamic identification with the object. In certain primitive languages articles of personal use have a gender denoting "alive" (the suffix of animation). With the

12 Cf. ibid., p. 19.
13 Condensed from Warren, *Buddhism in Translations*, p. 352.

abstracting attitude it is much the same, for here too the object is alive and autonomous from the beginning and in no need of empathy; on the contrary, it has such a powerful effect that the subject is forced into introversion. Its strong libido investment comes from its *participation mystique* with the subject's own unconscious. This is clearly expressed in the words of the Buddha: the universal fire is identical with the fire of libido, with the subject's burning passion, which appears to him as an object because it is not differentiated into a disposable function.

496   Abstraction thus seems to be a function that is at war with the original state of *participation mystique*. Its purpose is to break the object's hold on the subject. It leads on the one hand to the creation of art-forms, and on the other to knowledge of the object. Empathy too is as much an organ of artistic creation as of cognition. But it functions on a quite different level from abstraction. Just as the latter is based on the magical significance and power of the object, the basis of empathy is the magical significance of the subject, who gains power over the object by means of *mystical identification*. The primitive is in a similar position: he is magically influenced by the power of the fetish, yet at the same time he is the magician and accumulator of magical power who charges the fetish with potency. An example of this is the *churinga* rite of the Australian aborigines.[14]

497   The unconscious depotentiation that precedes the act of empathy gives the object a permanently lower value, as in the case of abstraction. Since the unconscious contents of the empathetic type are identical with the object and make it appear inanimate,[15] empathy is needed in order to cognize the nature of the object. One might speak in this case of a continual unconscious abstraction which "depsychizes" the object. All abstraction has this effect: it kills the independent activity of the object in so far as this is magically related to the psyche of the subject. The abstracting type does it quite consciously, as a defence against the magical influence of the object. The inertness of objects also explains the trustful relationship of the empath-

[14] Cf. Spencer and Gillen, *The Northern Tribes of Central Australia.*
[15] Because the unconscious contents of the empathetic type are themselves relatively unactivated.

etic type to the world; there is nothing that could exert a hostile influence or oppress him, since he alone gives the object life and soul, though to his conscious mind the converse would seem to be true. For the abstracting type, on the other hand, the world is filled with potent and dangerous objects that inspire him with fear and a consciousness of his own impotence; he withdraws from any too intimate contact with the world, in order to weave those thoughts and formulas with which he hopes to gain the upper hand. His psychology, therefore, is that of the under-dog, whereas the empathetic type faces the world with confidence—its inert objects hold no terrors for him. Naturally this sketch is schematic and makes no pretence to be a complete picture of the introverted or extraverted attitude; it merely emphasizes certain nuances which, nevertheless, are not without significance.

498   Just as the empathetic type is really taking an unconscious delight in himself through the object, so, without knowing it, the abstracting type is really reflecting himself when he reflects on the impressions which objects make upon him. For what the one projects into the object is himself, his own unconscious contents, and what the other thinks about his impression of the object is really his thoughts about his own feelings, which appear to him projected upon the object. It is evident, therefore, that both empathy and abstraction are needed for any real appreciation of the object as well as for artistic creation. Both are always present in every individual, though in most cases they are unequally differentiated.

499   In Worringer's view the common root of these two basic forms of aesthetic experience is "self-alienation"—the need to get outside oneself. Through abstraction and "in the contemplation of something immutable and necessary, we seek deliverance from the hazards of being human, from the seeming arbitrariness of ordinary organic existence."[16] Faced with the bewildering profusion of animate objects, we create an abstraction, an abstract universal image which conjures the welter of impressions into a fixed form. This image has the magical significance of a defence against the chaotic flux of experience. The abstracting type becomes so lost and sub-

[16] *Abstraction and Empathy*, p. 24.

merged in this image that finally its abstract truth is set above the reality of life; and because life might disturb the enjoyment of abstract beauty, it gets completely suppressed. He turns himself into an abstraction, he identifies with the eternal validity of the image and petrifies in it, because for him it has become a redeeming formula. He divests himself of his real self and puts his whole life into his abstraction, in which he is, so to speak, crystallized.

500 The empathetic type suffers a similar fate. Since his activity, his life is empathized into the object, he himself gets into the object because the empathized content is an essential part of himself. He becomes the object. He identifies himself with it and in this way gets outside himself. By turning himself into an object he desubjectivizes himself. Worringer says:

In empathizing this will to activity into another object, we *are* in the other object. We are delivered from our individual being as long as our inner urge for experience absorbs us into an external object, a form outside ourselves. We feel our individuality flowing into fixed bounds that contrast with the boundless diversity of individual consciousness. In this self-objectivation lies a self-alienation. This affirmation of our individual need for activity represents, at the same time, a restriction of its unlimited possibilities, a negation of its irreconcilable diversities. For all our inner urge to activity, we have to rest within the limits of this objectivation.[17]

501 Just as for the abstracting type the abstract image is a bulwark against the destructive effects of the unconsciously animated object,[18] so for the empathetic type the transference to the object is a defence against the disintegration caused by inner subjective factors, which for him consist in limitless fantasies and corresponding impulses to action. The extraverted neurotic clings as tenaciously to the object of his transference as, according to Adler, the introverted neurotic clings to his "guiding fiction." The introvert abstracts his "guiding fiction" from his good and bad experiences of objects, and relies on his formula to protect him from the limitless possibilities life offers.

502 Abstraction and empathy, introversion and extraversion, are mechanisms of adaptation and defence. In so far as they

17 Cf. ibid.

18 Friedrich Theodor Vischer, in his novel *Auch Einer*, gives an excellent description of "animated" objects.

make for adaptation, they protect a man from external dangers. In so far as they are directed functions,[19] they liberate him from fortuitous impulses; indeed they are an actual defence against them since they make self-alienation possible. As our daily psychological experience shows, there are very many people who are completely identified with their directed (or "valuable") function, among them the very types we are discussing. Identification with the directed function has an undeniable advantage in that a man can best adapt to collective demands and expectations; moreover, it also enables him to keep out of the way of his inferior, undifferentiated, undirected functions by self-alienation. In addition, "selflessness" is always considered a particular virtue from the standpoint of social morality. On the other hand, we also have to bear in mind the great disadvantage which identification with the directed function entails, namely, the degeneration of the individual. No doubt man can be mechanized to a very considerable extent, but not to the point of giving himself up completely, or only at the cost of the gravest injury. For the more he identifies with one function, the more he invests it with libido, and the more he withdraws libido from the other functions. They can tolerate being deprived of libido for even quite long periods, but in the end they will react. Being drained of libido, they gradually sink below the threshold of consciousness, lose their associative connection with it, and finally lapse into the unconscious. This is a regressive development, a reversion to the infantile and finally to the archaic level. Since man has spent only a few thousand years in a cultivated state, as opposed to several hundred thousand years in a state of savagery, the archaic modes of functioning are still extraordinarily vigorous and easily reactivated. Hence, when certain functions disintegrate by being deprived of libido, their archaic foundations in the unconscious become operative again.

503   This state brings about a dissociation of the personality, since the archaic modes of functioning have no direct connection with consciousness and no negotiable bridges exist between it and the unconscious. Consequently, the further the process of self-alienation goes, the further the unconscious

[19] On directed thinking, see *Symbols of Transformation*, Part I, ch. II.

functions sink down to the archaic level. The influence of the unconscious increases proportionately. It begins to provoke symptomatic disturbances of the directed function, thus producing that vicious circle characteristic of so many neuroses: the patient tries to compensate the disturbing influences by special feats on the part of the directed function, and the competition between them is often carried to the point of nervous collapse.

504   The possibility of self-alienation by identification with the directed function does not depend solely on a rigid restriction to the one function, but also on the fact that the directed function is itself a principle that makes self-alienation necessary. Thus every directed function demands the strict exclusion of everything not suited to its nature: thinking excludes all disturbing feelings, just as feeling excludes all disturbing thoughts. Without the repression of everything alien to itself, the directed function could never operate at all. On the other hand, since the self-regulation of the living organism requires by its very nature the harmonizing of the whole human being, consideration of the less favoured functions forces itself upon us as a vital necessity and an unavoidable task in the education of the human race.

VIII

THE TYPE PROBLEM IN MODERN PHILOSOPHY

1. WILLIAM JAMES' TYPES

505   The existence of two types has also been discovered in modern pragmatic philosophy, particularly in the philosophy of William James.[1] He says:

> The history of philosophy is, to a great extent, that of a certain clash of human temperaments. . . . Of whatever temperament a professional philosopher is, he tries, when philosophizing, to sink the fact of his temperament. . . . Yet his temperament really gives him a stronger bias than any of his more strictly objective premises. It loads the evidence for him one way or the other, making for a more sentimental or a more hard-hearted view of the universe, just as this fact or that principle would. He trusts his temperament. Wanting a universe that suits it, he believes in any representation of the universe that does suit it. He feels men of opposite temper to be out of key with the world's character, and in his heart considers them incompetent and "not in it," in the philosophic business, even though they may far excel him in dialectical ability.
>
> Yet in the forum he can make no claim, on the bare ground of his temperament, to superior discernment or authority. There arises thus a certain insincerity in our philosophic discussions; the potentest of all our premises is never mentioned.[2]

506   Whereupon James proceeds to the characterization of the two temperaments. Just as in the domain of manners and customs we distinguish conventional and easy-going persons, in politics authoritarians and anarchists, in literature purists and realists, in art classicists and romantics, so in philosophy, according to James, we find two types, the "rationalist" and the "empiricist." The rationalist is "your devotee of abstract and

[1] *Pragmatism: A New Name for Some Old Ways of Thinking.*
[2] Ibid., pp. 7f.

eternal principles." The empiricist is the "lover of facts in all their crude variety" (p. 9). Although no man can dispense either with facts or with principles, they nevertheless give rise to entirely different points of view according to whether the accent falls on one side or on the other.

507   James makes "rationalism" synonymous with "intellectualism," and "empiricism" with "sensationalism." Although in my opinion this equation is not tenable, we will follow James' line of thought for the time being, reserving our criticism until later. In his view, intellectualism is associated with an idealistic and optimistic tendency, whereas empiricism inclines to materialism and a very qualified and uncertain optimism. Intellectualism is always *monistic*. It begins with the whole, with the universal, and unites things; empiricism begins with the part and makes the whole into an *assemblage*. It could therefore be described as *pluralistic*. The rationalist is a man of feeling, but the empiricist is a hard-headed creature. The former is naturally disposed to a belief in free will, the latter to fatalism. The rationalist is inclined to be dogmatic, the empiricist sceptical (pp. 10ff.). James calls the rationalist *tender-minded*, the empiricist *tough-minded*. It is obvious that he is trying to put his finger on the characteristic mental qualities of the two types. Later, we shall examine this characterization rather more closely. It is interesting to hear what James has to say about the prejudices each type cherishes about the other (pp. 12f.):

They have a low opinion of each other. Their antagonism, whenever as individuals their temperaments have been intense, has formed in all ages a part of the philosophic atmosphere of the time. It forms a part of the atmosphere today. The tough think of the tender as sentimentalists and soft-heads. The tender feel the tough to be unrefined, callous, or brutal. . . . Each type believes the other to be inferior to itself.

James tabulates the qualities of the two types as follows:

Tender-minded	*Tough-minded*
Rationalistic (going by "principles")	Empiricist (going by "facts")
Intellectualistic	Sensationalistic
Idealistic	Materialistic

Optimistic	Pessimistic
Religious	Irreligious
Free-willist	Fatalistic
Monistic	Pluralistic
Dogmatical	Sceptical

508   This list touches on a number of problems we have met with in the chapter on realism and nominalism. The tender-minded have certain features in common with the realists, and the tough-minded with the nominalists. As I have pointed out, realism corresponds to introversion, and nominalism to extraversion. The controversy about universals undoubtedly forms part of that "clash of temperaments" in philosophy to which James alludes. These associations tempt one to think of the tender-minded as introverted and the tough-minded as extraverted, but it remains to be seen whether this equation is valid or not.

509   With my somewhat limited knowledge of James' writings, I have not been able to discover any more detailed definitions or descriptions of the two types, although he frequently refers to these two kinds of thinking, and incidentally describes them as "thin" and "thick." Flournoy[3] interprets "thin" as "mince, ténu, maigre, chétif," and "thick" as "épais, solide, massif, cossu." On one occasion, as we have seen, James calls the tender-minded "soft-heads." Both "soft" and "tender" suggest something delicate, mild, gentle, hence weak, subdued, and rather powerless, in contrast to "thick" and "tough," which are resistant qualities, solid and hard to change, suggesting the nature of matter. Flournoy accordingly elucidates the two kinds of thinking as follows:

It is the contrast between the abstract way of thinking—that is, the purely logical and dialectical way so dear to philosophers, but which failed to inspire James with any confidence and appeared to him fragile, hollow, and thin because too remote from particular objects—and the concrete way of thinking, which nourishes itself on the facts of experience and never leaves the solid earthy region of tortoise-shells or other positive data.[4]

510   We should not, however, conclude from this comment that James has a bias in favour of concrete thinking. He appreciates

3 *The Philosophy of William James.*
4 Ibid., pp. 24f.

both standpoints: "Facts are good, of course . . . give us lots of facts. Principles are good . . . give us plenty of principles." A fact never exists only as it is in itself, but also as we see it. When, therefore, James describes concrete thinking as "thick" and "tough," he is saying that for him this kind of thinking has something about it that is substantial and resistant, while abstract thinking appears to him weak, thin, and colourless, perhaps even (if we go along with Flournoy) sickly and decrepit. Naturally such a view is possible only for a person who has made an *a priori* connection between substantiality and concrete thinking—and that, as we have said, is just where the question of temperament comes in. When the empiricist attributes a resistant substantiality to his concrete thinking, from the abstract point of view he is deceiving himself, because substantiality or hardness is a property of external facts and not of empirical thinking. Indeed, the latter proves to be singularly feeble and ineffective; far from holding its own in the face of external facts, it is always running after them and depending on them, and, in consequence, hardly rises above the level of a purely classifying or descriptive activity. *Qua* thinking, therefore, is very weak and unself-reliant, because it has no stability in itself but only in objects, which gain ascendency over it as determining values. It is a thinking characterized by a succession of sense-bound representations, which are set in motion less by the inner activity of thought than by the changing stream of sense-impressions. A series of concrete representations conditioned by sensuous perceptions is not exactly what the abstract thinker would call thinking, but at best only passive apperception.

511   The temperament that favours concrete thinking and endows it with substantiality is thus distinguished by a preponderance of sensuously conditioned representations as contrasted with active apperception, which springs from a subjective act of the will and seeks to organize such representations in accordance with the intentions of a given *idea*. In a word, what counts for this temperament is the *object*: the object is empathized, it leads a quasi-independent existence in the ideational world of the subject, and comprehension follows as a kind of after-thought. It is therefore an extraverting temperament, for the thinking of the extravert is concretistic. Its

stability lies outside in the empathized object, which is why James calls it "tough." For anyone who espouses concrete thinking, i.e., the representation of facts, abstract thinking must appear feeble and ineffective, because he measures it by the stability of concrete, sense-bound objects. For the man who is on the side of abstraction, it is not the sensuously determined representation but the abstract idea that is the decisive factor.

512   Currently, an idea is held to be nothing more than the abstraction of a sum of experiences. One likes to think of the human mind as, originally, a *tabula rasa* that gradually gets covered with perceptions and experiences of life and the world. From this standpoint, which is the standpoint of empirical science in general, an idea cannot be anything else but an epiphenomenal, *a posteriori* abstraction from experiences, and consequently even feebler and more colourless than they are. We know, however, that the mind cannot be a *tabula rasa*, for epistemological criticism shows us that certain categories of thinking are given *a priori*; they are antecedent to all experience and appear with the first act of thought, of which they are its preformed determinants. What Kant demonstrated in respect of logical thinking is true of the whole range of the psyche. The psyche is no more a *tabula rasa* to begin with than is the mind proper (the thinking area). Naturally the concrete contents are lacking, but the potential contents are given *a priori* by the inherited and preformed functional disposition. This is simply the product of the brain's functioning throughout the whole ancestral line, a deposit of phylogenetic experiences and attempts at adaptation. Hence the new-born brain is an immensely old instrument fitted out for quite specific purposes, which does not only apperceive passively but actively arranges the experiences of its own accord and enforces certain conclusions and judgments. These patterns of experience are by no means accidental or arbitrary; they follow strictly preformed conditions which are not transmitted by experience as contents of apprehension but are the preconditions of all apprehension. They are ideas *ante rem*, determinants of form, a kind of pre-existent ground-plan that gives the stuff of experience a specific configuration, so that we may think of them, as Plato did, as *images*, as schemata, or as inherited functional

possibilities which, nevertheless, exclude other possibilities or at any rate limit them to a very great extent. This explains why even fantasy, the freest activity of the mind, can never roam into the infinite (although it seems that way to the poet) but remains anchored to these preformed patterns, these primordial images. The fairytales of the most widely separated races show, by the similarity of their motifs, the same tie. Even the images that underlie certain scientific theories—ether, energy, its transformations and constancy, the atomic theory, affinity, and so on—are proof of this restriction.

513   Just as concrete thinking is dominated and guided by sensuously conditioned representations, abstract thinking is dominated by "irrepresentable" primordial images lacking specific content. They remain relatively inactive so long as the object is empathized and thus made a determinant of thought. But if the object is not empathized, and loses its dominance over the thinking process, the energy denied to it accumulates in the subject. It is now the subject who is unconsciously empathized; the primordial images are awakened from their slumber and emerge as operative factors in the thinking process, but in irrepresentable form, rather like invisible stage managers behind the scenes. They are irrepresentable because they lack content, being nothing but activated functional possibilities, and accordingly they seek something to fill them out. They draw the stuff of experience into their empty forms, representing themselves *in* facts rather than representing facts. They clothe themselves with facts, as it were. Hence they are not, in themselves, a known *point d'appui*, as is the empirical fact in concrete thinking, but become experienceable only through the unconscious shaping of the stuff of experience. The empiricist, too, can organize this material and give it shape, but he models it as far as possible on a concrete idea he has built up on the basis of past experience.

514   The abstract thinker, on the other hand, uses an unconscious model, and only afterwards, from the finished product, does he experience the idea to which he has given shape. The empiricist is always inclined to assume that the abstract thinker shapes the stuff of experience in a quite arbitrary fashion from some colourless, flimsy, inadequate premise, judging the latter's mental processes by his own. But the actual premise,

the idea or primordial image, is just as unknown to the abstract thinker as is the theory which the empiricist will in due course evolve from experience after so and so many experiments. As I have shown in the first chapter,[5] the one type (in this case the empiricist) sees only the individual object and interests himself in its behaviour, while the other, the abstract thinker, sees mainly the similarities between objects, and disregards their singularity because he finds security in reducing the multiplicity of the world to something uniform and coherent. The empiricist finds similarities frankly tiresome and disturbing, something that actually hinders him from recognizing the object's singularity. The more the individual object is empathized, the more easily he discerns its singularity, and the more he loses sight of its similarities with other objects. If only he knew how to empathize other objects as well, he would be far more capable of sensing and recognizing their similarities than the abstract thinker, who sees them only from outside.

515   It is because he empathizes first one object and then another—always a time-consuming procedure—that the concrete thinker is very slow to recognize the similarities between them, and for this reason his thinking appears sluggish and viscid. But his empathy is fluid. The abstract thinker seizes on similarities quickly, puts general characteristics in the place of individual objects, and shapes the stuff of experience by his own mental activity, though this is just as powerfully influenced by the shadowy primordial image as the concrete thinker is by the object. The greater the influence the object has on thinking, the more it stamps its characteristics on the conceptual image. But the less the object works on the mind, the more the primordial idea will set its seal on experience.

516   The excessive importance attached to objects gives rise in science to a certain kind of theory favoured by specialists, which for instance cropped up in psychiatry in the form of the "brain mythology" mentioned in Chapter VI (par. 479). In all such theories an attempt is made to elucidate a very wide range of experience in terms of principles which, though applicable over a small area, are wholly inappropriate for other fields. Conversely, abstract thinking, by taking cognizance of individual facts only because of their similarities with others,

5 Supra, par. 69.

formulates a general hypothesis which, while presenting the leading idea in more or less pure form, has as little to do with the nature of concrete facts as a myth. When carried to extremes, therefore, both types of thinking create a mythology, the one expressed concretely in terms of cells, atoms, vibrations, etc., the other abstractly in terms of "eternal" ideas. At least extreme empiricism has the advantage of presenting the facts as purely as possible, just as extreme idealism reflects the primordial images as in a mirror. The theoretical results of the one are limited by its empirical material, just as the practical results of the other are confined to a presentation of the psychological idea. Because the contemporary scientific attitude is exclusively concretistic and empirical, it has no appreciation of the value of ideas, for facts rank higher than knowledge of the primordial forms in which the human mind conceives them. This swing towards concretism is a comparatively recent development, a relict of the Enlightenment. The results are indeed astonishing, but they have led to an accumulation of empirical material whose very immensity is productive of more confusion than clarity. The inevitable outcome is scientific separatism and specialist mythology, which spells death to universality. The predominance of empiricism not only means the suppression of active thinking; it also imperils the building of theories in any branch of science. The dearth of general viewpoints, however, caters to the construction of mythical theories, just as much as does the absence of empirical criteria.

517   I am therefore of the opinion that James' "tough-minded" and "tender-minded," as descriptive terms, are onesided and at bottom conceal a certain prejudice. Nevertheless, it should at least be clear from this discussion that his characterization deals with the same types which I have termed introverted and extraverted.

2. THE CHARACTERISTIC PAIRS OF OPPOSITES IN JAMES' TYPES

a. Rationalism versus Empiricism

518   I have already discussed this pair of opposites in the preceding section, conceiving it as the opposition between ideologism and empiricism. I avoided the term "rationalism"

because concrete empirical thinking is just as "rational" as active ideological thinking. Both forms are governed by reason. Moreover, there is not only a logical rationalism but a rationalism of feeling, for rationalism as such is a general psychological attitude to the rationality of feeling as well as thought. Conceiving rationalism in this way, I find myself at odds with the historical and philosophical view which uses "rationalistic" in the sense of "ideological" and sees in rationalism the supremacy of the idea. Certainly modern philosophers have stripped reason of its purely ideal character and are fond of describing it as a faculty, a drive, an intention, even a feeling or, indeed, a method. At any rate, psychologically considered, it is a certain attitude governed, as Lipps says, by the "sense of objectivity." Baldwin regards it as the "constitutive, regulative principle of mind."[6] Herbart conceives reason as "the capacity for reflection."[7] Schopenhauer says it has only one function, the forming of concepts, and from this one function "all the above-mentioned manifestations of reason which distinguish the life of man from that of the brutes may easily be explained. The application or non-application of this function is all that is meant by what men have everywhere and always called rational or irrational."[8] The "above-mentioned manifestations" refer to certain expressions of reason listed by Schopenhauer; they include "the control of the emotions and passions, the capacity for drawing conclusions and formulating general principles . . . the united action of several individuals . . . civilization, the state, also science, the storing up of experience," etc.[9] If, as Schopenhauer asserts, it is the function of reason to form concepts, it must possess the character of a particular psychic attitude whose function it is to form concepts through the activity of thought. It is entirely in this sense of an attitude that Jerusalem[10] conceives reason, as a disposition of the will which enables us to make use of reason in our decisions and to control our passions.

519   Reason, therefore, is the capacity to be reasonable, a definite attitude that enables us to think, feel, and act in accordance with objective values. From the empirical standpoint

[6] *Handbook of Psychology: Sense and Intellect*, p. 312.

[7] *Psychologie als Wissenschaft*, sec. 117.

[8] *The World as Will and Idea* (trans. Haldane and Kemp), I, p. 50.

[9] Ibid., p. 48.   [10] *Lehrbuch der Psychologie*, p. 195.

these objective values are the product of experience, but from the ideological standpoint they are the result of a positive act of rational evaluation, which in the Kantian sense would be the "capacity to judge and act in accordance with fundamental principles." For Kant, reason is the source of the idea, which he defines as a "rational concept whose object is not to be found in experience," and which contains the "archetype [*Urbild*] of all practical employment of reason . . . a regulative principle for the sake of thorough consistency in our empirical use of the rational faculty."[11] This is a genuinely introverted view, and it may be contrasted with the empirical view of Wundt, who declares that reason belongs to a group of complex intellectual functions which, with their "antecedent phases that give them an indispensable sensuous substrate," are lumped together "in one general expression."

It is self-evident that this concept "intellectual" is a survival from the old faculty psychology, and suffers, if possible, even more than such old concepts as memory, reason, fantasy, etc., from *confusion with logical points of view which have nothing to do with psychology*, so that the more various the psychic contents it embraces, the more indefinite and arbitrary it becomes. . . . If, from the standpoint of scientific psychology, there is no such thing as memory, reason, or fantasy, but only *elementary psychic processes and their connections with one another*, which from lack of discrimination one lumps together under those names, still less can there be "intelligence" or "intellectual functions" in the sense of a homogeneous concept corresponding to some strictly delimited datum. Nevertheless there remain cases where it is useful to avail oneself of these concepts borrowed from the inventory of faculty psychology, even though using them in a sense modified by the psychological approach. Such cases arise when we encounter complex phenomena of very heterogeneous composition, phenomena that demand consideration on account of the regularity of their combination and above all on practical grounds; or when the individual consciousness presents certain definite trends in its disposition and structure; or when the regularity of the combination necessitates an analysis of such complex psychic dispositions. *But in all these cases it is naturally incumbent on psychological research not to remain rigidly dependent on the general concepts thus formed, but to reduce them whenever possible to their simple factors.*[12]

11 *Logik*, I, sec. 1, par. 3, n. 2 (*Werke*, ed. Cassirer, VIII, p. 400).
12 *Grundzüge der physiologischen Psychologie*, III, pp. 582f.

520   Here speaks the extravert: I have italicized the passages that are specially characteristic. Whereas for the introvert "general concepts" like memory, reason, intelligence, etc. are "faculties," i.e., simple basic functions that comprise the multitude of psychic processes governed by them, for the extraverted empiricist they are nothing but secondary, derivative concepts, elaborations of elementary processes which for him are far more important. No doubt from this standpoint such concepts are not to be circumvented, but in principle one should "reduce them whenever possible to their simple factors." It is self-evident that for the empiricist anything except reductive thinking is simply out of the question, since for him general concepts are mere derivatives from experience. He recognizes no "rational concepts," no *a priori* ideas, because his passive, apperceptive thinking is oriented by sense impressions. As a result of this attitude, the object is always emphasized; *it* is the agent prompting him to insights and complicated ratiocinations, and these require the existence of general concepts which merely serve to comprise certain groups of phenomena under a collective name. Thus the general concept naturally becomes a secondary factor, having no real existence apart from language.

521   Science, therefore, can concede to reason, fantasy, etc. no right to independent existence as long as it maintains that the only things that really exist are elementary facts perceived by the senses. But when, as with the introvert, thinking is oriented by active apperception, reason, fantasy, and the rest acquire the value of basic functions, of faculties or activities operating from within, because for him the accent of value lies on the concept and not on the elementary processes covered and comprised by the concept. This type of thinking is synthetic from the start. It organizes the stuff of experience along the lines of the concept and uses it as a "filling" for ideas. Here the concept is the agent by virtue of its own inner potency, which seizes and shapes the experienced material. The extravert supposes that the source of this power is merely arbitrary choice, or else a premature generalizing of experiences which in themselves are limited. The introvert who is unconscious of the psychology of his own thought-processes, and who may even have adopted the vogue for empiricism as his guiding principle, is

defenceless in the face of this reproach. But the reproach is nothing but a projection of the extravert's psychology. For the active thinking type draws the energy for his thought-processes neither from arbitrary choice nor from experience, but from the idea, from the innate functional form which his introverted attitude has activated. He is not conscious of this source, since by reason of its *a priori* lack of content he can recognize the idea only after he has given shape to it, that is, from the form his thinking imposes on the data of experience. For the extravert, however, the object and the elementary process are important and indispensable because he unconsciously projects the idea into the object, and can reach the idea only through the accumulation and comparison of the empirical material. The two types are opposed in a remarkable way: the one shapes the material out of his own unconscious idea and thus comes to experience; the other lets himself be guided by the material which contains his unconscious projection and thus comes to the idea. There is something intrinsically irritating about this conflict of attitude, and, at bottom, it is the cause of the most heated and futile scientific discussions.

522　I trust that the foregoing sufficiently illustrates my view that rationalism, i.e., the elevation of reason into a principle, is as much a characteristic of empiricism as of ideologism. Instead of ideologism, we might have used the term "idealism," but the antithesis of this would be "materialism," and we could hardly say that the opposite of the materialist is the ideologist. The history of philosophy shows that the materialist can just as often be ideological in his thinking, that is, when he does not think empirically, but starts with the general idea of matter.

b. *Intellectualism* versus *Sensationalism*

523　Sensationalism connotes extreme empiricism. It postulates sense-experience as the sole and exclusive source of knowledge. The sensationalistic attitude is wholly oriented by objects of sense. James evidently means an intellectual rather than an aesthetic sensationalism, and for this reason "intellectualism" is not exactly an appropriate term for its opposite number. Psychologically speaking, intellectualism is an attitude that gives the main determining value to the intellect, to cognition on the conceptual level. But with such an attitude I can also be a sensationalist, for instance when my thinking is occupied with concrete concepts all derived from sense-experience. For the same reason, the empiricist may be intellectualistic. Intellectualism and rationalism are employed promiscuously in philosophy, so in this case too one would have to use ideologism as the antithesis of sensationalism, in so far as the latter is, in essence, only an extreme empiricism.

c. Idealism versus Materialism

524 One may have already begun to wonder whether by "sensationalism" James merely meant an extreme empiricism, i.e., an intellectual sensationalism as surmised above, or whether by "sensationalistic" he really meant "sensuous"—the quality pertaining to sensation as a function quite apart from the intellect. By "pertaining to sensation" I mean true sensuousness, not in the vulgar sense of *voluptas*, but a psychological attitude in which the orienting and determining factor is not so much the empathized object as the mere fact of sensory excitation. This attitude might also be described as reflexive, since the whole mentality depends on and culminates in sense-impressions. The object is neither cognized abstractly nor empathized, but exerts an effect by its very nature and existence, the subject being oriented exclusively by sense-impressions excited by the object. This attitude would correspond to a primitive mentality. Its antithesis and corollary is the intuitive attitude, which is distinguished by an immediate sensing or apprehension that depends neither on thinking nor on feeling but is an inseparable combination of both. Just as the object of sense *appears* before the perceiving subject, so the psychic content appears before the intuitive, as a quasi-hallucination.

525 That James should describe the tough-minded as both "sensationalistic" and "materialistic" (and "irreligious" to boot) makes it even more doubtful whether he had in mind the same type antithesis that I have. Materialism, as commonly understood, is an attitude oriented by "material" values—in other words, a kind of moral sensationalism. Hence James' charac-

terization would present a very unfavourable picture if we were to impute to these terms their common meaning. This is certainly not what James intended, and his own words about the types should suffice to remove any such misunderstanding. We are probably not wrong in assuming that what he had in mind was chiefly the philosophical meaning of those terms. In this sense materialism is certainly an attitude oriented by material values, but these values are factual rather than sensuous, referring to objective and concrete reality. Its antithesis is idealism, in the philosophical sense of a supreme valuation of the idea. It cannot be a moral idealism that is meant here, for then we would have to assume, contrary to James' intention, that by materialism he meant moral sensationalism. But if by materialism he meant an attitude oriented by factual values, we are once again in a position to find in this attitude the quality of extraversion, so that our doubts are dispelled. We have already seen that philosophical idealism corresponds to introverted ideologism. But moral idealism would not be especially characteristic of the introvert, for the materialist can be a moral idealist too.

d. *Optimism* versus *Pessimism*

526   I doubt very much whether this well-known antithesis of human temperaments can be applied to James' types. Is the empirical thinking of Darwin also pessimistic, for instance? Certainly Darwin is a pessimist for one who has an idealistic view of the world and sees the other type through the lens of his unconsciously projected feelings. But this does not mean that the empiricist himself takes a pessimistic view of the world. Or again, to follow the Jamesian typology, can it be said that the thinker Schopenhauer, whose view of the world is purely idealistic (like the pure idealism of the Upanishads), is by any chance an optimist? Kant himself, an extremely pure introverted type, is as remote from either optimism or pessimism as any of the great empiricists.

527   It seems to me, therefore, that this antithesis has nothing to do with James' types. There are optimistic introverts as well as optimistic extraverts, and both can be pessimists. But it is quite possible that James slipped into this error as a result of

an unconscious projection. From the idealist standpoint, a materialistic or empirical or positivist view of the world seems utterly cheerless and is bound to be felt as pessimistic. But the same view of the world seems optimistic to the man who has put his faith in the god "Matter." For the idealist the materialistic view severs the vital nerve, because his main source of strength—active apperception and realization of the primordial images—is sapped. Such a view of the world must appear completely pessimistic to him, as it robs him of all hope of ever again seeing the eternal idea embodied in reality. A world composed only of facts means exile and everlasting homelessness. So when James equates the materialistic with the pessimistic point of view, we may infer that he personally is on the side of idealism—an inference that might easily be corroborated by numerous other traits from the life of this philosopher. This might also explain why the tough-minded are saddled with the three somewhat dubious epithets "sensationalistic," "materialistic," "irreligious." The inference is further corroborated by that passage in *Pragmatism* where James likens the mutual aversion of the two types to a meeting between Bostonian tourists and the inhabitants of Cripple Creek.[13] It is a comparison hardly flattering to the other type, and it allows one to infer an emotional dislike which even a strong sense of justice could not entirely suppress. This little foible seems to me an amusing proof of the mutually irritating differences between the two types. It may seem rather petty to make such a point of these incompatibilities of feeling, but numerous experiences have convinced me that it is just such feelings as these, lurking in the background, that bias even the nicest reasoning and obstruct understanding. It is easy to imagine that the inhabitants of Cripple Creek might also view the Bostonian tourists with a jaundiced eye.

e. *Religiousness* versus *Irreligiousness*

528   The validity of this antithesis naturally depends on the definition of religiousness. If James conceives it entirely from

13 *Pragmatism*, p. 13. The Bostonians are noted for their high-brow aestheticism. Cripple Creek is a mining district in Colorado. "Each type believes the other to be inferior to itself; but disdain in the one case is mingled with amusement, in the other it has a dash of fear" (ibid.).

the idealist standpoint, as an attitude in which religious ideas (as opposed to feelings) play the dominant role, then he is certainly right to characterize the tough-minded as irreligious. But James' thought is so wide and so human that he can hardly have failed to see that a religious attitude can equally well be determined by feeling. He himself says: "But our esteem for facts has not neutralized in us all religiousness. It is itself almost religious. Our scientific temper is devout."[14]

529 Instead of reverence for "eternal" ideas, the empiricist has an almost religious belief in facts. It makes no difference, psychologically, whether a man is oriented by the idea of God or by the idea of matter, or whether facts are exalted into the determinants of his attitude. Only when this orientation becomes absolute does it deserve the name "religious." From such an exalted standpoint, facts are just as worthy of being absolutes as the idea, the primordial image, which is the imprint left on man's psyche by his collision for millions of years with the hard facts of reality. At any rate, absolute surrender to facts can never be described as irreligious from the psychological point of view. The tough-minded indeed have their empiricistic religion, just as the tender-minded have an idealistic one. It is also a phenomenon of our present cultural epoch that science is dominated by the object and religion by the subject, i.e., by the subjective idea—for the idea had to take refuge somewhere after having been ousted from its place in science by the object. If religion is understood as a phenomenon of our culture in this sense, then James is right in describing the empiricist as irreligious, but only in this sense. For since philosophers are not a separate class of men, their types will also extend beyond the philosopher to all civilized humanity. On these general grounds it is surely not permissible to class half of civilized humanity as irreligious. We also know from the psychology of primitives that the religious function is an essential component of the psyche and is found always and everywhere, however undifferentiated it may be.

530 In the absence of some such limitation of James' concept of "religion," we must once again assume that he was thrown off the rails by his emotions, as can happen all too easily.

[14] Ibid., p. 15.

f. *Indeterminism* versus *Determinism*

531   This antithesis is very interesting psychologically. It stands to reason that the empiricist thinks causally, the necessary connection between cause and effect being taken as axiomatic. The empiricist is oriented by the empathized object; he is, as it were, "actuated" by the external fact and impressed with a sense of the necessity of effect following cause. It is psychologically quite natural that the impression of the inevitability of the causal connection should force itself on such an attitude. The identification of the inner psychic processes with external facts is implied from the start, because in the act of empathy a considerable sum of the subject's activity, of his own life, is unconsciously invested in the object. The empathetic type is thereby assimilated to the object, although it feels as if the object were assimilated to him. But whenever the value of the object is emphasized, it at once assumes an importance which in its turn influences the subject, forcing him to a "dissimilation" from himself.[15] Human psychology is chameleon-like, as the practising psychologist knows from daily experience. So whenever the object predominates, an assimilation to the object takes place. Identification with the love-object plays no small role in analytical psychology, and the psychology of primitives swarms with examples of dissimilation in favour of the totem animal or ancestral spirit. The stigmatization of saints in medieval and even in recent times is a similar phenomenon. In the *imitatio Christi* dissimilation is exalted into a principle.

532   In view of this undoubted capacity of the human psyche for dissimilation, the carrying over of objective causal connections into the subject can readily be understood. The psyche then labours under the impression of the exclusive validity of the causal principle, and the whole armoury of the theory of knowledge is needed to combat the overmastering power of this impression. This is further aggravated by the fact that the very nature of the empirical attitude prevents one from believing in inner freedom, since any proof, indeed any possibility of proof, is lacking. What use is that vague, indefinable feeling of freedom in face of the overwhelming mass of objective

[15] See infra, Def. 7.

proofs to the contrary? The determinism of the empiricist, therefore, is a foregone conclusion, provided that he carries his thinking that far and does not prefer, as often happens, to live in two compartments—one for science, and the other for the religion he has taken over from his parents or from his surroundings.

533   As we have seen, idealism consists essentially in an unconscious activation of the idea. This activation may be due to an aversion for empathy acquired later in life, or it may be present at birth as an *a priori* attitude fashioned and favoured by nature (in my practical experience I have seen many such cases). In this latter case the idea is active from the beginning, though, because of its lack of content and its irrepresentability, it does not appear in consciousness. Yet, as an invisible inner dominant, it gains ascendency over all external facts and communicates a sense of its own autonomy and freedom to the subject, who, in consequence of his inner assimilation to the idea, feels independent and free in relation to the object. When the idea is the principal orienting factor, it assimilates the subject just as completely as the subject tries to assimilate the idea by shaping the stuff of experience. Thus, as in the case of his attitude to the object, the subject is dissimilated from himself, but this time in the reverse sense and in favour of the idea.

534   The inherited primordial image outlives all time and change, preceding and superseding all individual experience. It must thus be charged with immense power. When it is activated, it communicates a distinct feeling of power to the subject by assimilating him to itself through his unconscious inner empathy. This would account for his feeling of independence, of freedom, and of living forever (cf. Kant's threefold postulate: God, freedom, and immortality). When the subject feels within him the sway of the idea over the reality of facts, the idea of freedom naturally forces itself upon him. If his idealism is unalloyed, he is bound to believe in free will.

535   The antithesis here discussed is highly characteristic of our types. The extravert is distinguished by his craving for the object, by his empathy and identification with the object, his voluntary dependence on the object. He is influenced by the object in the same degree as he strives to assimilate it. The introvert is distinguished by his self-assertion vis-à-vis the object.

He struggles against any dependence on the object, he repels all its influences, and even fears it. So much the more is he dependent on the idea, which shields him from external reality and gives him the feeling of inner freedom—though he pays for this with a very noticeable power psychology.

g. *Monism* versus *Pluralism*

536   It follows from what we have already said that the idea-oriented attitude must tend towards monism. The idea always possesses an hierarchical character, no matter whether it is derived from a process of abstraction or exists *a priori* as an unconscious form. In the first case it is the apex of an edifice, so to speak, the terminal point that sums up everything that lies below it; in the second case it is the unconscious law-giver, regulating the possibilities and logical necessities of thought. In both cases the idea has a sovereign quality. Although a plurality of ideas may be present, one of them always succeeds in gaining the upper hand for a time and constellates the other psychic elements in a monarchic pattern. It is equally clear that the object-oriented attitude always tends towards a plurality of principles, because the multiplicity of objective qualities necessitates a plurality of concepts without which the nature of the object cannot be properly interpreted. The monistic tendency is a characteristic of introversion, the pluralistic of extraversion.

h. *Dogmatism* versus *Scepticism*

537   It is easy to see in this case too that dogmatism is the attitude *par excellence* that clings to the idea, although an unconscious realization of the idea is not necessarily dogmatic. It is none the less true that the forceful way in which an unconscious idea realizes itself gives outsiders the impression that the idea-oriented thinker starts out with a dogma that squeezes experience into a rigid ideological mould. It is equally clear that the object-oriented thinker will be sceptical about all ideas from the start, since his primary concern is to let every object and every experience speak for itself, undisturbed by general concepts. In this sense scepticism is a necessary condi-

tion of all empiricism. Here we have another pair of opposites that confirms the essential similarity between James' types and my own.

3. GENERAL CRITICISM OF JAMES' TYPOLOGY

538   In criticizing James' typology, I must first stress that it is almost exclusively concerned with the thinking qualities of the types. In a philosophical work one could hardly expect anything else. But the bias resulting from this philosophical setting easily leads to confusion. It would not be difficult to show that such and such a quality is equally characteristic of the opposite type, or even several of them. There are, for instance, empiricists who are dogmatic, religious, idealistic, intellectualistic, rationalistic, etc., just as there are ideologists who are materialistic, pessimistic, deterministic, irreligious, and so on. It is true, of course, that these terms cover extremely complex facts and that all sorts of subtle nuances have to be taken into account, but this still does not get rid of the possibility of confusion.

539   Taken individually, the Jamesian terms are too *broad* and give an approximate picture of the type antithesis only when taken as a whole. Though they do not reduce it to a simple formula, they form a valuable supplement to the picture of the types we have gained from other sources. James deserves credit for being the first to draw attention to the extraordinary importance of temperament in colouring philosophical thought. The whole purpose of his pragmatic approach is to reconcile the philosophical antagonisms resulting from temperamental differences.

540   Pragmatism is a widely ramifying philosophical movement, deriving from English philosophy,[16] which restricts the value of "truth" to its practical efficacy and usefulness, regard-

---

[16] F.C.S. Schiller, *Humanism*. [Schiller says (2nd edn., 1912, p. 5): "James first unequivocally advanced the pragmatist doctrine in connexion with what he called the 'Will to believe.' He had, however, laid the foundation of his doctrine long before in an article in *Mind* (1879)." James appears to have used the word first in an article in 1898 (see Oxf. Eng. Dict.), in which he wrote ". . . pragmatism, as he [C. S. Peirce] called it, when I first heard him enunciate it at Cambridge [Mass.] in the early '70's."—EDITORS.]

less of whether or not it may be contested from some other standpoint. It is characteristic of James to begin his exposition of pragmatism with this type antithesis, as if to demonstrate and justify the need for a pragmatic approach. Thus the drama already acted out in the Middle Ages is repeated. The antithesis at that time took the form of nominalism versus realism, and it was Abelard who attempted to reconcile the two in his "sermonism" or conceptualism. But since the psychological standpoint was completely lacking, his attempted solution was marred by its logical and intellectualistic bias. James dug deeper and grasped the conflict at its psychological root, coming up with a pragmatic solution. One should not, however, cherish any illusions about its value: pragmatism is but a makeshift, and it can claim validity only so long as no sources are discovered, other than intellectual capacities coloured by temperament, which might reveal new elements in the formation of philosophical concepts. Bergson, it is true, has drawn attention to the role of intuition and to the possibility of an "intuitive method," but it remains a mere pointer. Any proof of the method is lacking and will not be easy to furnish, notwithstanding Bergson's claim that his "élan vital" and "durée créatrice" are products of intuition. Aside from these intuitive concepts, which derive their psychological justification from the fact that they were current even in antiquity, particularly in Neoplatonism, Bergson's method is not intuitive but intellectual. Nietzsche made far greater use of the intuitive source and in so doing freed himself from the bonds of the intellect in shaping his philosophical ideas—so much so that his intuition carried him outside the bounds of a purely philosophical system and led to the creation of a work of art which is largely inaccessible to philosophical criticism. I am speaking, of course, of *Zarathustra* and not of the collection of philosophical aphorisms, which are accessible to philosophical criticism because of their predominantly intellectual method. If one may speak of an intuitive method at all, *Zarathustra* is in my view the best example of it, and at the same time a vivid illustration of how the problem can be grasped in a non-intellectual and yet philosophical way. As forerunners of Nietzsche's intuitive approach I would mention Schopenhauer and Hegel, the former because his intuitive feelings had such a decisive influence

320

on his thinking, the latter because of the intuitive ideas that underlie his whole system. In both cases, however, intuition was subordinated to intellect, but with Nietzsche it ranked above it.

541   The conflict between the two "truths" requires a pragmatic attitude if any sort of justice is to be done to the other standpoint. Yet, though it cannot be dispensed with, pragmatism presupposes too great a resignation and almost unavoidably leads to a drying up of creativeness. The solution of the conflict of opposites can come neither from the intellectual compromise of conceptualism nor from a pragmatic assessment of the practical value of logically irreconcilable views, but only from a positive act of creation which assimilates the opposites as necessary elements of co-ordination, in the same way as a co-ordinated muscular movement depends on the innervation of opposing muscle groups. Pragmatism can be no more than a transitional attitude preparing the way for the creative act by removing prejudices. James and Bergson are signposts along the road which German philosophy—not of the academic sort—has already trodden. But it was really Nietzsche who, with a violence peculiarly his own, struck out on the path to the future. His creative act goes beyond the unsatisfying pragmatic solution just as fundamentally as pragmatism itself, in acknowledging the living value of a truth, transcended the barren one-sidedness and unconscious conceptualism of post-Abelardian philosophy—and still there are heights to be climbed.

IX

THE TYPE PROBLEM IN BIOGRAPHY

542   As one might expect, biography too has its contribution to make to the problem of psychological types. For this we are indebted mainly to Wilhelm Ostwald, who, by comparing the biographies of a number of outstanding scientists, was able to establish a typical psychological pair of opposites which he termed the classic and romantic types.[1]

Whereas the former is characterized by the all-round perfection of each of his works, and at the same time by a rather retiring disposition and a personality that has but little influence on his immediate surroundings, the romantic stands out by reason of just the opposite qualities. His peculiarity lies not so much in the perfection of each individual work as in the variety and striking originality of numerous works following one another in rapid succession, and in the direct and powerful influence he has upon his contemporaries.

It should also be emphasized that the speed of mental reaction is a decisive criterion for determining to which type a scientist belongs. Discoverers with rapid reactivity are romantics, those with slower reactions are classics.[2]

543   The classic type is slow to produce, usually bringing forth the ripest fruit of his mind relatively late in life (p. 89). A never-failing characteristic of the classic type, according to Ostwald, is "the absolute need to stand unblemished in the public eye" (p. 94). As a compensation for his "lack of personal influence, the classic type is assured an all the more potent effect through his writings" (p. 100).

544   There seem, however, to be limitations to this effect, as the following episode from the biography of Helmholtz testifies. *A propos* Helmholtz's mathematical researches concerning the effects of induction shocks, his colleague Du Bois-Reymond

---

[1] *Grosse Männer.*   [2] Ibid., pp. 44f.

wrote to the scientist: "You must—please don't take this amiss —devote yourself much more carefully to the problem of abstracting yourself from your own scientific standpoint, and put yourself in the position of those who know nothing of what it is all about, or what it is you want to discuss." To which Helmholtz replied: "This time I really did take pains with my paper, and I thought that at last I might be satisfied with it." Ostwald comments: "He does not consider the reader's point of view at all, because, true to his classic type, he is writing for himself, so that the presentation seems irreproachable to him, while to others it is not." What Du Bois-Reymond says in the same letter to Helmholtz is entirely characteristic: "I read your treatise and the summary several times without understanding what you have actually done, or the way you did it. . . . Finally I discovered your method myself, and now I am gradually beginning to understand your paper."[3]

545   This is a thoroughly typical event in the life of the classic type who seldom or never succeeds in "setting like minds on fire with his own" (p. 100). It shows that the influence ascribed to him through his writings is as a rule posthumous, i.e., it appears after he has been disinterred from his works, as happened in the case of Robert Mayer. Moreover, his writings often seem unconvincing, uninspiring, lacking any direct personal appeal, because the way a man writes is, after all, just as much an expression of himself as the way he talks or lectures. Hence any influence the classic type exerts depends much less on the outwardly stimulating qualities of his writings than on the fact that these are all that finally remain of him, and that only from them can his achievement be reconstructed. It is also evident from Ostwald's description that the classic type seldom communicates what he is doing and the way he does it, but only the final result, regardless of the fact that his public has no notion how he arrived at it. Evidently the way and the method of working are of little importance to him just because they are most intimately linked with his personality, which is something he always keeps in the background.

546   Ostwald compares his two types with the four classical temperaments,[4] with special reference to the speed of reaction,

3 Ibid., p. 280.
4 P. 372. [Cf. infra, Appendix, pars. 883, 960.—EDITORS.]

which in his view is fundamental. Slow reactions are correlated with phlegmatic and melancholic temperaments, quick reactions with the sanguine and the choleric. He regards the sanguine and the phlegmatic as the average types, whereas the choleric and the melancholic seem to him morbid exaggerations of the basic character.

547   If one glances through the biographies of Humphry Davy and Liebig on the one hand, and Robert Mayer and Faraday on the other, it is easy to see that the former are distinctly romantic, sanguine, and choleric, while the latter are just as clearly classic, phlegmatic, and melancholic. This observation of Ostwald's seems to me entirely convincing, since the doctrine of the four temperaments was in all probability based on the same empirical principles as Ostwald's classic and romantic types. The four temperaments are obviously differentiations in terms of affectivity, that is, they are correlated with manifest affective reactions. But this is a superficial classification from the psychological point of view; it judges only by appearances. According to it, the man who is outwardly calm and inconspicuous in his behaviour has a phlegmatic temperament. He looks phlegmatic and is therefore classed as phlegmatic. In reality he may be anything but phlegmatic; he may have a profoundly sensitive, even passionate nature, his intense, introverted emotionality expressing itself through the greatest outward calm. Jordan, in his typology, takes this fact into account. He judges not merely from the surface impression, but from a deeper observation of human nature. Ostwald's criteria of distinction are based on appearances, like the old division into temperaments. His romantic type is characterized by a quick outward reaction; the classic type may react just as quickly, but within.

548   As one reads Ostwald's biographies, one can see at a glance that the romantic type corresponds to the extravert, and the classic type to the introvert. Humphry Davy and Liebig are perfect examples of the one, and Mayer and Faraday of the other. The outward reaction characterizes the extravert, just as the inward reaction is the mark of the introvert. The extravert has no especial difficulty in expressing himself; he makes his presence felt almost involuntarily, because his whole nature goes outwards to the object. He gives himself easily to the

324

world in a form that is pleasing and acceptable, and it is always understandable even when it is unpleasing. Because of his quick reactivity and discharge of emotion, valuable and worthless psychic contents will be projected together into the object; he will react with winsome manners as well as with dour thoughts and affects. For the same reason these contents will have undergone little elaboration and are therefore easily understood; the quick succession of immediate reactions produces a series of images that show the public the path he has followed and the means by which he has attained his result.

549   The introvert, on the other hand, who reacts almost entirely within, cannot as a rule discharge his reactions except in explosions of affect. He suppresses them, though they may be just as quick as those of the extravert. They do not appear on the surface, hence the introvert may easily give the impression of slowness. Since immediate reactions are always strongly personal, the extravert cannot help asserting his personality. But the introvert hides his personality by suppressing all his immediate reactions. Empathy is not his aim, nor the transference of contents to the object, but rather abstraction from the object. Instead of immediately discharging his reactions he prefers to elaborate them inwardly for a long time before finally coming out with the finished product. His constant endeavour is to strip the product of everything personal and to present it divested of all personal relationships. The matured fruit of prolonged inner labour, it emerges into the world in a highly abstract and depersonalized form. It is therefore difficult to understand, because the public lacks all knowledge of the preliminary stages and the way he attained his result. A personal relation to his public is also lacking, because the introvert in suppressing himself shrouds his personality from the public eye. But often enough it is just the personal relationship which brings about an understanding where mere intellectual apprehension fails. This must constantly be borne in mind when passing judgment on the introvert's development. As a rule one is badly informed about the introvert because his real self is not visible. His incapacity for immediate outward reaction keeps his personality hidden. His life therefore affords ample scope for fantastic interpretations and projections should his achievements ever make him an object of general interest.

550   So when Ostwald says that "early mental maturity" is characteristic of the romantic type, we must add that, though this is quite true, the classic type is just as capable of early maturity, but hides his products within himself, not intentionally of course, but from an incapacity for immediate expression. As a result of deficient differentiation of feeling, a certain awkwardness lingers on in the introvert, a real infantilism in his personal relations with other people. His outward personality is so uncertain and indefinite, and he himself is so sensitive in this respect, that he dares to appear before the public only with what in his own eyes is a perfect product. He prefers to let his work speak for him, instead of taking up the cudgels on its behalf. The natural result of such an attitude is a considerably delayed appearance on the world's stage, so that it is easy to accuse him of late maturity. But this superficial judgment overlooks the fact that the infantilism of the apparently early matured and outwardly differentiated extravert is all internal, in his relation to his inner world. It only reveals itself later in life, in some moral immaturity or, as is often the case, in an astonishing infantilism of thought. As Ostwald observes, conditions for development and growth are more favourable for the romantic than for the classic type. His convincing appearance before the public and his outward reactions allow his personal importance to be immediately recognized. In this way many valuable relations are quickly built up which enrich his work and give it *breadth* (p. 374), whereas the other remains hidden and his lack of personal relations limits any extension of his field of work, though his activity gains in *depth* and his work has a lasting value.

551   Both types are capable of *enthusiasm*. What fills the extravert's heart flows out of his mouth, but the enthusiasm of the introvert is the very thing that seals his lips. He kindles no flame in others, and so he lacks colleagues of equal calibre. Even if he had any desire to impart his knowledge, his laconic manner of expression and the mystified incomprehension it produces are enough to deter him from further efforts at communication, and it frequently happens that no one believes he has anything out of the ordinary to say. His manner of expression, his "personality," appear commonplace on a superficial view, whereas the romantic looks intrinsically "interesting" and

understands the art of pandering to this impression by fair means or foul. His very glibness provides a suitable background for brilliant ideas and helps the public over the gaps in his thinking. The emphasis Ostwald lays on the successful academic careers of the romantics is therefore very much to the point. The romantic empathizes his students and knows the right word at the right moment. But the classic type is sunk in his own thoughts and problems and completely overlooks the difficulties his students have in understanding him. Ostwald says of Helmholtz:[5]

In spite of his prodigious learning, wide experience, and richly creative mind, he was never a good teacher. He never reacted on the instant, but only after a long time. Confronted by a student's question in the laboratory, he would promise to think it over, and only after several days would he bring the answer. This turned out to be so remote from the predicament of the student that only in the rarest cases could the latter see any connection between the difficulty he had experienced and the nicely rounded theory of a general problem subsequently expounded to him. Not only was the immediate help lacking on which every beginner largely relies, but also any guidance adapted to the student's own personality, that would have helped him to outgrow the natural dependence of the beginner and win to complete mastery of his subject. All these deficiencies are directly due to the teacher's inability to react instantaneously to the student's needs, so that, when the desired reaction does come, its effect is entirely lost.

552   Ostwald's explanation in terms of the introvert's slowness to react does not seem to me sufficient. This is no sort of proof that Helmholtz possessed a slow reactivity. He merely reacted inwardly rather than outwardly. He had not empathized his student and so did not understand what he needed. His attitude was entirely directed to his own thoughts; consequently, he reacted not to the personal need of the student but to the thoughts which the student's question had aroused in himself, and he reacted so rapidly and thoroughly that he immediately perceived a further connection which, at that moment, he was incapable of evaluating and handing back in fully developed, abstract form. This was not because his thinking was too slow, but because it was impossible for him to grasp, all in a

[5] *Grosse Männer*, p. 377.

moment, the full extent of the problem he had divined. Not observing that the student had no inkling of any such problem, he naturally thought that this was what had to be dealt with, and not some extremely simple and trivial piece of advice which could have been given on the spot if only he had been able to see what the student needed in order to get on with his work. But, being an introvert, he had not empathized the other's psychology; his empathy had gone inwards to his own theoretical problems, and simply went on spinning the threads taken over from the student's problem while entirely ignoring his needs. From the academic standpoint, naturally, this peculiar attitude is highly unsuitable quite apart from the unfavourable impression it makes. The introverted teacher is to all appearances slow, somewhat eccentric, even thick-headed; because of this he is underestimated not only by the wider public but also by his own colleagues, until one day his thoughts are taken up and elaborated by other investigators.

553   The mathematician Gauss had such a distaste for teaching that he used to inform each of his students that his course of lectures would probably not take place at all, hoping in this way to disembarrass himself of the necessity of giving them. Teaching was repugnant to him because it meant having to "pronounce scientific results in his lectures without first having checked and polished every word of the text. To be obliged to communicate his findings to others without such verification must have felt to him as though he were exhibiting himself before strangers in his nightshirt" (p. 380). Here Ostwald puts his finger on a very essential point we have already mentioned— the introvert's dislike of anything other than entirely impersonal communications.

554   Ostwald points out that the romantic is usually compelled to terminate his career comparatively early because of increasing exhaustion. This fact, also, Ostwald attributes to the greater speed of reaction. Since in my opinion the speed of mental reaction is still far from having been explained scientifically, and there is as yet no proof that outward reactions are quicker than inward ones, it seems to me that the earlier exhaustion of the extraverted discoverer must be essentially connected not so much with the speed of reaction as with the outward reactions peculiar to his type. He begins to publish very

early, quickly makes a name for himself, and soon develops an intensive activity, both academically and as a writer; he cultivates personal relationships among a wide circle of friends and acquaintances and, in addition to all this, takes an unusual interest in the development of his pupils. The introverted pioneer begins to publish later; his works succeed one another at longer intervals, and are usually sparing in expression; repetitions of a theme are avoided unless something entirely new can be introduced into them. The pithy and laconic style of his scientific communications, frequently omitting all indications about the way he arrived at his results, prevents any general understanding or acceptance of his work, and so he remains unknown. His distaste for teaching does not bring him pupils; his lack of renown precludes relations with a large circle of acquaintances; as a rule he lives a retired life, not merely from necessity but also from choice. Thus he avoids the danger of expending himself too lavishly. His inward reactions draw him constantly back to the narrow path of his researches; these in themselves are very exacting, proving as time goes on to be so exhausting as to permit of no incidental expenditures on behalf of others. The situation is complicated by the fact that the public success of the romantic has an invigorating effect, but this is often denied to the classic type, who is therefore forced to seek his sole satisfaction in perfecting his research work. In the light of these considerations, the relatively premature exhaustion of the romantic genius, if demonstrable at all, seems to me to depend more on the outward reaction than on a quicker reactivity.

555   Ostwald does not pretend that his type division is absolute in the sense that every investigator can be shown at once to belong to one type or the other. He is, however, of the opinion that the "really great men" can definitely be classed in one or the other category with respect to speed of reaction, while "average people" much more frequently occupy the middle range (pp. 372f.). In conclusion I would like to observe that Ostwald's biographies contain material that has in part a very valuable bearing on the psychology of types, and strikingly exhibit the coincidence of the romantic with the extravert and the classic with the introvert.

329

X

GENERAL DESCRIPTION OF THE TYPES

1. INTRODUCTION

556   In the following pages I shall attempt a general description of the psychology of the types, starting with the two basic types I have termed introverted and extraverted. This will be followed by a description of those more special types whose peculiarities are due to the fact that the individual adapts and orients himself chiefly by means of his most differentiated function. The former I would call *attitude-types*, distinguished by the direction of their interest, or of the movement of libido; the latter I would call *function-types*.

557   The attitude-types, as I have repeatedly emphasized in the preceding chapters, are distinguished by their attitude to the object. The introvert's attitude is an abstracting one; at bottom, he is always intent on withdrawing libido from the object, as though he had to prevent the object from gaining power over him. The extravert, on the contrary, has a positive relation to the object. He affirms its importance to such an extent that his subjective attitude is constantly related to and oriented by the object. The object can never have enough value for him, and its importance must always be increased. The two types are so different and present such a striking contrast that their existence becomes quite obvious even to the layman once it has been pointed out. Everyone knows those reserved, inscrutable, rather shy people who form the strongest possible contrast to the open, sociable, jovial, or at least friendly and approachable characters who are on good terms with everybody, or quarrel with everybody, but always relate to them in some way and in turn are affected by them.

558   One is naturally inclined, at first, to regard such differences as mere idiosyncrasies of character peculiar to individ-

330

uals. But anyone with a thorough knowledge of human nature will soon discover that the contrast is by no means a matter of isolated individual instances but of typical attitudes which are far more common than one with limited psychological experience would assume. Indeed, as the preceding chapters may have shown, it is a fundamental contrast, sometimes quite clear, sometimes obscured, but always apparent when one is dealing with individuals whose personality is in any way pronounced. Such people are found not merely among the educated, but in all ranks of society, so that our types can be discovered among labourers and peasants no less than among the most highly differentiated members of a community. Sex makes no difference either; one finds the same contrast among women of all classes. Such a widespread distribution could hardly have come about if it were merely a question of a conscious and deliberate choice of attitude. In that case, one would surely find one particular attitude in one particular class of people linked together by a common education and background and localized accordingly. But that is not so at all; on the contrary, the types seem to be distributed quite at random. In the same family one child is introverted, the other extraverted. Since the facts show that the attitude-type is a general phenomenon having an apparently random distribution, it cannot be a matter of conscious judgment or conscious intention, but must be due to some unconscious, instinctive cause. As a general psychological phenomenon, therefore, the type antithesis must have some kind of biological foundation.

559   The relation between subject and object, biologically considered, is always one of adaptation, since every relation between subject and object presupposes the modification of one by the other through reciprocal influence. Adaptation consists in these constant modifications. The typical attitudes to the object, therefore, are processes of adaptation. There are in nature two fundamentally different modes of adaptation which ensure the continued existence of the living organism. The one consists in a high rate of fertility, with low powers of defence and short duration of life for the single individual; the other consists in equipping the individual with numerous means of self-preservation plus a low fertility rate. This biological difference, it seems to me, is not merely analogous to, but the actual founda-

tion of, our two psychological modes of adaptation. I must content myself with this broad hint. It is sufficient to note that the peculiar nature of the extravert constantly urges him to expend and propagate himself in every way, while the tendency of the introvert is to defend himself against all demands from outside, to conserve his energy by withdrawing it from objects, thereby consolidating his own position. Blake's intuition did not err when he described the two classes of men as "prolific" and "devouring."[1] Just as, biologically, the two modes of adaptation work equally well and are successful in their own way, so too with the typical attitudes. The one achieves its end by a multiplicity of relationships, the other by monopoly.

560   The fact that children often exhibit a typical attitude quite unmistakably even in their earliest years forces us to assume that it cannot be the struggle for existence in the ordinary sense that determines a particular attitude. It might be objected, cogently enough, that even the infant at the breast has to perform an unconscious act of psychological adaptation, in that the mother's influence leads to specific reactions in the child. This argument, while supported by incontestable evidence, becomes rather flimsy in face of the equally incontestable fact that two children of the same mother may exhibit contrary attitudes at an early age, though no change in the mother's attitude can be demonstrated. Although nothing would induce me to underrate the incalculable importance of parental influence, this familiar experience compels me to conclude that the decisive factor must be looked for in the disposition of the child. Ultimately, it must be the individual disposition which decides whether the child will belong to this or that type despite the constancy of external conditions. Naturally I am thinking only of normal cases. Under abnormal conditions, i.e., when the mother's own attitude is extreme, a similar attitude can be forced on the children too, thus violating their individual disposition, which might have opted for another type if no abnormal external influences had intervened. As a rule, whenever such a falsification of type takes place as a result of parental influence, the individual becomes neurotic later, and can be cured only by developing the attitude consonant with his nature.

[1] Supra, par. 460.

561   As to the individual disposition, I have nothing to say except that there are obviously individuals who have a greater capacity, or to whom it is more congenial, to adapt in one way and not in another. It may well be that physiological causes of which we have no knowledge play a part in this. I do not think it improbable, in view of one's experience that a reversal of type often proves exceedingly harmful to the physiological well-being of the organism, usually causing acute exhaustion.

2. THE EXTRAVERTED TYPE

562   In our description of this and the following types it is necessary, for the sake of clarity, to distinguish between the psychology of consciousness and the psychology of the unconscious. We shall first describe the phenomena of consciousness.

a. The General Attitude of Consciousness

563   Although it is true that everyone orients himself in accordance with the data supplied by the outside world, we see every day that the data in themselves are only relatively decisive. The fact that it is cold outside prompts one man to put on his overcoat, while another, who wants to get hardened, finds this superfluous. One man admires the latest tenor because everybody else does, another refuses to do so, not because he dislikes him, but because in his view the subject of universal admiration is far from having been proved admirable. One man resigns himself to circumstances because experience has shown him that nothing else is possible, another is convinced that though things have gone the same way a thousand times before, the thousand and first time will be different. The one allows himself to be oriented by the given facts, the other holds in reserve a view which interposes itself between him and the objective data. Now, when orientation by the object predominates in such a way that decisions and actions are determined not by subjective views but by objective conditions, we speak of an extraverted attitude. When this is habitual, we speak of an extraverted type. If a man thinks, feels, acts, and actually lives in a way that is *directly* correlated with the objective conditions and their demands, he is extraverted. His life makes it

perfectly clear that it is the object and not this subjective view that plays the determining role in his consciousness. Naturally he has subjective views too, but their determining value is less than that of the objective conditions. Consequently, he never expects to find any absolute factors in his own inner life, since the only ones he knows are outside himself. Like Epimetheus, his inner life is subordinated to external necessity, though not without a struggle; but it is always the objective determinant that wins in the end. His whole consciousness looks outward, because the essential and decisive determination always comes from outside. But it comes from outside only because that is where he expects it to come from. All the peculiarities of his psychology, except those that depend on the primacy of one particular psychological function or on idiosyncrasies of character, follow from this basic attitude. His interest and attention are directed to objective happenings, particularly those in his immediate environment. Not only people but things seize and rivet his attention. Accordingly, they also determine his actions, which are fully explicable on those grounds. The actions of the extravert are recognizably related to external conditions. In so far as they are not merely reactive to environmental stimuli, they have a character that is always adapted to the actual circumstances, and they find sufficient play within the limits of the objective situation. No serious effort is made to transcend these bounds. It is the same with his interest: objective happenings have an almost inexhaustible fascination for him, so that ordinarily he never looks for anything else.

564   The moral laws governing his actions coincide with the demands of society, that is, with the prevailing moral standpoint. If this were to change, the extravert's subjective moral guidelines would change accordingly, without this altering his general psychological habits in any way. This strict determination by objective factors does not mean, as one might suppose, a complete let alone ideal adaptation to the general conditions of life. In the eyes of the extravert, of course, an *adjustment* of this kind to the objective situation must seem like complete adaptation, since for him no other criterion exists. But from a higher point of view it by no means follows that the objective situation is in all circumstances a normal one. It can quite well

be temporarily or locally abnormal. An individual who adjusts himself to it is admittedly conforming to the style of his environment, but together with his whole surroundings he is in an abnormal situation with respect to the universally valid laws of life. He may indeed thrive in such surroundings, but only up to the point where he and his milieu meet with disaster for transgressing these laws. He will share the general collapse to exactly the same extent as he was adjusted to the previous situation. Adjustment is not adaptation; adaptation requires far more than merely going along smoothly with the conditions of the moment. (Once again I would remind the reader of Spitteler's Epimetheus.) It requires observance of laws more universal than the immediate conditions of time and place. The very adjustment of the normal extraverted type is his limitation. He owes his normality on the one hand to his ability to fit into existing conditions with comparative ease. His requirements are limited to the objectively possible, for instance to the career that holds out good prospects at this particular moment; he does what is needed of him, or what is expected of him, and refrains from all innovations that are not entirely self-evident or that in any way exceed the expectations of those around him. On the other hand, his normality must also depend essentially on whether he takes account of his subjective needs and requirements, and this is just his weak point, for the tendency of his type is so outer-directed that even the most obvious of all subjective facts, the condition of his own body, receives scant attention. The body is not sufficiently objective or "outside," so that the satisfaction of elementary needs which are indispensable to physical well-being is no longer given its due. The body accordingly suffers, to say nothing of the psyche. The extravert is usually unaware of this latter fact, but it is all the more apparent to his household. He feels his loss of equilibrium only when it announces itself in abnormal body sensations. These he cannot ignore. It is quite natural that he should regard them as concrete and "objective," since with his type of mentality they cannot be anything else—for him. In others he at once sees "imagination" at work. A too extraverted attitude can also become so oblivious of the subject that the latter is sacrificed completely to so-called objective demands—to the

335

demands, for instance, of a continually expanding business, because orders are piling up and profitable opportunities have to be exploited.

565   This is the extravert's danger: he gets sucked into objects and completely loses himself in them. The resultant functional disorders, nervous or physical, have a compensatory value, as they force him into an involuntary self-restraint. Should the symptoms be functional, their peculiar character may express his psychological situation in symbolic form; for instance, a singer whose fame has risen to dangerous heights that tempt him to expend too much energy suddenly finds he cannot sing high notes because of some nervous inhibition. Or a man of modest beginnings who rapidly reaches a social position of great influence with wide prospects is suddenly afflicted with all the symptoms of a mountain sickness.[2] Again, a man about to marry a woman of doubtful character whom he adores and vastly overestimates is seized with a nervous spasm of the oesophagus and has to restrict himself to two cups of milk a day, each of which takes him three hours to consume. All visits to the adored are effectively stopped, and he has no choice but to devote himself to the nourishment of his body. Or a man who can no longer carry the weight of the huge business he has built up is afflicted with nervous attacks of thirst and speedily falls a victim to hysterical alcoholism.

566   Hysteria is, in my view, by far the most frequent neurosis of the extraverted type. The hallmark of classic hysteria is an exaggerated rapport with persons in the immediate environment and an adjustment to surrounding conditions that amounts to imitation. A constant tendency to make himself interesting and to produce an impression is a basic feature of the hysteric. The corollary of this is his proverbial suggestibility, his proneness to another person's influence. Another unmistakable sign of the extraverted hysteric is his effusiveness, which occasionally carries him into the realm of fantasy, so that he is accused of the "hysterical lie." The hysterical character begins as an exaggeration of the normal attitude; it is then complicated by compensatory reactions from the uncon-

2 [For a detailed discussion of this case, see "The Tavistock Lectures," *Coll. Works*, vol. 18, pars. 161ff.—EDITORS.]

scious, which counteract the exaggerated extraversion by means of physical symptoms that force the libido to introvert. The reaction of the unconscious produces another class of symptoms having a more introverted character, one of the most typical being a morbid intensification of fantasy activity.

567 After this general outline of the extraverted attitude we shall now turn to a description of the modifications which the basic psychological functions undergo as a result of this attitude.

b. The Attitude of the Unconscious

568 It may perhaps seem odd that I should speak of an "attitude of the unconscious." As I have repeatedly indicated, I regard the attitude of the unconscious as compensatory to consciousness. According to this view, the unconscious has as good a claim to an "attitude" as the latter.

569 In the preceding section I emphasized the tendency to one-sidedness in the extraverted attitude, due to the ascendency of the object over the course of psychic events. The extraverted type is constantly tempted to expend himself for the apparent benefit of the object, to assimilate subject to object. I have discussed in some detail the harmful consequences of an exaggeration of the extraverted attitude, namely, the suppression of the subjective factor. It is only to be expected, therefore, that the psychic compensation of the conscious extraverted attitude will lay special weight on the subjective factor, and that we shall find a markedly egocentric tendency in the unconscious. Practical experience proves this to be the case. I do not wish to cite case material at this point, so must refer my readers to the ensuing sections, where I try to present the characteristic attitude of the unconscious in each function-type. In this section we are concerned simply with the compensation of the extraverted attitude in general, so I shall confine myself to describing the attitude of the unconscious in equally general terms.

570 The attitude of the unconscious as an effective complement to the conscious extraverted attitude has a definitely introverting character. It concentrates the libido on the subjective factor, that is, on all those needs and demands that are

337

stifled or repressed by the conscious attitude. As may be gathered from what was said in the previous section, a purely objective orientation does violence to a multitude of subjective impulses, intentions, needs, and desires and deprives them of the libido that is their natural right. Man is not a machine that can be remodelled for quite other purposes as occasion demands, in the hope that it will go on functioning as regularly as before but in a quite different way. He carries his whole history with him; in his very structure is written the history of mankind. This historical element in man represents a vital need to which a wise psychic economy must respond. Somehow the past must come alive and participate in the present. Total assimilation to the object will always arouse the protest of the suppressed minority of those elements that belong to the past and have existed from the very beginning.

571   From these general considerations it is easy to see why the unconscious demands of the extravert have an essentially primitive, infantile, egocentric character. When Freud says that the unconscious "can do nothing but wish" this is very largely true of the unconscious of the extravert. His adjustment to the objective situation and his assimilation to the object prevent low-powered subjective impulses from reaching consciousness. These impulses (thoughts, wishes, affects, needs, feelings, etc.) take on a regressive character according to the degree of repression; the less they are acknowledged, the more infantile and archaic they become. The conscious attitude robs them of all energy that is readily disposable, only leaving them the energy of which it cannot deprive them. This residue, which still possesses a potency not to be underestimated, can be described only as primordial instinct. Instinct can never be eradicated in an individual by arbitrary measures; it requires the slow, organic transformation of many generations to effect a radical change, for instinct is the energic expression of the organism's make-up.

572   Thus with every repressed impulse a considerable amount of energy ultimately remains, of an instinctive character, and preserves its potency despite the deprivation that made it unconscious. The more complete the conscious attitude of extraversion is, the more infantile and archaic the unconscious atti-

tude will be. The egoism which characterizes the extravert's unconscious attitude goes far beyond mere childish selfishness; it verges on the ruthless and the brutal. Here we find in full flower the incest-wish described by Freud. It goes without saying that these things are entirely unconscious and remain hidden from the layman so long as the extraversion of the conscious attitude is not extreme. But whenever it is exaggerated, the unconscious comes to light in symptomatic form; its egoism, infantilism, and archaism lose their original compensatory character and appear in more or less open opposition to the conscious attitude. This begins as an absurd exaggeration of conscious standpoint, aiming at a further repression of the unconscious, but usually it ends in a *reductio ad absurdum* of the conscious attitude and hence in catastrophe. The catastrophe may take an objective form, since the objective aims gradually become falsified by the subjective. I remember the case of a printer who, starting as a mere employee, worked his way up after years of hard struggle till at last he became the owner of a flourishing business. The more it expanded, the more it tightened its hold on him, until finally it swallowed up all his other interests. This proved his ruin. As an unconscious compensation of his exclusive interest in the business, certain memories of his childhood came to life. As a child he had taken great delight in painting and drawing. But instead of renewing this capacity for its own sake as a compensating hobby, he channelled it into his business and began wondering how he might embellish his products in an "artistic" way. Unfortunately his fantasies materialized: he actually turned out stuff that suited his own primitive and infantile taste, with the result that after a very few years his business went to pieces. He acted in accordance with one of our "cultural ideals," which says that any enterprising person has to concentrate everything on the one aim in view. But he went too far, and merely fell a victim to the power of his infantile demands.

573　　The catastrophe can, however, also be subjective and take the form of a nervous breakdown. This invariably happens when the influence of the unconscious finally paralyzes all conscious action. The demands of the unconscious then force themselves imperiously on consciousness and bring about a disastrous split which shows itself in one of two ways: either the subject no longer knows what he really wants and nothing interests him, or he wants too much at once and has too many interests, but in impossible things. The suppression of infantile and primitive demands for cultural reasons easily leads to a neurosis or to the abuse of narcotics such as alcohol, morphine, cocaine, etc. In more extreme cases the split ends in suicide.

574   It is an outstanding peculiarity of unconscious impulses that, when deprived of energy by lack of conscious recognition, they take on a destructive character, and this happens as soon as they cease to be compensatory. Their compensatory function ceases as soon as they reach a depth corresponding to a cultural level absolutely incompatible with our own. From this moment the unconscious impulses form a block in every way opposed to the conscious attitude, and its very existence leads to open conflict.

575   Generally speaking, the compensating attitude of the unconscious finds expression in the maintenance of the psychic equilibrium. A normal extraverted attitude does not, of course, mean that the individual invariably behaves in accordance with the extraverted schema. Even in the same individual many psychological processes may be observed that involve the mechanism of introversion. We call a mode of behaviour extraverted only when the mechanism of extraversion predominates. In these cases the most differentiated function is always employed in an extraverted way, whereas the inferior functions are introverted; in other words, the superior function is the most conscious one and completely under conscious control, whereas the less differentiated functions are in part unconscious and far less under the control of consciousness. The superior function is always an expression of the conscious personality, of its aims, will, and general performance, whereas the less differentiated functions fall into the category of things that simply "happen" to one. These things need not be mere slips of the tongue or pen and other such oversights, they can equally well be half or three-quarters intended, for the less differentiated functions also possess a slight degree of consciousness. A classic example of this is the extraverted feeling type, who enjoys an excellent feeling rapport with the people

around him, yet occasionally "happens" to express opinions of unsurpassable tactlessness. These opinions spring from his inferior and half-conscious thinking, which, being only partly under his control and insufficiently related to the object, can be quite ruthless in its effects.

576 The less differentiated functions of the extravert always show a highly subjective colouring with pronounced egocentricity and personal bias, thus revealing their close connection with the unconscious. The unconscious is continually coming to light through them. It should not be imagined that the unconscious lies permanently buried under so many overlying strata that it can only be uncovered, so to speak, by a laborious process of excavation. On the contrary, there is a constant influx of unconscious contents into the conscious psychological process, to such a degree that at times it is hard for the observer to decide which character traits belong to the conscious and which to the unconscious personality. This difficulty is met with mainly in people who are given to express themselves more profusely than others. Naturally it also depends very largely on the attitude of the observer whether he seizes hold of the conscious or the unconscious character of the personality. Generally speaking, a judging observer will tend to seize on the conscious character, while a perceptive observer will be more influenced by the unconscious character, since judgment is chiefly concerned with the conscious motivation of the psychic process, while perception registers the process itself. But in so far as we apply judgment and perception in equal measure, it may easily happen that a personality appears to us as both introverted and extraverted, so that we cannot decide at first to which attitude the superior function belongs. In such cases only a thorough analysis of the qualities of each function can help us to form a valid judgment. We must observe which function is completely under conscious control, and which functions have a haphazard and spontaneous character. The former is always more highly differentiated than the latter, which also possess infantile and primitive traits. Occasionally the superior function gives the impression of normality, while the others have something abnormal or pathological about them.

c. The Peculiarities of the Basic Psychological
Functions in the Extraverted Attitude

Thinking

577   As a consequence of the general attitude of extraversion, thinking is oriented by the object and objective data. This gives rise to a noticeable peculiarity. Thinking in general is fed on the one hand from subjective and in the last resort unconscious sources, and on the other hand from objective data transmitted by sense-perception. Extraverted thinking is conditioned in a larger measure by the latter than by the former. Judgment always presupposes a criterion; for the extraverted judgment, the criterion supplied by external conditions is the valid and determining one, no matter whether it be represented directly by an objective, perceptible fact or by an objective idea; for an objective idea is equally determined by external data or borrowed from outside even when it is subjectively sanctioned. Extraverted thinking, therefore, need not necessarily be purely concretistic thinking; it can just as well be purely ideal thinking, if for instance it can be shown that the ideas it operates with are largely borrowed from outside, i.e., have been transmitted by tradition and education. So in judging whether a particular thinking is extraverted or not we must first ask: by what criterion does it judge—does it come from outside, or is its origin subjective? A further criterion is the direction the thinking takes in drawing conclusions—whether it is principally directed outwards or not. It is no proof of its extraverted nature that it is preoccupied with concrete objects, since my thinking may be preoccupied with a concrete object either because I am abstracting my thought from it or because I am concretizing my thought through it. Even when my thinking is preoccupied with concrete things and could be described as extraverted to that extent, the direction it will take still remains an essential characteristic and an open question—namely, whether or not in its further course it leads back again to objective data, external facts, or generally accepted ideas. So far as the practical thinking of the business man, the technician, or the scientific investigator is concerned, its outer-directedness is obvious enough. But in the

case of the philosopher it remains open to doubt when his thinking is directed to ideas. We then have to inquire whether these ideas are simply abstractions from objective experience, in which case they would represent higher collective concepts comprising a sum of objective facts, or whether (if they are clearly not abstractions from immediate experience) they may not be derived from tradition or borrowed from the intellectual atmosphere of the time. In the latter case, they fall into the category of objective data, and accordingly this thinking should be called extraverted.

578   Although I do not propose to discuss the nature of introverted thinking at this point, reserving it for a later section (pars. 628–31), it is essential that I should say a few words about it before proceeding further. For if one reflects on what I have just said about extraverted thinking, one might easily conclude that this covers everything that is ordinarily understood as thinking. A thinking that is directed neither to objective facts nor to general ideas, one might argue, scarcely deserves the name "thinking" at all. I am fully aware that our age and its most eminent representatives know and acknowledge only the extraverted type of thinking. This is largely because all the thinking that appears visibly on the surface in the form of science or philosophy or even art either derives directly from objects or else flows into general ideas. For both these reasons it appears essentially understandable, even though it may not always be self-evident, and it is therefore regarded as valid. In this sense it might be said that the extraverted intellect oriented by objective data is actually the only one that is recognized. But—and now I come to the question of the introverted intellect—there also exists an entirely different kind of thinking, to which the term "thinking" can hardly be denied: it is a kind that is oriented neither by immediate experience of objects nor by traditional ideas. I reach this other kind of thinking in the following manner: when my thoughts are preoccupied with a concrete object or a general idea, in such a way that the course of my thinking eventually leads me back to my starting-point, this intellectual process is not the only psychic process that is going on in me. I will disregard all those sensations and feelings which become noticeable as a more or less disturbing accompaniment to my train of thought, and will

343

merely point out that this very thinking process which starts from the object and returns to the object also stands in a constant relation to the subject. This relation is a *sine qua non,* without which no thinking process whatsoever could take place. Even though my thinking process is directed, as far as possible, to objective data, it is still *my* subjective process, and it can neither avoid nor dispense with this admixture of subjectivity. Struggle as I may to give an objective orientation to my train of thought, I cannot shut out the parallel subjective process and its running accompaniment without extinguishing the very spark of life from my thought. This parallel process has a natural and hardly avoidable tendency to subjectify the objective data and assimilate them to the subject.

579   Now when the main accent lies on the subjective process, that other kind of thinking arises which is opposed to extraverted thinking, namely, that purely subjective orientation which I call introverted. This thinking is neither determined by objective data nor directed to them; it is a thinking that starts from the subject and is directed to subjective ideas or subjective facts. I do not wish to enter more fully into this kind of thinking here; I have merely established its existence as the necessary complement of extraverted thinking and brought it into clearer focus.

580   Extraverted thinking, then, comes into existence only when the objective orientation predominates. This fact does nothing to alter the logic of thinking; it merely constitutes that difference between thinkers which James considered a matter of temperament. Orientation to the object, as already explained, makes no essential change in the thinking function; only its appearance is altered. It has the appearance of being captivated by the object, as though without the external orientation it simply could not exist. It almost seems as though it were a mere sequela of external facts, or as though it could reach its highest point only when flowing into some general idea. It seems to be constantly affected by the objective data and to draw conclusions only with their consent. Hence it gives one the impression of a certain lack of freedom, of occasional short-sightedness, in spite of all its adroitness within the area circumscribed by the object. What I am describing is simply the impression this sort of thinking makes on the observer, who

must himself have a different standpoint, otherwise it would be impossible for him to observe the phenomenon of extraverted thinking at all. But because of his different standpoint he sees only its outward aspect, not its essence, whereas the thinker himself can apprehend its essence but not its outward aspect. Judging by appearances can never do justice to the essence of the thing, hence the verdict is in most cases depreciatory.

581   In its essence this thinking is no less fruitful and creative than introverted thinking, it merely serves other ends. This difference becomes quite palpable when extraverted thinking appropriates material that is the special province of introverted thinking; when, for instance, a subjective conviction is explained analytically in terms of objective data or as being derived from objective ideas. For our scientific consciousness, however, the difference becomes even more obvious when introverted thinking attempts to bring objective data into connections not warranted by the object—in other words, to subordinate them to a subjective idea. Each type of thinking senses the other as an encroachment on its own province, and hence a sort of shadow effect is produced, each revealing to the other its least favourable aspect. Introverted thinking then appears as something quite arbitrary, while extraverted thinking seems dull and banal. Thus the two orientations are incessantly at war.

582   One might think it easy enough to put an end to this conflict by making a clear distinction between objective and subjective data. Unfortunately, this is impossible, though not a few have attempted it. And even if it were possible it would be a disastrous proceeding, since in themselves both orientations are one-sided and of limited validity, so that each needs the influence of the other. When objective data predominate over thinking to any great extent, thinking is sterilized, becoming a mere appendage of the object and no longer capable of abstracting itself into an independent concept. It is then reduced to a kind of "after-thought," by which I do not mean "reflection" but a purely imitative thinking which affirms nothing beyond what was visibly and immediately present in the objective data in the first place. This thinking naturally leads directly back to the object, but never beyond it, not even to a

345

linking of experience with an objective idea. Conversely, when it has an idea for an object, it is quite unable to experience its practical, individual value, but remains stuck in a more or less tautological position. The materialistic mentality is an instructive example of this.

583   When extraverted thinking is subordinated to objective data as a result of over-determination by the object, it engrosses itself entirely in the individual experience and accumulates a mass of undigested empirical material. The oppressive weight of individual experiences having little or no connection with one another produces a dissociation of thought which usually requires psychological compensation. This must consist in some simple, general idea that gives coherence to the disordered whole, or at least affords the possibility of such. Ideas like "matter" or "energy" serve this purpose. But when the thinking depends primarily not on objective data but on some second-hand idea, the very poverty of this thinking is compensated by an all the more impressive accumulation of facts congregating round a narrow and sterile point of view, with the result that many valuable and meaningful aspects are completely lost sight of. Many of the allegedly scientific outpourings of our own day owe their existence to this wrong orientation.

The Extraverted Thinking Type

584   It is a fact of experience that the basic psychological functions seldom or never all have the same strength or degree of development in the same individual. As a rule, one or the other function predominates, in both strength and development. When thinking holds prior place among the psychological functions, i.e., when the life of an individual is mainly governed by reflective thinking so that every important action proceeds, or is intended to proceed, from intellectually considered motives, we may fairly call this a thinking type. Such a type may be either introverted or extraverted. We will first discuss the extraverted thinking type.

585   This type will, by definition, be a man whose constant endeavour—in so far, of course, as he is a pure type—is to make all his activities dependent on intellectual conclusions, which in the last resort are always oriented by objective data,

346

whether these be external facts or generally accepted ideas. This type of man elevates objective reality, or an objectively oriented intellectual formula, into the ruling principle not only for himself but for his whole environment. By this formula good and evil are measured, and beauty and ugliness determined. Everything that agrees with this formula is right, everything that contradicts it is wrong, and anything that passes by it indifferently is merely incidental. Because this formula seems to embody the entire meaning of life, it is made into a universal law which must be put into effect everywhere all the time, both individually and collectively. Just as the extraverted thinking type subordinates himself to his formula, so, for their own good, everybody round him must obey it too, for whoever refuses to obey it is wrong—he is resisting the universal law, and is therefore unreasonable, immoral, and without a conscience. His moral code forbids him to tolerate exceptions; his ideal must under all circumstances be realized, for in his eyes it is the purest conceivable formulation of objective reality, and therefore must also be a universally valid truth, quite indispensable for the salvation of mankind. This is not from any great love for his neighbour, but from the higher standpoint of justice and truth. Anything in his own nature that appears to invalidate this formula is a mere imperfection, an accidental failure, something to be eliminated on the next occasion, or, in the event of further failure, clearly pathological. If tolerance for the sick, the suffering, or the abnormal should chance to be an ingredient of the formula, special provisions will be made for humane societies, hospitals, prisons, missions, etc., or at least extensive plans will be drawn up. Generally the motive of justice and truth is not sufficient to ensure the actual execution of such projects; for this, real Christian charity is needed, and this has more to do with feeling than with any intellectual formula. "Oughts" and "musts" bulk large in this programme. If the formula is broad enough, this type may play a very useful role in social life as a reformer or public prosecutor or purifier of conscience, or as the propagator of important innovations. But the more rigid the formula, the more he develops into a martinet, a quibbler, and a prig, who would like to force himself and others into one mould. Here we have the two extremes between which the majority of these types move.

347

586   In accordance with the nature of the extraverted attitude, the influence and activities of these personalities are the more favourable and beneficial the further from the centre their radius extends. Their best aspect is to be found at the periphery of their sphere of influence. The deeper we penetrate into their own power province, the more we feel the unfavourable effects of their tyranny. A quite different life pulses at the periphery, where the truth of the formula can be felt as a valuable adjunct to the rest. But the closer we come to centre of power where the formula operates, the more life withers away from everything that does not conform to its dictates. Usually it is the nearest relatives who have to taste the unpleasant consequences of the extraverted formula, since they are the first to receive its relentless benefits. But in the end it is the subject himself who suffers most—and this brings us to the reverse side of the psychology of this type.

587   The fact that an intellectual formula never has been and never will be devised which could embrace and express the manifold possibilities of life must lead to the inhibition or exclusion of other activities and ways of living that are just as important. In the first place, all those activities that are dependent on feeling will become repressed in such a type—for instance, aesthetic activities, taste, artistic sense, cultivation of friends, etc. Irrational phenomena such as religious experiences, passions, and suchlike are often repressed to the point of complete unconsciousness. Doubtless there are exceptional people who are able to sacrifice their entire life to a particular formula, but for most of us such exclusiveness is impossible in the long run. Sooner or later, depending on outer circumstances or inner disposition, the potentialities repressed by the intellectual attitude will make themselves indirectly felt by disturbing the conscious conduct of life. When the disturbance reaches a definite pitch, we speak of a neurosis. In most cases it does not go so far, because the individual instinctively allows himself extenuating modifications of his formula in a suitably rationalistic guise, thus creating a safety valve.

588   The relative or total unconsciousness of the tendencies and functions excluded by the conscious attitude keeps them in an undeveloped state. In comparison with the conscious function they are inferior. To the extent that they are unconscious, they

become merged with the rest of the unconscious contents and acquire a bizarre character. To the extent that they are conscious, they play only a secondary role, though one of considerable importance for the over-all psychological picture. The first function to be affected by the conscious inhibition is feeling, since it is the most opposed to the rigid intellectual formula and is therefore repressed the most intensely. No function can be entirely eliminated—it can only be greatly distorted. In so far as feeling is compliant and lets itself be subordinated, it has to support the conscious attitude and adapt to its aims. But this is possible only up to a point; part of it remains refractory and has to be repressed. If the repression is successful, the subliminal feeling then functions in a way that is opposed to the conscious aims, even producing effects whose cause is a complete enigma to the individual. For example, the conscious altruism of this type, which is often quite extraordinary, may be thwarted by a secret self-seeking which gives a selfish twist to actions that in themselves are disinterested. Purely ethical intentions may lead him into critical situations which sometimes have more than a semblance of being the outcome of motives far from ethical. There are guardians of public morals who suddenly find themselves in compromising situations, or rescue workers who are themselves in dire need of rescue. Their desire to save others leads them to employ means which are calculated to bring about the very thing they wished to avoid. There are extraverted idealists so consumed by their desire for the salvation of mankind that they will not shrink from any lie or trickery in pursuit of their ideal. In science there are not a few painful examples of highly respected investigators who are so convinced of the truth and general validity of their formula that they have not scrupled to falsify evidence in its favour. Their sanction is: the end justifies the means. Only an inferior feeling function, operating unconsciously and in secret, could seduce otherwise reputable men into such aberrations.

589   The inferiority of feeling in this type also manifests itself in other ways. In keeping with the objective formula, the conscious attitude becomes more or less impersonal, often to such a degree that personal interests suffer. If the attitude is extreme, all personal considerations are lost sight of, even those

affecting the subject's own person. His health is neglected, his social position deteriorates, the most vital interests of his family—health, finances, morals—are violated for the sake of the ideal. Personal sympathy with others must in any case suffer unless they too happen to espouse the same ideal. Often the closest members of his family, his own children, know such a father only as a cruel tyrant, while the outside world resounds with the fame of his humanity. Because of the highly impersonal character of the conscious attitude, the unconscious feelings are extremely personal and oversensitive, giving rise to secret prejudices—a readiness, for instance, to misconstrue any opposition to his formula as personal ill-will, or a constant tendency to make negative assumptions about other people in order to invalidate their arguments in advance—in defence, naturally, of his own touchiness. His unconscious sensitivity makes him sharp in tone, acrimonious, aggressive. Insinuations multiply. His feelings have a sultry and resentful character—always a mark of the inferior function. Magnanimous as he may be in sacrificing himself to his intellectual goal, his feelings are petty, mistrustful, crotchety, and conservative. Anything new that is not already contained in his formula is seen through a veil of unconscious hatred and condemned accordingly. As late as the middle of the last century a certain doctor, famed for his humanitarianism, threatened to dismiss an assistant for daring to use a thermometer, because the formula decreed that temperature must be taken by the pulse.

590   The more the feelings are repressed, the more deleterious is their secret influence on thinking that is otherwise beyond reproach. The intellectual formula, which because of its intrinsic value might justifiably claim general recognition, undergoes a characteristic alteration as a result of this unconscious personal sensitiveness: it becomes rigidly dogmatic. The self-assertion of the personality is transferred to the formula. Truth is no longer allowed to speak for itself; it is identified with the subject and treated like a sensitive darling whom an evil-minded critic has wronged. The critic is demolished, if possible with personal invective, and no argument is too gross to be used against him. The truth must be trotted out, until finally it begins to dawn on the public that it is not so much a question of truth as of its personal begetter.

591   The dogmatism of the intellectual formula sometimes undergoes further characteristic alterations, due not so much to the unconscious admixture of repressed personal feelings as to a contamination with other unconscious factors which have become fused with them. Although reason itself tells us that every intellectual formula can never be anything more than a partial truth and can never claim general validity, in practice the formula gains such an ascendency that all other possible standpoints are thrust into the background. It usurps the place of all more general, less definite, more modest and therefore more truthful views of life. It even supplants that general view of life we call religion. Thus the formula becomes a religion, although in essentials it has not the slightest connection with anything religious. At the same time, it assumes the essentially religious quality of absoluteness. It becomes an intellectual superstition. But now all the psychological tendencies it has repressed build up a counter-position in the unconscious and give rise to paroxysms of doubt. The more it tries to fend off the doubt, the more fanatical the conscious attitude becomes, for fanaticism is nothing but over-compensated doubt. This development ultimately leads to an exaggerated defence of the conscious position and to the formation of a counter-position in the unconscious absolutely opposed to it; for instance, conscious rationalism is opposed by an extreme irrationality, and a scientific attitude by one that is archaic and superstitious. This explains those bigoted and ridiculous views well-known in the history of science which have proved stumbling-blocks to many an eminent investigator. Frequently the unconscious counter-position is embodied in a woman. In my experience this type is found chiefly among men, since, in general, thinking tends more often to be a dominant function in men than in women. When thinking dominates in a woman it is usually associated with a predominantly *intuitive* cast of mind.

592   The thinking of the extraverted type is *positive*, i.e., productive. It leads to the discovery of new facts or to general conceptions based on disparate empirical material. It is usually synthetic too. Even when it analyses it constructs, because it is always advancing beyond the analysis to a new combination, to a further conception which reunites the analysed material in a different way or adds something to it. One could call this

351

kind of judgment *predicative*. A characteristic feature, at any rate, is that it is never absolutely depreciative or destructive, since it always substitutes a fresh value for the one destroyed. This is because the thinking of this type is the main channel into which his vital energy flows. The steady flow of life manifests itself in his thinking, so that his thought has a progressive, creative quality. It is not stagnant or regressive. But it can become so if it fails to retain prior place in his consciousness. In that case it loses the quality of a positive, vital activity. It follows in the wake of other functions and becomes Epimethean, plagued by afterthoughts, contenting itself with constant broodings on things past and gone, chewing them over in an effort to analyse and digest them. Since the creative element is now lodged in another function, thinking no longer progresses: it stagnates. Judgment takes on a distinct quality of *inherence*: it confines itself entirely to the range of the given material, nowhere overstepping it. It is satisfied with more or less abstract statements which do not impart any value to the material that is not already inherent in it. Such judgments are always oriented to the object, and they affirm nothing more about an experience than its objective and intrinsic meaning. We may easily observe this type of thinking in people who cannot refrain from tacking on to an impression or experience some rational and doubtless very valid remark which in no way ventures beyond the charmed circle of the objective datum. At bottom such a remark merely says: "I have understood it because afterwards I can think it." And there the matter ends. At best such a judgment amounts to no more than putting the experience in an objective setting, where it quite obviously belonged in the first place.

593   But whenever a function other than thinking predominates in consciousness to any marked degree, thinking, so far as it is conscious at all and not directly dependent on the dominant function, assumes a negative character. If it is subordinated to the dominant function it may actually wear a positive aspect, but closer scrutiny will show that it simply mimics the dominant function, supporting it with arguments that clearly contradict the laws of logic proper to thinking. This kind of thinking is of no interest for our present discussion. Our concern is rather with the nature of a thinking which cannot sub-

ordinate itself to another function but remains true to its own principle. To observe and investigate this thinking is not easy, because it is more or less constantly repressed by the conscious attitude. Hence, in the majority of cases, it must first be retrieved from the background of consciousness, unless it should come to the surface accidentally in some unguarded moment. As a rule it has to be enticed with some such question as "Now what do you *really* think?" or "What is your private view of the matter?" Or perhaps one may have to use a little cunning, framing the question something like this: "What do you imagine, then, that *I* really think about it?" One should adopt this device when the real thinking is unconscious and therefore projected. The thinking that is enticed to the surface in this way has characteristic qualities, and it was these I had in mind when I described it as negative. Its habitual mode is best expressed by the two words "nothing but." Goethe personified this thinking in the figure of Mephistopheles. Above all it shows a distinct tendency to trace the object of its judgment back to some banality or other, thus stripping it of any significance in its own right. The trick is to make it appear dependent on something quite commonplace. Whenever a conflict arises between two men over something apparently objective and impersonal, negative thinking mutters "Cherchez la femme." Whenever somebody defends or advocates a cause, negative thinking never asks about its importance but simply: "What does *he* get out of it?" The dictum ascribed to Moleschott, "Der Mensch ist, was er isst" (man is what he eats, or, rendered more freely, what you eat you are), likewise comes under this heading, as do many other aphorisms I need not quote here.

594   The destructive quality of this thinking, as well as its limited usefulness on occasion, does not need stressing. But there is still another form of negative thinking, which at first glance might not be recognized as such, and that is *theosophical* thinking, which today is rapidly spreading in all parts of the world, presumably in reaction to the materialism of the recent past. Theosophical thinking has an air that is not in the least reductive, since it exalts everything to a transcendental and world-embracing idea. A dream, for instance, is no longer just a dream, but an experience "on another plane." The

hitherto inexplicable fact of telepathy is very simply explained as "vibrations" passing from one person to another. An ordinary nervous complaint is explained by the fact that something has collided with the "astral body." Certain ethnological peculiarities of the dwellers on the Atlantic seaboard are easily accounted for by the submergence of Atlantis, and so on. We have only to open a theosophical book to be overwhelmed by the realization that everything is already explained, and that "spiritual science" has left no enigmas unsolved. But, at bottom, this kind of thinking is just as negative as materialistic thinking. When the latter regards psychology as chemical changes in the ganglia or as the extrusion and retraction of cell-pseudopodia or as an internal secretion, this is just as much a superstition as theosophy. The only difference is that materialism reduces everything to physiology, whereas theosophy reduces everything to Indian metaphysics. When a dream is traced back to an overloaded stomach, this is no explanation of the dream, and when we explain telepathy as vibrations we have said just as little. For what are "vibrations"? Not only are both methods of explanation futile, they are actually destructive, because by diverting interest away from the main issue, in one case to the stomach and in the other to imaginary vibrations, they hamper any serious investigation of the problem by a bogus explanation. Either kind of thinking is sterile and sterilizing. Its negative quality is due to the fact that it is so indescribably cheap, impoverished, and lacking in creative energy. It is a thinking taken in tow by other functions.

Feeling

595   Feeling in the extraverted attitude is likewise oriented by objective data, the object being the indispensable determinant of the quality of feeling. The extravert's feeling is always in harmony with objective values. For anyone who has known feeling only as something subjective, the nature of extraverted feeling will be difficult to grasp, because it has detached itself as much as possible from the subjective factor and subordinated itself entirely to the influence of the object. Even when it appears not to be qualified by a concrete object, it is none the less still under the spell of traditional or generally accepted

values of some kind. I may feel moved, for instance, to say that something is "beautiful" or "good," not because I find it "beautiful" or "good" from my own subjective feeling about it, but because it is fitting and politic to call it so, since a contrary judgment would upset the general feeling situation. A feeling judgment of this kind is not by any means a pretence or a lie, it is simply an act of adjustment. A painting, for instance, is called "beautiful" because a painting hung in a drawing room and bearing a well-known signature is generally assumed to be beautiful, or because to call it "hideous" would presumably offend the family of its fortunate possessor, or because the visitor wants to create a pleasant feeling atmosphere, for which purpose everything must be felt as agreeable. These feelings are governed by an objective criterion. As such they are genuine, and represent the feeling function as a whole.

596   In precisely the same way as extraverted thinking strives to rid itself of subjective influences, extraverted feeling has to undergo a process of differentiation before it is finally denuded of every subjective trimming. The valuations resulting from the act of feeling either correspond directly with objective values or accord with traditional and generally accepted standards. This kind of feeling is very largely responsible for the fact that so many people flock to the theatre or to concerts, or go to church, and do so moreover with their feelings correctly adjusted. Fashions, too, owe their whole existence to it, and, what is far more valuable, the positive support of social, philanthropic, and other such cultural institutions. In these matters extraverted feeling proves itself a creative factor. Without it, a harmonious social life would be impossible. To that extent extraverted feeling is just as beneficial and sweetly reasonable in its effects as extraverted thinking. But these salutary effects are lost as soon as the object gains ascendency. The force of extraverted feeling then pulls the personality into the object, the object assimilates him, whereupon the personal quality of the feeling, which constitutes its chief charm, disappears. It becomes cold, "unfeeling," untrustworthy. It has ulterior motives, or at least makes an impartial observer suspect them. It no longer makes that agreeable and refreshing impression which invariably accompanies genuine feeling; instead, one suspects a pose, or that the person is acting, even though he

may be quite unconscious of any egocentric motives. Over-extraverted feeling may satisfy aesthetic expectations, but it does not speak to the heart; it appeals merely to the senses or —worse still—only to reason. It can provide the aesthetic padding for a situation, but there it stops, and beyond that its effect is nil. It has become sterile. If this process goes any further, a curiously contradictory dissociation of feeling results: everything becomes an object of feeling valuations, and innumerable relationships are entered into which are all at variance with each other. As this situation would become quite impossible if the subject received anything like due emphasis, even the last vestiges of a real personal standpoint are suppressed. The subject becomes so enmeshed in the network of individual feeling processes that to the observer it seems as though there were merely a feeling process and no longer a subject of feeling. Feeling in this state has lost all human warmth; it gives the impression of being put on, fickle, unreliable, and in the worst cases hysterical.

The Extraverted Feeling Type

597   As feeling is undeniably a more obvious characteristic of feminine psychology than thinking, the most pronounced feeling types are to be found among women. When extraverted feeling predominates we speak of an extraverted feeling type. Examples of this type that I can call to mind are, almost without exception, women. The woman of this type follows her feeling as a guide throughout life. As a result of upbringing her feeling has developed into an adjusted function subject to conscious control. Except in extreme cases, her feeling has a personal quality, even though she may have repressed the subjective factor to a large extent. Her personality appears adjusted in relation to external conditions. Her feelings harmonize with objective situations and general values. This is seen nowhere more clearly than in her love choice: the "suitable" man is loved, and no one else; he is suitable not because he appeals to her hidden subjective nature—about which she usually knows nothing—but because he comes up to all reasonable expectations in the matter of age, position, income, size and respectability of his family, etc. One could easily reject such a picture as ironical or cynical, but I am fully convinced

that the love feeling of this type of woman is in perfect accord with her choice. It is genuine and not just shrewd. There are countless "reasonable" marriages of this kind and they are by no means the worst. These women are good companions and excellent mothers so long as the husbands and children are blessed with the conventional psychic constitution.

598   But one can feel "correctly" only when feeling is not disturbed by anything else. Nothing disturbs feeling so much as thinking. It is therefore understandable that in this type thinking will be kept in abeyance as much as possible. This does not mean that the woman does not think at all; on the contrary, she may think a great deal and very cleverly, but her thinking is never *sui generis*—it is an Epimethean appendage to her feeling. What she cannot feel, she cannot consciously think. "But I can't think what I don't feel," such a type said to me once in indignant tones. So far as her feeling allows, she can think very well, but every conclusion, however logical, that might lead to a disturbance of feeling is rejected at the outset. It is simply not thought. Thus everything that fits in with objective values is good, and is loved, and everything else seems to her to exist in a world apart.

599   But a change comes over the picture when the importance of the object reaches a still higher level. As already explained, the subject then becomes so assimilated to the object that the subject of feeling is completely engulfed. Feeling loses its personal quality, and becomes feeling for its own sake; the personality seems wholly dissolved in the feeling of the moment. But since actual life is a constant succession of situations that evoke different and even contradictory feelings, the personality gets split up into as many different feeling states. At one moment one is this, at another something quite different—to all appearances, for in reality such a multiple personality is impossible. The basis of the ego always remains the same and consequently finds itself at odds with the changing feeling states. To the observer, therefore, the display of feeling no longer appears as a personal expression of the subject but as an alteration of the ego—a mood, in other words. Depending on the degree of dissociation between the ego and the momentary state of feeling, signs of self-disunity will become clearly apparent, because the originally compensatory attitude of the

357

unconscious has turned into open opposition. This shows itself first of all in extravagant displays of feeling, gushing talk, loud expostulations, etc., which ring hollow: "The lady doth protest too much." It is at once apparent that some kind of resistance is being over-compensated, and one begins to wonder whether these demonstrations might not turn out quite different. And a little later they do. Only a very slight alteration in the situation is needed to call forth at once just the opposite pronouncement on the selfsame object. As a result of these experiences the observer is unable to take either pronouncement seriously. He begins to reserve judgment. But since, for this type, it is of the highest importance to establish an intense feeling of rapport with the environment, redoubled efforts are now required to overcome this reserve. Thus, in the manner of a vicious circle, the situation goes from bad to worse. The stronger the feeling relation to the object, the more the unconscious opposition comes to the surface.

600   We have already seen that the extraverted feeling type suppresses thinking most of all because this is the function most liable to disturb feeling. For the same reason, thinking totally shuts out feeling if ever it wants to reach any kind of pure results, for nothing is more liable to prejudice and falsify thinking than feeling values. But, as I have said, though the thinking of the extraverted feeling type is repressed as an independent function, the repression is not complete; it is repressed only so far as its inexorable logic drives it to conclusions that are incompatible with feeling. It is suffered to exist as a servant of feeling, or rather as its slave. Its backbone is broken; it may not operate on its own account, in accordance with its own laws. But since logic nevertheless exists and enforces its inexorable conclusions, this must take place somewhere, and it takes place outside consciousness, namely in the unconscious. Accordingly the unconscious of this type contains first and foremost a peculiar kind of thinking, a thinking that is infantile, archaic, negative. So long as the conscious feeling preserves its personal quality, or, to put it another way, so long as the personality is not swallowed up in successive states of feeling, this unconscious thinking remains compensatory. But as soon as the personality is dissociated and dissolves into a succession of contradictory feeling states, the identity of the ego

358

is lost and the subject lapses into the unconscious. When this happens, it gets associated with the unconscious thinking processes and occasionally helps them to the surface. The stronger the conscious feeling is and the more ego-less it becomes, the stronger grows the unconscious opposition. The unconscious thoughts gravitate round just the most valued objects and mercilessly strip them of their value. The "nothing but" type of thinking comes into its own here, since it effectively depotentiates all feelings that are bound to the object. The unconscious thinking reaches the surface in the form of obsessive ideas which are invariably of a negative and depreciatory character. Women of this type have moments when the most hideous thoughts fasten on the very objects most valued by their feelings. This negative thinking utilizes every infantile prejudice or comparison for the deliberate purpose of casting aspersions on the feeling value, and musters every primitive instinct in the attempt to come out with "nothing but" interpretations. It need hardly be remarked that this procedure also mobilizes the collective unconscious and activates its store of primordial images, thus bringing with it the possibility of a regeneration of attitude on a different basis. Hysteria, with the characteristic infantile sexuality of its unconscious world of ideas, is the principal form of neurosis in this type.

Summary of the Extraverted Rational Types

601   I call the two preceding types rational or judging types because they are characterized by the supremacy of the reasoning and judging functions. It is a general distinguishing mark of both types that their life is, to a great extent, subordinated to rational judgment. But we have to consider whether by "rational" we are speaking from the standpoint of the individual's subjective psychology or from that of the observer, who perceives and judges from without. This observer could easily arrive at a contrary judgment, especially if he intuitively apprehended merely the outward behaviour of the person observed and judged accordingly. On the whole, the life of this type is never dependent on rational judgment alone; it is influenced in almost equal degree by unconscious irrationality. If observation is restricted to outward behaviour, without any concern for the internal economy of the individual's conscious-

ness, one may get an even stronger impression of the irrational and fortuitous nature of certain unconscious manifestations than of the reasonableness of his conscious intentions and motivations. I therefore base my judgment on what the individual feels to be his conscious psychology. But I am willing to grant that one could equally well conceive and present such a psychology from precisely the opposite angle. I am also convinced that, had I myself chanced to possess a different psychology, I would have described the rational types in the reverse way, from the standpoint of the unconscious—as irrational, therefore. This aggravates the difficulty of a lucid presentation of psychological matters and immeasurably increases the possibility of misunderstandings. The arguments provoked by these misunderstandings are, as a rule, quite hopeless because each side is speaking at cross purposes. This experience is one reason the more for basing my presentation on the conscious psychology of the individual, since there at least we have a definite objective footing, which completely drops away the moment we try to base our psychological rationale on the unconscious. For in that case the observed object would have no voice in the matter at all, because there is nothing about which he is more uninformed than his own unconscious. The judgment is then left entirely to the subjective observer—a sure guarantee that it will be based on his own individual psychology, which would be forcibly imposed on the observed. To my mind, this is the case with the psychologies of both Freud and Adler. The individual is completely at the mercy of the judging observer, which can never be the case when the conscious psychology of the observed is accepted as a basis. He after all is the only competent judge, since he alone knows his conscious motives.

602   The rationality that characterizes the conscious conduct of life in both these types involves a deliberate exclusion of everything irrational and accidental. Rational judgment, in such a psychology, is a force that coerces the untidiness and fortuitousness of life into a definite pattern, or at least tries to do so. A definite choice is made from among all the possibilities it offers, only the rational ones being accepted; but on the other hand the independence and influence of the psychic functions which aid the perception of life's happenings are con-

sequently restricted. Naturally this restriction of sensation and intuition is not absolute. These functions exist as before, but their products are subject to the choice made by rational judgment. It is not the intensity of a sensation as such that decides action, for instance, but judgment. Thus, in a sense, the functions of perception share the same fate as feeling in the case of the first type, or thinking in that of the second. They are relatively repressed, and therefore in an inferior state of differentiation. This gives a peculiar stamp to the unconscious of both our types: what they consciously and intentionally do accords with reason (*their* reason, of course), but what happens to them accords with the nature of infantile, primitive sensations and intuitions. At all events, what happens to these types is irrational (from their standpoint). But since there are vast numbers of people whose lives consist more of what happens to them than of actions governed by rational intentions, such a person, after observing them closely, might easily describe both our types as irrational. And one has to admit that only too often a man's unconscious makes a far stronger impression on an observer than his consciousness does, and that his actions are of considerably more importance than his rational intentions.

603   The rationality of both types is object-oriented and dependent on objective data. It accords with what is collectively considered to be rational. For them, nothing is rational save what is generally considered as such. Reason, however, is in large part subjective and individual. In our types this part is repressed, and increasingly so as the object gains in importance. Both the subject and his subjective reason, therefore, are in constant danger of repression, and when they succumb to it they fall under the tyranny of the unconscious, which in this case possesses very unpleasant qualities. Of its peculiar thinking we have already spoken. But, besides that, there are primitive sensations that express themselves compulsively, for instance in the form of compulsive pleasure-seeking in every conceivable form; there are also primitive intuitions that can become a positive torture to the person concerned and to everybody in his vicinity. Everything that is unpleasant and painful, everything that is disgusting, hateful, and evil, is sniffed out or suspected, and in most cases it is a half-truth calculated to provoke misunderstandings of the most poisonous

kind. The antagonistic unconscious elements are so strong that they frequently disrupt the conscious rule of reason; the individual becomes the victim of chance happenings, which exercise a compulsive influence over him either because they pander to his sensations or because he intuits their unconscious significance.

Sensation

604   Sensation, in the extraverted attitude, is pre-eminently conditioned by the object. As sense perception, sensation is naturally dependent on objects. But, just as naturally, it is also dependent on the subject, for which reason there is subjective sensation of a kind entirely different from objective sensation. In the extraverted attitude the subjective component of sensation, so far as its conscious application is concerned, is either inhibited or repressed. Similarly, as an irrational function, sensation is largely repressed when thinking or feeling holds prior place; that is to say, it is a conscious function only to the extent that the rational attitude of consciousness permits accidental perceptions to become conscious contents—in a word, registers them. The sensory function is, of course, absolute in the stricter sense; everything is seen or heard, for instance, to the physiological limit, but not everything attains the threshold value a perception must have in order to be apperceived. It is different when sensation itself is paramount instead of merely seconding another function. In this case no element of objective sensation is excluded and nothing is repressed (except the subjective component already mentioned).

605   As sensation is chiefly conditioned by the object, those objects that excite the strongest sensations will be decisive for the individual's psychology. The result is a strong sensuous tie to the object. Sensation is therefore a vital function equipped with the strongest vital instinct. Objects are valued in so far as they excite sensations, and, so far as lies within the power of sensation, they are fully accepted into consciousness whether they are compatible with rational judgments or not. The sole criterion of their value is the intensity of the sensation produced by their objective qualities. Accordingly, all objective processes which excite any sensations at all make their appearance in consciousness. However, it is only concrete, sensuously

perceived objects or processes that excite sensations for the extravert; those, exclusively, which everyone everywhere would sense as concrete. Hence the orientation of such an individual accords with purely sensuous reality. The judging, rational functions are subordinated to the concrete facts of sensation, and thus have all the qualities of the less differentiated functions, exhibiting negative, infantile, and archaic traits. The function most repressed is naturally the opposite of sensation —intuition, the function of unconscious perception.

The Extraverted Sensation Type

606   No other human type can equal the extraverted sensation type in realism. His sense for objective facts is extraordinarily developed. His life is an accumulation of actual experiences of concrete objects, and the more pronounced his type, the less use does he make of his experience. In certain cases the events in his life hardly deserve the name "experience" at all. What he experiences serves at most as a guide to fresh sensations; anything new that comes within his range of interest is acquired by way of sensation and has to serve its ends. Since one is inclined to regard a highly developed reality-sense as a sign of rationality, such people will be esteemed as very rational. But in actual fact this is not the case, since they are just as much at the mercy of their sensations in the face of irrational, chance happenings as they are in the face of rational ones. This type— the majority appear to be men—naturally does not think he is at the "mercy" of sensation. He would ridicule this view as quite beside the point, because sensation for him is a concrete expression of life—it is simply real life lived to the full. His whole aim is concrete enjoyment, and his morality is oriented accordingly. Indeed, true enjoyment has its own special morality, its own moderation and lawfulness, its own unselfishness and willingness to make sacrifices. It by no means follows that he is just sensual or gross, for he may differentiate his sensation to the finest pitch of aesthetic purity without ever deviating from his principle of concrete sensation however abstract his sensations may be. Wulfen's *Der Genussmensch: ein Cicerone im rücksichtslosen Lebensgenuss*[3] is the unvarnished confession

---

[3] ["The Sybarite: A Guide to the Ruthless Enjoyment of Life."—TRANS.]

of a type of this sort, and the book seems to me worth reading on that account alone.

607   On the lower levels, this type is the lover of tangible reality, with little inclination for reflection and no desire to dominate. To feel the object, to have sensations and if possible enjoy them—that is his constant aim. He is by no means unlovable; on the contrary, his lively capacity for enjoyment makes him very good company; he is usually a jolly fellow, and sometimes a refined aesthete. In the former case the great problems of life hang on a good or indifferent dinner; in the latter, it's all a question of good taste. Once an object has given him a sensation, nothing more remains to be said or done about it. It cannot be anything except concrete and real; conjectures that go beyond the concrete are admitted only on condition that they enhance sensation. The intensification does not necessarily have to be pleasurable, for this type need not be a common voluptuary; he is merely desirous of the strongest sensations, and these, by his very nature, he can receive only from outside. What comes from inside seems to him morbid and suspect. He always reduces his thoughts and feelings to objective causes, to influences emanating from objects, quite unperturbed by the most glaring violations of logic. Once he can get back to tangible reality in any form he can breathe again. In this respect he is surprisingly credulous. He will unhesitatingly connect a psychogenic symptom with a drop in the barometer, while on the other hand the existence of a psychic conflict seems to him morbid imagination. His love is unquestionably rooted in the physical attractions of its object. If normal, he is conspicuously well adjusted to reality. That is his ideal, and it even makes him considerate of others. As he has no ideals connected with ideas, he has no reason to act in any way contrary to the reality of things as they are. This manifests itself in all the externals of his life. He dresses well, as befits the occasion; he keeps a good table with plenty of drink for his friends, making them feel very grand, or at least giving them to understand that his refined taste entitles him to make a few demands of them. He may even convince them that certain sacrifices are decidedly worth while for the sake of style.

608   The more sensation predominates, however, so that the subject disappears behind the sensation, the less agreeable

does this type become. He develops into a crude pleasure-seeker, or else degenerates into an unscrupulous, effete aesthete. Although the object has become quite indispensable to him, yet, as something existing in its own right, it is none the less devalued. It is ruthlessly exploited and squeezed dry, since now its sole use is to stimulate sensation. The bondage to the object is carried to the extreme limit. In consequence, the unconscious is forced out of its compensatory role into open opposition. Above all, the repressed intuitions begin to assert themselves in the form of projections. The wildest suspicions arise; if the object is a sexual one, jealous fantasies and anxiety states gain the upper hand. More acute cases develop every sort of phobia, and, in particular, compulsion symptoms. The pathological contents have a markedly unreal character, with a frequent moral or religious streak. A pettifogging captiousness follows, or a grotesquely punctilious morality combined with primitive, "magical" superstitions that fall back on abstruse rites. All these things have their source in the repressed inferior functions which have been driven into harsh opposition to the conscious attitude, and they appear in a guise that is all the more striking because they rest on the most absurd assumptions, in complete contrast to the conscious sense of reality. The whole structure of thought and feeling seems, in this second personality, to be twisted into a pathological parody: reason turns into hair-splitting pedantry, morality into dreary moralizing and blatant Pharisaism, religion into ridiculous superstition, and intuition, the noblest gift of man, into meddlesome officiousness, poking into every corner; instead of gazing into the far distance, it descends to the lowest level of human meanness.

609   The specifically compulsive character of the neurotic symptoms is the unconscious counterpart of the easy-going attitude of the pure sensation type, who, from the standpoint of rational judgment, accepts indiscriminately everything that happens. Although this does not by any means imply an absolute lawlessness and lack of restraint, it nevertheless deprives him of the essential restraining power of judgment. But rational judgment is a conscious coercion which the rational type appears to impose on himself of his own free will. This coercion overtakes the sensation type from the unconscious, in the

form of compulsion. Moreover, the very existence of a judgment means that the rational type's relation to the object will never become an absolute tie, as it is in the case of the sensation type. When his attitude attains an abnormal degree of one-sidedness, therefore, he is in danger of being overpowered by the unconscious in the same measure as he is consciously in the grip of the object. If he should become neurotic, it is much harder to treat him by rational means because the functions which the analyst must turn to are in a relatively undifferentiated state, and little or no reliance can be placed on them. Special techniques for bringing emotional pressure to bear are often needed in order to make him at all conscious.

Intuition

610   In the extraverted attitude, intuition as the function of unconscious perception is wholly directed to external objects. Because intuition is in the main an unconscious process, its nature is very difficult to grasp. The intuitive function is represented in consciousness by an attitude of expectancy, by vision and penetration; but only from the subsequent result can it be established how much of what was "seen" was actually in the object, and how much was "read into" it. Just as sensation, when it is the dominant function, is not a mere reactive process of no further significance for the object, but an activity that seizes and shapes its object, so intuition is not mere perception, or vision, but an active, creative process that puts into the object just as much as it takes out. Since it does this unconsciously, it also has an unconscious effect on the object.

611   The primary function of intuition, however, is simply to transmit images, or perceptions of relations between things, which could not be transmitted by the other functions or only in a very roundabout way. These images have the value of specific insights which have a decisive influence on action whenever intuition is given priority. In this case, psychic adaptation will be grounded almost entirely on intuitions. Thinking, feeling, and sensation are then largely repressed, sensation being the one most affected, because, as the conscious sense function, it offers the greatest obstacle to intuition. Sensation is a hindrance to clear, unbiassed, naïve perception; its intrusive sensory stimuli direct attention to the physical surface, to the

366

very things round and beyond which intuition tries to peer. But since extraverted intuition is directed predominantly to objects, it actually comes very close to sensation; indeed, the expectant attitude to external objects is just as likely to make use of sensation. Hence, if intuition is to function properly, sensation must to a large extent be suppressed. By sensation I mean in this instance the simple and immediate sense-impression understood as a clearly defined physiological and psychic datum. This must be expressly established beforehand because, if I ask an intuitive how he orients himself, he will speak of things that are almost indistinguishable from sense-impressions. Very often he will even use the word "sensation." He does have sensations, of course, but he is not guided by them as such; he uses them merely as starting-points for his perceptions. He selects them by unconscious predilection. It is not the strongest sensation, in the physiological sense, that is accorded the chief value, but any sensation whatsoever whose value is enhanced by the intuitive's unconscious attitude. In this way it may eventually come to acquire the chief value, and to his conscious mind it appears to be pure sensation. But actually it is not so.

612   Just as extraverted sensation strives to reach the highest pitch of actuality, because this alone can give the appearance of a full life, so intuition tries to apprehend the widest range of *possibilities*, since only through envisioning possibilities is intuition fully satisfied. It seeks to discover what possibilities the objective situation holds in store; hence, as a subordinate function (i.e., when not in the position of priority), it is the auxiliary that automatically comes into play when no other function can find a way out of a hopelessly blocked situation. When it is the dominant function, every ordinary situation in life seems like a locked room which intuition has to open. It is constantly seeking fresh outlets and new possibilities in external life. In a very short time every existing situation becomes a prison for the intuitive, a chain that has to be broken. For a time objects appear to have an exaggerated value, if they should serve to bring about a solution, a deliverance, or lead to the discovery of a new possibility. Yet no sooner have they served their purpose as stepping-stones or bridges than they lose their value altogether and are discarded as burdensome

appendages. Facts are acknowledged only if they open new possibilities of advancing beyond them and delivering the individual from their power. Nascent possibilities are compelling motives from which intuition cannot escape and to which all else must be sacrificed.

The Extraverted Intuitive Type

613   Whenever intuition predominates, a peculiar and unmistakable psychology results. Because extraverted intuition is oriented by the object, there is a marked dependence on external situations, but it is altogether different from the dependence of the sensation type. The intuitive is never to be found in the world of accepted reality-values, but he has a keen nose for anything new and in the making. Because he is always seeking out new possibilities, stable conditions suffocate him. He seizes on new objects or situations with great intensity, sometimes with extraordinary enthusiasm, only to abandon them cold-bloodedly, without any compunction and apparently without remembering them, as soon as their range is known and no further developments can be divined. So long as a new possibility is in the offing, the intuitive is bound to it with the shackles of fate. It is as though his whole life vanished in the new situation. One gets the impression, which he himself shares, that he has always just reached a final turning-point, and that from now on he can think and feel nothing else. No matter how reasonable and suitable it may be, and although every conceivable argument speaks for its stability, a day will come when nothing will deter him from regarding as a prison the very situation that seemed to promise him freedom and deliverance, and from acting accordingly. Neither reason nor feeling can restrain him or frighten him away from a new possibility, even though it goes against all his previous convictions. Thinking and feeling, the indispensable components of conviction, are his inferior functions, carrying no weight and hence incapable of effectively withstanding the power of intuition. And yet these functions are the only ones that could compensate its supremacy by supplying the *judgment* which the intuitive type totally lacks. The intuitive's morality is governed neither by thinking nor by feeling; he has his own characteristic morality, which consists in a loyalty to his vision and in vol-

untary submission to its authority. Consideration for the welfare of others is weak. Their psychic well-being counts as little with him as does his own. He has equally little regard for their convictions and way of life, and on this account he is often put down as an immoral and unscrupulous adventurer. Since his intuition is concerned with externals and with ferreting out their possibilities, he readily turns to professions in which he can exploit these capacities to the full. Many business tycoons, entrepreneurs, speculators, stockbrokers, politicians, etc., belong to this type. It would seem to be more common among women, however, than among men. In women the intuitive capacity shows itself not so much in the professional as in the social sphere. Such women understand the art of exploiting every social occasion, they make the right social connections, they seek out men with prospects only to abandon everything again for the sake of a new possibility.

614   It goes without saying that such a type is uncommonly important both economically and culturally. If his intentions are good, i.e., if his attitude is not too egocentric, he can render exceptional service as the initiator or promoter of new enterprises. He is the natural champion of all minorities with a future. Because he is able, when oriented more to people than things, to make an intuitive diagnosis of their abilities and potentialities, he can also "make" men. His capacity to inspire courage or to kindle enthusiasm for anything new is unrivalled, although he may already have dropped it by the morrow. The stronger his intuition, the more his ego becomes fused with all the possibilities he envisions. He brings his vision to life, he presents it convincingly and with dramatic fire, he embodies it, so to speak. But this is not play-acting, it is a kind of fate.

615   Naturally this attitude holds great dangers, for all too easily the intuitive may fritter away his life on things and people, spreading about him an abundance of life which others live and not he himself. If only he could stay put, he would reap the fruits of his labours; but always he must be running after a new possibility, quitting his newly planted fields while others gather in the harvest. In the end he goes away empty. But when the intuitive lets things come to such a pass, he also has his own unconscious against him. The unconscious of the intuitive bears some resemblance to that of the sensation type.

Thinking and feeling, being largely repressed, come up with infantile, archaic thoughts and feelings similar to those of the countertype. They take the form of intense projections which are just as absurd as his, though they seem to lack the "magical" character of the latter and are chiefly concerned with quasi-realities such as sexual suspicions, financial hazards, forebodings of illness, etc. The difference seems to be due to the repression of real sensations. These make themselves felt when, for instance, the intuitive suddenly finds himself entangled with a highly unsuitable woman—or, in the case of a woman, with an unsuitable man—because these persons have stirred up the archaic sensations. This leads to an unconscious, compulsive tie which bodes nobody any good. Cases of this kind are themselves symptomatic of compulsion, to which the intuitive is as prone as the sensation type. He claims a similar freedom and exemption from restraint, submitting his decisions to no rational judgment and relying entirely on his nose for the possibilities that chance throws in his way. He exempts himself from the restrictions of reason only to fall victim to neurotic compulsions in the form of over-subtle ratiocinations, hairsplitting dialectics, and a compulsive tie to the sensation aroused by the object. His conscious attitude towards both sensation and object is one of ruthless superiority. Not that he means to be ruthless or superior—he simply does not see the object that everyone else sees and rides roughshod over it, just as the sensation type has no eyes for its soul. But sooner or later the object takes revenge in the form of compulsive hypochondriacal ideas, phobias, and every imaginable kind of absurd bodily sensation.

Summary of the Extraverted Irrational Types

616   I call the two preceding types irrational for the reasons previously discussed, namely that whatever they do or do not do is based not on rational judgment but on the sheer intensity of perception. Their perception is directed simply and solely to events as they happen, no selection being made by judgment. In this respect they have a decided advantage over the two judging types. Objective events both conform to law and are accidental. In so far as they conform to law, they are accessible to reason; in so far as they are accidental, they are not.

Conversely, we might also say that an event conforms to law when it presents an aspect accessible to reason, and that when it presents an aspect for which we can find no law we call it accidental. The postulate of universal lawfulness is a postulate of reason alone, but in no sense is it a postulate of our perceptive functions. Since these are in no way based on the principle of reason and its postulates, they are by their very nature irrational. That is why I call the perception types "irrational" by nature. But merely because they subordinate judgment to perception, it would be quite wrong to regard them as "unreasonable." It would be truer to say that they are in the highest degree *empirical*. They base themselves exclusively on experience—so exclusively that, as a rule, their judgment cannot keep pace with their experience. But the judging functions are none the less present, although they eke out a largely unconscious existence. Since the unconscious, in spite of its separation from the conscious subject, is always appearing on the scene, we notice in the actual life of the irrational types striking judgments and acts of choice, but they take the form of apparent sophistries, cold-hearted criticisms, and a seemingly calculating choice of persons and situations. These traits have a rather infantile and even primitive character; both types can on occasion be astonishingly naïve, as well as ruthless, brusque, and violent. To the rational types the real character of these people might well appear rationalistic and calculating in the worst sense. But this judgment would be valid only for their unconscious, and therefore quite incorrect for their conscious psychology, which is entirely oriented by perception, and because of its irrational nature is quite unintelligible to any rational judgment. To the rational mind it might even seem that such a hodge-podge of accidentals hardly deserves the name "psychology" at all. The irrational type ripostes with an equally contemptuous opinion of his opposite number: he sees him as something only half alive, whose sole aim is to fasten the fetters of reason on everything living and strangle it with judgments. These are crass extremes, but they nevertheless occur.

617   From the standpoint of the rational type, the other might easily be represented as an inferior kind of rationalist—when, that is to say, he is judged by what happens to him. For what happens to him is not accidental—here he is the master—

instead, the accidents that befall him take the form of rational judgments and rational intentions, and these are the things he stumbles over. To the rational mind this is something almost unthinkable, but its unthinkableness merely equals the astonishment of the irrational type when he comes up against someone who puts rational ideas above actual and living happenings. Such a thing seems to him scarcely credible. As a rule it is quite hopeless to discuss these things with him as questions of principle, for all rational communication is just as alien and repellent to him as it would be unthinkable for the rationalist to enter into a contract without mutual consultation and obligation.

618   This brings me to the problem of the psychic relationship between the two types. Following the terminology of the French school of hypnotists, psychic relationship is known in modern psychiatry as "rapport." Rapport consists essentially in a feeling of agreement in spite of acknowledged differences. Indeed, the recognition of existing differences, if it be mutual, is itself a rapport, a feeling of agreement. If in a given case we make this feeling conscious to a higher degree than usual, we discover that it is not just a feeling whose nature cannot be analysed further, but at the same time an insight or a content of cognition which presents the point of agreement in conceptual form. This rational presentation is valid only for the rational types, but not for the irrational, whose rapport is based not on judgment but on the parallelism of living events. His feeling of agreement comes from the common perception of a sensation or intuition. The rational type would say that rapport with the irrational depends purely on chance. If, by some accident, the objective situations are exactly in tune, something like a human relationship takes place, but nobody can tell how valid it is or how long it will last. To the rational type it is often a painful thought that the relationship will last just as long as external circumstances and chance provide a common interest. This does not seem to him particularly human, whereas it is precisely in this that the irrational type sees a human situation of particular beauty. The result is that each regards the other as a man destitute of relationships, who cannot be relied upon, and with whom one can never get on decent terms. This unhappy outcome, however, is reached only when

one makes a conscious effort to assess the nature of one's relationships with others. But since this kind of psychological conscientiousness is not very common, it frequently happens that despite an absolute difference of standpoint a rapport nevertheless comes about, and in the following way: one party, by unspoken projection, assumes that the other is, in all essentials, of the same opinion as himself, while the other divines or senses an objective community of interest, of which, however, the former has no conscious inkling and whose existence he would at once dispute, just as it would never occur to the other that his relationship should be based on a common point of view. A rapport of this kind is by far the most frequent; it rests on mutual projection, which later becomes the source of many misunderstandings.

619 Psychic relationship, in the extraverted attitude, is always governed by objective factors and external determinants. What a man is within himself is never of any decisive significance. For our present-day culture the extraverted attitude to the problem of human relationships is the principle that counts; naturally the introverted principle occurs too, but it is still the exception and has to appeal to the tolerance of the age.

3. THE INTROVERTED TYPE

a. The General Attitude of Consciousness

620 As I have already explained in the previous section, the introvert is distinguished from the extravert by the fact that he does not, like the latter, orient himself by the object and by objective data, but by subjective factors. I also mentioned[4] that the introvert interposes a subjective view between the perception of the object and his own action, which prevents the action from assuming a character that fits the objective situation. Naturally this is a special instance, mentioned by way of example and intended to serve only as a simple illustration. We must now attempt a formulation on a broader basis.

621 Although the introverted consciousness is naturally aware of external conditions, it selects the subjective determinants as

---

[4] Supra, par. 563.

the decisive ones. It is therefore oriented by the factor in perception and cognition which responds to the sense stimulus in accordance with the individual's subjective disposition. For example, two people see the same object, but they never see it in such a way that the images they receive are absolutely identical. Quite apart from the variable acuteness of the sense organs and the personal equation, there often exists a radical difference, both in kind and in degree, in the psychic assimilation of the perceptual image. Whereas the extravert continually appeals to what comes to him from the object, the introvert relies principally on what the sense impression constellates in the subject. The difference in the case of a single apperception may, of course, be very delicate, but in the total psychic economy it makes itself felt in the highest degree, particularly in the effect it has on the ego. If I may anticipate, I consider the viewpoint which inclines, with Weininger, to describe the introverted attitude as philautic, autoerotic, egocentric, subjectivistic, egotistic, etc., to be misleading in principle and thoroughly depreciatory. It reflects the normal bias of the extraverted attitude in regard to the nature of the introvert. We must not forget—although the extravert is only too prone to do so—that perception and cognition are not purely objective, but are also subjectively conditioned. The world exists not merely in itself, but also as it appears to me. Indeed, at bottom, we have absolutely no criterion that could help us to form a judgment of a world which was unassimilable by the subject. If we were to ignore the subjective factor, it would be a complete denial of the great doubt as to the possibility of absolute cognition. And this would mean a relapse into the stale and hollow positivism that marred the turn of the century—an attitude of intellectual arrogance accompanied by crudeness of feeling, a violation of life as stupid as it is presumptuous. By overvaluing our capacity for objective cognition we repress the importance of the subjective factor, which simply means a denial of the subject. But what is the subject? The subject is man himself—we are the subject. Only a sick mind could forget that cognition must have a subject, and that there is no knowledge whatever and therefore no world at all unless "I know" has been said, though with this statement one has already expressed the subjective limitation of all knowledge.

374

622   This applies to all the psychic functions: they have a subject which is just as indispensable as the object. It is characteristic of our present extraverted sense of values that the word "subjective" usually sounds like a reproof; at all events the epithet "merely subjective" is brandished like a weapon over the head of anyone who is not boundlessly convinced of the absolute superiority of the object. We must therefore be quite clear as to what "subjective" means in this inquiry. By the subjective factor I understand that psychological action or reaction which merges with the effect produced by the object and so gives rise to a new psychic datum. In so far as the subjective factor has, from the earliest times and among all peoples, remained in large measure constant, elementary perceptions and cognitions being almost universally the same, it is a reality that is just as firmly established as the external object. If this were not so, any sort of permanent and essentially unchanging reality would be simply inconceivable, and any understanding of the past would be impossible. In this sense, therefore, the subjective factor is as ineluctable a datum as the extent of the sea and the radius of the earth. By the same token, the subjective factor has all the value of a co-determinant of the world we live in, a factor that can on no account be left out of our calculations. It is another universal law, and whoever bases himself on it has a foundation as secure, as permanent, and as valid as the man who relies on the object. But just as the object and objective data do not remain permanently the same, being perishable and subject to chance, so too the subjective factor is subject to variation and individual hazards. For this reason its value is also merely relative. That is to say, the excessive development of the introverted standpoint does not lead to a better and sounder use of the subjective factor, but rather to an artificial subjectivizing of consciousness which can hardly escape the reproach "merely subjective." This is then counterbalanced by a de-subjectivization which takes the form of an exaggerated extraverted attitude, an attitude aptly described by Weininger as "misautic." But since the introverted attitude is based on the ever-present, extremely real, and absolutely indispensable fact of psychic adaptation, expressions like "philautic," "egocentric," and so on are out of place and objectionable because they arouse the

375

prejudice that it is always a question of the beloved ego. Nothing could be more mistaken than such an assumption. Yet one is continually meeting it in the judgments of the extravert on the introvert. Not, of course, that I wish to ascribe this error to individual extraverts; it is rather to be put down to the generally accepted extraverted view which is by no means restricted to the extraverted type, for it has just as many representatives among introverts, very much to their own detriment. The reproach of being untrue to their own nature can justly be levelled at the latter, whereas this at least cannot be held against the former.

623   The introverted attitude is normally oriented by the psychic structure, which is in principle hereditary and is inborn in the subject. This must not be assumed, however, to be simply identical with the subject's ego, as is implied by the above designations of Weininger; it is rather the psychic structure of the subject prior to any ego-development. The really fundamental subject, the self, is far more comprehensive than the ego, since the former includes the unconscious whereas the latter is essentially the focal point of consciousness. Were the ego identical with the self, it would be inconceivable how we could sometimes see ourselves in dreams in quite different forms and with entirely different meanings. But it is a characteristic peculiarity of the introvert, which is as much in keeping with his own inclination as with the general bias, to confuse his ego with the self, and to exalt it as the subject of the psychic process, thus bringing about the aforementioned subjectivization of consciousness which alienates him from the object.

624   The psychic structure is the same as what Semon calls "mneme"[5] and what I call the "collective unconscious." The individual self is a portion or segment or representative of something present in all living creatures, an exponent of the specific mode of psychological behaviour, which varies from species to species and is inborn in each of its members. The inborn mode of *acting* has long been known as *instinct,* and for the inborn mode of psychic apprehension I have proposed the term *archetype.*[6] I may assume that what is understood by in-

[5] *Die Mneme als erhaltendes Prinzip im Wechsel des organischen Geschehens* (trans. by L. Simon: *The Mneme*).

[6] "Instinct and the Unconscious," pars. 270ff.

stinct is familiar to everyone. It is another matter with the archetype. What I understand by it is identical with the "primordial image," a term borrowed from Jacob Burckhardt,[7] and I describe it as such in the Definitions that conclude this book. I must here refer the reader to the definition "Image."[8]

625   The archetype is a symbolic formula which always begins to function when there are no conscious ideas present, or when conscious ideas are inhibited for internal or external reasons. The contents of the collective unconscious are represented in consciousness in the form of pronounced preferences and definite ways of looking at things. These subjective tendencies and views are generally regarded by the individual as being determined by the object—incorrectly, since they have their source in the unconscious structure of the psyche and are merely released by the effect of the object. They are stronger than the object's influence, their psychic value is higher, so that they superimpose themselves on all impressions. Thus, just as it seems incomprehensible to the introvert that the object should always be the decisive factor, it remains an enigma to the extravert how a subjective standpoint can be superior to the objective situation. He inevitably comes to the conclusion that the introvert is either a conceited egoist or crack-brained bigot. Today he would be suspected of harbouring an unconscious power-complex. The introvert certainly lays himself open to these suspicions, for his positive, highly generalizing manner of expression, which appears to rule out every other opinion from the start, lends countenance to all the extravert's prejudices. Moreover the inflexibility of his subjective judgment, setting itself above all objective data, is sufficient in itself to create the impression of marked egocentricity. Faced with this prejudice the introvert is usually at a loss for the right argument, for he is quite unaware of the unconscious but generally quite valid assumptions on which his subjective judgment and his subjective perceptions are based. In the fashion of the times he looks outside for an answer, instead of seeking it behind his own consciousness. Should he become neurotic, it is the sign of an almost complete identity of the ego with the self; the importance of the self is reduced to nil, while the ego

7 [Cf. *Symbols of Transformation*, par. 45, n. 45.—EDITORS.]
8 [Especially pars. 746ff.—EDITORS.]

is inflated beyond measure. The whole world-creating force of the subjective factor becomes concentrated in the ego, producing a boundless power-complex and a fatuous egocentricity. Every psychology which reduces the essence of man to the unconscious power drive springs from this kind of disposition. Many of Nietzsche's lapses in taste, for example, are due to this subjectivization of consciousness.

b. The Attitude of the Unconscious

626   The predominance of the subjective factor in consciousness naturally involves a devaluation of the object. The object is not given the importance that belongs to it by right. Just as it plays too great a role in the extraverted attitude, it has too little meaning for the introvert. To the extent that his consciousness is subjectivized and excessive importance attached to the ego, the object is put in a position which in the end becomes untenable. The object is a factor whose power cannot be denied, whereas the ego is a very limited and fragile thing. It would be a very different matter if the self opposed the object. Self and world are commensurable factors; hence a normal introverted attitude is as justifiable and valid as a normal extraverted attitude. But if the ego has usurped the claims of the subject, this naturally produces, by way of compensation, an unconscious reinforcement of the influence of the object. In spite of positively convulsive efforts to ensure the superiority of the ego, the object comes to exert an overwhelming influence, which is all the more invincible because it seizes on the individual unawares and forcibly obtrudes itself on his consciousness. As a result of the ego's unadapted relation to the object—for a desire to dominate it is not adaptation—a compensatory relation arises in the unconscious which makes itself felt as an absolute and irrepressible tie to the object. The more the ego struggles to preserve its independence, freedom from obligation, and superiority, the more it becomes enslaved to the objective data. The individual's freedom of mind is fettered by the ignominy of his financial dependence, his freedom of action trembles in the face of public opinion, his moral superiority collapses in a morass of inferior relationships, and his desire to dominate ends in a pitiful craving to be loved. It is

now the unconscious that takes care of the relation to the object, and it does so in a way that is calculated to bring the illusion of power and the fantasy of superiority to utter ruin. The object assumes terrifying proportions in spite of the conscious attempt to degrade it. In consequence, the ego's efforts to detach itself from the object and get it under control become all the more violent. In the end it surrounds itself with a regular system of defences (aptly described by Adler) for the purpose of preserving at least the illusion of superiority. The introvert's alienation from the object is now complete; he wears himself out with defence measures on the one hand, while on the other he makes fruitless attempts to impose his will on the object and assert himself. These efforts are constantly being frustrated by the overwhelming impressions received from the object. It continually imposes itself on him against his will, it arouses in him the most disagreeable and intractable affects and persecutes him at every step. A tremendous inner struggle is needed all the time in order to "keep going." The typical form his neurosis takes is psychasthenia, a malady characterized on the one hand by extreme sensitivity and on the other by great proneness to exhaustion and chronic fatigue.

627 An analysis of the personal unconscious reveals a mass of power fantasies coupled with fear of objects which he himself has forcibly activated, and of which he is often enough the victim. His fear of objects develops into a peculiar kind of cowardliness; he shrinks from making himself or his opinions felt, fearing that this will only increase the object's power. He is terrified of strong affects in others, and is hardly ever free from the dread of falling under hostile influences. Objects possess puissant and terrifying qualities for him—qualities he cannot consciously discern in them, but which he imagines he sees through his unconscious perception. As his relation to the object is very largely repressed, it takes place via the unconscious, where it becomes charged with the latter's qualities. These qualities are mostly infantile and archaic, so that the relation to the object becomes primitive too, and the object seems endowed with magical powers. Anything strange and new arouses fear and mistrust, as though concealing unknown perils; heirlooms and suchlike are attached to his soul as by

379

invisible threads; any change is upsetting, if not positively dangerous, as it seems to denote a magical animation of the object. His ideal is a lonely island where nothing moves except what he permits to move. Vischer's novel, *Auch Einer*, affords deep insight into this side of the introvert's psychology, and also into the underlying symbolism of the collective unconscious. But this latter question I must leave to one side, since it is not specific to a description of types but is a general phenomenon.

c. The Peculiarities of the Basic Psychological Functions in the Introverted Attitude

Thinking

628   In the section on extraverted thinking I gave a brief description of introverted thinking (pars. 578–79) and must refer to it again here. Introverted thinking is primarily oriented by the subjective factor. At the very least the subjective factor expresses itself as a feeling of guidance which ultimately determines judgment. Sometimes it appears as a more or less complete image which serves as a criterion. But whether introverted thinking is concerned with concrete or with abstract objects, always at the decisive points it is oriented by subjective data. It does not lead from concrete experience back again to the object, but always to the subjective content. External facts are not the aim and origin of this thinking, though the introvert would often like to make his thinking appear so. It begins with the subject and leads back to the subject, far though it may range into the realm of actual reality. With regard to the establishment of new facts it is only indirectly of value, since new views rather than knowledge of new facts are its main concern. It formulates questions and creates theories, it opens up new prospects and insights, but with regard to facts its attitude is one of reserve. They are all very well as illustrative examples, but they must not be allowed to predominate. Facts are collected as evidence for a theory, never for their own sake. If ever this happens, it is merely a concession to the extraverted style. Facts are of secondary importance for this kind of thinking; what seems to it of paramount importance is the development and presentation of the subjective idea, of the initial symbolic image hovering darkly before the mind's eye.

Its aim is never an intellectual reconstruction of the concrete fact, but a shaping of that dark image into a luminous idea. It wants to reach reality, to see how the external fact will fit into and fill the framework of the idea, and the creative power of this thinking shows itself when it actually creates an idea which, though not inherent in the concrete fact, is yet the most suitable abstract expression of it. Its task is completed when the idea it has fashioned seems to emerge so inevitably from the external facts that they actually prove its validity.

629   But no more than extraverted thinking can wrest a sound empirical concept from concrete facts or create new ones can introverted thinking translate the initial image into an idea adequately adapted to the facts. For, as in the former case the purely empirical accumulation of facts paralyzes thought and smothers their meaning, so in the latter case introverted thinking shows a dangerous tendency to force the facts into the shape of its image, or to ignore them altogether in order to give fantasy free play. In that event it will be impossible for the finished product—the idea—to repudiate its derivation from the dim archaic image. It will have a mythological streak which one is apt to interpret as "originality" or, in more pronounced cases, as mere whimsicality, since its archaic character is not immediately apparent to specialists unfamiliar with mythological motifs. The subjective power of conviction exerted by an idea of this kind is usually very great, and it is all the greater the less it comes into contact with external facts. Although it may seem to the originator of the idea that his meagre store of facts is the actual source of its truth and validity, in reality this is not so, for the idea derives its convincing power from the unconscious archetype, which, as such, is eternally valid and true. But this truth is so universal and so symbolic that it must first be assimilated to the recognized and recognizable knowledge of the time before it can become a practical truth of any value for life. What would causality be, for instance, if it could nowhere be recognized in practical causes and practical effects?

630   This kind of thinking easily gets lost in the immense truth of the subjective factor. It creates theories for their own sake, apparently with an eye to real or at least possible facts, but always with a distinct tendency to slip over from the world of

ideas into mere imagery. Accordingly, visions of numerous possibilities appear on the scene, but none of them ever becomes a reality, until finally images are produced which no longer express anything externally real, being mere symbols of the ineffable and unknowable. It is now merely a mystical thinking and quite as unfruitful as thinking that remains bound to objective data. Whereas the latter sinks to the level of a mere representation of facts, the former evaporates into a representation of the irrepresentable, far beyond anything that could be expressed in an image. The representation of facts has an incontestable truth because the subjective factor is excluded and the facts speak for themselves. Similarly, the representation of the irrepresentable has an immediate, subjective power of conviction because it demonstrates its own existence. The one says "Est, ergo est"; the other says "Cogito, ergo cogito." Introverted thinking carried to extremes arrives at the evidence of its own subjective existence, and extraverted thinking at the evidence of its complete identity with the objective fact. Just as the latter abnegates itself by evaporating into the object, the former empties itself of each and every content and has to be satisfied with merely existing. In both cases the further development of life is crowded out of the thinking function into the domain of the other psychic functions, which till then had existed in a state of relative unconsciousness. The extraordinary impoverishment of introverted thinking is compensated by a wealth of unconscious facts. The more consciousness is impelled by the thinking function to confine itself within the smallest and emptiest circle—which seems, however, to contain all the riches of the gods—the more the unconscious fantasies will be enriched by a multitude of archaic contents, a veritable "pandaemonium" of irrational and magical figures, whose physiognomy will accord with the nature of the function that will supersede the thinking function as the vehicle of life. If it should be the intuitive function, then the "other side" will be viewed through the eyes of a Kubin or a Meyrink.[9] If it is the feeling function, then quite unheard-of and fantastic feeling relationships will be formed, coupled with contradictory and unintelligible value judgments. If it is the sensation function, the

---

[9] Kubin, *The Other Side*, and Meyrink, *Das grüne Gesicht*.

senses will nose up something new, and never experienced before, in and outside the body. Closer examination of these permutations will easily demonstrate a recrudescence of primitive psychology with all its characteristic features. Naturally, such experiences are not merely primitive, they are also symbolic; in fact, the more primordial and aboriginal they are, the more they represent a future truth. For everything old in the unconscious hints at something coming.

631   Under ordinary circumstances, not even the attempt to get to the "other side" will be successful—and still less the redeeming journey through the unconscious. The passage across is usually blocked by conscious resistance to any subjection of the ego to the realities of the unconscious and their determining power. It is a state of dissociation, in other words a neurosis characterized by inner debility and increasing cerebral exhaustion—the symptoms of psychasthenia.

The Introverted Thinking Type

632   Just as we might take Darwin as an example of the normal extraverted thinking type, the normal introverted thinking type could be represented by Kant. The one speaks with facts, the other relies on the subjective factor. Darwin ranges over the wide field of objective reality. Kant restricts himself to a critique of knowledge. Cuvier and Nietzsche would form an even sharper contrast.

633   The introverted thinking type is characterized by the primacy of the kind of thinking I have just described. Like his extraverted counterpart, he is strongly influenced by ideas, though his ideas have their origin not in objective data but in his subjective foundation. He will follow his ideas like the extravert, but in the reverse direction: inwards and not outwards. Intensity is his aim, not extensity. In these fundamental respects he differs quite unmistakably from his extraverted counterpart. What distinguishes the other, namely his intense relation to objects, is almost completely lacking in him as in every introverted type. If the object is a person, this person has a distinct feeling that he matters only in a negative way; in milder cases he is merely conscious of being *de trop*, but with a more extreme type he feels himself warded off as something definitely disturbing. This negative relation to the object, ranging from

indifference to aversion, characterizes every introvert and makes a description of the type exceedingly difficult. Everything about him tends to disappear and get concealed. His judgment appears cold, inflexible, arbitrary, and ruthless, because it relates far less to the object than to the subject. One can feel nothing in it that might possibly confer a higher value on the object; it always bypasses the object and leaves one with a feeling of the subject's superiority. He may be polite, amiable, and kind, but one is constantly aware of a certain uneasiness betraying an ulterior motive—the disarming of an opponent, who must at all costs be pacified and placated lest he prove himself a nuisance. In no sense, of course, is he an opponent, but if he is at all sensitive he will feel himself repulsed, and even belittled.

634   Invariably the object has to submit to a certain amount of neglect, and in pathological cases it is even surrounded with quite unnecessary precautionary measures. Thus this type tends to vanish behind a cloud of misunderstanding, which gets all the thicker the more he attempts to assume, by way of compensation and with the help of his inferior functions, an air of urbanity which contrasts glaringly with his real nature. Although he will shrink from no danger in building up his world of ideas, and never shrinks from thinking a thought because it might prove to be dangerous, subversive, heretical, or wounding to other people's feelings, he is none the less beset by the greatest anxiety if ever he has to make it an objective reality. That goes against the grain. And when he does put his ideas into the world, he never introduces them like a mother solicitous for her children, but simply dumps them there and gets extremely annoyed if they fail to thrive on their own account. His amazing unpracticalness and horror of publicity in any form have a hand in this. If in his eyes his product appears correct and true, then it must be so in practice, and others have got to bow to its truth. Hardly ever will he go out of his way to win anyone's appreciation of it, especially anyone of influence. And if ever he brings himself to do so, he generally sets about it so clumsily that it has just the opposite of the effect intended. He usually has bad experiences with rivals in his own field because he never understands how to curry their favour; as a rule he only succeeds in showing them how entirely su-

perfluous they are to him. In the pursuit of his ideas he is generally stubborn, headstrong, and quite unamenable to influence. His suggestibility to personal influences is in strange contrast to this. He has only to be convinced of a person's seeming innocuousness to lay himself open to the most undesirable elements. They seize hold of him from the unconscious. He lets himself be brutalized and exploited in the most ignominious way if only he can be left in peace to pursue his ideas. He simply does not see when he is being plundered behind his back and wronged in practice, for to him the relation to people and things is secondary and the objective evaluation of his product is something he remains unconscious of. Because he thinks out his problems to the limit, he complicates them and constantly gets entangled in his own scruples and misgivings. However clear to him the inner structure of his thoughts may be, he is not in the least clear where or how they link up with the world of reality. Only with the greatest difficulty will he bring himself to admit that what is clear to him may not be equally clear to everyone. His style is cluttered with all sorts of adjuncts, accessories, qualifications, retractions, saving clauses, doubts, etc., which all come from his scrupulosity. His work goes slowly and with difficulty.

635 　　In his personal relations he is taciturn or else throws himself on people who cannot understand him, and for him this is one more proof of the abysmal stupidity of man. If for once he is understood, he easily succumbs to credulous overestimation of his prowess. Ambitious women have only to know how to take advantage of his cluelessness in practical matters to make an easy prey of him; or he may develop into a misanthropic bachelor with a childlike heart. Often he is gauche in his behaviour, painfully anxious to escape notice, or else remarkably unconcerned and childishly naïve. In his own special field of work he provokes the most violent opposition, which he has no notion how to deal with, unless he happens to be seduced by his primitive affects into acrimonious and fruitless polemics. Casual acquaintances think him inconsiderate and domineering. But the better one knows him, the more favourable one's judgment becomes, and his closest friends value his intimacy very highly. To outsiders he seems prickly, unapproachable, and arrogant, and sometimes soured as a result of his anti-

social prejudices. As a personal teacher he has little influence, since the mentality of his students is strange to him. Besides, teaching has, at bottom, no interest for him unless it happens to provide him with a theoretical problem. He is a poor teacher, because all the time he is teaching his thought is occupied with the material itself and not with its presentation.

636   With the intensification of his type, his convictions become all the more rigid and unbending. Outside influences are shut off; as a person, too, he becomes more unsympathetic to his wider circle of acquaintances, and therefore more dependent on his intimates. His tone becomes personal and surly, and though his ideas may gain in profundity they can no longer be adequately expressed in the material at hand. To compensate for this, he falls back on emotionality and touchiness. The outside influences he has brusquely fended off attack him from within, from the unconscious, and in his efforts to defend himself he attacks things that to outsiders seem utterly unimportant. Because of the subjectivization of consciousness resulting from his lack of relationship to the object, what secretly concerns his own person now seems to him of extreme importance. He begins to confuse his subjective truth with his own personality. Although he will not try to press his convictions on anyone personally, he will burst out with vicious, personal retorts against every criticism, however just. Thus his isolation gradually increases. His originally fertilizing ideas become destructive, poisoned by the sediment of bitterness. His struggle against the influences emanating from the unconscious increases with his external isolation, until finally they begin to cripple him. He thinks his withdrawal into ever-increasing solitude will protect him from the unconscious influences, but as a rule it only plunges him deeper into the conflict that is destroying him from within.

637   The thinking of the introverted type is positive and synthetic in developing ideas which approximate more and more to the eternal validity of the primordial images. But as their connection with objective experience becomes more and more tenuous, they take on a mythological colouring and no longer hold true for the contemporary situation. Hence his thinking is of value for his contemporaries only so long as it is manifestly and intelligibly related to the known facts of the time.

Once it has become mythological, it ceases to be relevant and runs on in itself. The counterbalancing functions of feeling, intuition, and sensation are comparatively unconscious and inferior, and therefore have a primitive extraverted character that accounts for all the troublesome influences from outside to which the introverted thinker is prone. The various protective devices and psychological minefields which such people surround themselves with are known to everyone, and I can spare myself a description of them. They all serve as a defence against "magical" influences—and among them is a vague fear of the feminine sex.

Feeling

638   Introverted feeling is determined principally by the subjective factor. It differs quite as essentially from extraverted feeling as introverted from extraverted thinking. It is extremely difficult to give an intellectual account of the introverted feeling process, or even an approximate description of it, although the peculiar nature of this kind of feeling is very noticeable once one has become aware of it. Since it is conditioned subjectively and is only secondarily concerned with the object, it seldom appears on the surface and is generally misunderstood. It is a feeling which seems to devalue the object, and it therefore manifests itself for the most part negatively. The existence of positive feeling can be inferred only indirectly. Its aim is not to adjust itself to the object, but to subordinate it in an unconscious effort to realize the underlying images. It is continually seeking an image which has no existence in reality, but which it has seen in a kind of vision. It glides unheedingly over all objects that do not fit in with its aim. It strives after inner intensity, for which the objects serve at most as a stimulus. The depth of this feeling can only be guessed—it can never be clearly grasped. It makes people silent and difficult of access; it shrinks back like a violet from the brute nature of the object in order to fill the depths of the subject. It comes out with negative judgments or assumes an air of profound indifference as a means of defence.

639   The primordial images are, of course, just as much ideas as feelings. Fundamental ideas, ideas like God, freedom, and immortality, are just as much feeling-values as they are signifi-

cant ideas. Everything, therefore, that we have said about introverted thinking is equally true of introverted feeling, only here everything is felt while there it was thought. But the very fact that thoughts can generally be expressed more intelligibly than feelings demands a more than ordinary descriptive or artistic ability before the real wealth of this feeling can be even approximately presented or communicated to the world. If subjective thinking can be understood only with difficulty because of its unrelatedness, this is true in even higher degree of subjective feeling. In order to communicate with others, it has to find an external form not only acceptable to itself, but capable also of arousing a parallel feeling in them. Thanks to the relatively great inner (as well as outer) uniformity of human beings, it is actually possible to do this, though the form acceptable to feeling is extraordinarily difficult to find so long as it is still mainly oriented to the fathomless store of primordial images. If, however, feeling is falsified by an egocentric attitude, it at once becomes unsympathetic, because it is then concerned mainly with the ego. It inevitably creates the impression of sentimental self-love, of trying to make itself interesting, and even of morbid self-admiration. Just as the subjectivized consciousness of the introverted thinker, striving after abstraction to the nth degree, only succeeds in intensifying a thought-process that is in itself empty, the intensification of egocentric feeling only leads to inane transports of feeling for their own sake. This is the mystical, ecstatic stage which opens the way for the extraverted functions that feeling has repressed. Just as introverted thinking is counterbalanced by a primitive feeling, to which objects attach themselves with magical force, introverted feeling is counterbalanced by a primitive thinking, whose concretism and slavery to facts surpass all bounds. Feeling progressively emancipates itself from the object and creates for itself a freedom of action and conscience that is purely subjective, and may even renounce all traditional values. But so much the more does unconscious thinking fall a victim to the power of objective reality.

The Introverted Feeling Type

640   It is principally among women that I have found the predominance of introverted feeling. "Still waters run deep" is

very true of such women. They are mostly silent, inaccessible, hard to understand; often they hide behind a childish or banal mask, and their temperament is inclined to melancholy. They neither shine nor reveal themselves. As they are mainly guided by their subjective feelings, their true motives generally remain hidden. Their outward demeanour is harmonious, inconspicuous, giving an impression of pleasing repose, or of sympathetic response, with no desire to affect others, to impress, influence, or change them in any way. If this outward aspect is more pronounced, it arouses a suspicion of indifference and coldness, which may actually turn into a disregard for the comfort and well-being of others. One is distinctly aware then of the movement of feeling away from the object. With the normal type, however, this happens only when the influence of the object is too strong. The feeling of harmony, therefore, lasts only so long as the object goes its own moderate way and makes no attempt to cross the other's path. There is little effort to respond to the real emotions of the other person; they are more often damped down and rebuffed, or cooled off by a negative value judgment. Although there is a constant readiness for peaceful and harmonious co-existence, strangers are shown no touch of amiability, no gleam of responsive warmth, but are met with apparent indifference or a repelling coldness. Often they are made to feel entirely superfluous. Faced with anything that might carry her away or arouse enthusiasm, this type observes a benevolent though critical neutrality, coupled with a faint trace of superiority that soon takes the wind out of the sails of a sensitive person. Any stormy emotion, however, will be struck down with murderous coldness, unless it happens to catch the woman on her unconscious side—that is, unless it hits her feelings by arousing a primordial image. In that case she simply feels paralysed for the moment, and this in due course invariably produces an even more obstinate resistance which will hit the other person in his most vulnerable spot. As far as possible, the feeling relationship is kept to the safe middle path, all intemperate passions being resolutely tabooed. Expressions of feeling therefore remain niggardly, and the other person has a permanent sense of being undervalued once he becomes conscious of it. But this need not always be so, because very often he remains unconscious of the lack of feeling shown to him, in which case the unconscious demands of feeling will produce symptoms designed to compel attention.

641 Since this type appears rather cold and reserved, it might seem on a superficial view that such women have no feelings at all. But this would be quite wrong; the truth is, their feelings are intensive rather than extensive. They develop in depth. While an extensive feeling of sympathy can express itself in appropriate words and deeds, and thus quickly gets back to normal again, an intensive sympathy, being shut off from every means of expression, acquires a passionate depth that comprises a whole world of misery and simply gets benumbed. It may perhaps break out in some extravagant form and lead to an astounding act of an almost heroic character, quite unrelated either to the subject herself or to the object that provoked the outburst. To the outside world, or to the blind eyes of the extravert, this intensive sympathy looks like coldness, because usually it does nothing visible, and an extraverted consciousness is unable to believe in invisible forces. Such a misunderstanding is a common occurrence in the life of this type, and is used as a weighty argument against the possibility of any deeper feeling relation with the object. But the real object of this feeling is only dimly divined by the normal type herself. It may express itself in a secret religiosity anxiously guarded from profane eyes, or in intimate poetic forms that are kept equally well hidden, not without the secret ambition of displaying some kind of superiority over the other person by this means. Women often express a good deal of their feelings through their children, letting their passion flow secretly into them.

642 Although this tendency to overpower or coerce the other person with her secret feelings rarely plays a disturbing role in the normal type, and never leads to a serious attempt of this kind, some trace of it nevertheless seeps through into the personal effect they have on him, in the form of a domineering influence often difficult to define. It is sensed as a sort of stifling or oppressive feeling which holds everybody around her under a spell. It gives a woman of this type a mysterious power that may prove terribly fascinating to the extraverted man, for it touches his unconscious. This power comes from the deeply

felt, unconscious images, but consciously she is apt to relate it to the ego, whereupon her influence becomes debased into a personal tyranny. Whenever the unconscious subject is identified with the ego, the mysterious power of intensive feeling turns into a banal and overweening desire to dominate, into vanity and despotic bossiness. This produces a type of woman notorious for her unscrupulous ambition and mischievous cruelty. It is a change, however, that leads to neurosis.

643   So long as the ego feels subordinate to the unconscious subject, and feeling is aware of something higher and mightier than the ego, the type is normal. Although the unconscious thinking is archaic, its reductive tendencies help to compensate the occasional fits of trying to exalt the ego into the subject. If this should nevertheless happen as a result of complete suppression of the counterbalancing subliminal processes, the unconscious thinking goes over into open opposition and gets projected. The egocentrized subject now comes to feel the power and importance of the devalued object. She begins consciously to feel "what other people think." Naturally, other people are thinking all sorts of mean things, scheming evil, contriving plots, secret intrigues, etc. In order to forestall them, she herself is obliged to start counter-intrigues, to suspect others and sound them out, and weave counterplots. Beset by rumours, she must make frantic efforts to get her own back and be top dog. Endless clandestine rivalries spring up, and in these embittered struggles she will shrink from no baseness or meanness, and will even prostitute her virtues in order to play the trump card. Such a state of affairs must end in exhaustion. The form of neurosis is neurasthenic rather than hysterical, often with severe physical complications, such as anaemia and its sequelae.

Summary of the Introverted Rational Types

644   Both the foregoing types may be termed rational, since they are grounded on the functions of rational judgment. Rational judgment is based not merely on objective but also on subjective data. The predominance of one or the other factor, however, as a result of a psychic disposition often existing from early youth, will give the judgment a corresponding bias. A judgment that is truly rational will appeal to the objective and

the subjective factor equally and do justice to both. But that would be an ideal case and would presuppose an equal development of both extraversion and introversion. In practice, however, either movement excludes the other, and, so long as this dilemma remains, they cannot exist side by side but at best successively. Under ordinary conditions, therefore, an ideal rationality is impossible. The rationality of a rational type always has a typical bias. Thus, the judgment of the introverted rational types is undoubtedly rational, only it is oriented more by the subjective factor. This does not necessarily imply any logical bias, since the bias lies in the premise. The premise consists in the predominance of the subjective factor prior to all conclusions and judgments. The superior value of the subjective as compared with the objective factor appears self-evident from the beginning. It is not a question of *assigning* this value, but, as we have said, of a natural disposition existing before all rational valuation. Hence, to the introvert, rational judgment has many nuances which differentiate it from that of the extravert. To mention only the most general instance, the chain of reasoning that leads to the subjective factor seems to the introvert somewhat more rational than the one that leads to the object. This difference, though slight and practically unnoticeable in individual cases, builds up in the end to unbridgeable discrepancies which are the more irritating the less one is aware of the minimal shift of standpoint occasioned by the psychological premise. A capital error regularly creeps in here, for instead of recognizing the difference in the premise one tries to demonstrate a fallacy in the conclusion. This recognition is a difficult matter for every rational type, since it undermines the apparently absolute validity of his own principle and delivers him over to its antithesis, which for him amounts to a catastrophe.

645 The introvert is far more subject to misunderstanding than the extravert, not so much because the extravert is a more merciless or critical adversary than he himself might be, but because the style of the times which he himself imitates works against him. He finds himself in the minority, not in numerical relation to the extravert, but in relation to the general Western view of the world as judged by his feeling. In so far as he is a convinced participator in the general style, he undermines his

own foundations; for the general style, acknowledging as it does only the visible and tangible values, is opposed to his specific principle. Because of its invisibility, he is obliged to depreciate the subjective factor, and must force himself to join in the extraverted overvaluation of the object. He himself sets the subjective factor at too low a value, and his feelings of inferiority are his chastisement for this sin. Little wonder, therefore, that it is precisely in the present epoch, and particularly in those movements which are somewhat ahead of the time, that the subjective factor reveals itself in exaggerated, tasteless forms of expression bordering on caricature. I refer to the art of the present day.

646   The undervaluation of his own principle makes the introvert egotistical and forces on him the psychology of the underdog. The more egotistical he becomes, the more it seems to him that the others, who are apparently able, without qualms, to conform to the general style, are the oppressors against whom he must defend himself. He generally does not see that his chief error lies in not depending on the subjective factor with the same trust and devotion with which the extravert relies on the object. His undervaluation of his own principle makes his leanings towards egotism unavoidable, and because of this he fully deserves the censure of the extravert. If he remained true to his own principle, the charge of egotism would be altogether false, for his attitude would be justified by its effects in general, and the misunderstanding would be dissipated.

Sensation

647   Sensation, which by its very nature is dependent on the object and on objective stimuli, undergoes considerable modification in the introverted attitude. It, too, has a subjective factor, for besides the sensed object there is a sensing subject who adds his subjective disposition to the objective stimulus. In the introverted attitude sensation is based predominantly on the subjective component of perception. What I mean by this is best illustrated by works of art which reproduce external objects. If, for instance, several painters were to paint the same landscape, each trying to reproduce it faithfully, each painting will be different from the others, not merely because of differences in ability, but chiefly because of different ways

393

of seeing; indeed, in some of the paintings there will be a distinct psychic difference in mood and the treatment of colour and form. These qualities betray the influence of the subjective factor. The subjective factor in sensation is essentially the same as in the other functions we have discussed. It is an unconscious disposition which alters the sense-perception at its source, thus depriving it of the character of a purely objective influence. In this case, sensation is related primarily to the subject and only secondarily to the object. How extraordinarily strong the subjective factor can be is shown most clearly in art. Its predominance sometimes amounts to a complete suppression of the object's influence, and yet the sensation remains sensation even though it has become a perception of the subjective factor and the object has sunk to the level of a mere stimulus. Introverted sensation is oriented accordingly. True sense-perception certainly exists, but it always looks as though the object did not penetrate into the subject in its own right, but as though the subject were seeing it quite differently, or saw quite other things than other people see. Actually, he perceives the same things as everybody else, only he does not stop at the purely objective influence, but concerns himself with the subjective perception excited by the objective stimulus.

648   Subjective perception is markedly different from the objective. What is perceived is either not found at all in the object, or is, at most, merely suggested by it. That is, although the perception can be similar to that of other men, it is not immediately derived from the objective behaviour of things. It does not impress one as a mere product of consciousness—it is too genuine for that. But it makes a definite psychic impression because elements of a higher psychic order are discernible in it. This order, however, does not coincide with the contents of consciousness. It has to do with presuppositions or dispositions of the collective unconscious, with mythological images, with primordial possibilities of ideas. Subjective perception is characterized by the meaning that clings to it. It means more than the mere image of the object, though naturally only to one for whom the subjective factor means anything at all. To another, the reproduced subjective impression seems to suffer from the defect of not being sufficiently like the object and therefore to have failed in its purpose.

649   Introverted sensation apprehends the background of the physical world rather than its surface. The decisive thing is not the reality of the object, but the reality of the subjective factor, of the primordial images which, in their totality, constitute a psychic mirror-world. It is a mirror with the peculiar faculty of reflecting the existing contents of consciousness not in their known and customary form but, as it were, *sub specie aeternitatis*, somewhat as a million-year-old consciousness might see them. Such a consciousness would see the becoming and passing away of things simultaneously with their momentary existence in the present, and not only that, it would also see what was before their becoming and will be after their passing hence. Naturally this is only a figure of speech, but one that I needed in order to illustrate in some way the peculiar nature of introverted sensation. We could say that introverted sensation transmits an image which does not so much reproduce the object as spread over it the patina of age-old subjective experience and the shimmer of events still unborn. The bare sense impression develops in depth, reaching into the past and future, while extraverted sensation seizes on the momentary existence of things open to the light of day.

The Introverted Sensation Type

650   The predominance of introverted sensation produces a definite type, which is characterized by certain peculiarities. It is an irrational type, because it is oriented amid the flux of events not by rational judgment but simply by what happens. Whereas the extraverted sensation type is guided by the intensity of objective influences, the introverted type is guided by the intensity of the subjective sensation excited by the objective stimulus. Obviously, therefore, no proportional relation exists between object and sensation, but one that is apparently quite unpredictable and arbitrary. What will make an impression and what will not can never be seen in advance, and from outside. Did there exist an aptitude for expression in any way proportional to the intensity of his sensations, the irrationality of this type would be extraordinarily striking. This is the case, for instance, when an individual is a creative artist. But since this is the exception, the introvert's characteristic difficulty in expressing himself also conceals his irrationality. On the con-

trary, he may be conspicuous for his calmness and passivity, or for his rational self-control. This peculiarity, which often leads a superficial judgment astray, is really due to his unrelatedness to objects. Normally the object is not consciously devalued in the least, but its stimulus is removed from it and immediately replaced by a subjective reaction no longer related to the reality of the object. This naturally has the same effect as devaluation. Such a type can easily make one question why one should exist at all, or why objects in general should have any justification for their existence since everything essential still goes on happening without them. This doubt may be justified in extreme cases, but not in the normal, since the objective stimulus is absolutely necessary to sensation and merely produces something different from what the external situation might lead one to expect.

651   Seen from the outside, it looks as though the effect of the object did not penetrate into the subject at all. This impression is correct inasmuch as a subjective content does, in fact, intervene from the unconscious and intercept the effect of the object. The intervention may be so abrupt that the individual appears to be shielding himself directly from all objective influences. In more serious cases, such a protective defence actually does exist. Even with only a slight increase in the power of the unconscious, the subjective component of sensation becomes so alive that it almost completely obscures the influence of the object. If the object is a person, he feels completely devalued, while the subject has an illusory conception of reality, which in pathological cases goes so far that he is no longer able to distinguish between the real object and the subjective perception. Although so vital a distinction reaches the vanishing point only in near-psychotic states, yet long before that the subjective perception can influence thought, feeling, and action to an excessive degree despite the fact that the object is clearly seen in all its reality. When its influence does succeed in penetrating into the subject—because of its special intensity or because of its complete analogy with the unconscious image— even the normal type will be compelled to *act* in accordance with the unconscious model. Such action has an illusory character unrelated to objective reality and is extremely disconcerting. It instantly reveals the reality-alienating subjectivity of this

type. But when the influence of the object does not break through completely, it is met with well-intentioned neutrality, disclosing little sympathy yet constantly striving to soothe and adjust. The too low is raised a little, the too high is lowered, enthusiasm is damped down, extravagance restrained, and anything out of the ordinary reduced to the right formula—all this in order to keep the influence of the object within the necessary bounds. In this way the type becomes a menace to his environment because his total innocuousness is not altogether above suspicion. In that case he easily becomes a victim of the aggressiveness and domineeringness of others. Such men allow themselves to be abused and then take their revenge on the most unsuitable occasions with redoubled obtuseness and stubbornness.

652   If no capacity for artistic expression is present, all impressions sink into the depths and hold consciousness under a spell, so that it becomes impossible to master their fascination by giving them conscious expression. In general, this type can organize his impressions only in archaic ways, because thinking and feeling are relatively unconscious and, if conscious at all, have at their disposal only the most necessary, banal, everyday means of expression. As conscious functions, they are wholly incapable of adequately reproducing his subjective perceptions. This type, therefore, is uncommonly inaccessible to objective understanding, and he usually fares no better in understanding himself.

653   Above all, his development alienates him from the reality of the object, leaving him at the mercy of his subjective perceptions, which orient his consciousness to an archaic reality, although his lack of comparative judgment keeps him wholly unconscious of this fact. Actually he lives in a mythological world, where men, animals, locomotives, houses, rivers, and mountains appear either as benevolent deities or as malevolent demons. That they appear thus to him never enters his head, though that is just the effect they have on his judgments and actions. He judges and acts as though he had such powers to deal with; but this begins to strike him only when he discovers that his sensations are totally different from reality. If he has any aptitude for objective reason, he will sense this difference as morbid; but if he remains faithful to his irrationality, and is

397

ready to grant his sensations reality value, the objective world will appear a mere make-believe and a comedy. Only in extreme cases, however, is this dilemma reached. As a rule he resigns himself to his isolation and the banality of the world, which he has unconsciously made archaic.

654   His unconscious is distinguished chiefly by the repression of intuition, which consequently acquires an extraverted and archaic character. Whereas true extraverted intuition is possessed of a singular resourcefulness, a "good nose" for objectively real possibilities, this archaicized intuition has an amazing flair for all the ambiguous, shadowy, sordid, dangerous possibilities lurking in the background. The real and conscious intentions of the object mean nothing to it; instead, it sniffs out every conceivable archaic motive underlying such an intention. It therefore has a dangerous and destructive quality that contrasts glaringly with the well-meaning innocuousness of the conscious attitude. So long as the individual does not hold too aloof from the object, his unconscious intuition has a salutary compensating effect on the rather fantastic and overcredulous attitude of consciousness. But as soon as the unconscious becomes antagonistic, the archaic intuitions come to the surface and exert their pernicious influence, forcing themselves on the individual and producing compulsive ideas of the most perverse kind. The result is usually a compulsion neurosis, in which the hysterical features are masked by symptoms of exhaustion.

Intuition

655   Introverted intuition is directed to the inner object, a term that might justly be applied to the contents of the unconscious. The relation of inner objects to consciousness is entirely analogous to that of outer objects, though their reality is not physical but psychic. They appear to intuitive perception as subjective images of things which, though not to be met with in the outside world, constitute the contents of the unconscious, and of the collective unconscious in particular. These contents *per se* are naturally not accessible to experience, a quality they have in common with external objects. For just as external objects correspond only relatively to our perception of them, so

the phenomenal forms of the inner objects are also relative—products of their (to us) inaccessible essence and of the peculiar nature of the intuitive function.

656　Like sensation, intuition has its subjective factor, which is suppressed as much as possible in the extraverted attitude but is the decisive factor in the intuition of the introvert. Although his intuition may be stimulated by external objects, it does not concern itself with external possibilities but with what the external object has released within him. Whereas introverted sensation is mainly restricted to the perception, via the unconscious, of the phenomena of innervation and is arrested there, introverted intuition suppresses this side of the subjective factor and perceives the image that caused the innervation. Supposing, for instance, a man is overtaken by an attack of psychogenic vertigo. Sensation is arrested by the peculiar nature of this disturbance of innervation, perceiving all its qualities, its intensity, its course, how it arose and how it passed, but not advancing beyond that to its content, to the thing that caused the disturbance. Intuition, on the other hand, receives from sensation only the impetus to its own immediate activity; it peers behind the scenes, quickly perceiving the inner image that gave rise to this particular form of expression—the attack of vertigo. It sees the image of a tottering man pierced through the heart by an arrow. This image fascinates the intuitive activity; it is arrested by it, and seeks to explore every detail of it. It holds fast to the vision, observing with the liveliest interest how the picture changes, unfolds, and finally fades.

657　In this way introverted intuition perceives all the background processes of consciousness with almost the same distinctness as extraverted sensation registers external objects. For intuition, therefore, unconscious images acquire the dignity of things. But, because intuition excludes the co-operation of sensation, it obtains little or no knowledge of the disturbances of innervation or of the physical effects produced by the unconscious images. The images appear as though detached from the subject, as though existing in themselves without any relation to him. Consequently, in the above-mentioned example, the introverted intuitive, if attacked by vertigo, would never imagine that the image he perceived might in some way

399

refer to himself. To a judging type this naturally seems almost inconceivable, but it is none the less a fact which I have often come across in my dealings with intuitives.

658   The remarkable indifference of the extraverted intuitive to external objects is shared by the introverted intuitive in relation to inner objects. Just as the extraverted intuitive is continually scenting out new possibilities, which he pursues with equal unconcern for his own welfare and for that of others, pressing on quite heedless of human considerations and tearing down what has just been built in his everlasting search for change, so the introverted intuitive moves from image to image, chasing after every possibility in the teeming womb of the unconscious, without establishing any connection between them and himself. Just as the world of appearances can never become a moral problem for the man who merely senses it, the world of inner images is never a moral problem for the intuitive. For both of them it is an aesthetic problem, a matter of perception, a "sensation." Because of this, the introverted intuitive has little consciousness of his own bodily existence or of its effect on others. The extravert would say: "Reality does not exist for him, he gives himself up to fruitless fantasies." The perception of the images of the unconscious, produced in such inexhaustible abundance by the creative energy of life, is of course fruitless from the standpoint of immediate utility. But since these images represent possible views of the world which may give life a new potential, this function, which to the outside world is the strangest of all, is as indispensable to the total psychic economy as is the corresponding human type to the psychic life of a people. Had this type not existed, there would have been no prophets in Israel.

659   Introverted intuition apprehends the images arising from the *a priori* inherited foundations of the unconscious. These archetypes, whose innermost nature is inaccessible to experience, are the precipitate of the psychic functioning of the whole ancestral line; the accumulated experiences of organic life in general, a million times repeated, and condensed into types. In these archetypes, therefore, all experiences are represented which have happened on this planet since primeval times. The more frequent and the more intense they were, the more clearly focussed they become in the archetype. The

archetype would thus be, to borrow from Kant, the noumenon of the image which intuition perceives and, in perceiving, creates.

660   Since the unconscious is not just something that lies there like a psychic *caput mortuum*, but coexists with us and is constantly undergoing transformations which are inwardly connected with the general run of events, introverted intuition, through its perception of these inner processes, can supply certain data which may be of the utmost importance for understanding what is going on in the world. It can even foresee new possibilities in more or less clear outline, as well as events which later actually do happen. Its prophetic foresight is explained by its relation to the archetypes, which represent the laws governing the course of all experienceable things.

The Introverted Intuitive Type

661   The peculiar nature of introverted intuition, if it gains the ascendency, produces a peculiar type of man: the mystical dreamer and seer on the one hand, the artist and the crank on the other. The artist might be regarded as the normal representative of this type, which tends to confine itself to the perceptive character of intuition. As a rule, the intuitive stops at perception; perception is his main problem, and—in the case of a creative artist—the shaping of his perception. But the crank is content with a visionary idea by which he himself is shaped and determined. Naturally the intensification of intuition often results in an extraordinary aloofness of the individual from tangible reality; he may even become a complete enigma to his immediate circle. If he is an artist, he reveals strange, far-off things in his art, shimmering in all colours, at once portentous and banal, beautiful and grotesque, sublime and whimsical. If not an artist, he is frequently a misunderstood genius, a great man "gone wrong," a sort of wise simpleton, a figure for "psychological" novels.

662   Although the intuitive type has little inclination to make a moral problem of perception, since a strengthening of the judging functions is required for this, only a slight differentiation of judgment is sufficient to shift intuitive perception from the purely aesthetic into the moral sphere. A variety of this type is thus produced which differs essentially from the

aesthetic, although it is none the less characteristic of the introverted intuitive. The moral problem arises when the intuitive tries to relate himself to his vision, when he is no longer satisfied with mere perception and its aesthetic configuration and evaluation, when he confronts the questions: What does this mean for me or the world? What emerges from this vision in the way of a duty or a task, for me or the world? The pure intuitive who represses his judgment, or whose judgment is held in thrall by his perceptive faculties, never faces this question squarely, since his only problem is the "know-how" of perception. He finds the moral problem unintelligible or even absurd, and as far as possible forbids his thoughts to dwell on the disconcerting vision. It is different with the morally oriented intuitive. He reflects on the meaning of his vision, and is less concerned with developing its aesthetic possibilities than with the moral effects which emerge from its intrinsic significance. His judgment allows him to discern, though often only darkly, that he, as a man and a whole human being, is somehow involved in his vision, that it is not just an object to be perceived, but wants to participate in the life of the subject. Through this realization he feels bound to transform his vision into his own life. But since he tends to rely most predominantly on his vision, his moral efforts become one-sided; he makes himself and his life symbolic—adapted, it is true, to the inner and eternal meaning of events, but unadapted to present-day reality. He thus deprives himself of any influence upon it because he remains uncomprehended. His language is not the one currently spoken—it has become too subjective. His arguments lack the convincing power of reason. He can only profess or proclaim. His is "the voice of one crying in the wilderness."

663   What the introverted intuitive represses most of all is the sensation of the object, and this colours his whole unconscious. It gives rise to a compensatory extraverted sensation function of an archaic character. The unconscious personality can best be described as an extraverted sensation type of a rather low and primitive order. Instinctuality and intemperance are the hallmarks of this sensation, combined with an extraordinary dependence on sense-impressions. This compensates the rarefied air of the intuitive's conscious attitude, giving it a certain weight, so that complete "sublimation" is prevented. But if,

402

through a forced exaggeration of the conscious attitude, there should be a complete subordination to inner perceptions, the unconscious goes over to the opposition, giving rise to compulsive sensations whose excessive dependence on the object directly contradicts the conscious attitude. The form of neurosis is a compulsion neurosis with hypochondriacal symptoms, hypersensitivity of the sense organs, and compulsive ties to particular persons or objects.

Summary of the Introverted Irrational Types

664   The two types just described are almost inaccessible to judgment from outside. Being introverted, and having in consequence little capacity or desire for expression, they offer but a frail handle in this respect. As their main activity is directed inwards, nothing is outwardly visible but reserve, secretiveness, lack of sympathy, uncertainty, and an apparently groundless embarrassment. When anything does come to the surface, it is generally an indirect manifestation of the inferior and relatively unconscious functions. Such manifestations naturally arouse all the current prejudices against this type. Accordingly they are mostly underestimated, or at least misunderstood. To the extent that they do not understand themselves—because they very largely lack judgment—they are also powerless to understand why they are so constantly underestimated by the public. They cannot see that their efforts to be forthcoming are, as a matter of fact, of an inferior character. Their vision is enthralled by the richness of subjective events. What is going on inside them is so captivating, and of such inexhaustible charm, that they simply do not notice that the little they do manage to communicate contains hardly anything of what they themselves have experienced. The fragmentary and episodic character of their communications makes too great a demand on the understanding and good will of those around them; also, their communications are without the personal warmth that alone carries the power of conviction. On the contrary, these types have very often a harsh, repelling manner, though of this they are quite unaware and did not intend it. We shall form a fairer judgment of such people, and show them greater forbearance, when we begin to realize how hard it is to translate into intelligible language what is perceived within. Yet this for-

bearance must not go so far as to exempt them altogether from the need to communicate. This would only do them the greatest harm. Fate itself prepares for them, perhaps even more than for other men, overwhelming external difficulties which have a very sobering effect on those intoxicated by the inner vision. Often it is only an intense personal need that can wring from them a human confession.

665   From an extraverted and rationalistic standpoint, these types are indeed the most useless of men. But, viewed from a higher standpoint, they are living evidence that this rich and varied world with its overflowing and intoxicating life is not purely external, but also exists within. These types are admittedly one-sided specimens of nature, but they are an object-lesson for the man who refuses to be blinded by the intellectual fashion of the day. In their own way, they are educators and promoters of culture. Their life teaches more than their words. From their lives, and not least from their greatest fault—their inability to communicate—we may understand one of the greatest errors of our civilization, that is, the superstitious belief in verbal statements, the boundless overestimation of instruction by means of words and methods. A child certainly allows himself to be impressed by the grand talk of his parents, but do they really imagine he is educated by it? Actually it is the parents' lives that educate the child—what they add by word and gesture at best serves only to confuse him. The same holds good for the teacher. But we have such a belief in method that, if only the method be good, the practice of it seems to sanctify the teacher. An inferior man is never a good teacher. But he can conceal his pernicious inferiority, which secretly poisons the pupil, behind an excellent method or an equally brilliant gift of gab. Naturally the pupil of riper years desires nothing better than the knowledge of useful methods, because he is already defeated by the general attitude, which believes in the all-conquering method. He has learned that the emptiest head, correctly parroting a method, is the best pupil. His whole environment is an optical demonstration that all success and all happiness are outside, and that only the right method is needed to attain the haven of one's desires. Or does, perchance, the life of his religious instructor demonstrate the happiness which radiates from the treasure of the inner vi-

sion? The irrational introverted types are certainly no teachers of a more perfect humanity; they lack reason and the ethics of reason. But their lives teach the other possibility, the interior life which is so painfully wanting in our civilization.

d. The Principal and Auxiliary Functions

666   In the foregoing descriptions I have no desire to give my readers the impression that these types occur at all frequently in such pure form in actual life. They are, as it were, only Galtonesque family portraits, which single out the common and therefore typical features, stressing them disproportionately, while the individual features are just as disproportionately effaced. Closer investigation shows with great regularity that, besides the most differentiated function, another, less differentiated function of secondary importance is invariably present in consciousness and exerts a co-determining influence.

667   To recapitulate for the sake of clarity: the products of all functions can be conscious, but we speak of the "consciousness" of a function only when its use is under the control of the will and, at the same time, its governing principle is the decisive one for the orientation of consciousness. This is true when, for instance, thinking is not a mere afterthought, or rumination, and when its conclusions possess an absolute validity, so that the logical result holds good both as a motive and as a guarantee of practical action without the backing of any further evidence. This absolute sovereignty always belongs, empirically, to one function alone, and *can* belong only to one function, because the equally independent intervention of another function would necessarily produce a different orientation which, partially at least, would contradict the first. But since it is a vital condition for the conscious process of adaptation always to have clear and unambiguous aims, the presence of a second function of equal power is naturally ruled out. This other function, therefore, can have only a secondary importance, as has been found to be the case in practice. Its secondary importance is due to the fact that it is not, like the primary function, valid in its own right as an absolutely reliable and decisive factor, but comes into play more as an auxiliary or complementary function. Naturally only those functions can appear as auxiliary whose nature is not opposed to the dominant

function. For instance, feeling can never act as the second function alongside thinking, because it is by its very nature too strongly opposed to thinking. Thinking, if it is to be real thinking and true to its own principle, must rigorously exclude feeling. This, of course, does not do away with the fact that there are individuals whose thinking and feeling are on the same level, both being of equal motive power for consciousness. But in these cases there is also no question of a differentiated type, but merely of relatively undeveloped thinking and feeling. The uniformly conscious or uniformly unconscious state of the functions is, therefore, the mark of a primitive mentality.

668 Experience shows that the secondary function is always one whose nature is different from, though not antagonistic to, the primary function. Thus, thinking as the primary function can readily pair with intuition as the auxiliary, or indeed equally well with sensation, but, as already observed, never with feeling. Neither intuition nor sensation is antagonistic to thinking; they need not be absolutely excluded, for they are not of a nature equal and opposite to thinking, as feeling is—which, as a judging function, successfully competes with thinking—but are functions of perception, affording welcome assistance to thought. But as soon as they reached the same level of differentiation as thinking, they would bring about a change of attitude which would contradict the whole trend of thinking. They would change the judging attitude into a perceiving one; whereupon the principle of rationality indispensable to thought would be suppressed in favour of the irrationality of perception. Hence the auxiliary function is possible and useful only in so far as it *serves* the dominant function, without making any claim to the autonomy of its own principle.

669 For all the types met with in practice, the rule holds good that besides the conscious, primary function there is a relatively unconscious, auxiliary function which is in every respect different from the nature of the primary function. The resulting combinations present the familiar picture of, for instance, practical thinking allied with sensation, speculative thinking forging ahead with intuition, artistic intuition selecting and presenting its images with the help of feeling-values, philosophical intuition systematizing its vision into comprehensible thought by means of a powerful intellect, and so on.

670   The unconscious functions likewise group themselves in patterns correlated with the conscious ones. Thus, the correlative of conscious, practical thinking may be an unconscious, intuitive-feeling attitude, with feeling under a stronger inhibition than intuition. These peculiarities are of interest only for one who is concerned with the practical treatment of such cases, but it is important that he should know about them. I have frequently observed how an analyst, confronted with a terrific thinking type, for instance, will do his utmost to develop the feeling function directly out of the unconscious. Such an attempt is foredoomed to failure, because it involves too great a violation of the conscious standpoint. Should the violation nevertheless be successful, a really compulsive dependence of the patient on the analyst ensues, a transference that can only be brutally terminated, because, having been left without a standpoint, the patient has made his standpoint the analyst. But the approach to the unconscious and to the most repressed function is disclosed, as it were, of its own accord, and with adequate protection of the conscious standpoint, when the way of development proceeds via the auxiliary function—in the case of a rational type via one of the irrational functions. This gives the patient a broader view of what is happening, and of what is possible, so that his consciousness is sufficiently protected against the inroads of the unconscious. Conversely, in order to cushion the impact of the unconscious, an irrational type needs a stronger development of the rational auxiliary function present in consciousness.

671   The unconscious functions exist in an archaic, animal state. Hence their symbolic appearance in dreams and fantasies is usually represented as the battle or encounter between two animals or monsters.

XI

DEFINITIONS

⁶⁷² It may perhaps seem superfluous that I should add to my text a chapter dealing solely with definitions. But ample experience has taught me that, in psychological works particularly, one cannot proceed too cautiously in regard to the concepts and terms one uses: for nowhere do such wide divergences of meaning occur as in the domain of psychology, creating only too frequently the most obstinate misunderstandings. This drawback is due not only to the fact that the science of psychology is still in its infancy; there is the further difficulty that the empirical material, the object of scientific investigation, cannot be displayed in concrete form, as it were, before the eyes of the reader. The psychological investigator is always finding himself obliged to make extensive use of an indirect method of description in order to present the reality he has observed. Only in so far as elementary facts are communicated which are amenable to quantitative measurement can there be any question of a direct presentation. But how much of the actual psychology of man can be experienced and observed as quantitatively measurable facts? Such facts do exist, and I believe I have shown in my association studies[1] that extremely complicated psychological facts are accessible to quantitative measurement. But anyone who has probed more deeply into the nature of psychology, demanding something more of it as a science than that it should confine itself within the narrow limits of the scientific method, will also have realized that an experimental method will never succeed in doing justice to the nature of the human psyche, nor will it ever project anything like a true picture of the more complex psychic phenomena.

⁶⁷³ But once we leave the domain of measurable facts we are dependent on *concepts*, which have now to take over the role

[1] *Studies in Word-Association.*

408

of measure and number. The precision which measure and number lend to the observed fact can be replaced only by the *precision of the concept*. Unfortunately, as every investigator and worker in this field knows only too well, current psychological concepts are so imprecise and so ambiguous that mutual understanding is practically impossible. One has only to take the concept "feeling," for instance, and try to visualize everything this concept comprises, to get some sort of notion of the variability and ambiguity of psychological concepts in general. And yet the concept of feeling does express something characteristic that, though not susceptible of quantitative measurement, nevertheless palpably exists. One simply cannot resign oneself, as Wundt does in his physiological psychology, to a mere denial of such essential and fundamental phenomena, and seek to replace them by elementary facts or to resolve them into such. In this way an essential part of psychology is thrown overboard.

674   In order to escape the ill consequences of this overvaluation of the scientific method, one is obliged to have recourse to well-defined concepts. But in order to arrive at such concepts, the collaboration of many workers would be needed, a sort of *consensus gentium*. Since this is not within the bounds of possibility at present, the individual investigator must at least try to give his concepts some fixity and precision, and this can best be done by discussing the meaning of the concepts he employs so that everyone is in a position to see what in fact he means by them.

675   To meet this need I now propose to discuss my principal psychological concepts in alphabetical order, and I would like the reader to refer to these explanations in case of doubt. It goes without saying that these definitions and explanations are merely intended to establish the sense in which I myself use the concepts; far be it from me to affirm that this use is in all circumstances the only possible one or the absolutely right one.

676   1. ABSTRACTION, as the word itself indicates, is the drawing out or singling out of a content (a meaning, a general characteristic, etc.) from a context made up of other elements whose combination into a whole is something unique or individual and therefore cannot be compared with anything else.

Singularity, uniqueness, and incomparability are obstacles to cognition; hence the other elements associated with a content that is felt to be the essential one are bound to appear irrelevant.

677   Abstraction, therefore, is a form of mental activity that frees this content from its association with the irrelevant elements by distinguishing it from them or, in other words, *differentiating* it (v. *Differentiation*). In its wider sense, everything is *abstract* that is separated from its association with elements that are felt to have no relevance to its meaning.

678   Abstraction is an activity pertaining to the psychological *functions* (q.v.) in general. There is an abstract *thinking*, just as there is abstract *feeling, sensation,* and *intuition* (qq. v.). Abstract thinking singles out the rational, logical qualities of a given content from its intellectually irrelevant components. Abstract feeling does the same with a content characterized by its feeling-values; similarly with sensation and intuition. Hence, not only are there abstract thoughts but also abstract feelings, the latter being defined by Sully as intellectual, aesthetic, and moral.[2] To these Nahlowsky adds all religious feelings.[3] Abstract feelings would, in my view, correspond to the "higher" or "ideal" feelings of Nahlowsky. I put abstract feelings on the same level as abstract thoughts. Abstract sensation would be aesthetic as opposed to sensuous *sensation* (q.v.), and abstract intuition would be symbolic as opposed to fantastic *intuition* (v. *Fantasy* and *Intuition*).

679   In this work I also associate abstraction with the awareness of the psycho-energic process it involves. When I take an abstract attitude to an object, I do not allow the object to affect me in its totality; I focus my attention on one part of it by excluding all the irrelevant parts. My aim is to disembarrass myself of the object as a singular and unique whole and to abstract only a portion of this whole. No doubt I am aware of the whole, but I do not immerse myself in this awareness; my interest does not flow into the whole, but draws back from it, pulling the abstracted portion into myself, into my conceptual world, which is already prepared or constellated for the purpose of abstracting a part of the object. (It is only because of

2 Sully, *The Human Mind,* II, ch. 16.
3 Nahlowsky, *Das Gefühlsleben,* p. 48.

a subjective constellation of concepts that I am able to abstract from the object.) "Interest" I conceive as the energy or *libido* (q.v.) which I bestow on the object as a value, or which the object draws from me, maybe even against my will or unknown to myself. I visualize the process of abstraction as a withdrawal of libido from the object, as a backflow of value from the object into a subjective, abstract content. For me, therefore, abstraction amounts to an energic *devaluation of the object*. In other words, abstraction is an introverting movement of libido (v. *Introversion*).

680   I call an *attitude* (q.v.) *abstractive* when it is both introverting and at the same time *assimilates* (q.v.) a portion of the object, felt to be essential, to abstract contents already constellated in the subject. The more abstract a content is, the more it is *irrepresentable*. I subscribe to Kant's view that a concept gets more abstract "the more the differences of things are left out of it,"[4] in the sense that abstraction at its highest level detaches itself absolutely from the object, thereby attaining the extreme limit of irrepresentability. It is this pure "abstract" which I term an *idea* (q.v.). Conversely, an abstract that still possesses some degree of representability or plasticity is a *concrete* concept (v. *Concretism*).

681   2. AFFECT. By the term affect I mean a state of feeling characterized by marked physical innervation on the one hand and a peculiar disturbance of the ideational process on the other.[5] I use *emotion* as synonymous with affect. I distinguish —in contrast to Bleuler (v. *Affectivity*)—*feeling* (q.v.) from affect, in spite of the fact that the dividing line is fluid, since every feeling, after attaining a certain strength, releases physical innervations, thus becoming an affect. For practical reasons, however, it is advisable to distinguish affect from feeling, since feeling can be a voluntarily disposable function, whereas affect is usually not. Similarly, affect is clearly distinguished from feeling by quite perceptible physical innervations, while feeling for the most part lacks them, or else their intensity is so slight that they can be demonstrated only by the most delicate instruments, as in the case of psychogalvanic phenom-

4 Kant, *Logik*, I, par. 6. (*Werke*, ed. Cassirer, VIII, p. 403.)
5 Wundt, *Grundzüge der physiologischen Psychologie*, pp. 209ff.

ena.[6] Affect becomes cumulative through the sensation of the physical innervations released by it. This observation gave rise to the James-Lange theory of affect, which derives affect causally from physical innervations. As against this extreme view, I regard affect on the one hand as a psychic feeling-state and on the other as a physiological innervation-state, each of which has a cumulative, reciprocal effect on the other. That is to say, a component of sensation allies itself with the intensified feeling, so that the affect is approximated more to *sensation* (q.v.) and essentially differentiated from the feeling-state. Pronounced affects, i.e., affects accompanied by violent physical innervations, I do not assign to the province of feeling but to that of the sensation function.

682   3. AFFECTIVITY is a term coined by Bleuler. It designates and comprises "not only the affects proper, but also the slight feelings or feeling-tones of pain and pleasure."[7] Bleuler distinguishes affectivity from the sense-perceptions and physical sensations as well as from "feelings" that may be regarded as inner perception processes (e.g., the "feeling" of certainty, of probability, etc.) or vague thoughts or discernments.[8]

4. ANIMA/ANIMUS, v. SOUL; SOUL-IMAGE.

683   5. APPERCEPTION is a psychic process by which a new content is articulated with similar, already existing contents in such a way that it becomes understood, apprehended, or "clear."[9] We distinguish *active* from *passive* apperception. The first is a process by which the subject, of his own accord and from his own motives, consciously apprehends a new content with attention and assimilates it to other contents already constellated; the second is a process by which a new content forces itself upon consciousness either from without (through the senses) or from within (from the unconscious) and, as it were,

---

[6] Féré, "Note sur des modifications de la résistance électrique," pp. 217ff.; Veraguth, "Das psychogalvanische Reflexphänomen," pp. 387ff.; Binswanger, "On the Psychogalvanic Phenomenon in Association Experiments," in *Studies in Word-Association*, pp. 446ff.; Jung, "On the Psychophysical Relations of the Association Experiment."

[7] Bleuler, *Affektivität, Suggestibilität, Paranoia*, p. 6.

[8] Ibid., pp. 13f.

[9] Wundt, *Grundzüge der physiologischen Psychologie*, I, p. 322.

compels attention and enforces apprehension. In the first case the activity lies with the *ego* (q.v.); in the second, with the self-enforcing new content.

684   6. ARCHAISM is a term by which I designate the "oldness" of psychic contents or *functions* (q.v.). By this I do not mean qualities that are "archaistic" in the sense of being pseudo-antique or copied, as in later Roman sculpture or nineteenth-century Gothic, but qualities that have the character of *relics*. We may describe as archaic all psychological traits that exhibit the qualities of the primitive mentality. It is clear that archaism attaches primarily to the *fantasies* (q.v.) of the unconscious, i.e., to the products of unconscious fantasy activity which reach consciousness. An *image* (q.v.) has an archaic quality when it possesses unmistakable mythological parallels.[10] Archaic, too, are the associations-by-analogy of unconscious fantasy, and so is their symbolism (v. *Symbol*). The relation of *identity* (q.v.) with an object, or *participation mystique* (q.v.), is likewise archaic. *Concretism* (q.v.) of thought and feeling is archaic; also compulsion and inability to control oneself (ecstatic or trance states, possession, etc.). Fusion of the psychological functions (v. *Differentiation*), of thinking with feeling, feeling with sensation, feeling with intuition, and so on, is archaic, as is also the fusion of part of a function with its counterpart, e.g., positive with negative feeling, or what Bleuler calls ambitendency and ambivalence, and such phenomena as *colour hearing*.

6a. ARCHETYPE,[11] v. IMAGE, primordial: also IDEA.

685   7. ASSIMILATION is the approximation of a new content of consciousness to already constellated subjective material,[12] the similarity of the new content to this material being especially accentuated in the process, often to the detriment of its independent qualities.[13] Fundamentally, assimilation is a process of *apperception* (q.v.), but is distinguished from apperception

---

[10] Jung, *Symbols of Transformation*.

[11] [Note by Editors of the *Gesammelte Werke*: "The structure of the archetype was always central to Jung's investigations, but the formulation of the concept took place only in the course of the years."] [For a helpful survey of the development of the concept, see Jacobi, *Complex/Archetype/Symbol*.—EDITORS.]

[12] Wundt, *Logik*, I, p. 23.

[13] Lipps, *Leitfaden der Psychologie*, p. 104.

by this element of approximation to the subjective material. It is in this sense that Wundt says:[14]

This way of building up ideas [i.e., by assimilation] is most conspicuous when the assimilating elements arise through reproduction, and the assimilated ones through an immediate sense impression. For then the elements of memory-images are projected, as it were, into the external object, so that, particularly when the object and the reproduced elements differ substantially from one another, the finished sense impression appears as an illusion, deceiving us as to the real nature of things.

686   I use the term assimilation in a somewhat broader sense, as the approximation of object to subject in general, and with it I contrast *dissimilation*, as the approximation of subject to object, and a consequent alienation of the subject from himself in favour of the object, whether it be an external object or a "psychological" object, for instance an idea.

687   8. ATTITUDE. This concept is a relatively recent addition to psychology. It originated with Müller and Schumann.[15] Whereas Külpe[16] defines attitude as a predisposition of the sensory or motor centres to react to a particular stimulus or constant impulse, Ebbinghaus[17] conceives it in a wider sense as an effect of training which introduces the factor of habit into individual acts that deviate from the habitual. Our use of the concept derives from Ebbinghaus's. For us, attitude is a readiness of the psyche to act or react in a certain way. The concept is of particular importance for the psychology of complex psychic processes because it expresses the peculiar fact that certain stimuli have too strong an effect on some occasions, and little or no effect on others. To have an attitude means to be ready for something definite, even though this something is unconscious; for having an attitude is synonymous with an *a priori* orientation to a definite thing, no matter whether this be represented in consciousness or not. The state of readiness, which I conceive attitude to be, consists in the presence of a

14 Wundt, *Grundzüge*, III, p. 529.
15 "Ueber die psychologischen Grundlagen der Vergleichung gehobener Gewichte," pp. 37ff.
16 *Grundriss der Psychologie*, p. 44.
17 *Grundzüge der Psychologie*, I, pp. 681f.

certain subjective constellation, a definite combination of psychic factors or contents, which will either determine action in this or that definite direction, or react to an external stimulus in a definite way. Active *apperception* (q.v.) is impossible without an attitude. An attitude always has a point of reference; this can be either conscious or unconscious, for in the act of apperceiving a new content an already constellated combination of contents will inevitably accentuate those qualities or elements that appear to belong to the subjective content. Hence a selection or judgment takes place which excludes anything irrelevant. As to what is or is not relevant, this is decided by the already constellated combination of contents. Whether the point of reference is conscious or unconscious does not affect the selectivity of the attitude, since the selection is implicit in the attitude and takes place automatically. It is useful, however, to distinguish between the two, because the presence of two attitudes is extremely frequent, one conscious and the other unconscious. This means that consciousness has a constellation of contents different from that of the unconscious, a duality particularly evident in neurosis.

688   The concept of attitude has some affinity with Wundt's concept of *apperception*, with the difference that apperception includes the process of relating the already constellated contents to the new content to be apperceived, whereas attitude relates exclusively to the subjectively constellated content. Apperception is, as it were, the bridge which connects the already existing, constellated contents with the new one, whereas attitude would be the support or abutment of the bridge on the one bank, and the new content the abutment on the other bank. Attitude signifies *expectation*, and expectation always operates selectively and with a sense of direction. The presence of a strongly feeling-toned content in the conscious field of vision forms (maybe with other contents) a particular constellation that is equivalent to a definite attitude, because such a content promotes the perception and apperception of everything similar to itself and blacks out the dissimilar. It creates an attitude that corresponds to it. This automatic phenomenon is an essential cause of the one-sidedness of conscious *orientation* (q.v.). It would lead to a complete loss of equilibrium if there were no self-regulating, compensatory (v. *Compensation*) function

in the psyche to correct the conscious attitude. In this sense, therefore, the duality of attitude is a normal phenomenon, and it plays a disturbing role only when the one-sidedness is excessive.

689   Attitude in the sense of ordinary *attention* can be a relatively unimportant subsidiary phenomenon, but it can also be a general principle governing the whole psyche. Depending on environmental influences and on the individual's education, general experience of life, and personal convictions, a subjective constellation of contents may be habitually present, continually moulding a certain attitude that may affect the minutest details of his life. Every man who is particularly aware of the seamy side of existence, for instance, will naturally have an attitude that is constantly on the look-out for something unpleasant. This conscious imbalance is compensated by an unconscious expectation of pleasure. Again, an oppressed person has a conscious attitude that always anticipates oppression; he selects this factor from the general run of experience and scents it out everywhere. His unconscious attitude, therefore, aims at power and superiority.

690   The whole psychology of an individual even in its most fundamental features is oriented in accordance with his habitual attitude. Although the general psychological laws operate in every individual, they cannot be said to be characteristic of a particular individual, since the way they operate varies in accordance with his habitual attitude. The habitual attitude is always a resultant of all the factors that exert a decisive influence on the psyche, such as innate disposition, environmental influences, experience of life, insights and convictions gained through *differentiation* (q.v.), *collective* (q.v.) views, etc. Were it not for the absolutely fundamental importance of attitude, the existence of an individual psychology would be out of the question. But the habitual attitude brings about such great displacements of energy, and so modifies the relations between the individual *functions* (q.v.), that effects are produced which often cast doubt on the validity of general psychological laws. In spite of the fact, for instance, that some measure of sexual activity is held to be indispensable on physiological and psychological grounds, there are individuals who, without loss to themselves, i.e., without pathological effects or

any demonstrable restriction of their powers, can, to a very great extent, dispense with it, while in other cases quite insignificant disturbances in this area can have far-reaching consequences. How enormous the individual differences are can be seen most clearly, perhaps, in the question of likes and dislikes. Here practically all rules go by the board. What is there, in the last resort, that has not at some time given man pleasure, and what is there that has not caused him pain? Every instinct, every function can be subordinated to another. The ego instinct or power instinct can make sexuality its servant, or sexuality can exploit the ego. Thinking may overrun everything else, or feeling swallow up thinking and sensation, all depending on the attitude.

691   At bottom, attitude is an individual phenomenon that eludes scientific investigation. In actual experience, however, certain typical attitudes can be distinguished in so far as certain psychic functions can be distinguished. When a function habitually predominates, a typical attitude is produced. According to the nature of the differentiated function, there will be constellations of contents that create a corresponding attitude. There is thus a typical thinking, feeling, sensation, and intuitive attitude. Besides these purely psychological attitudes, whose number might very well be increased, there are also social attitudes, namely, those on which a collective idea has set its stamp. They are characterized by the various "-isms." These collective attitudes are very important, in some cases even outweighing the importance of the individual attitude.

692   9. COLLECTIVE. I term *collective* all psychic contents that belong not to one individual but to many, i.e., to a society, a people, or to mankind in general. Such contents are what Lévy-Bruhl[18] calls the *représentations collectives* of primitives, as well as general concepts of justice, the state, religion, science, etc., current among civilized man. It is not only concepts and ways of looking at things, however, that must be termed collective, but also *feelings*. Among primitives, the *représentations collectives* are at the same time collective feelings, as Lévy-Bruhl has shown. Because of this collective feeling-value he calls the *représentations collectives* "mystical," since they

18 *How Natives Think*, pp. 35ff.

417

are not merely intellectual but emotional.[19] Among civilized peoples, too, certain collective ideas—God, justice, fatherland, etc.—are bound up with collective feelings. This collective quality adheres not only to particular psychic elements or contents but to whole *functions* (q.v.). Thus the thinking function as a whole can have a collective quality, when it possesses general validity and accords with the laws of logic. Similarly, the feeling function as a whole can be collective, when it is identical with the general feeling and accords with general expectations, the general moral consciousness, etc. In the same way, sensation and intuition are collective when they are at the same time characteristic of a large group of men. The antithesis of collective is *individual* (q.v.).

693   10. COMPENSATION means *balancing, adjusting, supplementing*. The concept was introduced into the psychology of the neuroses by Adler.[20] He understands by it the functional balancing of the feeling of inferiority by a compensatory psychological system, comparable to the compensatory development of organs in organ inferiority.[21] He says:

With the breaking away from the maternal organism the struggle with the outer world begins for these inferior organs and organ systems, a struggle which must necessarily break out and declare itself with greater violence than in a normally developed apparatus. . . . Nevertheless, the foetal character supplies at the same time the heightened possibility of compensation and overcompensation, increases the capacity for adaptation to usual and unusual resistance, and ensures the development of new and higher forms, of new and higher achievements.[22]

The neurotic's feeling of inferiority, which according to Adler corresponds aetiologically to an organ inferiority, gives rise to an "auxiliary device,"[23] that is, a compensation, which consists in the setting up of a "guiding fiction" to balance the inferiority. The "guiding fiction" is a psychological system that endeavours to turn an inferiority into a superiority. The sig-

[19] Ibid., pp. 36f.
[20] *The Neurotic Constitution*. References to the theory of compensation, originally inspired by G. Anton, are also to be found in Gross.
[21] *Study of Organ Inferiority and Its Psychical Compensation*, p. 73.
[22] Cf. *The Neurotic Constitution*, p. 7.
[23] Cf. ibid., p. 14. [*Hilfskonstruktion*; see also p. xii.—TRANS.]

nificant thing about this conception is the undeniable and empirically demonstrable existence of a compensating function in the sphere of psychological processes. It corresponds to a similar function in the physiological sphere, namely, the self-regulation of the living organism.

694   Whereas Adler restricts his concept of compensation to the balancing of inferiority feelings, I conceive it as functional adjustment in general, an inherent self-regulation of the psychic apparatus.[24] In this sense, I regard the activity of the *unconscious* (q.v.) as a balancing of the one-sidedness of the general *attitude* (q.v.) produced by the function of *consciousness* (q.v.). Psychologists often compare consciousness to the eye: we speak of a visual field and a focal point of consciousness. The nature of consciousness is aptly characterized by this simile: only a limited number of contents can be held in the conscious field at the same time, and of these only a few can attain the highest grade of consciousness. The activity of consciousness is *selective*. Selection demands *direction*. But direction requires the *exclusion of everything irrelevant*. This is bound to make the conscious *orientation* (q.v.) one-sided. The contents that are excluded and inhibited by the chosen direction sink into the unconscious, where they form a counter-weight to the conscious orientation. The strengthening of this counterposition keeps pace with the increase of conscious one-sidedness until finally a noticeable tension is produced. This tension inhibits the activity of consciousness to a certain extent, and though at first the inhibition can be broken down by increased conscious effort, in the end the tension becomes so acute that the repressed unconscious contents break through in the form of dreams and spontaneous *images* (q.v.). The more one-sided the conscious attitude, the more antagonistic are the contents arising from the unconscious, so that we may speak of a real opposition between the two. In this case the compensation appears in the form of a counter-function, but this case is extreme. As a rule, the unconscious compensation does not run counter to consciousness, but is rather a balancing or supplementing of the conscious orientation. In dreams, for instance, the unconscious supplies all those contents that are

[24] Jung, "On the Importance of the Unconscious in Psychopathology," pars. 449ff.

constellated by the conscious situation but are inhibited by conscious selection, although a knowledge of them would be indispensable for complete adaptation.

695   Normally, compensation is an unconscious process, i.e., an unconscious regulation of conscious activity. In neurosis the unconscious appears in such stark contrast to the conscious state that compensation is disturbed. The aim of analytical therapy, therefore, is a realization of unconscious contents in order that compensation may be re-established.

696   11. CONCRETISM. By this I mean a peculiarity of thinking and feeling which is the antithesis of *abstraction* (q.v.). The actual meaning of *concrete* is "grown together." A concretely thought concept is one that has grown together or coalesced with other concepts. Such a concept is not abstract, not segregated, not thought "in itself," but is always alloyed and related to something else. It is not a differentiated concept, but is still embedded in the material transmitted by sense-perception. Concretistic *thinking* (q.v.) operates exclusively with concrete concepts and percepts, and is constantly related to *sensation* (q.v.). Similarly, concretistic *feeling* (q.v.) is never segregated from its sensuous context.

697   Primitive thinking and feeling are entirely concretistic; they are always related to sensation. The thought of the primitive has no detached independence but clings to material phenomena. It rises at most to the level of *analogy*. Primitive feeling is equally bound to material phenomena. Both of them depend on sensation and are only slightly differentiated from it. Concretism, therefore, is an *archaism* (q.v.). The magical influence of the fetish is not experienced as a subjective state of feeling, but sensed as a magical effect. That is concretistic feeling. The primitive does not experience the idea of divinity as a subjective content; for him the sacred tree is the abode of the god, or even the god himself. That is concretistic thinking. In civilized man, concretistic thinking consists in the inability to conceive of anything except immediately obvious facts transmitted by the senses, or in the inability to discriminate between subjective feeling and the sensed object.

698   Concretism is a concept which falls under the more general concept of *participation mystique* (q.v.). Just as the latter

represents a fusion of the individual with external objects, concretism represents a fusion of thinking and feeling with sensation, so that the object of one is at the same time the object of the other. This fusion prevents any differentiation of thinking and feeling and keeps them both within the sphere of sensation; they remain its servants and can never be developed into pure functions. The result is a predominance of the sensation factor in psychological *orientation* (q.v.). (Concerning the importance of this factor, v. *Sensation.*)

699   The disadvantage of concretism is the subjection of the functions to sensation. Because sensation is the perception of physiological stimuli, concretism either rivets the function to the sensory sphere or constantly leads back to it. This results in a bondage of the psychological functions to the senses, favouring the influence of sensuous facts at the expense of the psychic independence of the individual. So far as the recognition of facts is concerned this orientation is naturally of value, but not as regards the *interpretation* of facts and their relation to the individual. Concretism sets too high a value on the importance of facts and suppresses the freedom of the individual for the sake of objective data. But since the individual is conditioned not merely by physiological stimuli but by factors which may even be opposed to external realities, concretism results in a *projection* (q.v.) of these inner factors into the objective data and produces an almost superstitious veneration of mere facts, as is precisely the case with the primitive. A good example of concretistic feeling is seen in the excessive importance which Nietzsche attached to diet, and in the materialism of Moleschott ("Man is what he eats"). An example of the superstitious overvaluation of facts would be the hypostatizing of the concept of energy in Ostwald's monism.

700   12. CONSCIOUSNESS. By consciousness I understand the relation of psychic contents to the *ego* (q.v.), in so far as this relation is perceived as such by the ego.[25] Relations to the ego that are not perceived as such are *unconscious* (q.v.). Consciousness is the function or activity[26] which maintains the

[25] Natorp, *Einleitung in die Psychologie nach kritischer Methode*, p. 11. Cf. also Lipps, *Leitfaden der Psychologie*, p. 3.

[26] Riehl, *Zur Einführung in die Philosophie der Gegenwart*, p. 161. Riehl considers consciousness an "activity" or "process."

relation of psychic contents to the ego. Consciousness is not identical with the *psyche* (v. *Soul*), because the psyche represents the totality of all psychic contents, and these are not necessarily all directly connected with the ego, i.e., related to it in such a way that they take on the quality of consciousness. A great many psychic complexes exist which are not all necessarily connected with the ego.[27]

701   13. CONSTRUCTIVE. This concept is used by me in an equivalent sense to *synthetic*, almost in fact as an illustration of it. Constructive means "building up." I use *constructive* and *synthetic* to designate a method that is the antithesis of the *reductive* (q.v.).[28] The constructive method is concerned with the elaboration of the products of the unconscious (dreams, fantasies, etc.; v. *Fantasy*). It takes the unconscious product as a symbolic expression (v. *Symbol*) which anticipates a coming phase of psychological development.[29] Maeder actually speaks of a *prospective function* of the *unconscious* (q.v.), which half playfully anticipates future developments.[30] Adler, too, recognizes an anticipatory function of the unconscious.[31] It is certain that the product of the unconscious cannot be regarded as a finished thing, as a sort of end-product, for that would be to deny it any purposive significance. Freud himself allows the dream a teleological role at least as the "guardian of sleep,"[32] though for him its prospective function is essentially restricted to "wishing." The purposive character of unconscious tendencies cannot be contested *a priori* if we are to accept their analogy with other psychological or physiological functions. We conceive the product of the unconscious, therefore, as an expression oriented to a goal or purpose, but characterizing its objective in symbolic language.[33]

[27] Jung, "The Psychology of Dementia Praecox." [See also "A Review of the Complex Theory."—EDITORS.]

[28] Jung, *Two Essays on Analytical Psychology*, pars. 121ff.

[29] For a detailed example of this see my "On the Psychology and Pathology of So-called Occult Phenomena," esp. par. 136.

[30] *The Dream Problem*, p. 30.

[31] *The Neurotic Constitution*.

[32] *The Interpretation of Dreams* (Standard Edition, vol. 4), p. 233.

[33] Silberer (*Problems of Mysticism and Its Symbolism*, pp. 241ff.) expresses himself in a similar way in his formulation of *anagogic* significance.

702   In accordance with this conception, the constructive method of interpretation is not so much concerned with the primary sources of the unconscious product, with its raw materials, so to speak, as with bringing its symbolism to a general and comprehensible expression. The "free associations" of the subject are considered with respect to their aim and not with respect to their derivation. They are viewed from the angle of future action or inaction; at the same time, their relation to the conscious situation is carefully taken into account, for, according to the *compensation* (q.v.) theory, the activity of the unconscious has an essentially complementary significance for the conscious situation. Since it is a question of an anticipatory *orientation* (q.v.), the actual relation to the object does not loom so large as in the reductive procedure, which is concerned with actual relations to the object in the past. It is more a question of the subjective *attitude* (q.v.), the object being little more than a signpost pointing to the tendencies of the subject. The aim of the constructive method, therefore, is to elicit from the unconscious product a meaning that relates to the subject's future attitude. Since, as a rule, the unconscious can create only symbolic expressions, the constructive method seeks to elucidate the symbolically expressed meaning in such a way as to indicate how the conscious orientation may be corrected, and how the subject may act in harmony with the unconscious.

703   Thus, just as no psychological method of interpretation relies exclusively on the associative material supplied by the analysand, the constructive method also makes use of comparative material. And just as reductive interpretation employs parallels drawn from biology, physiology, folklore, literature, and other sources, the constructive treatment of an intellectual problem will make use of philosophical parallels, while the treatment of an intuitive problem will depend more on parallels from mythology and the history of religion.

704   The constructive method is necessarily *individualistic*, since a future collective attitude can develop only through the individual. The reductive method, on the contrary, is *collective* (q.v.), since it leads back from the individual to basic collective attitudes or facts. The constructive method can also be directly applied by the subject to his own material, in which

case it is an *intuitive* method, employed to elucidate the general meaning of an unconscious product. This elucidation is the result of an *associative* (as distinct from actively *apperceptive*, q.v.) addition of further material, which so enriches the symbolic product (e.g., a dream) that it eventually attains a degree of clarity sufficient for conscious comprehension. It becomes interwoven with more general associations and is thereby assimilated.

705   14. DIFFERENTIATION means the development of differences, the separation of parts from a whole. In this work I employ the concept of differentiation chiefly with respect to the psychological *functions* (q.v.). So long as a function is still so fused with one or more other functions—thinking with feeling, feeling with sensation, etc.—that it is unable to operate on its own, it is in an *archaic* (q.v.) condition, i.e., not differentiated, not separated from the whole as a special part and existing by itself. Undifferentiated thinking is incapable of thinking apart from other functions; it is continually mixed up with sensations, feelings, intuitions, just as undifferentiated feeling is mixed up with sensations and fantasies, as for instance in the sexualization (Freud) of feeling and thinking in neurosis. As a rule, the undifferentiated function is also characterized by ambivalence and ambitendency,[34] i.e., every position entails its own negation, and this leads to characteristic inhibitions in the use of the undifferentiated function. Another feature is the fusing together of its separate components; thus, undifferentiated sensation is vitiated by the coalescence of different sensory spheres (colour-hearing), and undifferentiated feeling by confounding hate with love. To the extent that a function is largely or wholly unconscious, it is also undifferentiated; it is not only fused together in its parts but also merged with other functions. Differentiation consists in the separation of the function from other functions, and in the separation of its individual parts from each other. Without differentiation direction is impossible, since the direction of a function towards a

---

[34] Bleuler, "Die negative Suggestibilität," *Psychiatrisch-neurologische Wochenschrift*, vol. 6, pp. 249ff.; *The Theory of Schizophrenic Negativism* (orig. in ibid., vol. 12, pp. 171, 189, 195); *Textbook of Psychiatry*, pp. 130, 382. [See also supra, par. 684.—EDITORS.]

goal depends on the elimination of anything irrelevant. Fusion with the irrelevant precludes direction; only a differentiated function is *capable* of being directed.

15. DISSIMILATION, V. ASSIMILATION.

706   16. EGO. By ego I understand a complex of ideas which constitutes the centre of my field of consciousness and appears to possess a high degree of continuity and identity. Hence I also speak of an *ego-complex*.[35] The ego-complex is as much a content as a condition of *consciousness* (q.v.), for a psychic element is conscious to me only in so far as it is related to my ego-complex. But inasmuch as the ego is only the centre of my field of consciousness, it is not identical with the totality of my psyche, being merely one complex among other complexes. I therefore distinguish between the ego and the *self* (q.v.), since the ego is only the subject of my consciousness, while the self is the subject of my total psyche, which also includes the unconscious. In this sense the self would be an ideal entity which embraces the ego. In unconscious *fantasies* (q.v.) the self often appears as supraordinate or ideal personality, having somewhat the relationship of Faust to Goethe or Zarathustra to Nietzsche. For the sake of idealization the archaic features of the self are represented as being separate from the "higher" self, as for instance Mephistopheles in Goethe, Epimetheus in Spitteler, and in Christian psychology the devil or Antichrist. In Nietzsche, Zarathustra discovered his shadow in the "Ugliest Man."

16a. EMOTION, V. AFFECT.

707   17. EMPATHY[36] is an *introjection* (q.v.) of the object. For a fuller description of the concept of empathy, see Chapter VII; also *projection*.

708   18. ENANTIODROMIA means a "running counter to." In the philosophy of Heraclitus[37] it is used to designate the play of

---

[35] "The Psychology of Dementia Praecox," *Psychiatric Studies,* index, s.v., "ego-complex."

[36] [This appeared as Def. 21, FEELING-INTO, in the Baynes translation.—EDITORS.]

[37] Stobaeus, *Eclogae physicae,* 1, 60: εἱμαρμένην δὲ λόγον ἐκ τῆς ἐναντιοδρομίας δημιουργὸν τῶν ὄντων. ("Fate is the logical product of enantiodromia, creator of all things.")

425

opposites in the course of events—the view that everything that exists turns into its opposite. "From the living comes death and from the dead life, from the young old age and from the old youth; from waking, sleep, and from sleep, waking; the stream of generation and decay never stands still."[38] "Construction and destruction, destruction and construction—this is the principle which governs all the cycles of natural life, from the smallest to the greatest. Just as the cosmos itself arose from the primal fire, so must it return once more into the same—a dual process running its measured course through vast periods of time, a drama eternally re-enacted."[39] Such is the enantiodromia of Heraclitus in the words of qualified interpreters. He himself says:

It is the opposite which is good for us.

Men do not know how what is at variance agrees with itself. It is an attunement of opposite tensions, like that of the bow and the lyre.

The bow ($\beta\iota\acute{o}s$) is called life ($\beta\acute{\iota}os$), but its work is death.

Mortals are immortals and immortals are mortals, the one living the others' death and dying the others' life.

For souls it is death to become water, for water death to become earth. But from earth comes water, and from water, soul.

All things are an exchange for fire, and fire for all things, like goods for gold and gold for goods.

The way up and the way down are the same.[40]

709   I use the term enantiodromia for the emergence of the unconscious opposite in the course of time. This characteristic phenomenon practically always occurs when an extreme, one-sided tendency dominates conscious life; in time an equally powerful counterposition is built up, which first inhibits the conscious performance and subsequently breaks through the conscious control. Good examples of enantiodromia are: the conversion of St. Paul and of Raymund Lully,[41] the self-identifi-

[38] Zeller, *A History of Greek Philosophy*, II, p. 17.
[39] Cf. Gomperz, *Greek Thinkers*, I, p. 64.
[40] Cf. Burnet, *Early Greek Philosophy*, pp. 133ff., Fragments 46, 45, 66, 67, 68, 22, 69.
[41] [Ramon Llull, 1234–1315. Cf. "The Psychology of Dementia Praecox," par. 89.—EDITORS.]

cation of the sick Nietzsche with Christ, and his deification and subsequent hatred of Wagner, the transformation of Swedenborg from an erudite scholar into a seer, and so on.

710   19. EXTRAVERSION is an outward-turning of *libido* (q.v.). I use this concept to denote a manifest relation of subject to object, a positive movement of subjective interest towards the object. Everyone in the extraverted state thinks, feels, and acts in relation to the object, and moreover in a direct and clearly observable fashion, so that no doubt can remain about his positive dependence on the object. In a sense, therefore, extraversion is a transfer of interest from subject to object. If it is an extraversion of thinking, the subject thinks himself into the object; if an extraversion of feeling, he feels himself into it. In extraversion there is a strong, if not exclusive, determination by the object. Extraversion is *active* when it is intentional, and *passive* when the object compels it, i.e., when the object attracts the subject's interest of its own accord, even against his will. When extraversion is habitual, we speak of the extraverted *type* (q.v.).

711   20. FANTASY.[42] By fantasy I understand two different things: 1. a *fantasm*, and 2. *imaginative activity*. In the present work the context always shows which of these meanings is intended. By fantasy in the sense of *fantasm* I mean a complex of ideas that is distinguished from other such complexes by the fact that it has no objective referent. Although it may originally be based on memory-images of actual experiences, its content refers to no external reality; it is merely the output of creative psychic activity, a manifestation or product of a combination of energized psychic elements. In so far as psychic energy can be voluntarily directed, a fantasy can be consciously and intentionally produced, either as a whole or at least in part. In the former case it is nothing but a combination of *conscious* elements, an artificial experiment of purely theoretical interest. In actual everyday psychological experience, fantasy is either set in motion by an intuitive attitude of expectation, or it is an irruption of *unconscious* contents into consciousness.

42 [This appeared as Def. 41, PHANTASY, in the Baynes translation.—EDITORS.]

712   We can distinguish between *active* and *passive* fantasy. *Active* fantasies are the product of *intuition* (q.v.), i.e., they are evoked by an *attitude* (q.v.) directed to the perception of unconscious contents, as a result of which the *libido* (q.v.) immediately invests all the elements emerging from the unconscious and, by association with parallel material, brings them into clear focus in visual form. *Passive* fantasies appear in visual form at the outset, neither preceded nor accompanied by intuitive expectation, the attitude of the subject being wholly passive. Such fantasies belong to the category of psychic *automatisms* (Janet). Naturally, they can appear only as a result of a relative dissociation of the psyche, since they presuppose a withdrawal of energy from conscious control and a corresponding activation of unconscious material. Thus the vision of St. Paul[43] presupposes that unconsciously he was already a Christian, though this fact had escaped his conscious insight.

713   It is probable that passive fantasies always have their origin in an unconscious process that is antithetical to consciousness, but invested with approximately the same amount of energy as the conscious attitude, and therefore capable of breaking through the latter's resistance. Active fantasies, on the other hand, owe their existence not so much to this unconscious process as to a conscious propensity to assimilate hints or fragments of lightly-toned unconscious complexes and, by associating them with parallel elements, to elaborate them in clearly visual form. It is not necessarily a question of a dissociated psychic state, but rather of a positive participation of consciousness.

714   Whereas passive fantasy not infrequently bears a morbid stamp or at least shows some trace of abnormality, active fantasy is one of the highest forms of psychic activity. For here the conscious and the unconscious personality of the subject flow together into a common product in which both are united. Such a fantasy can be the highest expression of the unity of a man's *individuality* (q.v.), and it may even create that individuality by giving perfect expression to its unity. As a general rule, passive fantasy is never the expression of a unified indi-

---

43 Acts 9:3ff.

428

viduality since, as already observed, it presupposes a considerable degree of dissociation based in turn on a marked conscious/unconscious opposition. Hence the fantasy that irrupts into consciousness from such a state can never be the perfect expression of a unified individuality, but will represent mainly the standpoint of the unconscious personality. The life of St. Paul affords a good example of this: his conversion to Christianity signified an acceptance of the hitherto unconscious standpoint and a repression of the hitherto anti-Christian one, which then made itself felt in his hysterical attacks. Passive fantasy, therefore, is always in need of conscious *criticism*, lest it merely reinforce the standpoint of the unconscious opposite. Whereas active fantasy, as the product of a conscious attitude *not* opposed to the unconscious, and of unconscious processes not opposed but merely compensatory to consciousness, does not require criticism so much as *understanding*.

715 In fantasies as in dreams (which are nothing but passive fantasies), a *manifest* and a *latent* meaning must be distinguished. The manifest meaning is found in the actual "look" of the fantasy image, in the direct statement made by the underlying complex of ideas. Frequently, however, the manifest meaning hardly deserves its name, although it is always far more developed in fantasies than in dreams, probably because the dream-fantasy usually requires very little energy to overcome the feeble resistance of the sleeping consciousness, with the result that tendencies which are only slightly antagonistic and slightly compensatory can also reach the threshold of perception. Waking fantasy, on the other hand, must muster considerable energy to overcome the inhibition imposed by the conscious attitude. For this to take place, the unconscious opposite must be a very important one in order to break through into consciousness. If it consisted merely of vague, elusive hints it would never be able to direct attention (conscious libido) to itself so effectively as to interrupt the continuity of the conscious contents. The unconscious opposite, therefore, has to depend on a very strong inner cohesion, and this expresses itself in an emphatic manifest meaning.

716 The manifest meaning always has the character of a visual and concrete process which, because of its objective unreality, can never satisfy the conscious demand for understanding.

Hence another meaning of the fantasy, in other words its interpretation or latent meaning, has to be sought. Although the existence of a latent meaning is by no means certain, and although the very possibility of it may be contested, the demand for understanding is a sufficient motive for a thorough-going investigation. This investigation of the latent meaning may be purely causal, inquiring into the psychological origins of the fantasy. It leads on the one hand to the remoter causes of the fantasy in the distant past, and on the other to ferreting out the instinctual forces which, from the energic standpoint, must be responsible for the fantasy activity. As we know, Freud has made intensive use of this method. It is a method of interpretation which I call *reductive* (q.v.). The justification of a reductive view is immediately apparent, and it is equally obvious that this method of interpreting psychological facts suffices for people of a certain temperament, so that no demand for a deeper understanding is made. If somebody shouts for help, this is sufficiently and satisfactorily explained when it is shown that the man is in immediate danger of his life. If a man dreams of a sumptuous feast, and it is shown that he went to bed hungry, this is a sufficient explanation of his dream. Or if a man who represses his sexuality has sexual fantasies like a medieval hermit, this is satisfactorily explained by a reduction to sexual repression.

717 But if we were to explain Peter's vision[44] by reducing it to the fact that, being "very hungry," he had received an invitation from the unconscious to eat animals that were "unclean," or that the eating of unclean beasts merely signified the fulfilment of a forbidden wish, such an explanation would send us away empty. It would be equally unsatisfactory to reduce Paul's vision to his repressed envy of the role Christ played among his fellow countrymen, which prompted him to identify himself with Christ. Both explanations may contain some glimmering of truth, but they are in no way related to the real psychology of the two apostles, conditioned as this was by the times they lived in. The explanation is too facile. One cannot discuss historical events as though they were problems of physiology or a purely personal *chronique scandaleuse*. That

44 Acts 10:10ff. and 11:4ff.

would be altogether too limited a point of view. We are therefore compelled to broaden very considerably our conception
of the latent meaning of fantasy, first of all in its causal aspect.
The psychology of an individual can never be exhaustively explained from himself alone: a clear recognition is needed of
the way it is also conditioned by historical and environmental
circumstances. His individual psychology is not merely a physiological, biological, or moral problem, it is also a contemporary problem. Again, no psychological fact can ever be exhaustively explained in terms of causality alone; as a living
phenomenon, it is always indissolubly bound up with the continuity of the vital process, so that it is not only something
evolved but also continually evolving and creative.

718   Anything psychic is Janus-faced—it looks both backwards
and forwards. Because it is evolving, it is also preparing the
future. Were this not so, intentions, aims, plans, calculations,
predictions and premonitions would be psychological impossi-
bilities. If, when a man expresses an opinion, we simply relate
it to an opinion previously expressed by someone else, this
explanation is quite futile, for we wish to know not merely
what prompted him to do so, but what he means by it, what his
aims and intentions are, and what he hopes to achieve. And
when we know that, we are usually satisfied. In everyday life
we instinctively, without thinking, introduce a final standpoint into an explanation; indeed, very often we take the final
standpoint as the decisive one and completely disregard the
strictly causal factor, instinctively recognizing the creative element in everything psychic. If we do this in everyday life, then
a scientific psychology must take this fact into account, and not
rely exclusively on the strictly causal standpoint originally
taken over from natural science, for it has also to consider the
purposive nature of the psyche.

719   If, then, everyday experience establishes beyond doubt the
final orientation of conscious contents, we have absolutely no
grounds for assuming, in the absence of experience to the contrary, that this is not the case with the contents of the unconscious. My experience gives me no reason at all to dispute this;
on the contrary, cases where the introduction of the final standpoint alone provides a satisfactory explanation are in the majority. If we now look at Paul's vision again, but this time from

431

the angle of his future mission, and come to the conclusion that Paul, though consciously a persecutor of Christians, had unconsciously adopted the Christian standpoint, and that he was finally brought to avow it by an irruption of the unconscious, because his unconscious personality was constantly striving toward this goal—this seems to me a more adequate explanation of the real significance of the event than a reduction to personal motives, even though these doubtless played their part in some form or other, since the "all-too-human" is never lacking. Similarly, the clear indication given in Acts 10:28 of a purposive interpretation of Peter's vision is far more satisfying than a merely physiological and personal conjecture.

720 To sum up, we might say that a fantasy needs to be understood both causally and purposively. Causally interpreted, it seems like a *symptom* of a physiological or personal state, the outcome of antecedent events. Purposively interpreted, it seems like a *symbol*, seeking to characterize a definite goal with the help of the material at hand, or trace out a line of future psychological development. Because active fantasy is the chief mark of the artistic mentality, the artist is not just a *reproducer* of appearances but a creator and educator, for his works have the value of symbols that adumbrate lines of future development. Whether the symbols will have a limited or a general social validity depends on the viability of the creative individual. The more abnormal, i.e., the less viable he is, the more limited will be the social validity of the symbols he produces, though their value may be absolute for the individual himself.

721 One can dispute the existence of the latent meaning of fantasy only if one is of the opinion that natural processes in general are devoid of meaning. Science, however, has extracted the meaning of natural processes in the form of natural laws. These, admittedly, are human hypotheses advanced in explanation of such processes. But, in so far as we have ascertained that the proposed law actually coincides with the objective process, we are also justified in speaking of the meaning of natural occurrences. We are equally justified in speaking of the meaning of fantasies when it can be shown that they conform to law. But the meaning we discover is satisfying, or to put it another way, the demonstrated law deserves its name,

only when it adequately reflects the nature of fantasy. Natural processes both conform to law and demonstrate that law. It is a law that one dreams when one sleeps, but that is not a law which demonstrates anything about the nature of the dream; it is a mere condition of the dream. The demonstration of a physiological source of fantasy is likewise a mere condition of its existence, not a law of its nature. The law of fantasy as a psychological phenomenon can only be a psychological law.

722 This brings us to the second connotation of fantasy, namely *imaginative activity*. Imagination is the reproductive or creative activity of the mind in general. It is not a special faculty, since it can come into play in all the basic forms of psychic activity, whether *thinking, feeling, sensation,* or *intuition* (qq.v.). Fantasy as imaginative activity is, in my view, simply the direct expression of psychic life,[45] of psychic energy which cannot appear in consciousness except in the form of images or contents, just as physical energy cannot manifest itself except as a definite physical state stimulating the sense organs in physical ways. For as every physical state, from the energic standpoint, is a dynamic system, so from the same standpoint a psychic content is a dynamic system manifesting itself in consciousness. We could therefore say that fantasy in the sense of a fantasm is a definite sum of libido that cannot appear in consciousness in any other way than in the form of an image. A fantasm is an *idée-force*. Fantasy as imaginative activity is identical with the flow of psychic energy.

723 21. FEELING.[46] I count feeling among the four basic psychological *functions* (q.v.). I am unable to support the psychological school that considers feeling a secondary phenomenon

[45] [Imaginative activity is therefore not to be confused with "active imagination," a psychotherapeutic method developed by Jung himself. Active imagination corresponds to the definitions of *active fantasy* in pars. 712–14. The method of active imagination (though not called by that name) may be found in "The Aims of Psychotherapy," pars. 101–6, "The Transcendent Function," pars. 166ff., "On the Nature of the Psyche," pars. 400–2, and *Two Essays on Analytical Psychology*, pars. 343ff., 366. The term "active imagination" was used for the first time in "The Tavistock Lectures" (delivered in London, 1935), first published as *Analytical Psychology: Its Theory and Practice* (1968), now in *Coll. Works,* vol. 18. The method is described there in pars. 391ff. Further descriptions occur in *Mysterium Coniunctionis*, esp. pars. 706, 749–54.—EDITORS.]

[46] [This appeared as Def. 20 in the Baynes translation.—EDITORS.]

dependent on "representations" or sensations, but in company with Höffding, Wundt, Lehmann, Külpe, Baldwin, and others, I regard it as an independent function *sui generis*.[47]

724   Feeling is primarily a process that takes place between the *ego* (q.v.) and a given content, a process, moreover, that imparts to the content a definite *value* in the sense of acceptance or rejection ("like" or "dislike"). The process can also appear isolated, as it were, in the form of a "mood," regardless of the momentary contents of consciousness or momentary sensations. The mood may be causally related to earlier conscious contents, though not necessarily so, since, as psychopathology amply proves, it may equally well arise from unconscious contents. But even a mood, whether it be a general or only a partial feeling, implies a valuation; not of one definite, individual conscious content, but of the whole conscious situation at the moment, and, once again, with special reference to the question of acceptance or rejection.

725   Feeling, therefore, is an entirely *subjective* process, which may be in every respect independent of external stimuli, though it allies itself with every sensation.[48] Even an "indifferent" sensation possesses a feeling-tone, namely that of indifference, which again expresses some sort of valuation. Hence feeling is a kind of *judgment*, differing from intellectual judgment in that its aim is not to establish conceptual relations but to set up a subjective criterion of acceptance or rejection. Valuation by feeling extends to *every* content of consciousness, of whatever kind it may be. When the intensity of feeling increases, it turns into an *affect* (q.v.), i.e., a feeling-state accompanied by marked physical innervations. Feeling is distinguished from affect by the fact that it produces no perceptible physical innervations, i.e., neither more nor less than an ordinary thinking process.

[47] For the history both of the theory and concept of feeling, see Wundt, *Outlines of Psychology*, pp. 33ff.; Nahlowsky, *Das Gefühlsleben in seinen wesentlichen Erscheinungen*; Ribot, *The Psychology of the Emotions*; Lehmann, *Die Hauptgesetze des menschlichen Gefühlslebens*; Villa, *Contemporary Psychology*, pp. 182ff.

[48] For the distinction between feeling and sensation, see Wundt, *Grundzüge der physiologischen Psychologie*, I, pp. 350ff.

726   Ordinary, "simple" feeling is *concrete* (q.v.), that is, it is mixed up with other functional elements, more particularly with sensations. In this case we can call it *affective* or, as I have done in this book, *feeling-sensation*, by which I mean an almost inseparable amalgam of feeling and sensation elements. This characteristic amalgamation is found wherever feeling is still an undifferentiated function, and is most evident in the psyche of a neurotic with differentiated thinking. Although feeling is, in itself, an independent function, it can easily become dependent on another function—thinking, for instance; it is then a mere concomitant of thinking, and is not repressed only in so far as it accommodates itself to the thinking processes.

727   It is important to distinguish *abstract* feeling from ordinary concrete feeling. Just as the abstract concept (v. *Thinking*) abolishes the differences between things it apprehends, abstract feeling rises above the differences of the individual contents it evaluates, and produces a "mood" or feeling-state which embraces the different individual valuations and thereby abolishes them. In the same way that thinking organizes the contents of consciousness under concepts, feeling arranges them according to their value. The more concrete it is, the more subjective and personal is the value conferred upon them; but the more abstract it is, the more universal and objective the value will be. Just as a completely abstract concept no longer coincides with the singularity and discreteness of things, but only with their universality and non-differentiation, so completely abstract feeling no longer coincides with a particular content and its feeling-value, but with the undifferentiated totality of all contents. Feeling, like thinking, is a *rational* (q.v.) function, since values in general are assigned according to the laws of reason, just as concepts in general are formed according to these laws.

728   Naturally the above definitions do not give the essence of feeling—they only describe it from outside. The intellect proves incapable of formulating the real nature of feeling in conceptual terms, since thinking belongs to a category incommensurable with feeling; in fact, no basic psychological function can ever be completely expressed by another. That being so, it is impossible for an intellectual definition to reproduce

435

the specific character of feeling at all adequately. The mere classification of feelings adds nothing to an understanding of their nature, because even the most exact classification will be able to indicate only the content of feeling which the intellect can apprehend, without grasping its specific nature. Only as many classes of feelings can be discriminated as there are classes of contents that can be intellectually apprehended, but feeling *per se* can never be exhaustively classified because, beyond every possible class of contents accessible to the intellect, there still exist feelings which resist intellectual classification. The very notion of classification is intellectual and therefore incompatible with the nature of feeling. We must therefore be content to indicate the limits of the concept.

729   The nature of valuation by feeling may be compared with intellectual *apperception* (q.v.) as an *apperception of value*. We can distinguish *active* and *passive* apperception by feeling. Passive feeling allows itself to be attracted or excited by a particular content, which then forces the feelings of the subject to participate. Active feeling is a transfer of value from the subject; it is an intentional valuation of the content in accordance with feeling and not in accordance with the intellect. Hence active feeling is a *directed* function, an act of the *will* (q.v.), as for instance loving as opposed to being in love. The latter would be *undirected*, passive feeling, as these expressions themselves show: the one is an activity, the other a passive state. Undirected feeling is *feeling-intuition*. Strictly speaking, therefore, only active, directed feeling should be termed *rational*, whereas passive feeling is *irrational* (q.v.) in so far as it confers values without the participation or even against the intentions of the subject. When the subject's attitude as a whole is oriented by the feeling function, we speak of a *feeling type* (v. *Type*).

730   21a. FEELING, A (OR FEELINGS). A feeling is the specific content or material of the feeling function, discriminated by *empathy* (q.v.).

731   22. FUNCTION (v. also INFERIOR FUNCTION). By a psychological function I mean a particular form of psychic activity that remains the same in principle under varying conditions. From the energic standpoint a function is a manifestation of

libido (q.v.), which likewise remains constant in principle, in much the same way as a physical force can be considered a specific form or manifestation of physical energy. I distinguish four basic functions in all, two rational and two irrational (qq.v.): *thinking* and *feeling*, *sensation* and *intuition* (qq.v.). I can give no *a priori* reason for selecting these four as basic functions, and can only point out that this conception has shaped itself out of many years' experience. I distinguish these functions from one another because they cannot be related or reduced to one another. The principle of thinking, for instance, is absolutely different from the principle of feeling, and so forth. I make a cardinal distinction between these functions and *fantasies* (q.v.), because fantasy is a characteristic form of activity that can manifest itself in all four functions. Volition or *will* (q.v.) seems to me an entirely secondary phenomenon, and so does *attention*.

732   23. IDEA. In this work the concept "idea" is sometimes used to designate a certain psychological element which is closely connected with what I term *image* (q.v.). The image may be either *personal* or *impersonal* in origin. In the latter case it is *collective* (q.v.) and is also distinguished by mythological qualities. I then term it a *primordial image*. When, on the other hand, it has no mythological character, i.e., is lacking in visual qualities and merely collective, I speak of an *idea*. Accordingly, I use the term idea to express the *meaning* of a primordial image, a meaning that has been abstracted from the *concretism* (q.v.) of the image. In so far as an idea is an *abstraction* (q.v.), it has the appearance of something derived, or developed, from elementary factors, a product of thought. This is the sense in which it is conceived by Wundt[49] and many others.

733   In so far, however, as an idea is the formulated meaning of a primordial image by which it was represented *symbolically* (v. *Symbol*), its essence is not just something derived or developed, but, psychologically speaking, exists *a priori*, as a given possibility for thought-combinations in general. Hence, in accordance with its essence (but not with its formulation), the idea is a psychological determinant having an *a priori*

---

49 "Was soll uns Kant nicht sein?," *Philosophische Studien*, VII, p. 13.

existence. In this sense Plato sees the idea as a prototype of things, while Kant defines it as the "archetype [*Urbild*] of all practical employment of reason," a transcendental concept which as such exceeds the bounds of the experienceable,[50] "a rational concept whose object is not to be found in experience."[51] He says:

Although we must say of the transcendental concepts of reason that *they are only ideas*, this is not by any means to be taken as signifying that they are superfluous and void. For even if they cannot determine any object, they may yet, in a fundamental and unobserved fashion, be of service to the understanding as a canon for its extended and consistent employment. The understanding does not thereby obtain more knowledge of any object than it would have by means of its own concepts, but for the acquiring of such knowledge it receives better and more extensive guidance. Further—what we need here no more than mention—concepts of reason may perhaps make a possible transition from the concepts of nature to the practical concepts, and in that way may give support to the moral ideas themselves.[52]

734   Schopenhauer says:

By Idea, then, I understand every definite and well-established stage in the objectivation of the Will, so far as the Will is a thing-in-itself and therefore without multiplicity, which stages are related to individual things as their eternal forms or prototypes.[53]

For Schopenhauer the idea is a visual thing, for he conceives it entirely in the way I conceive the primordial image. Nevertheless, it remains uncognizable by the individual, revealing itself only to the "pure subject of cognition," which "is beyond all willing and all individuality."[54]

735   Hegel hypostatizes the idea completely and attributes to it alone real being. It is the "concept, the reality of the concept, and the union of both."[55] It is "eternal generation."[56] Lasswitz

---

[50] Cf. Kant, *Critique of Pure Reason* (trans. Kemp Smith), p. 319.

[51] *Logik*, I, sec. 1, par. 3 (*Werke*, ed. Cassirer, VIII, p. 400). [Cf. supra, par. 519, n. 11.]

[52] *Critique of Pure Reason*, pp. 319ff.

[53] Cf. *The World as Will and Idea*, I, p. 168.

[54] Ibid., p. 302. See also infra, par. 752.

[55] *Einleitung in die Aesthetik* (*Sämtliche Werke*, XII), Part I, ch. 1, i.

[56] *The Logic of Hegel* (trans. Wallace), p. 356.

regards the idea as the "law showing the direction in which our experience should develop." It is the "most certain and supreme reality."[57] For Cohen, it is the "concept's awareness of itself," the "foundation" of being.[58]

736   I do not want to pile up evidence for the primary nature of the idea. These quotations should suffice to show that it can be conceived as a fundamental, *a priori* factor. It derives this quality from its precursor—the primordial, symbolic image. Its secondary nature as something abstract and derived is a result of the rational elaboration to which the primordial image is subjected to fit it for rational use. The primordial image is an autochthonous psychological factor constantly repeating itself at all times and places, and the same might be said of the idea, although, on account of its rational nature, it is much more subject to modification by rational elaboration and formulations corresponding to local conditions and the spirit of the time. Since it is derived from the primordial image, a few philosophers ascribe a transcendent quality to it; this does not really belong to the idea as I conceive it, but rather to the primordial image, about which a timeless quality clings, being an integral component of the human mind everywhere from time immemorial. Its autonomous character is also derived from the primordial image, which is never "made" but is continually present, appearing in perception so spontaneously that it seems to strive for its own realization, being sensed by the mind as an active determinant. Such a view, however, is not general, and is presumably a question of *attitude* (q.v., also Ch. VII).

737   The idea is a psychological factor that not only determines thinking but, as a practical idea, also conditions feeling. As a general rule, I use the term *idea* only when speaking of the determination of thought in a thinking type, or of feeling in a feeling type. On the other hand, it would be terminologically correct to speak of an *a priori* determination by the primordial image in the case of an undifferentiated function. The dual nature of the idea as something both primary and derived is responsible for the fact that I sometimes use it promiscuously with primordial image. For the introverted attitude the idea is the prime mover; for the extraverted, a product.

[57] *Wirklichkeiten: Beiträge zur Weltverständnis,* pp. 152, 154.
[58] *Logik der reinen Erkenntnis,* pp. 14, 18.

738   24. IDENTIFICATION. By this I mean a psychological process in which the personality is partially or totally *dissimilated* (v. *Assimilation*). Identification is an alienation of the subject from himself for the sake of the object, in which he is, so to speak, disguised. For example, identification with the father means, in practice, adopting all the father's ways of behaving, as though the son were the same as the father and not a separate individuality. Identification differs from *imitation* in that it is an *unconscious* imitation, whereas imitation is a conscious copying. Imitation is an indispensable aid in developing the youthful personality. It is beneficial so long as it does not serve as a mere convenience and hinder the development of ways and means suited to the individual. Similarly, identification can be beneficial so long as the individual cannot go his own way. But when a better possibility presents itself, identification shows its morbid character by becoming just as great a hindrance as it was an unconscious help and support before. It now has a dissociative effect, splitting the individual into two mutually estranged personalities.

739   Identification does not always apply to persons but also to things (e.g., a movement of some kind, a business, etc.) and to psychological functions. The latter kind is, in fact, particularly important.[59] Identification then leads to the formation of a secondary character, the individual identifying with his best developed function to such an extent that he alienates himself very largely or even entirely from his original character, with the result that his true *individuality* (q.v.) falls into the unconscious. This is nearly always the rule with people who have one highly differentiated function. It is, in fact, a necessary transitional stage on the way to *individuation* (q.v.).

740   Identification with parents or the closest members of the family is a normal phenomenon in so far as it coincides with the *a priori family identity*. In this case it is better not to speak of *identification* but of *identity* (q.v.), a term that expresses the actual situation. Identification with members of the family differs from identity in that it is not an *a priori* but a secondary phenomenon arising in the following way. As the individual emerges from the original family identity, the process of adaptation and development brings him up against obstacles that

[59] Supra, pars. 108f., 158ff.

cannot easily be mastered. A damming up of *libido* (q.v.) ensues, which seeks a regressive outlet. The regression reactivates the earlier states, among them the state of family identity. Identification with members of the family corresponds to this regressive revival of an identity that had almost been overcome. All identifications with persons come about in this way. Identification always has a purpose, namely, to obtain an advantage, to push aside an obstacle, or to solve a task in the way another individual would.

741   25. IDENTITY. I use the term *identity* to denote a psychological conformity. It is always an unconscious phenomenon since a conscious conformity would necessarily involve a consciousness of two dissimilar things, and, consequently, a separation of subject and object, in which case the identity would already have been abolished. Psychological identity presupposes that it is unconscious. It is a characteristic of the primitive mentality and the real foundation of *participation mystique* (q.v.), which is nothing but a relic of the original non-differentiation of subject and object, and hence of the primordial unconscious state. It is also a characteristic of the mental state of early infancy, and, finally, of the unconscious of the civilized adult, which, in so far as it has not become a content of consciousness, remains in a permanent state of identity with objects. Identity with the parents provides the basis for subsequent *identification* (q.v.) with them; on it also depends the possibility of *projection* (q.v.) and *introjection* (q.v.).

742   Identity is primarily an unconscious conformity with objects. It is not an *equation*, but an *a priori likeness* which was never the object of consciousness. Identity is responsible for the naïve assumption that the psychology of one man is like that of another, that the same motives occur everywhere, that what is agreeable to me must obviously be pleasurable for others, that what I find immoral must also be immoral for them, and so on. It is also responsible for the almost universal desire to correct in others what most needs correcting in oneself. Identity, too, forms the basis of suggestion and psychic infection. Identity is particularly evident in pathological cases, for instance in paranoic ideas of reference, where one's own

441

subjective contents are taken for granted in others. But identity also makes possible a consciously *collective* (q.v.), social *attitude* (q.v.), which found its highest expression in the Christian ideal of brotherly love.

743   26. IMAGE. When I speak of "image" in this book, I do not mean the psychic reflection of an external object, but a concept derived from poetic usage, namely, a figure of fancy or *fantasy-image*, which is related only indirectly to the perception of an external object. This image depends much more on unconscious fantasy activity, and as the product of such activity it appears more or less abruptly in consciousness, somewhat in the manner of a vision or hallucination, but without possessing the morbid traits that are found in a clinical picture. The image has the psychological character of a fantasy idea and never the quasi-real character of an hallucination, i.e., it never takes the place of reality, and can always be distinguished from sensuous reality by the fact that it is an "inner" image. As a rule, it is not a projection in space, although in exceptional cases it can appear in exteriorized form. This mode of manifestation must be termed *archaic* (q.v.) when it is not primarily pathological, though that would not by any means do away with its archaic character. On the primitive level, however, the inner image can easily be projected in space as a vision or an auditory hallucination without being a pathological phenomenon.

744   Although, as a rule, no reality-value attaches to the image, this can at times actually increase its importance for psychic life, since it then has a greater *psychological* value, representing an inner reality which often far outweighs the importance of external reality. In this case the *orientation* (q.v.) of the individual is concerned less with adaptation to reality than with adaptation to inner demands.

745   The inner image is a complex structure made up of the most varied material from the most varied sources. It is no conglomerate, however, but a homogeneous product with a meaning of its own. The image is a *condensed expression of the psychic situation as a whole*, and not merely, nor even predominately, of unconscious contents pure and simple. It undoubtedly does express unconscious contents, but not the whole of

them, only those that are momentarily constellated. This constellation is the result of the spontaneous activity of the unconscious on the one hand and of the momentary conscious situation on the other, which always stimulates the activity of relevant subliminal material and at the same time inhibits the irrelevant. Accordingly the image is an expression of the unconscious as well as the conscious situation of the moment. The interpretation of its meaning, therefore, can start neither from the conscious alone nor from the unconscious alone, but only from their reciprocal relationship.

746   I call the image *primordial* when it possesses an *archaic* (q.v.) character.[60] I speak of its archaic character when the image is in striking accord with familiar mythological motifs. It then expresses material primarily derived from the *collective unconscious* (q.v.), and indicates at the same time that the factors influencing the conscious situation of the moment are *collective* (q.v.) rather than personal. A *personal* image has neither an archaic character nor a collective significance, but expresses contents of the *personal unconscious* (q.v.) and a personally conditioned conscious situation.

747   The primordial image, elsewhere also termed *archetype*,[61] is always collective, i.e., it is at least common to entire peoples or epochs. In all probability the most important mythological motifs are common to all times and races; I have, in fact, been able to demonstrate a whole series of motifs from Greek mythology in the dreams and fantasies of pure-bred Negroes suffering from mental disorders.[62]

748   From[63] the scientific, causal standpoint the primordial image can be conceived as a mnemic deposit, an imprint or

[60] A striking example of an archaic image is that of the solar phallus, *Symbols of Transformation*, pars. 151ff.

[61] Jung, "Instinct and the Unconscious," pars. 270ff. See also supra, par. 624.

[62] [In a letter to Freud, Nov. 11, 1912, reporting on a recent visit to the United States, Jung wrote: "I analyzed fifteen Negroes in Washington, with demonstrations." He did this at St. Elizabeths Hospital (a government facility) through the cooperation of its director, Dr. William Alanson White; see *Symbols of Transformation*, par. 154 and n. 52. In late 1912 Jung had already written and partially published *Wandlungen und Symbole der Libido*, and he mentioned the research on Negroes only in its revision, *Symbols of Transformation* (orig. 1952). Cf. also "The Tavistock Lectures," par. 79.—EDITORS.]

[63] [This paragraph has been somewhat revised in *Gesammelte Werke*, vol. 6, and the translation reproduces the revisions.—EDITORS.]

engram (Semon), which has arisen through the condensation of countless processes of a similar kind. In this respect it is a precipitate and, therefore, a typical basic form, of certain ever-recurring psychic experiences. As a mythological motif, it is a continually effective and recurrent expression that reawakens certain psychic experiences or else formulates them in an appropriate way. From this standpoint it is a psychic expression of the physiological and anatomical disposition. If one holds the view that a particular anatomical structure is a product of environmental conditions working on living matter, then the primordial image, in its constant and universal distribution, would be the product of equally constant and universal influences from without, which must, therefore, act like a natural law. One could in this way relate myths to nature, as for instance solar myths to the daily rising and setting of the sun, or to the equally obvious change of the seasons, and this has in fact been done by many mythologists, and still is. But that leaves the question unanswered why the sun and its apparent motions do not appear direct and undisguised as a content of the myths. The fact that the sun or the moon or the meteorological processes appear, at the very least, in allegorized form points to an independent collaboration of the psyche, which in that case cannot be merely a product or stereotype of environmental conditions. For whence would it draw the capacity to adopt a standpoint outside sense perception? How, for that matter, could it be at all capable of any performance more or other than the mere corroboration of the evidence of the senses? In view of such questions Semon's naturalistic and causalistic engram theory no longer suffices. We are forced to assume that the given structure of the brain does not owe its peculiar nature merely to the influence of surrounding conditions, but also and just as much to the peculiar and autonomous quality of living matter, i.e., to a law inherent in life itself. The given constitution of the organism, therefore, is on the one hand a product of external conditions, while on the other it is determined by the intrinsic nature of living matter. Accordingly, the primordial image is related just as much to certain palpable, self-perpetuating, and continually operative natural processes as it is to certain inner determinants of psychic life and of life in general. The organism confronts light with a

444

new structure, the eye, and the psyche confronts the natural process with a symbolic image, which apprehends it in the same way as the eye catches the light. And just as the eye bears witness to the peculiar and spontaneous creative activity of living matter, the primordial image expresses the unique and unconditioned creative power of the psyche.

749   The primordial image is thus a condensation of the living process. It gives a co-ordinating and coherent meaning both to sensuous and to inner perceptions, which at first appear without order or connection, and in this way frees psychic energy from its bondage to sheer uncomprehended perception. At the same time, it links the energies released by the perception of stimuli to a definite meaning, which then guides action along paths corresponding to this meaning. It releases unavailable, dammed-up energy by leading the mind back to nature and canalizing sheer instinct into mental forms.

750   The primordial image is the precursor of the *idea* (q.v.), and its matrix. By detaching it from the *concretism* (q.v.) peculiar and necessary to the primordial image, reason develops it into a concept—i.e., an idea which differs from all other concepts in that it is not a datum of experience but is actually the underlying principle of all experience. The idea derives this quality from the primordial image, which, as an expression of the specific structure of the brain, gives every experience a definite form.

751   The degree of psychological efficacy of the primordial image is determined by the *attitude* (q.v.) of the individual. If the attitude is introverted, the natural consequence of the withdrawal of *libido* (q.v.) from the external object is the heightened significance of the internal object, i.e., thought. This leads to a particularly intense development of thought along the lines unconsciously laid down by the primordial image. In this way the primordial image comes to the surface indirectly. The further development of thought leads to the idea, which is nothing other than the primordial image intellectually formulated. Only the development of the counterfunction can take the idea further—that is to say, once the idea has been grasped intellectually, it strives to become effective in life. It therefore calls upon *feeling* (q.v.), which in this case is much less differentiated and more concretistic than thinking.

445

Feeling is impure and, because undifferentiated, still fused with the *unconscious*. Hence the individual is unable to unite the contaminated feeling with the idea. At this juncture the primordial image appears in the inner field of vision as a *symbol* (q.v.), and, by virtue of its concrete nature, embraces the undifferentiated, concretized feeling, but also, by virtue of its intrinsic significance, embraces the idea, of which it is indeed the matrix, and so unites the two. In this way the primordial image acts as a mediator, once again proving its redeeming power, a power it has always possessed in the various religions. What Schopenhauer says of the idea, therefore, I would apply rather to the primordial image, since, as I have already explained, the idea is not something absolutely *a priori*, but must also be regarded as secondary and derived (v. *Idea*).

752   In the following passage from Schopenhauer, I would ask the reader to replace the word "idea" by "primordial image," and he will then be able to understand my meaning.

It [the idea] is never cognized by the individual as such, but only by him who has raised himself beyond all willing and all individuality to the pure subject of cognition. Thus it is attainable only by the genius, or by the man who, inspired by works of genius, has succeeded in elevating his powers of pure cognition into a temper akin to genius. It is, therefore, not absolutely but only conditionally communicable, since the idea conceived and reproduced in a work of art, for instance, appeals to each man only according to the measure of his own intellectual worth.

The idea is the unity that falls into multiplicity on account of the temporal and spatial form of our intuitive apprehension.

The concept is like an inert receptacle, in which the things one puts into it lie side by side, but from which no more can be taken out than was put in. The idea, on the other hand, develops, in him who has comprehended it, notions which are new in relation to the concept of the same name: it is like a living, self-developing organism endowed with generative power, constantly bringing forth something that was not put into it.[64]

753   Schopenhauer clearly discerned that the "idea," or the primordial image as I define it, cannot be produced in the same

64 Cf. *The World as Will and Idea*, I, pp. 302f.

446

way that a concept or an "idea" in the ordinary sense can (Kant defines an "idea" as a concept "formed from notions").[65] There clings to it an element beyond rational formulation, rather like Schopenhauer's "temper akin to genius," which simply means a state of feeling. One can get to the primordial image from the idea only because the path that led to the idea passes over the summit into the counterfunction, feeling.

754   The primordial image has one great advantage over the clarity of the idea, and that is its vitality. It is a self-activating organism, "endowed with generative power." The primordial image is an inherited organization of psychic energy, an ingrained system, which not only gives expression to the energic process but facilitates its operation. It shows how the energic process has run its unvarying course from time immemorial, while simultaneously allowing a perpetual repetition of it by means of an apprehension or psychic grasp of situations so that life can continue into the future. It is thus the necessary counterpart of *instinct* (q.v.), which is a purposive mode of action presupposing an equally purposive and meaningful grasp of the momentary situation. This apprehension is guaranteed by the pre-existent primordial image. It represents the practical formula without which the apprehension of a new situation would be impossible.

26a. IMAGO V. SUBJECTIVE LEVEL.

755   27. INDIVIDUAL. The psychological individual is characterized by a peculiar and in some respects unique psychology. The peculiar nature of the individual psyche appears less in its elements than in its complex formations. The psychological individual, or his *individuality* (q.v.), has an *a priori* unconscious existence, but exists consciously only so far as a consciousness of his peculiar nature is present, i.e., so far as there exists a conscious distinction from other individuals. The psychic individuality is given *a priori* as a correlate of the physical individuality, although, as observed, it is at first unconscious. A conscious process of *differentiation* (q.v.), or *individuation* (q.v.), is needed to bring the individuality to con-

[65] *Critique of Pure Reason*, p. 314.

sciousness, i.e., to raise it out of the state of *identity* (q.v.) with the object. The identity of the individuality with the object is synonymous with its unconsciousness. If the individuality is unconscious, there is no psychological individual but merely a collective psychology of consciousness. The unconscious individuality is then projected on the object, and the object, in consequence, possesses too great a value and acts as too powerful a determinant.

756   28. INDIVIDUALITY. By individuality I mean the peculiarity and singularity of the individual in every psychological respect. Everything that is not *collective* (q.v.) is individual, everything in fact that pertains only to one individual and not to a larger group of individuals. Individuality can hardly be said to pertain to the psychic elements themselves, but only to their peculiar and unique grouping and combination (v. *Individual*).

757   29. INDIVIDUATION. The concept of individuation plays a large role in our psychology. In general, it is the process by which individual beings are formed and differentiated; in particular, it is the development of the psychological *individual* (q.v.) as a being distinct from the general, collective psychology. Individuation, therefore, is a process of *differentiation* (q.v.), having for its goal the development of the individual personality.

758   Individuation is a natural necessity inasmuch as its prevention by a levelling down to collective standards is injurious to the vital activity of the individual. Since *individuality* (q.v.) is a prior psychological and physiological datum, it also expresses itself in psychological ways. Any serious check to individuality, therefore, is an artificial stunting. It is obvious that a social group consisting of stunted individuals cannot be a healthy and viable institution; only a society that can preserve its internal cohesion and collective values, while at the same time granting the individual the greatest possible freedom, has any prospect of enduring vitality. As the individual is not just a single, separate being, but by his very existence presupposes a collective relationship, it follows that the process of individuation must lead to more intense and broader collective relationships and not to isolation.

448

759　　Individuation is closely connected with the *transcendent function* (v. *Symbol,* par. 828), since this function creates individual lines of development which could never be reached by keeping to the path prescribed by collective norms.

760　　Under no circumstances can individuation be the sole aim of psychological education. Before it can be taken as a goal, the educational aim of adaptation to the necessary minimum of collective norms must first be attained. If a plant is to unfold its specific nature to the full, it must first be able to grow in the soil in which it is planted.

761　　Individuation is always to some extent opposed to collective norms, since it means separation and differentiation from the general and a building up of the particular—not a particularity that is *sought out,* but one that is already ingrained in the psychic constitution. The opposition to the collective norm, however, is only apparent, since closer examination shows that the individual standpoint is not *antagonistic* to it, but only *differently oriented.* The individual way can never be directly opposed to the collective norm, because the opposite of the collective norm could only be another, but contrary, norm. But the individual way can, by definition, never be a norm. A norm is the product of the totality of individual ways, and its justification and beneficial effect are contingent upon the existence of individual ways that need from time to time to orient to a norm. A norm serves no purpose when it possesses absolute validity. A real conflict with the collective norm arises only when an individual way is raised to a norm, which is the actual aim of extreme individualism. Naturally this aim is pathological and inimical to life. It has, accordingly, nothing to do with individuation, which, though it may strike out on an individual bypath, precisely on that account needs the norm for its *orientation* (q.v.) to society and for the vitally necessary relationship of the individual to society. Individuation, therefore, leads to a natural esteem for the collective norm, but if the orientation is exclusively collective the norm becomes increasingly superfluous and morality goes to pieces. The more a man's life is shaped by the collective norm, the greater is his individual immorality.

762　　Individuation is practically the same as the development of consciousness out of the original state of *identity* (q.v.). It is thus an extension of the sphere of consciousness, an enriching of conscious psychological life.

763   30. INFERIOR FUNCTION. This term is used to denote the function that lags behind in the process of *differentiation* (q.v.). Experience shows that it is practically impossible, owing to adverse circumstances in general, for anyone to develop all his psychological functions simultaneously. The demands of society compel a man to apply himself first and foremost to the differentiation of the function with which he is best equipped by nature, or which will secure him the greatest social success. Very frequently, indeed as a general rule, a man identifies more or less completely with the most favoured and hence the most developed function. It is this that gives rise to the various psychological *types* (q.v.). As a consequence of this one-sided development, one or more functions are necessarily retarded. These functions may properly be called *inferior* in a psychological but not psychopathological sense, since they are in no way morbid but merely backward as compared with the favoured function.

764   Although the inferior function may be conscious as a phenomenon, its true significance nevertheless remains unrecognized. It behaves like many repressed or insufficiently appreciated contents, which are partly conscious and partly unconscious, just as, very often, one knows a certain person from his outward appearance but does not know him as he really is. Thus in normal cases the inferior function remains conscious, at least in its effects; but in a neurosis it sinks wholly or in part into the unconscious. For, to the degree that the greater share of *libido* (q.v.) is taken up by the favoured function, the inferior function undergoes a regressive development; it reverts to the *archaic* (q.v.) stage and becomes incompatible with the conscious, favoured function. When a function that should normally be conscious lapses into the unconscious, its specific energy passes into the unconscious too. A function such as feeling possesses the energy with which it is endowed by nature; it is a well-organized living system that cannot under any circumstances be wholly deprived of its energy. So with the inferior function: the energy left to it passes into the un-

conscious and activates it in an unnatural way, giving rise to *fantasies* (q.v.) on a level with the archaicized function. In order to extricate the inferior function from the unconscious by analysis, the unconscious fantasy formations that have now been activated must be brought to the surface. The conscious realization of these fantasies brings the inferior function to consciousness and makes further development possible.

765   31. INSTINCT. When I speak of instinct in this work or elsewhere, I mean what is commonly understood by this word, namely, an *impulsion* towards certain activities. The impulsion can come from an inner or outer stimulus which triggers off the mechanism of instinct psychically, or from organic sources which lie outside the sphere of psychic causality. Every psychic phenomenon is instinctive that does not arise from voluntary causation but from dynamic impulsion, irrespective of whether this impulsion comes directly from organic, extrapsychic sources, or from energies that are merely released by voluntary intention—in the latter case with the qualification that the end-result exceeds the effect voluntarily intended. In my view, all psychic processes whose energies are not under conscious control are instinctive. Thus *affects* (q.v.) are as much instinctive processes as they are *feeling* (q.v.) processes. Psychic processes which under ordinary circumstances are functions of the *will* (q.v.), and thus entirely under conscious control, can, in abnormal circumstances, become instinctive processes when supplied with unconscious energy. This phenomenon occurs whenever the sphere of consciousness is restricted by the repression of incompatible contents, or when, as a result of fatigue, intoxication, or morbid cerebral conditions in general, an *abaissement du niveau mental* (Janet) ensues—when, in a word, the most strongly feeling-toned processes are no longer, or not yet, under conscious control. Processes that were once conscious but in time have become *automatized* I would reckon among the automatic processes rather than the instinctive. Nor do they normally behave like instincts, since in normal circumstances they never appear as impulsions. They do so only when supplied with an energy which is foreign to them.

451

766   32. INTELLECT. I call *directed thinking* (q.v.) intellect.

767   33. INTROJECTION. This term was introduced by Avenarius[66] to correspond with *projection* (q.v.). The expulsion of a subjective content into an object, which is what Avenarius meant, is expressed equally well by the term projection, and it would therefore be better to reserve the term projection for this process. Ferenczi has now defined introjection as the opposite of projection, namely as an indrawing of the object into the subjective sphere of interest, while projection is an expulsion of subjective contents into the object. "Whereas the paranoiac expels from his ego emotions which have become disagreeable, the neurotic helps himself to as large a portion of the outer world as his ego can ingest, and makes this an object of unconscious fantasies."[67] The first mechanism is projection, the second introjection. Introjection is a sort of "diluting process," an "expansion of the circle of interest." According to Ferenczi, the process is a normal one.

768   Psychologically speaking, introjection is a process of *assimilation* (q.v.), while projection is a process of *dissimilation*. Introjection is an assimilation of object to subject, projection a dissimilation of object from subject through the expulsion of a subjective content into the object (v. *Projection, active*). Introjection is a process of *extraversion* (q.v.), since assimilation to the object requires *empathy* (q.v.) and an investment of the object with *libido* (q.v.). A *passive* and an *active* introjection may be distinguished: transference phenomena in the treatment of the neuroses belong to the former category, and, in general, all cases where the object exercises a compelling influence on the subject, while empathy as a process of adaptation belongs to the latter category.

769   34. INTROVERSION means an inward-turning of *libido* (q.v.), in the sense of a negative relation of subject to object. Interest does not move towards the object but withdraws from it into the subject. Everyone whose attitude is introverted thinks, feels, and acts in a way that clearly demonstrates that the subject is the prime motivating factor and that the object is of

66 *Der menschliche Weltbegriff*, pp. 25ff.

67 "Introjection and Transference," *First Contributions to Psychoanalysis*, pp. 47f.

secondary importance. Introversion may be intellectual or emotional, just as it can be characterized by *sensation* or *intuition* (qq.v.). It is *active* when the subject *voluntarily* shuts himself off from the object, *passive* when he is unable to restore to the object the libido streaming back from it. When introversion is habitual, we speak of an *introverted type* (q.v.).

770   35. INTUITION (L. *intueri*, 'to look at or into'). I regard intuition as a basic psychological *function* (q.v.). It is the function that mediates perceptions in an *unconscious way*. Everything, whether outer or inner objects or their relationships, can be the focus of this perception. The peculiarity of intuition is that it is neither sense perception, nor feeling, nor intellectual inference, although it may also appear in these forms. In intuition a content presents itself whole and complete, without our being able to explain or discover how this content came into existence. Intuition is a kind of instinctive apprehension, no matter of what contents. Like *sensation* (q.v.), it is an *irrational* (q.v.) function of perception. As with sensation, its contents have the character of being "given," in contrast to the "derived" or "produced" character of *thinking* and *feeling* (qq.v.) contents. Intuitive knowledge possesses an intrinsic certainty and conviction, which enabled Spinoza (and Bergson) to uphold the *scientia intuitiva* as the highest form of knowledge. Intuition shares this quality with *sensation* (q.v.), whose certainty rests on its physical foundation. The certainty of intuition rests equally on a definite state of psychic "alertness" of whose origin the subject is unconscious.

771   Intuition may be *subjective* or *objective*: the first is a perception of unconscious psychic data originating in the subject, the second is a perception of data dependent on subliminal perceptions of the object and on the feelings and thoughts they evoke. We may also distinguish *concrete* and *abstract* forms of intuition, according to the degree of participation on the part of sensation. Concrete intuition mediates perceptions concerned with the actuality of things, abstract intuition mediates perceptions of ideational connections. Concrete intuition is a reactive process, since it responds directly to the given facts; abstract intuition, like abstract sensation, needs a certain element of direction, an act of the will, or an aim.

453

772   Like sensation, intuition is a characteristic of infantile and primitive psychology. It counterbalances the powerful sense impressions of the child and the primitive by mediating perceptions of mythological images, the precursors of *ideas* (q.v.). It stands in a compensatory relationship to sensation and, like it, is the matrix out of which thinking and feeling develop as rational functions. Although intuition is an irrational function, many intuitions can afterwards be broken down into their component elements and their origin thus brought into harmony with the laws of reason.

773   Everyone whose general *attitude* (q.v.) is oriented by intuition belongs to the intuitive *type* (q.v.).[68] Introverted and extraverted intuitives may be distinguished according to whether intuition is directed inwards, to the inner vision, or outwards, to action and achievement. In abnormal cases intuition is in large measure fused together with the contents of the *collective unconscious* (q.v.) and determined by them, and this may make the intuitive type appear extremely irrational and beyond comprehension.

774   36. IRRATIONAL. I use this term not as denoting something *contrary* to reason, but something *beyond* reason, something, therefore, not grounded on reason. Elementary facts come into this category; the fact, for example, that the earth has a moon, that chlorine is an element, that water reaches its greatest density at four degrees centigrade, etc. Another irrational fact is *chance*, even though it may be possible to demonstrate a rational causation after the event.[69]

775   The irrational is an existential factor which, though it may be pushed further and further out of sight by an increasingly elaborate rational explanation, finally makes the explanation so complicated that it passes our powers of comprehension, the limits of rational thought being reached long before the whole of the world could be encompassed by the laws of reason. A

[68] The credit for having discovered the existence of this type belongs to Miss M. Moltzer. [Mary Moltzer, daughter of a Netherlands distiller, took up nursing as a personal gesture against alcoholic abuse and moved to Zurich. She studied under Jung, became an analytical psychologist, and was joint translator of his *The Theory of Psychoanalysis* (see vol. 4, p. 83 and par. 458). She attended the international congress of psychoanalysts at Weimar, 1911.—EDITORS.]

[69] Jung, "Synchronicity: An Acausal Connecting Principle."

completely rational explanation of an object that actually exists (not one that is merely posited) is a Utopian ideal. Only an object that is posited can be completely explained on rational grounds, since it does not contain anything beyond what has been posited by rational thinking. Empirical science, too, posits objects that are confined within rational bounds, because by deliberately excluding the accidental it does not consider the actual object as a whole, but only that part of it which has been singled out for rational observation.

776 In this sense *thinking* is a *directed function*, and so is *feeling* (qq.v.). When these functions are concerned not with a rational choice of objects, or with the qualities and interrelations of objects, but with the perception of accidentals which the actual object never lacks, they at once lose the attribute of directedness and, with it, something of their rational character, because they then accept the accidental. They begin to be irrational. The kind of thinking or feeling that is directed to the perception of accidentals, and is therefore irrational, is either *intuitive* or *sensational*. Both *intuition* and *sensation* (qq.v.) are functions that find fulfilment in the *absolute perception* of the flux of events. Hence, by their very nature, they will react to every possible occurrence and be attuned to the absolutely contingent, and must therefore lack all rational direction. For this reason I call them irrational functions, as opposed to thinking and feeling, which find fulfilment only when they are in complete harmony with the laws of reason.

777 Although the irrational as such can never become the object of science, it is of the greatest importance for a practical psychology that the irrational factor should be correctly appraised. Practical psychology stirs up many problems that are not susceptible of a rational solution, but can only be settled irrationally, in a way not in accord with the laws of reason. The expectation or exclusive conviction that there must be a rational way of settling every conflict can be an insurmountable obstacle to finding a solution of an irrational nature.

778 37. LIBIDO. By libido I mean *psychic energy*.[70] Psychic energy is the *intensity* of a psychic process, its *psychological*

[70] *Symbols of Transformation*, Part II, chs. II and III, and "On Psychic Energy," pars. 7ff.

value. This does not imply an assignment of value, whether moral, aesthetic, or intellectual; the psychological value is already implicit in its *determining* power, which expresses itself in definite psychic effects. Neither do I understand libido as a psychic *force,* a misconception that has led many critics astray. I do not hypostatize the concept of energy, but use it to denote intensities or values. The question as to whether or not a specific psychic force exists has nothing to do with the concept of libido. I often use "libido" promiscuously with "energy." The justification for calling psychic energy libido is fully gone into in the works cited in the footnote.

779   38. OBJECTIVE LEVEL. When I speak of interpreting a dream or fantasy on the objective level, I mean that the persons or situations appearing in it are referred to objectively real persons or situations, in contrast to interpretation on the *subjective level* (q.v.), where the persons or situations refer exclusively to subjective factors. Freud's interpretation of dreams is almost entirely on the objective level, since the dream wishes refer to real objects, or to sexual processes which fall within the physiological, extra-psychological sphere.

780   39. ORIENTATION. I use this term to denote the general principle governing an *attitude* (q.v.). Every attitude is oriented by a certain viewpoint, no matter whether this viewpoint is conscious or not. A power attitude (v. *Power-complex*) is oriented by the power of the *ego* (q.v.) to hold its own against unfavourable influences and conditions. A thinking attitude is oriented by the principle of logic as its supreme law; a sensation attitude is oriented by the sensuous perception of given facts.

781   40. PARTICIPATION MYSTIQUE is a term derived from Lévy-Bruhl.[71] It denotes a peculiar kind of psychological connection with objects, and consists in the fact that the subject cannot clearly distinguish himself from the object but is bound to it by a direct relationship which amounts to partial *identity* (q.v.). This identity results from an *a priori* oneness of subject and object. *Participation mystique* is a vestige of this primitive condition. It does not apply to the whole subject-object relation-

[71] *How Natives Think.*

ship but only to certain cases where this peculiar tie occurs. It is a phenomenon that is best observed among primitives, though it is found very frequently among civilized peoples, if not with the same incidence and intensity. Among civilized peoples it usually occurs between persons, seldom between a person and a thing. In the first case it is a transference relationship, in which the object (as a rule) obtains a sort of magical —i.e. absolute—influence over the subject. In the second case there is a similar influence on the part of the thing, or else an *identification* (q.v.) with a thing or the idea of a thing.

41. PERSONA, V. SOUL.

782   42. POWER-COMPLEX. I occasionally use this term to denote the whole complex of ideas and strivings which seek to subordinate all other influences to the *ego* (q.v.), no matter whether these influences have their source in people and objective conditions or in the subject's own impulses, thoughts, and feelings.

783   43. PROJECTION means the expulsion of a subjective content into an object; it is the opposite of *introjection* (q.v.). Accordingly it is a process of *dissimilation* (v. *Assimilation*), by which a subjective content becomes alienated from the subject and is, so to speak, embodied in the object. The subject gets rid of painful, incompatible contents by projecting them, as also of positive values which, for one reason or another—self-depreciation, for instance—are inaccessible to him. Projection results from the archaic *identity* (q.v.) of subject and object, but is properly so called only when the need to dissolve the identity with the object has already arisen. This need arises when the identity becomes a disturbing factor, i.e., when the absence of the projected content is a hindrance to adaptation and its withdrawal into the subject has become desirable. From this moment the previous partial identity acquires the character of projection. The term projection therefore signifies a state of identity that has become noticeable, an object of criticism, whether it be the self-criticism of the subject or the objective criticism of another.

784   We may distinguish *passive* and *active* projection. The passive form is the customary form of all pathological and

many normal projections; they are not intentional and are purely automatic occurrences. The active form is an essential component of the act of *empathy* (q.v.). Taken as a whole, empathy is a process of introjection, since it brings the object into intimate relation with the subject. In order to establish this relationship, the subject detaches a content—a feeling, for instance—from himself, lodges it in the object, thereby animating it, and in this way draws the object into the sphere of the subject. The active form of projection is, however, also an act of judgment, the aim of which is to separate the subject from the object. Here a subjective judgment is detached from the subject as a valid statement and lodged in the object; by this act the subject distinguishes himself from the object. Projection, accordingly, is a process of *introversion* (q.v.) since, unlike introjection, it does not lead to ingestion and assimilation but to differentiation and separation of subject from object. Hence it plays a prominent role in paranoia, which usually ends in the total isolation of the subject.

43a. PSYCHE, v. SOUL.

785   44. RATIONAL. The rational is the reasonable, that which accords with reason. I conceive reason as an *attitude* (q.v.) whose principle it is to conform thought, feeling, and action to objective values. Objective values are established by the everyday experience of external facts on the one hand, and of inner, psychological facts on the other. Such experiences, however, could not represent objective "values" if they were "valued" as such by the subject, for that would already amount to an act of reason. The rational attitude which permits us to declare objective values as valid at all is not the work of the individual subject, but the product of human history.

786   Most objective values—and reason itself—are firmly established complexes of ideas handed down through the ages. Countless generations have laboured at their organization with the same necessity with which the living organism reacts to the average, constantly recurring environmental conditions, confronting them with corresponding functional complexes, as the eye, for instance, perfectly corresponds to the nature of light. One might, therefore, speak of a pre-existent, metaphysical, universal "Reason" were it not that the adapted reaction of the

living organism to average environmental influences is the necessary condition of its existence—a thought already expressed by Schopenhauer. Human reason, accordingly, is nothing other than the expression of man's adaptability to average occurrences, which have gradually become deposited in firmly established complexes of ideas that constitute our objective values. Thus the laws of reason are the laws that designate and govern the average, "correct," adapted *attitude* (q.v.). Everything is "rational" that accords with these laws, everything that contravenes them is "irrational" (q.v.).

787   *Thinking* and *feeling* (qq.v.) are rational functions in so far as they are decisively influenced by *reflection*. They function most perfectly when they are in the fullest possible accord with the laws of reason. The irrational functions, *sensation* and *intuition* (qq.v.), are those whose aim is pure *perception*; for, as far as possible, they are forced to dispense with the rational (which presupposes the exclusion of everything that is outside reason) in order to attain the most complete perception of the general flux of events.

788   45. REDUCTIVE means "leading back." I use this term to denote a method of psychological interpretation which regards the unconscious product not as a *symbol* (q.v.) but *semiotically,* as a *sign* or *symptom* of an underlying process. Accordingly, the reductive method traces the unconscious product back to its elements, no matter whether these be reminiscences of events that actually took place, or elementary psychic processes. The reductive method is oriented backwards, in contrast to the *constructive* (q.v.) method, whether in the purely historical sense or in the figurative sense of tracing complex, differentiated factors back to something more general and more elementary. The interpretive methods of both Freud and Adler are reductive, since in both cases there is a reduction to the elementary processes of wishing or striving, which in the last resort are of an infantile or physiological nature. Hence the unconscious product necessarily acquires the character of an inauthentic expression to which the term "symbol" is not properly applicable. Reduction has a disintegrative effect on the real significance of the unconscious product, since this is either traced back to its historical antecedents and thereby

annihilated, or integrated once again with the same elementary process from which it arose.

789   46. SELF.[72] As an empirical concept, the self designates the whole range of psychic phenomena in man. It expresses the unity of the personality as a whole. But in so far as the total personality, on account of its unconscious component, can be only in part conscious, the concept of the self is, in part, only *potentially* empirical and is to that extent a *postulate*. In other words, it encompasses both the experienceable and the inexperienceable (or the not yet experienced). It has these qualities in common with very many scientific concepts that are more names than ideas. In so far as psychic totality, consisting of both conscious and unconscious contents, is a postulate, it is a *transcendental* concept, for it presupposes the existence of unconscious factors on empirical grounds and thus characterizes an entity that can be described only in part but, for the other part, remains at present unknowable and illimitable.

790   Just as conscious as well as unconscious phenomena are to be met with in practice, the self as psychic totality also has a conscious as well as an unconscious aspect. Empirically, the self appears in dreams, myths, and fairytales in the figure of the "supraordinate personality" (v. EGO), such as a king, hero, prophet, saviour, etc., or in the form of a totality symbol, such as the circle, square, *quadratura circuli*, cross, etc. When it represents a *complexio oppositorum*, a union of opposites, it can also appear as a united duality, in the form, for instance, of *tao* as the interplay of *yang* and *yin*, or of the hostile brothers, or of the hero and his adversary (arch-enemy, dragon), Faust and Mephistopheles, etc. Empirically, therefore, the self appears as a play of light and shadow, although conceived as a totality and unity in which the opposites are united. Since such a concept is irrepresentable—*tertium non datur*—it is transcendental on this account also. It would, logically consid-

---

[72] [This definition was written for the *Gesammelte Werke* edition. It may be of interest to note that the definition here given of the self as "the whole range of psychic phenomena in man" is almost identical with the definition of the psyche as "the totality of all psychic processes, conscious as well as unconscious" (par. 797). The inference would seem to be that every individual, by virtue of having, or being, a psyche, is potentially the self. It is only a question of "realizing" it. But the realization, if ever achieved, is the work of a lifetime.—EDITORS.]

ered, be a vain speculation were it not for the fact that it designates symbols of unity that are found to occur empirically.

791   The self is not a philosophical idea, since it does not predicate its own existence, i.e., does not hypostatize itself. From the intellectual point of view it is only a working hypothesis. Its empirical symbols, on the other hand, very often possess a distinct *numinosity*, i.e., an *a priori* emotional value, as in the case of the mandala,[73] "Deus est circulus . . . ,"[74] the Pythagorean tetraktys,[75] the quaternity,[76] etc. It thus proves to be an *archetypal idea* (v. *Idea; Image*), which differs from other ideas of the kind in that it occupies a central position befitting the significance of its content and its numinosity.

792   47. SENSATION. I regard sensation as one of the basic psychological *functions* (q.v.). Wundt likewise reckons it among the elementary psychic phenomena.[77] Sensation is the psychological function that mediates the perception of a physical stimulus. It is, therefore, identical with perception. Sensation must be strictly distinguished from *feeling* (q.v.), since the latter is an entirely different process, although it may associate itself with sensation as "feeling-tone." Sensation is related not only to external stimuli but to inner ones, i.e., to changes in the internal organic processes.

73 [Jung, "A Study in the Process of Individuation" and "Concerning Mandala Symbolism."—EDITORS.]

74 [The full quotation is "Deus est circulus cuius centrum est ubique, circumferentia vero nusquam" (God is a circle whose centre is everywhere and the circumference nowhere); see "A Psychological Approach to the Dogma of the Trinity," par. 229, n. 6. In this form the saying is a variant of one attributed to St. Bonaventure (*Itinerarium mentis in Deum*, 5): "Deus est figura intellectualis cuius centrum . . ." (God is an intelligible sphere whose centre . . .); see *Mysterium Coniunctionis*, par. 41, n. 42. For more documentation see Borges, "Pascal's Sphere."—EDITORS.]

75 [Concerning the *tetraktys* see *Psychology and Alchemy*, par. 189; "Commentary on The Secret of the Golden Flower," par. 31; *Psychology and Religion: West and East*, pars. 61, 90, 246.—EDITORS.]

76 [The quaternity figures so largely in Jung's later writings that the reader who is interested in its numerous significations, including that of a symbol of the self, should consult the indexes (s.v. "quaternity," "self") of *Coll. Works*, vols. 9, Parts I and II, 11, 12, 13, 14.—EDITORS.]

77 For the history of the concept of sensation see Wundt, *Grundzüge der physiologischen Psychologie*, I, pp. 350ff.; Dessoir, *Geschichte der neueren Psychologie*; Villa, *Contemporary Psychology*; Hartmann, *Die moderne Psychologie*.

793   Primarily, therefore, sensation is *sense perception*—perception mediated by the sense organs and "body-senses" (kinaesthetic, vasomotor sensation, etc.). It is, on the one hand, an element of ideation, since it conveys to the mind the perceptual image of the external object; and on the other hand, it is an element of feeling, since through the perception of bodily changes . it gives feeling the character of an *affect* (q.v.). Because sensation conveys bodily changes to consciousness, it is also a representative of physiological impulses. It is not identical with them, being merely a perceptive function.

794   A distinction must be made between sensuous or *concrete* (q.v.) sensation and *abstract* (q.v.) sensation. The first includes all the above-mentioned forms of sensation, whereas the second is a sensation that is abstracted or separated from the other psychic elements. Concrete sensation never appears in "pure" form, but is always mixed up with ideas, feelings, thoughts. Abstract sensation is a differentiated kind of perception, which might be termed "aesthetic" in so far as, obeying its own principle, it detaches itself from all contamination with the different elements in the perceived object and from all admixtures of thought and feeling, and thus attains a degree of purity beyond the reach of concrete sensation. The concrete sensation of a flower, on the other hand, conveys a perception not only of the flower as such, but also of the stem, leaves, habitat, and so on. It is also instantly mingled with feelings of pleasure or dislike which the sight of the flower evokes, or with simultaneous olfactory perceptions, or with thoughts about its botanical classification, etc. But abstract sensation immediately picks out the most salient sensuous attribute of the flower, its brilliant redness, for instance, and makes this the sole or at least the principal content of consciousness, entirely detached from all other admixtures. Abstract sensation is found chiefly among artists. Like every abstraction, it is a product of functional *differentiation* (q.v.), and there is nothing primitive about it. The primitive form of a function is always concrete, i.e., contaminated (v. *Archaism; Concretism*). Concrete sensation is a reactive phenomenon, while abstract sensation, like every abstraction, is always associated with the *will* (q.v.), i.e., with a sense of direction. The will that is directed to abstract

sensation is an expression and application of the *aesthetic sensation attitude*.

795 Sensation is strongly developed in children and primitives, since in both cases it predominates over thinking and feeling, though not necessarily over *intuition* (q.v.). I regard sensation as conscious, and intuition as unconscious, perception. For me sensation and intuition represent a pair of opposites, or two mutually compensating functions, like thinking and feeling. Thinking and feeling as independent functions are developed, both ontogenetically and phylogenetically, from sensation (and equally, of course, from intuition as the necessary counterpart of sensation). A person whose whole *attitude* (q.v.) is oriented by sensation belongs to the *sensation type* (q.v.).

796 Since sensation is an elementary phenomenon, it is given *a priori*, and, unlike thinking and feeling, is not subject to rational laws. I therefore call it an *irrational* (q.v.) function, although reason contrives to assimilate a great many sensations into a rational context. Normal sensations are proportionate, i.e., they correspond approximately to the intensity of the physical stimulus. Pathological sensations are disproportionate, i.e., either abnormally weak or abnormally strong. In the former case they are inhibited, in the latter exaggerated. The inhibition is due to the predominance of another function; the exaggeration is the result of an abnormal fusion with another function, for instance with undifferentiated thinking or feeling. It ceases as soon as the function with which sensation is fused is differentiated in its own right. The psychology of the neuroses affords instructive examples of this, since we often find a strong *sexualization* (Freud) of other functions, i.e., their fusion with sexual sensations.

797 48. SOUL. [Psyche, personality, persona, anima.] I have been compelled, in my investigations into the structure of the unconscious, to make a conceptual distinction between *soul* and *psyche*. By psyche I understand the totality of all psychic processes, conscious as well as unconscious. By soul, on the other hand, I understand a clearly demarcated functional complex that can best be described as a "personality." In order to make clear what I mean by this, I must introduce some further

463

points of view. It is, in particular, the phenomena of somnambulism, double consciousness, split personality, etc., whose investigation we owe primarily to the French school,[78] that have enabled us to accept the possibility of a plurality of personalities in one and the same individual.

[Soul as a functional complex or "personality"]

798   It is at once evident that such a plurality of personalities can never appear in a normal individual. But, as the above-mentioned phenomena show, the possibility of a dissociation of personality must exist, at least in the germ, within the range of the normal. And, as a matter of fact, any moderately acute psychological observer will be able to demonstrate, without much difficulty, traces of character-splitting in normal individuals. One has only to observe a man rather closely, under varying conditions, to see that a change from one milieu to another brings about a striking alteration of personality, and on each occasion a clearly defined character emerges that is noticeably different from the previous one. "Angel abroad, devil at home" is a formulation of the phenomenon of character-splitting derived from everyday experience. A particular milieu necessitates a particular *attitude* (q.v.). The longer this attitude lasts, and the more often it is required, the more habitual it becomes. Very many people from the educated classes have to move in two totally different milieus—the domestic circle and the world of affairs. These two totally different environments demand two totally different attitudes, which, depending on the degree of the ego's *identification* (q.v.) with the attitude of the moment, produce a duplication of character. In accordance with social conditions and requirements, the social character is oriented on the one hand by the expectations and demands of society, and on the other by the social aims and aspirations of the individual. The domestic character is, as a rule, moulded by emotional demands and an easy-going acquiescence for the sake of comfort and convenience; whence it frequently happens

[78] Azam, *Hypnotisme, double conscience, et altérations de la personnalité*; Prince, *The Dissociation of a Personality*; Landmann, *Die Mehrheit geistiger Persönlichkeiten in einem Individuum*; Ribot, *Die Persönlichkeit*; Flournoy, *From India to the Planet Mars*; Jung, "On the Psychology and Pathology of So-called Occult Phenomena."

that men who in public life are extremely energetic, spirited, obstinate, wilful and ruthless appear good-natured, mild, compliant, even weak, when at home and in the bosom of the family. Which is the true character, the real personality? This question is often impossible to answer.

799   These reflections show that even in normal individuals character-splitting is by no means an impossiblity. We are, therefore, fully justified in treating personality dissociation as a problem of normal psychology. In my view the answer to the above question should be that such a man has no real character at all: he is not *individual* (q.v.) but *collective* (q.v.), the plaything of circumstance and general expectations. Were he individual, he would have the same character despite the variation of attitude. He would not be identical with the attitude of the moment, and he neither would nor could prevent his *individuality* (q.v.) from expressing itself just as clearly in one state as in another. Naturally he is individual, like every living being, but unconsciously so. Because of his more or less complete identification with the attitude of the moment, he deceives others, and often himself, as to his real character. He puts on a *mask*, which he knows is in keeping with his conscious intentions, while it also meets the requirements and fits the opinions of society, first one motive and then the other gaining the upper hand.

[Soul as persona]

800   This mask, i.e., the *ad hoc* adopted attitude, I have called the *persona*,[79] which was the name for the masks worn by actors in antiquity. The man who identifies with this mask I would call "personal" as opposed to "individual."

801   The two above-mentioned attitudes represent two collective personalities, which may be summed up quite simply under the name "personae." I have already suggested that the real individuality is different from both. The persona is thus a functional complex that comes into existence for reasons of adaptation or personal convenience, but is by no means identical with the individuality. The persona is exclusively concerned with the relation to objects. The relation of the individ-

[79] *Two Essays on Analytical Psychology,* pars. 243ff.

ual to the object must be sharply distinguished from the relation to the subject. By the "subject" I mean first of all those vague, dim stirrings, feelings, thoughts, and sensations which flow in on us not from any demonstrable continuity of conscious experience of the object, but well up like a disturbing, inhibiting, or at times helpful, influence from the dark inner depths, from the background and underground vaults of consciousness, and constitute, in their totality, our perception of the life of the unconscious. The subject, conceived as the "inner object," *is* the unconscious. Just as there is a relation to the outer object, an outer attitude, there is a relation to the inner object, an inner attitude. It is readily understandable that this inner attitude, by reason of its extremely intimate and inaccessible nature, is far more difficult to discern than the outer attitude, which is immediately perceived by everyone. Nevertheless, it does not seem to me impossible to formulate it as a concept. All those allegedly accidental inhibitions, fancies, moods, vague feelings, and scraps of fantasy that hinder concentration and disturb the peace of mind even of the most normal man, and that are rationalized away as being due to bodily causes and suchlike, usually have their origin, not in the reasons consciously ascribed to them, but in perceptions of unconscious processes. Dreams naturally belong to this class of phenomena, and, as we all know, are often traced back to such external and superficial causes as indigestion, sleeping on one's back, and so forth, in spite of the fact that these explanations can never stand up to searching criticism. The attitude of the individual in these matters is extremely varied. One man will not allow himself to be disturbed in the slightest by his inner processes—he can ignore them completely; another man is just as completely at their mercy—as soon as he wakes up some fantasy or other, or a disagreeable feeling, spoils his mood for the whole day; a vaguely unpleasant sensation puts the idea into his head that he is suffering from a secret disease, a dream fills him with gloomy forebodings, although ordinarily he is not superstitious. Others, again, have only periodic access to these unconscious stirrings, or only to a certain category of them. For one man they may never have reached consciousness at all as anything worth thinking about, for another they are a worrying problem he broods on daily. One man takes them as physiological, another attributes them to the behaviour of his neighbours, another finds in them a religious revelation.

802   These entirely different ways of dealing with the stirrings of the unconscious are just as habitual as the attitudes to the outer object. The inner attitude, therefore, is correlated with just as definite a functional complex as the outer attitude. People who, it would seem, entirely overlook their inner psychic processes no more lack a typical inner attitude than the people who constantly overlook the outer object and the reality of facts lack a typical outer one. In all the latter cases, which are by no means uncommon, the persona is characterized by a lack of relatedness, at times even a blind inconsiderateness, that yields only to the harshest blows of fate. Not infrequently, it is just these people with a rigid persona who possess an attitude to the unconscious processes which is extremely susceptible and open to influence. Inwardly they are as weak, malleable, and "soft-centered" as they are inflexible and unapproachable outwardly. Their inner attitude, therefore, corresponds to a personality that is diametrically opposed to the outer personality. I know a man, for instance, who blindly and pitilessly destroyed the happiness of those nearest to him, and yet would interrupt important business journeys just to enjoy the beauty of a forest scene glimpsed from the carriage window. Cases of this kind are doubtless familiar to everyone, so I need not give further examples.

[Soul as anima]

803   We can, therefore, speak of an inner personality with as much justification as, on the grounds of daily experience, we speak of an outer personality. The inner personality is the way one behaves in relation to one's inner psychic processes; it is the inner attitude, the characteristic face, that is turned towards the unconscious. I call the outer attitude, the outward face, the *persona*; the inner attitude, the inward face, I call the *anima*.[80] To the degree that an attitude is habitual, it is a well-

80 [In the German text the word *Anima* is used only twice: here and at the beginning of par. 805. Everywhere else the word used is *Seele* (soul). In this translation *anima* is substituted for "soul" when it refers specifically to the feminine component in a man, just as in Def. 49 (SOUL-IMAGE) *animus* is substituted for "soul" when it refers specifically to the masculine component in a

knit functional complex with which the ego can identify itself more or less. Common speech expresses this very graphically: when a man has an habitual attitude to certain situations, an habitual way of doing things, we say he is quite *another man* when doing this or that. This is a practical demonstration of the autonomy of the functional complex represented by the habitual attitude: it is as though another personality had taken possession of the individual, as though "another spirit had got into him." The same autonomy that very often characterizes the outer attitude is also claimed by the inner attitude, the anima. It is one of the most difficult educational feats to change the persona, the outer attitude, and it is just as difficult to change the anima, since its structure is usually quite as well-knit as the persona's. Just as the persona is an entity that often seems to constitute the whole character of a man, and may even accompany him unaltered throughout his entire life, the anima is a clearly defined entity with a character that, very often, is autonomous and immutable. It therefore lends itself very readily to characterization and description.

804   As to the character of the anima, my experience confirms the rule that it is, by and large, *complementary* to the character of the persona. The anima usually contains all those common human qualities which the conscious attitude lacks. The tyrant tormented by bad dreams, gloomy forebodings, and inner fears is a typical figure. Outwardly ruthless, harsh, and unapproachable, he jumps inwardly at every shadow, is at the mercy of every mood, as though he were the feeblest and most impressionable of men. Thus his anima contains all those fallible human qualities his persona lacks. If the persona is intellectual, the anima will quite certainly be sentimental. The complementary character of the anima also affects the sexual character, as I have proved to myself beyond a doubt. A very feminine woman has a masculine soul, and a very masculine

---

woman. "Soul" is retained only when it refers to the psychic factor common to both sexes. The distinction is not always easy to make, and the reader may prefer to translate *anima/animus* back into "soul" on occasions when this would help to clarify Jung's argument. For a discussion of this question and the problems involved in translating *Seele* see *Psychology and Alchemy*, par. 9 n. 8. See also *Two Essays on Analytical Psychology*, pars. 296ff., for the relations between *anima/animus* and persona.—EDITORS.]

man has a feminine soul. This contrast is due to the fact that a man is not in all things wholly masculine, but also has certain feminine traits. The more masculine his outer attitude is, the more his feminine traits are obliterated: instead, they appear in his unconscious. This explains why it is just those very virile men who are most subject to characteristic weaknesses; their attitude to the unconscious has a womanish weakness and impressionability. Conversely, it is often just the most feminine women who, in their inner lives, display an intractability, an obstinacy, and a wilfulness that are to be found with comparable intensity only in a man's outer attitude. These are masculine traits which, excluded from the womanly outer attitude, have become qualities of her soul.

805   If, therefore, we speak of the *anima* of a man, we must logically speak of the *animus* of a woman, if we are to give the soul of a woman its right name. Whereas logic and objectivity are usually the predominant features of a man's outer attitude, or are at least regarded as ideals, in the case of a woman it is feeling. But in the soul it is the other way round: inwardly it is the man who feels, and the woman who reflects. Hence a man's greater liability to total despair, while a woman can always find comfort and hope; accordingly a man is more likely to put an end to himself than a woman. However much a victim of social circumstances a woman may be, as a prostitute for instance, a man is no less a victim of impulses from the unconscious, taking the form of alcoholism and other vices.

806   As to its common human qualities, the character of the anima can be deduced from that of the persona. Everything that should normally be in the outer attitude, but is conspicuously absent, will invariably be found in the inner attitude. This is a fundamental rule which my experience has borne out over and over again. But as regards its individual qualities, nothing can be deduced about them in this way. We can only be certain that when a man is identical with his persona, his individual qualities will be associated with the anima. This association frequently gives rise in dreams to the symbol of psychic pregnancy, a symbol that goes back to the *primordial image* (q.v.) of the hero's birth. The child that is to be born signifies the individuality, which, though present, is not yet conscious. For in the same way as the persona, the instrument of

469

adaptation to the environment, is strongly influenced by environmental conditions, the anima is shaped by the unconscious and its qualities. In a primitive milieu the persona necessarily takes on primitive features, and the anima similarly takes over the *archaic* (q.v.) features of the unconscious as well as its symbolic, prescient character. Hence the "pregnant," "creative" qualities of the inner attitude.

807   *Identity* (q.v.) with the persona automatically leads to an unconscious identity with the anima because, when the ego is not differentiated from the persona, it can have no conscious relation to the unconscious processes. Consequently, it *is* these processes, it is identical with them. Anyone who is himself his outward role will infallibly succumb to the inner processes; he will either frustrate his outward role by absolute inner necessity or else reduce it to absurdity, by a process of *enantiodromia* (q.v.). He can no longer keep to his individual way, and his life runs into one deadlock after another. Moreover, the anima is inevitably projected upon a real object, with which he gets into a relation of almost total dependence. Every reaction displayed by this object has an immediate, inwardly enervating effect on the subject. Tragic ties are often formed in this way (v. *Soul-image*).

808   49. SOUL-IMAGE [Anima /Animus].[81] The soul-image is a specific *image* (q.v.) among those produced by the unconscious. Just as the *persona* (v. *Soul*), or outer attitude, is represented in dreams by images of definite persons who possess the outstanding qualities of the persona in especially marked form, so in a man the soul, i.e., anima, or inner attitude, is represented in the unconscious by definite persons with the corresponding qualities. Such an image is called a "soul-image." Sometimes these images are of quite unknown or mythological figures. With men the anima is usually personified by the unconscious as a woman; with women the animus is personified as a man. In every case where the *individuality* (q.v.) is unconscious, and therefore associated with the soul, the soul-image has the character of the same sex. In all cases where there is an *identity* (q.v.) with the persona, and the soul accordingly is unconscious, the soul-image is transferred to a real person. This

[81] [See n. 80.—EDITORS.]

person is the object of intense love or equally intense hate (or fear). The influence of such a person is immediate and absolutely compelling, because it always provokes an affective response. The *affect* (q.v.) is due to the fact that a real, conscious adaptation to the person representing the soul-image is impossible. Because an objective relationship is non-existent and out of the question, the *libido* (q.v.) gets dammed up and explodes in an outburst of affect. Affects always occur where there is a failure of adaptation. Conscious adaptation to the person representing the soul-image is impossible precisely because the subject is unconscious of the soul. Were he conscious of it, it could be distinguished from the object, whose immediate effects might then be mitigated, since the potency of the object depends on the *projection* (q.v.) of the soul-image.

809   For a man, a woman is best fitted to be the real bearer of his soul-image, because of the feminine quality of his soul; for a woman it will be a man. Wherever an impassioned, almost magical, relationship exists between the sexes, it is invariably a question of a projected soul-image. Since these relationships are very common, the soul must be unconscious just as frequently—that is, vast numbers of people must be quite unaware of the way they are related to their inner psychic processes. Because this unconsciousness is always coupled with complete identification with the persona, it follows that this identification must be very frequent too. And in actual fact very many people are wholly identified with their outer attitude and therefore have no conscious relation to their inner processes. Conversely, it may also happen that the soul-image is not projected but remains with the subject, and this results in an identification with the soul because the subject is then convinced that the way he relates to his inner processes is his real character. In that event the persona, being unconscious, will be projected on a person of the same sex, thus providing a foundation for many cases of open or latent homosexuality, and of father-transferences in men or mother-transferences in women. In such cases there is always a defective adaptation to external reality and a lack of relatedness, because identification with the soul produces an attitude predominantly oriented to the perception of inner processes, and the object is deprived of its determining power.

810   If the soul-image is projected, the result is an absolute affective tie to the object. If it is not projected, a relatively un-adapted state develops, which Freud has described as *narcissism*. The projection of the soul-image offers a release from preoccupation with one's inner processes so long as the behaviour of the object is in harmony with the soul-image. The subject is then in a position to live out his persona and develop it further. The object, however, will scarcely be able to meet the demands of the soul-image indefinitely, although there are many women who, by completely disregarding their own lives, succeed in representing their husband's soul-image for a very long time. The biological feminine instinct assists them in this. A man may unconsciously do the same for his wife, though this will prompt him to deeds which finally exceed his capacities whether for good or evil. Here again the biological masculine instinct is a help.

811   If the soul-image is not projected, a thoroughly morbid relation to the unconscious gradually develops. The subject is increasingly overwhelmed by unconscious contents, which his inadequate relation to the object makes him powerless to as-similate or put to any kind of use, so that the whole subject-object relation only deteriorates further. Naturally these two attitudes represent the two extremes between which the more normal attitudes lie. In a normal man the soul-image is not dis-tinguished by any particular clarity, purity, or depth, but is apt to be rather blurred. In men with a good-natured and unag-gressive persona, the soul-image has a rather malevolent char-acter. A good literary example of this is the daemonic woman who is the companion of Zeus in Spitteler's *Olympian Spring*. For an idealistic woman, a depraved man is often the bearer of the soul-image; hence the "saviour fantasy" so frequent in such cases. The same thing happens with men, when the prosti-tute is surrounded with the halo of a soul crying for succour.

812   50. SUBJECTIVE LEVEL. When I speak of interpreting a dream or fantasy on the subjective level, I mean that the per-sons or situations appearing in it refer to subjective factors en-tirely belonging to the subject's own psyche. As we know, the psychic image of an object is never exactly like the object—at most there is a near resemblance. It is the product of sense per-

ception and *apperception* (q.v.), and these are processes that are inherent in the psyche and are merely stimulated by the object. Although the evidence of our senses is found to coincide very largely with the qualities of the object, our apperception is conditioned by unpredictable subjective influences which render a correct knowledge of the object extraordinarily difficult. Moreover, such a complex psychic factor as a man's character offers only a few *points d'appui* for pure sense perception. Knowledge of human character requires *empathy* (q.v.), reflection, *intuition* (q.v.). As a result of these complications, our final judgment is always of very doubtful value, so that the image we form of a human object is, to a very large extent, subjectively conditioned. In practical psychology, therefore, we would do well to make a rigorous distinction between the image or *imago* of a man and his real existence. Because of its extremely subjective origin, the *imago* is frequently more an image of a subjective functional complex than of the object itself. In the analytical treatment of unconscious products it is essential that the *imago* should not be assumed to be identical with the object; it is better to regard it as an image of the subjective relation to the object. That is what is meant by interpretation on the subjective level.

813 Interpretation of an unconscious product on the subjective level reveals the presence of subjective judgments and tendencies of which the object is made the vehicle. When, therefore, an object-imago appears in an unconscious product, it is not on that account the image of a real object; it is far more likely that we are dealing with a subjective functional complex (v. *Soul*, pars. 798ff.). Interpretation on the subjective level allows us to take a broader psychological view not only of dreams but also of literary works, in which the individual figures then appear as representatives of relatively autonomous functional complexes in the psyche of the author.

814 51. SYMBOL. The concept of a *symbol* should in my view be strictly distinguished from that of a *sign*. Symbolic and *semiotic* meanings are entirely different things. In his book on symbolism, Ferrero[82] does not speak of symbols in the strict sense, but of signs. For instance, the old custom of handing

[82] *I simboli in rapporto alla storia e filosofia del dicetto.*

473

over a piece of turf at the sale of a plot of land might be described as "symbolic" in the vulgar sense of the word, but actually it is purely semiotic in character. The piece of turf is a sign, or token, standing for the whole estate. The winged wheel worn by railway officials is not a *symbol* of the railway, but a *sign* that distinguishes the personnel of the railway system. A symbol always presupposes that the chosen expression is the best possible description or formulation of a relatively unknown fact, which is none the less known to exist or is postulated as existing. Thus, when the badge of a railway official is explained as a symbol, it amounts to saying that this man has something to do with an unknown system that cannot be differently or better expressed than by a winged wheel.

815   Every view which interprets the symbolic expression as an analogue or an abbreviated designation for a *known* thing is *semiotic*. A view which interprets the symbolic expression as the best possible formulation of a relatively *unknown* thing, which for that reason cannot be more clearly or characteristically represented, is *symbolic*. A view which interprets the symbolic expression as an intentional paraphrase or transmogrification of a known thing is *allegoric*. The interpretation of the cross as a symbol of divine love is *semiotic*, because "divine love" describes the fact to be expressed better and more aptly than a cross, which can have many other meanings. On the other hand, an interpretation of the cross is *symbolic* when it puts the cross beyond all conceivable explanations, regarding it as expressing an as yet unknown and incomprehensible fact of a mystical or transcendent, i.e., psychological, nature, which simply finds itself most appropriately represented in the cross.

816   So long as a symbol is a living thing, it is an expression for something that cannot be characterized in any other or better way. The symbol is alive only so long as it is pregnant with meaning. But once its meaning has been born out of it, once that expression is found which formulates the thing sought, expected, or divined even better than the hitherto accepted symbol, then the symbol is *dead*, i.e., it possesses only an historical significance. We may still go on speaking of it as a symbol, on the tacit assumption that we are speaking of it as it was before the better expression was born out of it. The way in which St.

Paul and the earlier speculative mystics speak of the cross shows that for them it was still a living symbol which expressed the inexpressible in unsurpassable form. For every esoteric interpretation the symbol is dead, because esotericism has already given it (at least ostensibly) a better expression, whereupon it becomes merely a conventional sign for associations that are more completely and better known elsewhere. Only from the exoteric standpoint is the symbol a living thing.

817　　An expression that stands for a known thing remains a mere sign and is never a symbol. It is, therefore, quite impossible to create a living symbol, i.e., one that is pregnant with meaning, from known associations. For what is thus produced never contains more than was put into it. Every psychic product, if it is the best possible expression at the moment for a fact as yet unknown or only relatively known, may be regarded as a symbol, provided that we accept the expression as standing for something that is only divined and not yet clearly conscious. Since every scientific theory contains an hypothesis, and is therefore an anticipatory description of something still essentially unknown, it is a symbol. Furthermore, every psychological expression is a symbol if we assume that it states or signifies something more and other than itself which eludes our present knowledge. This assumption is absolutely tenable wherever a consciousness exists which is attuned to the deeper meaning of things. It is untenable only when this same consciousness has itself devised an expression which states exactly what it is intended to state—a mathematical term, for instance. But for another consciousness this limitation does not exist. It can take the mathematical term as a symbol for an unknown psychic fact which the term was not intended to express but is concealed within it—a fact which is demonstrably not known to the man who devised the semiotic expression and which therefore could not have been the object of any conscious use.

818　　Whether a thing is a symbol or not depends chiefly on the *attitude* (q.v.) of the observing consciousness; for instance, on whether it regards a given fact not merely as such but also as an expression for something unknown. Hence it is quite possible for a man to establish a fact which does not appear in the least symbolic to himself, but is profoundly so to another consciousness. The converse is also true. There are undoubtedly products whose symbolic character does not depend merely on the attitude of the observing consciousness, but manifests itself spontaneously in the symbolic effect they have on the observer. Such products are so constituted that they would lack any kind of meaning were not a symbolic one conceded to them. Taken as a bare fact, a triangle with an eye enclosed in it is so meaningless that it is impossible for the observer to regard it as a merely accidental piece of foolery. Such a figure immediately conjures up a symbolic interpretation. This effect is reinforced by the widespread incidence of the same figure in identical form, or by the particular care that went into its production, which is an expression of the special value placed upon it.

819 Symbols that do not work in this way on the observer are either extinct, i.e., have been superseded by a better formulation, or are products whose symbolic nature depends entirely on the attitude of the observing consciousness. The attitude that takes a given phenomenon as symbolic may be called, for short, the *symbolic attitude*. It is only partially justified by the actual behaviour of things; for the rest, it is the outcome of a definite view of the world which *assigns meaning* to events, whether great or small, and attaches to this meaning a greater value than to bare facts. This view of things stands opposed to another view which lays the accent on sheer facts and subordinates meaning to them. For the latter attitude there can be no symbols whatever when the symbolism depends exclusively on the mode of observation. But even for such an attitude symbols do exist—those, namely, that prompt the observer to conjecture a hidden meaning. A bull-headed god can certainly be explained as a man's body with a bull's head on it. But this explanation can hardly hold its own against the symbolic explanation, because the symbolism is too arresting to be overlooked. A symbol that forcibly obtrudes its symbolic nature on us need not be a *living* symbol. It may have a merely historical or philosophical significance, and simply arouses intellectual or aesthetic interest. A symbol really lives only when it is the best and highest expression for something divined but not yet known to the observer. It then compels his unconscious participation and has a life-giving and life-enhancing effect. As Faust says: "How differently this new sign works upon me!"[83]

83 [*Goethe's Faust* (trans. MacNeice), p. 22.]

820   The living symbol formulates an essential unconscious factor, and the more widespread this factor is, the more general is the effect of the symbol, for it touches a corresponding chord in every psyche. Since, for a given epoch, it is the best possible expression for what is still unknown, it must be the product of the most complex and differentiated minds of that age. But in order to have such an effect at all, it must embrace what is common to a large group of men. This can never be what is most differentiated, the highest attainable, for only a very few attain to that or understand it. The common factor must be something that is still so primitive that its ubiquity cannot be doubted. Only when the symbol embraces that and expresses it in the highest possible form is it of general efficacy. Herein lies the potency of the living, social symbol and its redeeming power.

821   All that I have said about the social symbol applies equally to the individual symbol. There are individual psychic products whose symbolic character is so obvious that they at once compel a symbolic interpretation. For the individual they have the same functional significance that the social symbol has for a larger human group. These products never have an exclusively conscious or an exclusively unconscious source, but arise from the equal collaboration of both. Purely unconscious products are no more convincingly symbolic *per se* than purely conscious ones; it is the symbolic attitude of the observing consciousness that endows them both with the character of a symbol. But they can be conceived equally well as causally determined facts, in much the same way as one might regard the red exanthema of scarlet fever as a "symbol" of the disease. In that case it is perfectly correct to speak of a "symptom" and not of a "symbol." In my view Freud is quite justified when, from his standpoint, he speaks of *symptomatic*[84] rather than symbolic actions, since for him these phenomena are not symbolic in the sense here defined, but are symptomatic signs of a definite and generally known underlying process. There are, of course, neurotics who regard their unconscious products, which are mostly morbid symptoms, as symbols of supreme importance. Generally, however, this is not what happens. On the contrary,

[84] *The Psychopathology of Everyday Life.*

the neurotic of today is only too prone to regard a product that may actually be full of significance as a mere "symptom."

822   The fact that there are two distinct and mutually contradictory views eagerly advocated on either side concerning the meaning or meaninglessness of things shows that processes obviously exist which express no particular meaning, being in fact mere consequences, or symptoms; and that there are other processes which bear within them a hidden meaning, processes which are not merely derived from something but which seek to become something, and are therefore symbols. It is left to our discretion and our critical judgment to decide whether the thing we are dealing with is a symptom or a symbol.

823   The symbol is always a product of an extremely complex nature, since data from every psychic function have gone into its making. It is, therefore, neither *rational* nor *irrational* (qq.v.). It certainly has a side that accords with reason, but it has another side that does not; for it is composed not only of rational but also of irrational data supplied by pure inner and outer perception. The profundity and pregnant significance of the symbol appeal just as strongly to *thinking* as to *feeling* (qq.v.), while its peculiar plastic imagery, when shaped into sensuous form, stimulates *sensation* as much as *intuition* (qq.v.). The living symbol cannot come to birth in a dull or poorly developed mind, for such a mind will be content with the already existing symbols offered by established tradition. Only the passionate yearning of a highly developed mind, for which the traditional symbol is no longer the unified expression of the rational and the irrational, of the highest and the lowest, can create a new symbol.

824   But precisely because the new symbol is born of man's highest spiritual aspirations and must at the same time spring from the deepest roots of his being, it cannot be a onesided product of the most highly differentiated mental functions but must derive equally from the lowest and most primitive levels of the psyche. For this collaboration of opposing states to be possible at all, they must first face one another in the fullest conscious opposition. This necessarily entails a violent disunion with oneself, to the point where thesis and antithesis negate one another, while the ego is forced to acknowledge its absolute participation in both. If there is a subordination of one

part, the symbol will be predominantly the product of the other part, and, to that extent, less a symbol than a symptom— a symptom of the suppressed antithesis. To the extent, however, that a symbol is merely a symptom, it also lacks a redeeming effect, since it fails to express the full right of all parts of the psyche to exist, being a constant reminder of the suppressed antithesis even though consciousness may not take this fact into account. But when there is full parity of the opposites, attested by the ego's absolute participation in both, this necessarily leads to a suspension of the *will* (q.v.), for the will can no longer operate when every motive has an equally strong countermotive. Since life cannot tolerate a standstill, a damming up of vital energy results, and this would lead to an insupportable condition did not the tension of opposites produce a new, uniting function that transcends them. This function arises quite naturally from the regression of *libido* (q.v.) caused by the blockage. All progress having been rendered temporarily impossible by the total division of the will, the libido streams backwards, as it were, to its source. In other words, the neutralization and inactivity of consciousness bring about an activity of the unconscious, where all the differentiated functions have their common, archaic root, and where all contents exist in a state of promiscuity of which the primitive mentality still shows numerous vestiges.

825 From the activity of the unconscious there now emerges a new content, constellated by thesis and antithesis in equal measure and standing in a *compensatory* (q.v.) relation to both. It thus forms the middle ground on which the opposites can be united. If, for instance, we conceive the opposition to be sensuality versus spirituality, then the mediatory content born out of the unconscious provides a welcome means of expression for the spiritual thesis, because of its rich spiritual associations, and also for the sensual antithesis, because of its sensuous imagery. The ego, however, torn between thesis and antithesis, finds in the middle ground its own counterpart, its sole and unique means of expression, and it eagerly seizes on this in order to be delivered from its division. The energy created by the tension of opposites therefore flows into the mediatory product and protects it from the conflict which immediately breaks out again, for both the opposites are striving to get the

479

new product on their side. Spirituality wants to make something spiritual out of it, and sensuality something sensual; the one wants to turn it into science or art, the other into sensual experience. The appropriation or dissolution of the mediatory product by either side is successful only if the ego is not completely divided but inclines more to one side or the other. But if one side succeeds in winning over and dissolving the mediatory product, the ego goes along with it, whereupon an identification of the ego with the most favoured function (v. *Inferior Function*) ensues. Consequently, the process of division will be repeated later on a higher plane.

826 If, however, as a result of the stability of the ego, neither side succeeds in dissolving the mediatory product, this is sufficient demonstration that it is superior to both. The stability of the ego and the superiority of the mediatory product to both thesis and antithesis are to my mind correlates, each conditioning the other. Sometimes it seems as though the stability of the inborn *individuality* (q.v.) were the decisive factor, sometimes as though the mediatory product possessed a superior power that determines the ego's absolute stability. In reality it may be that the stability of the one and the superior power of the other are two sides of the same coin.

827 If the mediatory product remains intact, it forms the raw material for a process not of dissolution but of construction, in which thesis and antithesis both play their part. In this way it becomes a new content that governs the whole attitude, putting an end to the division and forcing the energy of the opposites into a common channel. The standstill is overcome and life can flow on with renewed power towards new goals.

828 I have called this process in its totality the *transcendent function*, "function" being here understood not as a basic function but as a complex function made up of other functions, and "transcendent" not as denoting a metaphysical quality but merely the fact that this function facilitates a transition from one attitude to another. The raw material shaped by thesis and antithesis, and in the shaping of which the opposites are united, is the living symbol. Its profundity of meaning is inherent in the raw material itself, the very stuff of the psyche, transcending time and dissolution; and its configuration by the opposites ensures its sovereign power over all the psychic functions.

829   Indications of the process of symbol-formation are to be found in the scanty records of the conflicts experienced by the founders of religion during their initiation period, e.g., the struggle between Jesus and Satan, Buddha and Mara, Luther and the devil, Zwingli and his previous worldly life; or the regeneration of Faust through the pact with the devil. In *Zarathustra* we find an excellent example of the suppressed antithesis in the "Ugliest Man."

52. SYNTHETIC, V. CONSTRUCTIVE.

830   53. THINKING. This I regard as one of the four basic psychological *functions* (q.v.). Thinking is the psychological function which, following its own laws, brings the contents of ideation into conceptual connection with one another. It is an *apperceptive* (q.v.) activity, and as such may be divided into *active* and *passive* thinking. Active thinking is an act of the *will* (q.v.), passive thinking is a mere occurrence. In the former case, I submit the contents of ideation to a voluntary act of judgment; in the latter, conceptual connections establish themselves of their own accord, and judgments are formed that may even contradict my intention. They are not consonant with my aim and therefore, for me, lack any sense of direction, although I may afterwards recognize their directedness through an act of active apperception. Active thinking, accordingly, would correspond to my concept of *directed thinking*.[85] Passive thinking was inadequately described in my previous work as "fantasy thinking."[86] Today I would call it *intuitive* thinking.

831   To my mind, a mere stringing together of ideas, such as is described by certain psychologists as *associative thinking*,[87] is not thinking at all, but mere ideation. The term "thinking" should, in my view, be confined to the linking up of ideas by means of a concept, in other words, to an act of judgment, no matter whether this act is intentional or not.

832   The capacity for directed thinking I call *intellect*; the capacity for passive or undirected thinking I call *intellectual intuition*. Further, I call directed thinking a *rational* (q.v.) function, because it arranges the contents of ideation under

---

[85] *Symbols of Transformation*, pars. 11 ff.
[86] Ibid., par. 20.
[87] [Cf. ibid., par. 18, citing James, *The Principles of Psychology*, II, p. 325.]

concepts in accordance with a rational norm of which I am conscious. Undirected thinking is in my view an *irrational* (q.v.) function, because it arranges and judges the contents of ideation by norms of which I am not conscious and therefore cannot recognize as being in accord with reason. Subsequently I may be able to recognize that the intuitive act of judgment accorded with reason, although it came about in a way that appears to me irrational.

833 Thinking that is governed by *feeling* (q.v.) I do not regard as intuitive thinking, but as a thinking dependent on feeling; it does not follow its own logical principle but is subordinated to the principle of feeling. In such thinking the laws of logic are only ostensibly present; in reality they are suspended in favour of the aims of feeling.

834 53a. THOUGHT. Thought is the specific content or material of the thinking function, discriminated by *thinking* (q.v.).

54. TRANSCENDENT FUNCTION, v. SYMBOL, pars. 825–28.

835 55. TYPE. A type is a specimen or example which reproduces in a characteristic way the character of a species or class. In the narrower sense used in this particular work, a type is a characteristic specimen of a general *attitude* (q.v.) occurring in many individual forms. From a great number of existing or possible attitudes I have singled out four; those, namely, that are primarily oriented by the four basic psychological *functions* (q.v.): *thinking, feeling, sensation, intuition* (qq.v.). When any of these attitudes is *habitual*, thus setting a definite stamp on the character of an *individual* (q.v.), I speak of a psychological type. These *function-types*, which one can call the thinking, feeling, sensation, and intuitive types, may be divided into two classes according to the quality of the basic function, i.e., into the *rational* and the *irrational* (qq.v.). The thinking and feeling types belong to the former class, the sensation and intuitive types to the latter. A further division into two classes is permitted by the predominant trend of the movement of *libido* (q.v.), namely *introversion* and *extraversion* (qq.v.). All the basic types can belong equally well to one or the other of these classes, according to the predominance of the introverted or

extraverted attitude.[88] A thinking type may belong either to the introverted or to the extraverted class, and the same holds good for the other types. The distinction between rational and irrational types is simply another point of view and has nothing to do with introversion and extraversion.

836   In my previous contributions to typology[89] I did not differentiate the thinking and feeling types from the introverted and extraverted types, but identified the thinking type with the introverted, and the feeling type with the extraverted. But a more thorough investigation of the material has shown me that we must treat the introverted and extraverted types as categories over and above the function-types. This differentiation, moreover, fully accords with experience, since, for example, there are undoubtedly two kinds of feeling types, the attitude of the one being oriented more by his feeling-experience [= introverted feeling type], the other more by the object [= extraverted feeling type].

837   56. UNCONSCIOUS. The concept of the *unconscious* is for me an *exclusively psychological* concept, and not a philosophical concept of a metaphysical nature. In my view the unconscious is a psychological borderline concept, which covers all psychic contents or processes that are not conscious, i.e., not related to the *ego* (q.v.) in any perceptible way. My justification for speaking of the existence of unconscious processes at all is derived simply and solely from experience, and in particular from psychopathological experience, where we have undoubted proof that, in a case of hysterical amnesia, for example, the ego knows nothing of the existence of numerous psychic complexes, and the next moment a simple hypnotic procedure is sufficient to bring the lost contents back to memory.

---

88 [Hence the types belonging to the introverted or extraverted class are called *attitude-types*. Cf. supra, par. 556, and *Two Essays on Analytical Psychology*, Part I, ch. IV.—EDITORS.]

89 "A Contribution to the Study of Psychological Types," infra, Appendix 1; "The Psychology of the Unconscious Processes," *Collected Papers on Analytical Psychology*, pp. 391ff., 401ff.; "The Structure of the Unconscious," *Two Essays on Analytical Psychology*, pars. 462, n. 8, and 482.

838   Thousands of such experiences justify us in speaking of the existence of unconscious psychic contents. As to the actual state an unconscious content is in when not attached to consciousness, this is something that eludes all possibility of cognition. It is therefore quite pointless to hazard conjectures about it. Conjectures linking up the unconscious state with cerebration and physiological processes belong equally to the realm of fantasy. It is also impossible to specify the range of the unconscious, i.e., what contents it embraces. Only experience can decide such questions.

839   We know from experience that conscious contents can become unconscious through loss of their energic value. This is the normal process of "forgetting." That these contents do not simply get lost below the threshold of consciousness we know from the experience that occasionally, under suitable conditions, they can emerge from their submersion decades later, for instance in dreams, or under hypnosis, or in the form of cryptomnesia,[90] or through the revival of associations with the forgotten content. We also know that conscious contents can fall below the threshold of consciousness through "intentional forgetting," or what Freud calls the *repression* of a painful content, with no appreciable loss of value. A similar effect is produced by a dissociation of the personality, i.e., the disintegration of consciousness as the result of a violent *affect* (q.v.) or nervous shock, or through the collapse of the personality in schizophrenia (Bleuler).

840   We know from experience, too, that sense perceptions which, either because of their slight intensity or because of the deflection of attention, do not reach conscious *apperception* (q.v.), none the less become psychic contents through unconscious apperception, which again may be demonstrated by hypnosis, for example. The same thing may happen with certain judgments or other associations which remain unconscious because of their low energy charge or because of the deflection of attention. Finally, experience also teaches that there are unconscious psychic associations—mythological *images* (q.v.), for instance—which have never been the object of con-

[90] Flournoy, *From India to the Planet Mars*; Jung, "On the Psychology and Pathology of So-called Occult Phenomena," pars. 139ff., and "Cryptomnesia."

sciousness and must therefore be wholly the product of unconscious activity.

841   To this extent, then, experience furnishes *points d'appui* for the assumption of unconscious contents. But it can tell us nothing about what might *possibly* be an unconscious content. It is idle to speculate about this, because the range of what *could* be an unconscious content is simply illimitable. What is the lowest limit of subliminal sense perception? Is there any way of measuring the scope and subtlety of unconscious associations? When is a forgotten content totally obliterated? To these questions there is no answer.

842   Our experience so far of the nature of unconscious contents permits us, however, to make one general classification. We can distinguish a *personal unconscious*, comprising all the acquisitions of personal life, everything forgotten, repressed, subliminally perceived, thought, felt. But, in addition to these personal unconscious contents, there are other contents which do not originate in personal acquisitions but in the inherited possibility of psychic functioning in general, i.e., in the inherited structure of the brain. These are the mythological associations, the motifs and images that can spring up anew anytime anywhere, independently of historical tradition or migration. I call these contents the *collective unconscious*. Just as conscious contents are engaged in a definite activity, so too are the unconscious contents, as experience confirms. And just as conscious psychic activity creates certain products, so unconscious psychic activity produces dreams, *fantasies* (q.v.), etc. It is idle to speculate on how great a share consciousness has in dreams. A dream presents itself to us: we do not consciously create it. Conscious reproduction, or even the perception of it, certainly alters the dream in many ways, without, however, doing away with the basic fact of the unconscious source of creative activity.

843   The functional relation of the unconscious processes to consciousness may be described as *compensatory* (q.v.), since experience shows that they bring to the surface the subliminal material that is constellated by the conscious situation, i.e., all those contents which could not be missing from the picture if everything were conscious. The compensatory function of the unconscious becomes more obvious the more one-sided the

conscious *attitude* (q.v.) is; pathology furnishes numerous examples of this.

844   57. WILL. I regard the will as the amount of psychic energy at the disposal of consciousness. Volition would, accordingly, be an energic process that is released by conscious motivation. A psychic process, therefore, that is conditioned by unconscious motivation I would not include under the concept of the will. The will is a psychological phenomenon that owes its existence to culture and moral education, but is largely lacking in the primitive mentality.

EPILOGUE

845   In our age, which has seen the fruits of the French Revolution—"Liberté, Egalité, Fraternité"—growing into a broad social movement whose aim is not merely to raise or lower political rights to the same general level, but, more hopefully, to abolish unhappiness altogether by means of external regulations and egalitarian reforms—in such an age it is indeed a thankless task to speak of the complete inequality of the elements composing a nation. Although it is certainly a fine thing that every man should stand equal before the law, that every man should have his political vote, and that no man, through hereditary social position and privilege, should have unjust advantage over his brother, it is distinctly less fine when the idea of equality is extended to other walks of life. A man must have a very clouded vision, or view human society from a very misty distance, to cherish the notion that the uniform regulation of life would automatically ensure a uniform distribution of happiness. He must be pretty far gone in delusion if he imagines that equality of income, or equal opportunities for all, would have approximately the same value for everyone. But, if he were a legislator, what would he do about all those people whose greatest opportunities lie not without, but within? If he were just, he would have to give at least twice as much money to the one man as to the other, since to the one it means much, to the other little. No social legislation will ever be able to overcome the psychological differences between men, this most necessary factor for generating the vital energy of a human society. It may serve a useful purpose, therefore, to speak of the heterogeneity of men. These differences involve such different requirements for happiness that no legislation, however perfect, could afford them even approximate satisfaction. No outward form of life could be devised, however equitable and just it might appear, that would not involve injustice for one or the other human type. That, in spite of this, every kind of enthusi-

487

ast—political, social, philosophical, or religious—is busily endeavouring to find those uniform external conditions which would bring with them greater opportunities for the happiness of all seems to me connected with a general attitude to life too exclusively oriented by the outer world.

846   It is not possible to do more than touch on this far-reaching question here, since such considerations lie outside the scope of this book. We are here concerned only with the psychological problem, and the existence of different typical attitudes is a problem of the first order, not only for psychology but for all departments of science and life in which man's psychology plays a decisive role. It is, for instance, obvious to anyone of ordinary intelligence that every philosophy that is not just a history of philosophy depends on a personal psychological premise. This premise may be of a purely individual nature, and indeed is generally regarded as such if any psychological criticism is made at all. The matter is then considered settled. But this is to overlook the fact that what one regards as an individual prejudice is by no means so under all circumstances, since the standpoint of a particular philosopher often has a considerable following. It is acceptable to his followers not because they echo him without thinking, but because it is something they can fully understand and appreciate. Such an understanding would be impossible if the philosopher's standpoint were determined only individually, for it is quite certain in that case that he would be neither fully understood nor even tolerated. The peculiarity of the standpoint which is understood and acknowledged by his followers must therefore correspond to a *typical* personal attitude, which in the same or a similar form has many representatives in a society. As a rule, the partisans of either side attack each other purely externally, always seeking out the chinks in their opponent's armour. Squabbles of this kind are usually fruitless. It would be of considerably greater value if the dispute were transferred to the psychological realm, from which it arose in the first place. The shift of position would soon show a diversity of psychological attitudes, each with its own right to existence, and each contributing to the setting up of incompatible theories. So long as one tries to settle the dispute by external compromises, one merely satisfies the modest demands of shallow minds that

have never yet been enkindled by the passion of a principle. A real understanding can, in my view, be reached only when the diversity of psychological premises is accepted.

847   It is a fact, which is constantly and overwhelmingly apparent in my practical work, that people are virtually incapable of understanding and accepting any point of view other than their own. In small things a general superficiality of outlook, combined with a none too common forbearance and tolerance and an equally rare goodwill, may help to build a bridge over the chasm which lack of understanding opens between man and man. But in more important matters, and especially those concerned with ideals, an understanding seems, as a rule, to be beyond the bounds of possibility. Certainly strife and misunderstanding will always be among the props of the tragicomedy of human existence, but it is none the less undeniable that the advance of civilization has led from the law of the jungle to the establishment of courts of justice and standards of right and wrong which are above the contending parties. It is my conviction that a basis for the settlement of conflicting views would be found in the recognition of different types of attitude—a recognition not only of the existence of such types, but also of the fact that every man is so imprisoned in his type that he is simply incapable of fully understanding another standpoint. Failing a recognition of this exacting demand, a violation of the other standpoint is practically inevitable. But just as the contending parties in a court of law refrain from direct violence and submit their claims to the justice of the law and the impartiality of the judge, so each type, conscious of his own partiality, should refrain from heaping abuse, suspicion, and indignity upon his opponent.

848   In considering the problem of typical attitudes, and in presenting them in outline, I have endeavoured to direct the eye of my readers to this picture of the many possible ways of viewing life, in the hope that I may have contributed my small share to the knowledge of the almost infinite variations and gradations of individual psychology. No one, I trust, will draw the conclusion from my description of types that I believe the four or eight types here presented to be the only ones that exist. This would be a serious misconception, for I have no doubt whatever that these attitudes could also be considered

and classified from other points of view. Indeed, there are indications of such possibilities in this book, as for instance Jordan's classification in terms of activity. But whatever the criterion for a classification of types may be, a comparison of the various forms of habitual attitudes will result in an equal number of psychological types.

849   However easy it may be to regard the existing attitudes from other viewpoints than the one here adopted, it would be difficult to adduce evidence against the existence of psychological types. I have no doubt at all that my opponents will be at some pains to strike the question of types off the scientific agenda, since the type problem must, to say the least of it, be a very unwelcome obstacle for every theory of complex psychic processes that lays claim to general validity. Every theory of complex psychic processes presupposes a uniform human psychology, just as scientific theories in general presuppose that nature is fundamentally one and the same. But in the case of psychology there is the peculiar condition that, in the making of its theories, the psychic process is not merely an object but at the same time the subject. Now if one assumes that the subject is the same in all individual cases, it can also be assumed that the subjective process of theory-making, too, is the same everywhere. That this is not so, however, is demonstrated most impressively by the existence of the most diverse theories about the nature of complex psychic processes. Naturally, every new theory is ready to assume that all other theories were wrong, usually for the sole reason that its author has a different subjective view from his predecessors. He does not realize that the psychology he sees is *his* psychology, and on top of that is the psychology of his type. He therefore supposes that there can be only one true explanation of the psychic process he is investigating, namely the one that agrees with his type. All other views—I might almost say all seven other views—which, in their way, are just as true as his, are for him mere aberrations. In the interests of the validity of his own theory, therefore, he will feel a lively but very understandable distaste for any view that establishes the existence of different types of human psychology, since his own view would then lose, shall we say, seven-eighths of its truth. For, besides his own theory, he would have to regard seven other theories of the same proc-

ess as equally true, or, if that is saying too much, at least grant
a second theory a value equal to his own.

850   I am quite convinced that a natural process which is very
largely independent of human psychology, and can therefore
be viewed only as an object, can have but one true explanation.
But I am equally convinced that the explanation of a complex
psychic process which cannot be objectively registered by any
apparatus must necessarily be only the one which that subjective process itself produces. In other words, the author of the
concept can produce only just such a concept as corresponds
to the psychic process he is endeavouring to explain; but it will
correspond only when the process to be explained coincides
with the process occurring in the author himself. If neither the
process to be explained, nor any analogy of it, were to be
found in the author, he would be confronted with a complete
enigma, whose explanation he would have to leave to the man
who himself experienced the process. If I have a vision, for instance, no objectively registering apparatus will enable me to
discover how it originated; I can explain its origin only as I
myself understand. But in this "as I myself understand it" lies
the partiality, for at best my explanation will start from the
way the visionary process presents itself to me. By what right
do I assume that the visionary process presents itself in the
same or a similar way to everyone?

851   With some show of reason, one will adduce the uniformity
of human psychology at all times and places as an argument in
favour of this generalization of a subjective judgment. I myself am so profoundly convinced of the uniformity of the
psyche that I have even summed it up in the concept of the collective unconscious, as a universal and homogeneous substra-
tum whose uniformity is such that one finds the same myth and
fairytale motifs in all corners of the earth, with the result that
an uneducated American Negro dreams of motifs from Greek
mythology[1] and a Swiss clerk re-experiences in his psychosis
the vision of an Egyptian Gnostic.[2] But this fundamental
homogeneity is offset by an equally great heterogeneity of the

1 [*Symbols of Transformation*, par. 154, and supra, par. 747 and n. 62.—EDITORS.]
2 [Vision of the solar phallus. *Symbols of Transformation*, pars. 151ff.; "The
Structure of the Psyche," pars. 31ff.; "The Concept of the Collective Unconscious," pars. 104ff.]

conscious psyche. What immeasurable distances lie between the consciousness of a primitive, a Periclean Athenian, and a modern European! What a difference even between the consciousness of a learned professor and that of his spouse! What, in any case, would our world be like if there existed a uniformity of minds? No, the notion of a uniformity of the conscious psyche is an academic chimera, doubtless simplifying the task of a university lecturer when facing his pupils, but collapsing into nothing in the face of reality. Quite apart from the differences among individuals whose innermost natures are separated by stellar distances, the types, as classes of individuals, are themselves to a very large extent different from one another, and it is to the existence of these types that we must ascribe the differences of views in general.

852   In order to discover the uniformity of the human psyche, I have to descend into the very foundations of consciousness. Only there do I find that in which all are alike. If I build my theory on what is common to all, I explain the psyche in terms of its foundation and origin. But that does nothing to explain its historical and individual differentiation. With such a theory I ignore the peculiarities of the conscious psyche. I actually deny the whole other side of the psyche, its differentiation from the original germinal state. I reduce man to his phylogenetic prototype, or I dissolve him into his elementary processes; and when I try to reconstruct him again, in the former case an ape will emerge, and in the latter a welter of elementary processes engaged in aimless and meaningless reciprocal activity.

853   No doubt an explanation of the psyche on the basis of its uniformity is not only possible but fully justified. But if I want to project a picture of the psyche in its totality, I must bear in mind the diversity of psyches, since the conscious individual psyche belongs just as much to a general picture of psychology as does its unconscious foundation. In my construction of theories, therefore, I can, with as much right, proceed from the fact of differentiated psyches, and consider the same process from the standpoint of differentiation which I considered before from the standpoint of uniformity. This naturally leads me to a view diametrically opposed to the former one. Everything which in that view was left out of the picture as an individual

492

variant now becomes important as a starting-point for further differentiations; and everything which previously had a special value on account of its uniformity now appears valueless, because merely collective. From this angle I shall always be intent on where a thing is going to, not where it comes from; whereas from the former angle I never bothered about the goal but only about the origin. I can, therefore, explain the same psychic process with two contradictory and mutually exclusive theories, neither of which I can declare to be wrong, since the rightness of one is proved by the uniformity of the psyche, and the rightness of the other by its diversity.

854 This brings us to the great difficulty which the reading of my earlier book[3] only aggravated, both for the scientific public and for the layman, with the result that many otherwise competent heads were thrown into confusion. There I made an attempt to present both views with the help of case material. But since reality neither consists of theories nor follows them, the two views, which we are bound to think of as divided, are united within it. Each is a product of the past and carries a future meaning, and of neither can it be said with certainty whether it is an end or a beginning. Everything that is alive in the psyche shimmers in rainbow hues. For anyone who thinks there is only one true explanation of a psychic process, this vitality of psychic contents, which necessitates two contradictory theories, is a matter for despair, especially if he is enamoured of simple and uncomplicated truths, incapable maybe of thinking both at the same time.

855 On the other hand, I am not convinced that, with these two ways of looking at the psyche—the reductive and constructive as I have called them[4]—the possibilities of explanation are exhausted. I believe that other equally "true" explanations of the psychic process can still be put forward, just as many in fact as there are types. Moreover, these explanations will agree as well or as ill with one another as the types themselves in their personal relations. Should, therefore, the existence of typical differences of human psyches be granted—and I confess I see no reason why it should not be granted—the

---

[3] *Symbols of Transformation.*
[4] "On Psychological Understanding," pars. 391ff. [Also *Two Essays on Analytical Psychology*, pars. 121ff.]

scientific theorist is confronted with the disagreeable dilemma of either allowing several contradictory theories of the same process to exist side by side, or of making an attempt, foredoomed at the outset, to found a sect which claims for itself the only correct method and the only true theory. Not only does the former possibility encounter the extraordinary difficulty of an inwardly contradictory "double-think" operation, it also contravenes one of the first principles of intellectual morality: *principia explicandi non sunt multiplicanda praeter necessitatem.*[5] But in the case of psychological theories the necessity of a plurality of explanations is given from the start, since, in contrast to any other scientific theory, the object of psychological explanation is consubstantial with the subject: one psychological process has to explain another. This serious difficulty has already driven thoughtful persons to remarkable subterfuges, such as the assumption of an "objective intellect" standing outside the psychic process and capable of contemplating the subordinate psyche objectively, or the similar assumption that the intellect is a faculty which can stand outside itself and contemplate itself. All these expedients are supposed to create a sort of extra-terrestrial Archimedean point by means of which the intellect can lift itself off its own hinges. I understand very well the profound human need for convenient solutions, but I do not see why truth should bow to this need. I can also understand that, aesthetically, it would be far more satisfactory if, instead of the paradox of mutually contradictory explanations, we could reduce the psychic process to the simplest possible instinctive foundation and leave it at that, or if we could credit it with a metaphysical goal of redemption and find peace in that hope.

856　　Whatever we strive to fathom with our intellect will end in paradox and relativity, if it be honest work and not *a petitio principii* in the interests of convenience. That an intellectual understanding of the psychic process must end in paradox and relativity is simply unavoidable, if only for the reason that the intellect is but one of many psychic functions which is intended by nature to serve man in constructing of his images of the ob-

[5] ["Explanatory principles are not to be multiplied beyond the necessary": Occam's Razor.—TRANSLATOR.]

jective world. We should not pretend to understand the world only by the intellect; we apprehend it just as much by feeling. Therefore the judgment of the intellect is, at best, only a half-truth, and must, if it is honest, also admit its inadequacy.

857   To deny the existence of types is of little avail in the face of the facts. In view of their existence, therefore, every theory of psychic processes has to submit to being evaluated in its turn as itself a psychic process, as the expression of a specific type of human psychology with its own justification. Only from these typical self-representations of the psyche can the materials be collected which will co-operate to form a higher synthesis.

APPENDIX

FOUR PAPERS ON PSYCHOLOGICAL TYPOLOGY

A CONTRIBUTION TO THE STUDY OF PSYCHOLOGICAL TYPES[1]

858   It is well known that in their general aspects hysteria and schizophrenia present a striking contrast, which is particularly evident in the attitude of the patients to the external world. In their relations to the object, the hysteric displays as a rule an intensity of feeling that surpasses the normal, while in the schizophrenic the normal level is not reached at all. The clinical picture is exaggerated emotivity in the one, and extreme apathy in the other, with regard to the environment. In their personal relations this difference is marked by the fact that we can remain in affective rapport with our hysterical patients, which is not the case in schizophrenia. The contrast between the two types of illness is also observable in the rest of their symptomatology. So far as the intellectual symptoms of hysteria are concerned, they are fantasy products which may be accounted for in a natural and human way by the antecedents and individual history of the patient; in schizophrenia, on the contrary, the fantasy products are more nearly related to dreams than to the psychology of the waking state. They have, moreover, a distinctly archaic character, the mythological creations of the primitive imagination being far more in evidence than the personal memories of the patient. Finally, the physical

---

1 [A lecture delivered at the Psychoanalytical Congress in Munich during September 1913 (the last time Jung and Freud met), but not published in German until 1960, as "Zur Frage der psychologischen Typen," in *Gesammelte Werke*, 6, Appendix, pp. 541ff. A French translation, incorporating the author's revisions, appeared in the *Archives de psychologie* (Geneva), XIII:52 (Dec. 1913), 289–99, and was translated into English by C. E. Long, as "A Contribution to the Study of Psychological Types," in *Collected Papers on Analytical Psychology* (London and New York, 1916), pp. 287ff. The present version is based on a comparison of the German original with the previous French and English translations.—EDITORS.]

symptoms so common in hysteria, which simulate well-known and impressive organic illnesses, are not to be found in the clinical picture of schizophrenia.

859   All this clearly indicates that hysteria is characterized by a centrifugal movement of libido, while in schizophrenia the movement is more centripetal. The reverse obtains, however, when the illness has fully established its compensatory effects. In the hysteric the libido is then hampered in its movement of expansion and is forced to regress upon itself; the patients cease to partake in the common life, are wrapped up in their daydreams, keep to their beds, remain shut up in their sickrooms, etc. During the incubation of his illness the schizophrenic likewise turns away from the outer world in order to withdraw into himself, but when the period of morbid compensation arrives, he seems constrained to draw attention to himself, to force himself upon the notice of those around him, by his extravagant, insupportable, or directly aggressive behaviour.

860   I propose to use the terms *extraversion* and *introversion* to describe these two opposite movements of libido, further qualifying them as *regressive* in pathological cases where delusional ideas, fictions, or fantastic interpretations, all inspired by emotivity, falsify the judgment of the patient about things or about himself. We speak of extraversion when he gives his whole interest to the outer world, to the object, and attributes an extraordinary importance and value to it. When, on the contrary, the objective world sinks into the shadow, at it were, or undergoes a devaluation, while the individual occupies the centre of his own interest and becomes in his own eyes the only person worthy of consideration, it is a case of introversion. I call *regressive extraversion* the phenomenon which Freud calls *transference*, when the hysteric projects upon the object his own illusions and subjective valuations. In the same way, I call *regressive introversion* the opposite phenomenon which we find in schizophrenia, when these fantastic ideas refer to the subject himself.

861   It is obvious that these two contrary movements of libido, as simple psychic mechanisms, may operate alternately in the same individual, since after all they serve the same purpose by different methods—namely, to minister to his well-being.

Freud has taught us that in the mechanism of hysterical extra-version the personality seeks to get rid of disagreeable mem-ories and impressions, and to free itself from its complexes, by a process of *repression*. The individual clings to the object in order to forget these painful contents and leave them behind him. Conversely, in the mechanism of introversion, the libido concentrates itself wholly on the complexes, and seeks to de-tach and isolate the personality from external reality. This psy-chological process is associated with a phenomenon which is not properly speaking "repression," but would be better ren-dered by the term "devaluation" of the objective world.

862 To this extent, extraversion and introversion are two modes of psychic reaction which can be observed in the same individual. The fact, however, that two such contrary dis-turbances as hysteria and schizophrenia are characterized by the predominance of the mechanism of extraversion or of intro-version suggests that there may also be normal human types who are distinguished by the predominance of one or other of the two mechanisms. And indeed, psychiatrists know very well that long before the illness is fully established, the hysterical patient as well as the schizophrenic is marked by the predomi-nance of his specific type, which reaches back into the earliest years of childhood.

863 As Binet has pointed out so aptly,[1a] a neurosis simply em-phasizes and throws into excessive relief the characteristic traits of a personality. It has long been known that the so-called hysterical character is not simply the product of the manifest neurosis, but predated it to a certain extent. And Hoch has shown the same thing by his researches into the his-tories of schizophrenic patients; he speaks of a "shut-in" per-sonality[2] which was present before the onset of the illness. If this is so, we may certainly expect to find the two types out-side the sphere of pathology. There are moreover numerous witnesses in literature to the existence of the two types of mentality. Without pretending to exhaust the subject, I will give a few striking examples.

864 So far as my limited knowledge goes, we have to thank William James for the best observations in this respect. He lays

[1a] [Reference cannot be traced.]

[2] ["Constitutional Factors in the Dementia Praecox Group" (1910).—EDITORS.]

down the principle: "Of whatever temperament a professional philosopher is, he tries, when philosophizing, to sink the fact of his temperament."[3] And starting from this idea, which is altogether in accord with the spirit of psychoanalysis, he divides philosophers into two classes: the "tender-minded" and the "tough-minded," or, as we might also call them, the "spiritually-minded" and the "materially-minded." The very terms clearly reveal the opposite movements of the libido. The first class direct their libido to the world of thought, and are predominantly introverted; the second direct it to material things and objective reality, and are extraverted.

865   James characterizes the "tender-minded" first of all as *rationalistic*, "going by principles."[4] They are the men of principles and systems; they aspire to dominate experience and to transcend it by abstract reasoning, by their logical deductions and purely rational concepts. They care little for facts, and the multiplicity of empirical phenomena hardly bothers or disconcerts them at all; they forcibly fit the data into their ideal constructions, and reduce everything to their *a priori* premises. This was the method of Hegel in settling beforehand the number of the planets. In the domain of pathology we again meet this kind of philosopher in paranoiacs, who, unperturbed by all factual evidence to the contrary, impose their delirious conceptions on the universe, and find a means of interpreting everything, and according to Adler "arranging" everything, in conformity with their preconceived system.

866   The other characteristics of this type which James enumerates follow logically from these premises. The "tender-minded" man is "intellectualistic, idealistic, optimistic, religious, free-willist, monistic, dogmatical."[5] All these qualities betray the almost exclusive concentration of libido upon his intellectual life. This concentration on the inner world of thought is nothing else than introversion. In so far as experience plays any role with these philosophers, it serves only as a fillip to abstraction, to the imperative need to fit the multiplicity and chaos of events into an order which, in the last resort, is the creation of purely subjective thinking.

---

[3] *Pragmatism*, p. 7. Cf. also supra, pars. 505ff.
[4] Ibid., p. 12.   [5] Ibid.

867   The "tough-minded" man, on the other hand, is empirical, "going by facts." Experience is his master, facts are his guide and they colour all his thinking. It is only tangible phenomena in the outside world that count. Thought is merely a reaction to external experience. For him principles are always of less value than facts; if he has any, they merely reflect and describe the flux of events, and are incapable of forming a system. Hence his theories are liable to inner contradiction and get overlaid by the accumulation of empirical material. Psychic reality limits itself for him to observation and to the experience of pleasure and pain; he does not go beyond that, nor does he recognize the rights of philosophical thought. Remaining on the ever-changing surface of the phenomenal world, he himself partakes of its instability; he sees all its aspects, all its theoretical and practical possibilities, but he never arrives at the unity of a settled system, which alone could satisfy the tender-minded. The tough-minded man is reductive. As James so excellently says: "What is higher is explained by what is lower and treated for ever as a case of 'nothing but'—nothing but something else of a quite inferior sort."[6]

868   From these general characteristics, the others which James points out logically follow. The tough-minded man is "sensationalistic," giving more value to the senses than to reflection. He is "materialistic and pessimistic," for he knows only too well the uncertainty and hopeless chaos of the course of things. He is "irreligious," being incapable of asserting the realities of his inner world against the pressure of external facts; a fatalist, because resigned; a pluralist, incapable of all synthesis; and finally a sceptic, as a last and inevitable consequence of all the rest.[7]

869   The expressions, therefore, used by James show clearly that the difference between the types is the result of a different localization of the libido, this "magical power" in the depth of our being, which, depending on the individual, is directed sometimes to our inner life, sometimes to the objective world. Contrasting the religious subjectivism of the solipsist with the contemporary empirical attitude, James says: "But our esteem for facts has not neutralized in us all religiousness. It is itself almost religious. Our scientific temper is devout."[8]

6 Ibid., p. 16.   7 Ibid., p. 12.   8 Ibid., p. 15.

870   A second parallel is furnished by Wilhelm Ostwald,[9] who divides men of genius into "classics" and "romantics." The romantics are distinguished by their rapid reactions, their abundant production of ideas, some of which are badly digested and of doubtful value. They are brilliant teachers, of a compelling ardour, and collect round them a large and enthusiastic circle of students, on whom they exert great personal influence. This type is obviously identical with our extraverted type. The classics, on the contrary, are slow to react; they produce with much difficulty, paralyzed by their own severe self-criticism; they have no love for teaching, and are in fact mostly bad teachers, lacking enthusiasm; living apart and absorbed in themselves, they exercise little direct personal influence, making scarcely any disciples, but producing works of finished perfection which often bring them only posthumous fame. This type is an unmistakable introvert.

871   We find a third, very valuable parallel in the aesthetic theory of Wilhelm Worringer.[10] Borrowing A. Riegl's expression "absolute artistic volition"[11] to designate the internal force which inspires the artist, he distinguishes two forms: abstraction and empathy. He speaks of the urge to abstraction and the urge to empathy, thereby making clear the libidinal nature of these two forms, the stirring of the *élan vital*. "In the same way," says Worringer, "as the urge to empathy finds its gratification in organic beauty, so the urge to abstraction discovers beauty in the inorganic, the negation of all life, in crystalline forms or, generally speaking, wherever the severity of abstract law reigns."[12] Empathy is a movement of libido towards the object in order to assimilate it and imbue it with emotional values; abstraction withdraws libido from the object, despoils it of all that could recall life; leaching out, as it were, its intellectual content, and crystallizing from the lye the typical elements that conform to law, which are either superimposed on the object or are its very antithesis. Bergson also makes use of these images of crystallization and rigidity to illustrate the nature of intellectual abstraction and clarification.

9 *Grosse Männer.* Cf. supra, pars. 542ff.

10 *Abstraction and Empathy.* Cf. supra, pars. 484ff.

11 Ibid., pp. 9f. [Worringer refers to Riegl, *Stilfragen* and *Spätrömische Kunstindustrie.*]

12 Cf. ibid., p. 4.

872   Worringer's "abstraction" represents that process which we have already encountered as a consequence of introversion—the exaltation of the intellect to offset the devaluation of external reality. "Empathy" corresponds to extraversion, as Theodor Lipps had already pointed out. "What I feel myself into is life in general, and life is power, inner work, effort, and accomplishment. To live, in a word, is to act, and to act is to experience the expenditure of my forces. This activity is by its very nature an activity of the will."[13] "Aesthetic enjoyment," says Worringer, "is objectified self-enjoyment,"[14] a formula that accords very well with our definition of extraversion. But Worringer's conception of aesthetics is not vitiated by any "tough-mindedness," and so he is fully capable of appreciating the value of psychological realities. Hence Worringer says: "The crucial factor is thus not so much the tone of the feeling as the feeling itself, the inner movement, the inner life, the subject's inner activity."[15] And again: "The value of a line or of a form consists in the vital value which it holds for us. It acquires its beauty only through the vital feeling which we unconsciously project into it."[16] These statements correspond exactly to my own view of the theory of libido, which seeks to maintain the balance between the two psychological opposites of extraversion and introversion.

873   The counterpole of empathy is abstraction. According to Worringer, "the urge to abstraction is the outcome of a great inner uneasiness inspired in man by the phenomena of the external world, and its religious counterpart is the strongly transcendental colouring of all ideas. We might describe this state as an immense spiritual dread of space. . . . This same feeling of fear may also be assumed to be the root of artistic creation."[17] We recognize in this definition the primary tendency towards introversion. To the introverted type the universe does not appear beautiful and desirable, but disquieting and even dangerous; he entrenches himself in his inner fastness, securing himself by the invention of regular geometrical figures full of repose, whose primitive, magical power assures him of domination over the surrounding world.

---

[13] Cited in ibid., p. 5.   [14] Ibid.
[15] Cf. ibid.   [16] Cf. ibid., p. 14.
[17] Cf. ibid., p. 15. [See supra, par. 488.]

874   "The urge to abstraction is the origin of all art," says Worringer.[18] This idea finds weighty confirmation in the fact that schizophrenics produce forms and figures showing the closest analogy with those of primitive humanity, not only in their thoughts but also in their drawings.

875   In this connection it would be unjust not to recall that Schiller attempted a similar formulation in his *naïve* and *sentimental* types.[19] The naïve poet *"is* Nature, the sentimental seeks her," he says. The naïve poet expresses primarily *himself,* while the sentimental is primarily influenced by the object. For Schiller, a perfect example of the naïve poet is Homer. "The naïve poet follows simple Nature and sensation and confines himself to a mere copying of reality."[20] "The sentimental poet," on the contrary "reflects on the impression objects make on him, and on that reflection alone depends the emotion with which he is exalted, and which likewise exalts us. Here the object is related to an idea, and on this relation alone depends his poetic power."[21] But Schiller also saw that these two types result from the predominance of psychological mechanisms which might be present in the same individual. "It is not only in the same poet," he says, "but even in the same work that these two categories are frequently found united."[22] These quotations show what types Schiller had in mind, and one recognizes their basic identity with those we have been discussing.

876   We find another parallel in Nietzsche's contrast between the *Apollinian* and the *Dionysian.*[23] The example which Nietzsche uses to illustrate this contrast is instructive—namely, that between dream and intoxication. In a dream the individual is shut up in himself, it is the most intimate of all psychic experiences; in intoxication he is liberated from himself, and, utterly self-forgetful, plunges into the multiplicity of the objective world. In his picture of Apollo, Nietzsche borrows the words of Schopenhauer: "As upon a tumultuous sea, unbounded in every direction, the mariner sits full of confidence in his frail barque, rising and falling amid the raging moun-

18 Cf. ibid.

19 "Über naive und sentimentalische Dichtung" (Cottasche Ausgabe, XVIII), pp. 205ff.

20 Ibid., p. 248.   21 Ibid., p. 249.   22 Ibid., p. 244.

23 Cf. supra, pars. 223ff.

tains of waves, so the individual man, in a world of troubles, sits passive and serene, trusting to the *principium individuationis*."[24] "Yes," continues Nietzsche, "one might say that the unshakable confidence in this principle, and the calm security of those whom it has inspired, have found in Apollo their most sublime expression, and one might describe Apollo himself as the glorious divine image of the principle of individuation."[25]

877   The Apollinian state, therefore, as Nietzsche conceives it, is a withdrawal into oneself, or introversion. Conversely the Dionysian state is the unleashing of a torrent of libido into things. "Not only," says Nietzsche, "is the bond between man and man reconfirmed in the Dionysian enchantment, but alienated Nature, hostile or enslaved, celebrates once more her feast of reconciliation with her prodigal son—Man. Liberally the earth proffers her gifts, and the wild beasts from rock and desert draw near peacefully. The car of Dionysos is heaped with flowers and garlands; panthers and tigers stride beneath his yoke. Transform Beethoven's Ode to Joy into a painting, and give free rein to your imagination as the awestruck millions prostrate themselves in the dust: thus you approach the Dionysian intoxication. Now is the slave free, now all the rigid, hostile barriers which necessity, caprice, or shameless fashion have set up between man and man are broken down. Now, with this gospel of universal harmony, each feels himself not only united, reconciled, merged with his neighbour, but one with him, as though the veil of Maya had been torn away, and nothing remained of it but a few shreds floating before the mystery of the Primal Unity."[26] Any commentary on this passage would be superfluous.

878   In concluding this series of examples drawn from outside my own special field of study, I would still like to mention a parallel from the sphere of linguistics, which likewise illustrates our two types. This is Franz Finck's hypothesis concerning the structure of language.[27] According to Finck, there are two main types of linguistic structure. The one is represented in general by the transitive verbs: I see him, I kill him, etc. The

[24] Cf. *The World as Will and Idea*, p. 455.
[25] Cf. *The Birth of Tragedy*, p. 125.
[26] Cf. ibid., pp. 26f.
[27] *Der deutsche Sprachbau als Ausdruck deutscher Weltanschauung.*

other is represented by the intransitive verbs: He appears before me, he dies at my feet. The first type clearly shows a centrifugal movement of libido going out from the subject; the second, a centripetal movement of libido coming in from the object. The latter, introverting type of structure is found particularly among the primitive languages of the Eskimos.

879   Finally, in the domain of psychiatry our two types have been described by Otto Gross.[28] He distinguishes two forms of inferiority: a type with a diffuse and shallow consciousness, and another with a contracted and deep consciousness. The first is characterized by the weakness, the second by the intense activity, of the "secondary function." Gross recognized that the secondary function is closely connected with affectivity, from which it is not difficult to see that once again our two types are meant. The relation he established between manic-depressive insanity and the type with a shallow consciousness shows that we are dealing with extraversion, while the relation between the psychology of the paranoiac and the type with a contracted consciousness indicates the identity with introversion.

880   After the foregoing considerations it will come as a surprise to nobody to learn that in the domain of psychoanalysis we also have to reckon with the existence of these two psychological types. On the one side we have a theory which is essentially reductive, pluralistic, causal, and sensualistic. This is the theory of Freud, which is strictly limited to empirical facts, and traces back complexes to their antecedents and to more simple elements. It regards psychological life as consisting in large measure of reactions, and accords the greatest role to sensation. On the other side we have the diametrically opposed theory of Adler,[29] which is thoroughly intellectualistic, monistic, and finalistic. Here psychological phenomena are not reduced to antecedent and more simple elements, but are conceived as "arrangements," as the outcome of intentions and aims of a complex nature. Instead of the *causa efficiens* we have the *causa finalis*. The previous history of the patient and the concrete influences of the environment are of much less importance than his dominating principles, his "guiding fic-

28 *Die zerebrale Sekundärfunktion.* Cf. supra, pars. 461 ff.
29 *The Neurotic Constitution.*

tions." It is not his striving for the object and his subjective pleasure in it that are the determining factors, but the securing of the individual's power in the face of the hostile environmental influences.

881   While the dominant note in Freudian psychology is a centrifugal tendency, a striving for pleasure in the object, in Adler's it is a centripetal striving for the supremacy of the subject, who wants to be "on top," to safeguard his power, to defend himself against the overwhelming forces of existence. The expedient to which the type described by Freud resorts is the infantile transference of subjective fantasies into the object, as a compensatory reaction to the difficulties of life. The characteristic recourse of the type described by Adler is, on the contrary, "security," "masculine protest," and the stubborn reinforcement of the "guiding fiction."

882   The difficult task of creating a psychology which will be equally fair to both types must be reserved for the future.

PSYCHOLOGICAL TYPES[1]

883 From ancient times there have been numerous attempts to reduce the manifold differences between human individuals to definite categories, and on the other hand to break down the apparent uniformity of mankind by a sharper characterization of certain typical differences. Without wishing to go too deeply into the history of these attempts, I would like to call attention to the fact that the oldest categories known to us originated with physicians. Of these perhaps the most important was Claudius Galen, the Greek physician who lived in the second century A.D. He distinguished four basic temperaments: the sanguine, the phlegmatic, the choleric, and the melancholic. The underlying idea goes back to the fifth century B.C., to the teachings of Hippocrates, that the human body was composed of the four elements, air, water, fire, and earth. Corresponding to these elements, four substances were to be found in the living body, blood, phlegm, yellow bile, and black bile; and it was Galen's idea that, by the varying admixture of these four substances, men could be divided into four classes. Those in whom there was a preponderance of blood belonged to the sanguine type; a preponderance of phlegm produced the phlegmatic; yellow bile produced the choleric, and black bile the melancholic. As our language shows, these differences of temperament have passed into history, though they have, of course, long since been superseded as a physiological theory.

1 [A lecture delivered at the International Congress of Education, Territet, Switzerland, 1923, and published as "Psychologische Typen," in the *Zeitschrift für Menschenkunde* (Kampen a. Sylt), I:1 (May 1925), 45–65. First translated into English in *Problems of Personality, Studies presented to Dr. Morton Prince* (London and New York, 1925), pp. 289–302; retranslated by H. G. and C. F. Baynes in *Contributions to Analytical Psychology* (London and New York, 1928), pp. 295ff. The present translation is made from the republication in *Gesammelte Werke*, 6, Appendix, pp. 552ff., in consultation with the Baynes version.—EDITORS.]

884   To Galen undoubtedly belongs the credit for having created a psychological classification of human beings which has
endured for two thousand years, a classification based on perceptible differences of *emotionality* or *affectivity*. It is interesting to note that the first attempt at a typology was concerned
with the emotional behaviour of man—obviously because affectivity is the commonest and most striking feature of behaviour in general.

885   Affects, however, are by no means the only distinguishing
mark of the human psyche. Characteristic data can be expected from other psychological phenomena as well, the only
requirement being that we perceive and observe other functions as clearly as we do affects. In earlier centuries, when the
concept "psychology" as we know it today was entirely lacking,
all psychic functions other than affects were veiled in darkness,
just as they still seem to be scarcely discernible subtleties for
the great majority of people today. Affects can be seen on the
surface, and that is enough for the unpsychological man—the
man for whom the psyche of his neighbour presents no problem. He is satisfied with seeing other people's affects; if he
sees none, then the other person is psychologically invisible to
him because, apart from affects, he can perceive nothing in the
other's consciousness.

886   The reason why we are able to discover other functions
besides affects in the psyche of our fellow men is that we ourselves have passed from an "unproblematical" state of consciousness to a problematical one. If we judge others only by
affects, we show that our chief, and perhaps only, criterion is
affect. This means that the same criterion is also applicable to
our own psychology, which amounts to saying that our psychological judgment is neither objective nor independent but is
enslaved to affect. This truth holds good for the majority of
men, and on it rests the psychological possibility of murderous
wars and the constant threat of their recurrence. This must always be so as long as we judge the people "on the other side"
by our own affects. I call such a state of consciousness "unproblematical" because it has obviously never become a problem to itself. It becomes a problem only when a doubt arises
as to whether affects—including our own affects—offer a satisfactory basis for psychological judgments. We are always

inclined to justify ourselves before anyone who holds us responsible for an emotional action by saying that we acted only on an outburst of affect and are not usually in that condition. When it concerns ourselves we are glad to explain the affect as an exceptional condition of diminished responsibility but are loath to make the same allowance for others. Even if this is a not very edifying attempt to exculpate our beloved ego, there is still something positive in the feeling of justification such an excuse affords: it is an attempt to distinguish oneself from one's own affect, and hence one's fellow man from *his* affect. Even if my excuse is only a subterfuge, it is nevertheless an attempt to cast doubt on the validity of affect as the sole index of personality, and to appeal to other psychic functions that are just as characteristic of it as the affect, if not more so. When a man judges us by our affects, we readily accuse him of lack of understanding, or even injustice. But this puts us under an obligation not to judge others by their affects either.

887   For this purpose the primitive, unpsychological man, who regards affects in himself and others as the only essential criterion, must develop a problematical state of consciousness in which other factors besides affects are recognized as valid. In this problematical state a paradoxical judgment can be formed: "I am this affect" and "this affect is not me." This antithesis expresses a splitting of the ego, or rather, a splitting of the psychic material that constitutes the ego. By recognizing myself as much in my affect as in something else that is not my affect, I differentiate an affective factor from other psychic factors, and in so doing I bring the affect down from its original heights of unlimited power into its proper place in the hierarchy of psychic functions. Only when a man has performed this operation on himself, and has distinguished between the various psychic factors in himself, is he in a position to look around for other criteria in his psychological judgment of others, instead of merely falling back on affect. Only in this way is a really objective psychological judgment possible.

888   What we call "psychology" today is a science that can be pursued only on the basis of certain historical and moral premises laid down by Christian education during the last two thousand years. A saying like "Judge not, that ye be not judged," inculcated by religion, has created the possibility of a will which strives, in the last resort, for simple objectivity of

judgment. This objectivity, implying no mere indifference to others but based on the principle of excusing others as we do ourselves, is the prerequisite for a just judgment of our fellow men. You wonder perhaps why I dwell so insistently on this question of objectivity, but you would cease to wonder if ever you should try to classify people in practice. A man of pronounced sanguine temperament will tell you that at bottom he is deeply melancholic; a choleric, that his only fault consists in his having always been too phlegmatic. But a classification in the validity of which I alone believe is about as helpful as a universal church of which I am the sole member. We have, therefore, to find criteria which can be accepted as binding not only by the judging subject but also by the judged object.

889   In complete contrast to the old system of classification by temperaments, the new typology begins with the explicit agreement neither to allow oneself to be judged by affect nor to judge others by it, since no one can declare himself finally identical with his affect. This creates a problem, because it follows that, where affects are concerned, the general agreement which science demands can never be reached. We must, therefore, look around for other factors as a criterion—factors to which we appeal when we excuse ourselves for an emotional action. We say perhaps: "Admittedly I said this or that in a state of affect, but of course I was exaggerating and no harm was meant." A very naughty child who has caused his mother a lot of trouble might say: "I didn't mean to, I didn't want to hurt you, I love you too much."

890   Such explanations appeal to the existence of a different kind of personality from the one that appeared in the affect. In both cases the affective personality appears as something inferior that seized hold of the real ego and obscured it. But often the personality revealed in the affect is a higher and better one, so much so that, regrettably, one cannot remain on such a pinnacle of perfection. We all know those sudden fits of generosity, altruism, self-sacrifice, and similar "beautiful gestures" for which, as an ironical observer might remark, one does not care to be held responsible—perhaps a reason why so many people do so little good.

891   But whether the affective personality be high or low, the affect is considered an exceptional state whose qualities are represented either as a falsification of the "real" personality or

as not belonging to it as an authentic attribute. What then is this "real" personality? Obviously, it is partly that which everyone distinguishes in himself as separate from affect, and partly that in everyone which is dismissed as inauthentic in the judgment of others. Since it is impossible to deny the pertinence of the affective state to the ego, it follows that the ego is the same ego whether in the affective state or in the so-called "authentic" state, even though it displays a differential attitude to these psychological happenings. In the affective state it is unfree, driven, coerced. By contrast, the normal state is a state of free will, with all one's powers at one's disposal. In other words, *the affective state is unproblematical, while the normal state is problematical: it comprises both the problem and possibility of free choice.* In this latter state an understanding becomes possible, because in it alone can one discern one's motives and gain self-knowledge. Discrimination is the *sine qua non* of cognition. But discrimination means splitting up the contents of consciousness into discrete functions. Therefore, if we wish to define the psychological peculiarity of a man in terms that will satisfy not only our own subjective judgment but also the object judged, we must take as our criterion that state or attitude which is felt by the object to be the conscious, normal condition. Accordingly, we shall make his conscious motives our first concern, while eliminating as far as possible our own arbitrary interpretations.

892 Proceeding thus we shall discover, after a time, that in spite of the great variety of conscious motives and tendencies, certain groups of individuals can be distinguished who are characterized by a striking conformity of motivation. For example, we shall come upon individuals who in all their judgments, perceptions, feelings, affects, and actions feel external factors to be the predominant motivating force, or who at least give weight to them no matter whether causal or final motives are in question. I will give some examples of what I mean. St. Augustine: "I would not believe the Gospel if the authority of the Catholic Church did not compel it."[2] A dutiful daughter: "I could not allow myself to think anything that would be displeasing to my father." One man finds a piece of modern music

---

[2] *Contra epistolam Manichaei,* V, 6 (Migne, *P.L.,* vol. 42, col. 176).

beautiful because everybody else pretends it is beautiful. Another marries in order to please his parents but very much against his own interests. There are people who contrive to make themselves ridiculous in order to amuse others; they even prefer to make butts of themselves rather than remain unnoticed. There are not a few who in everything they do or don't do have but one motive in mind: what will others think of them? "One need not be ashamed of a thing if nobody knows about it." There are some who can find happiness only when it excites the envy of others; some who make trouble for themselves in order to enjoy the sympathy of their friends.

893   Such examples could be multiplied indefinitely. They point to a psychological peculiarity that can be sharply distinguished from another attitude which, by contrast, is motivated chiefly by internal or subjective factors. A person of this type might say: "I know I could give my father the greatest pleasure if I did so and so, but I don't happen to think that way." Or: "I see that the weather has turned out bad, but in spite of it I shall carry out my plan." This type does not travel for pleasure but to execute a preconceived idea. Or: "My book is probably incomprehensible, but it is perfectly clear to me." Or, going to the other extreme: "Everybody thinks I could do something, but I know perfectly well I can do nothing." Such a man can be so ashamed of himself that he literally dares not meet people. There are some who feel happy only when they are quite sure nobody knows about it, and to them a thing is disagreeable just because it is pleasing to everyone else. They seek the good where no one would think of finding it. At every step the sanction of the subject must be obtained, and without it nothing can be undertaken or carried out. Such a person would have replied to St. Augustine: "I would believe the Gospel if the authority of the Catholic Church did *not* compel it." Always he has to prove that everything he does rests on his own decisions and convictions, and never because he is influenced by anyone, or desires to please or conciliate some person or opinion.

894   This attitude characterizes a group of individuals whose motivations are derived chiefly from the subject, from inner necessity. There is, finally, a third group, and here it is hard to say whether the motivation comes chiefly from within or with-

out. This group is the most numerous and includes the less differentiated normal man, who is considered normal either because he allows himself no excesses or because he has no need of them. The normal man is, by definition, influenced as much from within as from without. He constitutes the extensive middle group, on one side of which are those whose motivations are determined mainly by the external object, and, on the other, those whose motivations are determined from within. I call the first group *extraverted,* and the second group *introverted.* The terms scarcely require elucidation as they explain themselves from what has already been said.

895 Although there are doubtless individuals whose type can be recognized at first glance, this is by no means always the case. As a rule, only careful observation and weighing of the evidence permit a sure classification. However simple and clear the fundamental principle of the two opposing attitudes may be, in actual reality they are complicated and hard to make out, because every individual is an exception to the rule. Hence one can never give a description of a type, no matter how complete, that would apply to more than one individual, despite the fact that in some ways it aptly characterizes thousands of others. Conformity is one side of a man, uniqueness is the other. Classification does not explain the individual psyche. Nevertheless, an understanding of psychological types opens the way to a better understanding of human psychology in general.

896 Type differentiation often begins very early, so early that in some cases one must speak of it as innate. The earliest sign of extraversion in a child is his quick adaptation to the environment, and the extraordinary attention he gives to objects and especially to the effect he has on them. Fear of objects is minimal; he lives and moves among them with confidence. His apprehension is quick but imprecise. He appears to develop more rapidly than the introverted child, since he is less reflective and usually without fear. He feels no barrier between himself and objects, and can therefore play with them freely and learn through them. He likes to carry his enterprises to the extreme and exposes himself to risks. Everything unknown is alluring.

897   To reverse the picture, one of the earliest signs of introversion in a child is a reflective, thoughtful manner, marked
shyness and even fear of unknown objects. Very early there
appears a tendency to assert himself over familiar objects, and
attempts are made to master them. Everything unknown is regarded with mistrust; outside influences are usually met with
violent resistance. The child wants his own way, and under no
circumstances will he submit to an alien rule he cannot understand. When he asks questions, it is not from curiosity or a
desire to create a sensation, but because he wants names,
meanings, explanations to give him subjective protection
against the object. I have seen an introverted child who made
his first attempts to walk only after he had learned the names of
all the objects in the room he might touch. Thus very early in
an introverted child the characteristic defensive attitude can
be noted which the adult introvert displays towards the object;
just as in an extraverted child one can very early observe a
marked assurance and initiative, a happy trustfulness in his
dealings with objects. This is indeed the basic feature of the
extraverted attitude: psychic life is, as it were, enacted outside
the individual in objects and objective relationships. In extreme cases there is even a sort of blindness for his own individuality. The introvert, on the contrary, always acts as though
the object possessed a superior power over him against which
he has to defend himself. His real world is the inner one.

898   Sad though it is, the two types are inclined to speak very
badly of one another. This fact will immediately strike anyone
who investigates the problem. And the reason is that the
psychic values have a diametrically opposite localization for
the two types. The introvert sees everything that is in any way
valuable for him in the subject; the extravert sees it in the object. This dependence on the object seems to the introvert a
mark of the greatest inferiority, while to the extravert the preoccupation with the subject seems nothing but infantile auto-
eroticism. So it is not surprising that the two types often come
into conflict. This does not, however, prevent most men from
marrying women of the opposite type. Such marriages are very
valuable as psychological symbioses so long as the partners do
not attempt a mutual "psychological" understanding. But this

phase of understanding belongs to the normal development of every marriage provided the partners have the necessary leisure or the necessary urge to development—though even if both these are present real courage is needed to risk a rupture of the marital peace. In favourable circumstances this phase enters automatically into the lives of both types, for the reason that each type is an example of one-sided development. The one develops only external relations and neglects the inner; the other develops inwardly but remains outwardly at a standstill. In time the need arises for the individual to develop what has been neglected. The development takes the form of a differentiation of certain functions, to which I must now turn in view of their importance for the type problem.

899 The conscious psyche is an apparatus for adaptation and orientation, and consists of a number of different psychic functions. Among these we can distinguish four basic ones: *sensation, thinking, feeling, intuition*. Under sensation I include all perceptions by means of the sense organs; by thinking I mean the function of intellectual cognition and the forming of logical conclusions; feeling is a function of subjective valuation; intuition I take as perception by way of the unconscious, or perception of unconscious contents.

900 So far as my experience goes, these four basic functions seem to me sufficient to express and represent the various modes of conscious orientation. For complete orientation all four functions should contribute equally: thinking should facilitate cognition and judgment, feeling should tell us how and to what extent a thing is important or unimportant for us, sensation should convey concrete reality to us through seeing, hearing, tasting, etc., and intuition should enable us to divine the hidden possibilities in the background, since these too belong to the complete picture of a given situation.

901 In reality, however, these basic functions are seldom or never uniformly differentiated and equally at our disposal. As a rule one or the other function occupies the foreground, while the rest remain undifferentiated in the background. Thus there are many people who restrict themselves to the simple perception of concrete reality, without thinking about it or taking feeling values into account. They bother just as little about the possibilities hidden in a situation. I describe such people as

sensation types. Others are exclusively oriented by what they think, and simply cannot adapt to a situation which they are unable to understand intellectually. I call such people *thinking types.* Others, again, are guided in everything entirely by feeling. They merely ask themselves whether a thing is pleasant or unpleasant, and orient themselves by their feeling impressions. These are the *feeling types.* Finally, the *intuitives* concern themselves neither with ideas nor with feeling reactions, nor yet with the reality of things, but surrender themselves wholly to the lure of possibilities, and abandon every situation in which no further possibilities can be scented.

902   Each of these types represents a different kind of one-sidedness, but one which is linked up with and complicated in a peculiar way by the introverted or extraverted attitude. It was because of this complication that I had to mention these function-types, and this brings us back to the question of the one-sidedness of the introverted and extraverted attitudes. This one-sidedness would lead to a complete loss of psychic balance if it were not compensated by an unconscious counterposition. Investigation of the unconscious has shown, for example, that alongside or behind the introvert's conscious attitude there is an unconscious extraverted attitude which automatically compensates his conscious one-sidedness.

903   Though one can, in practice, intuit the existence of a general introverted or extraverted attitude, an exact scientific investigator cannot rest content with an intuition but must concern himself with the actual material presented. We then discover that no individual is simply introverted or extraverted, but that he is so in one of his functions. Take a thinking type, for example: most of the conscious material he presents for observation consists of thoughts, conclusions, reflections, as well as actions, affects, valuations, and perceptions of an intellectual nature, or at least the material is directly dependent on intellectual premises. We must interpret the nature of his general attitude from the peculiarity of this material. The material presented by a feeling type will be of a different kind, that is, feelings and emotional contents of all sorts, thoughts, reflections, and perceptions dependent on emotional premises. Only from the peculiar nature of his feelings shall we be able to tell to which of the attitude-types he belongs. That

519

is why I mention these function-types here, because in individual cases the introverted and extraverted attitudes can never be demonstrated *per se;* they appear only as the peculiarity of the predominating conscious function. Similarly, there is no general attitude of the unconscious, but only typically modified forms of unconscious functions, and only through the investigation of the unconscious functions and their peculiarities can the unconscious attitude be scientifically established.

904 It is hardly possible to speak of typical unconscious functions, although in the economy of the psyche one has to attribute *some* function to the unconscious. It is best, I think, to express oneself rather cautiously in this respect, and I would not go beyond the statement that the unconscious, so far as we can see at present, has a compensatory function to consciousness. What the unconscious is in itself is an idle speculation. By its very nature it is beyond all cognition. We merely postulate its existence from its products, such as dreams and fantasies. But it is a well-established fact of scientific experience that dreams, for example, practically always have a content that could correct the conscious attitude, and this justifies us in speaking of a compensatory function of the unconscious.

905 Besides this general function, the unconscious also possesses functions that can become conscious under other conditions. The thinking type, for instance, must necessarily repress and exclude feeling as far as possible, since nothing disturbs thinking so much as feeling, and the feeling type represses thinking, since nothing is more injurious to feeling than thinking. Repressed functions lapse into the unconscious. Just as only one of the four sons of Horus had a human head,[3] so as a rule only one of the four basic functions is fully conscious and differentiated enough to be freely manipulable by the will, the others remaining partially or wholly unconscious. This "unconsciousness" does not mean that a thinking type, for instance, is not conscious of his feelings. He knows his feelings very well, in so far as he is capable of introspection, but he denies them any validity and declares they have no influence over him. They therefore come upon him against his will, and being spontaneous and autonomous, they finally appropriate to them-

---

[3] [Cf. *Psychology and Alchemy*, par. 314, n. 143, and fig. 102.]

selves the validity which his consciousness denies them. They are activated by unconscious stimulation, and form indeed a sort of counterpersonality whose existence can be established only by analysing the products of the unconscious.

906 When a function is not at one's disposal, when it is felt as something that disturbs the differentiated function, suddenly appearing and then vanishing again fitfully, when it has an obsessive character, or remains obstinately in hiding when most needed—it then has all the qualities of a quasi-unconscious function. Other peculiarities may be noted: there is always something inauthentic about it, as it contains elements that do not properly belong to it. Thus the unconscious feelings of the thinking type are of a singularly fantastic nature, often in grotesque contrast to the excessively rationalistic intellectualism of his conscious attitude. His conscious thinking is purposive and controlled, but his feeling is impulsive, uncontrolled, moody, irrational, primitive, and just as archaic as the feelings of a savage.

907 The same is true of every function that is repressed into the unconscious. It remains undeveloped, fused together with elements not properly belonging to it, in an archaic condition —for the unconscious is the residue of unconquered nature in us, just as it is also the matrix of our unborn future. The undeveloped functions are always the seminal ones, so it is no wonder that sometime in the course of life the need will be felt to supplement and alter the conscious attitude.

908 Apart from the qualities I have mentioned, the undeveloped functions possess the further peculiarity that, when the conscious attitude is introverted, they are extraverted and vice versa. One could therefore expect to find extraverted feelings in an introverted intellectual, and this was aptly expressed by just such a type when he said: "Before dinner I am a Kantian, but after dinner a Nietzschean." In his habitual attitude, that is to say, he is an intellectual, but under the stimulating influence of a good dinner a Dionysian wave breaks through his conscious attitude.

909 It is just here that we meet with a great difficulty in diagnosing the types. The observer sees both the manifestations of the conscious attitude and the autonomous phenomena of the unconscious, and he will be at a loss as to what he should

ascribe to the conscious and what to the unconscious. A differential diagnosis can be based only on a careful study of the qualities of the observed material. We must try to discover which phenomena result from consciously chosen motives and which are spontaneous; and it must also be established which of them are adapted, and which of them have an unadapted, archaic character.

910 It will now be sufficiently clear that the qualities of the main conscious function, i.e., of the conscious attitude as a whole, are in strict contrast to those of the unconscious attitude. In other words, we can say that between the conscious and the unconscious there is normally an opposition. This opposition, however, is not perceived as a conflict so long as the conscious attitude is not too one-sided and not too remote from that of the unconscious. But if the contrary should be the case, then the Kantian will be disagreeably surprised by his Dionysian counterpart, which will begin to develop highly unsuitable impulses. His consciousness will then feel obliged to suppress these autonomous manifestations, and thus the conflict situation is created. Once the unconscious gets into active opposition to consciousness, it simply refuses to be suppressed. It is true that certain manifestations which consciousness has marked down are not particularly difficult to suppress, but then the unconscious impulses simply seek other outlets that are less easy to recognize. And once these false safety valves are opened, one is already on the way to neurosis. The indirect outlets can, of course, each be made accessible to understanding by analysis and subjected again to conscious suppression. But that does not extinguish their instinctual dynamism; it is merely pushed still further into the background, unless an understanding of the indirect route taken by the unconscious impulses brings with it an understanding of the one-sidedness of the conscious attitude. The one should alter the other, for it was just this one-sidedness that activated the unconscious opposition in the first place, and insight into the unconscious impulses is useful only when it effectively compensates that one-sidedness.

911 The alteration of the conscious attitude is no light matter, because any habitual attitude is essentially a more or less conscious ideal, sanctified by custom and historical tradition, and

founded on the bedrock of one's innate temperament. The conscious attitude is always in the nature of a *Weltanschauung*, if it is not explicitly a religion. It is this that makes the type problem so important. The opposition between the types is not merely an external conflict between men, it is the source of endless inner conflicts; the cause not only of external disputes and dislikes, but of nervous ills and psychic suffering. It is this fact, too, that obliges us physicians constantly to widen our medical horizon and to include within it not only general psychological standpoints but also questions concerning one's views of life and the world.

912   Within the space of a lecture I cannot, of course, give you any idea of the depth and scope of these problems. I must content myself with a general survey of the main facts and their implications. For a fuller elaboration of the whole problem I must refer you to my book *Psychological Types*.

913   Recapitulating, I would like to stress that each of the two general attitudes, introversion and extraversion, manifests itself in a special way in an individual through the predominance of one of the four basic functions. Strictly speaking, there are no introverts and extraverts pure and simple, but only introverted and extraverted function-types, such as thinking types, sensation types, etc. There are thus at least eight clearly distinguishable types. Obviously one could increase this number at will if each of the functions were split into three subgroups, which would not be impossible empirically. One could, for example, easily divide thinking into its three well-known forms: intuitive and speculative, logical and mathematical, empirical and positivist, the last being mainly dependent on sense perception. Similar subgroups could be made of the other functions, as in the case of intuition, which has an intellectual as well as an emotional and sensory aspect. In this way a large number of types could be established, each new division becoming increasingly subtle.

914   For the sake of completeness, I must add that I do not regard the classification of types according to introversion and extraversion and the four basic functions as the only possible one. Any other psychological criterion could serve just as well as a classifier, although, in my view, no other possesses so great a practical significance.

3

A PSYCHOLOGICAL THEORY OF TYPES[1]

915   Character is the fixed individual form of a human being. Since this form is compounded of body and mind, a general characterology must teach the significance of both physical and psychic features. The enigmatic oneness of the living organism has as its corollary the fact that bodily traits are not merely physical, nor mental traits merely psychic. The continuity of nature knows nothing of those antithetical distinctions which the human intellect is forced to set up as aids to understanding.

916   The distinction between mind and body is an artificial dichotomy, an act of discrimination based far more on the peculiarity of intellectual cognition than on the nature of things. In fact, so intimate is the intermingling of bodily and psychic traits that not only can we draw far-reaching inferences as to the constitution of the psyche from the constitution of the body, but we can also infer from psychic peculiarities the corresponding bodily characteristics. It is true that the latter process is far more difficult, not because the body is less influenced by the psyche than the psyche by the body, but for quite another reason. In taking the psyche as our starting-point, we work from the relatively unknown to the known; while in the opposite case we have the advantage of starting from something known, that is, from the visible body. Despite all the psychology we think we possess today, the psyche is still infinitely more obscure to us than the visible surface of the body. The psyche is still a foreign, barely explored country of

---

1 [A lecture delivered at the Congress of Swiss Psychiatrists, Zurich, 1928, and published as "Psychologische Typologie" in *Seelenprobleme der Gegenwart* (Zurich, 1931), pp. 101ff., reprinted in *Gesammelte Werke*, 6, Appendix, pp. 568ff. Translated into English by W. S. Dell and Cary F. Baynes as "A Psychological Theory of Types," in *Modern Man in Search of a Soul* (London and New York, 1933), pp. 85ff., which version is reproduced here with minor modifications.— EDITORS.]

which we have only indirect knowledge, mediated by conscious functions that are open to almost endless possibilities of deception.

917   This being so, it seems safer to proceed from outside inwards, from the known to the unknown, from the body to the psyche. Thus all attempts at characterology have started from the outside world; astrology, in ancient times, even started from interstellar space in order to arrive at those lines of fate whose beginnings lie in the human heart. To the same class of interpretations from outward signs belong palmistry, Gall's phrenology, Lavater's physiognomy, and—more recently—graphology, Kretschmer's physiological types, and Rorschach's klexographic method. As we can see, there are any number of paths leading from outside inwards, from the physical to the psychic, and it is necessary that research should follow this direction until the elementary psychic facts are established with sufficient certainty. But once having established these facts, we can reverse the procedure. We can then put the question: What are the bodily correlatives of a given psychic condition? Unfortunately we are not yet far enough advanced to give even an approximate answer. The first requirement is to establish the primary facts of psychic life, and this is far from having been accomplished. Indeed, we have only just begun the work of compiling an inventory of the psyche, not always with great success.

918   Merely to establish the fact that certain people have this or that physical appearance is of no significance if it does not allow us to infer a psychic correlative. We have learned something only when we have determined what psychic attributes go with a given bodily constitution. The body means as little to us without the psyche as the latter without the body. But when we try to infer a psychic correlative from a physical characteristic, we are proceeding—as already stated—from the known to the unknown.

919   I must, unfortunately, stress this point, since psychology is the youngest of the sciences and therefore the one that suffers most from preconceived opinions. The fact that we have only recently discovered psychology tells us plainly enough that it has taken us all this time to make a clear distinction between ourselves and the content of our minds. Until this could

be done, it was impossible to study the psyche objectively. Psychology, as a science, is actually our most recent acquisition; up to now it has been just as fantastic and arbitrary as was natural science in the Middle Ages. It was believed that psychology could be created as it were by decree—a prejudice under which we are still labouring. Psychic life is, after all, what is most immediate to us, and apparently what we know most about. Indeed, it is more than familiar, we yawn over it. We are irritated by the banality of its everlasting commonplaces; they bore us to extinction and we do everything in our power to avoid thinking about them. The psyche being immediacy itself, and we ourselves being the psyche, we are almost forced to assume that we know it through and through in a way that cannot be doubted or questioned. That is why each of us has his own private opinion about psychology and is even convinced that he knows more about it than anyone else. Psychiatrists, because they must struggle with their patients' relatives and guardians whose "understanding" is proverbial, are perhaps the first to become aware as a professional group of that blind prejudice which encourages every man to take himself as his own best authority in psychological matters. But this of course does not prevent the psychiatrist also from becoming a "know-all." One of them even went so far as to confess: "There are only two normal people in this city—Professor B. is the other."

920 Since this is how matters stand in psychology today, we must bring ourselves to admit that what is closest to us, the psyche, is the very thing we know least about, although it seems to be what we know best of all, and furthermore that everyone else probably understands it better than we do ourselves. At any rate that, for a start, would be a most useful heuristic principle. As I have said, it is just because the psyche is so close to us that psychology has been discovered so late. And because it is still in its initial stages as a science, we lack the concepts and definitions with which to grasp the facts. If concepts are lacking, facts are not; on the contrary, we are surrounded—almost buried—by facts. This is in striking contrast to the state of affairs in other sciences, where the facts have first to be unearthed. Here the classification of primary data results in the formation of descriptive concepts covering cer-

tain natural orders, as, for example, the grouping of the elements in chemistry and of plant families in botany. But it is quite different in the case of the psyche. Here an empirical and descriptive method merely plunges us into the ceaseless stream of subjective psychic happenings, so that whenever any sort of generalizing concept emerges from this welter of impressions it is usually nothing more than a symptom. Because we ourselves are psyches, it is almost impossible to us to give free rein to psychic happenings without being dissolved in them and thus robbed of our ability to recognize distinctions and make comparisons.

921 This is one difficulty. The other is that the more we turn from spatial phenomena to the non-spatiality of the psyche, the more impossible it becomes to determine anything by exact measurement. It becomes difficult even to establish the facts. If, for example, I want to emphasize the unreality of something, I say that I merely "thought" it. I say: "I would never even have had this thought unless such and such had happened; and besides, I never think things like that." Remarks of this kind are quite usual, and they show how nebulous psychic facts are, or rather, how vague they appear subjectively— for in reality they are just as objective and just as definite as any other events. The truth is that I actually did think such and such a thing, regardless of the conditions and provisos I attach to this process. Many people have to wrestle with themselves in order to make this perfectly obvious admission, and it often costs them a great moral effort. These, then, are the difficulties we encounter when we draw inferences about the state of affairs in the psyche from the known things we observe outside.

922 My more limited field of work is not the clinical study of external characteristics, but the investigation and classification of the psychic data which may be inferred from them. The first result of this work is a phenomenology of the psyche, which enables us to formulate a corresponding theory about its structure. From the empirical application of this structural theory there is finally developed a psychological typology.

923 Clinical studies are based on the description of symptoms, and the step from this to a phenomenology of the psyche is comparable to the step from a purely symptomatic pathology

to the pathology of cellular and metabolic processes. That is to say, the phenomenology of the psyche brings into view those psychic processes in the background which underlie the clinical symptoms. As is generally known, this knowledge is obtained by the application of analytical methods. We have today a working knowledge of the psychic processes that produce psychogenic symptoms, and have thus laid the foundations for a theory of complexes. Whatever else may be taking place in the obscure recesses of the psyche—and there are notoriously many opinions about this—one thing is certain: it is the complexes (emotionally-toned contents having a certain amount of autonomy) which play the most important part here. The term "autonomous complex" has often met with opposition, unjustifiably, it seems to me, because the active contents of the unconscious do behave in a way I cannot describe better than by the word "autonomous." The term is meant to indicate the capacity of the complexes to resist conscious intentions, and to come and go as they please. Judging by all we know about them, they are psychic entities which are outside the control of the conscious mind. They have been split off from consciousness and lead a separate existence in the dark realm of the unconscious, being at all times ready to hinder or reinforce the conscious functioning.

924　　A deeper study of the complexes leads logically to the problem of their origin, and as to this a number of different theories are current. Theories apart, experience shows that complexes always contain something like a conflict, or at least are either the cause or the effect of a conflict. At any rate the characteristics of conflict—shock, upheaval, mental agony, inner strife—are peculiar to the complexes. They are the "sore spots," the *bêtes noires*, the "skeletons in the cupboard" which we do not like to remember and still less to be reminded of by others, but which frequently come back to mind unbidden and in the most unwelcome fashion. They always contain memories, wishes, fears, duties, needs, or insights which somehow we can never really grapple with, and for this reason they constantly interfere with our conscious life in a disturbing and usually a harmful way.

925　　Complexes obviously represent a kind of inferiority in the broadest sense—a statement I must at once qualify by saying that to have complexes does not necessarily indicate inferiority. It only means that something discordant, unassimilated, and antagonistic exists, perhaps as an obstacle, but also as an incentive to greater effort, and so, perhaps, to new possibilities of achievement. In this sense, therefore, complexes are focal or nodal points of psychic life which we would not wish to do without; indeed, they should not be missing, for otherwise psychic activity would come to a fatal standstill. They point to the unresolved problems in the individual, the places where he has suffered a defeat, at least for the time being, and where there is something he cannot evade or overcome—his weak spots in every sense of the word.

926   These characteristics of the complex throw a significant light on its origin. It obviously arises from the clash between a demand of adaptation and the individual's constitutional inability to meet the challenge. Seen in this light, the complex is a valuable symptom which helps us to diagnose an individual disposition.

927   Experience shows us that complexes are infinitely varied, yet careful comparison reveals a relatively small number of typical primary forms, which are all built upon the first experiences of childhood. This must necessarily be so, because the individual disposition is already a factor in infancy; it is innate, and not acquired in the course of life. The parental complex is therefore nothing but the first manifestation of a clash between reality and the individual's constitutional inability to meet the demands it makes upon him. The primary form of the complex cannot be other than a parental complex, because the parents are the first reality with which the child comes into conflict.

928   The existence of a parental complex therefore tells us little or nothing about the peculiar constitution of the individual. Practical experience soon teaches us that the crux of the matter does not lie in the presence of a parental complex, but rather in the special way in which the complex works itself out in the individual's life. And here we observe the most striking variations, though only a very small number can be attributed to the special nature of the parental influence. There are often several children who are exposed to the same influence, and yet each of them reacts to it in a totally different way.

929   I therefore turned my attention to these differences, telling myself that it is through them that the peculiarities of the individual dispositions may be discerned. Why, in a neurotic family, does one child react with hysteria, another with a compulsion neurosis, the third with a psychosis, and the fourth apparently not at all? This problem of the "choice of neurosis," which Freud was also faced with, robs the parental complex as such of its aetiological significance, and shifts the inquiry to the reacting individual and his special disposition.

930   Although Freud's attempts to solve this problem leave me entirely dissatisfied, I am myself unable to answer the question. Indeed, I think it premature to raise the question of the choice of neurosis at all. Before we tackle this extremely difficult problem we need to know a great deal more about the way the individual reacts. The question is: How does a person react to an obstacle? For instance, we come to a brook over which there is no bridge. It is too broad to step across, so we must jump. For this purpose we have at our disposal a complicated functional system, namely, the psychomotor system. It is fully developed and needs only to be triggered off. But before this happens, something of a purely psychic nature takes place: a decision is made about what is to be done. This is followed by those crucial events which settle the matter in some way and vary with each individual. But, significantly enough, we rarely if ever recognize these events as characteristic, for as a rule we do not see ourselves at all or only as a last resort. That is to say, just as the psychomotor apparatus is habitually at our disposal for jumping, there is an exclusively psychic apparatus ready for use in making decisions, which functions by habit and therefore unconsciously.

931   Opinions differ widely as to what this apparatus is like. It is certain only that every individual has his accustomed way of making decisions and dealing with difficulties. One person will say he jumped the brook for fun; another, that there was no alternative; a third, that every obstacle he meets challenges him to overcome it. A fourth did not jump the brook because he dislikes useless effort, and a fifth refrained because he saw no urgent necessity to get to the other side.

932   I have purposely chosen this commonplace example in order to demonstrate how irrelevant such motivations seem.

They appear so futile that we are inclined to brush them aside and to substitute our own explanation. And yet it is just these variations that give us valuable insights into the individual psychic systems of adaptation. If we observe, in other situations of life, the person who jumped the brook for fun, we shall probably find that for the most part everything he does or omits to do can be explained in terms of the pleasure it gives him. We shall observe that the one who jumped because he saw no alternative goes through life cautiously and apprehensively, always deciding *faute de mieux*. And so on. In all these cases special psychic systems are in readiness to execute the decisions. We can easily imagine that the number of these attitudes is legion. The individual attitudes are certainly as inexhaustible as the variations of crystals, which may nevertheless be recognized as belonging to one or another system. But just as crystals show basic uniformities which are relatively simple, these attitudes show certain fundamental peculiarities which allow us to assign them to definite groups.

933   From earliest times attempts have been made to classify individuals according to types, and so to bring order into the chaos. The oldest attempts known to us were made by oriental astrologers who devised the so-called trigons of the four elements—air, water, earth, and fire. The air trigon in the horoscope consists of the three aerial signs of the zodiac, Aquarius, Gemini, Libra; the fire trigon is made up of Aries, Leo, Sagittarius. According to this age-old view, whoever is born in these trigons shares in their aerial or fiery nature and will have a corresponding temperament and fate. Closely connected with this ancient cosmological scheme is the physiological typology of antiquity, the division into four temperaments corresponding to the four humours. What was first represented by the signs of the zodiac was later expressed in the physiological language of Greek medicine, giving us the classification into the phlegmatic, sanguine, choleric, and melancholic. These are simply designations for the secretions of the body. As is well known, this typology lasted at least seventeen hundred years. As for the astrological type theory, to the astonishment of the enlightened it still remains intact today, and is even enjoying a new vogue.

934   This historical retrospect may serve to assure us that our

modern attempts to formulate a theory of types are by no means new and unprecedented, even though our scientific conscience does not permit us to revert to these old, intuitive ways of thinking. We must find our own answer to this problem, an answer which satisfies the need of science. And here we meet the chief difficulty of the problem of types—that is, the question of standards or criteria. The astrological criterion was simple and objective: it was given by the constellations at birth. As to the way characterological qualities could be correlated with the zodiacal signs and the planets, this is a question which reaches back into the grey mists of prehistory and remains unanswerable. The Greek classification according to the four physiological temperaments took as its criteria the appearance and behaviour of the individual, exactly as we do today in the case of physiological typology. But where shall we seek our criterion for a psychological theory of types?

935 Let us return to the example of the four people who had to cross a brook. How and from what standpoints are we to classify their habitual motivations? One person does it for fun, another does it because not to do it is more troublesome, a third doesn't do it because he has second thoughts, and so on. The list of possibilities seems both endless and useless for purposes of classification.

936 I do not know how other people would set about this task. I can only tell you how I myself have tackled it, and I must bow to the charge that my way of solving the problem is the outcome of my personal prejudice. This objection is so entirely true that I would not know how to defend myself. I can only point happily to old Columbus, who, following his subjective assumptions, a false hypothesis, and a route abandoned by modern navigation, nevertheless discovered America. Whatever we look at, and however we look at it, we see only through our own eyes. For this reason science is never made by one man, but many. The individual merely offers his own contribution, and it is only in this sense that I dare to speak of *my* way of seeing things.

937 My profession has always obliged me to take account of the peculiarities of individuals, and the special circumstance that in the course of I don't know how many years I have had to treat innumerable married couples and have been faced

with the task of making husband and wife plausible to each other has emphasized the need to establish certain average truths. How many times, for instance, have I not had to say: "Look here, your wife has a very active nature, and it cannot be expected that her whole life should centre on housekeeping." That is a sort of statistical truth, and it holds the beginnings of a type theory: there are active natures and passive natures. But this time-worn truth did not satisfy me. My next attempt was to say that some persons are reflective and others are unreflective, because I had observed that many apparently passive natures are in reality not so much passive as given to forethought. They first consider a situation and then act, and because they do this habitually they miss opportunities where immediate action without reflection is called for, thus coming to be prejudged as passive. The persons who did not reflect always seemed to me to jump headfirst into a situation without any forethought, only to reflect afterwards that they had perhaps landed themselves in a swamp. Thus they could be considered "unreflective," and this seemed a more appropriate word than "active." Forethought is in certain cases a very important form of activity, a responsible course of action as compared with the unthinking, short-lived zeal of the mere busybody. But I soon discovered that the hesitation of the one was by no means always forethought, and that the quick action of the other was not necessarily want of reflection. The hesitation equally often arises from a habitual timidity, or at least from a customary shrinking back as if faced with too great a task; while immediate action is frequently made possible by a predominating self-confidence in relation to the object. This observation caused me to formulate these typical differences in the following way: there is a whole class of men who, at the moment of reaction to a given situation, at first draw back a little as if with an unvoiced "No," and only after that are able to react; and there is another class who, in the same situation, come out with an immediate reaction, apparently quite confident that their behaviour is self-evidently right. The former class would therefore be characterized by a negative relation to the object, and the latter by a positive one.

938   The former class corresponds to the *introverted* and the second to the *extraverted* attitude. But these two terms in

themselves signify as little as the discovery of Molière's *bourgeois gentilhomme* that he ordinarily spoke in prose. They acquire meaning and value only when we know all the other characteristics that go with the type.

939   One cannot be introverted or extraverted without being so in every respect. For example, to be "introverted" means that everything in the psyche happens as it must happen according to the law of the introvert's nature. Were that not so, the statement that a certain individual is "introverted" would be as irrelevant as the statement that he is six feet tall, or that he has brown hair, or is brachycephalic. These statements contain no more than the facts they express. The term "introverted" is incomparably more exacting. It means that the consciousness as well as the unconscious of the introvert must have certain definite qualities, that his general behaviour, his relation to people, and even the course of his life show certain typical characteristics.

940   Introversion or extraversion, as a typical attitude, means an essential bias which conditions the whole psychic process, establishes the habitual mode of reaction, and thus determines not only the style of behaviour but also the quality of subjective experience. Not only that, it determines the kind of compensation the unconscious will produce.

941   Once we have established the habitual mode of reaction it is bound to hit the mark to a certain extent, because habit is, so to speak, the central switchboard from which outward behaviour is regulated and by which specific experiences are shaped. A certain kind of behaviour brings corresponding results, and the subjective understanding of these results gives rise to experiences which in turn influence our behaviour, in accordance with the saying "Every man is the maker of his own fate."

942   While there can be little doubt that the habitual mode of reaction brings us to the central point, the delicate question remains as to whether or not we have satisfactorily characterized it by the term "introverted" or "extraverted." There can be a honest difference of opinion about this even among those with an intimate knowledge of this special field. In my book on types I have put together everything I could find in support of my views, though I expressly stated that I do not imagine mine to be the only true or possible typology.

534

943 The contrast between introversion and extraversion is simple enough, but simple formulations are unfortunately the most open to doubt. They all too easily cover up the actual complexities and so deceive us. I speak here from my own experience, for scarcely had I published the first formulation of my criteria[2] when I discovered to my dismay that somehow or other I had been taken in by them. Something was amiss. I had tried to explain too much in too simple a way, as often happens in the first joy of discovery.

944 What struck me now was the undeniable fact while people may be classed as introverts or extraverts, this does not account for the tremendous differences between individuals in either class. So great, indeed, are these differences that I was forced to doubt whether I had observed correctly in the first place. It took nearly ten years of observation and comparison to clear up this doubt.

945 The question as to where the tremendous differences among individuals of the same type came from entangled me in unforeseen difficulties which for a long time I was unable to master. To observe and recognize the differences gave me comparatively little trouble, the root of my difficulties being now, as before, the problem of criteria. How was I to find suitable terms for the characteristic differences? Here I realized for the first time how young psychology really is. It is still little more than a chaos of arbitrary opinions and dogmas, produced for the most part in the study or consulting room by spontaneous generation from the isolated and Jove-like brains of learned professors, with complete lack of agreement. Without wishing to be irreverent, I cannot refrain from confronting the professor of psychology with, say, the psychology of women, of the Chinese, or of the Australian aborigines. Our psychology must get down to brass tacks, otherwise we simply remain stuck in the Middle Ages.

946 I realized that no sound criteria were to be found in the chaos of contemporary psychology, that they had first to be created, not out of thin air, but on the basis of the invaluable preparatory work done by many men whose names no history of psychology will pass over in silence.

947 Within the limits of a lecture I cannot possibly mention all the separate observations that led me to pick out certain

[2] Supra, pars. 858ff.

psychic functions as criteria for the differences under discussion. I will only state very broadly what the essential differences are, so far as I have been able to ascertain them. An introvert, for example, does not simply draw back and hesitate before the object, but he does so in a quite definite way. Moreover he does not behave just like every other introvert, but again in a way peculiar to himself. Just as the lion strikes down his enemy or his prey with his fore-paw, in which his specific strength resides, and not with his tail like the crocodile, so our habitual mode of reaction is normally characterized by the use of our most reliable and efficient function, which is an expression of our particular strength. However, this does not prevent us from reacting occasionally in a way that reveals our specific weakness. According to which function predominates, we shall seek out certain situations while avoiding others, and shall thus have experiences specific to ourselves and different from those of other people. An intelligent man will adapt to the world through his intelligence, and not like a sixth-rate pugilist, even though now and then, in a fit of rage, he may make use of his fists. In the struggle for existence and adaptation everyone instinctively uses his most developed function, which thus becomes the criterion of his habitual mode of reaction.

948   How are we to sum up these functions under general concepts, so that they can be distinguished from the welter of merely individual events? A rough typization of this kind has long since existed in social life, in the figures of the peasant, the worker, the artist, the scholar, the fighter, and so forth, or in the various professions. But this sort of typization has little or nothing to do with psychology, for, as a well-known savant once maliciously remarked, there are certain scholars who are no more than "intellectual porters."

949   A type theory must be more subtle. It is not enough, for example, to speak of intelligence, for this is too general and too vague a concept. Almost any kind of behaviour can be called intelligent if it works smoothly, quickly, effectively and to a purpose. Intelligence, like stupidity, is not a function but a modality; the word tells us no more than *how* a function is working, not *what* is functioning. The same holds true of moral and aesthetic criteria. We must be able to designate what it is that functions outstandingly in the individual's habitual way

of reacting. We are thus forced to revert to something that at first glance looks alarmingly like the old faculty psychology of the eighteenth century. In reality, however, we are only returning to ideas current in daily speech, perfectly accessible and comprehensible to everyone. When, for instance, I speak of "thinking," it is only the philosopher who does not know what it means; no layman will find it incomprehensible. He uses the word every day, and always in the same general sense, though it is true he would be at a loss if suddenly called upon to give an unequivocal definition of thinking. The same is true of "memory" or "feeling." However difficult it is to define these purely psychological concepts scientifically, they are easily intelligible in current speech. Language is a storehouse of concrete images; hence concepts which are too abstract and nebulous do not easily take root in it, or quickly die out again for lack of contact with reality. But thinking and feeling are such insistent realities that every language above the primitive level has absolutely unmistakable expressions for them. We can therefore be sure that these expressions coincide with quite definite psychic facts, no matter what the scientific definition of these complex facts may be. Everyone knows, for example, what consciousness means, and nobody can doubt that it coincides with a definite psychic condition, however far science may be from defining it satisfactorily.

950 And so it came about that I simply took the concepts expressed in current speech as designations for the corresponding psychic functions, and used them as my criteria in judging the differences between persons of the same attitude-type. For instance, I took thinking, as it is generally understood, because I was struck by the fact that many people habitually do more thinking than others, and accordingly give more weight to thought when making important decisions. They also use their thinking in order to understand the world and adapt to it, and whatever happens to them is subjected to consideration and reflection or at least subordinated to some principle sanctioned by thought. Other people conspicuously neglect thinking in favour of emotional factors, that is, of feeling. They invariably follow a policy dictated by feeling, and it takes an extraordinary situation to make them reflect. They form an unmistakable contrast to the other type, and the dif-

ference is most striking when the two are business partners or
are married to each other. It should be noted that a person
may give preference to thinking whether he be extraverted or
introverted, but he will use it only in the way that is characteristic of his attitude-type, and the same is true of feeling.

951   The predominance of one or the other of these functions
does not explain all the differences that occur. What I call the
thinking and feeling types comprise two groups of persons who
again have something in common which I cannot designate except by the word *rationality*. No one will dispute that thinking
is essentially rational, but when we come to feeling, weighty
objections may be raised which I would not like to brush aside.
On the contrary, I freely admit that this problem of feeling has
been one that has caused me much brain-racking. However, as
I do not want to overload my lecture with the various existing
definitions of this concept, I shall confine myself briefly to my
own view. The chief difficulty is that the word "feeling" can be
used in all sorts of different ways. This is especially true in
German, but is noticeable to some extent in English and
French as well. First of all, then, we must make a careful distinction between feeling and *sensation*, which is a sensory function. And in the second place we must recognize that a feeling
of regret is something quite different from a "feeling" that the
weather will change or that the price of our aluminum shares
will go up. I have therefore proposed using *feeling* as a proper
term in the first example, and dropping it—so far as its psychological usage is concerned—in the second. Here we should
speak of *sensation* when sense impressions are involved, and
of *intuition* if we are dealing with a kind of perception which
cannot be traced back directly to conscious sensory experience.
Hence I define sensation as perception via conscious sensory
functions, and intuition as perception via the unconscious.

952   Obviously we could argue until Doomsday about the fitness of these definitions, but ultimately it is only a question of
terminology. It is as if we were debating whether to call a certain animal a leopard or a panther, when all we need to know
is what name we are giving to what. Psychology is virgin territory, and its terminology has still to be fixed. As we know,
temperature can be measured according to Réaumur, Celsius,
or Fahrenheit, but we must indicate which system we are
using.

953   It is evident, then, that I take feeling as a function *per se* and distinguish it from sensation and intuition. Whoever confuses these last two functions with feeling in the strict sense is obviously not in a position to acknowledge the rationality of feeling. But once they are distinguished from feeling, it becomes quite clear that feeling values and feeling judgments—indeed, feelings in general—are not only rational but can also be as logical, consistent and discriminating as thinking. This may seem strange to the thinking type, but it is easily explained when we realize that in a person with a differentiated thinking function the feeling function is always less developed, more primitive, and therefore contaminated with other functions, these being precisely the functions which are not rational, not logical, and not discriminating or evaluating, namely, sensation and intuition. These two are by their very nature opposed to the rational functions. When we think, it is in order to judge or to reach a conclusion, and when we feel it is in order to attach a proper value to something. Sensation and intuition, on the other hand, are perceptive functions—they make us aware of what is happening, but do not interpret or evaluate it. They do not proceed selectively, according to principles, but are simply receptive to what happens. But "what happens" is essentially irrational. There is no inferential method by which it could ever be proved that there must be so and so many planets, or so and so many species of warm-blooded animals. Irrationality is a vice where thinking and feeling are called for, rationality is a vice where sensation and intuition should be trusted.

954   Now there are many people whose habitual reactions are irrational because they are based either on sensation or on intuition. They cannot be based on both at once, because sensation is just as antagonistic to intuition as thinking is to feeling. When I try to assure myself with my eyes and ears of what is actually happening, I cannot at the same time give way to dreams and fantasies about what lies around the corner. As this is just what the intuitive type must do in order to give the necessary free play to his unconscious or to the object, it is easy to see that the sensation type is at the opposite pole to the intuitive. Unfortunately, time does not allow me to go into the interesting variations which the extraverted or introverted attitude produces in the irrational types.

955   Instead, I would like to add a word about the effects regularly produced on the other functions when preference is given to one function. We know that a man can never be everything at once, never quite complete. He always develops certain qualities at the expense of others, and wholeness is never attained. But what happens to those functions which are not consciously brought into daily use and are not developed by exercise? They remain in a more or less primitive and infantile state, often only half conscious, or even quite unconscious. These relatively undeveloped functions constitute a specific inferiority which is characteristic of each type and is an integral part of his total character. The one-sided emphasis on thinking is always accompanied by an inferiority of feeling, and differentiated sensation is injurious to intuition and vice versa.

956   Whether a function is differentiated or not can easily be recognized from its strength, stability, consistency, reliability, and adaptedness. But inferiority in a function is often not so easy to recognize or to describe. An essential criterion is its lack of self-sufficiency and consequent dependence on people and circumstances, its disposing us to moods and crotchetiness, its unreliable use, its suggestible and labile character. The inferior function always puts us at a disadvantage because we cannot direct it, but are rather its victims.

957   Since I must restrict myself here to a mere sketch of the ideas underlying a psychological theory of types, I must forgo a detailed description of each type. The total result of my work in this field up to the present is the establishing of two general attitude-types, extraversion and introversion, and four function-types, thinking, feeling, sensation, and intuition. Each of these function-types varies according to the general attitude and thus eight variants are produced.

958   I have often been asked, almost accusingly, why I speak of four functions and not of more or fewer. That there are exactly four was a result I arrived at on purely empirical grounds. But as the following consideration will show, these four together produce a kind of totality. Sensation establishes what is actually present, thinking enables us to recognize its meaning, feeling tells us its value, and intuition points to possibilities as to whence it came and whither it is going in a given situation. In this way we can orient ourselves with respect to

the immediate world as completely as when we locate a place geographically by latitude and longitude. The four functions are somewhat like the four points of the compass; they are just as arbitrary and just as indispensable. Nothing prevents our shifting the cardinal points as many degrees as we like in one direction or the other, or giving them different names. It is merely a question of convention and intelligibility.

959 But one thing I must confess: I would not for anything dispense with this compass on my psychological voyages of discovery. This is not merely for the obvious, all-too-human reason that everyone is in love with his own ideas. I value the type theory for the objective reason that it provides a system of comparison and orientation which makes possible something that has long been lacking, a critical psychology.

PSYCHOLOGICAL TYPOLOGY[1]

960   Ever since the early days of science, it has been a notable endeavour of the reflective intellect to interpose gradations between the two poles of the absolute similarity and dissimilarity of human beings. This resulted in a number of types, or "temperaments" as they were then called, which classified similarities and dissimilarities into regular categories. The Greek philosopher Empedocles attempted to impose order on the chaos of natural phenomena by dividing them into the four elements: earth, water, air, and fire. It was above all the physicians of ancient times who applied this principle of order, in conjunction with the related doctrine of the four qualities, dry, moist, cold, warm, to human beings, and thus tried to reduce the bewildering diversity of mankind to orderly groups. Of these physicians one of the most important was Galen, whose use of these teachings influenced medical science and the treatment of the sick for nearly seventeen hundred years. The very names of the Galenic temperaments betray their origin in the pathology of the four "humours." *Melancholic* denotes a preponderance of black bile, *phlegmatic* a preponderance of phlegm or mucus (the Greek word *phlegma* means fire, and phlegm was regarded as the end-product of inflammation), *sanguine* a preponderance of blood, and *choleric* a preponderance of choler, or yellow bile.

961   Our modern conception of "temperament" has certainly become much more psychological, since in the course of man's development over the last two thousand years the "soul" has freed itself from any conceivable connection with cold agues and fevers, or secretions of mucus and bile. Not even the doc-

[1] [First published as "Psychologische Typologie" in *Süddeutsche Monatshefte*, XXXIII:5 (Feb. 1936), 264–72. Reprinted in *Gesammelte Werke*, 6, Appendix, pp. 587ff., from which the present version is newly translated.—EDITORS.]

tors of today would equate a temperament, that is, a certain kind of emotional state or excitability, directly with the constitution of the blood or lymph, although their profession and their exclusive approach to human beings from the side of physical illness tempt them, more often than the layman, to regard the psyche as an end-product dependent on the physiology of the glands. The "humours" of present-day medicine are no longer the old body-secretions, but the more subtle hormones, which influence "temperament" to an outstanding degree, if we define this as the sum-total of emotional reactions. The whole make-up of the body, its constitution in the broadest sense, has in fact a very great deal to do with the psychological temperament, so much that we cannot blame the doctors if they regard psychic phenomena as largely dependent on the body. Somewhere the psyche is living body, and the living body is animated matter; somehow and somewhere there is an undiscoverable unity of psyche and body which would need investigating psychically as well as physically; in other words, this unity must be as dependent on the body as it is on the psyche so far as the investigator is concerned. The materialism of the nineteenth century gave the body first place and relegated the psyche to the rank of something secondary and derived, allowing it no more substantiality than that of a so-called "epiphenomenon." What proved to be a good working hypothesis, namely, that psychic phenomena are conditioned by physical processes, became a philosophical presumption with the advent of materialism. Any serious science of the living organism will reject this presumption; for on the one hand it will constantly bear in mind that living matter is an as yet unsolved mystery, and on the other hand it will be objective enough to recognize that for us there is a completely unbridgeable gulf between physical and psychic phenomena, so that the psychic realm is no less mysterious than the physical.

962   The materialistic presumption became possible only in recent times, after man's conception of the psyche had, in the course of many centuries, emancipated itself from the old view and developed in an increasingly abstract direction. The ancients could still see body and psyche together, as an undivided unity, because they were closer to that primitive world where no moral rift yet ran through the personality, and the

pagan could still feel himself indivisibly one, childishly innocent and unburdened by responsibility. The ancient Egyptians
could still enjoy the naïve luxury of a negative confession of
sin: "I have not let any man go hungry. I have not made anyone weep. I have not committed murder," and so on. The
Homeric heroes wept, laughed, raged, outwitted and killed
each other in a world where these things were taken as natural
and self-evident by men and gods alike, and the Olympians
amused themselves by passing their days in a state of amaran-
thine irresponsibility.

963   It was on this archaic level that pre-philosophical man
lived and experienced the world. He was entirely in the grip
of his emotions. All passions that made his blood boil and his
heart pound, that accelerated his breathing or took his breath
away, that "turned his bowels to water"—all this was a manifestation of the "soul." Therefore he localized the soul in the
region of the diaphragm (in Greek *phren*, which also means
mind)[2] and the heart. It was only with the first philosophers
that the seat of reason began to be assigned to the head. There
are still Negroes today whose "thoughts" are localized principally in the belly, and the Pueblo Indians "think" with their
hearts—"only madmen think with their heads," they say.[3] On
this level consciousness is essentially passion and the experience of oneness. Yet, serene and tragic at once, it was just this
archaic man who, having started to think, invented that dichotomy which Nietzsche laid at the door of Zarathustra: the
discovery of pairs of opposites, the division into odd and even,
above and below, good and evil. It was the work of the old
Pythagoreans, and it was their doctrine of moral responsibility
and the grave metaphysical consequences of sin that gradually,
in the course of the centuries, percolated through to all strata
of the population, chiefly owing to the spread of the Orphic
and Pythagorean mysteries. Plato even used the parable of the
white and black horses[4] to illustrate the intractability and
polarity of the human psyche, and, still earlier, the mysteries
proclaimed the doctrine of the good rewarded in the Here-

---

[2] [As Onians (*The Origins of European Thought*, pp. 26ff.) has shown, *phrenes*
in Homer were the lungs.—EDITORS.]

[3] [Jung, *Memories, Dreams, Reflections*, p. 248.]

[4] [*Phaedrus* 246, 253–54.]

after and of the wicked punished in hell. These teachings cannot be dismissed as the mystical humbug of "backwoods" philosophers, as Nietzsche claimed, or as so much sectarian cant, for already in the sixth century B.C. Pythagoreanism was something like a state religion throughout Graecia Magna. Also, the ideas underlying its mysteries never died out, but underwent a philosophical renaissance in the second century B.C., when they exercised the strongest influence on the Alexandrian world of thought. Their collision with Old Testament prophecy then led to what one can call the beginnings of Christianity as a world religion.

964   From Hellenistic syncretism there now arose a classification of man into types which was entirely alien to the "humoral" psychology of Greek medicine. In the philosophical sense, it established gradations between the Parmenidean poles of light and darkness, of above and below. It classified men into *hylikoi, psychikoi,* and *pneumatikoi*—material, psychic, and spiritual beings. This classification is not, of course, a scientific formulation of similarities and dissimilarities; it is a critical system of values based not on the behaviour and outward appearance of man as a phenotype, but on definitions of an ethical, mystical, and philosophic kind. Although it is not exactly a "Christian" conception it nevertheless forms an integral part of early Christianity at the time of St. Paul. Its very existence is incontrovertible proof of the split that had occurred in the original unity of man as a being entirely in the grip of his emotions. Before this, he was merely alive and there, the plaything of experience, incapable of any reflective analysis concerning his origins and his destination. Now, suddenly, he found himself confronted by three fateful factors and endowed with body, soul, and spirit, to each of which he had moral obligations. Presumably it was already decided at birth whether he would pass his life in the hylic or the pneumatic state, or in the indeterminate centre between the two. The ingrained dichotomy of the Greek mind had now become acute, with the result that the accent shifted significantly to the psychic and spiritual, which was unavoidably split off from the hylic realm of the body. All the highest and ultimate goals lay in man's moral destination, in a spiritual, supramundane end-state, and the separation of the hylic realm broadened into a

cleavage between world and spirit. Thus the original, suave wisdom expressed in the Pythagorean pairs of opposites became a passionate moral conflict. Nothing, however, is so apt to challenge our self-awareness and alertness as being at war with oneself. One can hardly think of any other or more effective means of waking humanity out of the irresponsible and innocent half-sleep of the primitive mentality and bringing it to a state of conscious responsibility.

965   This process is called cultural development. It is, at any rate, a development of man's powers of discrimination and capacity for judgment, and of consciousness in general. With the increase of knowledge and enhanced critical faculties the foundations were laid for the whole subsequent development of the human mind in terms of intellectual achievement. The particular mental product that far surpassed all the achievements of the ancient world was science. It closed the rift between man and nature in the sense that, although he was separated from nature, science enabled him to find his rightful place again in the natural order. His special metaphysical position, however, had to be jettisoned—so far as it was not secured by belief in the traditional religion—whence arose the notorious conflict between "faith and knowledge." At all events, science brought about a splendid rehabilitation of matter, and in this respect materialism may even be regarded as an act of historical justice.

966   But one absolutely essential field of experience, the human psyche itself, remained for a very long time the preserve of metaphysics, although increasingly serious attempts were made after the Enlightment to open it up to scientific investigation. They began, tentatively, with the sense perceptions, and gradually ventured into the domain of associations. This line of research paved the way for experimental psychology, and it culminated in the "physiological psychology" of Wundt. A more descriptive kind of psychology, with which the medical men soon made contact, developed in France. Its chief exponents were Taine, Ribot, and Janet. It was characteristic of this scientific approach that it broke down the psyche into particular mechanisms or processes. In face of these attempts, there were some who advocated what we today would call a "holistic" approach—the systematic observation of the psyche

as a whole. It seems as if this trend originated in a certain type of biography, more particularly the kind that an earlier age, which also had its good points, used to describe as "curious lives." In this connection I think of Justinus Kerner and his *Seeress of Prevorst*, and the case of the elder Blumhardt and his medium Gottliebin Dittus.[5] To be historically fair, however, I should not forget the medieval *Acta Sanctorum*.[6]

967   This line of research has been continued in more recent investigations associated with the names of William James, Freud, and Theodore Flournoy. James and his friend Flournoy, a Swiss psychologist, made an attempt to describe the whole phenomenology of the psyche and also to view it as a totality. Freud, too, as a doctor, took as his point of departure the wholeness and indivisibility of the human personality, though, in keeping with the spirit of the age, he restricted himself to the investigation of instinctive mechanisms and individual processes. He also narrowed the picture of man to the wholeness of an essentially "bourgeois" collective person, and this necessarily led to philosophically onesided interpretations. Freud, unfortunately, succumbed to the medical man's temptation to trace everything psychic to the body, in the manner of the old "humoral" psychologists, not without rebellious gestures at those metaphysical preserves of which he had a holy dread.

968   Unlike Freud, who after a proper psychological start reverted to the ancient assumption of the sovereignty of the physical constitution, trying to turn everything back in theory into instinctual processes conditioned by the body, I start with the assumption of the sovereignty of the psyche. Since body and psyche somewhere form a unity, although in their manifest natures they are so utterly different, we cannot but attribute to the one as to the other a substantiality of its own. So long as we have no way of knowing that unity, there is no alternative but to investigate them separately and, for the present, treat them as though they were independent of each other, at least in their structure. That they are not so, we can see for ourselves every day. But if we were to stop at that, we

5 [Zündel, *Pfarrer J. C. Blumhardt: Ein Lebensbild.*]
6 [Görres, *Die christliche Mystik.*]

would never be in a position to make out anything about the psyche at all.

969   Now if we assume the sovereignty of the psyche, we exempt ourselves from the—at present—insoluble task of reducing everything psychic to something definitely physical. We can then take the manifestations of the psyche as expressions of its intrinsic being, and try to establish certain conformities or types. So when I speak of a psychological typology, I mean by this the formulation of the structural elements of the psyche and not a description of the psychic emanations of a particular type of constitution. This is covered by, for instance, Kretschmer's researches into body-structure and character.

970   I have given a detailed description of a purely psychological typology in my book *Psychological Types*. My investigation was based on twenty years of work as a doctor, which brought me into contact with people of all classes from all the great nations. When one begins as a young doctor, one's head is still full of clinical pictures and diagnoses. In the course of the years, impressions of quite another kind accumulate. One is struck by the enormous diversity of human individuals, by the chaotic profusion of individual cases, the special circumstances of whose lives and whose special characters produce clinical pictures that, even supposing one still felt any desire to do so, can be squeezed into the straitjacket of a diagnosis only by force. The fact that the disturbance can be given such and such a name appears completely irrelevant beside the overwhelming impression one has that all clinical pictures are so many mimetic or histrionic demonstrations of certain definite character traits. The pathological problem upon which everything turns has virtually nothing to do with the clinical picture, but is essentially an expression of character. Even the complexes, the "nuclear elements" of a neurosis, are beside the point, being mere concomitants of a certain characterological disposition. This can be seen most easily in the relation of the patient to his parental family. He is, let us say, one of four siblings, is neither the eldest nor the youngest, has had the same education and conditioning as the others. Yet he is sick and they are sound. The anamnesis shows that a whole series of influences to which the others were exposed as well as he, and

from which indeed they all suffered, had a pathological effect on him alone—at least to all appearances. In reality these influences were not aetiological factors in his case either, but prove to be false explanations. The real cause of the neurosis lies in the peculiar way he responded to and assimilated the influences emanating from the environment.

971 By comparing many such cases it gradually became clear to me that there must be two fundamentally different general attitudes which would divide human beings into two groups— provided the whole of humanity consisted of highly differentiated individuals. Since this is obviously not the case, one can only say that this difference of attitude becomes plainly observable only when we are confronted with a comparatively well-differentiated personality; in other words, it becomes of practical importance only after a certain degree of differentiation has been reached. Pathological cases of this kind are almost always people who deviate from the familial type and, in consequence, no longer find sufficient security in their inherited instinctual foundation. Weak instincts are one of the prime causes of the development of an habitual one-sided attitude, though in the last resort it is conditioned or reinforced by heredity.

972 I have called these two fundamentally different attitudes *extraversion* and *introversion*. Extraversion is characterized by interest in the external object, responsiveness, and a ready acceptance of external happenings, a desire to influence and be influenced by events, a need to join in and get "with it," the capacity to endure bustle and noise of every kind, and actually find them enjoyable, constant attention to the surrounding world, the cultivation of friends and acquaintances, none too carefully selected, and finally by the great importance attached to the figure one cuts, and hence by a strong tendency to make a show of oneself. Accordingly, the extravert's philosophy of life and his ethics are as a rule of a highly collective nature with a strong streak of altruism, and his conscience is in large measure dependent on public opinion. Moral misgivings arise mainly when "other people know." His religious convictions are determined, so to speak, by majority vote.

973 The actual subject, the extravert as a subjective entity, is, so far as possible, shrouded in darkness. He hides it from him-

self under veils of unconsciousness. The disinclination to submit his own motives to critical examination is very pronounced. He has no secrets he has not long since shared with others. Should something unmentionable nevertheless befall him, he prefers to forget it. Anything that might tarnish the parade of optimism and positivism is avoided. Whatever he thinks, intends, and does is displayed with conviction and warmth.

974   The psychic life of this type of person is enacted, as it were, outside himself, in the environment. He lives in and through others; all self-communings give him the creeps. Dangers lurk there which are better drowned out by noise. If he should ever have a "complex," he finds refuge in the social whirl and allows himself to be assured several times a day that everything is in order. Provided he is not too much of a busybody, too pushing, and too superficial, he can be a distinctly useful member of the community.

975   In this short essay I have to content myself with an allusive sketch. It is intended merely to give the reader some idea of what extraversion is like, something he can bring into relationship with his own knowledge of human nature. I have purposely started with a description of extraversion because this attitude is familiar to everyone; the extravert not only lives in this attitude, but parades it before his fellows on principle. Moreover it accords with certain popular ideals and moral requirements.

976   *Introversion*, on the other hand, being directed not to the object but to the subject, and not being oriented by the object, is not so easy to put into perspective. The introvert is not forthcoming, he is as though in continual retreat before the object. He holds aloof from external happenings, does not join in, has a distinct dislike of society as soon as he finds himself among too many people. In a large gathering he feels lonely and lost. The more crowded it is, the greater becomes his resistance. He is not in the least "with it," and has no love of enthusiastic get-togethers. He is not a good mixer. What he does, he does in his own way, barricading himself against influences from outside. He is apt to appear awkward, often seeming inhibited, and it frequently happens that, by a certain brusqueness of manner, or by his glum unapproachability, or some kind of malapropism, he causes unwitting offence to peo-

ple. His better qualities he keeps to himself, and generally does everything he can to dissemble them. He is easily mistrustful, self-willed, often suffers from inferiority feelings and for this reason is also envious. His apprehensiveness of the object is not due to fear, but to the fact that it seems to him negative, demanding, overpowering or even menacing. He therefore suspects all kinds of bad motives, has an everlasting fear of making a fool of himself, is usually very touchy and surrounds himself with a barbed wire entanglement so dense and impenetrable that finally he himself would rather do anything than sit behind it. He confronts the world with an elaborate defensive system compounded of scrupulosity, pedantry, frugality, cautiousness, painful conscientiousness, stiff-lipped rectitude, politeness, and open-eyed distrust. His picture of the world lacks rosy hues, as he is over-critical and finds a hair in every soup. Under normal conditions he is pessimistic and worried, because the world and human beings are not in the least good but crush him, so he never feels accepted and taken to their bosom. Yet he himself does not accept the world either, at any rate not outright, for everything has first to be judged by his own critical standards. Finally only those things are accepted which, for various subjective reasons, he can turn to his own account.

977   For him self-communings are a pleasure. His own world is a safe harbour, a carefully tended and walled-in garden, closed to the public and hidden from prying eyes. His own company is the best. He feels at home in his world, where the only changes are made by himself. His best work is done with his own resources, on his own initiative, and in his own way. If ever he succeeds, after long and often wearisome struggles, in assimilating something alien to himself, he is capable of turning it to excellent account. Crowds, majority views, public opinion, popular enthusiasm never convince him of anything, but merely make him creep still deeper into his shell.

978   His relations with other people become warm only when safety is guaranteed, and when he can lay aside his defensive distrust. All too often he cannot, and consequently the number of friends and acquaintances is very restricted. Thus the psychic life of this type is played out wholly within. Should any difficulties and conflicts arise in this inner world, all doors

and windows are shut tight. The introvert shuts himself up with his complexes until he ends in complete isolation.

979   In spite of these peculiarities the introvert is by no means a social loss. His retreat into himself is not a final renunciation of the world, but a search for quietude, where alone it is possible for him to make his contribution to the life of the community. This type of person is the victim of numerous misunderstandings—not unjustly, for he actually invites them. Nor can he be acquitted of the charge of taking a secret delight in mystification, and that being misunderstood gives him a certain satisfaction, since it reaffirms his pessimistic outlook. That being so, it is easy to see why he is accused of being cold, proud, obstinate, selfish, conceited, cranky, and what not, and why he is constantly admonished that devotion to the goals of society, clubbableness, imperturbable urbanity, and selfless trust in the powers-that-be are true virtues and the marks of a sound and vigorous life.

980   The introvert is well enough aware that such virtues exist, and that somewhere, perhaps—only not in his circle of acquaintances—there are divinely inspired people who enjoy undiluted possession of these ideal qualities. But his self-criticism and his awareness of his own motives have long since disabused him of the illusion that he himself would be capable of such virtues; and his mistrustful gaze, sharpened by anxiety, constantly enables him to detect on his fellow men the ass's ear sticking up from under the lion's mane. The world and men are for him a disturbance and a danger, affording no valid standard by which he could ultimately orient himself. What alone is valid for him is his subjective world, which he sometimes believes, in moments of delusion, to be the objective one. We could easily charge these people with the worst kind of subjectivism, indeed with morbid individualism, if it were certain beyond a doubt that only one objective world existed. But this truth, if such it be, is not axiomatic; it is merely a half truth, the other half of which is the fact that the world *also* is as it is seen by human beings, and in the last resort by the individual. There is simply no world at all without the knowing subject. This, be it never so small and inconspicuous, is always the other pier supporting the bridge of the phenomenal world. The appeal to the subject therefore has the same validity as the

appeal to the so-called objective world, for it is grounded on psychic reality itself. But this is a reality with its own peculiar laws which are not of a secondary nature.

981   The two attitudes, extraversion and introversion, are opposing modes that make themselves felt not least in the history of human thought. The problems to which they give rise were very largely anticipated by Friedrich Schiller, and they underlie his *Letters on the Aesthetic Education of Man*.[7] But since the concept of the unconscious was still unknown to him, he was unable to reach a satisfactory solution. Moreover philosophers, who would be the best equipped to go more closely into this question, do not like having to submit their thinking function to a thorough psychological criticism, and therefore hold aloof from such discussions. It should, however, be obvious that the intrinsic polarity of such an attitude exerts a very great influence on the philosopher's own point of view.

982   For the extravert the object is interesting and attractive *a priori*, as is the subject, or psychic reality, for the introvert. We could therefore use the expression "numinal accent" for this fact, by which I mean that for the extravert the quality of positive significance and value attaches primarily to the object, so that it plays the predominant, determining, and decisive role in all psychic processes from the start, just as the subject does for the introvert.

983   But the numinal accent does not decide only between subject and object; it also selects the conscious function of which the individual makes the principal use. I distinguish four functions: *thinking, feeling, sensation,* and *intuition.* The essential function of sensation is to establish that something exists, thinking tells us what it means, feeling what its value is, and intuition surmises whence it comes and whither it goes. Sensation and intuition I call irrational functions, because they are both concerned simply with what happens and with actual or potential realities. Thinking and feeling, being discriminative functions, are rational. Sensation, the *fonction du réel*, rules out any simultaneous intuitive activity, since the latter is not concerned with the present but is rather a sixth sense for hidden possibilities, and therefore should not allow itself to be

---

[7] Supra, pars. 101 ff.

unduly influenced by existing reality. In the same way, thinking is opposed to feeling, because thinking should not be influenced or deflected from its purpose by feeling values, just as feeling is usually vitiated by too much reflection. The four functions therefore form, when arranged diagrammatically, a cross with a rational axis at right angles to an irrational axis.

984   The four orienting functions naturally do not contain everything that is in the conscious psyche. Will and memory, for instance, are not included. The reason for this is that the differentiation of the four orienting functions is, essentially, an empirical consequence of typical differences in the functional attitude. There are people for whom the numinal accent falls on sensation, on the perception of actualities, and elevates it into the sole determining and all-overriding principle. These are the fact-minded men, in whom intellectual judgment, feeling, and intuition are driven into the background by the paramount importance of actual facts. When the accent falls on thinking, judgment is reserved as to what significance should be attached to the facts in question. And on this significance will depend the way in which the individual deals with the facts. If feeling is numinal, then his adaptation will depend entirely on the feeling value he attributes to them. Finally, if the numinal accent falls on intuition, actual reality counts only in so far as it seems to harbour possibilities which then become the supreme motivating force, regardless of the way things actually are in the present.

985   The localization of the numinal accent thus gives rise to four function-types, which I encountered first of all in my relations with people and formulated systematically only very much later. In practice these four types are always combined with the attitude-type, that is, with extraversion or introversion, so that the functions appear in an extraverted or introverted variation. This produces a set of eight demonstrable function-types. It is naturally impossible to present the specific psychology of these types within the confines of an essay, and to go into its conscious and unconscious manifestations. I must therefore refer the interested reader to the aforementioned study.

986   It is not the purpose of a psychological typology to classify human beings into categories—this in itself would be pretty

pointless. Its purpose is rather to provide a critical psychology which will make a methodical investigation and presentation of the empirical material possible. First and foremost, it is a critical tool for the research worker, who needs definite points of view and guidelines if he is to reduce the chaotic profusion of individual experiences to any kind of order. In this respect we could compare typology to a trigonometric net or, better still, to a crystallographic axial system. Secondly, a typology is a great help in understanding the wide variations that occur among individuals, and it also furnishes a clue to the fundamental differences in the psychological theories now current. Last but not least, it is an essential means for determining the "personal equation" of the practising psychologist, who, armed with an exact knowledge of his differentiated and inferior functions, can avoid many serious blunders in dealing with his patients.

987   The typological system I have proposed is an attempt, grounded on practical experience, to provide an explanatory basis and theoretical framework for the boundless diversity that has hitherto prevailed in the formation of psychological concepts. In a science as young as psychology, limiting definitions will sooner or later become an unavoidable necessity. Some day psychologists will have to agree upon certain basic principles secure from arbitrary interpretation if psychology is not to remain an unscientific and fortuitous conglomeration of individual opinions.

CORRELATION OF PARAGRAPH NUMBERS

CORRELATION OF PARAGRAPH NUMBERS

As the Gesammelte Werke edition of *Psychologische Typen* (1960; 2nd edn., 1967) follows a different system of paragraph numbering from the Collected Works edition, the following table gives the equivalents between the two. Paragraphs 1–7 are numbered alike in both.

Collected Works	Gesammelte Werke	Collected Works	Gesammelte Werke	Collected Works	Gesammelte Werke
CHAPTER I		47	39	84	81/82
1	1	48/49	40	85	82
		50	41	86/87	83
......	......	51	42	88	84
8–11	8	52	43	89/90	85
12/13	9	53	44	91/92	86
14	10	54	45	93*	87/88
15/16	11	55	46/47	94	89
17	12	56	48/49	95	90
18	13/14	57	50/51	96	91
19	15/16	58	52	97	92
20	17	59	53	98	93
21/22	18	60	54	99	94
23	19	61	55	100	95
24–26	20	62	56		
27	21	63	57/58	CHAPTER II	
28	22	64	59	101	96
29	23	65	59–62	102	97/98
30	24	66	63	103	98
31	25	67	64	104	99
32	26	68	65	105	100/101
33	27	69/70	66	106	102/103
34	28	71	67	107	104
35	29	72	68	108	105
36	30	73	69	109	106
37/38	31	74	70	110	107/108
39	32	75	71	111	108
40	33	76	72	112	109
41	34	77/78	73	113	109/110
42/43	35	79	74	114	111/112
44	36	80/81	75	115	113/114
45	37	82	76–79	116	115
46	38/39	83	80		

* Last sentence from 1950 Swiss edn., p. 85.

Collected Works	Gesammelte Werke	Collected Works	Gesammelte Werke	Collected Works	Gesammelte Werke
117	116	176	167	236	219
118	117	177	168	237	220
119	118	178	169	238	221
120	119/120	179	170	239	222
121/122	121	180	171	240	223
123/124	122	181/182	172	241	224
125/126	123	183	173	242	225
127	124	184	174		
128	125/126	185	175	CHAPTER IV	
129	127	186	176		
130	128	187	177/178	243	226
131	128/129	188	178	244	227
132	129	189	179	245–247	228
133	129/130	190/191	180	248	229
134	131	192	181	249	230
135	132	193	182	250	231
136	133	194	183	251–253	232
137	134	195	184	254	233
138–140	135	196–198	185	255	234
141	136	199/200	186	256	235/236
142/143	137	201	187	257	237
144	138	202/203	188	258	238
145	139	204/205	189	259	239
146	140	206	190	260	240
147/148	141	207	191	261	241–243
149	142	208	192	262	244/245
150	143	209	193	263	246
151	144	210	194	264	247
152	145	211	195–196	265	248–252
153	146	212	197	266	253
154	147	213/214	198	267/268	254
155	148	215/216	199	269	255
156	149	217	200	270	256
157	150/151	218	201	271	257
158	152	219	202	272	258
159	153	220	203	273	259
160	154	221	204	274	260
161	155	222	205		
162	156			CHAPTER V	
163	157	CHAPTER III		275	261
164	158	223/224	206	276	262
165	159	225	207–209	277	263/264
166/167	160	226/227	210	278	265/266
168	161	228/229	211	279	267
169	161/162	230	212	280	267–269
170	162	231	213	281	270/271
171	162/163	232	214	282	272–274
172/173	164	233	215	283	275
174	165	234	216/217	284	276
175	166	235	218	285	276–280

Collected Works	Gesammelte Werke	Collected Works	Gesammelte Werke	Collected Works	Gesammelte Werke
286/287	281	343	373	397/398	445
288	282	344	374/375	399/400	447
289	283	345	375	401	446
290–292	284	346	376	402	448/449
293	285	347	377	403	449
294	286	348	378	404	450
295	287–289	349	379–385	405/406	451
296	290	350	386/387	407	452
297	291–294	351	388/390	408	453
298	295	352	391–393	409	454/455
299	296	353	394	410/411	455
300	297	354	395/397	412/413	456
301	298	355	398	414/415	457
302	299	356	399	416	458–460
303	300	357	400	417	461
304	301/302	358	401	418	461/462
305	303/304	359	402–404	419/420	463
306	305/306	360	405	421	464/465
307–309	307	361	406/407	422	465
310	308	362	408–411	423/424	466
311	309	363	412–414	425	466/467
312	310	364*	415	426	468
313	311	365	416	427	469
314	312	366/367	417	428	470–473
315	313	368	418	429	474
316/317	314	369	419	430/431	475
318/319	315	370	420	432	476/477
320	316	371/372	421	433	478
321	317	373	421–423	434	479
322	318	374	423	435	480/481
323	318/319	375	424	436/437	482
324	320/321	376	425	438	483
325	322	377	425/426	439	484–486
326	323	378	427	440	487
327	324/325	379	428	441	488–490
328	326–336	380	429	442	491
329	337–347	381	430/431	443	492–495
330	348	382	431/432	444	496
331	349–354	383/384	433	445	497–501
332	355	385	434	446	502
333	356/357	386	435	447	502–510
334	358–362	387	436	448/449	511
335	363/364	388	436/437	450	512
336	365–367	389	438	451	513/514
337	367/368	390	439	452	515–517
338	369	391	440/441	453	518/519
339	370	392/393	442	454/455	520
340/341	371	394/395	443	456	521/522
342	372	396	444/445	457	523

* Quotations referred to in G. W. 6, p. 121, n. 120 added.

Collected Works	Gesammelte Werke	Collected Works	Gesammelte Werke	Collected Works	Gesammelte Werke
458	524	508	574	561	626
459	525	509	575	562	627
460	526	510	575/576	563	628/629
		511	577	564	629/632
CHAPTER VI		512	578	565	633
461/462	527	513	579	566/567	634
463	528/529	514	580/581	568	635
464	529	515	581	569	636
465	529–531	516	581/582	570/571	637
466	532	517	583	572	638
467	533/534	518	584	573/574	639
468	534–536	519	585	575	640
469	537	520	586	576	641
470	538	521	586/587	577	642-644
471	539	522	588	578	645/646
472	540	523	589	579	646
473	541	524	590	580	647/648
474	542	525	591	581	648
475	543	526/527	592	582	649
476	544	528/529	593	583	650
477	545	530	594	584	651
478	546	531	595	585	652
479	547/548	532	596	586	653
480	549	533/534	597	587	654
481	549/550	535	598	588	655
482	551	536	599/600	589	656
483	552	537	601/602	590	657
		538/539	603	591	658/659
CHAPTER VII		540	603–605	592	660
484/485	553	541	606	593	661
486	554			594	662
487	554/555	CHAPTER IX		595	663
488	555/556	542–544	607	596	663/664
489/490	557	545	608	597/598	665
491	558/559	546/547	609	599	666
492	559	548	610	600	667–669
493	560–562	549	611	601	670
494	563	550	612/613	602	671/672
495	564	551	614/615	603	673
496/497	565	552	616	604/605	674
498/499	566	553	617	606	675
500/501	567	554	618	607	676
502	568/569	555	619/620	608	677
503/504	570			609	678
		CHAPTER X		610/611	679
CHAPTER VIII		556	621	612	680
		557	622	613	681/682
505	571	558	622/623	614	683
506	572	559	624	615	684/685
507	572/573	560	625	616	686/687
				617	688

Collected Works	Gesammelte Werke	Collected Works	Gesammelte Werke	Collected Works	Gesammelte Werke
618/619	689	CHAPTER XI		719	866
620	691	672	741	720	867
621	692	673	742	721	868
622	692–694	674	743	722	869
623	695	675	744	723–725	801
624/625	696	676	745	726	802
626	697/698	677	746	727	803
627	699	678	747	728	804
628	700	679	748	729	805/806
629	701	680	749	730	809
630	702	681	750	731	807
631	703	682	751	732	811
632	704	......	752	733	812
633	705	683	753	734	813
634	705/706	684	754	735	814–816
635	706	......	755	736	817
636	707	685	756	737	818
637	708	686	757	738	819
638	709	687	781	739/740	820
639	710/711	688/689	782	741	821
640	712	690	783	742	822
641	713	691	784	......	823
642	714	692	838	743	759
643	715	693	839	744	760
644	716	694	840	745	761
645/646	717	695	841	746	762/763
647	718/719	696	842	747	764
648/649	720	697	843	748	765
650	721	698	844	749	766
651	722	699	845	750	767
652	723	700	758	751	768
653	724	701	846	752	768–771
654	725	702	847	753	772
655	726	703	848	754	773
656	726	704	849	755	829
657	727	705	778	756	824
658	728	......	779	757/758	825
659/660	729	706	810	759	826
661	730	707	780	760	827
662	731	708	793–797	761/762	828
663	732	709	798	763	852
664	733	710	799	764	852/853
665	734	711	858	765	911/912
666	735	712	859	766	830
667	736	713	859/860	767	831
668	737	714	861	768	832
669	738	715	862	769	833
670	739	716	863	770/771	834
671	740	717	864	772/773	835
		718	865	774–776	836
				777	837

Collected Works	Gesammelte Werke	Collected Works	Gesammelte Werke	Collected Works	Gesammelte Werke
778	850	830	774	APPENDIX 2	
779	854	831	775	883	951
780	855	832	776	884	952
781	856	833	777	885	953
......	857	834	808	886–888	954
782	851	835	913	889	955
783	870	836	914	890	956
784	871	837/838	915	891	957/958
......	872	839	915/916	892/893	958
785	873	840	917	894	959
786	874	841	918	895	960
787	875	842	919	896	961
788	876	843	920	897	962
789–791	891	844	921	898	962/963
792	786/787			899	964
793	787			900	965
794/795	788	EPILOGUE		901	966
796	790–792	845/846	922	902	967
797	877	847/848	923	903	968
798	878	849	924	904	969
799/800°	879	850	925	905/906	970
801	880/881	851–853	926	907	971
802	882	854	927	908	972
803	883	855	928	909	973
804/805	884	856	929	910	974
806	885	857	930	911	975
807	886			912	976
808	887			913	977
809	888	APPENDIX 1		914	978
810	889	858/859	931		
811	890	860	932	APPENDIX 3	
812	892	861/862	933	915/916	979
813	893	863	934	917	980/981
814	894	864/865	935	918	982
815	895	866	936	919	983
816	896	867/868	937	920	984
817	897	869	938	921	985/986
818	898	870	939	922	987
819	899/900	871	940	923	988
820	901	872	941/942	924	989
821/822	902	873	943/944	925	990
823	903	874	944	926	991
824	903/904	875	945	927	992
825	905	876/877	946	928	993
826	906	878	947	929	994
827	907	879	948	930	995
828/829	908	880/881	949	931	996
......	909	882	950	932	997/998
......	910				

° Last sentence from 1950 Swiss edn., p. 631.

Collected Works	Gesammelte Werke	Collected Works	Gesammelte Werke	Collected Works	Gesammelte Werke
933	999	953	1022	971	1040
934	1000/1001	954	1023	972	1041
935	1002	955	1024	973	1042
936	1003	956	1025	974	1043/1044
937	1004	957	1026/1027	975	1045
938	1005/1006	958	1028/1029	976	1046
939	1007	959	1030	977	1047
940	1008			978	1048
941	1009			979	1049/1050
942	1010	APPENDIX 4		980	1051
943	1011			981	1052
944	1012	960/961	1031	982	1053
945	1013	962	1032	983	1054
946	1014	963	1033	984	1055
947	1015	964	1034	985	1056
948	1016/1017	965	1035	986	1057
949	1018	966/967	1036	987	1058
950	1019	968	1037		
951	1020	969	1038		
952	1021	970	1039		

BIBLIOGRAPHY

BIBLIOGRAPHY

ADLER, ALFRED. *The Neurotic Constitution.* Translated by Bernard Glueck and John E. Lind. New York, 1916. (Original: *Über den nervösen Charakter.* Wiesbaden, 1912.)

──────. *Study of Organ Inferiority and Its Physical Compensation.* Translated by Smith Ely Jelliffe. (Nervous and Mental Disease Monographs, 24.) New York, 1917. (Original: *Studie über Minderwertigkeit von Organen.* Vienna, 1907.)

AMBROSE, SAINT, Bishop of Milan. *De institutione Virginis.* In MIGNE, *P.L.*, vol. 16, cols. 305–334.

AMBROSE, SAINT (pseudo-). *Expositio beati Ambrosii Episcopi super Apocalypsin.* Paris, 1554.

ANGELUS, SILESIUS. See SCHEFFLER, JOHANN.

ANQUETIL DU PERRON, A. H. *Oupnek'hat (id est, Secretum legendum . . . in Latinum conversum.* Strasbourg, 1801–2. 2 vols.

ANSELM, SAINT, Archbishop of Canterbury. *An Address (Proslogion)* In: EUGENE R. FAIRWEATHER (ed. and trans.). *A Scholastic Miscellany: Anselm to Ockham.* (Library of Christian Classics, 10.) Philadelphia and London, 1956.

ATHANASIUS, SAINT, Bishop of Alexandria. *Life of Saint Antony.* In: E. A. WALLIS BUDGE. *The Book of Paradise.* (Lady Meux MS., no. 6.) London, 1904. 2 vols. (Vol. I, pp. 3–76.)

Atharva Veda. See: *Atharva-Veda Samhita.* Translated by William Dwight Whitney and Charles Rockwell Lanman. (Harvard Oriental Series, 7, 8.) Cambridge, Mass., 1905. 2 vols.

AUGUSTINE, SAINT, Bishop of Hippo. *Contra epistolam Manichaei.* In MIGNE, *P.L.*, vol. 42, cols. 173–206.

──────. *Sermones.* In MIGNE, *P.L.*, vol. 38.

AVENARIUS, RICHARD. *Der menschliche Weltbegriff.* Leipzig, 1891.

AZAM, C. M. ÉTIENNE EUGÈNE. *Hypnotisme, double conscience, et altérations de la personnalité.* Paris, 1887.

BALDWIN, JAMES MARK. *Handbook of Psychology: Senses and Intellect*. London and New York, 1890.

BARLACH, ERNST. *Der tote Tag*. Berlin, 1912; 2nd edn., 1918.

BARTSCH, KARL (ed.). *Meisterlieder der Kolmarer Handschrift*. (Bibliothek des Literarischen Vereins in Stuttgart, 68.) Stuttgart, 1862.

BERGAIGNE, ABEL. *La Religion védique d'après les hymnes du Rig-Veda*. Vol. III. (Bibl. de l'École des hautes études, 54.) Paris, 1883.

Bhagavad Gita. See: *The Song of God: Bhagavad-Gita*. Translated by Swami Prabhavananda and Christopher Isherwood. London, 1947.

Bhagavata Purana. Translated by Manmatha Nath Dutt. Calcutta, 1895–96. 5 parts.

BINSWANGER, LUDWIG. "On the Psychogalvanic Phenomena in Association Experiments." In: C. G. JUNG (ed.). *Studies in Word-Association*. Translated by M. D. Eder. London, 1918; New York, 1919.

BJERRE, PAUL. "Zur Radikalbehandlung der chronischen Paranoia," *Jahrbuch für psychoanalytische und psychopathologische Forschungen* (Vienna), III (1911), 795–847.

BLAKE, WILLIAM. *The Complete Writings of William Blake*. Edited by Geoffrey Keynes. London, 1966.

BLEULER, EUGEN. "Die negative Suggestibilität, ein psychologisches Prototyp des Negativismus," *Psychiatrisch-neurologische Wochenschrift* (Halle), VI (1904), 249–69.

―――. "Affectivity, Suggestibility, Paranoia" (translated by Charles Ricksher), *New York State Hospitals Bulletin* (Utica, N.Y.), V (1912), pp. 481ff. (Original: *Affektivität, Suggestibilität, Paranoia*. Halle, 1906.)

―――. *Textbook of Psychiatry*. Translated by A. A. Brill. New York and London, 1924. (Original: *Lehrbuch der Psychiatrie*. Berlin, 1916.)

―――. *The Theory of Schizophrenic Negativism*. Translated by William A. White. (Nervous and Mental Disease Monograph Series, 11.) New York, 1912. (Original: "Zur Theorie des schizophrenen Negativismus," *Psychiatrisch-neurologische Wochenschrift* (Halle), XII (1910–11), 171, 189, 195.)

BORGES, JORGE LUIS. "Pascal's Sphere." In: *Other Inquisitions.* Translated by Ruth L. C. Simms. Austin, Tex., 1964. (Original: "La esfera de Pascal," in *Otras Inquisiciones.* (Obras Completas, 8.) Buenos Aires, 1960.)

Brihadaranyaka Upanishad. See HUME.

BUBER, MARTIN. *Ekstatische Konfessionen.* Jena, 1909.

BUDGE, E. A. WALLIS. *The Gods of the Egyptians.* London, 1904. 2 vols.

————. See also ATHANASIUS, SAINT.

BURNET, JOHN. *Early Greek Philosophy.* 4th edn., London, 1930.

Chhandogya Upanishad. See HUME.

COHEN, HERMANN. *Logik der reinen Erkenntnis.* Berlin, 1902.

Colmar Manuscript. See BARTSCH, KARL.

DANTE ALIGHIERI. *The Divine Comedy. The Inferno, Purgatorio, and Paradiso.* Translated by Lawrence Grant White. New York, 1948.

DESSOIR, MAX. *Geschichte der neueren deutschen Psychologie.* Vol. I: *Von Leibniz bis Kant.* Berlin, 1894; 2nd edn., 1902.

DEUSSEN, PAUL. *Allgemeine Geschichte der Philosophie.* Leipzig, 1894–1917. 2 vols. in 6 parts.

DIONYSIUS THE AREOPAGITE (pseudo-). *On the Divine Names and The Mystical Theology.* Translated by C. E. Rolt. London and New York, 1920.

EBBINGHAUS, HERMANN. *Grundzüge der Psychologie.* 2nd edn., Leipzig, 1905–13. 2 vols.

EBERSCHWEILER, ADOLF. "Untersuchungen über die sprachliche Komponente der Assoziation," *Allgemeine Zeitschrift für Psychiatrie* (Berlin), LXV (1908), 240–71.

ECKHART, MEISTER. [*Works.*] Translated by C. de B. Evans. London, 1924–31. 2 vols.

EUSEBIUS, Bishop of Caesarea. *The Ecclesiastical History and the Martyrs of Palestine.* Translated by H. J. Lawlor and J.E.L. Oulton. London, 1927–28. 2 vols.

FÉRÉ, CHARLES. "Note sur des modifications de la résistance électrique sous l'influence des excitations sensorielles et des émotions," *Comptes-rendus hebdomadaires des séances et memoires de la Société de Biologie* (Paris), ser. 8, V (1888), 217–19.

FERENCZI, SANDOR. "Introjection and Transference." In: *First Contributions to Psycho-Analysis.* Translated by Ernest Jones. London, 1952. (Pp. 35–93.) (Original: "Introjektion und Übertragung," *Jahrbuch für psychoanalytische und psychopathologische Forschungen* (Vienna), II (1910).)

FERRERO, GUGLIELMO. *I simboli in rapporto alla storia e filosofia del diritto.* Turin, 1893. (French translation: *Les Lois psychologiques du symbolisme.* Paris, 1895.)

FICHTE, IMMANUEL HERMANN VON. *Psychologie.* Leipzig, 1864–73. 2 vols.

FINCK, FRANZ NIKOLAUS. *Der deutsche Sprachbau als Ausdruck deutscher Weltanschauung.* Marburg, 1899.

FLOURNOY, THÉODORE. *From India to the Planet Mars.* Translated by D. B. Vermilye. New York, 1900. (Original: *Des Indes à la planète Mars.* 3rd edn., Paris, 1900.)

———. "Une Mystique moderne," *Archives de psychologie* (Geneva), XV (1915), 1–224.

———. "Nouvelles observations sur un cas de somnambulisme avec glossolalie," *Archives de psychologie* (Geneva), I (1901), 101–255.

———. *The Philosophy of William James.* Translated by Edwin B. Holt and William James, Jr. London, 1917.

FRANCE, ANATOLE. *Le Jardin d'Epicure.* 4th edn., Paris, 1895.

FREUD, SIGMUND. *The Interpretation of Dreams.* (Complete Psychological Works, 4 and 5.) Translated by James Strachey. London, 1953. 2 vols. (Original: *Die Traumdeutung.* 1900.)

———. *The Psychopathology of Everyday Life.* (Complete Psychological Works, 6.) Translated by Alan Tyson. London, 1960. (Original: *Zur Psychopathologie des Alltagsleben.* 1901.)

FROBENIUS, LEO. *Das Zeitalter des Sonnengottes.* (Only vol. I published.) Berlin, 1904.

Garuda-Purana. Translated by E. Wood and S. V. Subrahmanyam. (Sacred Books of the Hindus, 26 and 27.) Allahabad, 1911. 2 vols.

GOETHE, JOHANN WOLFGANG. *Werke.* (Gedenkausgabe.) Edited by Ernst Beutler. Zurich, 1948–54. 24 vols. (For *Die Geheimnisse*, see vol. 3, pp. 273–83; *Pandora*, vol. 6, pp. 406–443; *Prometheus*, vol. 1, pp. 320–21, and vol. 4, pp. 185–98; Correspondence with Schiller, vol. 20.)

———. *Faust, Part One* and *Part Two.* Translated by Philip Wayne. Harmondsworth and Baltimore, 1956, 1959.

————. *Goethe's Faust*. Parts I and II. An abridged version translated by Louis MacNeice. London and New York, 1952.

GOMPERZ, THEODOR. *Greek Thinkers*. Translated by Laurie Magnus and G. G. Berry. London, 1901–12. 4 vols. (Original: *Griechische Denker*. 3rd edn., Leipzig, 1911–12.)

GÖRRES, JOHAN JOSEPH VON. *Die christliche Mystik*. Regensburg and Landshut, 1836–42. 4 vols.

GROSS, OTTO. *Die zerebrale Sekundärfunktion*. Leipzig, 1902. (See also an unsigned review of the book in *Archives de psychologie* (Geneva), III (1903), 397–99.)

————. *Über psychopathische Minderwertigkeit*. Vienna, 1909.

HARNACK, ADOLF VON. *History of Dogma*. Translated from the 3rd German edition. (Theological Translation Library, 2, 7–12.) London, 1896–1905. 7 vols. (Original: *Lehrbuch der Dogmengeschichte*. 1888–94.)

HARTMANN, EDUARD VON. *Die moderne Psychologie*. (Ausgewählte Werke, 13.) Leipzig, 1901.

HASE, CARL AUGUST VON. *A History of the Christian Church*. Translated by Charles E. Blumenthal and Conway P. Wing. New York, 1855. (Original: *Kirchengeschichte*. 10th edn., Leipzig, 1877.)

HEGEL, GEORG WILHELM FRIEDRICH. *The Logic of Hegel*. Translated by William Wallace. 2nd edn., Oxford, 1892.

————. *Einleitung in die Aesthetik*. (Sämtliche Werke, Jubiläumsausgabe, edited by Hermann Glockner, 12.) Stuttgart, 1927.

HEINE, HEINRICH. *Deutschland*. (Original: 1834.) Cf.: *Germany*. (Works, translated by Charles Godfrey Leland, 5.) New York, 1892. (P. 81.)

HERBART, JOHANN FRIEDRICH. *Psychologie als Wissenschaft, neu gegründet auf Erfahrung, Metaphysik und Mathematik*. (Sämtliche Werke, edited by G. Hartenstein, 6, pt. 2.) Leipzig, 1850. (Cf.: *A Text-book in Psychology*. Translated by Margaret K. Smith. New York, 1894.)

HERMAS. *The Shepherd*. In: *The Apostolic Fathers*. With an English translation by Kirsopp Lake. (Loeb Classical Library.) London and New York, 1917. 2 vols. (Vol. 2, pp. 6–305.)

HOCH, AUGUST. "Constitutional Factors in the Dementia Praecox Group," *Review of Neurology and Psychiatry* (Edinburgh), VIII:8 (Aug., 1910).

HÖLDERLIN, JOHANN CHRISTIAN FRIEDRICH. See: *Hölderlin: His Poems.* Translated by Michael Hamburger. 2nd edn., London and New York, 1952.

HUME, ROBERT ERNEST (trans.). *The Thirteen Principal Upanishads.* 2nd edn., revised, London and New York, 1934.

INOUYE, TETSUJIRO. "Die japanische Philosophie," in *Allgemeine Geschichte der Philosophie,* by W. Wundt and others. (Die Kultur der Gegenwart, edited by Paul Hinneberg, Part I, sec. V.) Berlin and Leipzig, 2nd edn., 1923.

Isha Upanishad. See HUME.

JACOBI, JOLANDE. *Complex/Archetype/Symbol in the Psychology of C. G. Jung.* Translated by Ralph Manheim. New York (Bollingen Series) and London, 1959.

JAMES, WILLIAM. *Pragmatism: A New Name for Some Old Ways of Thinking.* London and New York, 1911.

———. *The Principles of Psychology.* New York, 1890. 2 vols.

JERUSALEM, WILHELM. *Lehrbuch der Psychologie.* 5th edn., Vienna and Leipzig, 1912.

JODL, FRIEDRICH. *Lehrbuch der Psychologie.* 3rd edn., Stuttgart and Berlin, 1908. 2 vols.

JORDAN, FURNEAUX. *Character as Seen in Body and Parentage.* 3rd edn., London, 1896.

JULIAN, "the Apostate." *Works.* Translated by Wilmer Cave Wright. (Loeb Classical Library.) Vol. I. London and New York, 1913. ("Hymn to King Helios," pp. 353–435; "Hymn to the Mother of the Gods," pp. 443–503.)

JUNG, CARL GUSTAV.* "The Aims of Psychotherapy." In *Collected Works,* 16.

———. *Aion: Researches into the Phenomenology of the Self. Collected Works,* 9, ii.

———. *Collected Papers on Analytical Psychology.* Edited by Constance E. Long. London and New York, 1916; 2nd edn., 1917.

———. "Commentary on *The Secret of the Golden Flower,*" in *Collected Works,* 13.

*For details of *The Collected Works of C. G. Jung,* see list at the end of this volume.

JUNG, CARL GUSTAV. "The Concept of the Collective Unconscious."
In *Collected Works*, 9, i.

———. "Concerning Mandala Symbolism." In *Collected Works*,
9, i.

———. "The Content of the Psychoses." In *Collected Works*, 3.

———. "Cryptomnesia." In *Collected Works*, 1.

———. "Flying Saucers: A Modern Myth of Things Seen in the
Sky." In *Collected Works*, 10.

———. "Instinct and the Unconscious." In *Collected Works*, 8.

———. *Letters*. Selected and edited by Gerhard Adler, in collaboration with Aniela Jaffé. Translated by R.F.C. Hull. Princeton
(Bollingen Series) and London, 1973, 1975. 2 vols.

———. *Memories, Dreams, Reflections*. Recorded and edited by
Aniela Jaffé. Translated by Richard and Clara Winston. New
York and London, 1963. (Edns. separately paginated.)

———. *Mysterium Coniunctionis. Collected Works*, 14.

———. "On the Importance of the Unconscious in Psychopathology." In *Collected Works*, 3.

———. "On the Nature of the Psyche." In *Collected Works*, 8.

———. "On Psychic Energy." In *Collected Works*, 8.

———. "On Psychological Understanding." In *Collected Works*, 3.

———. "On the Psychology and Pathology of So-called Occult Phenomena." In *Collected Works*, 1.

———. "On Psychophysical Relations of the Association Experiment." In *Collected Works*, 2.

———. *The Practice of Psychotherapy. Collected Works*, 16.

———. *Psychiatric Studies. Collected Works*, 1.

———. "A Psychological Approach to the Dogma of the Trinity."
In *Collected Works*, 11.

———. "The Psychological Aspects of the Kore." In *Collected
Works*, 9, i.

———. "Psychological Aspects of the Mother Archetype." In *Collected Works*, 9, i.

———. *Psychology and Alchemy. Collected Works*, 12.

———. *Psychology and Religion: West and East. Collected Works*,
11.

———. "The Psychology of the Child Archetype." In *Collected
Works*, 9, i.

JUNG, CARL GUSTAV. "The Psychology of Dementia Praecox." In *Collected Works*, 3.

――――. *Psychology of the Unconscious: A Study of the Transformations and Symbolisms of the Libido.* Translated by Beatrice M. Hinkle. New York, 1916; London, 1917. (Original: *Wandlungen und Symbole der Libido.* Vienna, 1912.) Revised as *Symbols of Transformation,* q.v.

――――. "The Psychology of the Unconscious Processes." In *Collected Papers on Analytical Psychology,* q.v.

――――. "A Review of the Complex Theory." In *Collected Works,* 8.

――――. "The Structure of the Psyche." In *Collected Works,* 8.

――――. "The Structure of the Unconscious." In *Collected Works,* 7. (Revised version in the 2nd edn., 1966.)

――――. *Studies in Word-Association.* Under the direction of C. G. Jung. Translated by M. D. Eder. London, 1918; New York, 1919. (Jung's contributions, retranslated, in *Collected Works,* 2.)

――――. "A Study in the Process of Individuation." In *Collected Works,* 9, i.

――――. *Symbols of Transformation. Collected Works,* 5. Cf. JUNG, *Psychology of the Unconscious.*

――――. "Synchronicity: An Acausal Connecting Principle." In *Collected Works,* 8.

――――. "The Tavistock Lectures (On the Theory and Practice of Analytical Psychology)." In *Collected Works,* 18.

――――. "The Theory of Psychoanalysis." In *Collected Works,* 4.

――――. "The Transcendent Function." In *Collected Works,* 8.

――――. "Transformation Symbolism in the Mass." In *Collected Works,* 11.

――――. *Two Essays on Analytical Psychology. Collected Works,* 7.

―――― and FREUD, SIGMUND. *The Freud/Jung Letters.* Edited by William McGuire. Translated by Ralph Manheim and R.F.C. Hull. Princeton (Bollingen Series) and London, 1974.

KANT, IMMANUEL. *Critique of Practical Reason and Other Writings in Moral Philosophy.* Translated and edited by Lewis White Beck. Chicago, 1949.

――――. *Immanuel Kant's Critique of Pure Reason.* Translated by Norman Kemp Smith. London and New York, 1929.

————. *Logik.* In: *Werke.* Edited by Ernst Cassirer. Berlin, 1912–22. 11 vols. (Vol. 8, pages 325–452.)

Katha Upanishad. See HUME.

Kaushitaki Upanishad. See HUME.

KERNER, JUSTINUS. *The Seeress of Prevorst.* Translated by Mrs. Catherine Crowe. New York, 1859.

KING, CHARLES WILLIAM. *The Gnostics and Their Remains, Ancient and Medieval.* London, 1864; 2nd edn., 1887.

KÖHLER, HEINRICH KARL ERNST VON. "Einleitung über die Gemmen mit dem Namen der Künstler, vom wirklichen Staatsrath von Köhler in Skt. Petersburg," in: K. A. BÖTTIGER (ed.). *Archaeologie und Kunst.* Breslau, 1828.

KÖNIG, [FRIEDRICH] EDUARD. *Ahasver, "der Ewige Jude."* Gütersloh, 1907.

KUBIN, ALFRED. *The Other Side.* Translated by Denver Lindley. New York, 1967. (Original: *Die andere Seite.* Munich, 1909.)

KÜLPE, OSWALD. *Grundriss der Psychologie.* Leipzig, 1893.

Lalita-Vistara, The; or Memoirs of the Early Life of Shakya Sinha. Translated from the Sanskrit by Rajendralala Mitra. (Bibliotheca Indica, Asiatic Society of Bengal, n.s., 455, 473, 575.) Calcutta, 1881–86. 3 vols.

LANDMANN, S. *Die Mehrheit geistiger Persönlichkeiten in einem Individuum.* Stuttgart, 1894.

LASSWITZ, KURD. *Wirklichkeiten. Beiträge zur Weltverständnis.* Leipzig, 1900.

Laws of Manu, The. Translated by Georg Bühler. (Sacred Books of the East, 25.) Oxford, 1886.

LEHMANN, ALFRED GEORG LUDWIG. *Die Hauptgesetze des menschlichen Gefühlslebens.* 2nd edn., Leipzig, 1914.

LÉVY-BRUHL, LUCIEN. *How Natives Think.* Translated by Lilian A. Clare. London, 1926. (Original: *Les Fonctions mentales dans les sociétés inférieures.* Paris, 1912.)

LIPPS, THEODOR. *Aesthetik: Psychologie des Schönen und der Kunst.* Hamburg, 1903–6. 2 vols.

————. *Leitfaden der Psychologie.* 3rd edn., Leipzig, 1909.

Lyra Germanica: Second Series. Translated from the German by Catherine Winkworth. London, 1858. (Pp. 53f.)

577

MAEDER, A. *The Dream Problem.* Translated by Frank Mead Hallock and Smith Ely Jelliffe. (Nervous and Mental Disease Monograph Series, 22.) New York, 1916. (Original: "Über das Traumproblem," *Jahrbuch für psychoanalytische und psychopathologische Forschungen* (Vienna), V (1913), 647–86.)

Mahabharata. Translated by Manmatha Nath Dutt. Calcutta, 1895–1905. 17 vols.

Manuscripts. Oxford, Bodleian Library, Digby MS. 65. By Godfrey, Prior of St. Swithin's, Winchester. 13th century.

———. See also BARTSCH.

MATTER, JACQUES. *Histoire critique du gnosticisme.* Paris, 1828. 2 vols.

MEYRINK, GUSTAV. *The Golem.* Translated by Madge Pemberton. London, 1928. (Original: *Der Golem.* Leipzig, 1915.)

———. *Das grüne Gesicht; eine Roman.* Leipzig, 1916.

MIGNE, JACQUES PAUL (ed.). *Patrologiae cursus completus.* [*P.L.*] Latin Series. Paris, 1844–64. 221 vols. [*P.G.*] Greek Series. Paris, 1857–66. 166 vols.

MÜLLER, G. E., and SCHUMANN, F. "Über die psychologischen Grundlagen der Vergleichung gehobener Gewichte." In: *Archiv für die gesamte Physiologie,* ed. E.F.W. Pflüger ("Pflüger's Archiv," Bonn), XLV (1889), 37–112.

NAHLOWSKY, JOSEPH WILHELM. *Das Gefühlsleben in seinen wesentlichsten Erscheinungen und Beziehungen.* 3rd edn., Leipzig, 1907.

NATORP, PAUL. *Einleitung in die Psychologie nach kritischer Methode.* Freiburg im Breisgau, 1888.

NEUMANN, ERICH. *The Origins and History of Consciousness.* Translated by R.F.C. Hull. New York (Bollingen Series) and London, 1954.

NIETZSCHE, FRIEDRICH. *The Birth of Tragedy.* Translated by William A. Haussmann. (Complete Works, 1.) Edinburgh and London, 1909.

———. *The Joyful Wisdom.* Translated by Thomas Common, with poetry rendered by Paul V. Cohn and Maude D. Petre. (Complete Works, 10.) Edinburgh and London, 1910.

———. *Thus Spake Zarathustra.* Translated by Thomas Common and revised by Oscar Levy and John L. Beevers. London, 1931.

————. "The Use and Abuse of History," in *Thoughts Out of Season*, part II. Translated by Adrian Collins. (Complete Works, 5.) Edinburgh and London, 1915.

NUNBERG, HERMANN. "On the Physical Accompaniments of Association Processes." In: C. G. JUNG (ed.). *Studies in Word-Association*. Translated by M. D. Eder. London, 1918; New York, 1919. (Pp. 531–60.)

OLDENBERG, HERMANN. *Die Religion des Veda*. Berlin, 1894; 2nd edn., 1917.

————. "Zur Religion und Mythologie des Veda." In: *Nachrichten von der königlichen Gesellschaft der Wissenschaften zu Göttingen*, Philologisch-historische Klasse. Berlin, 1916. (Pp. 167–225.)

ONIANS, RICHARD BROXTON. *The Origins of European Thought*. 2nd edn., Cambridge, 1954.

OSTWALD, FRIEDRICH WILHELM. *Grosse Männer*. 3/4th edn., Leipzig, 1919.

Pañcavimsha Brahmana. Translated by W. Caland. (Bibliotheca Indica, 252.) Calcutta, 1931.

PLATO. *The Symposium*. Translated by W. Hamilton. (Penguin Classics.) Harmondsworth, 1956.

PLUTARCH. *Adversus Colotem*. See: Plutarch's *Moralia*, vol. XIV. (Loeb Classical Library.) London and Cambridge, Mass., 1967.

PORPHYRY. See: *The Organon, or Logical Treatises, of Aristotle, with the Introduction of Porphyry*. Translated by Octavius Freire Owen. London, 1853. 2 vols.

POWELL, JOHN WESLEY. "Sketch of the Mythology of the North American Indians." In: *First Annual Report of the Bureau of Ethnology to the Secretary of the Smithsonian Institution, 1897–80*. Washington, 1881. (Pp. 19–56.)

PRINCE, MORTON. *The Dissociation of a Personality: A Biographical Study in Abnormal Psychology*. New York, 1906.

Ramayana. Translated by Manmatha Nath Dutt. Calcutta, 1892–94. 7 vols.

RÉMUSAT, CHARLES F. M. DE. *Abélard*. Paris, 1845. 2 vols.

RIBOT, THÉODULE ARMAND. *Die Persönlichkeit. Pathologisch-psychologische Studien*. Berlin, 1894.

RIBOT, THÉODULE ARMAND. *The Psychology of the Emotions.* London, 1897. (Original: *Psychologie der Gefühle.* Altenburg, 1903.)

RIEGL, ALOIS. *Spätrömische Kunstindustrie.* Vienna, 1901.

———. *Stilfragen.* Berlin, 1893.

RIEHL, ALOIS. *Zur Einführung in die Philosophie der Gegenwart.* 4th edn., Leipzig and Berlin, 1913.

Rig Veda. See: *The Hymns of the Rigveda.* Translated by Ralph H. T. Griffith. Benares, 2nd edn., 1896–97. 2 vols. Also: *Vedic Hymns.* Translated by F. Max Müller and Hermann Oldenberg. (Sacred Books of the East, 32, 46.) Oxford, 1891–97.

ROUSSEAU, JEAN-JACQUES. *Emile; or, Education.* Translated by Barbara Foxley. (Everyman's Library.) London and New York, 1911.

SALZER, ANSELM. *Die Sinnbilder und Beiworte Mariens in der deutschen Literatur und lateinischen Hymnenpoesie des Mittelalters.* Linz, 1886.

SCHÄRF KLUGER, RIVKAH. *Satan in the Old Testament.* Translated by Hildegard Nagel. Evanston, 1967.

SCHEFFLER, JOHANN (Angelus Silesius). "Cherubinischer Wandersmann." In: *Johann Schefflers Sämmtliche Poetische Werke.* Edited by David August Rosenthal. Regensburg, 1862. 2 vols.

SCHILLER, F.C.S. *Humanism; Philosophical Essays.* 2nd edn., London, 1912.

SCHILLER, JOHANN CHRISTOPH FRIEDRICH VON. *Letters to Goethe.* See GOETHE, *Werke*, Gedenkausgabe, of which the Schiller-Goethe correspondence forms vol. 20.

———. *On the Aesthetic Education of Man, in a Series of Letters.* Translated by Reginald Snell. New Haven and London, 1954. (Original: "Über die ästhetische Erziehung des Menschen." In: *Sämtliche Werke,* q.v., vol. 18, pp. 1–164.)

———. "The Diver." Cf. *Poems.* Translated by E. P. Arnold-Forster. London, 1901.

———. *Sämtliche Werke.* Cottasche Ausgabe. Stuttgart and Tübingen, 1826.

———. "Über naive und sentimentalische Dichtung." In: *Sämtliche Werke,* q.v., vol. 18, pp. 205–348.

———. "Über die notwendigen Grenzen beim Gebrauch schöner Formen." In: *Sämtliche Werke,* q.v., vol. 18, pp. 165–204.

SCHOPENHAUER, ARTHUR. *The World as Will and Idea.* Translated by R. B. Haldane and J. Kemp. London, 1883. 3 vols. (Original: *Die Welt als Wille und Vorstellung.* (Sämtliche Werke, ed. by Eduard Grisebach, 6.) Leipzig, 1891.)

SCHULTZ, WOLFGANG. *Dokumente der Gnosis.* Jena, 1910.

SEMON, RICHARD. *The Mneme.* Translated by L. Simon. London, 1921. (Original: *Die Mneme als erhaltendes Prinzip im Wechsel des organischen Geschehens.* Leipzig, 1904.)

Shatapatha Brahmana. Translated by Julius Eggeling. (Sacred Books of the East, 12, 26, 41, 43, 44.) Oxford, 1882–1900. 5 vols.

Shvetashvatara Upanishad. See HUME.

SILBERER, HERBERT. *Problems of Mysticism and Its Symbolism.* Translated by Smith Ely Jelliffe. New York, 1917. (Original: *Probleme der Mystik und ihrer Symbolik.* Vienna and Leipzig, 1904.)

Song of Tishtriya, The. See *Tir Yasht.*

SPENCER, SIR WALTER R., and GILLEN, FRANCIS JAMES. *The Northern Tribes of Central Australia.* London, 1904.

SPITTELER, CARL. *Prometheus and Epimetheus: a Prose Epic.* Translated by James Fullarton Muirhead. London, 1931. (Original: 1880–81.)

STATIUS. *Thebaid.* See: *Works.* With a translation by J. H. Mozley. (Loeb Classical Library.) London and New York, 1928. 2 vols. (Vol. I.)

STOBAEUS, JOHANNES. *Eclogarum physicarum et ethicorum Libri duo.* Edited by Thomas Gaisford. Oxford, 1850. 2 vols.

SULLY, JAMES. *The Human Mind; a Text-book of Psychology.* London, 1892. 2 vols.

SYNESIUS. *De Insomniis.* In: *Iamblichus De Mysteriis Aegyptiorum* . . . etc. Translated by Marsilio Ficino. Venice, 1497. See also: "Concerning Dreams" ("De Insomniis"). In: *The Essays and Hymns of Synesius of Cyrene.* Translated by Augustine Fitz-Gerald. London, 1930. 3 vols. (II, pp. 326ff.)

Taittiriya Aranyaka. With Sayana's commentary. Edited by Baba Shastri Phadke. (Anandashrama Sanskrit Series, 36.) Poona, 1897–98. 2 vols.

Taittiriya Brahmana. With the commentary of Vedarthaprakasa of Sayana. Edited by Narayana Balakrishna Godbole. (Anandashrama Sanskrit Series, 37.) Poona, 1898. 3 vols.

Taittiriya Samhita. See: ARTHUR BERRIEDALE KEITH (trans.). *The Veda of the Black Yajus School, entitled Taittiriya Sanhita.* (Harvard Oriental Series, 18, 19.) Cambridge, Mass., 1914. 2 vols.

Taittiriya Upanishad. See HUME.

TALBOT, P. AMAURY. *In the Shadow of the Bush.* London, 1912.

Tao Te King. See WALEY.

TAYLOR, HENRY OSBORN. *The Medieval Mind.* London, 1911. 2 vols.

Tejobindu (Teyovindu) Upanishad. See: *Minor Upanishads.* With text, introduction, English rendering, and commentary. Mayavati (Advaita Ashrama), 1928. (Pp. 35–42.)

TERTULLIAN. *De carne Christi.* See: *Tertullian's Treatise on the Incarnation.* The text with translation by Ernest Evans. London, 1956.

———. *De testimonio animae.* See: *The Writings of Tertullian.* Vol. I: *Apologetic and Practical Treatises.* Translated by C. Dodgson. (Library of the Fathers of the Holy Catholic Church.) Oxford, 1842.

———. *Liber adversus Judaeos.* In MIGNE, *P.L.*, vol. 2, cols. 595–642. For translation, see: S. THELWALL. *The Writings of Tertullianus.* (Ante-Nicene Christian Library, 11, 15, 18.) Edinburgh, 1869–70. 3 vols. (III, pp. 201–88.)

THOMAS AQUINAS. *Scriptum supra libros Sententiarum magistri Petri Lombardi.* Edited by P. F. Mandonnet. Paris, 1929–47. 5 vols.

Tir Yasht. In: *The Zend-Avesta,* Part II. Translated by James Darmesteter. (Sacred Books of the East, 23.) Oxford, 1883. (Pp. 92ff.)

Vajasanayi Samhita. See: *The Texts of the White Yajurveda.* Translated by P.T.H. Griffith. Benares, 1899.

VERAGUTH, OTTO. "Das psycho-galvanische Reflex-Phänomen," *Monatsschrift für Psychologie und Neurologie* (Berlin), XXI (1907), 387–425.

VILLA, GUIDO. *Contemporary Psychology.* Translated by H. Manacorda. London, 1903. (Original: *Einleitung in die Psychologie der Gegenwart.* Leipzig, 1902.)

VISCHER, FRIEDRICH THEODOR VON. *Auch Einer.* 9th edn., Leipzig, 1902.

WALEY, ARTHUR (trans.). *The Way and Its Power; A Study of the Tao Tê Ching.* London, 1934.

WANG YING-MING. *Instructions for Practical Living and Other Neo-Confucian Writings.* Translated by Wing-tsit Chan. (Records of Civilization: Sources and Studies, Columbia University, 68.) New York and London, 1963.

WARNECK, JOHANNES GUSTAV. *Die Religion der Batak.* (Religions-Urkunden der Völker, ed. Julius Böhmer, Part IV, Vol. I.) Leipzig, 1909.

WARREN, HENRY CLARKE. *Buddhism in Translations.* (Harvard Oriental Series, 3.) Cambridge, Mass., 1900.

WEBER, ALBRECHT. *Indische Studien.* Vol. 9. Leipzig, 1865.

WERNICKE, CARL. *Grundriss der Psychiatrie in klinischen Vorlesungen.* Leipzig, 1894–1900. 3 vols.

WORRINGER, WILHELM ROBERT. *Abstraction and Empathy.* Translated by Michael Bullock. London, 1953. (Original: *Abstraktion und Einfühlung.* 3rd edn., Munich, 1911.)

WULFEN, WILLEM VAN (pseud. of Willem van Vloten). *Der Genussmensch: Ein Cicerone im rücksichtslosen Lebensgenuss.* 3rd edn., Munich, 1911.

WUNDT, WILHELM. *Grundzüge der physiologischen Psychologie.* 5th edn., Leipzig, 1902/3. 3 vols. For translation, see: *Principles of Physiological Psychology.* Translated from the 5th German edn. by Edward Bradford Titchener. London and New York, 1904. (Vol. I only published.)

———. *Logik.* 3rd edn. Stuttgart, 1906–8. 3 vols.

———. *Outlines of Psychology.* Translated by Charles Hubbard Judd. 2nd revised English edn. Leipzig, London, and New York, 1902. (Original: *Grundriss der Psychologie.* 5th edn., Leipzig, 1902.)

———. "Was soll uns Kant nicht sein?" In: *Philosophische Studien.* Edited by W. Wundt. Leipzig, 1883–1903. 20 vols. (VII, pp. 1ff.)

ZELLER, EDUARD. *A History of Greek Philosophy from the Earliest Period to the Time of Socrates.* Translated by S. F. Alleyne. London, 1881. 2 vols. (Original: *Die Philosophie der Griechen in ihrer geschichtlichen Entwicklung dargestellt.* Tübingen, 1856–68. 5 vols.)

ZÜNDEL, FRIEDRICH. *Pfarrer J. C. Blumhardt: Ein Lebensbild.* Zurich and Heilbronn, 1880.

INDEX

INDEX

A

abaissement du niveau mental, 123,
451
Abegg, Emil, 209n
Abelard, Peter, 39, 46–52, 63–64,
320
abstract, as idea, 411
abstracting: attitude of consciousness, and introvert, 91–93, 149,
184, 292–93; —, Buddhist, 294;
type, 295–97
abstraction, 29, 409–11 (Def.); from
object in introvert, 48, 149, 292–
95, 297, 325, 330; Worringer's
concept, 289, 291–94, 504–6
Acta Sanctorum, 547
activity, and character, 148–49
Adam, 22
adaptation, 18, 158–59, 279, 285,
378, 420; and adjustment, 334f;
as aim, 449; collective, 100, 298;
by differentiated function, 106,
206, 330, 518, 536, 540; of extravert, 334–35; failure of, 471;
individual systems of, 531; to inner world, 185, 442; by intuition,
145, 366; passive, 252; phylogenetic attempts at, 304; rapid, 275,
280; to reality/object, 63, 119,
145, 167, 185, 206, 252, 442; religion as, 185
adjustment, 334f
Adler, Alfred, 360, 379, 418–19, 422,
459, 502, 508–9; "guiding fiction"
concept, 297, 418; theory contrasted with Freud's, 60–62
aesthetic: attitude, see attitude s.v.;
condition, 137&n, 128; mood,
122–23, 127; types, 145, 151&n
aestheticism, 121&n, 141&n, 142–43

aesthetics, 140, 289–99, 505; and
empathy, 289–92
affect (s), 239, 269, 274, 411–12
(Def.), 513–14; control of, 149;
deliverance from, 199; differentiated, 159; and feeling, 462;
inferiority of, 239, 273, 573; as
instinctive process, 112, 144, 451;
origin of, 471; Schiller on, 98,
101; symptom of disharmony, 89
affectivity, 101, 275, 412 (Def.), 508,
511; ego and, 90–91; extravert
and, 90, 145, 158; of introvert,
149–50, 155, 159, 165; sensuousness and, 95, 97; and types, 149,
151; see also feeling-sensation
Africa, West, creation myth of, 217
Agni (fire), 203–4, 208–9&n, 210–
11
aggressiveness, 397, 500
Ahasuerus legend, 268
alcoholism, 336, 340, 469
Alexandria, 14
All-oneness, 34, 36
altruism, 349, 549
ambitendency/ambivalence, 413,
424
Ambrose, St., 232–33
Ambrose, pseudo-, 232n
Amfortas, 70, 219–20
amnesia, 483
anaemia, 391
analysis, 62, 420, 473, 522, 528
ananda, 119, 218, 249
anarchism, 191
Anastasius I, Pope, 16
ancestral spirits, 141, 316
Angelus Silesius (Johann Scheffler),
256&n, 257&n

anima, 221, 223, 463, 467*n*, 467–72
(Def.); *see also* soul-image
anima naturaliter christiana, 13-14,
18
animals: battle of, in dreams, 407;
and conscience, 179*n*; distinguished from man, 270, 308; love
of, as compensation, 278; part of
man's psyche, 213, 219, 270; symbol of crude strength, 269; as
totem, 141, 316; without soul,
179; as union of opposites, 262
  SPECIFIC ANIMALS: bird, 271;
bull, 204, 209; cow, 204, 210;
crocodile, 536; dragon, 263, 265,
460; goat, 230; horse, 208*n*, 211,
544; lamb, 185, 190; lion, 536;
pig, 18; sheep, 230; whale, 263,
271
animus, 467*n*–468*n*, 470–72
Anquetil du Perron, A. H., 120
Anselm of Canterbury, 39–40, 42–43
Anthony, St., 54–56
anthropophagy, 28
Antinomians, 17
Antiphon of Rhamnos, 28
antiquity, 320, 542–43; chaos of, 76;
Christianity and, *see* Christianity;
and neurotic disturbances, 109;
overvalued, 73, 82; paganism of,
186; psychology and, 8, 10; and
Renaissance, 185; Schiller and,
see Schiller *s.v.*
Antisthenes, 27–28, 33, 36
Antitactae, 17, 252
Anton, Gabriel, 418*n*
apocatastasis, 263, 271
Apollinian impulse, 137–46, 507;
and dreaming, 138, 144, 506; reconciliation with Dionysian, 140–
41
Apollo, 138–39, 141, 506–7
apperception, 412–13 (Def.)
approfondissement, 276, 280
a priori: foundations of unconscious, 400; *see also* idea(s) *s.v.*
Aquinas, St. Thomas, 42
archaic man in ourselves, 86

archaism, 413 (Def.)
archetype(s), 376–77, 381, 400–401,
413&*n*, 443 (Def.), 461 (*Urbild*);
Kant's term, 309, 438; *see also*
engram(s); primordial image
Archontics, 17
Aristotle, 39
Arius/Arian heresy, 20–21
art: Apollinian/Dionysian, 137; mediating role of, 140; Oriental,
293–94; of present day, 393; of
primitives, 293; and subjective
factor, 393–94; western, 291
artist: as introverted intuitive type,
401; and abstract sensation, 462
asceticism, Christian, 207
Ass Festival (*Zarathustra*), 185
assimilation, 413–14 (Def.); of object, empathy and, 290, 292; *see
also* extraverted type *s.v.*
association(s), 274–78, 287, 546;
free, 423
assonances, 274
Astarte, 269*n*
astrology, 525, 531–32
Athanasius, St., Bishop of Alexandria, 54
Atharva Veda, see Vedas
Athene, 176; Phidias' statue of, 28
Athens, 27–28
Atlantis, 354
atman/Atman, 118, 198–200, 215,
244
Atreus, 27*n*; Atrides, 137
attitude(s) 414–17 (Def.); abstracting, of consciousness, *see* abstracting; aesthetic, 107, 121, 142, 289;
collective, 10, 184–85; —, undifferentiated, 184; Epimethean, 179,
183–84; negation as, 191; Promethean ideal and abstract, 179,
183–84; religion as, 185: renewal
of, 193; -types, 330–31, 483*n*, 519,
540, 549, 554 (*see also* extraverted type; introverted type); of
unconscious, 337*ff*, 378*ff*, 520
Augustine, St., 14, 22, 232–34, 514–
15

F

J

35–36, 49; medieval, 47–51; and realism, 26, 33, 36, 39–40, 47–48, 50, 282, 320; and tough-minded, 302

"nothing but" type of thinking, 187, 353, 359, 503

Nous, 207

number, Apollo and, 138

numinal accent, 533–54

Nunberg, Hermann, 112*n*

Nutt, Alfred, 237*n*

O

Obatala and Odudua, 217

object: and collective values, 189; conflict with, 89; dynamic animation of, 294, 297&*n*, extraverted cultural ideal and, 73; Freudian psychology and, 61–62; Luther-Zwingli controversy and, 66; naïve or sentimental poets and, 130–34; nominalism and, 50; spell/magical power of, 226–27, 295, 365, 379–80; and subject, identity of, 238–39; subjection to, 246; yoga and, 119; *see also* abstraction; empathy; extraverted type; introverted type, *ss. vv.*

objective: level, 456 (Def.); psychology, 8–10; and subjective, confused, 30

obsessive ideas, 359

Ocampo, Victoria, xv

Occam's razor, 41, 494*n*

Oedipus, 28

Old Kule (Barlach), 259, 263

old woman/Ecclesia, 228–29, 231, 238

Oldenberg, Hermann, 209*n*

Om mani padme hum, 178

one-sidedness, 74, 80, 207–8, 226, 337, 415–16, 519, 522

Onians, Richard Broxton, 544*n*

ontological argument, 40–45

opposite(s), pairs of: beauty and, 84, 121; Brahmanic view of, 195–99; cancellation of, 117; conflict

of, 213, 217; detachment from, 123; dissolution of individuality into, 108–9; energy and, 202; liberation/deliverance/release from, 118, 194–95, 199, 216; mediation between, 115, 218; —, and symbol, 111–12, 479 (*see also* transcendent function); and middle way, 194; natural combination of, 265; in pagan unconscious, 188; play of, 89; Pythagorean, 544, 546; and redemption, *see* redemption; release of repression and, 107; renunciation of, 219; Schiller on, *see* Schiller *s.v.*; self and, 114&*n*, 460; separation/splitting apart of, 46, 89, 258; solution of conflict of, by creative act, 321; *tao* and, 120, 216–17; tension of, 199, 207, 217, 219; union/reconciliation of, 77, 105–6, 109, 111–12, 139, 197, 215, 217, 220–21, 262, 270–71; —, Brahman is, 198–99; —, and will, 115; yogi and, 202

optimism, 313–14

orientation, 456 (Def.), 518

Origen, 11–12, 14–19, 27; self-castration, 15–17, 27

Orphic mysteries, 544

Ostwald, F. W., 192, 322–24, 326–29, 421, 504; *Grosse Männer*, 322*n*, 323*n*, 327*n*, 504*n*

"other side," 382–83

P

paganism, 185–86

palmistry, 525

Pañcavimsha Brahmana, see Brahmanas

Pandora, 175–84, 187, 258–59, 266, 271

paranoia, 277, 502, 508

parental: complex, 124, 529–30; imago, 201; influence, and child's attitude, 332

Paris and Helen, 125

THE COLLECTED WORKS OF

C. G. JUNG

EDITORS: SIR HERBERT READ, MICHAEL FORDHAM, AND GER-
HARD ADLER; *EXECUTIVE EDITOR*, WILLIAM McGUIRE. *TRANS-
LATED BY* R.F.C. HULL, EXCEPT WHERE NOTED.

In the following list, dates of original publication are given in pa-
rentheses (of original composition, in brackets). Multiple dates indicate
revisions.

(*continued*)

(*continued*)

(*continued*)

C. G. JUNG SPEAKING: Interviews and Encounters
Edited by William McGuire and R.F.C. Hull

C. G. JUNG: Word and Image
Edited by Aniela Jaffé

THE ESSENTIAL JUNG
Selected and introduced by Anthony Storr

THE GNOSTIC JUNG
Selected and introduced by Robert A. Segal

PSYCHE AND SYMBOL
Selected and introduced by Violet S. de Laszlo

Notes of C. G. Jung's Seminars:

DREAM ANALYSIS ([1928–30] 1984)
Edited by William McGuire

NIETZSCHE'S *ZARATHUSTRA* ([1934–39] 1988)
Edited by James L. Jarrett (2 vols.)

ANALYTICAL PSYCHOLOGY ([1925] 1989)
Edited by William McGuire

THE PSYCHOLOGY OF KUNDALINI YOGA ([1932] 1996)
Edited by Sonu Shamdasani

INTERPRETATION OF VISIONS ([1930–34]1996)
Edited by Claire Douglas